One-Design & Offshore Yachtsman

ENCYCLOPEDIA OF SAILING

ONE-DESIGN
& OFFSHORE YACHTSMAN

1817

ENCYCLOPEDIA
OF SAILING

By the Editors of

One-Design & Offshore Yachtsman

HARPER & ROW, PUBLISHERS

New York, Evanston, San Francisco, London

Contents

Contents

Section III. Catalog of One-Design and Offshore Sailboats, 105

Section IV. The Art of Sailing, 165

Section V. Sailing Is Fun, 229

quette—Good Manners Afloat—Increase Your Knowledge of the Weather—Visual Indications of the Weather—*Storm Signals*—Radio Weather Reports—Weather Maps —Weather Instruments—*How to Use a Barometer*—*The Beaufort Numbers*—Sailing and the Weather—Tides and Their Effects—Sailing Tactics in Bad Weather—*Luffing Through a Puff*—*Sailing in Very Strong Winds*—*Reefing Procedures*—*Heaving To in Bad Weather*—Sailing in a Fog—Sound Signals in Fog—Sailing Emergencies—Capsizing and Righting—*Righting a Capsized Catamaran*—Going Aground—Man Overboard—Fire Afloat—Being Lost—First Aid—*Seasickness*—*Artificial Respiration*— First Aid for Your Yacht—*Rigging Repairs*—*Loss or Disablement of a Rudder*—*Hull Repair*—*Collision*—*Taking On Water*—*Plugged Head*—*Lighting Problems*—*Engine Failure*—Distress Signals—Abandoning Ship—Sailboat Maintenance—Going Out of Commission—*Selection of Storage*—*Proper Shoring or Cradle Supports*—*Stripping and Cleaning*—*Preparing Engines for Winter Storage*—*Winter Cover*—Fitting Out— *Painting Your Boat*—*General Inspection*—*Preparing the Engine*—*Electrical System*— *Tuning the Rigging*—*Launching*—*Sail Care*—Midseason Care.

Section VI. The Lure of Racing, 315

Class-boat Racing—Sailing Instructions—Racing Courses—*Establishment of a Racing Course*—Scoring Yacht Races—*Low-point System*—*High-point System*—*New Olympic Scoring System*—*Old Olympic Scoring System*—*Snipe Scoring System*—Yacht Racing Rules—*North American Yacht Racing Union's Racing Rules*—Know Your Racing Committee—Racing Tactics—The Start—*Planning the Start*—*Selecting the Starting Position*—*Starting Technique*—*Match-race Starts*—The Windward Leg— Rounding Marks—Reaching and Running—Wind and Racing—*Light-weather Technique*—*Heavy-weather Technique*—Against the Current—Frostbite Racing—Team Racing—*Racing Tactics*—Protests and Appeals—Selecting Your Crew—*The Corinthians*—Crewman's Checklist—Handicap and Distance Racing—Measurement Rules and Time Allowance—*The Cruising Club of America Measurement Rule*—*The International Offshore Rating Rule*—*The Midget Ocean Racing Club Rule*—*The Off Soundings Club Rule*—*The Storm Trysail Club Rule*—Time-allowance Tables—Relative-speed Handicap Systems—*Pacific Handicap Racing Fleet Rule*—*Portsmouth System*—Distance-racing Tips and Strategy—*Equipment Lists*—*Offshore-racing Numbering System*—*The Crew*—*Before the Race*—*Sailing Tactics*.

Section VII. Sailing Competition, 391

The America's Cup—Olympic Games—Pan-American Games—Newport-Bermuda Race—Onion Patch Trophy—Annapolis—Newport Race—Transpacific Race—Transatlantic Race—La Coupe Internationale du Cercle de la Voile de Paris (C.V.P.) —Coupe Internationale Atlantique (Half-Ton Cup)—Quarter-Ton Cup—Admiral's Cup—Fastnet Race—Captain James Cook Trophy—International Catamaran Challenge Cup Trophy (Little America's Cup)—The Canada's Cup—Chicago-Mackinac Race—Acapulco Race—World Ocean Racing Championship—Ensenada Race—Congressional Cup—Southern Ocean Racing Conference—Other Major Distance Sailing Races—One-Design Sailing Championships—*Yachting*'s One-of-a-Kind Regatta—America's Teacup—Sears Cup (Junior Sailing Championship)—Adams Trophy (Women's North American Sailing Championship)—Clifford D. Mallory Cup (North American

Section VIII. Glossary of Sailing Terms, 445

Acknowledgments

As with the magazine, the compilation of this volume required the help of many people. Members of the staff of *One-Design & Offshore Yachtsman* who were exceedingly cooperative were Bruce Kirby, George A. Eddy, Theodore A. Jones, William A. King, and Barbara J. Fengler. Contributing editors of this publication who were also helpful include Peter Barrett, Robert Smith, Jack Knights, and Dr. Stuart Walker. Most of the line art in this book was done by Mark Smith, *One-Design & Offshore Yachtsman*'s assistant editor.

Although the vast majority of the material in this book appeared in one form or another in *One-Design & Offshore Yachtsman,* some material was contributed from other sources. We would like to thank, for instance, Frances Krupka, Sohei Hohri, Thomas J. Lipton, Inc., Wall Rope Works, Grumman Allied Industries, Inc., United States Coast Guard, New York Yacht Club, Yacht Racing Association of Long Island Sound, Cruising Club of America, Inc., United States Department of Commerce, H. A. Bruno & Associates, Inc., San Diego Yacht Club, Bermuda News Bureau, United States Naval Academy, San Francisco Yacht Club, Royal Ocean Racing Club, Cercle de la Voile de Paris, United States Naval Institute, Leonard M. Fowle, Royal Bermuda Yacht Club, Midget Ocean Racing Club, William N. Wallace, Miami-Metro News Bureau, Royal Canadian Yacht Club of Toronto, Manhasset Bay Yacht Club, Walter Kidde and Company, Inc., Charles Booz, Du Pont Company, Canor Plarex, Inc., Hard Sails, Inc., Bahamas News Bureau, Charles Ulmer, Inc., Lands' End Publishing Corp., Martini & Rossi, Inc., Raytheon Company, and the American Sailing Council. In addition, we thank Jackie Lersch, Hettie Jackman, and Marie Mastromardo, who had the task of typing this huge manuscript.

Special thanks are due to William Davies of Harper & Row, Publishers, for his toil and zest in making this project possible.

THE EDITORS

One-Design & Offshore Yachtsman
ENCYCLOPEDIA OF SAILING

SECTION I

The History of Sailing

Sailing has played an important part in this country's heritage—both in commerce and in sport. Naval architects and shipbuilders became world-renowned for the beauty and speed of their tall ships that sailed the oceans of the world. Full-rigged clipper ships such as the *Flying Cloud* set speed records for passages from New York to London, San Francisco, and the Orient. Continuing in this tradition, American yacht designers and manufacturers have seen their boats gain international popularity and racing supremacy.

Enthusiasm in sailing as a sport grew steadily after amateur skippers such as Commodore Harold S. Vanderbilt successfully defended the America's Cup during the 1930's. The boats used in those races against England were the majestic J class sloops that measured up to 135 feet in length. Today the America's Cup is raced in 12-Meter sloops, averaging 65 feet in length. These boats are the ultimate in precision design for closed-course match racing. Sailed entirely by amateur crews, the "Twelves" have continued America's domination of this most famous international competition since the first race in 1851.

Amateur sailors from the United States have entered many other sailing events all over the world including the Olympics, international classboat championships, the One-Ton Cup competition in Europe, international team racing at Cowes, England, and many ocean races. This sport has become so important to many boat owners that the well-known 57-foot ocean racing yacht *Ondine* has sailed over 500,000 miles in her twelve-year career.

Up until 1945 sailors were still few in number compared with today. Different classes of sailboats were also few in number, which made them easy to recognize by their design and sail insignia. Such well-known classes as Star, Penguin, Snipe, Comet, and Inland Lake Scow became popular, and class racing began to grow on a national basis. Ownership of a boat generally tied in with membership in a yacht club, but there were not the organized racing and cruising schedules such as we have today. More important, most boats were built of wood, which required regular maintenance and upkeep.

Since 1945 many new materials have been devised to make boating easier and less expensive. Fiberglass was introduced and quickly accepted by boatbuilders and boat owners alike. Fiberglass was generally found easier to use because basically all a builder needed was a mold of the desired hull. He did not have to use wood-plank construction. He could therefore build boats on a mass-production basis, economically cheaper and faster. Boat owners liked fiberglass because it required less upkeep and less expense. Aluminum as a hull material also gained recognition, particularly in larger sailing yachts.

Along with these new hulls came the introduction of synthetic sail material—first nylon and then Dacron—replacing the cotton duck which had been used for over a hundred years. Sails of cotton were subject to mildew and rot unless they were frequently washed in fresh water. They were also subject to stretch and shrinkage. Today's synthetic sails are rot-free, can be made of lighter-weight cloth, are stretch-resistant, and have better lasting quality.

As these new materials were developed, aluminum was introduced to replace wooden masts and stainless-steel rigging replaced galvanized stays and shrouds. So, the important breakthroughs came in only a few years' time, and because of them boating was on the way to becoming the biggest participation sport in America.

Each year many new kinds of sailboats are designed and offered to sailing enthusiasts. These boats come in all sizes and styles, from sailboards and sailing dinghies to cruising sailboats that families can live on during vacations. This means that sailors can choose almost exactly the size and style of boat they want. In fact, there are now over 1,000 *different* classes of sailboats (see Section III) and over 400,000 sailboat owners, of whom over half have racing sailboats. The term class refers to a particular design, and all boats in a class must be built to the same design specifications. Also, in class racing, there are strict regulations governing what sailors can and cannot use on their boats. Violations of rig and equipment rules will disqualify a boat in a race.

The number of people participating in sailing in the United States is now estimated at over three million, and there are an estimated 42 million enjoying boating of all kinds, with over nine million boat owners. With so many people enjoying sailing, it is easy to see that the sport is not just an individual activity. It is a family and group affair because it is shared by parents and their children, family friends, and other sailors who are members of boating organizations. Actually the feeling of friendliness is one of the unique qualities of sailors, particularly when they are on the water. People in sailboats wave to people in other sailboats even if they do not know them. It is this *esprit de corps* that makes sailing so much fun.

Sailing is, of course, a sport that demands ability, intelligence—and complete command of one's boat. Its enjoyment depends not only upon the physical and technical competence of the helmsman but also upon the elements, such as wind and tide. These factors make good sailing a genuine achievement. But the techniques and requirements of sailing will be discussed in detail in later sections of this book. For now, let us see how sailing began as a sport.

EARLY HISTORY OF SAILING

Pleasure craft, or what we now know as yachts, have existed among maritime nations from the most remote period, but the records of these gorgeous vessels of antiquity have perished, except in fragments to be found scattered here and there among the writings of ancient authors. For example, one of the most ancient pleasure craft, and the most beautiful and renowned of which any definite description has been preserved, was the royal barge, or galley, of Cleopatra, Queen of Egypt thirty years before the Christian era. We are indebted to Plutarch for the following description:

Crossing the Mediterranean to Cilicia, where Anthony then was, she [Cleopatra] came up the River Cydnus in a vessel, the stern whereof was gold, the sails of purple silk, and the oars of silver, which gently kept time to the sound of music.

She placed herself under a rich canopy of cloth-of-gold, habited like Venus rising out of the sea, with beautiful boys about her, like cupids, fanning her; and her women, representing the Nereids and Graces, leaned negligently on the sides and shrouds of the vessel, while troops of virgins, richly drest, marched on the banks of the river burning incense and rich perfumes, which were covered with an infinite number of people, gazing on in wonder and admiration. The Queen's success with Anthony was answerable to her expectations.

No record appears to exist of the dimensions of this vessel, but judging from the length of the voyage, the number of attendants and servants probably required by Cleopatra, and their equipment and stores, and judging from the statement that the galley was "laden with the most magnificent offerings and presents of all kinds," it is reasonable to suppose that this craft must have been of a considerable tonnage.

Of other ancient vessels we have some knowledge, though not as much as could be wished. The *Haw Ting,* or flower boats, of the Chinese, with their rich ornamental carvings and silken draperies of vermilion and gold, sweet with the perfume of sandalwood; the Greek and Roman galleys, which one historian, not overgallant, compares to women —equally greedy of ornament; the galley race for royal prizes between the *Dolphin, Centaur,* and *Chimara,* immortalized by Virgil—all these are of interest. It is also interesting to note that the word "regatta" is Italian in origin; it was taken from the name of the gondolas that participated in the races of Venice, which have been famous since 1171. "Yacht" is an English word, coming from the Dutch *jaght,* or *jaght schip,* meaning "to put on speed" or "to hunt." The Dutch gave these names to the small, fast cargo boats that plied the canals of the Lowlands three hundred years ago.

In fact, an intelligent approach to the introduction of yachts and sailing for pleasure into America and England makes it necessary to turn to Holland, where they originated. Philip II of Spain maintained his hold upon Flanders and Brabant, but in 1580 the seven other provinces formed themselves into the Republic of the United Netherlands, and by their situation were naturally led to commercial pursuits. In these they rapidly excelled. Amsterdam rose to be a city of the first rank—the center of commerce in Europe—and Holland grew in wealth and influence until it not only held its own against Spain, but invaded Spain's most valuable monopolies.

From remote times the people of Holland have been celebrated for their skill and industry upon the ocean. They were the first to develop the whale and herring fisheries, which proved not only a source of great wealth but were the nursery of a splendid race of seamen. The country itself was rescued from the ocean by embankments, which were constructed with unceasing toil and skill, and was drained by innumerable pumps, driven by windmills. And upon this ground, lying below the level of the sea, was founded the most prosperous community in Europe.

It was quite natural, therefore, that a refined and wealthy people as the Hollanders were, living in a country situated upon an inland sea and intersected by waterways and canals—the highways of commerce and travel—should have had both their private and public conveyance by water. This was what the people did have; and this conveyance was the *jaght* or *jaght schip.*

Actually, the word *jaght* grew in stature as time went along, and often signified a splendidly equipped state or private vessel handsomely and comfortably furnished; also a small private vessel, owned partly for pleasure, partly for trade use; or a vessel attached to a squadron, fitted with accommodations for an admiral or other officer, used to communicate with the vessels of a fleet or with the shore, carrying dispatches or keeping watch on an enemy's ship. A *jaght,* or yacht, might also be a vessel engaged upon an expedition, alone or in company with other vessels. And yet, with this wide range of uses, there was something distinctive about the seventeenth-century yacht of Holland—she could never be mistaken for anything else.

When yachts were first used and built in Holland is not known; probably at a very early date. Naturally, from the nature of the country, they were a necessity, as were the private carriages and public coaches in other countries before the days of steam; and the various types of yachts used in Holland were as numerous as their employment. We should feel deeply indebted to the Dutch artists of that period, upon whose canvas yachts have frequently been portrayed.

When Charles I of England was beheaded by the Puritans, Charles II barely escaped into exile after his defeat by Cromwell at the Battle of Worcester in 1651. During his exile in Holland, Charles II discovered the popular Dutch pastime of *jaghting*. On his restoration to the throne of England in 1660, his Dutch friends presented him with the yacht *Mary*. In due course, she came to England, together with her name.

The dimensions of the *Mary* were: length of keel, 52 feet; breadth, 19 feet; draught, 10 feet; and 100 tons burden. The length of keel, or "as she treads the ground," is given in all the measurements of yachts at that period, to which should be added from ten to fifteen percent for the length overall. The *Mary* carried eight guns and a crew of thirty men.

In 1661 Charles added two more yachts to his royal fleet—the *Bezan* and *Catherine*. The following year the naval yards at Lambeth, England, turned out the 25-ton royal yacht *Jamie*. The King himself was at the helm of the *Jamie* when she raced the Duke of York's speedy Dutch yacht *Anne* from Greenwich to Gravesend and back for a side bet of 100 pounds. The King's yacht won.

The English nobility followed the royal example, and yachting soon became popular. In fact, the first private yacht in England appears to have been the *Charlotte,* owned by Sir William Batten, of the Admiralty. The English chronicler Samuel Pepys, in his *Diary,* records, under the date of September 3, 1663, that he "boarded her early in the morning at Greenwich, accompanied by Batten and Lady Batten, who, for pleasure were going to the Downes"; and the wind being fresh, he predicts that "they will be sick enough, as my lady is mighty troublesome on the water." And Pepys was correct, for, on September 5, he records: "Sir William Batten was fain to put ashore at Queensborough with my Lady, who has been so sick she swears never to go to sea again." This sounds modern, and perhaps no complaint connected with yachting is so familiar or has been repeated more frequently and persistently than this. No doubt like most of us Lady Batten sailed again, and many times, on board the *Charlotte.*

The world's first yacht club, the Water Club of Cork Harbour, Ireland, was formed in 1720, a few years before the precursor of the Royal Yacht Club. Actually new organizations were established as the sport de-

veloped, and each contributed to the design of new boats. The Cumberland Fleet, later to be known as the Royal Thames Yacht Club, was incorporated in 1775; and in 1812 the present Royal Yacht Club was formed under the name of the Royal Yacht Squadron. In fact, the first time that the words "yacht" and "club" were put together was at Cowes on the Isle of Wight, a favored summer resort, where English yacht owners gathered. On June 1, 1815, a group of them met in London and formed a Cowes organization simply called the Yacht Club.

The formation of the Yacht Club marked a new era in yachting history, for until then, as just stated, the word "yacht" had never been used in connection with a club or its vessels. Probably no club has ever been founded with a more distinguished membership, and certainly no club has kept to its traditions more faithfully. In 1820 the name of the club was changed to the Royal Yacht Club, and in 1821 the colors were changed to a red ensign with the letters RYC and a crown and foul anchor, also a red burgee. In 1829 the Lords of the Admiralty issued warrants for yachts of the Royal Yacht Club to carry the St. George's ensign; a white burgee with a red cross and yellow crown in the center was accordingly adopted, and these are still the colors of the club. In 1833 the name was again changed to the Royal Yacht Squadron. It is a singular fact that for the first ten years of its existence, the club had no flag officers, and it was not until 1825 that Lord Yarborough became the first commodore, and so continued until his death in 1846.

Some years elapsed, after the Yacht Club was established, before racing became a feature of yachting at Cowes. The yachts composing its fleet were fine seagoing vessels, built, rigged, and manned in imitation of vessels of a similar class in the Royal Navy, and were often commanded by Naval officers on leave of absence. Speed was regarded as of less importance than good seamanship at the reviews of the fleet, which were occasionally held in The Solent, or keeping the decks, guns, spars, and rigging in shipshape and man-of-war fashion. These yachts were the floating summer homes of their owners, who were frequently accompanied by their families, while the pleasant life on board was

Yachts belonging to the Royal Yacht Club off Cowes Castle, Isle of Wight, in the 1830's.

conducted with the decorum, refinement, and comfort of an English home.

It is interesting to note that, while there must have been some races between individual yacht owners, the first open sailing match on the Thames of which any record appears was sailed during the summer of 1749 and was won by the *Princess Augusta,* a small yacht or pleasure boat owned by George Bellas, a Registrar in Doctors Commons. The course was from Greenwich to the Nore and return; the prize was a silver cup presented by the Prince of Wales, afterward King George III. It appears that this youthful patron of sport had already presented a cup which was rowed for from Whitehall to Putney, in celebration of his eleventh birthday, on June 4 of the same year, when it was intimated that he might also present a prize to be sailed for by yachts or pleasure boats on the Thames.

A short account of this sailing match was published at the time in the *Gentleman's Magazine,* which records that twelve vessels started though not mentioning their names, but relates that the *Princess Augusta* "in the going down to Woolwich was a mile before the rest, and at the Hope three miles, but in coming up by the shifting of the winds and

the situation they were all in, two shot by her at Gravesend; notwithstanding which she came in first by ten minutes, which was the next day at forty minutes past two in the afternoon. The Prince of Wales with five or six attendants in his Chinese barge and the rowers in Chinese habits drove gently before for some time and a crowd of boats about him, the people frequently huzzaing, at which he pulled off his hat. It was almost a perfect calm and not the least damage happened, though the river seemed overspread with sailing yachts, galleys, and small boats." Mr. Bellas "on receiving the prize generously gave the value of it among the men that had worked the boat."

On June 28, 1775, a new entertainment called a regatta, introduced from Venice into England, was held on the Thames. As we have seen, rowing and sailing matches had been held on the Thames among watermen for many years, but this first regatta was probably more in the nature of a social function or fete, not unlike the Henley Regatta of the present day, although on a less extensive scale. At this regatta "several very respectable gentlemen, proprietors of sailing vessels and pleasure boats on the river, agreed at their annual meeting at Battersea, to draw up their boats in line off Ranelagh Gardens, in order that they might be able to witness the rowing matches, without interfering with them." These men were probably the first to organize a yacht club on the Thames.

Yacht racing in England really dates from the year 1775; and while many a man, at various times and places, has been called the "father of yachting," there can be no doubt that the Duke of Cumberland is justly entitled the "father of yacht racing." He was a brother of King George III, an admiral in the Royal Navy, and greatly interested in yachts and yachting.

On July 6, 1775, a notice appeared in the *Public Advertiser*—a newspaper published in London—which read as follows: "A silver Cup, the gift of His Royal Highness the Duke of Cumberland, is to be sailed for on Tuesday the 11th Inst. from Westminster Bridge to Putney Bridge and back, by Pleasure Sailing Boats, and constantly lying above London Bridge. Any gentleman inclined to enter his Boat may be informed of particulars by applying to Mr. Roberts, Boatbuilder, Lambeth, at any time before Saturday Noon Next."

This match, however, was not sailed until July 13, owing to the weather. When it did occur, the cup, valued at twenty guineas, was won by the *Aurora,* which belonged to Mr. Parkes, "late of Ludgate Hill." And "His Royal Highness, who honored the sport with his presence, filled the Cup with wine, drank out of it, and delivered it to Mr. Parkes." This, though not the first open sailing match held in England, was the germ of yacht racing as we know it at the present.

YACHTING COMES TO THE NEW WORLD

Sailing and sailboat racing soon became popular in other European countries. The inclination to go down to the sea solely for enjoyment was not lacking with the American colonist, but indulgence in the pastime was so rare that it was slow in becoming a recognized sport. The early sailing craft had various functions, not the least of which was its use as an easy means of transportation in a country without roads. It required less exertion, less expense, and often less time to go from Boston to New York by sea than by a bridle path through the woods of Massachusetts and Connecticut. No one in the years before the Revolution ever regarded his general utility boat as a yacht.

One of the first Americans to push off shore for pleasure was the redoubtable John Paul Jones, who was making a leisurely cruise up the coast in his sloop, fishing and shooting, when he arrived in New York as the news of the Battle of Lexington was received. He says in his journal that he intended to keep on to Boston through the Sounds; but he ended two years of comparative leisure and headed for the glory he was to attain as the greatest sea fighter of his time.

Six months after Jones went back to his Virginia plantation with his slaves Cato and Scipio, a Boston physician, Dr. John Jeffries, obtained permission from the British authorities to go down the harbor to shoot and fish. The pass issued to him is the first license to go sailing for pleasure.

While John Paul Jones and Dr. John Jeffries were more or less concerned with the side benefits of pleasure boating, it remained for a dapper Salem, Massachusetts, sea captain and successful merchant, George Crowninshield, Jr., to lift the pastime to another plane of endeavor and to build boats in America solely for enjoyment.

It was some years after Crowninshield had built his 22-ton sloop *Jefferson* in 1801 before the staid citizens of Essex County could understand why anyone, even with sufficient means to gratify a whim, could sail round Massachusetts Bay without some commercial object in view. Yet Crowninshield did not devote all his time to yachting, for he kept his *Jefferson* well stocked at all times and ready for any emergency. Since he ran out of Salem on several occasions to aid and succor helpless mariners, we could consider him a "local" coast guard.

For a score of years George Crowninshield was a picturesque and energetic figure on the North Shore. With his Hessian boots and

Italian artist painted *Cleopatra's Barge* in the harbor of Genoa.

thin gold tassels, his handsome coat and beautifully decorated waistcoat, his pigtail and bell-crowned beaver, made of the skin of the animal and not of silk, seated in a two-wheeled vehicle called a curricle, Captain George created a sensation, and every time he drove through the streets of the town he received an ovation. No one was jealous or scornful, for they knew that he had jumped overboard three times to save lives and dashed into several burning buildings on similar errands of mercy, to say nothing of riding over to Marblehead on the guns which Salem sent to help defend the *Constitution* after she had been chased in by the British fleet. Perhaps his most noteworthy exploit was his trip to Halifax under a flag of truce to secure the bodies of Lawrence and Ludlow of the *Chesapeake*.

It was when he built his *Cleopatra's Barge* at a cost of more than $50,000 and thus placed yachting in the privileged class that his friends and neighbors began to question his sanity. When the famous hermaphrodite brig, designed and built by Retire Becket at Salem, but with her fittings, rigging, and gear all the product of Captain Crowninshield's original-

ity, was launched on October 17, 1816, fully rigged, Salem had a holiday, and for the next six months she was the greatest attraction that Essex County had ever known.

Pictures of *Cleopatra's Barge,* striped on the starboard side and herringboned on the port, have long been familiar, and volumes could be written of her remarkable voyage to the Mediterranean in the summer of 1817 and of her reception at scores of ports. The British watched her, however, because of the rumor that she had been built expressly to rescue Napoleon from St. Helena.

She was commanded by Captain Benjamin Crowninshield, a cousin of the owner, known in Salem as "Philosopher Ben," and had a crew of ten men before the mast, two mates, a steward and a cook. Every man on board was a qualified navigator, and when at Genoa a famous German astronomer questioned this fact, the Negro cook was called into the cabin. With a chicken in one hand and a carving knife in the other, he was able to demonstrate his ability and declare that in the 3,000-mile trip across the Atlantic he was only six miles off his course when the brig sighted Cadiz. Salem boys in those days began to learn navigation at the age of ten.

A year after his return from Europe on his *Cleopatra's Barge*, Captain George Crowninshield died suddenly at his home in Salem. The brig, together with half interest in his *Jefferson* and his ship *America*, were sold at auction, the first two becoming merchantmen. *Cleopatra's Barge* after a voyage to Rio Janeiro was sent to the Northwest coast and while in the Pacific was purchased by King Kamehameha of the Sandwich Islands. A few years later she was driven on the rocks on the island of Oahu, where, so well was she built, she withstood the big surges for months, being finally hauled off to end her days as the first American cruising yacht in the Pacific.

The honor of initiating the first yacht race in America is generally given to Robert Bennett Forbes, a skillful Boston yachtsman and boat designer. The story goes something like this: While rounding Cape Cod on August 3, 1835, in the schooner *Sylph*, which Commodore Forbes had designed for John P. Cushing and which he commanded, the schooner *Wave* of New York, owned by John C. Stevens, was encountered on Nantucket Shoals. At the suggestion of Commodore Forbes there was a brief and perhaps indecisive brush, followed by two more the next day in Vineyard Sound, also inspired by the Boston yachtsman. As these races were subsequently reported in public prints, we have in them our first recorded yacht races.

Most of the early yachts were not built for speed. Actually, one of the first yachts to be built for speed as well as pleasure was the schooner *Northern Light*, the pride of Boston in the 1840's, whose fame was sung in prose and rhyme up and down the waterfront for a dozen years. Her owner, Colonel William P. Winchester, for whom the Massachusetts town was named, although he never resided in it, was one of the merchant princes of Boston. His father amassed a fortune in army contracts during the second war with England, and for years the firm of E. A. & W. Winchester practically controlled the pig products of the country.

Northern Light was a 62-foot-overall schooner, the product of a young Danish naval constructor, Louis Winde, and built by Whitmore & Holbrook in Boston. Winde may be regarded as our first yacht designer, and

although his adopted country was somewhat tardy in recognizing his genius, his native land was not, for eight of his models are in the naval museum in Copenhagen.

For years *Northern Light,* with her gay bunting and colorful crew, was cheered every time she left her dock at Ripley's Wharf, opposite the Navy Yard. In order that his friends might not soil their onshore clothes, Winchester supplied red shirts, white pants, and straw hats with white ribbons bearing "Northern Light" in gilt letters.

Despite the boasts of her Boston supporters, *Northern Light* did not engage in any race until she joined *Belle* and *Lancet* at Newport in August, 1844. Then she was too late for the race round Conanticut Island, but she had a brush with *Cygnet* the next day, and although many Bostonians claimed a victory, Colonel Winchester subsequently admitted that he was beaten.

He sold *Northern Light* late in 1849 to Elton R. Smylie and Basilus Argyus of Boston, Francis I. Gould of Lexington, and George McHall of Derry, New Hampshire, who fitted her out for the California gold fields. She was lost a few months later while trying to negotiate the Straits of Magellan.

Another Bostonian who was well known in the early American yachting scene was Benjamin Cutler Clark. He began sailing around the bay in a little half-decked craft known as the *Mary*. In 1832 he ordered a more pretentious boat, the *Mermaid,* built by Whitmore & Holbrook, an 11-ton schooner, said to have been the first decked yacht in Boston Harbor. But even this boat became too small for Mr. Clark's widening view of yachting. Selling it to Colonel Winchester, he obtained from Whitmore & Holbrook a new yacht, the *Raven,* which for twenty years was one of the best-known pleasure craft in Massachusetts Bay. She was one of the first to fly her owner's merchant, or house, flag, a red swallowtail with a white Greek cross, a custom that was subsequently adopted by other yachting families, notably the Forbes with their flag of white and blue diamonds, the Atkinsons with their blue flag and red Greek cross, and the Welds with their famous black horse.

Raven sailed in numerous races, but her most notable one was that of July 19, 1845, the first regatta to be held in Massachusetts

Bay. It took place off Nahant and was promoted by that enterprising hotel proprietor, Paran Stevens. The schooner *Cygnet* led at the finish, but gave way to *Raven* on time allowance.

Actually, the history of yachting in America really begins with the career of the Stevens brothers. Few men in the country's history have contributed so many progressive ideas to the welfare of the United States as Colonel John Stevens and his three energetic sons, John Cox, Edwin Augustus, and Robert Livingston Stevens. All four were so far ahead of their times that many of their pet projects and inventions were rejected as impractical, only to be adopted enthusiastically without semblance of credit decades and even a century later. In fact, it is difficult to recount their pleasure-boat activities and the impetus which their deeds and example gave to yachting without some brief reference to their accomplishments for the public good.

Colonel Stevens, treasurer of New Jersey during the Revolution, never owned a yacht, but he enjoyed sailing with his boys in the lower Hudson below his stone house, the Castle, which he had built on the heights of Hoboken. As early as 1791 he assisted in inventing a steamboat, which was patented under the laws which he helped establish. He constructed a screw-propeller steamboat in 1802, a side-wheeler, the *Phoenix,* in 1807, which he was obliged to send to the Delaware, as Fulton had a monopoly of the Hudson. Stevens in 1811 established a steam ferry between New York and Hoboken, the first in the world, and with his sons he obtained rights and built the Camden & Amboy Railroad, the initial steam railroad in the country.

His son Robert, while on his way to Europe in 1830 to obtain a locomotive for the new railroad, whittled out the model for a "T" rail, which has been used ever since, and continued his father's studies of an iron warship with a double turret, besides inventing a percussion shell for smooth-bore cannon.

Robert L. Stevens' contribution to yachting was the sloop *Maria,* designed for his brother John, which was built in the nearby yard of William Capes at Hoboken. She was the largest single-masted yacht the world had ever known, 110 feet overall, and embodied such progressive innovations as hollow mast

and boom, a track on the mast for her mainsail, instead of hoops, cross-cut sails, outside lead ballast, two centerboards, rubber compressors on the mainsheet traveler, and she was sheathed in copper. She cost $100,000, twice as much as *Cleopatra's Barge.*

Edwin Augustus Stevens was closely associated with his father and brother Robert in securing capital to float their numerous enterprises. His principal individual gift was the Stevens Institute of Technology, and he endowed the Hoboken High School. Like his brothers, he was an ardent yachtsman, but it was the oldest brother, John Cox Stevens, who came to be called the "father of American yachting."

It was aboard John Stevens' yacht *Gimcrack*—anchored off the Battery at the foot of Manhattan Island in July, 1844—that it was first decided to form the New York Yacht Club. However, this organization is not the oldest yacht club in America—out at Detroit a little body of men had formed the Detroit Boat Club in 1839, since which time the Detroit Boat Club has had a continuous existence. A month or so after the New York Yacht Club was established, a little group of Bermudians formed the Royal Bermuda Yacht Club. Five years later the Southern Yacht Club sprang up in New Orleans, and the following year the Springfield Yacht and Canoe Club was established in Springfield, Massachusetts. But a "boat club" and a "yacht and canoe club" imply activity in smaller craft and lack the courageous outlook of the New York Yacht Club, which from its very beginning has been an organization of large yachts.

There were also three older organizations, all of them short-lived. The Knickerbocker Boat Club, founded in 1811, died the next year. The New York Boat Club, organized in 1830, had such a short and undistinguished career that there is no record of its demise. The Boston Yacht Club (first of the name), founded in 1835, lasted about two years.

It is hard to picture yachting in 1844. It was the day of the big square-riggers, the clipper ships, the coasting schooners. Bowsprits and figureheads projected over South Street and Front Street; New York and Brooklyn were small, independent cities. Staten Island and New Jersey were unspoiled country, and

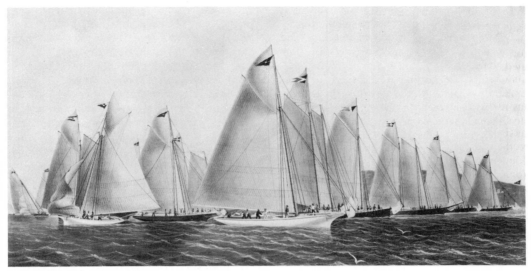

The start of a regatta of the New York Yacht Club in 1854.

New York Bay and the Hudson River were a yachtsman's paradise. Probably there are few places in the world that afforded such gorgeous sailing as New York Harbor. Swept by a strong prevailing southwesterly wind, unhampered by traffic, free from smoke, it was as enticing then as it is impossible today.

In the summer of 1845, the New York Yacht Club, under Commodore John C. Stevens (he was elected to this position in the spring of the year), held its first club regatta, thus initiating what was to become an annual event. On July 16, nine yachts gathered in the Upper New York Bay to sail a course described as "From a Stakeboat off Robbin's Reef, to a stakeboat off Stapleton, Staten Island, thence to and around the Southwest Spit buoy [in the Lower Bay], returning over the same course." Time allowances were figured on Custom House measurements, and were to be 45 seconds per ton. There were no allowances for rig. The starters were as follows:

Name	Rig	Tonnage	Owner
La Coquille	Schooner	27	John C. Jay
Cygnet	Schooner	45	William Edgar
Sybil	Schooner	42	C. B. Miller
Spray	Schooner	37	Hamilton Wilkes
Minna	Schooner	30	James M. Waterbury
Gimcrack	Schooner	25	John C. Stevens
Newburgh	Sloop	33	H. Robinson
Ida	Sloop	17	James Rogers
Lancet	Sloop	20	George B. Rollins

Seven of these nine owners were charter members of the club, the newcomers being C. B. Miller and H. Robinson.

This regatta proved a great event in the sporting life of the city, and was witnessed by thousands—all New Yorkers who could get there, apparently, being on the water to view the yachts sail. The prizes awarded were purchased with the entrance money, which was $25 per starter. The only records of the race that have been kept show that but three of the nine starters were timed as finishing, Cygnet winning in 5 hours 23 minutes 15 seconds; Sybil being second in 5 hours 25 minutes 25 seconds; and Gimcrack third, 5 hours 30 minutes 30 seconds.

Since the new club got off to such a good start, Commodore Stevens decided that a clubhouse was in order and generously gave the new organization a piece of land on which to build, located on the water at the Elysian Fields, Hoboken, New Jersey, just across the Hudson from what was then the residential district of New York City. This property was just to the north of Castle Point, Hoboken, the residence of the Stevens family, which later became Stevens Institute. Here the club's first home was built, and it was opened to the members on July 15, 1846. W. P. Stephens, in his History of American Yachting, gives the year as 1845, but the club records indicate it was 1846, although plans for the new clubhouse were probably started in 1845.

The building is described by Philip Hone, a club member who kept a diary of his daily doings, as "a handsome Gothic cottage in a pleasant grove." It was large enough to enable forty-three diners to sit down to a turtle dinner (apparently a club specialty) in 1846. (This building was moved in 1904 to Glen Cove, Long Island, and later became a part of Mystic Seaport Village in Connecticut.)

In the autumn of 1846, the New York Yacht Club gave a regatta in which it was required that the crews of the yachts (pilots excepted) should all be club members instead of paid hands, as was then customary. It was the first "Corinthian" regatta, and was sailed on October 6 over a special course which did not go below the Narrows in New York Harbor. There were only six starters, one of which was the *Maria*—Robert L. Stevens' yacht. As this was her first race, there was great interest in the outcome. There was a strong southwester blowing on the day of the race and *Maria*, with her great size, won easily. The schooner *Siren* was second, almost an hour behind.

Interest in the *Maria* was so keen, and her owners so confident in her ability, that a match was made between her and the schooner *Coquette* for $1,000 a side. In those days men backed their opinions with hard cash. It was to be an ocean race, sailed outside, the course being from a buoy at the entrance of Gedney's Channel to a stakeboat twenty-five miles to windward and return. This was the club's first race over an ocean course. There were to be many in later years. It was sailed on October 10, 1846. There was a strong northeast breeze blowing and *Maria* started with two reefs in her mainsail and the bonnet off the jib. The *Coquette*, which carried full sail, won the race, described at the time as a close one, by over twenty-five minutes. Incidentally, the history of the early races are delightfully detailed. A surprisingly large number of yachts got into trouble, and the records tell us that such a yacht ran aground and injured her keel, that another sprung her bowsprit, a third lost her topmast, and so on. Nowadays, a dismal "d.n.f.," meaning "did not finish," leaves us in doubt as to whether the skipper was tired or seasick, or the ship incapacitated in an epic encounter with the seas.

The years between 1847 and 1851 were

John Cox Stevens.

largely "growing years" for the New York Yacht Club and were devoted to organizing the club's racing program, revising the classification of yachts, and overhauling the time allowances. In 1847 the racing fleet was divided into two classes according to size, but not by rig, and a third class was provided for boats not enrolled in the club. Undoubtedly some of the latter class were working or commercial vessels such as the North River sloops, which were already famous for their speed. Time allowances were altered to 35 seconds per ton for yachts of the first class, 45 seconds per ton for second-class boats, and 40 seconds for the "outsiders." The big sloop *Maria* dominated the club fleet, and in spite of being dismasted in the Annual Regatta of 1848, her superiority, and that of a new smaller sloop, the 39-ton *Una*, designed by George Steers, was so obvious that for the next few years the number of entries showed a marked decline. The older yachts were already being outbuilt. All this, however, showed progress both in designing and in more equitable methods of handicapping.

It is important to note that for many years organized yachting was in the hands of the New York Yacht Club. Most of the prominent clubs in the country were founded much later than the New York Yacht Club. The Brooklyn Yacht Club, which was very important in the old days, was founded ten years later, in 1854. The Southern YC (1849), Carolina YC (1853), Buffalo YC (1860), Neenah-Nodway YC (1861), Riverton YC and Raritan YC (1865), Atlantic YC (1866), Columbia YC (1867), South Boston YC (1868), and Boston YC, Portland (Maine) YC, San Francisco YC, and Savannah Y and CC (1869) all date from before 1870, and from then on expansion was rapid. Some of the best known and most influential clubs were established in the next three decades, some with big yachts and fancy trappings, others providing more informal racing for small local boats. These included: Eastern YC (1870), Seawanhaka Corinthian YC (1871), Madison YC (1871), Toms River YC (1871), Milwaukee YC (1871), Santa Barbara YC (1872), Knickerbocker YC (1874), Lake Geneva YC (1874), Chicago YC (1875), Florida (Jacksonville) YC (1876), New Bedford YC (1877), Monmouth Boat Club (1879), Larchmont YC (1880), Buffalo Canoe Club (1882), American YC (1883), Annapolis YC (1886), San Francisco Corinthian YC (1886), San Diego YC (1886), Biscayne Bay YC (1887), Corinthian (Marblehead) YC (1888), Riverside YC (1888), Bay Head YC (1888), Indian Harbor YC (1889), Manhassett Bay YC (1891), Seattle YC (1892), Philadelphia Corinthian YC, Mantoloking YC (1897), and Los Angeles YC (1899). All of these clubs, splendid organizations that they are, certainly are old enough and sufficiently well established to achieve national and international importance. It is significant that of the more than five hundred yacht clubs in the United States, the New York Yacht Club is the only club known all over the world and everywhere regarded as *the* yacht club of the United States.

WINNING THE AMERICA'S CUP

Probably no trophy in the world has caused such a stir among men and nations as the pregnant pitcher that is bolted to the base of a glass case in the Trophy Room of the New York Yacht Club. It is impossible to measure the millions of dollars to say nothing of the time, physical energy, and the up-tight emotions that have been expended on this baroque bit of silver in the past hundred years. Twenty-one challenges have brought out the pride and prejudice of yachtsmen as well as their skills and, despite American domination of this series, nothing has dulled the burning enthusiasm this classic competition continues to evoke.

It all started when the British indicated they would welcome the participation of an American yacht in a regatta to be held at the time of their World's Fair in 1851. Commodore Stevens of the New York Yacht Club quickly formed a syndicate consisting of his brother Edwin, George Schuyler, J. Beekman Finlay, Hamilton Wilkes, and Colonel James A. Hamilton. The group engaged thirty-year-old George Steers to design the schooner which was built at William H. Brown's shipyard on the East River at Twelfth Street in New York City, at a cost of $30,000.

A successful designer of pilot boats, Steers departed from conventional design and gave the new hull a sharp clipper bow, a straight run aft, and raked masts. The boat measured 93 feet 6 inches on the waterline, and had a beam of 22 feet 6 inches and a draft of 9 feet. She was launched on May 3, 1851, and christened *America,* as befitting a vessel that would represent this country in foreign competition.

Under command of veteran pilot-boat captain Dick Brown, *America* departed New York for Le Havre on June 21. The twelve in crew did not include syndicate members who made the trans-Atlantic passage by steamer. Under working sails (her good racing canvas was below) the schooner made the crossing in twenty days.

Commodore Stevens met the boat in the French port where she was cleaned up, painted, and fitted with her unusually flat (for those days) suit of sails. On July 31 she set sail for Cowes and arrived there that night but anchored off because of fog. The following morning the reputedly fast English cutter *Laverock* appeared to escort *America* into the harbor. The skipper of the British vessel drew Captain Brown into a race, which the Yankee

Captain Dick Brown.

make a wager against this unusually designed boat.

America lay at Cowes for weeks without a match, so Stevens and his syndicate finally decided to start in a race that was being held around the Isle of Wight for the Royal Yacht Squadron's Hundred Guineas Cup. At least they would have one race even if they could not win any cash from it. The course was one notoriously unfair to strangers without local knowledge, owing to tidal and other conditions. *America* started the race (rather late) against fourteen of the fastest British schooners and sloops, some much bigger than she, others much smaller. On August 22 the start was made at anchor at 10 A.M. *America* got away slowly and momentarily was left in the wake of the fleet. Then she picked up speed and overhauled the British boats one by one until she gained the lead. She lost this to *Volante,* a cutter, when the wind dropped off Ventnor on the southeast side of the island. The breeze freshened and *America* swept by *Volante* and was never headed. She finished at 8:37 P.M., eight minutes ahead of *Aurora.* There were no time allowances.

Stevens and his friends came home with the Hundred Guineas Cup and little else except

schooner won by a quarter of a mile. This not only astounded the British yachtsmen but led them to decline the challenge offered by Commodore Stevens. No one was about to

The schooner *America.*

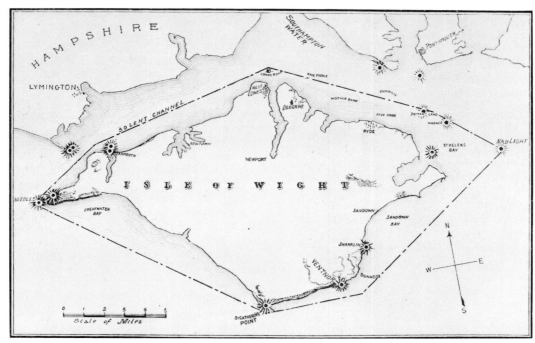

On this course (clockwise from Cowes Road) *America* defeated fourteen yachts of the Royal Yacht Squadron and captured the Squadron Cup (Hundred Guineas Cup) on August 22, 1851.

America as she appeared in 1890 after being rerigged by Edward Burgess.

$25,000 they got for selling the schooner in England. Her fine-lined clipper model and her flat-cut cotton sails—both new to English yachtsmen—started a new mode in British yacht design. Subsequently she was a British yacht, a Confederate blockade runner, a Federal naval dispatch boat in the Civil War, a naval training vessel, then a yacht again, under various owners and through various fortunes. Finally she was donated by a group of public-spirited yachtsmen to the Naval Academy at Annapolis, where she raced again in the 1870's with midshipmen crews.

The Hundred Guineas Cup sat on Commodore Stevens' shelf for six years gathering dust. He and his associates were beginning to feel their years and decided that the cup ought to stand for something permanent in yachting, so in 1857 they deeded it to the New York Yacht Club as a permanent trophy for which any foreign yacht club might challenge, under a set of terms that were obviously sporting in intent but left a lot of room for interpretation. Another eleven years passed before even an intimation of a challenge was received. The first challenger was James Ashbury, owner of the English schooner yacht *Cambria.*

Ashbury wanted a two-boat match, but the New York Yacht Club said that the America's Cup, as it was now known, had been won the hard way, by one American yacht sailing against a British fleet over a course that favored the local talent, and if Ashbury wanted it he would have to win it back the same way.

Cambria came over and on August 8, 1870, raced against fourteen American yachts, ranging from seagoing schooners like herself to light centerboard racing sloops, over a course in Lower New York Bay. The schooner *Magic* won; old *America,* sailed by a Naval Academy crew, was fourth, and *Cambria* finished eighth (tenth on corrected time).

Ashbury built a new schooner, *Livonia,* and

The schooner *Magic.*

Columbia defeats *Livonia* on October 18, 1871.

opened negotiations again. This time he wrested from the New York Yacht Club a concession that he need race against only one boat at a time, but they reserved the right to name their boat the morning of each race, agreeing to race four out of seven instead of one race. The schooner *Columbia* gave *Livonia* two pastings, one on an inside and one on an ocean course off the Hook. In the third race *Columbia*, a light racing machine compared to *Livonia*, broke her steering gear, finishing 19 minutes after the challenger, so they called up the reserves, meaning the schooner *Sappho*, which won twice by margins of about half an hour and settled that match.

After the lapse of five years Canada made the first of two abortive attempts to win the cup. The Royal Canadian Yacht Club of Toronto entered a syndicate-owned schooner, *Countess of Dufferin*, a boat similar to the prevailing shallow-draft American type of yacht. She was handicapped by a lack of funds, being roughly built and with poor sails.

The New York schooner *Madeleine* took her by margins of 11 and 27 minutes over the inside and outside courses. Canada tried again in 1881, with *Atalanta*, which was the smallest boat (70 feet overall) and the first sloop to challenge for the cup. *Atalanta*, towed down through the Erie Canal, was another rough job. She was met by the iron sloop *Mischief*, the first really scientifically designed America's Cup defender, turned out by A. Cary Smith. *Mischief* disposed of *Atalanta* in two races by margins of about 28 and 38 minutes.

Following this, George L. Schuyler, sole survivor of the owners of the *America*, drafted a new deed of gift in 1882, intended to iron out some of the loopholes in the original one. Among other things it specified that the holding club must meet the challenger with one yacht, that the challenger must proceed to the country holding the cup under sail on her own bottom, barred a defeated yacht from challenging within a year, and specified that a challenge could come only from a club having its home waters on the sea or an arm of the sea, which eliminated Toronto as a potential threat.

Schuyler also stipulated that races be sailed

"with a yacht or vessel propelled by sails alone and that every challenger's boat be designed and constructed in the country of that challenging yacht club, and that each defender's boat be designed and constructed in the defender's country."

The deed has been modified legally to update and clarify conditions for the international matches. For example, in 1962 the word "designed" was construed as allowing the use of a design facility, such as a towing tank, and that the word "built" included components, fittings, and sails. It was also stated that if these items were not obtainable in the country of the challenging club, the New York Yacht Club would consider a request for permission to obtain them in any country other than that of the defending club. But at no time has there been any deviation from Schuyler's basic principle that the cup should represent a nation against nation competition. This should not be confused with Olympic sailing matches, which *are* between nations but are *only* a test of the skills of skippers and crews in boats that can be built and equipped anywhere in the world. United States Olympic teams frequently face foreign competitors who have the best American-made boats and sails. And conversely, United States competition frequently use boats, spars, and sails imported from Europe.

The next three races for the cup might be called the Burgess-Paine, or Boston, period. All three defenders, *Puritan* in 1885, *Mayflower* in 1886, and *Volunteer* in 1887, were designed by Edward Burgess (father of W. Starling Burgess, later designer of *Enterprise* and *Rainbow* and codesigner of *Ranger* with Olin Stephens) and owned either principally or wholly by General Charles J. Paine, of Boston, whose son, Frank Paine, designed the famous cup boat *Yankee* in 1930.

Puritan, Mayflower, and *Volunteer* were typically American centerboard boats, though not of the extreme shallow-draft type of earlier years, and the challengers that raced them—*Genesta, Galatea,* and *Thistle*—were typically deep, narrow British cutters. The nearest any of them came to winning a race was when *Puritan* fouled *Genesta* at a start and the committee told the challenger to go on and sail the course. Sir Richard Sutton,

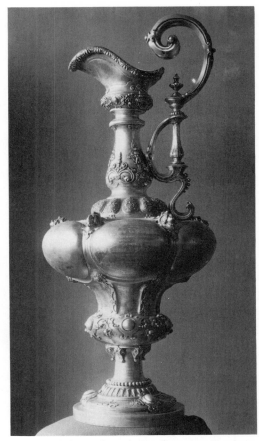

Hundred Guineas Cup—better known as the America's Cup.

Genesta's owner, declined, saying he came for a race, not a sail-over. It was a sporting gesture. *Puritan* took the next two races.

The following year Lieutenant Paddy Henn brought over *Galatea,* which lost two straight to *Mayflower,* and in 1887 *Thistle,* from the Royal Clyde Yacht Club in Scotland, was as summarily disposed of by *Volunteer.*

Six years elapsed, during which Schuyler accommodated the New York Yacht Club by signing a third deed of gift, still in force. This document is pretty airtight if the New York Yacht Club wants to stand on its rights, but it contains a "mutual consent" clause which has been interpreted with increasing liberality to meet modern conditions in a sporting spirit.

Lord Dunraven was the next challenger, with *Valkyrie II* in 1893. With her successful

Four American boats were built for the 1893 America's Cup challenge. Two were designed by Nathanael Herreshoff: *Vigilant* (left) and *Colonia* (right).

opponent, *Vigilant,* began the long ascendancy of Nathanael G. Herreshoff as designer and builder of a long series of cup defenders for New York Yacht Club syndicates headed by C. Oliver Iselin and others. The defender *Vigilant* was of the comparatively modern type with long overhangs, which Herreshoff later developed into the fast but freakish fin-keel type that culminated in the 143-footer *Reliance* in 1903, and which has since been modified into the more normal and desirable but equally speedy Class J yacht. In another respect conditions changed, for all races were held in the open sea, off Sandy Hook, where local knowledge of Lower Bay conditions did not give the defenders any advantage.

Lord Dunraven proved himself a contentious sea lawyer, not to say a chronic belly-acher, even before the first race. When he went home after *Vigilant* had beaten *Valkyrie II* in three straight races—only one of them close—he left a not-too-pleasant impression behind him. He did not really hit the top of his form until 1895, when he came back with *Valkyrie III* to suffer three straight defeats from *Defender.* This time Dunraven accused Oliver Iselin and the New York Yacht Club of practically everything but piracy—cheating on *Defender*'s measurement was just one of the things he charged. Actually, the series should have been close and highly instructive, but it ended in a row due to a protest by the American yacht in the second race; *Valkyrie III* seemingly won by a close margin from *Defender,* crippled through a foul at the start. The handling of the protest was unsatisfactory to Lord Dunraven, and in the final race *Valkyrie III*, starting under lower sails only, withdrew after crossing the starting line and went back to port. Lord Dunraven took his yacht home in a huff. He subsequently charged the club with trickery in the ballasting of the *Defender,* charges which were completely refuted. At the time he made the

charges he was still an honorary member of the club, an honor of which he was later deprived. The controversy with Lord Dunraven was the most serious and regrettable episode in the long history of America's Cup racing.

THE BIG-SCHOONER ERA

Spurred by *America*'s success in England in 1851, another invasion of British waters was made two years later, when the sloop *Silvie,* owned by Louis A. Depau, one of the founders of the New York Yacht Club, sailed across. The records of her visit are incomplete but show that she was defeated by the British cutter *Julia* in a close race. She is said to have been the first racing sloop to cross the Atlantic. Incidentally, *America* was the first *racing* yacht to cross the Atlantic Ocean and call at foreign ports. Unfortunately, however, international sailing was curtailed, first by Britain's Crimean War (1854–1855) and then by the American Civil War (1861–1865).

In 1855, being in failing health and feeling the weight of advancing years, Commodore Stevens, who had led the New York Yacht Club since its founding eleven years before, resigned as senior flag officer. William Edgar, another of the original members, was elected in his stead. Two years later John Cox Stevens passed away and yachting lost one of its most progressive and colorful figures.

Commodore Edgar carried on until 1859, thus continuing the policies of the men who founded the club and carrying on the traditions of what might be called the *Gimcrack* era, after the gallant little vessel in which the club was born. It was in the last year of Edgar's term of office that the club sailed its first real ocean race, the forerunner of many blue-water sailing events that the club has sponsored since then. This was a race around Long Island, starting from off the clubhouse at Elysian Fields, passing out by Sandy Hook, thence around Montauk, with the finish at Throggs Neck, at the western end of the Sound. It was a famous race, with eight starters, four sloops, and four schooners. The entry list is interesting because it marks the passing of the "old guard" of the club's active sailors. Commodore Edgar, with the *Widgeon,* was the only old name on the list, all the others being relative newcomers, who were to carry on the sport thereafter. These included James Gordon Bennett, Jr., son of the owner of the New York *Herald*. He was the first of a new type of yachtsman who were later to dominate the activities of the club with larger and more expensive yachts. Bennett's sloop *Rebecca* was first in this race but she was disqualified for going through Plum Gut instead of through the Race, so the prize went to the sloop *Minna* owned by S. W. Thomas, while W. A. Stebbins' *Silvie* took the trophy for schooners.

As previously stated, all racing was suspended during the Civil War. But once it ended, yachting entered what W. P. Stephens, in his history of American yachting, called the "Big Schooner Era." In fact, the Civil War was hardly over before the big-schooner boys were at it again, and in 1865 the first race to

The inquiry was held in the model room of the NYYC. Here, on December 27, Joseph H. Choate, counsel for Iselin, questions Lord Dunraven (right). The investigating committee ruled that the evidence completely disproved the charges of fraud.

A breezy day outside. *Columbia, Sappho,* and *Palmer.*

Cape May was sailed. This was a match race between J. G. Bennett's schooner *Henrietta* and Franklin Osgood's *Fleetwing,* the course being from Sandy Hook Lightship to Cape May. The latter won, but *Henrietta* sailed two other long races that summer, beating the schooner *Palmer* in one and the *Restless* in the other.

The following year, 1866, saw the first transatlantic yacht race, an outstanding event in yachting history, and one which set a tradition for racing yachts over ocean courses. The affair was the result of a bet, probably made after too much "turtle soup," at the New York Yacht Club, between the Osgood brothers' keel schooner *Fleetwing* and Pierre Lorillard, Jr.'s centerboarder *Vesta,* a new schooner launched that spring, for a race from Sandy Hook Lightship to the Needles, Isle of Wight, England, a distance of some 3,100 miles. On learning of this wager, young James Gordon Bennett applied for admission to the affair, which was accorded him; his entry was the schooner *Henrietta,* built in 1861 and a veteran of the Civil War. In order to be sure of getting enough wind, it was

agreed to sail the race in December and with summer racing rigs. The stakes were $30,000 a boat, winner to take all. Incidentally, the stakes were held by Leonard W. Jerome, maternal grandfather of Winston Churchill.

It was a foolhardy affair—although the starters all completed the course—six seamen were washed overboard at night from the *Fleetwing.* The race started December 11 and was won by the *Henrietta,* sailed by Captain "Bully" Samuels, formerly of the packet ship *Dreadnaught.* The winner finished at 3:55 P.M. Christmas Day, making the crossing in 13 days 21 hours 45 minutes, beating *Fleetwing* by 8 hours 15 minutes, the *Vesta* coming in 40 minutes later.

The vogue for large schooners brought out the *Sappho* in 1868, and she went to England that summer and was badly beaten in a race around the Isle of Wight by James Ashbury's schooner *Cambria* and three other British yachts. It was probably due to this victory that Ashbury made the first challenge for the America's Cup in 1870. As was previously detailed, he lost to the United States schooner *Magic.*

After sailing several races subsequently in our waters, Ashbury left our shores in a friendly spirit, promising to return with another challenge soon, which he did the next year with the schooner *Livonia*. While *Cambria,* a heavy ocean-going vessel, was well beaten, she did have one important "win" to her credit. On her way across the Atlantic to sail for the Cup, she defeated James G. Bennett's schooner *Dauntless* in a close race from Ireland to Sandy Hook. *Cambria* took 23 days on the passage, and *Dauntless* was only 1 hour 17 minutes behind her, in what was the first yacht race across the Atlantic sailed in a westerly direction.

In 1861 James Gordon Bennett, Jr., was elected to the commodoreship of the New York Yacht Club. At that time there were two groups in the club, one made up of those who sailed and raced their own yachts, and were interested in yacht design and the development of types and rigs, and the other composed of owners of the larger yachts who left the handling and the racing of them to their professional skippers and crews. The latter were wealthy men who owned the fleet of great schooners that was making the club and the sport famous, and often they lived aboard their vessels. This group, headed by Bennett, was then in power. It was a colorful group, interested in their own sport rather than in the development of yachting as a whole. It was at this time that the first-mentioned group formed a new yacht club for Corinthian members—sailing enthusiasts who were largely interested in handling their own yachts. Locating on Oyster Bay, Long Island Sound, they called the new organization the Seawanhaka Yacht Club. Many of its members retained their membership in both clubs.

However, Commodore Bennett did much for the club during his commodoreship. Having recently inherited the New York *Herald* from his father, he was able to have this leading newspaper publicize the sport of yachting. The racing among the big schooners of the fleet was spectacular and exciting, and the general public around New York became yachting conscious. All of this helped the sport in general and the prestige of the New York Yacht Club in particular. Besides this, Commodore Bennett was ever ready to do his utmost to promote yachting of every description and spared neither time nor money in these endeavors.

Bennett donated two challenge cups, one known as the Cape May Cup and the other as the Brenton's Reef Challenge Cup, for races over an ocean course, and these were first sailed for in 1872. In 1885 the British cutter *Genesta* won them both and took them to England. The latter was brought back to the club in 1893 by the *Navahoe,* and the Cape May Cup was returned to the club in 1897 by the Prince of Wales after his *Britannia* had won it in 1893. Neither of these cups are in competition today.

Schooners dating from 1851 through 1876 had short rigs with the area of sail spread out fore and aft, rather than high in the air. This put a lot less strain on sails, gear, rigging, spars, and hull. Later schooners were designed with taller rigs which were, naturally, more efficient. Actually, the end of the "big" short-rigged schooner era came with the capsizing of the *Mohawk*. This vessel—in her time considered the largest yacht afloat—was 140 feet long with a 120-foot waterline; her sails covered a distance of 235 feet from the end of her main boom to the tip of her bowsprit. Her main topsail yard was 163 feet from the water's surface. She was aptly described as looking "like a snake with a frog in its belly." On July 20, 1876, while getting under way from her anchorage, she capsized and sank, taking five lives, including the owner William T. Garner and his wife.

It was the fate of the *Mohawk* that really caused the change in the design of the schooner. Eventually, in 1881, the gaff-headed sloop rig appeared in America's Cup competition and sailboat racing in general. From this time through 1920 all Cup contenders used the gaff-headed sloop rig. Hulls became lighter, longer, deeper, and larger. Taller rigs put great strains on the boat and its gear. The mainsail became the main driving sail.

By this, we do not mean that schooners were not popular. But they were smaller and much better designed. Because of his success in designing the America's Cup winners—*Puritan, Mayflower,* and *Volunteer*—Edward Burgess jumped to fame as a designer. While *Mayflower* was being built, the schooner *Sachem* was also taking shape as the first of a large fleet of two-stickers designed by this naval architect, and they furnished fine racing. Most of this fleet were owned by Bostonians, and for this reason the bulk of their racing was done east of Cape Cod. These were *Quickstep, Oenone, Marguerite, Merlin, Constellation,* and others. To these must be added the non-Burgess schooners *Sea Fox, Iroquois,* and the foreign-built *Miranda. Mayflower* and *Volunteer* were also changed to schooners and this great fleet dominated racing for several years, easily outclassing the then-existing schooners.

At the same time that the schooners were making their appearance, Burgess turned out four 40-foot sloops in 1888 that were the first of what was to become a famous class. The next season eleven more "forties" appeared, seven from designs by Burgess, two from the board of McVey, and one each by Cary Smith and William Gardner. In 1890 Burgess brought three more into the class. Perhaps the most famous of these "forties" that linger in memory are the *Babboon* and the *Gossoon,* both owned by that famous yachtsman Charles Francis Adams and his brother George. Altogether eighteen boats were built to the class. The 40-footers were highly important in the history of yachting because among their owners were several men who were to play prominent and important parts in the future—such as Edwin D. Morgan, August Belmont, Royal Phelps Carroll, and Charles H. W. Foster. Also it was in this class that the great professional racing skip-

per Charles Barr won his spurs sailing the British cutter *Minerva* to a long string of victories. Later he was at the helm of many America's Cup defenders.

The forties were followed in 1891 by the 46-foot class, an outgrowth of the former class, which started off with eight boats and one existing yacht, the *Jessica.* Four of these new yachts were by Burgess. It looked as if the class were good for several years of hot racing, but one of the yachts, the only one designed by Nathanael Herreshoff, of Bristol, Rhode Island, proved such a sensation, and so outclassed the others, that she "killed" the class for racing almost at its birth. This was the *Gloriana,* and she and her designer played a revolutionary part in yacht development. In this year also, Edward Burgess died, and a great designer passed into history.

With *Gloriana* the talents of Herreshoff became known to yachtsmen, and the following year the Bristol designer brought out *Wasp,* to the same 46-foot class, and she was a distinct improvement on the earlier yacht. These two remarkable boats discouraged active racing in the class, though *Wasp* and *Gloriana* had many private battles for some years to come, and Nathanael Herreshoff became the favorite designer with major yachtsmen. His success with the big America's Cup defender *Vigilant,* which beat *Valkyrie II* in 1893, brought him international fame, and for twenty-seven years every Cup challenger was defeated by a Herreshoff creation.

START OF SMALL-BOAT SAILING

While the period from the end of the Civil War to the turn of the century, as noted previously, is often called the era of the big schooners, it was also the start of small-boat sailing. In fact, the sandbagger was the first small-boat type that found wide popularity among people who were not necessarily "swells," or yacht-club members of means. Wealth and yachts do complement one another, but there also are ways to find pleasure on the water at a minimal expense. Sandbagger sailors were among the first Americans to discover this—and to reap the benefits.

The sandbagger was a shallow, wide-beam,

centerboard sloop carrying a tremendous amount of sail, and the resulting problem of ballasting gave the craft its name. Canvas or burlap bags of sand, weighing fifty pounds each, were carried on deck and shifted from side to side by the crew as the boat tacked. The sandbags prevented the boat from tipping over, and the technique required a strong, numerous, and indefatigable crew. Actually the sandbagger was directly related to a work boat, the so-called New York sloop, which was used as a fishing vessel for almost half a century. The New York boats were developed in the 1830's, once the centerboard had been accepted as a safe and sane feature for craft sailed in shallow waters. The model spread rapidly. By the 1880's, with the growth of the fisheries, the shoal centerboard sloop—New York style—could be found all along the Atlantic Coast, in the Gulf of Mexico, and in San Francisco Bay.

The pleasure sandbagger was the national type of small sailboat in America in the last half of the nineteenth century, and its kind spread from the northeast coast into southern waters and the lakes of the Middle West. Its rig was simple: a jib, a gaff-rigged mainsail with a long, long boom reaching far beyond the square stern, and a bowsprit almost as lengthy. Half of the hull was decked over, and the cockpit had a U-shaped bench around the sides and across the stern to provide sitting room for the big crew. The beam was great; there was plenty of room for pleasure sailing or racing on protected waters.

The sandbagger, then, was the ancestor of today's small, inexpensive boat, such as the sailing dinghy. And among those Americans who had little time or money for pleasure boats, the sandbagger prospered because it served two purposes: fishing and yachting. Many a vessel with shortened rig spent its weekdays oystering or tending fish lines, and its weekends as a racing machine.

The catboat, another popular small sailboat and a type existing to this day, had similar work-boat origins. The catboat first appeared on Narragansett Bay and flourished in New England waters, notably off Cape Cod, beginning in the 1870's. The catboat differed from the sandbagger in having a sensible rig: a single, moderate-sized mainsail provided the propulsion. It was so simple that the thick, strong mast had no shrouds for support and just a single headstay. The hull was fat, and centerboard-equipped, like the sandbagger, but considerably more rounded and not nearly so beamy. This made for a more seaworthy vessel, a safe, practical sailer for the workingman.

A traditional difficulty of the yachting fraternity is its constitutional inability to let well enough alone. The sight of something inherently good often stirs an impulse to improve it. So it was with the catboat. Objections centered on its slowness in light air, and the speed-up remedies were numerous. The cats

began to take on the vicious sailing characteristics of the older sandbaggers. Beginning around 1900, more sail was added, resulting in taller masts and longer booms and gaffs. In extreme cases the main boom extended so far beyond the stern that the boat had to be brought alongside a pier or another vessel in order to reef the mainsail; it was the only way the outermost reef points could be reached and tied. The graceful curves gradually disappeared and "catboat" came to mean a powerful box-shaped hull with a large outboard rudder. It was an extremely swift sailing craft on protected waters, but look out in a squall! Capsizing was common and sailors occasionally drowned.

Sailing soon acquired a poor reputation and was viewed as a dangerous sport by nonnautical people. The catboat fell into disrepute, and around 1925 began a decline in popularity that has continued unabated. There is nothing wrong, however, with the kind of catboat that follows sensible design: moderate beam, round bottom, small sail area, and small rudder. This breed of catboat will always have friends who swear by it.

A third type of small boat popular in America over the last thirty-five years of the nineteenth century was the canoe, and for that we owe thanks to a retired British army officer, Captain John Macgregor, who was a courageous sailor and a prolific writer on the subject of his accomplishments afloat. In 1865 he built the first of a long series of canoes called *Rob Roy*. This one was a 15-footer of the Eskimo kayak type, and Macgregor paddled her about the English Channel to the surprise of many who expected he would drown.

Macgregor found a ready market for his published adventures, and he expanded them, traveling in various *Rob Roys* through the rivers and canals of Europe. His trips and his prose enjoyed a big following, and when the captain paddled through town he attracted large, cheering crowds. He was widely read in America, and the popularity of canoeing shot upward in the 1870's and 1880's. Adventure and economy seemed to be the appeal. In *Forest and Stream*, the leading outdoor magazine of the era, yachting editor W. P. Stephens wrote that one could "cruise under sail or paddle, according to weather, carrying stores, a tent, bedding, to a canoe club rendezvous." Sail and paddle races were the attraction at the rendezvous, followed by a cruise home.

Stephens was an avid canoeist and supporter of the New York Canoe Club, which was founded in 1871, six years after the Royal Canoe Club inspired by Macgregor in England. Like Macgregor, Stephens found an audience for articles on the sport. *Forest and Stream* and Stephens published page after page of build-it-yourself plans and advice, and the double-ended, 15-foot sailing canoe with twin masts and sails enjoyed a vogue. *Forest and Stream* told how it could be built out of wood and canvas for $15.

The popularity of canoeing established a rapport between British and American yachtsmen, a communication that resulted in the founding of a racing event for small boats that gained wide renown. The prize was the Seawanhaka International Challenge Trophy, a $500 silver cup that became to some yachtsmen every bit as important as the America's Cup.

In 1895 William Willard Howard of the New York Canoe Club learned through correspondence that J. Arthur Brand of England's Minima Yacht Club planned to bring to this country his small sailboat, *Spruce III.* Howard and several of his friends thought it would be fitting to entertain Brand with a series of races. Members of the Seawanhaka Corinthian Yacht Club at Oyster Bay obliged and put up the challenge trophy. The series would be on a match basis, the prizes going to the boat winning three out of five races. Alternate windward-leeward and triangular courses, each twelve miles long, were to be run by competing boats.

By the late 1880's there had developed on England's Solent a full range of small yachts that raced and were rated by a simple formula: $L \times SA \div 6,000$. L equaled the boat's waterline length and SA its sail area. The formula separated different boats into classes called half-rater, single-rater, twin-rater, and $2\frac{1}{2}$-rater. The general dimensions of the half-rater were a boat with a waterline length of 15 feet and a sail area of 200 square feet since L (15) times SA (200) divided by 6,000 equaled $\frac{1}{2}$. By this formula, Brand's boat, *Spruce III,* was a half-rater.

There were no comparable small sailing craft in America, and six new boats were built for the Seawanhaka Cup races under a rating rule similar to the English one. Class designations in accordance with this rule were worked out as follows: the sum of the waterline length plus the square root of the sail area divided in half. For example, a boat with a 15-foot length and a sail area of 225 square feet would have a rating of 15, based on the equation $\frac{15 + \sqrt{225}}{2} = 15$. Consequently, instead of half-raters, the American boats were referred to as 15-footers.

By the summer of 1895, when he finally appeared on the scene, Brand had supplanted *Spruce III* with a new contender, *Spruce IV,* which was also a half-rater. After some trial races, a shoal centerboard yacht called *Ethelwynn* was chosen to race the English invader. W. P. Stephens had designed and hastily built *Ethelwynn,* and she won the Seawanhaka Cup, three races to two.

Seawanhaka Cup competition was thus launched and it quickly bloomed, even though a Canadian, G. Herrick Duggan, was to dominate it through the first decade of its existence. (The deed of gift for the Seawanhaka Cup followed that of the America's Cup, and a recognized yacht club of any foreign nation could challenge.) Duggan challenged in 1896, the year following the cup's inception, and he represented the Royal St. Lawrence Yacht Club of Montreal. His yacht *Glencairn* won the prize by taking three straight races from the defender, *El Heirie,* designed and sailed by Clinton Crane, a twenty-three-year-old naval architect two years out of Harvard.

The trials to select the defender had been run off Oyster Bay, and the entry list showed how rapidly the club system had grown. There were twenty-eight original starters in the trials representing seventeen different yacht clubs spread from Fall River, Massachusetts, to Brooklyn, New York.

After *El Heirie,* a wide, flat scow with a sharp bow, had won the trials, Crane had a finisher from the Steinway piano company come out from New York to work on the boat's bottom prior to the cup series. After all, the bottom was mahogany, like the top of a Steinway grand, and Crane hoped for a superlatively smooth, easy-riding finish. The Steinway man did an excellent job, but *El Heirie* was no competition for *Glencairn*. The Canadian scow was shorter on the waterline and it carried more sail. Furthermore, the hull was lighter and the sails had better shapes. The result was more speed on almost every point of sailing.

The original scows were copied from the bateau type of hull, with its flat floor and sides, and square bilges. It soon became evident that if the flat floor were given a rocker shape from bow to stern, the waterline length might be made very short. But if the boat were inclined in the water on one edge, by means of such movable ballast as a crewman weighing 200 pounds, then the actual waterline would be greatly increased. And it was an axiom in boats that the longer the waterline, the greater the speed. At the same time, the heeling of the hull served to reduce the width of the boat that was actually in the water, a condition satisfying another requirement for speed: reduction of the wetted surface of the hull, minimizing resistance.

The result, with a heeling scow, was a long, narrow, canoe-shaped hull going through the water rather than a wide, square box, as is the case with a conventional hull, such as a catboat's. When a conventional sloop or catboat is at rest on a mooring, the hull's waterline is at maximum. Not so with a scow. When at anchor, the rocker-shaped hull has its minimum waterline.

Duggan was among the first to appreciate these factors, and others, like Crane, copied his scow designs. Eventually, extreme scows were evolved, boats that could be heeled safely at a much greater angle than desirable in normal yachts. W. P. Stephens, who disapproved of scows as being "unhealthy" types, described the Seawanhaka Cup scows of the late 1890's as "the most grotesque collection of craft ever seen in civilized waters." But his asperity went unheeded. Success commanded respect and inspired emulation.

Duggan managed to stay ahead of the United States challengers as the Royal St. Lawrence Yacht Club successfully defended the Seawanhaka Cup year after year. *Dominion,* Duggan's defender of 1898, had an overall length of 37 feet, but a waterline length of a mere 17½ feet.

Small boats made their entry in sailing circles in the age of big yachts, but they really made their advance after the turn of the century.

THE BIRTH OF THE ONE-DESIGN

The term "one-design" for sailboats means that all boats of the class have been constructed to the same set of specifications and measurements. In other words, each boat in a class is as similar to her sister ship in sailing characteristics and dimensions as possible. This means that within a class success in racing depends upon the skill of the skipper rather than upon his ability to pay for expensive refinements built into his craft. It also means you may race in competition on an even basis—no handicapping system required.

The principle of one-design had been known since the 1890's, but it was not until 1900 that the idea aroused interest and was given support. In that year the first of the New York Yacht Club's one-design classes came into being. This was composed of the four famous 70-footers that furnished excel-

lent racing for a few years and were followed by five other one-design classes during the next thirty years. These did much to increase interest in racing at a time when open class racing yachts were being rapidly outbuilt. The "seventies" were the largest size sloops of one design ever produced. They were designed and built at Herreshoff's and were owned by five prominent members of the club, Vice Commodore August Belmont, Cornelius Vanderbilt, William K. Vanderbilt, Jr., and Harry Payne Whitney in partnership with Herman B. Duryea. In its first season the class did most of its racing off Newport, where it was the chief attraction of the club cruise that year, and one of the yachts, August Belmont's *Mineola,* won the Astor Cup for sloops. The other three were named *Rainbow, Virginia,* and *Yankee.*

The one-design idea was further stimulated

Two early stars—*Astrea* (118) and *Corona* (117) race on English Bay, Vancouver, Canada.

a few years later when, in 1905, the club sponsored and Nat Herreshoff turned out the celebrated class of thirty-footers, which was to provide some of the finest small-boat racing ever seen and was destined to become famous the world over. Eighteen of these speedy and seaworthy little yachts were built for members of the club. The class was raced for many years, and there are several of them around and still racing.

The biggest advancement in one-design boat theory, however, came in 1922, with the founding of the Star Class Association of America by George A. Corry. Actually, at the instigation of Corry and his friends around Port Washington, a man named Francis Sweisguth drew the lines for the Star in 1911, generally copying and enlarging on the Bug, a little sloop introduced in 1907. Sweisguth was a designer in the naval architecture firm of William Gardner, and although Sweisguth's name is not associated with any other yachting designs, he did nobly with the Star.

The hull was 22 feet 7½ inches long and its characteristics were a low freeboard, hard chines, a slightly rounded bottom, and a thin fin keel with a cast-iron bulb at the base weighing from 870 to 900 pounds. The hull is the same to this day, and Stars are raced all over the world in greater numbers than

ever before. Other dimensions are a beam of 5 feet 8¼ inches (4 feet 6 inches at the chine) and a draft of 3 feet 4 inches.

The rigging has been modernized twice. Originally, Stars had a gaff mainsail. This was changed in 1915 to a short Marconi rig, eliminating the gaff, and in 1930 to a taller Marconi rig. The boom overhanging the stern was cut down, and the rig brought entirely inboard. Two hundred eighty square feet of sail is now supported on a slender wood or aluminum mast stayed with the lightest stainless-steel wire. The Star has a tiny cockpit for the helmsman and single crew. In heavy weather it is a wet boat, and it has never been anything except a racing machine.

Between 1911 and 1922, 111 Stars were built and raced on Long Island Sound, Narragansett Bay, Lake Erie, the Detroit River, and, for the first time in 1922, on the West Coast at Los Angeles. The class organization had been perfected largely by Corry's friend George Elder. The boats were divided into local fleets. A measurement rule was written. A monthly magazine and a yearbook were published. And the class provided its own organization in running regattas, taking over from yacht clubs, which up to that time never had to cope with running races for dozens of evenly matched yachts.

Barnegat Bay Sneakbox.

International Canoe.

The first national championship between winners of local fleet eliminations was held in 1922, and Stars became international with the establishment of a fleet at Vancouver, British Columbia, in 1923. Soon there were fleets at Havana, Cuba; New Zealand; Pearl Harbor, Hawaii; England's Solent; and Cannes, France. By 1931 Stars were also racing in Venezuela, Algeria, Germany, the Scandinavian countries, Switzerland, Spain, Portugal, and Italy.

The success of the Star has inspired other one-design classes in the years since 1911. In 1921 the Cape Cod Shipbuilding Company of Wareham, Massachusetts, began producing an 18-foot centerboard sloop called the Cape Cod Baby Knockabout. It was designed by the founder of the company, Charles Gurney, and it proved to be a good performer and a safe one. The Knockabouts were almost impossible to tip over. When a gust hit, they would heel far enough to spill the wind out of the sails, then come up again and head into the wind. Small rudders helped. They came out of the water when the boat heeled over, so that it naturally headed up to windward. The materials were excellent. The hull was framed of white oak and planked in white cedar. Nothing was fancy about these sloops, not even the price. The company turned them out by the hundreds, the price at one point going as low as $175. And if the purchaser wished to sail down Buzzards Bay from the factory, he was given a "sail-away" box lunch, gratis.

The Barnegat Bay Sneakbox was another early one-design class. It evolved from the early nineteenth-century Sneakboxes used for shallow-water gunning by duck hunters. The name probably came from the term "sink-box," meaning a floating duckblind which, when camouflaged with marsh grass, could be used to sneak up on unwary ducks. J. Howard Perrine produced a formal design in the early 1900's, a 15-foot gaff-rigged centerboard sloop that weighed only 350 pounds and could sail in as little as six inches of water. In subsequent years over 3,000 boats of this type were sold, but no national association was ever formed to promote them. The successor boat, the 14-foot Sneakbox, is a modern one-design class on New Jersey's Barnegat Bay.

The American Canoe Association, founded in 1880, established rules for decked sailing canoes and some uniformity of design. In the early 1890's a man named Paul Butler developed some features for canoes, which later became standard on many small one-design sailboats. He invented the thwartship sliding seat for hiking, so that the weight of the helmsman could serve as stabilizing ballast when the seat projected out of the hull. He put a crosshead extension on the tiller so the boat could be steered at the windward end of the hiking seat. He developed an "automatic" jam cleat that eliminated the slower and somewhat clumsy technique of tying half-hitch knots to secure sheets. And he made the cockpits self-bailing, so that water taken inboard ran out of the boat.

Nat Herreshoff, who could produce an excellent design for any type of vessel, drew the lines and built the Herreshoff Twelves, fat little gaff-rigged sloops that came out in 1914 as a one-design class. They were 15 feet 8½ inches long (12 feet on the waterline). The Twelves became popular on Buzzards Bay. Their modern successor is known as the Bull's Eye class, and it carries on as a $2,000 fiberglass boat.

One of the most popular one-design classes, the Snipe, appeared in 1931, and boat number 15,000 was built in 1969. The beginning came at a meeting of the West Coast Racing Association at Sarasota, Florida, in March, 1931. The delegates decided the time had come to introduce a small boat which could be trailered about the state much the same as outboard racing hulls were. William F. Crosby, of *Rudder* magazine, was present and he promised to deliver such a design. In the July issue of the magazine the plans appeared and the boat was called the Snipe in keeping with *Rudder*'s policy of naming all boats it introduced after sea birds. Crosby received credit for the design, and the issue in which it appeared was soon out of print.

A fourteen-year-old boy named Jimmy Brown, of Pass Christian, Mississippi, built the first Snipe with the help of his father and was given Number 1. The Snipe was intended to be home-built for under $100. It is 15½ feet long, with a centerboard, weighs 440

pounds, and has a sail area of 116 square feet in a sloop rig. When racing, it is sailed by two people. The Snipe design spread rapidly; by 1971 there were more than 510 fleets in thirty-two nations.

The Comet class began the year after the Snipes, in 1932. C. Lowndes Johnson of Easton, Maryland, was asked by Mrs. Elliott Wheeler to design a small sailboat for her sons, one that would be inexpensive, easy to handle, and competitive enough for the handicap races at nearby Oxford. Ralph Wiley built the first one in Oxford for $120. *Yachting* magazine published the plans and Dr. John Eiman and Dr. Wilbur Haines introduced the boat to their summer resort, Stone Harbor, New Jersey. They also founded the national class organization and helped promote the popularity of Comets, increasing their number into the thousands.

The Comet is like a small Star (except that it has a centerboard instead of a keel) and was called in its early days the Star Junior. Its overall length is 16 feet, sail area 130 square feet, weight not less than 300 pounds.

Sailing in Knockabouts, Stars, Snipes, Comets, and other one-design classes became very popular in the early 1930's, and many boatowners wished that the season could be extended beyond the traditional closing date in the fall. It was several such die-hards, gathered in the men's bar of the Larchmont Yacht Club on a hot July afternoon, who planted the seeds of the first "frostbite" regatta. One challenged another to a race in sailing dinghies on New Year's Day and was accepted. As the months passed and word of the event went around, others clamored to be let in. They were. The first regatta took place on January 2, 1932, off the Knickerbocker Yacht Club in Manhasset Bay, off Long Island Sound. Since that time frostbite regattas (see page 367) have been a popular sport for one-design sailors in cold-weather regions.

OCEAN RACING BECOMES THE THING

Ocean racing became popular in the early 1900's, too. This was due in part to Captain Joshua Slocum's famous around-the-world trip in a 37-foot sloop, the *Spray*. Sailing by

himself, Slocum left Boston on April 24, 1895, and arrived at Newport, Rhode Island, on June 27, 1898. A few days later, the Yankee shipmaster arrived back at his starting spot.

In 1900 his book, *Sailing Alone Around the World,* was published. It was a success and it served to impress Joshua Slocum's mark on the world of men, ships, and the sea. He inspired many others to take to the sea on long, romantic voyages, and in every decade since there have been sailors scattered all over the world, sailing about in small boats. Most profess to have read Slocum, but few have been as able seamen as he. A number have lost their lives trying to be.

Just after the turn of the century, the New York Yacht Club was largely responsible for the success of the fastest ocean yacht race ever sailed, when it handled the American end of a race from Sandy Hook to the Lizard, England, in 1905, for a trophy put up by Kaiser Wilhelm II—at that time not as unpopular as he became nine years later when Germany entered World War I.

The race brought together eleven yachts, representing three nations, ranging from the ship-rigged *Valhalla* to the schooner *Fleur de Lys,* smallest entry in the fleet. Eight of these were American yachts, all flying the NYYC burgee, two were British, and the schooner *Hamburg* was also British but German-owned and sailed. Starting on May 17, the race was sailed in record time, the big three-masted schooner *Atlantic,* owned by Wilson Marshall, winning in 12 days 4 hours, from start to finish, over a course of 3,014 nautical miles. This record has stood unbeaten for sixty years. Incidentally, the Kaiser's trophy, supposedly of gold, was given by Marshall to the Red Cross during the trying days of World War I, to be sold to provide funds for that organization of mercy. It is said to have netted $125,000 as the result of several auctions for it. Later, it was broken up and, instead of pure gold, it was said to be gold-plated over a base metal.

Thomas Fleming Day, the famous editor of *Rudder,* organized the first Bermuda Race in 1906, but he obtained only three entries— *Tamerlane, Gauntlett,* and *Lila.* The three contenders left Gravesend Bay in Brooklyn on May 25. *Lila,* a 40-foot yawl, was dismasted in a squall shortly after the start and put back to refit. *Tamerlane,* a 38-foot yawl, returned with her, but not *Gauntlett. Gauntlett* was a 28-foot cutter sailed by a crew of three—Mr. and Mrs. George W. Robinson

and John W. Dunlap. The threesome failed to see the dismasting and so pressed on to Bermuda, 675 miles to the southeast.

Tamerlane and *Lila* started out again three days later, but *Lila* quit after two days. Surprisingly enough, *Tamerlane* won the race, finishing a whole day ahead of *Gauntlett,* which had experienced a hard, stormy passage. *Tamerlane*'s time was 126 hours 9 minutes. The Bermuda Race record—set in 1956 over a slightly shorter course by *Bolero,* a 73-foot yawl—is 70 hours 11 minutes 40 seconds. In fifty years, the track record was lowered by 56 hours.

Twelve entries started the second Bermuda Race in 1907, but it did not catch on as an annual event. And finally after the 1910 race, which showed only two starters, it was abandoned. In 1923 the race was revived and the response was good. From then on it flourished as no other ocean race has.

The 1923 Bermuda fleet enlisted seventeen schooners, three yawls, one ketch, and one cutter. All were gaff-rigged except a New York Forty called *Memory,* which had the relatively new and untried Marconi rig. Many were sure she could not stand a good blow and that her mast would come down before she cleared the Gulf Stream. It did not.

The winner was *Malabar IV,* a schooner designed and owned by John Alden, a naval architect from Boston. Alden sailed in thirteen Bermuda Races—his first in 1910, his last in 1954—and won three outright: with *Malabar IV* in 1923, *Malabar VII* in 1926, and *Malabar X* in 1932. In all, he built thirteen *Malabar*s for himself, each of which was sold to one of a crowd of eager customers at the end of the season.

On the West Coast, the "big" ocean race is the Transpacific—2,225 miles from California to Hawaii. It began the same year as the Bermuda—1906—and like the Bermuda it did not flourish at first. There was a hiatus between 1913 and 1922, and the event was not put on its regular biennial basis until 1926. There was a race to Tahiti from San Francisco in 1925. This was a course of 3,700 miles. The longest "normal" ocean race so far held—4,200 miles each—were the races from Havana, Cuba, to San Sebastian, Spain, in 1951 and 1955. However, in 1969 there was a round the world single-handed race held over a distance of more than 30,000 miles.

The idea for the Tahiti race started at a lunch in the San Francisco Yacht Club one day in November, 1924. L. A. Norris made the proposal, and by dessert there were three entries. A fourth was added later, and away they went on June 10, 1925. The competitors were the 107-foot Norris schooner, *Mariner; Eloise,* an 85-foot schooner; *Idalia,* a 75-foot schooner; and *Shawnee,* a 73-foot ketch. Norris, who had sailed to Tahiti many times, took issue with the sailing charts that recommended a course to the east of the Pacific's feared doldrums. These are a vast area of calm and cat's-paws, broken by occasional thunder squalls, that overlaps the direct route to Tahiti. Instead of bearing east to avoid it, Norris sailed *Mariner* right through the doldrums, thereby gaining the advantage of the shortest great-circle route. He reached Tahiti in 20 days 11 hours—a full week ahead of the second boat, *Idalia.*

The Middle West's "ocean" race, from Chicago to Mackinac Island, 333 miles up Lake Michigan, is even older than the Transpacific or Bermuda events. The first one was held in 1898. As with the Transpac, the yachts in the early years were imports bought from eastern owners, at first large schooners and sloops. In the 1890's the Chicago yachtsmen often cruised to Mackinac Island and the islands adjacent to the Straits of Mackinac. In the winter of 1898 several skippers were sitting around a potbellied stove at the Chicago Yacht Club and boasting about how fast they could sail to Mackinac. Challenges and counterchallenges brought about the first race that summer. There were two sloops and three schooners; the winner was William Cameron's sloop *Vanenna.* The event was sailed on a boat-for-boat basis without handicaps, and *Vanenna*'s elapsed time came to 51 hours.

The race was not run again until 1904, when the Chicago Yacht Club made it an annual affair. The big topsail sloops won most of the prizes, particularly *Vencedor,* owned by Fred Price of the Columbia Yacht Club. *Vencedor* had a disastrous ending, however, running aground on Fisherman's Island, off Charlevoix, Michigan, during a whole gale

in the 1911 race. A powerboat took the crew off safely. That also was the year the 100-foot schooner *Amorita* set an elapsed-time record of 31 hours 14 minutes 30 seconds.

The 1911 passage, which saw the wind reach a measured hurricane velocity of 82 miles per hour, dampened the ardor of Lake Michigan yachtsmen, and entries fell off after that. Only five boats competed in 1914 and seven in 1916. The race was suspended during World War I and revived in 1921, continuing each year since, and even running through World War II.

The Chicago-Mackinac and its sister race in Lake Huron—the Port Huron, Michigan–Mackinac Island event—have presented to yachtsmen every variety of weather from long calms to exasperating squalls and damaging gales. Only eight of forty-two starters were able to finish the 1937 Chicago-Mackinac Race, owing to a 75-mile-per-hour storm. Those who have sailed in the oceans and on the Great Lakes say that they cannot tell the difference when the wind blows up, except for the taste of the water slamming into their faces.

On the Southern Ocean-Racing Circuit the water is definitely salty, but it also can be warm. The original race, organized principally for northern yachtsmen vacationing in the South during the winter, was from St. Petersburg, Florida, to Havana, first run in 1930. This 284-mile event was climaxed by a gala welcome in Havana, but the coming of Fidel Castro's government has changed all that. Since 1960 the race has been run around the Florida peninsula, outside the Keys, then north to Fort Lauderdale, a distance of 403 miles.

An event claimed by many yachtsmen to be the best ocean race of all is the 184-mile Miami-Nassau contest. Instead of a straight-line course, such as those run in the Bermuda and Transpacific races, the Miami-Nassau has three legs to it, with turning marks at Great Isaacs light and Great Stirrup light to add zest. The Miami-Nassau event was first run in 1934, and like the St. Petersburg-Havana competition, almost all the contenders were yachts from the Great Lakes or the Northeast that were wintering in the South.

THE AMERICA'S CUP CONTINUES ON

While racing in smaller boats was the trend in the period from 1900 to 1941, the "big" prize in all sailing was still the America's Cup. After the Lord Dunraven affair in 1895, it was a pleasant surprise to the New York Yacht Club when Sir Thomas Lipton came forward with a challenge for a race in 1899. Subsequently, Lipton became something of a burr in the yacht club's hair, but they were glad to see him when he brought the first *Shamrock* over and lost three races to *Columbia*.

After that it got to be sort of a habit. Lipton would build a new *Shamrock* and send her over, and the New York Yacht Club would beat her. The old *Columbia* won the trials

against the new American boat and defeated *Shamrock II* in 1901, and the huge fin-keeler *Reliance* with her 17,000 square feet of sail, turned back *Shamrock III*'s challenge in 1903.

After that came the longest gap since the first challenge—1903 to 1914. Meanwhile yachting progressed. The extreme fin-keelers had been legislated out and the Universal Rule framed to produce a more useful all-around type of boat. Amateurs had come to the fore instead of the old professional racing skippers, many of whom, including the famous Charley Barr, had died.

Lipton's fourth challenge came in 1914, and the boats were ready to go into the Cup series when the war broke out. They were

Resolute defeats *Shamrock IV*.

laid up, and it was not until 1920 that the challenge was renewed and *Resolute* and *Shamrock IV* came to the line. Amateurs were in command for the first time, Sir William Burton in *Shamrock* and Charles Francis Adams in *Resolute*. For the first time in history it looked as though the perennial fear that the challenger had the best boat might be well grounded. *Shamrock IV* took the first race when *Resolute*'s halyard broke and won the second by two and a half minutes. Then Adams took two races. The day of what would have been the deciding race the wind was blowing pretty hard—not too hard for real boats, but these racing machines were pretty fragile.

The experts generally agreed that *Shamrock* would have stood up better and gone faster in the hard going, but when the committee asked Lipton if he would agree to a postponement (which suited *Resolute*'s afterguard very well) he assented. That cooked his goose, for when they did hold that race the breeze was light and *Resolute* won it easily. It was the closest call the New York Yacht Club ever had in defending the Cup.

Ten years later, in 1930, Lipton made a last attempt. The season was marked chiefly by the close racing of the four American boats—*Enterprise, Weetamoe, Yankee,* and *Whirlwind*—in the trials and by Harold S. Vanderbilt's eventual triumph with *Enterprise*. When it came to the Cup series the highly touted *Shamrock V* turned out to be a dud. She could not touch *Enterprise* under any conditions and her crew apparently did not even bother to try very hard once they saw how things were going.

The race marked several advances in yachting, however. For the first time J class yachts were employed. That is, the boats were designed to the J class rule, which specified a load waterline of from 75 to 87 feet with a rating not to exceed 76 feet. With yachts built to exactly the same rating, time allowances were eliminated, making more interesting racing for the contestants and a much better show for the crowd. Also the boats had to be built to Lloyd's scantling requirements, which meant that both hulls had to be amply strong and heavy for ocean work, thus eliminating the challenger's previous disadvantage of having to build a boat heavy enough to stand the

The J boat *Shamrock V*.

ocean passage while the defender could be skinned down on weight. In 1930 the ocean courses off Newport were adopted to get away from steamer traffic and other undesirable conditions off Sandy Hook. Much of the secrecy that had hitherto surrounded challenger and defender were swept aside, and designers and skippers exchanged ideas and visits before the races.

It is interesting to note that when *Shamrock V* lost her last race for the America's Cup to the *Enterprise,* a spontaneous outpouring of good will toward Thomas Lipton resulted in a flood of dollars to buy him a loving cup bigger than the one he would have got if he had won. Within ten days many thousands of dollars had come in, and two months later the Tiffany-designed cup surmounted by Shamrock leaves was ready. The inscription read: "In the name of the hundreds and thousands of Americans and well-wishers of Sir Thomas Johnstone Lipton, Bart., K.C.V.O."

Enterprise of 1930 was also very important in the development of yachting. Both she and *Shamrock V,* the last boat backed by Sir

Sir Thomas Johnstone Lipton.

Thomas Lipton, carried jib-headed rigs, the first in America's Cup racing. *Enterprise* was called a mechanical ship by virtue of the extent to which she used below-deck winches, but an innovation which became the norm was her use of an aluminum-alloy mast. Her ultralight spar was a major contribution to her success, bringing her to the top in the final trial series off Newport. Hardly a boat is built today without a light-alloy spar.

Enterprise also carried a wide "Park Avenue" boom, while *Shamrock V* carried a tranversely bending boom. Both controlled the draft in the lower part of the mainsail. Actually the history of these booms suggests a slightly ironic phase of yacht design, reflected in a saying about "greener grass." In the succeeding match between *Rainbow* and *Endeavour* in 1934, it was the American *Rainbow* which carried the bending boom and the English *Endeavour* had the "Park Avenue" type. *Rainbow* contributed rod rigging to the technical history of the sport. This has since become almost universally adopted in larger boats intended primarily for racing.

For the 1934 series T. O. M. Sopwith appeared on the scene as the new English challenger, and he brought over the boat *Endeavour,* designed by Charles E. Nicholson, that was far faster than anything of her class ever seen. Vanderbilt had *Rainbow*, which was not nearly as fast as *Endeavour*. *Endeavour* won two races straight, and the Cup seemed to be bound abroad. But Sopwith was not the skipper that Vanderbilt was and he did not have as good a crew. Mistakes in tactics and inferior helmsmanship cost Sopwith races he should have won, and an incident involving a protest which the New York Yacht Club disallowed did not improve the state of his mind and nerves. When it was over he found himself bound for home with a faster boat but without the Cup.

He shouldered the blame for the fiasco (without entirely forgiving Vanderbilt and the New York Yacht Club over the disposition of the protest), built *Endeavour II,* a faster boat than *Endeavour,* and came back in 1937. But the results were more decisive. *Ranger,* Harold Vanderbilt's yacht, turned back *Endeavour II,* four races to none. With the 1937 series, sixteen matches had been sailed for the famous trophy since 1870. In these sixteen matches a total of fifty completed races were sailed. Of these, forty-five were won by the various American defenders, the remaining five being divided as follows: one to *Livonia* (1871), two to *Shamrock IV* (1920), and two to *Endeavour* (1934). Most of the American victories were by a wide margin. *Genesta* (1885) lost a fairly close race, and *Shamrock II* (1901) lost two that were really close. One of *Valkyrie II's* (1893) defeats was also close, while all of the *Rainbow-Endeavour* races (1934) were close. As regards protests, there were only three up through 1937, not counting the disqualification of the *Puritan* in the 1885 series, which the challenger refused to accept. All in all, fifty races with but three protests was quite a record.

One last invasion of British waters was to occur before war put a stop to the sport. This was when Vanderbilt took his new 12-Meter *Vim* to England in 1939, to race her against the British Twelves. Here he met T. O. M. Sopwith's *Tomahawk* and several other good British 12-Meter yachts. *Vim*'s overseas record was nearly as good as that of *Ranger* here in 1937. Luckily, the English racing season finished in time for *Vim* to leave Britain on her return trip before Hitler invaded Poland. On her arrival here she raced in September against a fine trio of Twelves, *Nyala, Seven Seas,* and *Gleam.* This class carried on for another season and then the proximity of war ended all racing except in the one-design small classes.

AFTER WORLD WAR II

During the twenty years that passed before the next challenge, there were many suggestions to revive America's Cup competition. The large Universal Rule boats had become too expensive to build and keep in racing shape—the J's in particular. An amendment ordered by the Supreme Court of the State of New York changed the deed of gift in 1956 to bring America's Cup contenders down to practical postwar size. Since yachts of the 12-Meter class had a minimum waterline length of approximately 44 feet, it seemed impractical and unnecessarily limiting to require the challenger to "sail on her own bottom" to the match. This was the major change in the original agreement between George L. Schuyler (then the sole surviving owner of the Cup) and the New York Yacht Club. Otherwise, the deed stands as it was written in 1887.

In the 1958 Cup series off Newport, *Columbia* defeated the British challenger *Sceptre* with relative ease—four races to zero. The next challenge—in 1962—came from the Royal Sydney Yacht Club on behalf of a syndicate headed by Sir Frank Packer. The Australian *Gretel* made a good fight of the series, winning one race from the defender *Weatherly* and coming close in another.

One serious handicap the challenger has been faced with is the lack of adequate competition prior to the match. Each of the defenders since 1881 has engaged in a serious elimination series before being selected. These have ranged from a brief three-race series to the summer-long series of preliminary, observation, and final trials we have today. To overcome this handicap, the British had an elimination series in the waters off Newport in 1964. It was a hotly contested battle between *Sovereign* and *Kurrewa V.* Unfortunately for them, both boats were the same and there was no clear yardstick against which they could measure their performance. Both boats were clearly inferior to any of the potential defenders, so the elimination series was meaningless. Actually, *Constellation,* the American defender, won the series four to zero and by such overwhelming margins that the victory lost some of its flavor. In fact, *Sovereign*—the challenger—set a record, losing one race by 20 minutes 24 seconds, the worst drubbing in cup race history since 1866.

The 1967 series between Australia's *Dame Pattie* and United States' *Intrepid* was another easy victory for the defender. But the 1970 match between *Intrepid* and *Gretel II* was a different story. As one writer stated, "Australia has given the old trophy a new luster and has put the color back into 12-Meter racing."

After *Gretel II* defeated *France* in four races to zero to gain the right to challenge for the cup, things began to happen. Actually, before the challenge round started, the Australians claimed *Intrepid*'s gap, or "notch," that existed between the sternpost and the rudderpost evaded the spirit of the 12-Meter measurement rule. But the New York Yacht Club denied the protest.

As for the series itself, *Intrepid* won the first race, a race in which *Gretel II* lost a crewman overboard, and had to go back and pick him up, but the event brought a protest from both boats involving Rules 34 and 36. Both protests were disallowed by NYYC. The second race, with *Gretel II* leading, was canceled just after the third mark because of fog. When the second race was finally run to completion, *Gretel II* seemingly won. *Intrepid* protested the results under Rule 42.1(*e*).

The protest was heard the following day and the result: *Intrepid*'s protest was upheld and *Gretel II* was disqualified. The decision,

The *Dame Pattie* led *Intrepid* at the start of the first race, but lost the series 4–0.

which was greeted with snide questions by many of the American and Australian newspapermen covering the event, almost caused a minor international incident. The facts were not really in dispute; the only point at issue was the application of the rules. Had the gun gone off 10 seconds later the whole position would have been different, but it did not and it was not. The Australians were naturally bitterly disappointed. With this race in the bag they would have been even in the series in a boat clearly faster in light conditions and in no disastrous shape in heavy. With the race not just removed from them but added to the defenders, they found themselves back at an all-too-familiar 2–0.

Intrepid won the third race, while *Gretel II* picked up the next. In the fifth race, the inevitable occurred: *Intrepid* won by over a minute and half. But *Gretel II* had proved that the defender is not always invincible, thus giving heart to those boats who will challenge in the future.

International competition in the period

since World War II has increased greatly. Of course, some events took years to develop. For example, Olympic yachting, with its international glamor appeal, is now attracting more competitors in this country. Adverse weather conditions forced the cancellation of all the scheduled yachting events at the first of the modern Olympic Games in Greece in 1896. The first Olympic yachting championships were contested at Paris in 1900—but it was not until 1928 that a U.S. team competed for the coveted Olympic yachting medals. Prior to World War II, there were an average of five yachting events on each Olympic program. There were none in 1904 and an astronomical fifteen classes in 1920. There are six competitive classes in the 1972 Olympics: Dragon, Finn, Flying Dutchman, Soling, Star, and Tempest. The American record in Olympic yachting is a good one, with a consistent run of medal winners since the postwar revival of the competition in 1948. The United States International Sailing Association now raises money to pay the team's complete expenses. A sister organization, the United States Olympic Yachting Committee, conducts the trial series to select the crews.

Small-boat sailing increased between the World Wars. Today, the modern classifications of sailing yachts consist of different one-design classes built to race; cruising yachts for racing, cruising, or both; day sailers with neither competitive intentions nor overnight cruising abilities; and catamarans. Within these four broad classifications, there is great variety.

Actually, the number of different one-design classes is beyond strict account. In fact the variety of one-design classes (see Section III) in this country is astonishing. Hulls may be of traditional wood planking (Stars, Internationals, Lightnings), of plywood (Blue Jays, Penguins, El Toro dinghies), of molded plywood (Thistles, Ravens, Luders 16's), or of fiberglass (Mobjacks, Flying Scots, Bull's Eyes). Some of the older wooden-hull classes (Snipe, Comet) now permit construction in fiberglass, and the two types race competitively, a compliment to the stringent class rules regarding measurements and weights. Most one-design classes are small in size, with hulls below 25 feet in overall

The two largest classes of sailboats in the United States. There are over 75,000 Sunfish and 50,000 Sailfish sailing today.

length; centerboards are preferred to keels. Notable keel classes are the 210's and 110's, the Stars, and the Internationals.

Currently there are several classes of boats with planing hulls. These lift out of the water in a reasonable breeze, thereby reducing drag and increasing speed. Although planing hulls are far from new, they have become popular with speed-minded young sailors of the present generation. The advocates of modern planing hulls, like the Flying Dutchman, 5-0-5, and Finn monotype classes, are vocal and sincere.

One-design classes come and go. It is no trick to invent a new class, but quite an undertaking to establish it on a semipermanent basis, with a broad fleet representation in the different sailing areas, and a national class organization. George Corry's Star is more than sixty years old, but the class has issued more new numbers in recent years than ever before. The Star remains fashionable and its magnificent class organization has a lot to do with this fact. There are over 4,800 Stars racing actively, 3,200 of them in the United States. The old adage of the class still applies: "No matter where you go, it's not diffi-cult to find someone who can beat you."

The Snipes, now in their fifth decade, and the Lightnings, in their third, continue to grow on a worldwide basis, too, and have withstood the challenges of the modern planing classes. The longevity of the Stars, Snipes, and Lightnings seems to make this point: A good class organization run by dedicated officers attracts the best kind of competitive sailor, who in turn perpetuates the class.

One-design yacht racing against skilled competition means, under ideal conditions, an event of 1 to 3 hours' duration, sailed around a course from 4 to 15 miles long, and including 3 to 5 legs. This can be enjoyable and rewarding fun, although the demands on the racing skipper are many. He must concentrate throughout the race and constantly reevaluate several factors that bear upon his next tactical decision: wind shifts, tide or current influences, sail trim, centerboard adjustment, crew placement, competitors' positions, the relevance, if any, of similar situations in past races, and the choice of future moves and each one's probability of success or failure.

A CHANGE IN THE SAILING SCENE

As previously stated, it was between the wars that ocean racing in relatively small boats became a major phase of yachting. Simple, seaworthy, fast, and peculiarly American, the Alden-designed fisherman-type schooners led in this area, especially after his Bermuda Race win in *Malabar IV* in 1924. The ability of these boats, and their ease of handling, available at a relatively modest cost, brought many owners into cruising and ocean racing who must have had little taste for the plush yachts of the New York Yacht Club and similar organizations.

The wide category of modern cruising yachts is generally designed for what the name suggests—sailing from port to port, with facilities on board to house and feed the passengers and crew. Theoretically, racing is a secondary consideration, but no aspect of yachting in the past decade has shown a greater growth of popularity than cruiser competition. To qualify as a bona fide cruising yacht, a boat should have a built-in head, berths for at least two, an inboard or outboard motor, a galley and icebox, a cuddy or cabin, and hopefully, a self-draining cockpit.

With family togetherness rating as highly as it does these days, boat designers have tried to pack as many amenities into their cruisers as possible, while holding the product to an attractive price level. Especially on the West Coast, one-design sailing has become popular in good-sized ocean-racing classes. Big boats race on a one-design basis in Southern California, and the increased use of fiberglass has hastened the trend. The Cal-40 class, designed by Bill Lapworth, started an interesting new match race round-robin on a boat-for-boat basis.

Day sailers, again, are literally named. They are suitable for daylight cruising or racing, but must put into port at nightfall since they lack the comforts of home. Technically, most one-designs could be classified as day sailers.

Catamarans are not yet fully established, although they are becoming more numerous all the time. And for exuberance and enthusiasm it is hard to match the men who sail these swift boats. Many claim they have sailed a cat as fast as 25 knots. Catamarans are not permitted in the Bermuda Race or other major distance events. The powers that be still hold to an old prejudice that the twin-hulled craft are not seaworthy. Still, *Aikaine,* a 46-foot cat, has twice sailed in the Transpacific Race as an unofficial competitor and "beaten" everyone to Honolulu. It would seem that the cats are proving themselves to be entirely seaworthy and practical as cruising boats or day racers.

A consuming American interest in anything can be satisfied only by the widest possible range of products. The ever-increasing popularity of boating, and the special impetus given by fiberglass, have meant a steady demand for new designs—and a considerable stimulus for the normally rather quiet and specialized field of naval architecture. Today there are dozens of successful boat designers across the United States.

One-design boats have made sailing a competitive sport. Beyond winning local fleet honors, one-design skippers may aim for national or international championships in their individual classes, Mallory Trophy competition against the best from other classes on a local, regional, or national basis, and the Olympic games. Most classes have national championships sailed at a yacht club where a particular class is strongly represented. In large classes, like Lightning and Thistle, preliminary eliminations are sailed on local waters and only winners go to the finals. In smaller classes, all entries are welcome at the "nationals."

Winning a major trophy requires a great deal of skill. For instance, Mallory Trophy competition begins on an association level. The Inter-Lake Yachting Association or the Southern Massachusetts Yacht Racing Association, for example, invites prominent class skippers each summer to sail in a round-robin series held at a local yacht club using a fleet of class boats. The winner then proceeds to a regional elimination involving champions from other associations—Southern Massachu-

Catamarans such as this Shark class (left) and trimarans such as this Triumph class (right) began to be popular in the 1960's.

setts, Buzzards Bay, Massachusetts Bay, and Maine, for example. The winner of the regional elimination in turn goes to the finals, which are held at different sailing centers in the United States and Canada each year. There are always eight finalists, and eight races are sailed in a fleet of one-design boats. The crews exchange boats after each race so that any inequity in hull or sails will be shared by all. About 200 skippers try for the Mallory prize.

With the increase of one-design racing events and the betterment of the type of competition, a new type of sailor has emerged. In the early days of sailing, the hero of the sport stood at the wheel of an ocean-racing schooner or an America's Cup yacht. Today, most of the big names come from the ranks of the one-designs. Even sailors like Briggs Cunningham, Bus Mosbacher, Bob Bavier, Arthur Knapp, Corny Shields, and Bill Cox, who went on to America's Cup fame, came originally from one-designs, and the roster of champions grows each year. In every class, the man who wins the class championship that year is king in the eyes of his fellow owners, but there are some topnotchers, who have shown extra consistency in staying

ahead, whose names are known wherever sailors gather. Harry C. "Bud" Melges has won the North American Yacht Racing Union men's championship, the Mallory Cup, more times than any other skipper, and he is generally unbeatable in his first love, scows. He has been an Olympic sailor in Flying Dutchmen, and is probably the single most successful small-boat skipper in action in the United States today.

There are many who would contest this, however. In no particular order there are: Tom Allen, who won the Lightning World Championship the first three times it was held, plus several North American titles; Runnie Colie, seven times Penguin champ, and a top scow sailor as well; Dick Stearns, Lowell North, Malin Burnham, and Joe Duplin of the Star class; Pete Bordes in Thistles, Pete Barrett in Finns, and Richard Tillman in Snipes and Finns. Others who have done well no matter what the class include Sandy Douglass, George O'Day, Eric Olsen, Bob Lippincott, Harry Sindle, Buddy Friedrichs, and Bruce Goldsmith.

Catamarans have produced such special stars as Van Clark and Bob Smith, and the ladies have had their own leaders, like Mrs.

Allegra Knapp Mertz, Jerie Clark, Mrs. Jane Pegel, Mrs. Timmie Schneider Larr, Mrs. Betty Foulk, and Mrs. Jan Chance O'Malley.

Each year new topnotchers fight their way into this select company, as one-design sailing breeds more and more dedicated, scientific-minded, hard-nosed competitors. We must remember that sailing is the same sport that Crowninshield pursued and the one that has given America a grand heritage since the time of *Cleopatra's Barge*. Ours has been and is a nation of sailors.

SECTION II

Sailboats and Sailing Gear

American preeminence in sailing is legendary. In less than two hundred years, the boat-building industry has attained a level of sailing technology that commands the respect and attention of the nations of the world. Perhaps the most glorious time of sail was during the wonderful clipper-ship days of the nineteenth century, when majestic multisparred ships raced to Europe or around Cape Horn, establishing the United States as a great seafaring nation. Today, sailors in small boats recapture the thrilling speed and dignity of the sailing clippers of old. There are hundreds of different types of sailboats made in the United States, some of them by the same shipyards that once built the sleek clippers.

The first thing a newcomer to sailing will discover is that sailors seem to have a language all their own (see Section VIII). They talk about sloops, ketches, catboats, schooners, and yawls. These are different kinds of sailboats distinguished by the number of masts, their size and location, and the sail plan. However, all sailboats, although having different rigs, have one thing in common: they all use the wind for power.

BASIC SAILBOAT RIGS

The first feature of a sailing yacht to be identified will be her "rig," this being the largest thing about her and the first thing to be seen as her sails lift over the horizon. In addition, the rig, which is a combination of mast and sails, usually determines her classification.

Today there are two general types of craft: single-masted and double-masted; and two sail plans: jib-headed (Bermudian) and gaff-headed. Let us first consider the general types of sailboats.

Catboat. Has a single mast, forward in the boat, and carries a single sail called the "mainsail" (*mains'l*). This type rig is the simplest and easiest with which to learn. However, this rig can be awkward to handle in strong winds, and coming about (going from one tack to the other) is sometimes difficult. Many of the familiar small sailing dinghies are cat-rigged. In Europe, catboats are often referred to as "una"-rigged boats.

Sloop. Has a single mast, and in addition to the mainsail carries one or more foresails (jibs) forward of the mast. The sloop gives better control than the catboat because the

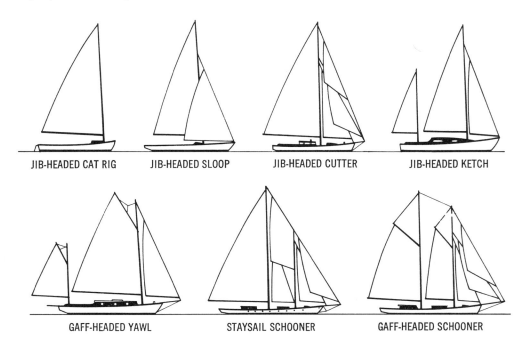

JIB-HEADED CAT RIG　　JIB-HEADED SLOOP　　JIB-HEADED CUTTER　　JIB-HEADED KETCH

GAFF-HEADED YAWL　　STAYSAIL SCHOONER　　GAFF-HEADED SCHOONER

Popular sailboat rigs.

The Great Pelican (2) is a gaff-rigged catboat, while the San Francisco Pelican (501) is a gaff-rigged sloop.

sail area is broken up into two or more sails, which makes handling easier. If properly designed, this is the fastest of the rigs. In addition to the working headsails, light sails —such as a genoa jib and a spinnaker—can be set when racing. The hull of a sloop is leaner than that of a cat and has more overhang. Its fastest point of sailing is with the wind on the beam.

Cutter. Has one mast, but it is stepped (placed) proportionately farther aft than the mast of a conventional sloop. That is, in most sloops, a mast stepped at two-fifths of the waterline length from the forward end of the waterline is now common, whereas one-third of this length used to be usual; and the mast of a cutter may be nearly amidships, or at any rate more than the two-fifths of the waterline length from forward, which was once general practice.

The cutter arrangement permits a variety of sails to be employed. Generally, her regular suit of sails calls for two jibs, the inner called a *staysail,* flying under the jibsail. In such an arrangement, the mainsail is usually smaller than on a sloop of similar size, but

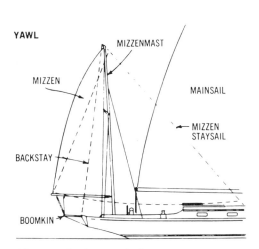

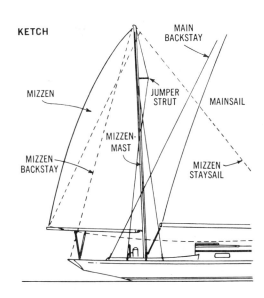

Mizzen and mizzenmast plans.

the total sail area because of double head-sails is generally greater. Since a variety of sail combinations may be carried for all types of weather, the cutter is regarded as a good cruising boat.

Yawl. This is a handy rig, with the sails divided on two masts. The shorter of the two is called the *mizzenmast,* and is stepped aft of the rudderpost. The same light sails carried on the sloop and the cutter may be set, plus a hard-pulling mizzen staysail. In ordinary weather the mizzen sail is useful on all points of sailing except on a very broad reach, where it may disturb the flow of air to the mainsail. (To increase speed, when running or reaching, an extra staysail can be rigged from the top of the mizzenmast and cleated down to the deck or cabin top.) In bad weather the mainsail may be reefed or even furled entirely, yet the boat will remain in good balance with jib and mizzen sail (often called the *jigger*) or heave to with only the mizzen sail up. In addition, at an anchorage, a raised jigger will keep the craft steady and head to the wind.

The yawl can drop its mizzen and sail as a sloop. This is possible because the mizzen sail is quite small, and the craft is so designed to sail as a sloop, if necessary, when beating.

Ketch. Similar to the yawl, except that the mizzenmast is proportionately larger and is stepped forward of the rudderpost. This makes a fine, easily handled cruising boat with the sails divided into handy sizes. The rig is a favorite among deep-sea voyagers. Its only disadvantage is that the mizzenmast comes either in the middle of the cockpit, where it obstructs working and lounging space, or against the after-cabin bulkhead, where it interferes with access to the cabin.

Schooner. This rig is seldom designed today. It requires a larger crew than the others, but when the wind is coming in abeam and sails are set full, the boat really races through the water. There are many fine, used schooners available, with countless variations of rig; almost all are two-masted and the aftermast is always the taller. The most common rig carries two jibs, a gaff foresail with a small "fisherman's staysail" over it, and the mainsail. A great variety of other sails can be used, from a spinnaker to a "golliwobbler"— a large fisherman's staysail set between the masts.

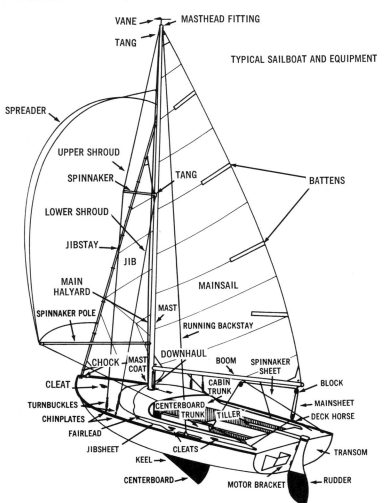

TYPICAL SAILBOAT AND EQUIPMENT

Parts and equipment of a typical sailboat.

SAIL PLANS

Foresails, that is, sails set forward of the mainmast, are always triangular in fore-and-aft rigged craft, which means with sails set in a line from bow to stern and not across the boat. (We are not concerned with square-rigged craft in this book.) Different types of foresails will be described later in this chapter.

Mainsails and mizzen sails can be either (1) jib-headed (also called Marconi or Bermudian) or (2) gaff-headed.

Jib-headed Mainsail. This type of sail is essentially a triangle. But note that it is long on the luff, relatively short on the foot. In the strictest sense, this sail is not a perfect triangle, for the leech is cut on a long, gentle curve between head and clew to give it extra fullness—and therefore provide extra drive for the boat—when reaching or running. You will see this extra fullness, called the "roach," in the drawing; it is that portion of the sail between the dotted line and the leech. And while we are speaking of the roach, we might as well point out the battens. A sail's roach has a tendency to either sag or flap, depending upon the state of the wind; to prevent this, battens are inserted in special pockets along the leech. Battens are narrow,

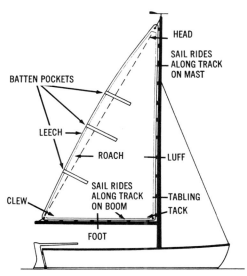

Jib-headed mainsail arrangement.

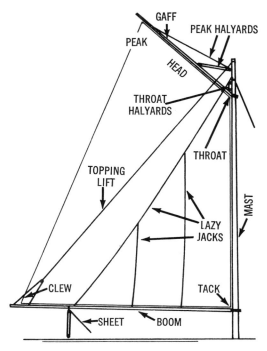

Gaff-headed mainsail arrangement.

smooth and thin, but fairly stiff slats of wood, aluminum, or plastic. Once inside their pockets, some battens are tied fast to secure.

The jib-headed type of mainsail is one of the most popular in use. It is an efficient sail and easy to handle. Only one halyard, or line, is needed to raise and lower it.

For most small, single-masted sailboats today the jib-headed mainsail is the principal source of power. In certain rigs, such as the catboat and sailing dinghy, it is the only sail. In both the catboat and sailing dinghy, the mast is stepped, or mounted, far forward—much more so than in a sloop. And since both these craft carry just a mainsail, it is usually larger, proportionately, than that carried by a sloop-type rig of comparable size.

Gaff-headed Mainsail. Compare the outline of this sail with that of the jib-headed type. The gaff-headed mainsail is a rectangle—more or less—and as such has four sides and four corners. Luff, foot, and leech remain the same as for a jib-headed mainsail; but here you have an additional side, and this is called the "head." The two bottom corners—tack and clew—are the same as for a triangular sail; but the uppermost corner now becomes the peak, while the other upper corner, that adjacent to the mast, is called the "throat." This sail is not as high, proportionately, as the jib-headed mainsail; but its foot, proportionately, is longer.

With its fourth side, or head, the gaff-headed mainsail calls for the use of an additional spar, known as a "gaff" (from which the sail gets its name). The function of the gaff is to aid in raising and lowering the sail, an operation which requires two halyards instead of one, as in the case of the jib-headed mainsail. One of these ropes, the throat halyard, raises the sail's throat; the peak halyard raises its peak. Aloft, the gaff helps hold the sail in position.

Although the gaff-headed mainsails have been around a lot longer than the jib-headed, there are nowhere near as many of them in use nowadays on small, single-masted boats. This type of mainsail has certain advantages, such as being easier to reef (that is, reduce its area) in a strong wind; but it is not as efficient as the jib-headed type; and, since there are two halyards and a spar involved, it is not as easy to handle. A few small sailboats, however, still employ a gaff rig.

Gunter Mainsail. There are two other mainsail patterns that were at one time popular in small boats, the *gunter* and the *lug*. The former represents a stage in development from

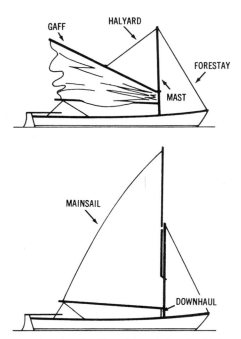

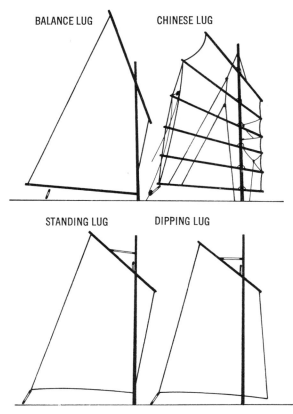

Gunter-rigged mainsail and how it is raised into position. The halyard draws gaff up mast (left), raises it vertically (right) to point where sail is fully extended.

Main lugsail types.

the gaff mainsail to jib-headed type. The major difference between gaff-headed mainsail and the gunter—which is also a four-sided sail—is that the angle between the luff (the forward edge) and the head is much wider, making it more nearly triangular. That is, when the spar to which the head of the sail is laced (which, although serving the same purpose as a gaff, is more usually called a *yard* in gunter-rigged boats) is set up tight, it looks almost like an extension of the mast itself. The angle between the mast and yard being such a small one, the set of the sail resembles a jib-headed mainsail.

Lateen Sail. Another sail type that has recently become fairly popular in the United States and Canada—thanks to its use on boardboats, catamarans, and sailing canoes —is the lateen. The lateen sail is a triangular one which is designed to be hoisted with its head secured to a long spar or yard at about a 45 degree angle to the mast. The lateen sail originated in the Mediterranean–Indian Ocean area and still is most common there.

Lug Mainsail. Lugsails are held aloft by a yard and there are three basic types—the standing lug, the balanced lug, and the dipping lug. These names help to describe the differences between each type. For instance, the standing lug has a yard and generally a boom. Very little sail is forward of the mast. The balanced lug also has a yard and boom but a good deal more sail is forward of the mast. It acts like a headsail in balancing the area aft of the mast. The dipping lug has a yard but no boom. The bottom edge, or foot, of the sail is said to be loose-footed. The dipping lug is so called because the yard has to be dipped and sometimes lowered when moving the sail across from one side of the boat to the other.

Aspect Ratio. Another factor in identification of rigs is the *aspect ratio*. This term is used to describe the relationship the height of a sail (luff) bears to its length at the foot.

The Windsurfer boat uses a leg-of-mutton sail arrangement. That is a triangular sail, used with a boom as shown.

A sail with a short luff and a long foot is said to have a low aspect ratio; one with a high luff and short foot has a high aspect ratio. A sail not high at the luff and not too short at the foot has a moderate aspect ratio. Actually, the aspect ratio is an important help in identification, as certain classes and yachts have an aspect ratio which is individual to the class or boat. Furthermore, the aspect ratio of a rig may afford some clue to year or build of the craft. Older boats, unless rerigged as they sometimes are, usually have a rather low aspect ratio. Yachts built immediately before World War II had higher rigs, and the aspect ratio probably came to its maximum (sometimes exceeding 3:1) in yachts built in the years immediately following the war. The tendency since then has been toward more moderate aspect ratios, though the early 1970's have seen a move to rather high aspect ratios in offshore racers.

The commonest rig for small sailing yachts today is the jib-headed, or Bermudian, sloop. As is mentioned in Section III, most present-day one-design class boats are of this type.

CENTERBOARD VERSUS KEEL

Sailboat hulls are divided into two definite types—*centerboard* and *keel*. The main function of both these devices is to furnish lateral resistance to keep the boat from sliding sidewise through the water. There the resemblance ends.

Centerboard. The conventional centerboard hull is shallow and has a wood, fiberglass, or metal plate which moves up and down through a well or trunk on the centerline. Standard centerboards, the most commonly used type, are fitted with pins at their forward, lower corners. At the after, upper corner of each, there is a line or chain arranged to control, about one third of the way down, the depth of the centerboard. It is most important that the centerboard box or trunk be well constructed and properly designed since it must withstand racking side pressures. While the slot in the bottom of the boat under the trunk should permit easy raising and lowering of the board, it should not be so

wide as to permit the board to wobble. Such wobble will slow the boat's progress.

When sailing in very shoal water or before the wind, and when at anchor, the centerboard is raised up into the trunk so that little, if any, of it projects below the bottom of the sailboat. However, no boat will sail well when the centerboard is up unless dead before the wind. For stability this type of boat relies on its wide beam and the weight of the crew. A centerboard craft can be easily capsized, but this is counteracted by the knowledge that it will not sink if swamped. Furthermore, it is relatively inexpensive to build and maintain, and its light weight and fairly flat bottom make it easy to trailer. The draft of centerboard sailboats can be as little as 3 inches. If an underwater object is hit, normally the board will swing up out of harm's way.

Daggerboard. Another style of centerboard which is often found in small class boats is the dagger type. This type requires a trunk

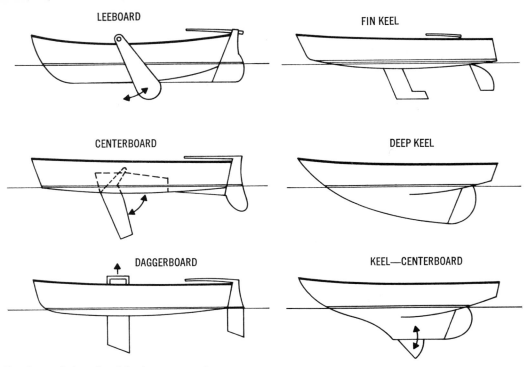

LEEBOARD

FIN KEEL

CENTERBOARD

DEEP KEEL

DAGGERBOARD

KEEL—CENTERBOARD

Popular centerboard and keel arrangements.

and slot, but it is not hinged. It is bodily lowered or raised. In fact, it can be entirely lifted out when the boat is not being sailed. Adjustments are provided so that the depth of the daggerboard below the bottom can be controlled, and often the slot and trunk are somewhat longer than the daggerboard so that the latter can be shifted forward or aft to provide perfect balance in relation to the center of sail pressure. Less cockpit space is required for a daggerboard trunk and thus there is more room for movement in the cockpit. But the center of lateral resistance moves in a much narrower range with a daggerboard since it can only go one way—straight down. In addition, should an underwater object be hit, the boat may come to a jarring halt and the board may be damaged.

Leeboard. Only a few small dinghies—mainly of European design—have leeboards to offer lateral resistance. These boards, which pivot on the sides of the boats, do a good job to minimize leeway when sailing upwind.

Keel Boats. The keel in a small sailboat is built as an integral part of the hull and has

a ballast weight attached to its bottom. There are two basic types of keels: fin keel and deep, or full, keel. The majority of the keel sloops described in Section III are fin type. In the simplest form, this type of keel has the appearance of a dagger centerboard that has been lowered all the way and fixed in place. Generally it is an iron casting with a cigar-shaped bottom, which is actually ballast. But, the fin-type keel cannot be lowered or raised. Whatever its distance below water, that is the minimum depth of water in which you can sail.

The deep, or full, keel is usually triangular-shaped when viewed from the side. The apex of the triangle is at the bow and the base is aft. Lead or iron ballast, in the form of a casting, is attached at some point along the bottom of the keel. This type of keel has a great deal of lateral-plane area, is very strong, and is very stable due to the fact that ballast is positioned low. Actually, the longer the keel, the easier it is to hold a course for long periods with little effort. But, the long-keel yacht offers greater resistance to turns and makes it difficult to tack up a tight chan-

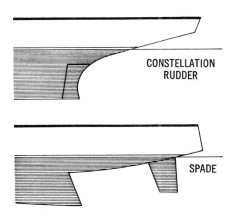

Contemporary rudder styles.

keel boats are finding some acceptance in shallow-water regions in the United States, such as the Chesapeake Bay area.

If you have a choice between a sailboat with a keel and one with a centerboard, it should be remembered that each is a good craft if used under the circumstances for which it was designed. In an area where the water is uniformly deep, the keel boat is generally preferable. If the water is thin, the centerboard type is the best craft. The latter is also better if extreme speed is desired.

In larger keel-type boats, the ballast ratio is rather important. Usually expressed as a percentage, this is the ratio of the keel-ballast weight to the displacement, or total weight of the yacht. Internal ballast may be included in the ratio, though usually its weight is of insignificant importance. The ballast ratio should be as high as possible, for it confers the sail-carrying power that is one of the most vital elements in performance. In practice the highest attainable ballast ratios are limited severely. In a few class racers ratios may reach 70 percent. In the modern cruiser-racer it is conventional to claim a ratio of 35 to 50 percent.

Centerboard/Keel Design. Some of the newer class sailboats have a combination centerboard/keel. This design style, while offering many of the advantages of both the centerboard and keel types, is more popular with the cruising sailor than with the racing skipper.

nel or turn at a tack. For this reason, weekend cruisers and racers prefer a short-keel sailboat with the rudder attached to the keel, or aft of keel. (The latter type is called a *spade rudder*.)

The chief disadvantages of keel boats are that they may sink if swamped and are exceedingly difficult to transport. To overcome the latter, several English boat builders have produced twin-keel craft. All other factors being equal, they require less water and have less rolling tendencies downwind. If caught aground in outgoing tide, the standard keel boat may roll over on her side, while the twin-keel craft remains upright. These new twin-

TYPES OF HULLS

The hull shapes commonly used on all small class sailboats are classified as flat-, V-, round-, and arc-bottomed. In the following discussion, remember that we are considering the hull shape bow on, not as it looks when viewed from one side. When you look at a beached boat from one side, the profile is relatively the same irrespective of whether it is flat-, V-, round-, or arc-bottomed.

The flat-bottomed hull, which is sometimes called a flattie, is possibly the most popular with beginners, but is least attractive from just about every viewpoint. This type of hull is suitable only on protected waters and is employed mainly in dinghies. When it is used

in a moderate sea, it has a tendency to pound or bounce. Actually its major virtue is ease of construction, particularly if the bottom is planked athwartships rather than fore-and-aft. With the exception of the modified flat-bottom—which can be identified by the abnormal flare of the sides—this type of hull has few sailing virtues.

The V-bottomed hull, which has a hard chine, avoids most of the difficulties of the flat-bottomed hull. It is stable, seaworthy, and has good speed.

The round-bottomed hull—also known as round-bilge construction—is the strongest and lends itself to a better appearance. Under

Hull shapes of keel-type boats (left to right): triangular, wine glass, champagne glass, arc of a circle, and twin.

normal conditions, it does not have quite as much stability as a V-bottomed hull. It may not be able to carry as much sail without heeling objectionably, but its stability can be increased by proper use of ballast, less sail, or by greater skill on the part of the skipper. This type of hull is fast, but there is no proof that it is really faster than the V-bottom in small-sized sailboats.

The arc-bottom, which is also known as double chine, is fairly uncommon, except in the Comet, Lightning, and Star classes. In all basic elements it is similar to the V-bottom and its characteristics are also similar. But this type of hull is more expensive to construct.

In addition to the standard types of hulls, there are two other one-design class shapes that should be mentioned. They are the scows and the multihulls such as catamarans. Scows are beamy, slightly round-bottomed, extremely shallow-draft "skimming-dish"-type sailboats, and are of light construction. This type of hull is most suitable for protected waters such as lakes or bays. Catamarans are fully described later in this section.

Planing Hulls. As is discussed in the rating of sailboats for handicapped racing in Section VI, the longer the boat and the more sail area it flies, the faster it goes. But while a small boat may not in actual fact go as fast as a larger craft, it *seems* to go a great deal

A scow (Class W) (left) and shallow-draft boardboats or sailboard (Glastron Alpha Class) (right).

faster since the occupants are much nearer to the water. In many cases it can go faster for its length than a larger boat. This is because many of the modern craft are able to plane. Planing happens when the bow waves become sufficiently strong to lift the fore part of the boat right out of the water. When this occurs the wetted area of the hull is drastically reduced and with it the friction that holds the boat back. The result is an increase in speed. Generally, lighter weight in a boat means a faster boat, and so new ideas and sailing techniques have been devised as new strong lightweight materials have been introduced. One of the most exciting designs of recent years is the planing hull, which is gaining rapidly in popularity all over the world. Basically, this refers to a lightweight hull which, on gaining a certain speed in proper sea and wind conditions, begins bodily to rise up over its own bow wave onto a plane. In so doing, it displaces less than its own weight in water as it moves. And when this type of boat is planing, it really moves. Boats of the Eighteen Footer class in Sydney Harbor, Australia, have gone as fast as 20 knots downwind. To control these lightweight hulls a crewman uses either a trapeze, hiking straps, hiking boards, or other means of distributing his weight out over the windward side of the boat. The reason for this positioning of weight is to keep the boat in as near an upright position as possible, which is necessary to achieve planing. Sailing in these hulls is, to many enthusiasts, a supreme exhilaration, where precision timing and balance are needed during every minute of the "ride."

Keel boats, which use a fixed ballast, are seldom able to plane because the weight which gives them stability makes it very difficult to raise them onto their own bow wave. (For displacement hulls which do not plane or skim over the water, the maximum speed of a hull expressed in knots is about 1.4 times the square root of the waterline length. A boat 25 feet on the waterline has $1.4 \times \sqrt{25} = 1.4 \times 5 = 7.0$ knots maximum speed.) But most centerboards of more than 12 feet are ballasted in a most economical way by human weight, which can be lifted from one side of the boat to the other and can even be draped over the side to exert extra leverage to keep the boat level—the best position for planing. Therefore, once the necessary

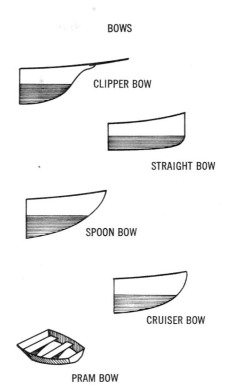

BOWS

CLIPPER BOW

STRAIGHT BOW

SPOON BOW

CRUISER BOW

PRAM BOW

Bow shapes (top to bottom): clipper bow; straight bow; spoon bow; cruise bow; and pram bow.

speed is reached, there is a good chance that the boat will climb out of the water, and plane. Of course some classes, such as Flying Dutchmen, 505's, International 14's, Finns, scows, etc., plane more easily than others.

Bow Designs. In addition to the underwater sections, the shape of the bow, stern, and sheer influence the behavior of the craft. The *clipper bow,* once the most common of all, had a very fine entry to water which made it fast. Its long, slender body section makes it rather expensive to build, and this type of bow is now virtually extinct. The *spoon bow,* which was developed from the clipper bow's slender section, gives fine speed and for this reason it is frequently used for racing yachts. The *straight bow* is almost a semicircle and, while it has a less fine entry and little or no hollow weight forward, it is very buoyant when carrying weight in the bow. It is used frequently in small sailing craft. The so-called *cruiser bow,* which is now popular in the design of cruising yachts, is really a compromise

STERNS

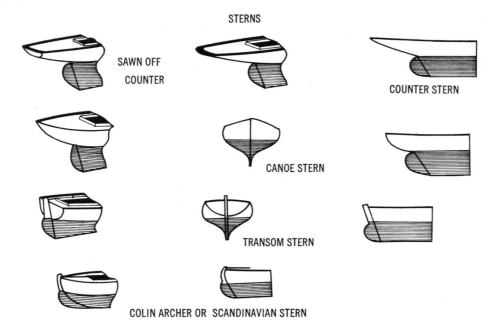

SAWN OFF
COUNTER

COUNTER STERN

CANOE STERN

TRANSOM STERN

COLIN ARCHER OR SCANDINAVIAN STERN

Various stern shapes.

between straight and spoon bows. The *pram bow,* which is cheap and easy to construct, is used primarily for small dinghies.

Stern Designs. The commonest form of stern for cruiser-racers is the *counter* of moderate length. This is the type of stern that projects beyond the rudderpost, giving an overhang which makes the boat's length overall some feet longer than her waterline length. A *canoe stern* is a pointed affair of canoe shape. The curve in profile of this type of stern takes various forms but usually it is in the nature of a parabola, and the overhanging length is relatively short. With both the counter or canoe stern, the rudder usually works through a rudder trunk.

The *transom stern* is a straight or slightly sloped one onto which the rudder is hung externally by means of fittings called gudgeons and pintles. In a sailing dinghy, a rudder is always detachable and can also have a hinged blade. Usually in the upper end of the rudder stock is a slot into which is fixed the curved piece of wood called the tiller, by means of which the rudder is moved from side to side and the boat steered. Many sailing yachts are also fitted with wheel steering. Another type of stern is the *Scandinavian.*

This is similar to the canoe stern, except that the overhang is shorter and the rudder is hung externally, the stock nowhere entering the hull. The accessibility of the rudder is one advantage of this form of stern. While the most serious faults of the transom stern are undue fullness and heaviness, that of the Scandinavian type can be excessive narrowness and lack of buoyancy.

Sheerline Styles. The sheerline is the outline at the top edge of the hull when you look at it from the side. Actually, the sheer governs to some extent the freeboard, or height of the hull, above the water. With a heavily sprung, boldly swinging sheer the freeboard will be low amidships unless it is excessively high at bow and stern. It was once believed, and the belief persists, that a *bold sheer* makes a seaworthy boat, and it was usual for cruisers to have sheerlines of this nature, while racing boats had flat sheerlines. In recent years sheerlines have flattened, and the older sheer with its high ends and low freeboard amidships has been replaced by flatter lines giving more average freeboard and a drier craft.

Straight and reverse sheer have recently been introduced. In fact, one of the most distinctive trends in modern yacht design has

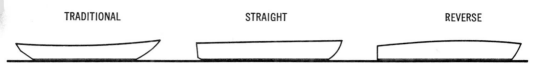

TRADITIONAL STRAIGHT REVERSE

Sheerlines in use today are generally conventional (traditional) and reverse sheers. A few boats still employ a straight sheer.

been the general increase in freeboard, many small cruisers and ocean racers having today nearly twice the freeboard amidships of older boats equal in length. This is, of course, partly the result of the more flatly curving sheers, and one of the reasons for them. The reverse curve, or hogged sheer, allows a roomier, drier boat with more headroom below.

A parallel development, and one found especially in small craft, is the broken sheerline, in which the coachroof is, in effect, extended to the side of the hull and made integral with it. This allows more room to be obtained inside the hull or cuddy.

Hull Design Measurements

There are five principal measurements of interest to every sailor. They are the craft's (1) length, (2) beam, (3) draft, (4) freeboard, and (5) displacement.

Length. The length of a sailboat is usually described in three ways:

1. *Length Overall* (LOA). From the foremost part of the bow in a straight line to the furthest point aft.

2. *Length at the Waterline* (LWL). Length of the hull at the surface of the water with the boat upright.

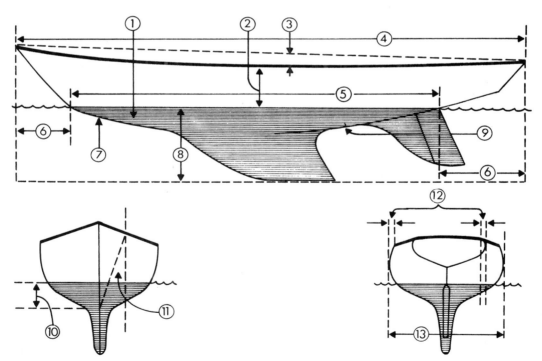

Descriptive terms for the hull: 1. entrance; 2. freeboard; 3. sheer; 4. length overall; 5. load waterline; 6. overhangs; 7. forefoot; 8. draft; 9. run; 10. deadrise; 11. flare; 12. tumble home; 13. beam.

3. *Sailing Length*. Effective waterline length of a boat when heeling. This normally is greater than the upright waterline length (LWL), particularly in a boat with long bow and stern overhang. Remember that in sailing hulls the principal value of overhangs, apart from adding to the sailing length and potential speed, lies in the reserve buoyancy forward and aft that they provide, which damps pitching and promotes dryness.

Beam. The beam is, of course, the maximum width of the hull. Under sail the amount of propulsive power that may be effectively deployed is a function of stability, i.e., stability provides sail-carrying power. Big beam, so long as other stability characteristics are satisfactory, enables a yacht to carry a given amount of sail for longer as the wind increases. Actually, the type of stability obtained by beam, as opposed to weight of ballast, is stiffness, or a strong resistance to initial inclinations and a quickness in returning to the upright once inclined. These effects are not harmful in sailing craft, in which violent angular velocities are damped by the steadying effect of the sails. Thus sailing craft with considerable beam are liable to be harder to balance on the helm and rather more temperamental to handle than the narrower. Length-beam ratio on the average sailing craft is approximately three (LOA) to one (beam).

Draft. The draft of a sailboat is her depth below waterline and it varies with size, shape, and position of her keel or centerboard. Under sail, the ultimate stability is increased by deep draft, since the ballast keel may be hung at a great depth and hence have a longer righting lever arm. This effect is, however, partially offset by the fact that the hydrodynamic force resisting leeway, which is a heeling force, operates at a greater depth and hence also has a longer lever arm. That is, the keel, together with the submerged lateral area of the hull, is a hydrofoil producing the "lift" —which is the force resisting leeway mentioned above—and the hull-keel combination obeys the same laws as other hydrofoils or airfoils. Draft gives a high aspect ratio to a keel and hence, under sailing conditions, a bigger lift drag ratio, which means a superior resistance to leeway, i.e., a smaller leeway angle. In shoal-draft yachts without center-

board, weatherliness is sacrificed to the convenience of drawing only a little water. In yachts with centerboards the low aspect of the fixed keel is compensated by the higher aspect ratio achieved when the board is lowered. Excluding centerboard craft, draft is about ⅕ waterline length.

Freeboard. The freeboard is the vertical distance, at any point on a boat's hull, from the load waterline to the deck. It provides headroom inside the hull and promotes dryness on deck. In a sailing yacht it has the particular value of allowing a bigger angle of heel to be attained before the lee rail and deck become awash, at which point a sudden and appreciable increase in resistance occurs owing to the inharmonious shape of the hull that then becomes immersed.

Freeboard has an important effect on stability in two contrary ways. By raising the height of the deck and all the eights upon it, the center of gravity of the craft is lifted and stability reduced. On the other hand, once the hull is well heeled or rolling heavily, high freeboard gives additional buoyant support at the bigger angles of heel, and though it may slightly reduce the initial stiffness of the boat, with correct design it increases the range of stability, which is the more important quality.

Displacement. Displacement is the weight of water that is displaced by a floating body. Expressed in pounds or tons, the displacement is identical to the weight of the body itself. A displacement hull, as the name implies, displaces a volume of water equal to the weight of the boat. A planing hull at planing speeds displaces less than its own weight of water, the difference being supported by dynamic lift on the bottom of the hull. In effect, a displacement hull moves through the water; a planing hull (when planing) moves over it. Except for the smaller planing-type racing classes, sailboats are truly displacement types.

Hull Stability. A sailboat must be designed to be fairly efficient over the usable range of wind speed and heading. This involves design compromise. For example, a sailboat going to windward requires "transverse stability" to resist the lateral component of the wind, which tends to heel her over. This stability is a function of both hull form and vertical weight distribution, and usually is achieved, as previously stated, by either a beamy hull, one with

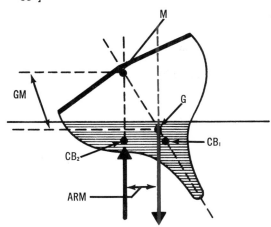

Hull stability. Remember that arm × displacement equals righting moment.

It can be seen by studying the diagram that there are actually two ways that the arm can be lengthened: (1) by increasing the beam or changing the hull shape to make the center of buoyancy move outboard, because it is the geometric center of the immersed hull, or (2) by lowering or increasing the keel ballast to lower the center of gravity.

The actual measure of stability is the righting moment, which is the length of the righting arm times the displacement of the boat. Thus it is possible for a light-displacement boat with a slightly longer lever arm than a heavy boat to be more tender than the heavy boat. The metacentric height (GM), shown in the illustration, varies according to the height of the center of gravity and the lateral location of the center of buoyancy. The metacentric height on most keel racing-cruisers measures, depending on the size, between less than 2½ feet to more than 3½ feet with the smaller boats having the lower heights. The figures for centerboarders are usually somewhat less. The center of gravity is slightly above, on, or slightly below the LWL on most racing-cruisers.

Hull Construction Materials

Apart from shape, another characteristic of hulls is their construction. Today, boats are built of planked wood, plywood, or fiberglass plastics. A few have aluminum hulls. Incidentally, as you will find in Section III, some classes specify the construction materials allowed.

Wooden Sailboats. In carvel or wooden-planking construction, the long, wooden planks are screwed, nailed, or riveted flush to the hull's frame, with the planks running fore and aft on the sides, and the bottom planking either from side to side across the cruiser or lengthwise, depending on the design. The planks are fitted edge to edge, with the outer edges outgauged (beveled) so that the seams can be calked. (The reason for this outgauge space is to give planking room to expand when the wood swells in the water. Without the spacing, the air-dried but porous wood would warp, buckle, and check.) Oakum or cotton is used to calk this seam, with a synthetic-rubber sealer filling the crack to make it watertight.

a heavy ballast keel, or some combination of both. But those very qualities militate against the boat's performance in light airs and downwind. No one boat can be equally efficient for every condition. Intended use, crew size, cruising range, expected normal wind speeds, limiting harbor drafts, etc., must all be considered in setting the displacement and hull proportions of a sailboat.

The key to sailboat design, in any case, is transverse stability, the tendency of a craft to return from a heeled position to an upright position. Of course, all sailboats must have sufficient stability for sail-carrying power. They need stiffness to stand up to their rigs and sail at low or optimum angles of heel in fresh winds. Furthermore, racing-cruisers need the reserved or ultimate stability for safety, to prevent capsizing or rolling over.

The drawing here illustrates the importance of beam and ballast in a boat's design and shows how these righting forces operate. The center of gravity (G) is fixed on the boat's centerline, but the center of buoyancy, also on the centerline when the boat is upright (at CB_1), moves to the side (to CB_2) when the boat is heeled. The distance between the upward force acting through the heeled center of buoyancy (CB_2) and the downward force acting through the center of gravity, is the righting arm. This arm changes in length as the angle of heel changes and the center of buoyancy moves toward or away from the boat's centerline. The longer the righting arm, the more righting force is exerted on the hull.

The advantages of carvel construction are the ready availability and relative cheapness of materials. Commonly used woods are pine, fir, and cedar, although some hulls of this type are made of more expensive woods such as teak and mahogany. It is also a fairly inexpensive method of construction. The disadvantage of carvel construction is in its excessive weight, since the wood must be of sufficient thickness to hold the calking materials. In other words, you are paying for thicker wood, not required for hull strength but for water integrity. While this type of construction is very durable, it requires recalking and considerable maintenance. Because of these disadvantages, carvel is now the least popular for boat construction.

Strip-planking is a type of carvel construction that is commonly used on many boats today. Strip-planking utilizes a method similar to tongue-and-groove matching with a sealer in the seams. Generally speaking, strip-planking produces inexpensive, lightweight, sleek and sturdy hulls, but it requires a good deal of maintenance to keep it in top shape.

Plywood Sailboats. Plywood craft utilize two types of material: the sheet and the molded. In recent years, sheet plywood has largely taken the place of wood-planked hulls in smaller sailboats. This type of construction requires a framework or skeleton similar to that in carvel-planked boats except perhaps for somewhat fewer frames. But because big plywood panels will cover wide areas, they shorten construction time, and reduce the seam area and the number of fastenings required. Cross-grained bonding of the veneers makes a construction material that is split-proof, virtually punctureproof, and dimensionally stable. This means greater strength with less weight at a sizable reduction in cost. Joints are end-butted and glued so that calking troubles are reduced to a minimum. The principal drawback of plywood hulls is the bending limitation of the material, which controls the degree of sharpness to which the planking may be curved.

Sheet-plywood hulls are easy to repair. Simply fit in a new square of plywood of the size needed, backed up by any necessary battens to prevent leaking; or in the case of less severe damage, leave the injured piece in, covering it with a butt block from the inside.

The International 14 class boat shown here is of molded plywood. Boats in class are also made of fiberglass.

Being wood, plywood hulls require scraping and painting.

Molded-plywood Hulls. All modern plywood boats are not built of sheet plywood. The molded-plywood hull was introduced just before World War II and is still used in the manufacture of smaller boats. In this manufacturing process, the hull is "planked" upside down over a solid wood mold. Each "plank" consists of a single ply, and has been previously cut to shape from a pattern, to fit its exact place on the boat. The "planks" are laid on diagonally, stapled to the mold. Then waterproof glue (resin glue of the hot-press type) is applied. Next comes another layer of piles or "plank," diagonally opposite to the first layer. As many as five or seven layers are put on in this manner, each running more or less crisscross to the layer under and above it. More layers may be used in certain parts of the hull, where more strength is needed. Once all the piles are on and stapled, the hull and mold are placed in an autoclave (heated oven), where the glue is permanently set under pressure. The resulting hull is a single, strong bottom of molded plywood.

Molded-plywood sailboat hulls, because of their absence of framing and their thin, molded skin, are extremely lightweight, strong, and require less upkeep than the conventional wood hull. Also, the molded hull has more "give" to it than the sheet-plywood boat has. This quality of "give" is important. A sailboat will hit something sometime, and when it does a hull that can bend at point of contact, providing of course it snaps back into position immediately afterward, is preferable to one that can only crack, dent, or break. But the compound-curve surfaces of molded sailboats do not lend themselves well to neat repairs.

Plastic Sailboats. One of the greatest accomplishments of yacht designers in the 1950's was their quick acceptance and application of a new material—fiberglass molded in layers of polyester-plastic resin. The molding process allows complete freedom in the choice of hull shape; a freedom which, as previously noted, is lacking when materials such as wood and plywood are employed. The plastic reinforced with fiberglass is probably the strongest and most durable of any material used in boat construction. Most plastic hulls are color-impregnated, which means that they are the same color through the entire thickness of the material. Thus scratches do not require retouching with paint. The material is also immune to teredos (sea worms), termites, fungi, and bacteria; it does not rot, and water absorption is low.

While maintenance costs are greatly reduced with plastic hulls, it should be pointed out that this material is not completely indestructible. Because of the great impact strength, the material will not dent or take an out-of-shape set—there are no internal stresses. Fiberglass will often deflect on impact and return to its original shape; if it does puncture or break, it can be repaired easily. Although plastic hulls do not require paint for preservation, they do need it for antifouling when used in salt water and certain freshwater areas. Also, the topsides of a fiberglass-plastic boat may need paint for color, because the molded-in color will gradually fade with

exposure to sunlight. Since fiberglass hulls do not have the buoyance of wood, flotation gear (a compartment containing buoyant material) is provided in most small sailboats presently marketed. But all in all, fiberglass is *the* most popular of all boat construction materials.

Actually an elementary knowledge of fiberglass construction is mandatory for the boat buyer. Fiberglass laminates consist basically of two components: the reinforcing material and the resin which hardens around the reinforcing. The reinforcing takes several forms: mat (random fibers), fabric (clothlike weave), and roving (coarse weave). Application methods differ among builders: some lay up the hull and deck shells in the molds by hand from layers of roving, mat, and cloth, while others spray on a mixture of random fibers and resin from a "chopper gun." But the experts disagree about the merits of the two construction methods. Some feel that the hand laid-up hulls of cloth and roving are superior in tensile strength to chopper-gun hulls. They claim that you cannot develop the same tensile strength with a chopper. To get structural integrity you have to insure a good, tense glass layup and you get it with woven material.

Other experts feel that the two methods are about equal, and a few go as far as stating that some chopper methods are superior to hand layups. But they quickly emphasize the importance of control in both methods. The builder is alloying the material, he is not buying sheets of plywood or planks or sheet-metal. The big problem is the fact that the builder is making the alloy. Buyers should look at it in those terms. It is not so much the materials, but the one who does it.

There are three main problem areas to watch for in the actual construction of the hull—stress concentrations, joints, and attachments. Stress concentrations are those areas where the bulkheads, stiffeners, and air tanks join the actual glass hull or deck. Since fiberglass is a flexible material, the hull can be expected to "work," or flex, under sail, but obviously anything rigid like a bulkhead is not going to move and will cause a stress concentration on that part of the shell. Good construction eliminates as many of these hard spots as possible by spreading the loads across large areas. The hull-to-deck joint is the single worst problem area in glass boats. Quality builders not only attach the hull to the deck with fasteners, but take the trouble to go back and bond it with fiberglass. Attachments are where any piece of hardware joins the shell. Mast steps, winch bases, centerboard trunks, and even the smallest cleats should be carefully reinforced to take the loads which they will carry under racing conditions.

Most experts agree that it is tough for the nonexpert buyer to walk into a showroom and determine a fiberglass boat's properties. One knowledgeable man we asked suggested that the buyer find an unpainted hull area and check to see the general quality. Are there any edges that would indicate thickness? Are all the joints bonded together? Is the overall appearance workmanlike? He also pointed out that flexibility (like tire-kicking) is no criteria, since many shells will bend easily, even though the construction is quite strong.

Another expert friend of ours suggested that the buyer use his native intelligence and also buy a builder's reputation. He added that he had a standard way of making a visual judgment: "I automatically tend to give high grades to any builder who is going to make a neat, tidy boat throughout. You stick your head underneath the deck and you see a lot of shredded wheat hanging down and all this garbage and you cut your hand to pieces on it—then I say, well gee, if he does that where I can reasonably see it, how has he built the rest of it? This does not automatically condemn it, but certainly the guy ought to get credit for doing a neat job."

The most obvious method of inspection is visual. Many flaws in the construction of a boat can be seen by transmitted light through the hull or deck surfaces. A good laminate will be evenly translucent, while dry areas (with not enough resin content) will appear lighter or white and air bubbles will show up darker. Minor defects in the colored gelcoat surface are usually apparent, but the problem areas are in sharp corners where the reinforcing backup laminates fail to meet the gelcoat, leaving a bubble that will soon break. Tapping the hull is also a good test of a fiberglass layup. A good laminate when tapped sharply by a hard object will make a crisp, clear sound, while a dull or muffled sound indicates the presence of air bubbles, delamination, or uncured resins.

Used boats present the opportunity to pick out deficiencies more readily. Our expert suggests looking inside the hull for whitish areas which would suggest water migration indicative of poor construction. While he felt that major structural problems in glass boats were extremely rare, he said, "With a decent builder who has been on the market for a couple of years, all your used-boat problems will be hardware, fittings, and machinery. Unless the builder does a really bad job, 99 percent of the problems will be non-fiberglass and in that last one percent, most of it will be in the gelcoat. But a structural panel failure is very remote."

Many racing dinghies (and larger yachts) are turning to foam or balsa cores for strength in hulls and decks. One of our experts said that foam cores have lower shear and compressive strengths than balsa, besides being a very unstable material to control in production. But another pointed out that while balsa came out ahead on a cost/performance basis, you had to accept problems along with the advantages. Balsa is an organic material and must be properly sealed to prevent water migration, rot, and weight increase. The consensus was that either method must be used carefully to avoid complications, but that core reinforcing did provide a solution to the inherent flexibility of large, flat fiberglass surfaces, as in the case of boats originally designed for plywood construction.

The difference between a "fair" hull and a "smooth" hull also came up. A fair hull has an overall lack of bulges or ridges, while a smooth hull has only a skin slickness but the shape is marred by flaws. Any skipper can get a smooth hull if he wet-sands and polishes enough, but fair hulls are a must for speed. Sighting down the side of the hull will usually tell how good the mold was and how fair the hull is. Attachment point for bulkheads and air tanks should not produce hard ridges on the outer surface of the hull.

Every class boat should come with either a measurement certificate or a guarantee that the boat will measure in—otherwise you may end up with an expensive day sailer. If you plan to race competitively, compare the boat's actual weight against the class minimums before you accept it.

Check the underwater surfaces—keel and rudder on larger boats and centerboard and

Aluminum hulls come in various sizes. The 16-foot Grumman Flyer (left) and the *Carina* (right), winner of the 1970 Newport-Bermuda, have aluminum hulls. Actually, aluminum is used more in bigger boats than in smaller sailing craft. It has a very fine race record.

rudder on smaller ones—for overall fairness, shape, and quality. Rarely does a builder offer the ideal shape on the underwater fins, but make sure that it is at least reasonably efficient. You will probably be reshaping the board and rudder anyway. In larger boats with spade rudders, try to find out how the rudder post attaches to the foam-constructed rudder. A number of steering losses in recent ocean races could have been avoided if owners had known how flimsy the rudder assembly was. In general, the buyer should exercise the same care he takes in selecting any other expensive item (like an automobile) at which he cannot become an expert. Look at all the accessible areas and study the general quality of the workmanship. Talk to owners of sister boats and see what problems they have had. If the manufacturer is not well established,

get an expert's opinion. Also remember that several classes now allow combining fiberglass with wood construction to obtain the good characteristics of each. In other words, these classes allow a wood-planked or plywood hull to be covered with fiberglass cloth material.

Aluminum Sailboats. The efficient strength-to-weight ratio of aluminum coupled with its inherent resistance to corrosion makes it a good boatbuilding material, economically feasible in small sailboats. It is easily formed into attractive shapes, and strategically located extrusions reinforce the hull, making it a sturdy and rigid package. Maintenance of aluminum boats is also minimal. But in spite of these advantages, aluminum sailboats have never been popular and only a few classes are made of this material.

SAILS

The technology of sails has undergone more change in the past thirty years than in the previous thousand. The turning point dates from the advent of man-made fibers which can be made as strong as steel or as stretchy as rubber, giving sailors the power to specify whatever they want in a sail. In the past no such choice was possible. Sailors took whatever was at hand for sails.

History of Sails. In early Egypt, Persia, and Babylonia, sails were made from woven rushes, reeds, and grass. Then the Phoenicians developed sails of flax. The Greeks were the first to develop hemp for sails, preferring it for an ability to withstand water and rot. Durability was further increased by a coating of tar. At various other times in history, virtually every fibrous material, including silk, has been tried for sails. Cotton's use was a relatively late chapter in man's search for a better natural fiber.

As late as 1851, cotton sails were virtually unknown in Europe. That was the year that the schooner yacht *America* sailed to victory in England. The win was credited in part to the flat American sails of cotton, which made the *America* very close-winded. The opposing British fleet was outfitted with sails of flax (very baggy). Cotton sails were accepted as more efficient because the fiber could be spun into finer thread, making for more uniformity and a tighter weave.

With this beginning, it is small wonder that one of the subsequent defenses of the America's Cup also made fiber history. In 1937, the J boat *Ranger* flew the first sail of a man-made fiber (rayon) against the British challenger *Endeavour II*. And the *Ranger,* with her rayon genoa jib, won easily.

The experience of *Ranger* showed the potential of chemistry in evolving still other fibers for sails. Just two years later nylon appeared, but it was not accepted at first by sailmakers. However, man-made fiber developments accelerated rapidly after World War II. In 1949 Du Pont introduced the world's first acrylic fiber—Orlon—and American yachtsmen were the first to discover its advantages as a replacement for nylon spinnakers and jibs. It helped win championships in

the Star, Comet, and 110 classes that year. In 1953 the United States became the first to commercially produce a polyester fiber. Known at first under the experimental code as "Fiber V" and later as Dacron polyester, it was quickly accepted by sailmakers as a superior sail material. In fact, from the beginning, its racing performance was outstanding. One of the most dramatic was the experience of the Cuban Cardenas in the 1954 Star world's championships off Cascais, Portugal. While few expected him to do much better than tenth place, he arrived for the series with the only sails of Dacron polyester and won first place, largely by superior boat speed to windward. In the 1955 ocean-racing season, R. S. Nye used an inventory of Dacron aboard his 53-foot yawl *Carina* and won the Fastnet.

Nearly all of today's sails are made from Dacron. (Known in Great Britain as *Terylene,* in France as *Tergal,* in Japan as *Tetoron,* and in Russia as *Lavsan,* this material, independent of the many trade names—arising from patent and other legal considerations rather than chemical composition—is all basically the same.) Dacron polyester is highly resistant to rot, mildew, and stretch. In addition, it is smooth, relatively nonporous, and it needs little, if any, gradual breaking in, as was necessary with new sails made of cotton. A new cotton sail had to be handled gently. At first, it had to be used in light breezes only, and it was never let stretch extremely tight on its mast or boom until it had been used for a considerable length of time. A new Dacron sail, however, can be stretched reasonably tight and can be carried in all but the strongest winds. It should set properly, have the correct shape, and almost fit its spars the first time it is used. In time, its luff and foot may grow slightly longer from being constantly stretched tight, but the lengthening will be very slight compared to a cotton sail.

The other most commonly used synthetic sailcloth is nylon. This has most of the major advantages of Dacron, except one. Nylon is not resistant to stretch. In fact, it is highly elastic, a characteristic which is very bad for all sails except certain downwind sails, such

Various types of light sails: (top left) a Santana 37 under a genoa jib; (top right) *Carina* (the famous 1955 transatlantic winner in 1955 and forerunner of the present *Carina*) with a mizzen staysail; (bottom left) a Cal-40 with a parachute spinnaker and spinnaker staysail; and (bottom right) a Morgan 33 with a reaching jib, or drifter.

as the drifter and spinnaker. The big advantage in nylon for these sails is that it is very strong and is made in very light weights, as light as half an ounce per yard. Elasticity of sail cloth is detrimental to any sail that is carried to windward, especially in strong winds, because the sail stretches out of shape and loses its proper curvature. However, for balloonlike downwind sails this loss of shape is not really harmful, and it is more important to use lightweight cloth which is definitely advantageous in light airs.

Classification of Sails. Yacht sails may be grouped into three general classifications: working sails, storm sails, and light sails. The first group includes mainsails, mizzens, and moderate-sized jibs or forestaysails of moderate weight which are carried most of the time for ordinary or everyday sailing. Storm sails are small, extra-heavy sails used in heavy weather. These include the storm trysail, a small triangular sail, usually not attached to the boom, which is set in place of the mainsail, and the spitfire, or small, heavy storm jib. Light sails are racing sails made of lighter-weight cloth than that used for working sails. The most common light sails are genoa jibs, spinnakers, drifters, spinnaker staysails, and mizzen staysails, or mizzen spinnakers, which are actually balloonlike mizzen staysails.

The well-known Swedish yachtsman Sven Salén is given credit for inventing the genoa jib. It was first shown to the sailing world at a regatta in Genoa, hence its name. The genoa, or jenny, has a long foot which overlaps the mainsail. It is an effective sail for reaching and beating to windward because of its great area and the strong driving effect it creates due to its overlap. It comes in various sizes and weights and is carried when racing in all breezes, except perhaps the very lightest airs, up to strong winds. Most racing boats carry genoa jibs of different weights and sizes.

The spinnaker is a balloonlike, triangular sail carried when the true wind is abaft the beam. It is made from very light cloth and is an essential sail for racing. The spinnaker can be tricky to handle, trim, and steer by; its use is fully covered in the next section.

The drifter, or ghoster, is a lightweight jib for reaching in very light airs. It is cut high at the clew so that it will fill easily in the lightest airs and so that it can be sheeted to the main boom. It is often cut fuller or with a deeper belly than a genoa, and the drifter's leech, or after edge, is nearly straight, without having concave curvature as is the case with a genoa's leech.

The spinnaker staysail is a balloonlike forestaysail of lightweight cloth which is set beneath the spinnaker. In a good breeze, a well-designed spinnaker will rise, or lift, so that its foot is high above the deck. The spinnaker staysail, sometimes called the cheater, simply fills in the gap under the lifted spinnaker.

The mizzen staysail, of course, is carried only by boats having mizzens—yawls or ketches. It is set forward of the mizzen and is sheeted to the mizzen boom. The mizzen spinnaker is set identically, but its shape is that of a spinnaker.

Weight of Sail Material. A standard and exact scale is used to determine the gradations of synthetic materials when they are used for sailmaking. The gradations are in weight, measured in ounces per yard in length of material that comes 28½ inches wide. The weight ranges from 1.2 ounces to 15 ounces. Although Dacron is much stronger than cotton, other factors in addition to strength must be considered when determining the weight of the cloth to be employed. This is particularly true for mainsails; not only the size of the boat but her primary use must be taken into account.

Spinnakers are the exceptions. For these sails the more strength and the less body the better. Although boats which carry several spinnakers should have one or two of heavier weight for heavy winds, generally speaking, the lighter the spinnaker the more effective it will be. This has not proven true with working sails. Experimentation with mainsails on some of the smaller classes (sails as nearly identical as they could be made except for weight) have demonstrated frequently that the heavier sails outperform the lighter ones.

Most expert sailmakers feel that the buyer should not concern himself with the many varieties and weights of sailcloth. Leave the decisions to the reputable sailmaker; he will give you the best sail possible because he just cannot afford to have a bad sail with his emblem on it. Most agree, however, that it

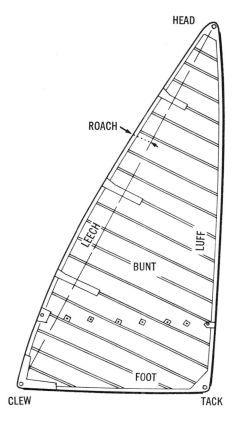

Sail parts and names.

would be wise for the buyer to discuss the particular cloth used in his sail with the sailmaker to gain a working knowledge of what to expect from it. To help in this matter, the following table gives recommended weight of cloth (in ounces per yard, 28½ inches wide) under "average" conditions:

Working Sail Area, Square Feet	Working Sail Weights	Genoa Weights*	Nylon Spinnaker Weights	Storm Sails
Up to 150	4	3	1.2	
150–360	5	4	1.2	
360–420	6	4	1.2	
420–550	8	4–7	1.2	8
550–1000	9	4–7	1.2–1.5	10
1000–1500	9–10	6–7	1.2–1.5	12
1500–2000	12–13¾	6–12	1.2–1.5	15

* As stated earlier, in the more highly competitive racing classes, boats will usually carry genoa jibs of different weights and sizes (generally four) as indicated in the table above for all sail areas between 420 and 2,000 square feet.

Cut of Sail Material. The four standard methods are named from the way in which the panels of cloth run in sails. They are (1) crosscut, (2) miter, (3) vertical, and (4) Scottish cut.

Most mainsails today are crosscut. That is, the length of the sail material is laid at right angles to the leech, which is the same as the direction of pull of the mainsheet. Thus, the seams and airflow run in the same direction and there appears to be a better airflow.

For many years, practically all jibs, both working and genoa, were diagonal, or miter cut. The seams of material are laid at right angles to the leech and to the foot of the sail. They meet a line that bisects the angle of the clew. It is made this way to withstand the single line pull coming at the clew. In the early 1970's many sailmakers got away from mitered jibs and turned to crosscut construction.

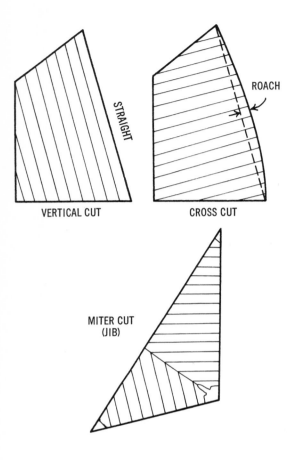

VERTICAL CUT   CROSS CUT

MITER CUT
(JIB)

STRAIGHT

ROACH

Common sail cuts.

The vertical cut, which is the oldest method of construction, is primarily employed for a lugsail or gaff mainsail and mizzen because it reduces bagginess in the area of the roach and leech. The cloths of this cut run parallel to the leech.

In the Scottish—which is similar to the miter cut in that the sail is divided into two parts—the cloths run parallel to the leech and foot. The Scottish cut is seldom seen today.

As you can see in the various illustrations in this book, there are several ways used to cut the material to make a spinnaker. Often, alternating cloths are used—principally for distinctive decorative purposes, often for ready identification.

Sailmaking

Most new sailboats, especially the larger ones, are sold *without* sails and their cost is not usually included in the price of the boat. This permits the owner to purchase them from a sailmaker of his own choosing. It is the general consensus of most sailing experts that buying sails as original equipment with the boat is fine if you know exactly what you are getting. But all the sailmakers agree that "production-line" sails are inferior in shape and often in quality to the custom sails produced singly. Some builders offer sails as standard equipment, but the quality suffers when the sailmaker must make them in lots of 50 at a time. Production sails tend to be compromises—designed for use in all areas, all weather, by all calibers of sailors. With racing, this is particularly true since the hotter the class, the less likely that you will be offered a package deal. The experts agree that the customer who orders a particular sail through a dealer would get the same quality as if he orders it at the loft, but they emphasize that the buyer should still contact the loft. In that way, the sailmaker can decide upon the buyer's particular needs more effectively than by talking to the dealer.

The sailmaker will need information about you, your sailing area, your boat, and your sailing style. If you are an experienced sailor, he can give you a stretchy rope luff in your jib instead of the safer wire luff. He will want to know what kind of rigging you have, how stiff your mast and boom are, and in what weather conditions you expect to sail.

How to Buy Sails. When buying small-boat sails, it is wise to talk to the winning skippers in your class and determine what kind of sails they are using. As you are buying the boat, you will be deciding on the kind of mast and boom, the type of deck equipment (like fairleads and travelers), and other details that will have a direct bearing upon your suit of sails. A bendy mast and boom require a drafty sail, while a stiff spar will take a flatter sail. The weight of your crew, especially in overpowered classes like Flying Dutchman and International 14's, will determine your spar stiffness; a heavy crew can use a rigid spar in strong winds, while a light crew will need a bendy mast to ease the gusts. The conditions

Some spinnakers have distinctive designs, such as the Dragon class boat, left, while the Countess 44 has a specially designed venturi-type spinnaker.

of your own sailing area will vary the sail cut, since a sail made for blustery San Francisco Bay is far removed from one designed for drifting in Long Island Sound. Your own peculiar sailing style will also affect your choice. If you regularly pinch on the beats, you will want a flatter sail, while those who foot off for speed want fuller sails.

In the bigger boats, the choices are just as varied. One of the first decisions is which sails should you get? Many expert sailmakers suggest the purchase of sails which give you the most advantageous club rating. Once you have decided on a rating (usually determined mainly by genoa size), you have to fill out your complement of racing sails. Again the experts choose to disagree—some feeling that no fewer than nine sails would be a minimum inventory for a 35- to 40-foot ocean racer, while others feel that nothing more than a main, a genoa, and a chute are necessary. A heavy genoa, a light genoa, a medium-weight spinnaker and staysail, plus the main (with a zipper foot) would probably be a good starting inventory. From that point, the

buyer can head toward "specialty" sails for his own area, such as drifters or low-hoist heavy-weather genoas. Obviously, you must look at your future plans for the boat—are you going to race closed-course events? Short offshore races? Or long-distance hauls like the Transpac? The closed-course racer requires a much smaller sail locker than a competitor in a transatlantic race who will meet all weather conditions. The experts emphasize that they should know your future plans when you buy your first sails, so that you will not duplicate or overlap when you add more later. Too many buyers order an "all-purpose" genoa, which later is too close to either a heavy or light jenny to be of any use. And many buyers, who know they will not be getting more sails for several years, buy a special-purpose sail such as a superlight spinnaker, which is then rarely used. Be realistic about your needs —do not rush out and buy every sail that is offered. You can always add more sails when you decide you need them and at a time when you know more about your boat.

The sailmaker should be familiar with your

Sail windows, as shown in Jet class boats, can be very handy.

boat. Besides the basic sail plan or measurement certificate, he should know the sailing characteristics of the boat, its actual weight, and the designed stability. He should probably sail aboard to study the positions of fairleads, shrouds, and spreaders—all of which will help him give you the best sail for your particular boat. Most sailmakers have sets of (stock) sails on hand for trial runs.

There is, of course, a great deal of controversy about the design of sails. The location and amount of draft (airfoil), the weight of material, the method of cutting and roping, and a hundred other details affect the final product. To the racing skipper, whose principal aim is winning, many of these factors are of interest as topics of debate, but to the sailmaker, whose job is to produce winning sails for a variety of skippers on a variety of boats, all of them are vital. The sailmaker must attempt to find working answers to all of the many problems presented, and his ability to do so is the measure of his success.

Sails do not age in use like a pair of shoes. In fact, it is well known that sails of Dacron polyester take a certain set after a season's use and often become more resistant to dis-

tortion. This unique stability of polyester sail fabrics made it possible to develop roller-reefing booms and roller-furling jibs. This same quality led to the development of devices to change the shape of sails under way so that a single sail could be made to do the job formerly done by a whole wardrobe of sails—baggy ones for light airs and flat ones for use in a blow. This included a range of edge-tensioning devices: roping in luff and foot, zippers in the foot, for flattening the sail by removing excess fabric, fabric tapes instead of cable in the luff of jibs so that tension and shape could be controlled, and grommets fastened in the luff of the sail near the junction of boom and mast—a "Cunningham hole"—which would be used to pull additional tension into the luff. Bending booms and masts added to this arsenal of tugging and pulling devices, all of which depended on the ability of modern fabrics to resist their destructive effects. Along the leech of a 12-Meter mainsail, these forces can reach 5,000 pounds exerted on a fabric which is only slightly heavier than that used in slacks or a golf jacket.

While Dacron fabric has long life, purchase "used" sails with a great deal of care. It is wise to check the reputation of the sailmaking loft on the condition of used sails, along with their apparent age, to obtain a general idea of value. Usually sailmakers suggest "eyeballing" the sails for draft position, tight leeches, stretching, and overall appearance while the sails are drawing. With the sails down, check for badly worn jib snaps, wear around the spreader areas and clews, deterioration of grommets or luff wires, and cloth appearance. They all agree that it is foolish to plan on having old sails cut down for storm sails, since the cloth weakens with age. Checking the boat's recent racing record will also give an idea of how effective the sails are. Do not always accept the marine surveyor's opinion on sail condition in a used boat, since he often counts the sails, checks the general wear, and appraises their value only on that basis. Know what area the sails were intended for, heavy air or light air. If your sailing conditions are different, plan to get new sails for racing.

Selection of a Sailmaker. Selection of a sailmaker is important. A local sailmaker with a good reputation in your class is the best answer. Choosing a sail loft close to home means you can get all necessary servicing performed easily; the sailmaker can see the sails on the boat and he knows your sailing conditions. Talking to local skippers will give you a feel for the top two or three lofts that build competitive sails for your boat. Sailmakers agree that some lofts are better at certain sails than others, so do not take a chance on a loft that does not regularly produce your boat's sails, regardless of the loft's reputation. A good reputation in other classes does not necessarily mean good sails for your boat. For this reason, skippers of the top racing sailboat classes follow the rule of buying from a sailmaker who has personal experience in that boat. Recognizing this, many of the top sailmakers have worked hard to become champions. They may be relatively unknown to nonracing sailors, depend-ing on word of mouth to build their circle of customers.

Cruising sailors, on the other hand, are more interested in convenience, hence, prefer a sailmaker who is near home port and is available to give personal advice. Of the hundred sailmakers in the United States, the largest portion operate this regional type of business. They know the winds of their particular area—Chesapeake Bay, the Gulf Coast, or Long Island Sound—and they take pride in knowing the right sail combinations needed. They will measure a boat personally, like a custom tailor, and make special adjustments after the sail is delivered. Some sailmakers are skilled engineers and can advise on design work needed in rerigging. But the selection of the ideal sailmaker depends on verifying his talents and matching them to the particular job needed.

RIGGING

To carry all of the sail considered necessary, masts are fitted into the hull; and since the load or thrust of the sails is transmitted to the hull through the masts, they must be strong and well supported. Solid wood masts and spars—originally made of grown timbers or their limbs—were traditional for centuries. In the 1920's, laminated spars—made of planks of wood glued together—were developed. Later, it was discovered that *hollow, laminated* spars were lighter and even stronger. In the new age of the sail, hollow aluminum-alloy spars are light and are not corroded by salt, and they are now generally used in place of laminated spars.

In addition to a very substantial support of the mast, rigging is employed to help in supporting and distributing the stresses to the hull proper. All rigging of whatever kind used to support and stay the masts is called "standing rigging," as opposed to the various lines which are used to raise or lower the sails and to control their position, which is termed the "running rigging."

The Standing Rigging

The headstay, the backstay, and the shrouds, which all support the mast, are standing rigging. They "stand" permanently, as long as the mast is up. (In larger craft the standing rigging, once set up, is rarely adjusted during the season. Small dinghy owners may have to strip down and set up rigging for each trip.)

The headstay runs from the bow of the hull to a point high up on the mast, or, on some boats, to her very peak. The backstay runs from the top of the mast to the stern. The stays running from the side of the boat to the mast are called shrouds. All stays attach to the boat's hull by means of turnbuckles, adjustable threaded links with eyes that are rotated to tighten or slacken the stays. The turnbuckles secure the shrouds to metal chain plates built into the hull. Spreaders are small metal struts extending from both sides of the mast aloft. The shrouds lead over the ends of these struts and then to the mast at an angle, providing a stronger rig.

Types of Standing Rigging. The larger the sailboat, the more support her mast must have. The standing rigging then multiplies. A second headstay, most often called a jibstay, is added; it secures farther down the mast. A second set of shrouds ends at the base of the spreaders. For additional support, a second or even third set of spreaders may be added. Strength at the top of the mast may be provided by a jumper strut, facing forward, with

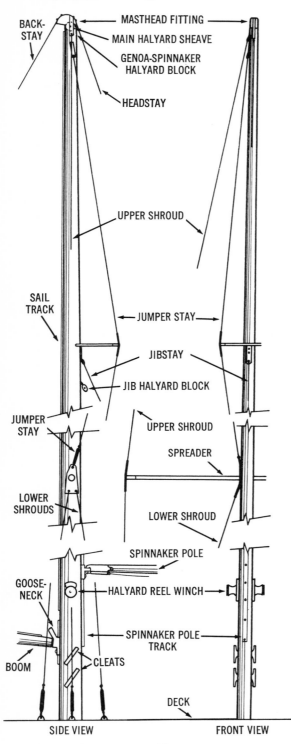

BACK-
STAY

MASTHEAD FITTING

MAIN HALYARD SHEAVE

GENOA-SPINNAKER
HALYARD BLOCK

HEADSTAY

UPPER SHROUD

SAIL
TRACK

JUMPER STAY

JIBSTAY

JIB HALYARD BLOCK

JUMPER
STAY

UPPER SHROUD

SPREADER

LOWER
SHROUDS

LOWER SHROUD

SPINNAKER POLE

GOOSE-
NECK

HALYARD REEL WINCH

SPINNAKER POLE
TRACK

BOOM

CLEATS

DECK

SIDE VIEW   FRONT VIEW

Typical sailboat mast assembly.

its accompanying jumper stays. There are
many standing-rigging variations employed
aboard modern sailboats, but the *masthead*
and *seven-eighths* rigs are the most popular.
The masthead, as previously noted, is the
ultimate of simplicity and is used primarily
with sloops. Running backstays are eliminated, and the forestay is supported by single
or twin standing backstays. The mast must
be proportioned to suit the rig, with a deep
fore-and-aft section and only a slight taper
to the masthead. If the jib is fitted with a
club, making it self-trimming, the masthead
sloop provides a rig in which no gear needs
to be tended when short tacking.

The term seven-eighths is applied to rigs
in which the fore triangle is almost, but not
quite, mastheaded, and the top of the mast,
above the high forestay, is bare of rigging
except for the standing backstay. The shrouds
are terminated at the level of the forestay,
jumper stays being eliminated.

Parts of Standing Rigging. Athwartships,
as previously mentioned, the masts are supported by stays known as shrouds. The object
of spreaders is solely to increase the angle
between the shrouds and the mast and thereby,
for any applied loading on the mast due to
the sails, to reduce the tension in the weather
shrouds and the compression they put in the
mast.

The prime object of standing rigging,
apart from assuring the safety of the mast, is
to make sail-carrying stays as straight as
possible when under their full load of canvas
working to windward. The worth of standing
rigging lies in the attainment of this ideal as
nearly as possible. Complete attainment is
impossible, since it would entail infinite ten-
sions in some members of the rigging; also a
perfectly straight and incompressible mast,
and no stretch in any wire rope.

The upper, or the only (as the case may
be), forestay is the one of principal importance, the most heavily loaded wire rope in
the rigging. With the masthead rig, the primary support for this stay comes from the single or twin standing backstays. The latter, led
to either side of the counter or transom, provide some lateral support as well, for the masthead tends to droop to leeward under sail
pressure.

With some smaller yachts—when you sail

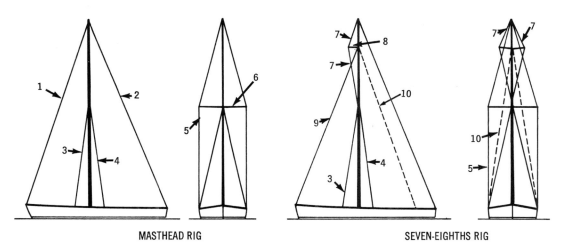

MASTHEAD RIG   SEVEN-EIGHTHS RIG

1. HEADSTAY   2. PERMANENT BACKSTAY   3. FORWARD LOWER SHROUD   4. AFTER LOWER SHROUD   5. UPPER SHROUD
6. SPREADER   7. JUMPER STAY   8. JUMPER STRUT   9. JIBSTAY   10. RUNNING BACKSTAYS

Two types of standing rigging.

with the wind aft—the sail and boom, of course, should be as far forward as possible and the boom should be nearly at right angles to the mast in the fore-and-aft line. If backstays were fixed permanently from the mast to the side of the hull, the sail and boom would catch against them and prevent this. To overcome the difficulty backstays are often made to move at deck level, and they are known as sliding, or *running,* backstays. The backstay slides fore and aft on a wire stay or length of track. Sometimes, in place of two running backstays, boats with an inboard rig are often fitted with a single *fixed* backstay. This makes it easier to handle the boat

under way. If it is necessary to carry this backstay a little further aft to clear the mainsail, this is done with a bumpkin. A single standing backstay is often split aft to avoid interfering with the rudder head and tiller.

In the smallest craft, running backstays may be eliminated, the load in the forestay being carried in the standing backstay through the jumper stays. In craft of any size, and certainly offshore cruisers and racers, this support is inadequate, and running backstays (runners) are essential. Remember that the masthead sloop is generally without runners; this is considered one of the chief justifications for the rig. But in some bigger sloops

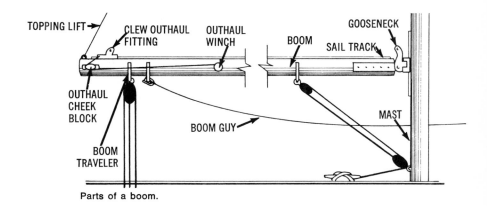

Parts of a boom.

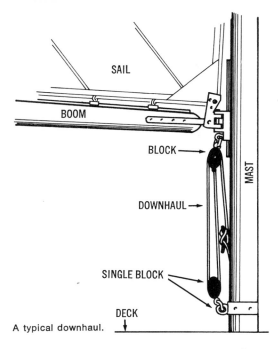

A typical downhaul.

of this type runners may be fitted together with a portable inner forestay to control the otherwise considerable length of unsupported mast; and certainly, if without runners, the masthead sloop requires as much drift as possible between the lower shrouds. A portable inner forestay is also useful when setting a storm staysail.

When under sail in a fresh wind the forestay is the most heavily loaded wire in the ship. Forestays may be double or single. The advantages of the former are security and quickness of sail changing, and in cruising yachts the former is an important consideration, for in the absence—which so often occurs nowadays—of any other forward staying the whole rig becomes dependent on the one highly stressed forestay. The failure of a rigging screw or swage then means disaster. Disadvantages of twin forestays are weight and windage, both increased by twin halyards; complexity; the slightly twisting load they put into the mast; the liability of the idle stay to take away some tension from the one in action; and the possibility of a hank closing round both stays and jamming the sail aloft.

Some boats do not require stays, and the masts are described as unstayed. The un-

stayed mast, like a tree, carries little compression loading and is stepped as a fixed-ended column and proportioned to withstand the bending stresses only. The Finn class has a mast of this type, and for centuries so have many of the largest Chinese junks, but in yachts of any size it is very rare indeed.

On modern boats the rigging nearly always consists of wire rope; stainless steel is the most popular material. Because of its stiffness, resistance to stretch, and great strength for size, 1×19 construction wire (one solid strand of 19 wires) is the most suitable for standing rigging. But you should investigate the variety of rigs and rigging for areas you plan to sail. Several builders offer up to six different mast options depending upon the local wind conditions. Most offer a "heavy-air" package, which usually includes a larger wire size, a heavier mast section, and sometimes items like double lower shrouds or running backstays. Larger wire sizes are recommended not only in windy areas, but in hot, humid conditions like Hawaii or Texas where the dampness tends to corrode rigging quickly. Most builders feel that the trend will be toward more options in rig size, so buyers should find out what is, and will be, available for their boats.

As previously stated, your sailmaker can offer expert assistance in choosing a mast and boom section (if you have a choice) that will suit you and your crew for your sailing conditions. A look at other spars will show you how they have been rigged, and talking to racing sailors in your class will give you an idea of how to tune the mast. Many sailmakers distribute information sheets on various classes, offering their suggestions on rig and tune. In Section IV we have a simple introduction to the *generally* accepted rules.

The Running Rigging

As the name implies, running rigging is constantly being adjusted. It does not remain fixed like standing rigging. Running rigging is the term given to the lines (ropes) by which the sails are hoisted, set, and trimmed. To trim is to adjust the sails when the wind changes or the boat alters course. To hoist and to trim are two different operations. They require two main types of running rigging for each function: (1) halyards for hoisting sail; and (2) sheets for trimming sail.

Halyards. The halyards hoist aloft the head of the sail and therefore need to be connected with the top of the mast. This is done in one of two ways: (1) the halyard is rove through a block attached to the mast by a strap or shackled to a mast band (rove is the past tense of the verb "to reave"—to pass a rope through a hole or block); (2) the halyard is passed over a sheave and down through a hollow mast to deck level. A mainsail is hoisted with a main halyard. This halyard passes over a sheave let into the top of the mast and then either inside or outside the mast down to deck level. Halyards that are led inside a hollow mast are known as *internal halyards*. The main is usually to the port side of the mast, while the jib halyard, which is used to hoist the jib or genoa, is to the starboard. If a boat has a spinnaker, then a spinnaker halyard is used. Flag halyards, signal halyards, or lines are required to hoist the burgee and all flags.

Internal halyards, widely accepted in one-design boats, were, up to a short time ago, generally considered unacceptable for cruising boats. The reason is reliability. If a one-design boat breaks a halyard in a race, that is the end of the race, almost invariably. Reaving a new one and finishing anywhere but last is out of the question, and it makes little difference whether the halyard is accessible or not. On an offshore racer, however, it is imperative that a broken halyard be repaired and rereaved. There is no chance to beach the boat and tack the sail to the mast. You would not want to if you could; there comes a time at sea when you want a sail down even more urgently than you might have wanted it up. But recently, internal halyards have come into vogue on offshore racers as a result of increasing competition, and in conjunction with aluminum masts. Wire halyards for mainsails and headsails *are* reliable, making the risk of losing one very slight.

Even spinnaker halyards are going inside from a few feet below the masthead to a few feet above the winch to reduce windage. Spinnaker halyards can be rereaved without too much difficulty as the block is outside anyway. Care must be exercised in the design stage to be sure the mast is not weakened by making too many holes in the same area. Staggering the entry and exit points up and down the spar usually takes care of this.

Racing boats that are rigged for the several varieties of sails often have a special halyard for each of the sails so that in shifting from one sail to another, no sail need be taken in until the other is drawing. The multiple halyards and sheets present a problem that only a trained crew can solve. All sorts of stunts to identify the running gear have been tried. Lettered tags work fairly well in daylight. Racing cruisers sailing in total darkness usually have the halyards identified by small metal tags of different shapes. Of course, the positions of the different lengths of running rigging and the cleats to which they are belayed follow a standard pattern. Even the crew of the smallest sailing craft should know the location of every line and cleat.

Sheets. Sheets are the lines used to trim the sails when under way. They take their names from the sails which they control; thus the mainsail is controlled by the mainsheet. Even on large boats, the mainsheet is always a single line running into the cockpit, but the common arrangement on the jib finds double sheets, one each for port and starboard sides. The mainsheet controls the in-and-out movement of the boom and, therefore, the sail itself. On small boats your mainsheet may be simply a line passing directly from the boom to a cleat close to your helm, or to pegs or cleats next to the tiller. On larger boats the sheets will pass through one or more blocks, and frequently one of these blocks moves on a slide, or traveler, running crosswise on the deck abaft the helm. The jib sheet may also be a single line sliding on a traveler, but more likely it will comprise two separate lines, each running from the clew down through a fairlead or a small pulley fastened to the deck and back to the helm where it is made fast near the tiller or wheel.

It would be preposterous to assume that a good sheeting system could make a poor crew more effective or a slow boat fast, but it is a fact that a poor sheeting system can make a good crew ineffective or a fast boat slow. A good sheet lead can make a poor sail set better, and it goes without saying that a

A tackle may be rigged from the rail to the boom to control leach twist if a traveler is not used.

poor sheet lead can make a good sail look like a sack of potatoes. There are several ways in which sheets directly affect boat speed; most important is the lead and the way it controls sail shape.

The mainsheet has relinquished some of its in-and-out control functions to the traveler in high-performance one-designs, and travelers under the end of the boom are beginning to catch on in cruising boats. In the latter, however, their only function is to take the twist out of the mainsail's leach. If a traveler is not used it may be necessary to add a tackle from the rail to the boom.

Dacron rope is the most popular today because it is stronger than manila or cotton, has less stretch, and will not rot. Since the running rigging is the lifeblood of any sailing vessel, it must be kept in impeccable condition and be constantly checked for wear.

Travelers. When we consider sail trim, we must not only consider the in-and-out adjustment of the sheet, but also the location of its lead. A sheet lead is usually a block (pulley) on the deck or rail through which the sheet is led. Most leads are mounted in such a way that their location (fore and aft or athwartships) can be changed slightly to give the sheet the most favorable angle of trim for various sailing conditions. This altering of location is usually accomplished by the block being attached to a slide on a

track, although sometimes a lead block slides on a low, athwartships metal bar called a traveler, or horse. Actually, long and easily adjusted travelers give control over the all-important leach area of the mainsail. As the leach of the sail is the only one of the three sides which is not directly controlled by being fastened to a spar, it deserves a great deal of attention. Too loose a leach, especially in light airs, will take all the drive and "feel" out of the boat, whereas too tight a leach, especially in heavy air, will increase heeling moment and weather helm, and if it is really tight it might result in a portion of the sail giving negative drive. Provided the sail is properly cut for all-round conditions, proper use of the traveler will result in the mainsail maintaining the right fore-and-aft contour for all types of wind.

In light winds, when the heeling moment is not a factor, a full sail is required for drive. Under such conditions the helmsman must avoid putting strain on the leach as this will cause the mast to bend aft (in most classes), thus flattening the sail. To avoid putting tension on the leach, the traveler should be kept amidships and the sheet slacked so that the only strain comes from the weight of the boom. Some helmsmen actually pull the traveler slightly to windward under certain conditions to be absolutely sure no tensioning (or flattening) strain is being exerted on the sail. However, if the lead were kept amidships or to windward when the wind increased, the boom would begin to lift too much and the leach would take a great curve off to leeward. This would result in the top of the sail falling off to leeward and luffing; the boat would lose its forward drive and feel. So, as the wind increases, the traveler should be allowed to slide to leeward. Then the sheet will begin to put tension on the leach, taking the twist out of the sail so that it is working in the same plane all the way up. As the wind rises further, tension can be exerted with the sheet, thus pulling the top of the mast aft and reducing the draft in the sail. The stronger the wind blows the flatter the sail should be (as a general rule), so the traveler should be allowed to slide more and the sheet should be pulled harder to take more and more draft out of the sail.

The Boom Vang. Frequently described as

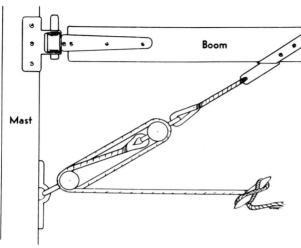

A simple boom-vang arrangement.

Shaping with a boom vang is the best way to keep mainsail leech straight during strong, puffy winds when the mainsheet has to be slacked quickly from time to time to spill wind. Otherwise, a boom vang is seldom used in windward sailing, since downward pull of mainsheet will keep leech straight enough. However, in courses across the wind and downwind a boom vang should be in constant use to keep leech straight and boom under control, since on these points of sailing the boom hangs farther out and the mainsheet cannot pull hard enough to control it.

the most important single piece of equipment on a racing boat, the boom vang (or kicking strap) has earned this reputation on two counts: it makes the boat go faster, and it makes jibing in heavy weather a relatively safe maneuver.

The boom vang affects a boat's speed by helping to control the shape of the mainsail. A tight vang on a reach means that the sail will not twist, or fall off to leeward at the top. The leech is kept firm and the sail will swing out like a door when the sheet is slacked. Without a kicking strap the boom would lift, causing the leech to sag off, especially at the top. This twist in the sail means that the top part will be luffing when the bottom is trimmed right, or that the bottom part will be trimmed too far in when the top is kept from luffing. In other words, when there is a good breeze blowing, a sail without a boom vang is not efficient; it does not develop maximum forward drive throughout its height.

In light weather, with no sea running, a vang has no work to do, as the weight of the boom is usually sufficient to prevent it from lifting and allowing the sail to fall off at the top. But the vang helps even in light stuff when there is a leftover slop tossing the boat around. It will keep the boom from leaping about and help keep what wind there is where it belongs—in the sail.

On boats in which the mainsheet leads from the end of the boom, the vang is useful when going to windward in a blow as it can be used to bend the boom down in the middle, thus reducing the draft in the sail. However, a mainsheet leading from the center of the boom will do this job far more effectively than the vang.

There are classes in which a kicking strap can be of use only part of the time. In the Stars, for instance, the boom is so close to the deck that it is impossible to fit the normal vang, and this class must therefore be content with a less efficient "go-fast" tackle which is led to one of three or four fixed points on the deck. For a beam reach it is in one place, for a broad reach in another, and for a run in yet another. The idea is the same—to pull the boom down and improve the shape of the sail; but quick trimming or slacking of the sail or sharp luffing becomes virtually impossible with such a rig. And of course the Stars are therefore without the benefit of the vang when jibing, which accounts for the many photographs of these boats with the mainsail wrapped around the spreaders, and which also speaks very highly for Star sailors who consistently jibe in heavy weather *without* wrapping their sails around their spreaders. Recently many Stars have been using a curved track for their vangs so all maneuvering can be done with the vang left on.

In some smaller classes where daggerboards are used, skippers must make a choice between jibing with no vang or jibing with

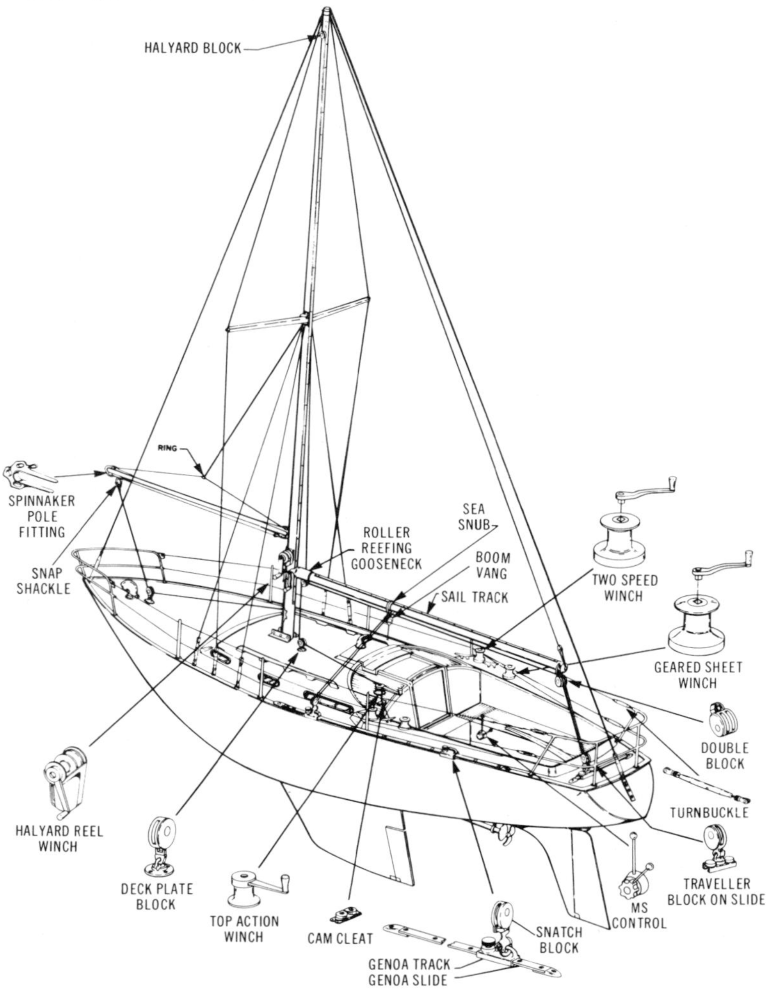

HALYARD BLOCK

RING

SPINNAKER
POLE
FITTING

SNAP
SHACKLE

ROLLER
REEFING
GOOSENECK

SEA
SNUB

BOOM
VANG

SAIL TRACK

TWO SPEED
WINCH

GEARED SHEET
WINCH

DOUBLE
BLOCK

TURNBUCKLE

HALYARD REEL
WINCH

DECK PLATE
BLOCK

TOP ACTION
WINCH

CAM CLEAT

GENOA TRACK
GENOA SLIDE

SNATCH
BLOCK

MS
CONTROL

TRAVELLER
BLOCK ON SLIDE

Typical cruiser-racer sailboat rigging.

the board almost full down. Neither is an inviting prospect, but, because the dagger-board sticks up so far when raised it is impossible to jibe without having the vang hit the board—which would result in either a rapid capsize, a broken board, or a broken boom, and maybe all three at the same instant. Most helmsmen in these classes (the Windmill, for example) choose to lower the board and jibe with the vang set up.

Other Running Rigging. Other parts of a boat's running rigging include topping lifts, downhauls, and guys. There are two types of topping lifts, one for the main boom (only on larger boats), the other for the spinnaker pole. The former merely takes the weight off

the boom when the mainsail is not set, while the lift on the spinnaker pole runs from the middle of this pole to a block on the mast, then to the deck. As for the downhauls, the main one, at the inboard end of the boom, pulls down on the tack of the mainsail, thereby making sure that the desired tight fit along the luff of the sail is obtained. The spinnaker downhaul runs from the midsection or outboard end of the pole through a block on the deck and then to the cockpit. This lowers the pole and gives a crew member in the cockpit control over its outboard end. A guy is employed also to help control the spinnaker.

The Rigging Fittings

The many items of hardware aboard a sailboat are called *fittings*. Starting at the bow of a small sailboat, you will find the headstay fitting and its turnbuckle, which secures the headstay. On the foredeck lies a cleat for either or both the mooring line and the docking line, and the bow chock, through which these lines pass. Near the mast, the jib sheets attach to the clew by means of a shackle which snaps shut. Around the mast at deck level a group of fittings can be found. Halyard cleats are located here, either on deck or below it, in which case the halyards run through the deck. Then there are cleats for the main downhaul, spinnaker guy, and topping lift. Also here is the gooseneck fitting that secures the boom to the mast.

On larger boats you will find it necessary to have means for providing additional power for the control of the halyards and sheets. Power can always be gained by adding blocks to the tackles, but such multiplication of power involves an equal reduction in the speed of hoisting and sheeting. Most sails are hoisted on wire halyards, rather than on the older cordage lines rove through two or more sheaves to provide power. Wire running rigging cannot be belayed around a cleat. Sometimes such rigging has a rope tail spliced to the wire, the line portion being used for hauling and belaying. It is impossible for a man to haul in wire running rigging by hand; the diameter is too small to grasp. Rope large enough to be grasped comfortably is often out of proportion to its job. For these reasons, the use of hand winches is becoming more and more popular even though they add to the cost of rigging gear and increase the number of toe-breakers on deck. The larger boats sometimes have electrically driven winches for halyards and sheets.

Winches. To be fast and efficient, a good winch must be strong (using the best materials available) and it must minimize friction (requiring good engineering and careful workmanship). That means spending money; it is axiomatic. As in anything worthwhile, cheap winches are likely to be cheap winches that are not up to the job they must do. In addition to having sufficient power, a well-designed winch should have a minimum of internal resistance. If the drum is hard to spin because of excess friction or a stiff gear train, then it will be hard to turn when tailing a sheet. Less hand-over-hand trimming can be done before the handle must be cranked, and even though the power is available through the winch handle, the final trimming will be slower and more difficult.

The foregoing points concern winches as they are used to trim headsails on the wind. Because the strain is greatest on the wind, windward work requirements dictate the size and type of the primary winches. Spinnaker sheets and guys use the same winches, but their demands are not so great. Many boat owners install a second pair of winches which can be used as interim winches when setting or taking in the spinnaker. The secondary winches are also useful for vangs and changing sheet leads, and they may be one or two sizes smaller than the primary pair.

Winch sizes are usually designated by number—#0 or #1 being the smallest. Some manufacturers assign arbitrary numbers, but generally the higher the number the more powerful the winch. Power ratios (overall mechanical advantage disregarding friction losses) vary from 8:1 to over 60:1, in one, two, or three speeds. However, power ratio should not be the sole criterion for selecting a winch. Elaborate gearing can slow the freewheeling of the drum, resulting in slower trimming. Selection should be based on the overall effectiveness of the winch—how fast it can trim the sail, not how easily it can tear the clew out of a genoa.

Location of Winches. Next in importance to proper selection is the placement of the winch. The winch grinder should be able to put his back into his work and the tailer should be able to grab great handfuls of sheet as it spins off the winch. (That is why you signed on a crew with muscles.) For best results the handle should be at belly-button height with the grinder *standing* next to the winch. Few cockpits are so arranged to afford the luxury of the space this arrangement requires, but it is well worthwhile and hardly a luxury if racing is the primary objective. The winch must also be placed so the handle will make a full revolution without hitting lifelines or the cabin house. Nothing will discourage a crew member faster than bashing his knuckles against a steel stanchion.

The sheet lead must also be considered when positioning a winch. The winch drum is designed to promote an even progression of turns riding up from the bottom of the drum and off at the top. Unless the lead is from a slightly downward angle or at right angles to the drum axis, overriding turns will jam on the drum. Cleats are often ignored and placed in awkward positions without regard to the winches. Rather than bolt a cleat to the cockpit coaming in a vertical plane, it is better to mount it horizontally on a block adjacent to the winch. Here the sheet tender can see what he is doing, he can follow the lead directly from winch to cleat (avoiding confusion as to which line goes to which sail), and he can often slack the sheet on the cleat to ease the strain when making fine trim adjustments.

Halyard winches are not as vital as sheet winches, and their position is dictated more by halyard leads than ideal working position. Nevertheless, many builders and designers place them indiscriminately without regard to the user. For best muscle efficiency halyard winches should be between 30 and 36 inches above the deck area the crew stands on to use them.

The current trend toward internal halyards has some designers placing halyard winches on deck, 12-Meter fashion. This removes them from the wind stream and lowers the weight. Both advantages override crew convenience in this area.

Cordage and Ropework

During manufacture and procurement, the word *rope* is generally applied to all sizes and types of rope, both fiber and wire. Sizes of wire and fiber ropes usually are designated by diameter in inches. It is interesting to note that the United States Navy defines *rope* as wire rope, *line* as fiber rope. The sailing fraternity, on the other hand, defines *rope* as becoming line only when used in a boat operation including standing and running rigging, anchor line, mooring lines, etc., and as *rope* when employed to secure an object.

Cordage, in marine usage, is a collective term that includes all cord, twine, line, rope, and string made from twisted synthetic or vegetable fibers. Cord, string, and twine are loosely spoken of as small line. Small cordage is usually known on shipboard as *small stuff*. It is designated either by the number of threads that it contains, such as 12- or 15-thread, or by its use, such as *ratline stuff, seizing stuff,* or *marline*. Generally the term *fiber rope* refers to heavy lines having three or more strands; as a rule, in marine usage all fiber cordage larger than 1½ inch in circumference or more than 21 threads is called fiber rope. Fiber rope larger than 5 inches in circumference is called hawser. When ordering wire and fiber rope, the desired diameter or circumference must be specified.

Types of Fiber Rope. Fiber rope is so named because it is made from natural or synthetic fibers, including manila, nylon, Dacron, etc. In the days of the square-riggers, rope used aboard ship was almost invariably hemp or manila. Today, with synthetics supplementing natural fibers, it is different. Properties of the various fibers differ. One may be superior in tensile strength, another in elasticity, a third in resistance to abrasion, still another in its soft, smooth handling qualities. Characteristics of leading fiber ropes are as follows:

Manila rope will function satisfactorily in virtually any use as a line—provided it is top-quality manila. But you may need larger, heavier manila than would be required if a synthetic line were used.

Nylon rope is more than twice as strong as manila, size for size, permitting use of smaller, lighter lines that are smoother and easier to handle. It is also quite elastic. This quality is fine in mooring and anchor lines where shock absorption is desirable.

Dacron rope is nearly as strong as nylon, but has less stretch in it. This makes Dacron suitable for sheets and halyards, or other places where strength is desirable but stretchiness would be a disadvantage.

Polyethylene rope is made in different grades, the strongest being about the same as Dacron. Its main quality is that it floats, making it an ideal line for heaving, and for the dinghy painter.

Here are representative strengths in pounds of different fiber yacht ropes:

Diameter, Inches	Manila	Nylon	Dacron	Polyethylene
¼	600	1,800	1,725	1,050
⅜	1,350	4,000	3,650	2,150
½	2,650	7,300	6,200	3,900
⅝	4,400	10,900	9,300	6,000
¾	5,400	15,600	13,000	8,000
⅞	7,700	21,400	17,500	10,500
1	9,000	27,000	23,300	14,000

Wire Rope. Wire ropes are fabricated almost exclusively from steel wire and can be broadly divided into two types: flexible steel wire rope for use as halyards, hoists, etc., and the heavier, less flexible types used for standing rigging. The flexible types are usually formed of thin strands of wire cable laid round a fiber core (the 6 × 12 and 6 × 18 are typical). Ropes used for standing rigging as previously mentioned are usually solid—that is, there is no fiber core (the 1 × 19 is typical). Wire rope may be made from various kinds of alloys and may be either galvanized, uncoated, or stainless steel. Galvanized wire rope is used as standing rigging for sailboats and in places on board where rope is not subjected to excessive wear; uncoated wire rope is used for running rigging. Stainless-steel wire ropes may be used for both standing and running rigging. Vinyl- and nylon-coated cables are good for running rigging too.

Wire-rope Sizes. As previously stated, the size of wire rope is designated by its diameter in inches. To measure wire rope correctly, place it in the micrometer so that the outermost points of the strands will be touching the jaws of the micrometer. Because of friction and tension, the diameter of a used wire rope will be 1/8 to 1/64 inch less than a new one of the same original size. Wire rope is also designated by the number of strands per rope and the number of wires per strand. Typical weights and breaking strengths of 1 × 19 stainless-steel wire rope are as follows:

Size	1 × 19 Breaking Strength	Weight per Foot
3/64	375	.0055
1/16	500	.0085
3/32	1,200	.020
1/8	2,100	.035
5/32	3,300	.055
3/16	4,700	.077
7/32	6,300	.102
1/4	8,200	.135
9/32	10,300	.170
5/16	12,500	.210
3/8	17,500	.300

The sailor's selection of wire-rope size and construction should be influenced by the use he makes of his boat. If he sails for quiet relaxation and pleasure, his selections may be different from those made by the avid racer. The wire-rope manufacturer can make recommendations based on good engineering practice and experience. Because of considerations of weight and space, or his own experience, the sailor may see fit to modify such recommendations.

The advantages of wire rope are fairly obvious: it is many times stronger than comparable sizes of fiber, requires less maintenance, and is virtually stretch free. On the other hand, even the flexible types are less flexible than fiber, and splicing and manipulation requires a high degree of skill.

WHAT KIND OF SAILBOAT TO BUY?

It has been more or less reliably estimated that United States builders now offer over 1,000 different kinds of sailboats (see Section III) to the bewildered buyer. No wonder, then, that some people spend several years in sifting, looking, thumping, and sailing their way through as many of these 1,000 boats as physically possible, hoping that somehow one of them will "feel just right for me."

While it is not quite so easy to buy the right boat as it is to buy, say, an automobile, it need not be a hit-or-miss, wide-ranging search. If you analyze what it is that you need from a boat, at least 950 of those 1,000 possibles will be automatically eliminated, perhaps even 999 of them. The controlling idea in your analysis is *use*—the use to which you will put the boat you buy; and this includes the conditions under which she will be used.

As was stated in Section I, there are three basic types of sailing yachts available: catamarans, racer-day sailers, and racer-cruisers.

A Rhodes 19 (left) is a typical day-sailer, while the Ericson can be classed as a racer-cruiser.

The latter two—catamarans will be discussed later in this section—are monohulled, and their construction and equipment have just been described.

The Racer-Cruiser or Cruising Sailboat. The racer-cruiser (also called cruising auxiliary, when equipped with an engine—or cruising sailboat) is a great favorite all over the world. The cabin provides shelter for the youngsters on day sails and longshore accommodations for periods ranging from a weekend in the small sizes to more extended voyages in 30-footers and up. They are stiff, able, and sea-worthy, and can negotiate a lot of rough water in safety. While many auxiliary and cruising sailboats are considered one-designs and do have associations, quite often—unlike the smaller class boats—there are not suffi-cient numbers in a given area for even-up racing. (Open-design or one-of-kinds are also available in this basic type of craft.) To over-come the problem of insufficient boats, most yacht clubs have a program of handicapped racing for cruising sailboats, so the cruiser or auxiliary is not excluded from active compe-tition (see Section VI for details). If the

skipper and crew are experienced enough, and your boat can pass the race-committee re-quirements, you can participate in the classic offshore races such as the Bermuda, Nassau, Mackinac, Ensenada, and Honolulu events. Midget ocean racers, which are sailing cruis-ers under thirty feet, are becoming very popu-lar, and the reasons for this popularity are given later in this section.

The Racer–Day Sailer. Racer–day sailer one-design classes are the most popular of the sailing craft. They are the least expensive but they still provide tremendous fun. Whether you want a pleasant, easy day sail with your family or a devil-take-the-hindmost race, you can get it from this type of boat. If racing is your prime interest, inquire at local yacht clubs and find out what the active one-design classes are. There is no use having a racing boat if there is no competition. One-of-kind or open-design boats are seldom avail-able in racer–day sailer types. For complete information on the racer–day sailer or day sailer–racer see Section III. (Since most boats are designed with a prime purpose, either racing or leisurely day sailing, and a secondary purpose, either racing or day sailing, you must decide on the primary reason for buying the craft.) Incidentally, regardless of his original plans, the buyer of a class sailboat *nearly* always comes to the point where he is at least casually involved with racing.

On this matter of use, one must consider first *who* will use the boat. If you are a young man with a big bank account, then you have only yourself to please, and whether you fancy a 9-foot board boat or a 12-Meter you need worry only about whether it is going to suit *you*. If, on the other hand, you have wife and children, then you really should take their needs and interests into account, too, or *you* will not enjoy the boat fully. A hot (but probably cramped and uncomfortable) racing machine may please you, but the accusing eyes of the family you leave at the dock will tend to dampen that pleasure. It will be better to sail a boat that is kind to people, even if you give up something in performance. Remember that there is keen racing even in small boats. The 11-foot Penguin, a class of thousands around the world, offers excellent competition at a cost of less than $750. These and other sailboats are frequently sailed the year round, even in northern states. The hardy sailors who race in the winter up north are known as "frostbiters" (see Section VI for further details). Of course, some one-designs are better for the beginner than others. For this reason, it is a good idea to talk to members of a class and find out the level of competition of that class before purchasing any craft.

But the one-design class does not have to be raced to have fun. One-design sailors have a wide choice of boats, too. You can find boats suitable for racing as well as day sailing. But, if you want to go day sailing comfortably, or if you are a beginner in racing, or especially if you want your family to learn to like sailing, do not pick too extreme a racing type of boat. Buy a one-design boat of the day-sailer type with a comfortable cockpit to sit in, not one where you have to hang out over the rail and perform acrobatics to keep it right side up. A boat on the heavy and beamy side is better for the afternoon-sailing family, or for the beginner, than the ultrafast types. Even though you do not want to race at first, you may later. In other words,

with a one-design class sailboat, you can sail for fun and still race in competition if you wish.

Points to Consider When Buying a Sailboat. When considering a boat from a point of view of comfort, incidentally, one fact often overlooked is that a small boat is only half as roomy in a fresh breeze as it may be pictured on a builder's brochure sailing in a 6-knot breeze. The obvious reason is that when the breeze picks up, six people might have to get up on the windward rail when there is really only room for two or three. A boat with cockpit seating for six at the mooring is really only comfortable for three or four if you sail a lot in brisk breezes.

It is quite certain, as previously stated, that you will get no racing in home waters unless there are boats to race with. Thus, it is fundamental to tour the waterfront and see what kinds of boats are being raced where you intend to sail. Unless you want to try organizing a new racing fleet (and many people have done it successfully), then you must immediately limit yourself to boats of classes being raced where you sail—or, plan to join the turnpike-regatta circuit, trailing frequently to out-of-town regattas (and this, too, is something that lots of people do, even prefer). If the turnpike-regatta idea appeals to you, then, again, it is a good idea to get in touch with the national secretary of the particular class that interests you and see how far away you are from regular competitive events in the class.

Another factor which immediately eliminates many of the 600 potential choices you might make is that of mooring or launching facilities available to you. For example, if it is going to be necessary for you to dry-sail the boat from a "mooring" space in your garage, you must plan on launching from a ramp every time you use the boat—then you will have to unstep the mast and rudder and tie all the loose equipment down for the over-the-road trip from water to home every time you want to take a casual evening sail. If you have to go through all this with a big, heavy brute of a boat (anything over 700 or 800 pounds) with towering mast and a maze of heavy rigging, it will soon get to the point where you will prefer to stay home and prune the roses.

Dry sailing from a more highly developed facility, conversely, can be the most convenient of all ways to sail. Such a facility will have an enclosed, paved trailer-parking area, electric hoists, no overhead power lines to hit with the mast as you push the trailer around, on-the-spot locker space, and other niceties which allow you to sail almost any kind of a boat up to 25 or 30 feet, keel or centerboard, with no fuss at all. Just bend on sails, push trailer to hoist, and you are over the side ready to sail. Such facilities are rare, however, and so if you have to dry-sail, give some thought to the weight of the boat and trailer and the difficulty of getting the mast stepped before leaping into a type of boat which will eventually seem like drudgery rather than fun.

Still another limiting factor is local wind and sea conditions. These conditions include not only the typical weights of wind and the size and steepness of the seas you can expect, but also the temperatures of water and air. For instance, if you are going to sail in Biscayne Bay, off Miami, the prospect of getting wet, either through capsize or just from green water and spray coming aboard in a breeze, is not too great a problem. On the other hand very cold water can represent a real danger in terms of safety. In such conditions a keel boat may be the only safe choice if one is responsible for the safety of children or adults who may not be in the best physical condition.

Prevailing wind conditions may limit your choice, too. In an area such as San Francisco Bay, where there's almost always a fresh breeze, a stable, beamy boat with plenty of freeboard and a moderate ratio of sail area to weight is most practical for comfortable day sailing and racing. In Long Island Sound, where typical summer month winds are much lighter, one needs more sail area and an easily driven hull in order to avoid endless hours of slatting around, swatting flies, and getting nowhere.

In waters where there is a lot of steep chop, built-in buoyancy and automatic bailers not only add to convenience and comfort, but, more importantly, to safety.

The matter of safety is paramount, but not as simple as it seems. One might suppose that a heavy, lightly rigged keel boat would be the ultimate in safety, and so she is, provided you keep her from filling with water. Once filled, however, she will go down like a stone and leave you there, hopefully snug in a life jacket, with a long swim ahead. A seemingly frail, planing centerboard boat weighing only 200 or 300 pounds and carrying clouds of sail on a tall rig can be just as safe, or a safer boat, provided she is well sailed. She may take a lot of water as she crashes and skims along in a squall, but if transom flaps and automatic bailers are open, she casts it off just about as fast. In the event of a capsize, her built-in buoyancy will keep her floating high enough in the water so that she will be reasonably easy to right and sail home. However, all this requires some agility, strength, and stamina and is *not* recommended for people who might tire easily. In icy water you will have to get her righted and sailing again right *now,* or your strength will all be gone in a few minutes.

Ways of Obtaining a Sailboat

There are four ways in which you can get the sailing yacht of your choice:

1. Build it from plans and raw materials.
2. Build one from a preplanned, precut, material-supplied kit.
3. Purchase a secondhand or used boat.
4. Buy a new boat ready to sail.

Each method listed is progressively more expensive, but as the cost goes up the work required to get the boat afloat decreases. We indicate here a rough guide comparing costs for a 13½-foot, sheet-plywood, centerboard sloop of the Blue Jay class:

Raw materials plus plans—up to $400
Kits—$450 up
Used—$500 to $1,200
New—$1,400 to $1,600

To this one should add that it will take from 50 to 150 hours of labor to build a Blue Jay from scratch, depending on how skillful one is with wood and tools. (Plans cost $15 per set plus a $15 fee for each additional boat from one set of plans.) Kit boats of this class require 25 to 75 hours to assemble.

Building Your Own Sailboat. A man who builds his own boat in his spare time, rather than having it built by a boat manufacturer, will save from one-third to three-quarters of the cost of a class sailboat. Added to money saved is the fun of building your boat and then, on the water, the thrill that comes when you first sail the creation of your own hands and skill. But before rushing headlong into a sailboat-building project, ask yourself if you are a fine enough and patient enough craftsman to execute the intricate work properly. It is far wiser to decide regretfully against building your own boat than to end up with a misshapen, half-finished skeleton in your garage or backyard. It is much more pleasant to recognize your own limitations beforehand than to erect an embarrassing monument to your ineptness that is good for nothing but firewood. Remember that a class boat must be built exactly to plans and specifications. The plans of most small one-design class boats can be obtained from the secretary of the class.

Kit Boats. A few designs of class boats are available in kit form. These kits, manufactured by some of the finest boatbuilding firms in the country, have been designed under class rules for easy construction by the average person. Full step-by-step instructions have been prepared for each kit, all the difficult work of laying out and building the frames, keel or centerboard, stem, planking, etc. has been eliminated. The job is simplified so that the boat can be assembled with ordinary hand tools and requires no previous boatbuilding experience or technical knowledge.

When building a boat from scratch, fully detailed plans are usually obtained from the class secretary for a set fee ($10 and up) per set. This fee must be paid for every boat built, whether by amateur or professional, and is often referred to as a "number tax," since each and every class usually must pay it or be legally liable for infringement of the design. It also covers registration, the designer's royalty, the actual cost of the plans themselves and—in some class associations—the first year's membership.

Secondhand Boats. Secondhand boats are usually purchased from a private party or through a yacht broker. The private party forces you to assume a "buyer beware" stance, while the broker relieves you of many of the headaches, especially in larger boats.

Private-party deals are most common in smaller one-design classes, where the yacht-club bulletin board and newspaper classifieds serve to pass the word. Brokers usually shy away from small boats anyway, since the small commission makes them hardly worth the effort. The drawback that many people see in a broker is his 10 percent commission, feeling that they could purchase the same boat more inexpensively from a private party. The broker, however, does quite a bit for his fee. He makes sure that the title to the boat is clear, that no liens are upon the boat, and he takes care of the complete title transfer, which is often complex, especially in the case of documented yachts. He organizes the marine survey and will assist in obtaining insurance and financing. So the broker earns his commission—but should you use his services? The consensus of experts is when dealing with smaller boats—no; but when you get to the larger sailboats, he is usually worth his fee.

In a used racing boat, there is a nebulous value often put on a "racing record." Similar to good will when selling a business, a racing record is based entirely on past performance and sometimes just does not work for the new owner. A racing record is still the most valuable key to the relative value of a used racing sailboat though. In a smaller boat, even a moderately good recent record shows that the boat is still competitive. In ocean racers, it shows that the boat will sail to its rating at least under certain conditions. But how much should you pay for this racing record? A record is not as valuable in strictly controlled one-design classes where a boat is the duplicate of the rest of the fleet, but in high-performance and development classes, the racing record is worth nearly as much as the replacement cost of the boat. In larger boats, the racing record again is a mirror of the owner's skill, but if the boat is custom-built, the record can be expensive. Each prospective buyer will have to decide how much the record is worth. Talk to other skippers and get their opinions of the boat's value. Determine what the exact replacement cost of the boat is and then see if you could take another similar hull and bring it up to the faster boat's standards. In some cases, a boat specially built at the factory would be impossible for a private party to duplicate—thus the value of the boat will be dependent solely upon the buyer's desire for it.

Most smaller one-designs are sold without the expense of a marine survey. The buyer merely checks the boat over on his own and determines its condition, or calls on a more experienced friend for advice. In larger boats, surveys are often a very wise investment since there are so many potential problem areas. Most insurance men and brokers agree that the quality of marine surveyors varies widely. Even though all surveyors are licensed and bonded, some are conscientious, while others are slipshod. Before you select a surveyor, contact your insurance agent, who will have a list of approved surveyors. A marine survey will give you a good idea of the actual condition of the hull, sails, and equipment, but this is generally from a technical standpoint and few surveyors will offer opinions as to the boat's racing ability. So the buyer can only expect to find out the condition of the boat, not its speed, from a surveyor.

A buyer should ask several questions when looking at a used sailboat. The first should be: "Why is the owner selling?" Many times it is a matter of the owner moving into a larger boat for family or personal reasons, but sometimes it is because the boat is no longer competitive. If the owner is buying a newer version of the same boat—be suspicious. Even in the strictest one-design classes, there are old models. Often deck arrangements and hull tolerances are changed legally —leaving the owners of older boats at a disadvantage. So talk to a new-boat dealer and see if he has, or is expecting, a newer version of that used boat.

Used-boat prices *usually* include a reasonably good sail inventory, a trailer, extra racing gear such as winches, cam cleats, bailers, anchor and line, paddle, pillows, compass, life jackets, masthead fly, etc., etc. Look at the equipment and sails carefully and determine their condition. Often a boat will need a new suit of sails, sheets, and a new bottom job— expenses that can bring the used-boat price up to that of a new one.

Buying a New Sailboat. Actually, buying a new sailboat is the easiest and safest way to obtain your craft. You go to a local showroom, pick out the class boat you want, per-

haps take a trial sail, and then buy it. If there are no dealers carrying the class boat you want, you may order it by mail directly from the manufacturer and it will be shipped to you by freight. If a new boat is bought from a professional builder, he should be asked to notify the class secretary of the sale, and the purchaser should also write, giving the boatbuilder's name and date of transaction. If that boat has paid its number tax, there is no charge for registering it in the owner's name. The transfer will, however, not be officially recorded until the tax has been paid. It is the responsibility of the builder to pay the number tax, so purchasers should make sure that the tax has been paid. But, before a boat—whether purchased ready-made, assembled from a kit, or built from scratch—can take part in a class race, it must be inspected and approved by a member of that association (generally a member of the class measurement committee) to make sure that it conforms to class specifications, and to grant a measurement certificate. Once approved, a number is assigned by the class association and is sewn on the mainsail along with the class insignia. This is the number under which the boat races regardless of how many times the craft may change ownership. If a boat is purchased or sold secondhand, notice should be sent to the secretary by both parties. There is usually a nominal fee charged for changing the name of registration.

Class Membership

Ownership of a class boat and membership in a class association have many advantages. In addition to the way in which these associations enforce their class rules and promote well-run, well-organized racing, they also serve to bring sailors with common interests together socially at class meetings and regattas, and they protect the value of any boat in the class. By strict enforcement of the rules and maintaining standards, by registering boats and keeping a record of them, the association protects the buyer and seller when a class boat changes hands, and tends to keep the value of boats up over the years. A one-design is generally a wise boating investment if suited to the sailing area and if other boats of the same class are nearby. Actually, as previously stated, a well-maintained, one-design racing sailboat depreciates very little through the years, and many built in the fifties are selling for more now than they cost new. The open-design sailboats and power-boats depreciate in value and in relative performance just as automobiles do. But the one-design boat retains its value. This is usually true if the boat has a good racing record. This competitive factor is very important in the price of a used boat. Also, a numerous class in an area will be more in demand because of the greater racing competition it offers than a class with only a few boats.

Parenthetically, it may be noted that if the boat you buy is one of a vigorous local racing fleet, whatever investment you make is bound to be a fairly good one. You will not be able to resell your boat for more than you have invested unless you are very lucky, but you will be pleasantly surprised at how little she depreciates and, spreading it over the years you sail her, the cost will be negligible.

Another "people" consideration, beyond who might go sailing with you as passengers, is the requirement for a racing crew of the boat you are thinking about. There are a number of racing classes which require at least three strong, active, and expert crewmen to handle jib, runners, spinnaker, and mainsheet and to make all the smaller adjustments. If you are starting from scratch in such a class, it might be well to join a crew, rather than buy a boat, at least for one season. Otherwise, as you spend a good part of each summer week on the phone trying to round up a halfway competent crew for Saturday, and sail with them one or two evenings prior to the race getting them to at least remember what strings are attached to what sails, you will have moments when you wish you had bought a single-hander.

Also to be considered is the physical strength and agility required of even a single crewman on a given boat. If your most likely crew is to be a preteen son or daughter, then any boat with a jib of more than 65 or 75 feet of area is pretty much out of the question. A crew job that is physically too demanding is one of the best ways in the world to sour a child on sailing for life. Furthermore, you as skipper will have misgivings about starting a race if the wind is blowing

harder than 15 to 18 miles per hour. It is lots better to sail a boat that is well within the physical capabilities of the crew than it is to sail one which is just at the limit.

Midget Ocean Racers

In the last five years, the "midget ocean racer"—racing, cruising, day-sailing boats of 18 to 30 feet—have burst onto the United States sailing scene in unbelievable numbers. There are several reasons for this:

First, fiberglass construction has brought costs per foot of boats in this size range down drastically (in "real" money, at least, discounting any inflation). Also, fiberglass construction requires less framing and other structural members, and these little boats may be surprisingly roomy.

Second, most of the gifted naval architects in the country have given thought to the small ocean racer and have come up with able, comfortable, and fast designs.

Third, the economics of boatbuilding and boat ownership are such that while a 50-foot yacht is only twice as long as a 25-footer, only one in, say, 10,000 United States families may be inclined to spend the amount necessary for the 50-footer, but one in 10 families find the 25-footer within reach if they want a boat badly enough. There are several reasons why you might want a boat of this type:

1. They are generally moderately rigged, stable, and easy for two average people to sail. Many may be single-handed comfortably.

2. The good ones are able sea boats and one need have no hesitation about taking on some fairly extended cruises.

3. Often they are trailable. One can trail to cruising waters quite a distance from the home port and not only have a boat to sail when he gets there but a home to live in and even a place to heat the baby's bottle, if that's desired.

4. There is good racing available for such boats along the East Coast, Gulf Coast, Great Lakes, and West Coast, though not much on inland waters. A few of these designs have developed strong one-design class organizations and have 50 to 100 starters crossing the line in their championship regattas. Others are raced under CCA, MORC, or MORF

The Cutlass class was one of the first popular MORC boats in the United States.

An outboard can be handy to have aboard, even if sailors do not like to admit it.

handicap rules (see Section VI).

5. These midget ocean racers are often a good solution to the skipper whose family is growing too big for the class boat he is sailing, or for the man who wants to do some cruising as well as racing. However, one should not be dazzled by the prospect of extended offshore passages in the "28-footer which sleeps six." Six on the 28-footer is fine for an overnight, or when the weather is nice and a couple of them may sleep on deck. But have you ever spent 48 hours huddled in a small cabin with five others, cold winds and torrents of rain forcing you to keep all hatches buttoned up tight? It's better to stay home.

The interior is often left to the wife, yet it is a major factor in a racing crew's efficiency. Most builders point out that they have been forced to adopt the dinette interior as a result of public demand. The dinette models appear roomier and more useful in the showroom or at the mooring, but under way it is rarely used. For long-distance racing or cruising, pilot berths in the main cabin keep the crew sleeping in the midsection of the hull with less motion, while the dinette style forces them to sleep in the ends of the boat. Some builders note that they will install a nondinette interior for any customer who prefers it. More on cabin interiors can be found in Section V.

Wheel steering is now being offered on boats as small as 28 feet, and the buyer must make another decision. Nearly every sailor we polled favored the tiller for general sensitivity and racing "feel," but they agreed that in many long races the wheel's mechanical advantage is a blessing. Most competitive ocean racers up to about 40 feet are well-enough balanced to handle with a tiller. With the wheel, you tend to lose the feel of the boat, but the ease of steering is increased, especially downwind in heavy air.

As a rule, when one buys a class boat of 25 feet or more in length, she usually comes with the engine installed, and one must pretty much assume that the engine is well put in. There has been a tendency among several boatbuilders to make small cruiserracers available with the power optional. This, in many cases, reduces the cost as much as two thousand dollars. Then the engine may be installed at a later date should the owner wish. In any case, if you wish to add power, check her original builder for his recommendations. Should these not be available, try to find a yard or mechanic familiar with sailboat installations. Mechanics used only to working on power cruisers just cannot be trusted with the planning or installing of an exhaust system or a line at all complicated. Nor is the average engine dealer likely to be up on the finer points of sailboat installations. You can, however, get worthwhile advice from the engine's manufacturer. The average manufacturer will plan the entire layout for you, if you will supply him with the hull plan and particulars of the boat. Many have booklets on sailboat installation. Regardless of the circumstances, here are two rules to be sure to follow: (1) Select your engine intelligently, but be a real stickler as to how it is installed; and (2) follow through by giving your engine every chance to do its best. Do not baby it or hesitate to use it, for disuse rather than actual running is responsible for so many engine ailments. Just see that your way of using it and of looking after its needs offset those disadvantages inherent to a sailboat installation.

When engines are offered, gasoline fueling is considered as standard equipment with the diesel as an option; and here again the eventual use of the boat will be the deciding factor. The diesel is more efficient, cheaper to operate, more rugged, and fuel is readily available in all cruising areas. The diesel's disadvantages are more weight and considerably more initial expense. The diesel is considered safer as the fuel is far less volatile.

Some smaller cruiser-racers and the larger racer–day sailers have facilities for outboard motor power (1½ to 10 horsepower in size). An outboard well, ballast-compensated, is designed into the hull of some of these boats, while others have motor brackets available.

Financing a Sailboat. So popular is sailing today that most banks and commercial-loan firms will finance your new sailboat (sometimes secondhand ones, too) in much the same way as a new automobile. Financing can be arranged through the dealer, or directly with your own bank or other lending institution. A down payment of from 20 to 30 per cent of the purchase price is required by most companies. Interest rates and duration of contracts vary with the amount of money extended. You can also find that loans are obtainable for sailboat repairs, overhauls, and insurance, by using your boat as security.

CATAMARANS AND MULTIHULLS

The catamaran is one of the oldest types of craft known to the civilized world. The word is of Malayan origin: *catu* (to tie)–*maran* (log). Centuries ago, the Polynesians would tie two huge canoes together and actually transport entire villages from island to island. The tribal fathers felt that this boat was far more seaworthy than any with a single hull.

The design somehow became lost in antiquity with the exception of some limited native activity in the Hawaiian Islands. During the late 1800's, the famous Nathanael Herreshoff startled the yachting world with a "modern" catamaran and had the audacity to enter it into the New York Yacht Club cruise. The yacht's performance was so crushing to the conventional boats that he was barred from further club racing. The "unmaneuverable" V-shaped hulls on this boat were later improved by his son, L. Francis, with the introduction of a centerboard in each hull.

Development in catamarans was slow until about 1952, when a major design breakthrough was accomplished by the Prout brothers in England. Notably, the change from the V-shaped hull cross-section to a U-shaped one with a centerboard so improved the maneuverability of this craft that it became practical and popular in Europe immediately. A well-designed small cat (20-foot and under) will not snap about as readily as a monohull but the little it sacrifices in this maneuver is replaced by rapid acceleration, breathtaking speed, and performance.

Yachting magazine's One-of-a-Kind Regattas have been the springboard for the acceptance of the modern catamaran in the United States. In 1959 the close boat-for-boat second-place finish of the 17-foot Tiger Cat (235 square feet of sail plus a Lightning spinnaker) behind the 38-foot A-Scow (2,000 square feet of sail with spinnaker), considered the fastest monohull in the world, startled American yachtsmen. The outstanding first-place performance of Van Alan Clark's *Beverly,* four years later, left little doubt as to the speed of the catamaran. By the end of 1963 the consistent and convincing performance of the twin-hull yacht eliminated the "odd" label. Yachting enthusiasts are not only accepting catamarans but are demanding

Malibu outriggers were forerunners of today's multihulls. They are, of course, still a major class boat.

The Tiger Cat class (left) was the first popular small catamaran in the United States, while the Beverly-International Class C Catamaran made sailors take notice because of her speed. An International Class C Catamaran is 25 feet long (maximum) and 14 feet in beam and has a total sail and spar area of 300 square feet.

them. In recent years the trimaran—a three-hulled craft—has entered the sailing scene.

For those unfamiliar with the modern sailing catamaran, the craft consists of two separate hull units rather than the one hull of a conventional boat. When turned upside down, the "cat," as it usually is called, gives the appearance of two planing hulls joined side by side with an indention or a tunnel in the place of the keel of the standard type of construction. Viewed from broad abeam, the catamaran looks almost like an ordinary boat. However, when viewed from the bow, the tunnel between the two hulls can be clearly seen. The majority of the present designs tend toward the use of modified V forms for the two hulls, though some designers stick to the older plan which looks like two pontoons with a tunnel between. There are several variations from these two basic designs—all, however, use the principle of the air passage between two basic hulls. The purpose of the tunnel is to generate lift and produce a smooth, faster ride. The hulls are constructed from fiberglass, wood, or plywood—sheet and molded plywood.

Speed of Catamarans. The big question: Are two hulls better than one? The sailing catamarans, like the other hull designs discussed earlier in this section, have assets and drawbacks, but the assets are rather impressive. When they first made their appearance in numbers, sailing cats were treated as a novelty craft; that was, until they consistently outraced monohull sailboats. For instance, there was an old conception that multihulls would not go well to windward or tack easily. This, of course, has been dispelled with events such as this: One day a recent Larchmont Race Week furnished a good sailing breeze from the southwest, and the committee sent the cats around the same 12-mile, windward-leeward course as the larger craft. The winning catamaran covered this distance in less time than the leading boats in all other classes—about ½ minute better than the 33-foot International One-Design, over 2½ minutes better than the 210, nearly 4 minutes ahead of the Raven, and 13½ minutes before the Star. This is all the more noteworthy because the type of course did not permit the cats to reach, and thus show their best speed. Off the wind, speed of 20 knots have frequently been recorded.

A multihull can be designed to have plenty of cabin space as well as cruising range. The PI-30 (a 30-foot craft) is shown here.

Of course the first thing that comes to mind: Why all the speed from a catamaran? First, its twin hulls give it virtually the speed of two boats with not much more wetted surface area than one. Since resistance at high speeds is primarily a matter of wave formation, the narrower the hulls and the straighter the run, the faster you will go. For water does not like to be pushed apart, or bent. Comparisons of narrowness (potential speed) are easily made by relating a hull's waterline beam to its waterline length. A beam that is one-twelfth of length gives good performance. A beam that is one-thirteenth of length would be even faster; a waterline beam one-eighth of length would be noticeably wide for a catamaran.

With regard to having a straight run, you want the water to be bent as little as possible aft of amidships, not only along the keel but also at the waterline. Hence the desirability of transom sterns of approximately full beam. Other considerations contributing to high-speed catamaran performance are: (1) the sharpness of entry at each bow; (2) sufficient distance between the hulls to minimize interference of bow waves; (3) sufficient vertical clearance between the water and the underside of the "cockpit" to prevent "belly drag"; and last, but not least, (4) the matter of total weight aboard—for, surprisingly, light weight helps at high speeds much more than in light air. Among monohull sailboats, the bigger they are the faster they go, and the smaller they are the slower they go. Likewise with catamarans—but even more so. For, as you cut down on overall length, you soon come to a size that ceases to benefit from being a catamaran. The joker here, of course, is that you and your crew weigh just as much aboard the little catamaran. Hence, to support your weight, the beam of each hull of the small cat must be relatively much fatter than one-twelfth of its length. So you no longer have truly narrow hulls with sharp entries. Furthermore, whatever surface waves there are will bother any small cat out of all proportion to its slightly smaller size, and especially with regard to the way a small cat "hobby horses" while going to windward.

Good performance in light air is achieved by reducing underwater resistance, and increasing sail power. Underwater resistance at slow speeds is primarily a matter of the number of square inches of "wetted area." Since the least amount of wetted area for a given displacement is in the shape of a hemisphere, it follows that the least amount of wetted area for a catamaran will be obtained if the underwater cross section of each hull is in the shape of a semicircle, and the underwater profile of each hull rises toward both bow and stern. Wetted area is also reduced by lightweight construction, and on some catamarans by having the extension tillers arranged in such a way that the skipper as well as the crew can move his weight forward.

To increase sail power for light air, good catamarans have three features: (1) larger actual sail area than a monohull of comparable size; (2) full-length battens that give shape to the mainsail even in a calm; and (3) a streamlined mast that rotates from tack to tack.

In recent years the highly sophisticated C-class catamarans have turned to "wing masts." This is a thick, wide mast which may make up as much as ⅓ the area of the sail. Though heavy, it allows even greater speeds for these already fast boats. Experiments are under way with completely rigid masts.

Other Advantages of Catamarans. Speed is not the only advantage of multihulls. Their tremendous stability in all kinds of weather made sailors take notice. As has already been discussed, a monohull, or conventional sailing hull, obtains its stability from two factors: displacement and freeboard. As a general rule, the greater the displacement and the higher the freeboard, the more stability the craft has. The multihull, on the other hand, relies almost exclusively on only its wide beam for its self-preservation. It has practically no displacement—one of the major reasons that it is able to accelerate so rapidly. It has very little weight and low freeboard.

If you compare the beam of a 16-foot one-design Comet and the average 16-foot catamaran, you will find that the Comet has a beam of 5 feet and the catamaran 7 feet 6 inches. In other words, the Comet's beam is a little more than one-third of its length, while the catamaran's beam is very nearly one-half of its length. Not only this, but the outside edges of the catamarans are so much more buoyant than those of a conventional hull. If an ordinary sailboat is heeled to the point where the leeward gunwale goes under the water, the boat's cockpit will start to fill unless it is protected by side decking. You do not have this worry with a catamaran since there is no cockpit, in the true sense of the word, to fill. The helmsman and crew, of course, sit on a deck supported between the twin hulls. In cruising-type catamarans and trimarans, cabin facilities are available.

Most catamarans are equipped with a dagger-type centerboard. Some catamarans are equipped with drop rudders which can be lowered or raised to the required depth by the helmsman at any time, even while sailing. Other cats have fixed rudders. The twin rudders are controlled by a single tiller and can be operated from either side of the craft.

As previously stated, most good catamarans are fitted with fully battened mainsails. This helps to insure the correct airfoil shape, eliminates slatting and flutter, and enables the use of an extensive roach. To suit their ample beam, cats are often fitted with a fairly long slide along which the mainsheet block is free to travel. The purpose of this is to make it possible to keep the boom well down when sailing free before the wind and to control more exactly the angle of the mainsail. This arrangement usually allows the amount of travel to be controlled from either side of the catamaran. When short tacking, the amount of slack allowed should be cut to 6 inches on either side of the boat's centerline. On some catamarans there are special arrangements for adjusting the tension on the luff of the jib by means of a downhaul on the tack.

To make catamarans transportable, specially designed trailers are available. The beams of almost all catamarans are within maximum highway limitations. Some of the smaller catamarans can be mounted on a car-top carrier.

EQUIPMENT REQUIREMENTS

If your yacht operates on any body of water classed as "navigable" by the Federal government, you must comply with equipment regulations of the Motorboat Act of 1940. "Navigable water" is any body of water which is a part of the Atlantic or Pacific Oceans, the Gulf of Mexico, the Great Lakes, and all rivers and their tributaries, upstream to the first lockless dam, which empty into these waters. The navigable waters of the United States also include waterways that are navigable in fact and are interstate in nature regardless of direct connection with the oceans or the Great Lakes. (Lake Tahoe is an example of this.) When on navigable waters, any Coast Guard patrol vessel or craft may stop you at any time and come aboard to see if you are properly equipped in accordance with Federal law. The chart below shows the "minimum" that must be carried by motorboats up to 65 feet. (Boats without engines on board do not fall under the Motorboat Act, but it is highly recommended that they carry the equipment listed below applicable to their craft. Auxiliary sailboats and sailboats with outboard motors are considered to be motorboats according to the Motorboat Act.)

SAFETY EQUIPMENT REQUIRED ABOARD*

Class	Life Preserver	Fire Extinguisher†	Horn or Whistle	Bell	Bilge Ventilation	Flame Arrestors
A (boats less than 16 feet long)	For each person on board: 1 Coast Guard approved life preserver, ring buoy, buoyant vest, or buoyant cushion	One	None	None	Bilge, fuel tank, and engine compartment ventilators	Every engine must have a carburetor flame arrestor
1 (16–25 feet)	Same as Class A	One	One, audible ½ mile	None	Same as Class A	Same as Class A
2 (26–39 feet)	Same as Class A	Two	One, audible 1 mile	One	Same as Class A	Same as Class A
3 (40–64 feet)	Same as Class A, but life preserver or ring buoy only	Three	Same as 2	One	Same as Class A	Same as Class A

* Applies to sailboats with auxiliary power; all sailboats, however, must carry life preservers as noted above, plus a signaling device such as a horn or whistle.
† Carbon tetrachloride extinguishers are no longer approved.

While the legal requirements of boat equipment may not be mandatory for sailboat owners—none of which *must* be carried by sailboats that do not have motor power—there are many items which should be carried and used even though there is no compulsion to do so. The law does not say you must carry an anchor. Yet what sailor would think of starting off on any kind of a sail without this item?

Anchor and Anchor Lines

Experts generally agree that the choice of an anchor depends on a number of considerations, including weight and shape of the hull, type of water bed generally encountered, usual weather conditions, and the purpose for which it is most often used. For instance, the kedge is for larger boats and is best in sheltered and currentless locations. It is very heavy and is often called a deadweight type. The lightweight twin-fluke (Danforth) has good holding power once dug in, but it tends to slide over the bottom in weedy areas. It is light in weight and is currently the most popular type on yachts not equipped with winches or other ground tackle to raise or lower the "hook." Suggested working sizes of Danforth-type anchors are as follows:

Boat Length, Feet	Beam, Feet	Standard Working*	High-Tensile Working*
10	4	2½	—
15	5	4	—
20	6	8	5
25	6½	8	12
30	7	13	12
35	8	22	18
40	9	22	18
50	11	40	28
60	12	65	60

* For storm or heavy-duty anchor, use one anchor size larger, while for lunch (light-duty) hook, one size smaller. Your yacht should carry two anchors—one light-duty one for short stops such as for lunch, swimming, etc.; and a working-duty one for overnight stops—and a cruising boat may even carry a storm or heavy-duty anchor.

The mushroom type is good for permanent moorings in soft and yielding bottoms. In the lighter-weight sizes, it makes a good temporary anchor for small fishing boats. The CQR plow-type anchor is used mostly on larger boats because of its heavy weight, and it is a good holder. The Northill is fine for all-round use, although it has its limitations in soft mud, and its free arm will sometimes foul the slack line. It is rather lightweight. The Navy stockless, or patent, type has almost the same characteristics as the fluke type but is heavier. Comparison of holding power of four major types of yacht anchors:

Danforth, Pounds	Yachtsman's Kedge, Pounds	Stockless, Pounds	Mushroom, Pounds
2½	22	60	75
4	35	70	100
8	60	100	180
13	140	210	400
22	225	340	650
40	270	400	800

Whatever the type of anchor, the secret of successful anchoring rests on two things: making the length (scope) of anchor line (rode) as long as possible, and keeping the anchor off its side so that its flukes can penetrate the bottom. Rope is generally preferred for anchoring boats up to 50 feet in length, with chain or cable used for larger boats. For cruising sailboats, 6 to 10 feet of chain is recommended as part of any anchor rode. The chain leader helps keep the line on bottom and avoids chafing. Following are recommended anchor lines:

Overall Length of Sailboat, Feet	Anchor Used	Length of Anchor Lines, Feet	Manila Rope Diameter, Inches	Nylon Rope Diameter, Inches
Under 20	Light	100	½	⅜
	Working	100	½	⅜
20–25	Light	125	½	⅜
	Working	200	⅝	½
25–30	Light	150	¾	9/16
	Working	200	¾	9/16
30–40	Light	150	1	¾
40–50	Working	250	1⅛	13/16
	Light	200	1¼	⅞
	Working	300	1½	1⅛
50–65	Light	200	1⅜	1
	Working	300	1⅝	1⅛

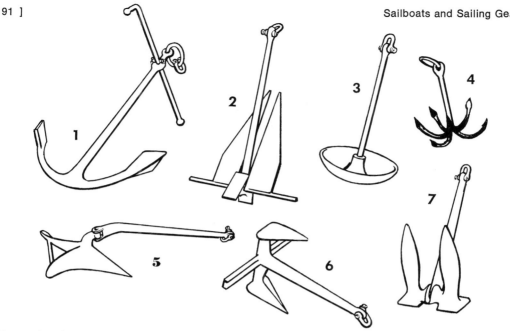

Types of anchors: 1. yachtsman's; 2. Danforth; 3. mushroom; 4. grapnel; 5. CQR plow; 6. Northill; 7. Navy stockless, or patent.

For maximum holding power it is important to have a length of anchor line out that is equal to many times the depth of the water —seven times is a safe minimum. It is a good idea to mark your line so that you can be sure that you will anchor with enough scope. Every fathom (6 feet) paint a mark on the line. Anchor-line markers are also available commercially. When you lower the anchor to the bottom, note the depth by the number of marks paid out, then continue until you have the desired length of line out. The effectiveness of an anchor at different ratios of scope to depth is as follows:

2 to 1—13%	5 to 1—65%	8 to 1—77%
3 to 1—46%	6 to 1—72%	9 to 1—82%
4 to 1—54%	7 to 1—75%	10 to 1—85%

The best method of attaching the anchor to the line, or rode, is a splice over a galvanized thimble (stainless steel if your anchor is stainless) fastened with a galvanized (or stainless) shackle. Next in order of preference is the fisherman's bend—two round turns and two half hitches, with the first hitch passed through the loop of the turns. (See Section IV for complete information on tying

knots.) The minimum "approved" hitch is the anchor bowline—two round turns and a regular bowline. Anything less will brand you as a novice. At the boat end of the line, a tight hitch is essential. Use a conventional hitch on a cleat (it should be simple, secure,

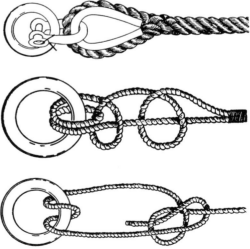

Method of attaching anchor to anchor line (top to bottom): the eye splice, timble and shackle; the fisherman's bend; and the anchor bowline.

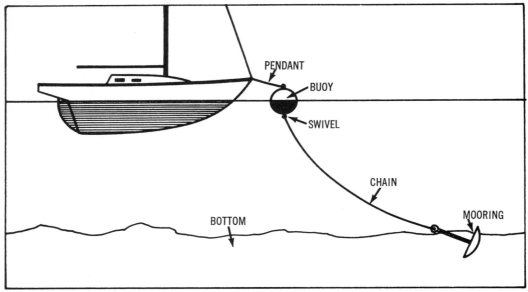

Permanent mooring arrangement.

and easy to cast off). For a bit, two round turns and two half hitches, or a clove hitch with a stopping hitch or two are excellent. Beware of the clove hitch without stoppers; it may slip under strain.

Chafe must be considered at the boat end as well. Chocks, bobstays, bow pulpit supports, even the boat's stem may chafe through a rode in short order. Areas of possible chafe should be protected with rubber hose, servings, canvas sleeves, or even old rags in an emergency. Do not forget that the rode will stretch under tension, and allow for this when applying chafe gear. Secure the chafe protectors to the line so they do not work away from the point they protect.

Permanent Moorings

What constitutes a proper mooring is as controversial as the weather. Actually, all manner of things are in use as anchors for permanent moorings—old flywheels, old engines, odds and ends of junk bound together in cement, old oil drums filled with cement and many others. All of these have limited holding power value beyond their weight, and even this is compromised for the more bulky types because of the buoyant effect of the displaced water. Furthermore, when such anchors are once set they are never lifted, and

this absence of a check on the condition of mooring chain, including its attachment to the anchor, is a prime cause of failure.

The mushroom type is the popularly accepted permanent mooring. In design, it is ideal for 360-degree swing, being free of projections which might foul the chain, and it has good holding qualities. Local advice from experienced yachtsmen, club dock captains, service yards, or the harbormaster will tell you the weight of mooring anchor for your size and type of boat. A rule of thumb of 10 pounds of mushroom for every foot of boat length is fairly safe in a protected harbor. One authority suggests: for a boat up to 25 feet long overall, 150 to 200 pounds; up to 35 feet, 200 to 300 pounds; up to 45 feet, 300 to 400 pounds; and up to 55 feet length overall, 450 to 550 pounds.

Scope is vital in permanent moorings, too. Most authorities would call 3 to 1 the irreducible minimum, and all will agree that 5 to 1 is a lot safer. Sometimes in crowded ports two anchors are set out in opposite directions so that the boat lies between and above them.

Only solid forged-link galvanized chain should be used. Shackles should be screw type with the pin set up with a wrench and wired in. Use wire of the same metal as the shackle to avoid electrolysis—never a copper wire on a steel shackle, for instance. A swivel must be used in the chain to avoid its kinking up as the boat swings, and should be extra heavy because of wear. If the chain goes up to a float, rather than directly to the rope pendant, and the latter is secured to the top of the float, chain and pendant must be connected by a solid steel rod running through the float.

Nylon rope is popular for mooring pendants, as is the case with anchor lines, because it is strong, has great elasticity, which eases the jerks on the mooring in a sea, outlasts manila, and will not absorb water. A main fault is that nylon is so slippery that it is hard to make a splice in it that won't pull out. It is usually wiser to have a yard do your splicing. But when you make the splice, be sure each strand is tucked at least five or six times instead of the usual three for manila, and that the ends of the strands are then secured with a sailmaker's needle-whipping. As to diameter, see what other boats like yours in your harbor use—then make yours a bit heavier. And put chafing gear on where it leads through chocks or might rub on stem or bobstay.

As to other materials: Dacron is strong, but less springy than nylon. Manila of somewhat heavier diameter than the synthetics is good but will not last as long. Cotton or ordinary hemp should never be used. Stainless steel deteriorates due to electrolysis or galvanic action and can also cut through softer bronze mooring cleats or chocks in a gale, and should never be used. Whatever the material, a thimble must be spliced into the end of the pendant that shackles to the chain or buoy. Chocks should be of a depth and a design to prevent the mooring pendant jumping out of them in a sea and so placed that the line leads fair in the direction of normal pull. Bitts let through the deck and toed into the keel structure are probably the strongest. Bitts or cleats must never be screwed to the deck, but must be bolted through the deck and through a butt block or backing block under it.

Lights

If you sail after dark you must display the proper lights in accord with either the International Rules or the Inland Rules. The latter prescribe the correct lighting for inland waters, the Great Lakes, and western rivers, while the International Rules meet the requirements of both inland rules and the high seas. Thus, if you plan to sail on inland waterways and open seas, equip your craft according to the International Rules.

Navigation-light regulations for all vessels use the "point" (abbreviated to "pt.") system. This term is based on the understanding that a light with a completely circular globe —which can be seen from every angle—is said to be a 32-pt. light. Therefore, the globe of a 10-pt. light covers $^{10}/_{32}$, or $^{5}/_{16}$, of a circle; a 12-pt. light, $^{12}/_{32}$, or $^{3}/_{8}$, of a circle; and a 20-pt. light, $^{20}/_{32}$, or $^{5}/_{8}$, of a circle.

Lights aboard all vessels must be displayed from sunset to sunrise. Under International Rules, there is a lighting option that enables a sailing vessel under sail to carry (in addition to her normal side lights and 12-point stern light) a 20-point red light over a 20-point green light at the masthead, sufficiently separated so as to be clearly distinguished and visible for 2 miles. This option has been added because normal side lights are often obscured by sails. The rule also says that a vessel may, if necessary in order to attract attention, in addition to the lights which she is required to carry, show a flare-up light. In other words, it is often wise to shine a flashlight on the sails when converging with another vessel at night.

Also under International Rules, powerboats of 40 gross tons or over must carry separate side lights, visible for 2 miles, and a 20-point white light, visible 5 miles. Sailing vessels of 20 gross tons or over must carry separate side lights, visible 2 miles. Under sail, only boats of less than 20 tons or under 40 feet may use a combination lantern. Also a boat under sail alone on the Great Lakes is not required to display a stern light. Such boats should also carry a flashlight or spotlight to throw a white light on a sail when being overtaken.

If you are in shallow water and decide to anchor at night, you must turn off the running lights and display an anchor light (except if under 65 feet length overall in special anchorage areas). An anchor light or riding light is a white, 32-point light displayed on the forward part of the vessel.

LIGHTS REQUIRED ON BOATS UNDERWAY—BETWEEN SUNSET AND SUNRISE

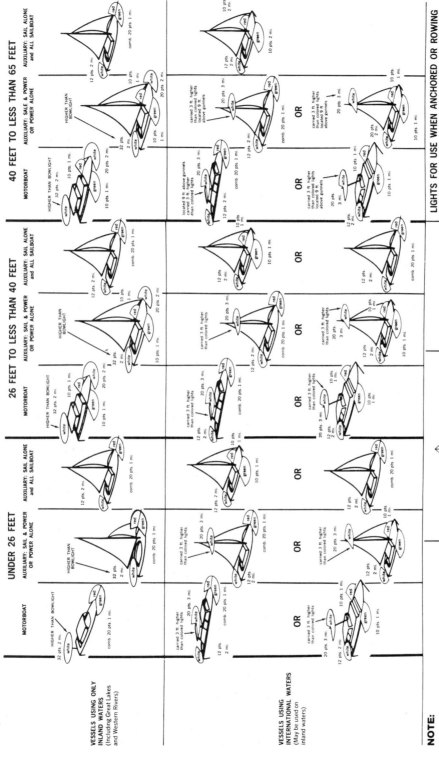

LIGHTS FOR USE WHEN ANCHORED OR ROWING

POWER BOATS under 65 feet and all Sailing Vessels at anchor must display anchor lights except those under 65 feet in "special anchorage areas." An anchor light is a white light visible to a boat approaching from any direction.

ROWING BOATS: Rowing boats whether under oars or sail, shall have ready at hand a lantern showing a white light which shall be temporarily exhibited in sufficient time to prevent collision.

NOTE:

EXCEPTIONS: (1) Western River Rules. Sidelights for vessels under sail must be visible for 3 miles. (2) Great Lakes. On the Great Lakes sailing vessels show a white light (in lieu of a stern light) upon that portion of the vessel which is being approached by another vessel.

DEFINITION: "10 pts. 1 mi." means that the light can be seen through an arc of 10 points (see diagram at right), for a distance of 1 mile by another vessel.

IMPORTANT: LIGHTS MUST BE PLACED HIGH ENOUGH THAT THEIR LIGHT WILL NOT BE BLOCKED BY PERSONS OR PARTS OF THE BOAT OR IT'S EQUIPMENT.

NAYRU Offshore Gear List

Every skipper in this new age of sail should have aboard equipment besides that required by law. In recent years a lot of safety requirements have been written into the circulars of ocean and longshore racers, and they are equally good if you are cruising. In fact, the North American Yacht Racing Union has established *minimum* equipment and accommodations standards for offshore racing events in North America. The following list is intended to provide uniform racing and is *not* intended to replace but merely to supplement requirements established by governmental bodies.

The detailed minimum equipment and accommodations standards have been arranged in groups to conform to four categories of offshore events as follows:

1. Long-distance offshore races in open ocean where the vessel must be completely self-sufficient—perhaps for extended periods —and capable of withstanding heavy storms.
2. Distance races of extended duration along shoreline or in large, relatively unprotected bays or lakes which require a high degree of self-sufficiency of crew and yacht.
3. Medium-distance races which extend overnight or across open water which is relatively protected.
4. Short day races close to shore or in protected waters. These category numbers appear in parentheses in the following six equipment and accommodation standard groups:

Group A. Hull and Cabin

1. Completely strong and watertight hull capable of withstanding solid water and knockdowns without significant leakage (1,2,3).
2. Hatches, companionways, and ports essentially watertight and capable of being closed securely with strong hardware (1,2,3).
3. Structurally strong, essentially watertight, self-bailing cockpit permanently incorporated as a structural part of the hull (1,2,3,4).
4. Cockpit companionways, if below main deck level, capable of being blocked off to deck level by solid, essentially leakproof and rigidly secured, if not permanent, means (1,2,3).
5. Maximum cockpit volume over lowest coamings not to exceed 6% × LOA × maximum beam × freeboard aft. Cockpit floor at least 0.02 × LWL above LWL (1,2).
6. Cockpit drains adequate to drain cockpit quickly and not less in combined area than the equivalent of two ¾-inch diameter drains. Yachts built after January 1, 1971, must have combined area of drains not less than the equivalent of four ¾-inch drains (1,2,3).
7. Rigid and strong coverings for all windows more than 2 square feet in area (1,2,3).
8. Sea cocks or valves on all underwater openings except for integral deck scuppers. This does not apply to openings in the hull to accommodate the shaft, speed indicator, depth finder, etc. However, a satisfactory means of closing these openings shall be provided when it becomes necessary to do so (1,2).
9. Lifelines and pulpits:
   a. Fixed bow pulpit (forward of headstay) and stern pulpit (unless lifelines are arranged in such a way as to adequately substitute for a stern pulpit). Pulpits and stanchions must be throughbolted or welded. Taut double lifelines with upper lifeline of wire to be secured to pulpits and stanchions. Pulpits and upper lifeline must not be less than 24 inches above the deck at any point. Stanchions shall not be spaced more than 7 feet apart, except in the way of shrouds when lifelines are permanently attached to shrouds. Lower lifelines need not be extended through pulpits. Lifelines need not be affixed to the bow pulpit if they terminate at or pass through adequately braced stanchions 24 inches high set inside of and overlapping the bow pulpit (1,2).
   b. Taut single-wire lifeline securely attached with a minimum height of not less than 18 inches (3).
10. Approved running lights which will remain unobstructed by sails and when the yacht is heeled in heavy weather (1,2,3).

Group B. Accommodations

1. Permanently installed toilet (1,2,3).
2. Permanently installed bunks (1,2,3).
3. Permanently installed stove having

safely accessible remote fuel-shutoff control (1,2).

4. Stove (3).

5. Galley facilities including permanently installed sink (1,2,3).

6. Permanently installed water tanks which must be capable of dividing water supply into at least two separate containers (1).

7. Permanently installed water tank plus at least one additional container capable of holding 5 gallons (2,3).

8. Suitable water containers (4).

Group C. General Equipment

1. USCG approved (or equivalent) fire extinguishers as required by USCG (or country of registry) rules, readily accessible in different parts of the yacht, but not fewer than 3 (1,2).

2. USCG approved (or equivalent) fire extinguishers as required by USCG (or country of registry) rules, readily accessible, but at least one (3,4).

3. Two manually operated bilge pumps, one of which must be operable with all cockpit seats and hatches and all cabin hatches and companionways closed (1,2,3).

4. One manual bilge pump operable with all cockpit seats and hatches closed (4).

5. Two suitable anchors and cables (1,2,3).

6. One suitable anchor and cable (4).

7. Water-resistant flashlights and signaling light (1,2,3).

8. First-aid kit and manual (1,2,3,4).

9. Manually operated foghorn (1,2,3,4).

10. Radar reflector (1,2,3).

11. Set of international code flags and code book (1,2).

12. Shut-off valves on all fuel tanks (1,2,3,4).

Group D. Navigation Equipment

1. Properly installed, adjusted marine compass (1,2,3,4).

2. Spare compass (1,2,3).

3. Suitable charts, light lists, and equipment for piloting (1,2,3).

4. Sextant, tables, and accurate timepiece (1).

5. Radio direction finder (1,2).

6. Radio receiver to receive 150 to 400 kc, broadcast, and 2 to 4 mc bands (1,2,3).

7. Lead line (1,2,3).

8. Speedometer or log (1,2,3).

Group E. Emergency Equipment

1. Spare running lights and power source (1,2).

2. Storm trysail and storm jib (1,2).

3. Heavy-weather jib and reefing equipment for mainsail (3,4).

4. Emergency steering equipment (1,2).

5. Bolt or rigging cutters (1,2,3).

6. Suitable tools and spare parts (1,2,3).

7. Yacht's name on miscellaneous buoyant equipment such as life jackets, oars, cushions, etc. (1,2).

8. Radio transmitter, minimum power 35 watts AM, 20 watts FM, moisture-proofed, with emergency antenna system if regular system depends upon the mast (1,2).

Group F. Safety Equipment

1. USCG (or country of registry) approved life jackets for each member of crew (1,2,3,4).

2. Whistles (referee or siren type) on life jackets (1,2,3).

3. Safety belts (harness type) for each member of crew (1,2,3).

4. Covered life boat(s) or raft(s) rated to accommodate the entire crew and equipped with emergency provisions (1).

5. Life boat(s) or raft(s) rated to accommodate the entire crew (2,3).

6. Inflatable rafts must have automatic inflating device, at least two separate air chambers, and must have been inspected, tested, and approved within three years by the manufacturer or other competent authority (1,2,3).

7. Horseshoe-type life rings equipped with whistles (referee or siren type), dye marker, and drogues:

    a. Two horseshoe life rings with high-intensity automatic water lights each attached with 25 feet of floating line to a pole with a flag; the pole to be of a length and so ballasted that the flag will fly at least 8 feet off the water in calm conditions (1).

    b. Two horseshoe life rings, one equipped as in 8*a* (2).

    c. One horseshoe life ring with high-intensity water light or 18-inch diameter USCG approved ring buoy with high-intensity water light (3).

    d. One horseshoe life ring or 18-inch

diameter USCG approved ring buoy (4).

8. Flare gun (Very pistol or equivalent) and flares, stowed in a waterproof container (1,2,3).

   a. Twelve red and 4 white parachute flares (1).

   b. Six red and 2 white parachute flares (2,3).

9. Heaving line (50-foot minimum, floating type) readily accessible to cockpit (1,2,3).

Safety Gear. Some of the equipment listed above deserves brief comment. The large life rings should be placed in holders, usually on the lifelines, near the helmsman, since there is always a man stationed at the helm. Never lash a life ring to its holder. The horseshoe life buoy is generally thought to be the best type. The buoyed pole with a counterweight and flag is a very important item at sea where there are large waves, because the flag can be seen above the wave tops. The pole should be attached to a life ring, and if a man falls overboard, both pole and ring are thrown over the side instantly. The weighted pole will also tend to prevent the life ring from drifting excessively. It is often a good idea to attach a small drogue (a canvas, cone-shaped sea anchor) to a life ring that is not attached to a pole, in order to decrease drift. Obviously, water lights attached to life rings are essential at night. Electric water lights vary in design, but the usual type is equipped with a battery-powered light that shuts off when it is hung upside down. However, the light is buoyed and weighted in such a way that when it is thrown overboard, it rights itself and turns itself on.

Safety belts are indispensable for your crew in rough weather at sea, especially at night. It is generally agreed that the best belt is one that fits on the chest and is equipped with shoulder straps. Attached to the front of the belt is a short, stout line with a large snap-hook at its end. The belted crewman snaps the hook onto a convenient part of the rigging or lifelines when he needs to work with both hands. The crew should always use safety belts when they leave the cockpit at night or when in a rough sea.

The radar reflector is very important at night and especially in fog. Its purpose is to warn large ships, or any radar-equipped vessel, of your presence. Obviously, the reflector is essential in or near shipping lanes. A multisurface folding metal box hung high in the rigging or mast makes a good reflector.

The crew of an ocean cruiser should always be conscious of the watertightness of the hull. In bad weather or even in fair weather, a boat can be rolled over on her beam ends by a sudden squall. If ports, ventilators, and hatches are not closed and secured, the boat can quickly fill with water and perhaps sink. This has happened. Sea cocks (barrel-type valves in pipes where they go through the hull) on all through-hull openings should be shut in bad weather. Hinged cockpit seat-locker lids should be latched shut, because during a severe knockdown, they can fall or float open. Portholes and hatches should be dogged down in bad weather, and vulnerable ventilators should be provided with a quick means of closing, even if they are only covered with small canvas bags.

Navigation Charts and Equipment

Long before it is time to cast off, obtain the National Ocean Survey (formerly the United States Coast and Geodetic Survey) and United States Army Corps of Engineers catalog sheets (see Section V). Circle chart numbers for all waters where you are likely to be sailing during the season, and order the charts. Make some type of arrangement so that these charts can be cut to workable size and stored in a combination chart board-holder. One can be made with waterproof plywood covers with bronze bolts as fasteners. The board provides a fine surface for laying out courses with a course protractor or parallel rulers. Also, if your boat does not have a bulkhead rack for rulers, dividers, protractor, and tide and current tables, install one. In addition, you might place an old "railroad" type pocket watch next to the chart table or bulkhead rack as an inexpensive and practical substitute for a chronometer. Since most men no longer carry them, the pawnshops are full of excellent watches which can be purchased inexpensively. The daily error on such watches is fairly constant so that an accurate rating card can be made. The watch can be employed for piloting, and for timing runs between landmarks or aids to navigation. For ocean runs, it might even be used for keeping track of Greenwich time for celestial navigation.

The safety of your craft and all aboard can depend upon the accuracy of your compass, so the best you can obtain is none too good. Do not attempt to adapt compasses intended for other services, such as aeronautical or automotive; such instruments seldom meet all of the requirements for marine use. For complete details on marine compasses, see Section V.

Sounding Devices. There are other items you should have aboard to help you navigate safely. For example, when you sail in deep water it makes little difference how deep the water under the keel is. But when you get into shallower water it is helpful to know that the depths are sufficient for the draft of the boat. Several methods are in common use, particularly in the inland-waterway regions where shoaling frequently changes certain depths almost overnight. The time-tested and well-known sounding lead is one of the generally used methods, while a still simpler method is to use a sounding pole. The lead line is nothing more than a heavy weight secured to a line. This is dropped overboard and the depth of the water read off the graduated line. Special marking devices are used so that the depths can be quickly and accurately read. The sounding pole is nothing more than a long stick with the draft of the boat prominently marked. The user stands on the bow of the boat and sounds as the boat moves along. Touching bottom, he can warn the helmsman away from danger spots.

Larger sailing vessels with ample electrical power supply may be fitted with an electronic depth finder, or echo device, which transmits an impulse to the bottom, picks it up again on the return, and then translates the minute time element into fathoms or feet. This type of depth finder consists of two parts: an indicator unit, and a "transducer" that is a combination fist-sized loudspeaker and microphone which is attached to your boat. The indicator unit generates an electrical "bang" that the transducer shoots to the bottom. When the echo bounces back, the transducer

picks it up; and the indicator unit measures the round-trip time and translates it to depth in feet. Deep-sea models show fathoms. There are also recorders which chart the bottom contour on a moving strip of paper, making a constant record of the ground you have been over. Echo sounders require very little electric current and many of them are transistorized, powered by their own self-contained batteries. Some models are portable; you can take them aboard a dinghy. Others operate from the boat battery. If you are a fairly good boat carpenter you should be able to do the installing yourself. But, proceed with caution, as an incorrect installation may cause serious damage.

Radio Direction Finder. Another navigational instrument, the radio direction finder is regarded by sailors as an invaluable piece of emergency equipment. The RDF actually takes the place of the visual instrument through which you sight to get the bearings of navigational markers. It is used in the same way, the main difference being that it "sees" radio waves instead of light waves. Instead of telling by eye when the instrument is lined up on the target, you do it by ear. When the RDF is "on the beam," the loudness of a signal drops down to a "null" (minimum signal). Some RDF's have a meter that helps you judge when you have the pointer aimed correctly. Then you read the bearing of the station from a pelorus and plot the bearing line on your chart, just as if it were staring you smack in the eye. Besides taking bearings for chart navigation, you can also use the RDF to "home" on a station, such as a light vessel or a radio station on a point of land or at a harbor entrance. To do this you set the RDF on the bearing line running through the bow of the boat, then steer to keep the radio station in the "null." The simplest RDF's cover just one band—from approximately 200 to 400 kilocycles—where marine- and airways-beacon stations are located. Two-band sets also cover the standard broadcast band. Many broadcast stations are just as good to navigate by as the marine radio beacons. Three-band outfits tune the marine radiotelephone band in addition. This feature has two advantages: you can take bearings on radiotelephone-equipped boats and you can use the receiver for radiotelephone standby watch on 2182 kc.

Radiotelephone. While not a navigational device, the radiotelephone is nevertheless very useful in bad weather, and is a very valuable safety instrument. With it you can talk directly with other boats, shore stations, and vessels of the Coast Guard, and through commercial telephone facilities (paying a small toll charge) to your home, office, shipyard, or any other party on land. Use is restricted to water craft, so you are not competing with taxicabs or oil trucks for air time. Intership channels are reserved for safety, operational, and "ship's-business" conversations. There is also a special distress frequency, monitored by other boats and the Coast Guard.

Marine radiotelephones come in a sufficient number of shapes, sizes, operating ranges, and prices to meet all requirements. Whether you cruise to Calcutta, commute to Catalina, or just putter around Puget Sound, you can get a radiotelephone with a range that will keep you in touch with anyone you wish to reach. The smallest equipment has transmitting power of from 15 to 30 watts. From three to five communicating channels are provided. With a three-channel telephone, you can switch to the International Calling and Distress frequency (2182 kc), a ship-to-ship channel (2638 kc), and a shore telephone channel. If your set has more channels you can add the Coast Guard frequency (2670 kc), the shore-telephone frequencies of additional seaports, or a second ship-to-ship frequency (2738 kc). When you buy a telephone you choose the channels you want. These channels are pretuned and the frequencies are precisely controlled by crystals, so all you do is turn a knob to make the shift from one frequency to another. In addition to the talking channels, many marine radiotelephone receivers also tune the standard broadcast band, which enables you to listen to radio programs, news, and weather reports. The ship-to-shore radio's use is controlled by the Federal Communications Commission. The radio must have a station license and a call sign; only a licensed operator (usually the skipper) may operate it, and he is re-

quired to log all his calls. The FCC demands that its own radio channel be monitored. For further details on the use of the radiotelephone as a safety device see Section V.

Radar and Loran. Two electronic devices that are found only on *large* ocean sailing cruisers are radar and loran. The former paints a living chart of your surroundings (out to several miles distant) on a small TV-like "scope" tube, regardless of fog, rain, or darkness. Other boats as well as prominent buoys, beacons, and land objects are shown as lighted areas on the scope. When a skipper is properly trained in its use, radar is the happiest sight for sore-eyed harbor navigators ever invented.

The traditional method of navigation offshore, of course, is to put your eye to a sextant and measure the altitude of the sun, moon, stars, or planets. The main trouble with this (aside from the mathematics involved) is that you can sail days without seeing either heavenly bodies or the horizon. Consequently, many skippers turn to loran as a supplementary navigational aid. Government-operated loran stations spread a grid of radio lines of position over the face of the earth. With a loran receiver you can pick up and identify these lines, fair weather or foul. You twist a few knobs, line up a pair of "pips" on a scope tube, read a number from a dial, and look in a table or on a loran chart to find the loran line you are sitting on. By getting two crossed lines of position, you can obtain an accurate "fix."

Other Necessary Items. Three more items, less sophisticated than the electronic gear just mentioned, that fall into the near-necessity category are barometer, portable radio, and binoculars. A barometer and radio help to keep you informed of the weather. Binoculars are most useful in spotting buoys, landmarks, and other navigational aids, and in addition they will add a great deal to your awareness and enjoyment of life afloat. There are other pieces of gear in this near-necessity class; they will be covered later in this book. Also, to complete the commissioning of your sailboat, you will need such items as personal gear, galley equipment, boatkeeping gear, etc. These items will also be discussed in later sections.

A HOME FOR YOUR SAILBOAT

During the sailing season you can keep your craft at your dock if you live on the waterfront; at an offshore mooring; or at boatyard, marina, or yacht club. The latter three must be paid for.

The Yacht Club. If you plan to race, membership in a class association is a must. Since many of the classes are affiliated locally with yacht clubs and because many yacht clubs hold regattas, it is usually desirable to become a member of a club.

Yacht clubs vary in size, services, activities, and costs. Some are informal groups that pool their resources to buy a patched-up dock and an old shed in which to store gear. They seek new members to reduce individual costs or to get equipment that all can use. Then there are huge, nonprofit organizations with million-dollar properties that include swimming pools, tennis courts, and a Hollywoodian clubhouse. Somewhere in between is the typical American yacht club. It offers group lessons in sailing, swimming, safety and seamanship to old and young; winter programs in sailing education; dances and dinners; and a summer calendar of races, cruises, and social functions. You can judge for yourself how vital to your sailing pleasure such clubs are. But, remember that the facilities of a yacht club are for the exclusive use of its members and their guests. Usually, members of other recognized yacht clubs may use the facilities of clubs of which they are not members only if they are visiting the harbor in a yacht, never if they approach by land—in a car, for instance. (It is not, however, true that membership in a recognized yacht club automatically gives you the right to use facilities of any other club when you are cruising. Some clubs have exchange-visiting privileges, and very few clubs would deny you a vacant mooring in bad weather.) It is *not* proper for members of one club to use the facilities of another club in the same harbor if they are not also members of the second club. Club courtesies to visiting yachtsmen usually include the services of the launch, the use of bathroom facilities in the club, and dining-room privileges. However, it is only polite for the boatowner to go ashore first in his own dinghy,

and ascertain which privileges are available by speaking to the steward or manager of the club. The guest book should be signed at this time.

If you join a yacht club, participate in all its activities. It is true that most club work is done by a dedicated minority. Joining it will present you with some of the most rewarding contacts of your life. From club service it is a logical step to interclub or association duties. Here, on the "inside" of boating, you will meet the vast complex that makes up your marine fraternity, a complex truly international in scope and embracing with equal vigor commercial and pleasure boating. You may learn, to your surprise, that personalities and groups you once believed hostile to boating interests often are dedicated to increasing its safety, preserving its intent, and expanding its facilities.

Many yacht clubs have long waiting lists of people who want to join. The number of new clubs has not kept up with the increased number of boats in use, which accounts for the long prospective-membership lists. The greatly increasing interest in sailing, plus the lack of yacht-club facilities, has led many sailors to form their own organizations, where sailing is the prime activity. In many areas local communities have organized sailing programs and clubs. If you like to head up committees you might gather a group of friends and neighbors and start your own sailing club.

The Marina. The fastest growing development in the age of the sail is marinas, both municipally and privately owned. The concept of a modern marina encompasses a wide latitude, but the owner of a recreational craft has come to expect more than the basics in service and facilities from the establishment he chooses as home port. The size, shape, and functions of a marina today are highly flexible, and along with equipment and construction details vary according to the needs and desires of boat owners in the immediate area. Yachtsmen, however, have come to expect certain features and services at a marina, no matter what the size. These include berthing space; dockside electricity; fresh water and telephone outlets; available fuel, groceries, and other supplies; laundry service and garbage disposal; parking space; showers and rest rooms and access to marine stores; and boat hauling and repair and storage service. (But select a marina—either public or private—carefully; some are excellent, while others are little more than busy, noisy service stations.)

The Boatyard. Most boatyards rent lockers and dock space or mooring to customers who use the yard for winter storage as well as to those who use it only for the summer. The facilities in a boatyard are usually limited and very informal but generally quite satisfactory. There is a lavatory, there may be showers, and there are usually a couple of rowboats handy for getting to and from your mooring. Boatyards generally offer dockage or moorage at the lowest possible cost. If you do not keep your boat home during the winter and have to pay for winter storage, year-round cost at a boatyard is generally less than anywhere else. Another advantage is that you have repair and maintenance service close at hand if you should ever need it. But, one word of caution: your boatyard is not likely to permit you to do unlimited work on your boat, nor to bring in outside labor. Have things understood before you store your boat there.

The Offshore Mooring. When choosing an offshore mooring site, be sure it is protected from the wind as much as possible; out of the direct surge of waves from large areas of open water; not in the main channel of a stream or tidal flow, or beneath the mouth of a feeder stream, dry wash, or gulley where flash floods may suddenly occur. Also make sure your mooring is not in a channel or fairway; if possible, it should be an authorized anchorage or mooring area. You should make arrangements for launching and perhaps storing a dinghy at a point on shore near where the boat is moored so that you can easily get to and back from it. For this reason it is usually a good idea to moor the boat near a friend's waterfront cottage, near a yacht club, marina, boatyard, or public park. In many places mooring spots can be rented for fees ranging from $10 to $100 per season.

Trailers. Light, strong, standard trailers for sailboats have brought many landlocked sailors to lakes and rivers previously inaccessible. Actually, the importance of trailers in spreading sailboating popularity cannot be overemphasized. They not only facilitate intersectional and national regattas, but also permit those who do not belong to a yacht club and have no mooring for their boat to get into the act. The garage becomes the boat's home port—waters anywhere can be its racing course. That is, some sailors keep their craft on trailers all year long, launching and hauling whenever they wish to use their boat. A modern sailboat can be launched, rigged, and ready to sail in less than 20 minutes.

It is interesting to note that many racing one-designs spend as much as 95 percent of their life resting on a trailer. The buyer should be sure it is the best. The hull should be supported evenly with the loads spread over as large an area as possible. The trailer springs should be adjusted for the boat's weight, not its size (a Snipe needs a much stiffer springing than the larger, but lighter, Flying Dutchman). But do not set the springs too tight, because you can deform any hull by bouncing on the road. If you plan to travel on one of the racing circuits, consider getting a large-wheeled trailer to ease the strain on your car. Welded trailers are generally superior to bolted-together models, but each must be periodically inspected so that you will not break down on the road.

When you go dry sailing, follow these eight basic tips:

1. Be sure your trailer is able to handle the weight of your boat and whatever gear you may store in the boat. Stay within the maximum capacity specified by the manufacturer.

2. Check the laws governing the use of small-boat trailers in your state and other states you plan to travel through.

3. Be sure your trailer is equipped with proper lights and reflectors.

4. Practice turning and backing up with your trailer attached to your car before driving in heavy traffic. Avoid sudden braking when towing the rig.

5. Balance your boat properly on the trailer, placing most of the weight over the wheels with a slight off-balance toward the

car. About 10 percent of the total weight should be on the trailer hitch. A weaving trailer indicates improper balance.

6. Check tire pressures against the manufacturer's recommendations before starting out. In general, trailer tires need more pressure than car tires.

7. When backing the trailer into the water, have someone guide you and tell you when to stop. Cars do not float too well.

8. Use a designated launching ramp, avoiding muddy or sandy areas.

Insurance

It is only common sense to protect your sailboat investment with insurance. But the first thing to look for is a competent, knowledgeable marine insurance agent. The fact that you have had one agent for your home, business, and automobile insurance for 20 years does not qualify him to carry your marine insurance. Marine underwriting is highly specialized and you will always get more for your insurance dollar from a professional in that field. True, most insurance companies have changed from the old "perils of the sea" policies, which excluded coverage of racing activities, to the newer "all-risk" policies. The all-risk policy covers you while racing. It does not include personal property aboard the boat, but this would usually fall under your homeowner's insurance anyway. When looking for a basic hull coverage, make sure that racing sails such as spinnakers and spars are covered while racing. If they are not, find out how expensive it will be to include them.

You should insure your boat for at least 80 percent of its replacement value, since insuring it for less will be just as expensive. If you have an older boat, a rule of thumb for insurance valuation is to decide what your boat is worth on the market right now and insure it for that figure. Replacement value is the deciding factor in newer sailboats.

If you have a smaller one-design that you plan to trail to other racing areas, make sure the hull is covered while on the highway. Most all-risk policies contain a "land-transportation exposure" section which insures your boat within a radius of from 300 to 500 miles from its home port. If you plan to travel

cross country, find out how expensive the additional coverage will be. On ocean cruiser-racers, make sure that your normal sailing areas are within the policy's coverage zone.

All items pertaining to the boat, excluding personal belongings, will be covered under a basic hull policy. This includes sails, spars, and electronic equipment if they are listed on the policy. Excluded from most policies are skin-diving gear, cameras, and fishing equipment. Most marine policies of less than $10,000 insurance have a deductible of $50, while $10,000 to $25,000 policies carry a $100-deductible clause. Liability coverage will often be included in your homeowner's package policy for boats under 26 feet and less than 16 mph speed capability. But do not just assume that you will not need a marine liability policy with a small boat, because you will not be covered in a number of common situations. The homeowner's policy is much less comprehensive than a marine policy and it does not offer protection under the Longshoreman and Harbor Workers Act against an injury to someone working for you on the boat. It also would not cover anyone who borrowed your boat, but you as owner would still be liable. A comprehensive marine protection and indemnity (P&I) policy is generally inexpensive, and the difference between a $50,000/$100,000 policy and a $100,000/$300,000 policy is often as little as $4. The marine liability policy covers everyone aboard except the owner, so it is often wise to leave your wife off the boat registration so that she will be insured.

Most insurance agents have only minimal equipment requirements for new boats, the most basic being the U.S. Coast Guard requirements. Nearly all insurance companies, though, offer discounts for extras such as ship-to-shore radios (2½ percent off), diesel instead of gasoline engines (10 percent off), RDF's, fathometers, and CO_2 fire systems. Fiberglass hulls, Power Squadron or Coast Guard Auxiliary training, and owner experience will also add up to a sizable reduction in yearly premiums. Used sailboats generally have to have a marine survey by a reputable surveyor that is acceptable to the insurance company, but recently built (within five years) glass sailboats are often accepted without a survey. Sails are insured on a pro-rata basis, meaning that they will depreciate in replacement value each year. Few if any agents offer a specific life expectancy for a sail, an improvement over the flat three-year lifetime in the past; the use of the sail, its condition at the time of loss, and many other factors are considered in the determination of value.

Most marine insurance policies are figured for the specific period of time during which the boat will be in use. As previously stated, many policies also state specific limits within which the boat will be operated. This is determined by where you use your boat, how much of the year it is in the water, how much protection and indemnity (liability) coverage you want, and, of course, the value of your boat. Yachts insured for $10,000 and over may be covered for any twelve 15-day periods, not necessarily consecutive. Yacht policies may be written for any period of navigation up to 12 months by applying the proper rate adjustment. Policies written for a specific period of navigation are subject to "layup" credit for any 15 consecutive days the boat is not used during this time, but these only apply to yachts with a hull value of $10,000 and over.

In general, you should look for an agent familiar with *sailboats* and make sure that your hull and liability policies will cover you adequately.

Before Getting Under Way

As with everything in our modern day, there is, to a degree, government regulation of sailing. For instance, all boats powered by motors of more than 10 horsepower plying the navigable waters of the United States must be registered and numbered according to the Federal Boating Act of 1958; documented boats are excepted. That is, a boat must be registered in the state where it operates most. (This includes the time it is berthed.) The numbering fee may be charged

either by the state or the Coast Guard. The law provides for reciprocity between states in recognizing the validity of a number awarded by another state or by the Coast Guard. Although Federal laws are to be enforced by Federal enforcement agents and state laws by the law-enforcement officers of that state or its political subdivisions, this act specifically provides that "nothing herein shall preclude enforcement of both state and Federal laws pursuant to agreements or other arrangements" between the Coast Guard and any state designed to "insure that there shall be the fullest cooperation in the enforcement of both state and Federal statutes, rules and regulations relating to recreation boating." The intent of the law is the promotion of boating safety, to provide coordination and cooperation between the states and with the Federal government in the interest of uniformity of boating laws, and to encourage the highest degree of reciprocity and comity among the several jurisdictions. Nothing in this act interferes with, abrogates, or limits the jurisdiction of any state, and any state system for numbering which is not incompatible with the Federal numbering system will be approved as provided for in the act. The certificate of registration must be on board whenever the boat is in use.

As for the identification numbers themselves, the following regulations must be remembered:

1. Paint or otherwise permanently attach your numbers to the bow so that they will be clearly visible and legible.

2. They should be of the *plain block design* not less than 3 inches high.

3. The numbers must be of a *solid color* that contrasts with the background.

4. The hyphens or spaces separating the numerals from the letters must be equal to the width of a letter except I, or any numeral except 1.

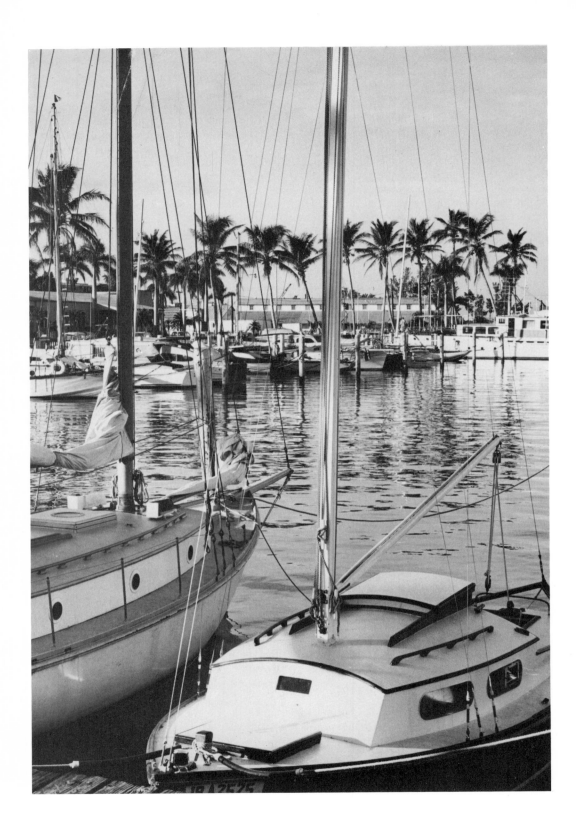

SECTION III

Catalog of One-Design and Offshore Sailboats

In this section we have divided the more popular sailboat designs into two major categories: *one-design* (Olympic, keel-boat, centerboard, and multihull classes), and *offshore*.

In Section II it was stated that all boats in a given one-design class are built as similar to each other as possible. With the possible exception of fiberglass hulls, it is almost impossible to build two boats absolutely alike, no matter how hard you try. But they are one-design. Measurements are held to within strict tolerances. These tolerances can be of help to the amateur, but they can also be used by professional builders, following one extreme or another of the allowable tolerances, to create slightly different boats. This has been the cause of controversy in some classes, and to overcome this some associations kept the building to tolerances known only to the boat's designer and the association's chief measurer. Cheating or chiseling on such points is kept to a minimum by the refusal of a measurement certificate. Some classes are the exclusive property of a single builder and can then be built similar in every detail.

In addition to construction changes, there are sometimes varied ways to change the rig or fittings of a one-design boat to make it go a bit faster than the other craft of the same class. For example, aluminum centerboards, streamlined and slotted masts, lighter frames, variable-area rudders, and hosts of other seemingly minor changes will undoubtedly increase the speed of a boat that has these improvements over one that does not. Actually, one of the most difficult problems in any one-design class is just that; to remain one-design. Many classes start with that ideal, and gradually little deviations and changes creep in, none apparently large enough to matter, but in the aggregate appreciable. Then the fight for "improvements" begins, and holding the line becomes increasingly difficult. Eventually it is found that the topnotchers of the class have incorporated numbers of variations which the rank and file feel they must copy if they are to stay in the running. A person, product, or organization blind to change is doomed, since change is inherent in, indeed almost synonymous with, life. Any knowledgeable and understanding sailor, on having a reasonable experience with almost any boat ever built, could suggest improvements. The object of the class is, however, to encourage competition among boats as closely identical as it is reasonably possible to build them. There is a very definite place for the development classes in which variations and innovations are allowed, even encouraged, and a useful purpose is served by such classes, but as the objectives of a one-design and of a development class are different, they should be kept separate.

One-design principles are generally em-

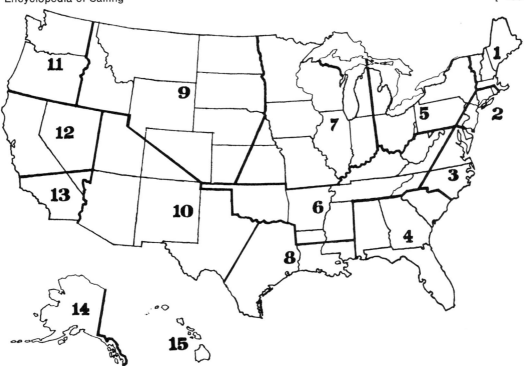

The map is for reference when consulting the individual boat listings in this section. The numbers, which follow "area" in the paragraphs, indicate regions of the United States where most fleets in that particular class are found today.

ployed in the construction of offshore, or cruising-racing, boats. In offshore craft, however, an owner's individual requirements, the amount of gear placed aboard, and his choice of sails make it more difficult to maintain one-design principles as a basis to even-up racing. Most boats of this style are raced in handicap events (see Section VI).

Specifications are given in the order: length overall × beam × draft (with centerboard up). The abbreviation SA is used to indicate sail area. Where possible, spinnaker information indicates the status of this sail according to class rule. Again, class rules, and not popular practice, dictate the kinds of hiking assists permitted and the materials indicated for hull and spars; consequently, several classes are listed as allowing *any material* for construction. All sailboats are sloop rigged unless otherwise noted.

Class rules again are in primary focus in the descriptions of *buoyancy* characteristics. First, rules may not require additional buoy-

ancy—*none added*. If buoyancy is required, the rules may not permit the water-removal equipment necessary to make the boat truly self-rescuing—*positive flotation*. Finally, a class may permit (or require) its members sufficient buoyancy and bailing devices to make their boats *self-rescuing*. As we define it, a boat is self-rescuing if it can be swamped, righted, and continue a race competitively.

Number of *crew* listed reflects the minimum permitted by class rules.

The *rules* of each one-design class limit the degree and area of innovation within that class. If the rules allow no modification of hull shape, standing rigging, or sail plan, it is rated *one-design*. If, in any of these categories, the rules permit tolerances wide enough to encourage innovation, the category is labeled open. In such cases, those categories not mentioned are one-design.

The map here is for reference when consulting the individual boat listings in this section. The numbers, which follow *area* in the paragraphs, indicate regions of the United States where most fleets in that particular class are found today.

Price lists only *approximate* price when new.

Most of the more popular one-designs are represented by associations. We have omitted addresses because these change each year with the election of different secretaries. But, as a rule, the builders of the various classes keep in close contact with the secretaries of the associations of the types they construct. A letter to the National Association of Engine and Boat Manufacturers, Inc., 420 Lexington Avenue, New York, N.Y. 10017, will give you the address of the association you desire.

As suggested in Section II, it is a good idea for prospective sailboat owners to write to the class association of interest for more information. In many cases class handbooks are available (either free or at a small charge) which list detailed requirements for building, measuring, and racing a particular one-design boat. It is always best to join a class through a local fleet when possible, thus assuring racing competition and perhaps the benefit of a local sailing-instruction program. Most one-design fleets are affiliated with yacht clubs, and often have a local spokesman who carries on correspondence with the national secretary. Detailed information on local fleets is usually available from the particular one-design class secretary.

Olympic Classes

The following are the classes of boats that will be raced in the 1972 Olympic games in Germany:

Dragon. Specs: 29′2″ × 6′5″ × 3′11″. SA: 267; spinnaker: 325. Hiking assists: none. Hull: wood. Spars: wood. Buoyancy: none added. Kits not available, plans available. Crew: 3. Area: 5, 7, 8, 11–13. Number: U.S. 250; world 2,000. Rules: one-design. Price: $7,000. Designer: Johan Anker

Finn. Specs: 14′9″ × 4′10″ × 2′–3″. SA: 114; no spinnaker. Catboat. Hiking assists: straps. Hull: wood or fiberglass. Spars: wood. Buoyancy: self-rescuing. Kits available, plans not available. Crew: 1. Area: 1–13. Number: U.S. 900; world 4,000. Rules: rigging

Dragon

Flying Dutchman

open. Price: $1,400. Designer: Rickard Sarby

Flying Dutchman. Specs: 19′10″ × 5′7″ × 3′8″. SA: 200; spinnaker: 190. Hiking assists: straps, trapeze. Hull: any material. Spars: any material. Buoyancy: self-rescuing. Kits, plans available. Crew: 2. Area: 1–15. Number: U.S. 1,300; world 4,200. Rules: standing rigging, sail plan open. Price: $2,000. Designer: Uffa van Essen

Soling. Specs: 26′9″ × 6′3″ × 4′3″. SA: 233; spinnaker: 350. Hiking assists: straps.

Soling

Hull: fiberglass. Spars: aluminum. Buoyancy: self-rescuing. Kits available, plans not available. Crew: 3. Area: 1–15. Number: U.S. 475; world 2,000. Rules: one-design. Price: $4,000–$5,200. Designer: Jan Linge

Star. Specs: 22′7½″ × 5′8″ × 3′4″. SA: 285; no spinnaker. Hiking assists: straps. Hull: wood or fiberglass. Spars: wood. Buoyancy: positive flotation. Kits not available, plans available. Crew: 2. Area: 1–15. Number: U.S. 1,500; world 3,000. Rules: standing rigging open. Price: $3,500–$5,000. Designer: Francis Sweisguth

Tempest. Specs: 21′11¾″ × 6′5½″ × 3′7″. SA: 247; spinnaker: 225. Hiking assists: straps, trapeze. Hull: fiberglass. Spars: metal. Buoyancy: self-rescuing. Kits, plans not available. Crew: 2. Area: 1–3, 5, 7, 8, 12, 13.

Star

Number: U.S. 275; world 600. Rules: standing rigging open. Price: $3,300. Designer: Ian Proctor

Keel-Boat Classes

The following boats in this group have either a full keel or are of the fin type:

Atlantic. Specs: 30′7″ × 6′6″ × 4′9″. SA: 383; spinnaker: 880. Hiking assists: none. Hull: wood or fiberglass. Spars: wood. Buoyancy: required in fiberglass boats. Kits, plans not available. Crew: 2 or 3. Area: 1, 2. Number: U.S. 90. Rules: sail plan open. Price: $5,600. Designer: W. Starling Burgess

Bluenose. Specs: 23′6″ × 6′2″ × 3′6″. SA: 212; spinnaker permitted. Hiking assists: none. Hull: fiberglass. Spars: aluminum. Buoyancy: none. Kits, plans not available. Crew: 2. Area: 1, 2, 5, 12, 13. Number: U.S. 150. Rules: one-design. Price: $3,295. Designer: W. J. Rove

Bull's Eye. Specs: 15′8½″ × 5′10″ × 2′5″. SA: 140; spinnaker permitted. Hiking assists: none. Hull: fiberglass. Spars: aluminum. Buoyancy: self-rescuing. Kits, plans not available. Crew: 2. Area: 1–5. Number: U.S. 600.

Bull's Eye

Cape Cod Mercury

Etchells 22

Rules: one-design. Price: $2,475. Designer: Nathanael Herreshoff

Cape Cod Mercury. Specs: 15′ × 5′5″ × 2′6″ with keel (× 3′3″–6″ with centerboard). SA: 110; spinnaker: 150. Hiking assists: straps. Hull: fiberglass. Spars: aluminum. Buoyancy: positive flotation. Kits, plans not available. Crew: 2. Area: 1–4. Number: U.S. 1,000. Rules: one-design. Price: $1,600 to $2,000. Designer: Sparkman & Stephens

Ensign. Specs: 22′6″ × 7′ × 3′. SA: 290; spinnaker: 375. Hiking assists: none. Hull: fiberglass. Spars: aluminum. Buoyancy: flotation tanks. Kits, plans not available. Crew: 2 or 3. Area: 1, 2, 5, 7, 8, 10. Number: U.S. 1,400. Rules: one-design. Price: $3,600. Designer: Carl Alberg

Etchells 22. Specs: 30′6″ × 6′11½″ × 4′6″. SA: 316; spinnaker: 408. Hiking assists:

none. Hull: fiberglass. Spars: aluminum. Buoyancy: positive flotation. Kits, plans not available. Crew: 3. Area: 2, 11. Number: U.S. 48. Rules: one-design. Price: $6,700. Designer: E. W. Etchells

5.5-Meter. Specs: (approx.) 32' × 6'3" × 4'5". SA: 300; spinnaker permitted. Hiking assists: straps. Hull: wood. Spars: wood or aluminum. Buoyancy: none added. Kits not available, plans available. Crew: 3. Area: 2, 3. Number: U.S. 75; world 400. Rules: hull open, rigging open. Price: $10,000 up. Designer: open

Flying Fifteen. Specs: 20' × 5' × 2'6". SA: 160; spinnaker: 133. Hiking assists:

Flying Fifteen

straps. Hull: wood or fiberglass. Spars: wood or metal. Buoyancy: self-rescuing. Kits and plans available from England. Crew: 2. Area: 1, 2, 12, 13. Number: U.S. 50; world: 1,200. Rules: one-design. Price: $2,500. Designer: Uffa Fox

Herreshoff S. Specs: 27'6" × 7'2" × 4'10". SA: 426; spinnaker permitted. Hiking assists: none. Hull: wood. Spars: wood. Buoyancy: none. Kits, plans not available. Crew: 3. Area: 1–3, 15. Number: U.S. 80. Rules: one-design. Price: $4,000. Designer: Nathanael Herreshoff

International One-Design. Specs: 33'2" ×

6'9" × 5'4". SA: 430; spinnaker permitted. Hiking assists: none. Hull: wood. Spars: wood. Buoyancy: none. Kits, plans not available. Crew: 4–6. Area: 1, 2, 12. Number: U.S. 79; world 174. Rules: one-design. Price: $10,000. Designer: Bjarne Aas

International 110. Specs: 24' × 4'2" × 2'9". SA: 167; spinnaker: 200. Hiking assists:

International 110

straps, trapeze. Hull: wood or fiberglass. Spars: wood or aluminum. Buoyancy: positive flotation. Kits and plans available. Crew: 2. Area: 1–13. Number: U.S. 600; world 625. Rules: one-design. Price: $3,500. Designer: Ray Hunt

International 210. Specs: 29'9½" × 5'10" × 3'10". SA: 305; spinnaker: 400. Hiking assists: none. Hull: wood or fiberglass. Spars: wood. Buoyancy: positive flotation. Kits, plans not available. Crew: 3. Area: 1, 2, 7, 12, 15. Number: U.S. 302; world 312. Rules: one-design. Price: $4,950. Designer: Ray Hunt

International 21. Specs: 21' × 5'9" × 3'4". SA: 200; spinnaker permitted. Hiking assists: none. Hull: wood or fiberglass. Spars: aluminum. Buoyancy: flotation tanks. Kits, plans not available. Crew: 3. Area: 1–3, 5, 7. Number: U.S. 62. Rules: one-design. Price: $2,975. Designer: Hodgdon Bros.

Luders 16. Specs: 26'4" × 5'9" × 4'. SA:

Luders 16

Rainbow

260; spinnaker permitted. Hiking assists: none. Hull: wood or fiberglass. Spars: wood or metal. Buoyancy: none. Kits, plans not available. Crew: 3–4. Area: 2, 7, 8, 13. Number: U.S. 275; world 300. Rules: standing rigging open. Price: $4,800. Designer: A. E. Luders, Jr.

Mercury. Specs: 18′ × 5′4″ × 3′. SA: 177; spinnaker: 100. Hiking assists: straps. Hull: wood or fiberglass. Spars: wood. Buoyancy: optional. Kits, plans available. Crew: 2. Area: 7, 11–13, 15. Number: U.S. 450; world 475. Rules: one-design. Price: $2,295. Designer: Ernest Nunes

Orion. Specs: 19′ × 6′9″ × 4′6″–1′8″ with keel-centerboard (× 5′3″–1′ with centerboard). SA: 200; spinnaker not permitted. Hiking assists: none. Hull: fiberglass. Spars: metal. Buoyancy: positive flotation. Kits, plans not available. Crew: 2. Area: 1, 2, 4. Number: U.S. 300. Rules: one-design. Price: $2,500. Designer: Robert Baker

Rainbow. Specs: 24′2″ × 6′3″ × 3′6″. SA: 278; spinnaker: 365. Hiking assists: none. Hull: fiberglass. Spars: aluminum. Buoyancy: self-rescuing. Kits, plans not available. Crew: 3. Area: 2, 3, 5, 7, 8, 12. Number: U.S. 300; world 350. Rules: one-design. Price: $2,995. Designer: Sparkman & Stephens

Rhodes 18. Specs: 18′ × 6′3″ × 2′8″ with keel (× 4′7″ with centerboard). SA: 196; spinnaker: 197. Hiking assists: none. Hull: wood or fiberglass. Spars: wood or aluminum. Buoyancy: positive flotation. Kits, plans not available. Crew: 3. Area: 1, 2. Number: U.S. 650. Rules: one-design. Price: $1,835 (keel), $1,930 (centerboard). Designer: Philip L. Rhodes

Rhodes 19. Specs: 19′2″ × 7′ × 3′3″. SA: 176; spinnaker permitted. Hiking assists: none. Hull: fiberglass. Spars: aluminum. Buoyancy: flotation tanks. Kits not available, plans not available. Crew: 2. Area: 1–4, 7, 8, 11–13. Number: U.S. 2,000. Rules: one-design. Price: $2,495. Designer: Philip L. Rhodes

Schock 25. Specs: 25′ × 7′ × 4′. SA: 222; spinnaker: 300. Hiking assists: none. Hull: fiberglass. Spars: aluminum. Buoyancy: self-rescuing. Kits, plans not available. Crew: 3. Area: 12, 13. Number: U.S. 90. Rules: one-design. Price: $5,000. Designer: W. D. Schock

Shields. Specs: 30′2½″ × 6′5¼″ × 4′9″. SA: 498; spinnaker: 580. Hiking assists: none. Hull: fiberglass. Spars: aluminum. Buoyancy: positive flotation. Kits, plans not available. Crew: 2. Area: 1–3, 7, 12, 13. Number: U.S. 184; world 187. Rules: one-design. Price: $7,500. Designer: Sparkman & Stephens

Shields

Victory

22-Square Meter. Specs (approx.): 37′ × 6′6″ × 4′6″. SA: 232; spinnaker: 600. Hiking assists: none. Hull: wood. Spars: wood. Buoyancy: none. Kits, plans not available. Crew: 3–4. Area: 7. Number: U.S. 50; world 300. Rules: hull design to measurement formula. Price: $8,000–$8,500. Designer: open

Victory. Specs: 21′ × 6′4″ × 3′. SA: 185; spinnaker permitted. Hiking assists: none. Hull: fiberglass. Spars: aluminum. Buoyancy: flotation tanks. Kits, plans not available. Crew: 2. Area: 6, 8, 10, 12, 13. Number: U.S. 580; world 600. Rules: one-design. Price: $2,000. Designer: Ted Carpentier

Vineyard 21. Specs: 21′ × 5′6″ × 4′. SA: 211; spinnaker permitted. Hiking assists: straps. Hull: wood or fiberglass. Spars: wood. Buoyancy: positive flotation. Kits, plans not available. Crew: 4. Area: 1. Number: U.S. 45. Rules: one-design. Price: $4,400. Designer: Erford Burt

Westerly Nimrod. Specs: 17′9″ × 6′5½″ × 4′8″ (retractable keel). SA: 166; spinnaker permitted. Hiking assists: none. Hull: fiberglass. Spars: aluminum. Buoyancy: flotation

tanks. Kits, plans not available. Crew: 2. Area: 2, 5, 7. Number: U.S. 50; world 250. Rules: one-design. Price: $2,550. Designer: Ian Proctor

Zephyr. Specs: 20′ × 4′ × 32″. SA: 115. Hiking assists: straps. Hull: wood. Spars: wood. Buoyancy: none. Kits, plans not available. Crew: 2. Area: 12. Number: U.S. 100. Rules: one-design. Price: $1,975. Designer: Thrall & Freitag

Zip. Specs: 17′ × 6′2″ × 2′. SA: 130; spinnaker: 75. Hiking assists: none. Hull: fiberglass. Spars: aluminum. Buoyancy: positive flotation. Kits, plans not available. Crew: 1. Area: 2, 4. Number: U.S. 1,580. Rules: one-design. Price: $1,995. Designer: John Ek

Centerboard Classes

The centerboard sailboats listed here may be of the standard type or of the daggerboard type:

Albacore. Specs: 15′ × 5′4″ × 4′9″–9″. SA: 125; spinnaker not permitted. Hiking assists: straps. Hull: wood or fiberglass. Spars: material optional. Buoyancy: self-rescuing. Kits available, plans not available. Crew: 2 or 3. Area: 2–5, 7, 8, 12. Number: U.S. 750; world 5,000. Rules: standing rigging open. Price: $1,300. Designer: Uffa Fox

Amflite 14. Specs: 13'10" × 4½" × 2'6"–4½". SA: 75; no spinnaker. Catboat. Hiking assists: none. Hull: fiberglass. Spars: aluminum. Buoyancy: self-rescuing. Kits, plans not available. Crew: 1. Area: 1–15. Number: U.S. 120. Rules: one-design. Price $520. Designer: AMF Alcort

Arrow. Specs: 18' × 6'4" × 4'2"–14". SA: 175; spinnaker not permitted. Hiking assists: straps. Hull: wood or fiberglass. Spars: wood or aluminum. Buoyancy: positive flotation. Kits not available, plans available. Crew: 2. Area: 7. Number: U.S. 125. Rules: standing rigging open. Price: $2,290. Designer: J. Deering

Banshee. Specs: 16'1" × 5'2" × 3'8"–6". SA: 145; spinnaker: 145. Hiking assists: straps and trapeze. Hull: fiberglass. Spars: aluminum. Buoyancy: positive flotation. Kits, plans not available. Crew: 2. Area: 1–4. Number: U.S. 100; world 450. Rules: one-design. Price: $1,175. Designer: E. Santarelli

Barnegat Bay Sneakbox. Specs: 12'(14', 15') × 5' × 3'3½"–8". SA: 156; spinnaker permitted. Hiking assists: none. Hull: wood or fiberglass. Spars: wood or aluminum. Buoyancy: none. Kits, plans not available. Crew: 1. Area: 1, 2. Number: U.S. 3,000. Rules: one-design. Price: $800 ($1,200, $1,500). Designer: various

Barnegat 17. Specs: 16'7" × 6' × 3'6"–8". SA: 145; spinnaker permitted. Hiking assists: straps. Hull: fiberglass. Spars: aluminum. Buoyancy: positive flotation. Kits, plans not available. Crew: 2. Area: 2, 3. Number: U.S. 150. Rules: one-design. Price: $1,600. Designer: Howard Siddons

Beetle Cat. Specs: 12'4" × 6' × 2'6"–6". SA: 100; no spinnaker. Catboat. Hiking assists: none. Hull: wood. Spars: wood. Buoyancy: none. Kits, plans not available. Crew: 2. Area: 1–3. Number: U.S. 3,000. Rules: one-design. Price: $950. Designer: John Beetle

Blue Jay

Blue Jay. Specs: 13'6" × 5'2" × 3'6"–6". SA: 90; spinnaker: 55. Hiking assists: straps. Hull: wood or fiberglass. Spars: wood, aluminum. Buoyancy: positive flotation. Kits, plans available. Crew: 2. Area: 1–12. Number: U.S. 5,100; world 5,500. Rules: one-design. Price: $1,300–$1,800. Designer: Sparkman & Stephens

Bonito. Specs: 14'6" × 4' × 2'5"–4". SA: 88; no spinnaker. Catboat. Hiking assists: straps. Hull: fiberglass. Spars: aluminum-fi-

Beetle Cats

berglass. Buoyancy: self-rescuing. Kits, plans not available. Crew: 1. Area: 1–13. Number: U.S. 600; world 1,500. Rules: one-design. Price: $599. Designer: J. Pearson

Butterball. Specs: 9′6″ × 5′4″ × 2′5½″–5″. SA: 49; no spinnaker. Catboat. Hiking assists: none. Hull: wood. Spars: wood. Buoyancy: positive flotation. Kits not available, plans available. Crew: 2. Area: 4. Number: U.S. 45; world 88. Rules: one-design. Price: $400. Designer: R. T. Miller

Butterfly. Specs: 12′ × 4′6″ × 2′6″–3″. SA: 75; no spinnaker. Catboat. Hiking assists: none. Hull: fiberglass. Spars: aluminum. Buoyancy: self-rescuing. Kits, plans not available. Crew: 2. Area: 5, 7. Number: U.S. 3,100. Rules: one-design. Price: $635. Designer: John Barnett

C-Lark. Specs: 14′ × 5′9″ × 3′6″–6″. SA: 131; spinnaker permitted. Hiking assists: straps. Hull: fiberglass. Spars: aluminum. Buoyancy: self-rescuing. Kits, plans not available. Crew: 2. Area: 11, 13. Number: U.S. 585. Rules: one-design. Price: $1,195. Designer: Don Clark

Cadet. Specs: 10′7″ × 4′2″ × 2′6″–6½″. SA: 56; spinnaker: 38. Hiking assists: straps. Hull: wood. Spars: aluminum. Buoyancy: positive flotation. Kits, plans available. Crew: 2. Number: world 3,000. Rules: one-design. Price: $700. Designer: Jack Holt

Cape Cod Knockabout. Specs: 18′ × 6′ × 4′2″–14″. SA: 187; spinnaker: 150. Hiking assists: straps. Hull: wood or fiberglass (new). Spars: wood or aluminum. Buoyancy: self-rescuing. Kits, plans not available. Crew: 2. Area: 1, 2. Number: U.S. 2,918. Rules: one-design. Price: $2,850. Designer: Guerney & Fox

Cape Dory 10. Specs: 10′6″ × 4′1″ × 2′5″–5½″. SA: 68; no spinnaker. Catboat. Hiking assists: none. Hull: fiberglass. Spars: aluminum. Buoyancy: positive flotation. Kits, plans not available. Crew: 2. Area: 1–7. Number: U.S. 1,500. Rules: one-design. Price: $600. Designer: Andrew Vavolotis

Cape Dory 14. Specs: 14′6″ × 4′3″ × 3′–6″. SA: 85; no spinnaker. Catboat. Hiking assists: none. Hull: fiberglass. Spars: aluminum. Buoyancy: positive flotation. Kits, plans not available. Crew: 2. Area: 1–7. Number: U.S. 500. Rules: one-design. Price: $775. Designer: Andrew Vavolotis

Caprice. Specs: 14′8″ × 6½″ × 3′10″–7″. SA: 123; spinnaker: 170. Hiking assists: straps. Hull: fiberglass. Spars: aluminum. Buoyancy: self-rescuing. Kits, plans not available. Crew: 2. Area: 2, 3, 5. Number: U.S. 100; world 280. Rules: one-design. Price: $1,495. Designer: Cuthbertson & Cassian

Celebrity. Specs: 19′9″ × 6′4″ × 3′3″–6″. SA: 172; no spinnaker. Hiking assists: none. Hull: fiberglass. Spars: wood. Buoyancy: positive flotation. Kits, plans not available. Crew: 2. Area: 2, 3, 5, 7. Number: U.S. 720. Rules: one-design. Price: $2,350. Designer: unknown

Chickadee. Specs: 10′8″ × 3′1″ × 2′2″–3″. SA: 40; spinnaker: 15. Hiking assists: straps. Hull: fiberglass. Spars: wood. Buoyancy: self-rescuing. Kits, plans not available. Crew: 1. Area: 1–3. Number: U.S. 100. Rules: one-design. Price: $300. Designer: Bengt Johnson

Comet

Comet. Specs: 16′ × 5′ × 3′6″–3½″. SA: 130; no spinnaker. Hiking assists: straps. Hull: wood or fiberglass. Spars: wood or aluminum. Buoyancy required in fiberglass boats. Kits not available, plans available.

Crew: 2. Area: 1–5, 7. Number: U.S. 3,700; world 3,920. Rules: one-design. Price: $1,800. Designer: Lowndes Johnson

Contender. Specs: 16′ × 4′8″ × 4′4″–3′5″. SA: 120; no spinnaker. Catboat. Hiking assists: straps, trapeze. Hull: fiberglass. Spars: aluminum. Buoyancy: positive flotation. Kits and plans available. Crew: 1. Area: 2–5, 7, 8, 12, 13. Number: U.S. 60; world 300. Rules: one-design. Price: $1,200–$1,600. Designer: Robert Miller

Coronado 15. Specs: 15′4″ × 5′8″ × 3′6″–3″. SA: 135; spinnaker permitted. Hiking assists: straps. Hull: fiberglass. Spars: aluminum. Buoyancy: self-rescuing. Kits, plans not available. Crew: 2. Area: 8, 10–13. Number: U.S. 600; world 700. Rules: one-design. Price: $1,095. Designer: Ed Edgar and Frank Butler

Cottontail. Specs: 15′10″ × 5′1″ × 3′–5″. SA: 140; spinnaker: 150. Hiking assists: trapeze, straps. Hull: fiberglass. Spars: aluminum. Buoyancy: positive flotation. Kits, plans not available. Crew: 2. Area: 1, 2, 5. Number: U.S. 100. Rules: standing rigging open. Price: $1,400. Designer: Robert Matteson

Cygnus. Specs: 20′ × 6′10″ × 4′4″–8″. SA: 180; no spinnaker. Hiking assists: straps. Hull: fiberglass. Spars: aluminum. Buoyancy: positive flotation. Kits available, plans not available. Crew: 2, 3. Area: 1, 2, 5, 7. Number: U.S. 12; world 145. Rules: standing rigging open. Price: $2,200. Designer: George Hinterhoeller

Dabchick. Specs: 12′ × 3′10″ × 2′8″–5″. SA: 60; no spinnaker. Hiking assists: straps. Hull: wood or fiberglass. Spars: wood or aluminum. Buoyancy: self-rescuing. Kits, plans available. Crew: 1. Area: 6. Number: U.S. 65; world 1,700. Rules: one-design. Price: $450. Designer: Jack Koper

Day Sailer. Specs: 16′9″ × 6′6″ × 4′8″–7″. SA: 145; spinnaker permitted. Hiking assists: none. Hull: fiberglass. Spars: aluminum. Buoyancy: self-rescuing. Kits, plans not available. Crew: 2. Area: 1–15. Number: U.S. 4,560. Rules: one-design. Price: $1,900. Designer: Uffa Fox

Demon. Specs: 15′3″ × 5′3″ × 3′2″–7″. SA: 116; spinnaker: 135. Hiking assists: straps. Hull: fiberglass. Spars: aluminum. Buoyancy: self-rescuing. Kits, plans not available. Crew: 2. Area: 6, 7, 9. Number: U.S.

199. Rules: one-design. Price: $1,170. Designer: Advance Corp.

Discoverer. Specs: 17′7″ × 6′4″ × 4′6″–9″. SA: 165; no spinnaker. Hiking assists: none. Hull: fiberglass. Spars: aluminum. Buoyancy: positive flotation. Kits, plans not available. Crew: 2. Area: 1, 2, 3. Number: U.S. 140. Rules: one-design. Price: $1,975. Designer: Annapolis Sailboat Builders

Duster. Specs: 13′9″ × 5′4″ × 4′6″–3″. SA: 117; no spinnaker. Catboat. Hiking assists: straps, trapeze. Hull: wood or fiberglass. Spars: wood. Buoyancy: self-rescuing. Kits not available, plans available. Crew: 1. Area: 2, 5. Number: U.S. 388. Rules: one-design. Price: $900. Designer: Owen Merrill

Dyer Dhow. Specs: 9′ × 4′5″ × 1′9″–3″. SA: 45; no spinnaker. Catboat. Hiking assists: none. Hull: fiberglass. Spars: wood or aluminum. Buoyancy: positive flotation. Kits, plans not available. Crew: 1. Area: 1–15. Number: U.S. 2,800. Rules: one-design. Price: $650. Designer: William Dyer

El Toro

Dyer Dink. Specs: 10′ × 4′3″ × 3′6″–6″. SA: 66; no spinnaker. Catboat. Hiking assists: none. Hull: fiberglass. Spars: wood. Buoyancy: positive flotation. Kits not available, plans available. Crew: 1. Area: 1–15. Number: U.S. 1,000. Rules: one-design. Price: $700. Designer: Philip L. Rhodes

El Toro. Specs: 7′11″ × 3′10″ × 1′9″–3″. SA: 38; no spinnaker. Catboat. Hiking assists: straps. Hull: wood or fiberglass. Spars: wood. Buoyancy: positive flotation. Kits, plans available. Crew: 1. Area: 1–15. Number: U.S. 7,000; world 7,500. Rules: one-design. Price: $250–$500. Designer: Macgregor

Enterprise

Enterprise. Specs: 13′3″ × 5′3″ × 3′3″–7″. SA: 113; spinnaker: 90. Hiking assists: straps. Hull: wood or fiberglass. Spars: wood or fiberglass. Buoyancy: self-rescuing. Kits,

plans available. Crew: 2. Area: 1–4, 12, 13. Number: U.S. 800; world 15,000. Rules: one-design. Price: $800, wood; $1,100, fiberglass. Designer: Jack Holt

Explorer. Specs: 17′ × 6′4″ × 4′6″–9″. SA: 147, spinnaker: 134. Hiking assists: straps. Hull: fiberglass. Spars: aluminum. Buoyancy: self-rescuing. Kits, plans not available. Crew: 2, 3. Area: 1–3, 8. Number: U.S. 600. Rules: one-design. Price: $2,200. Designer: Talman Bigelow

Falcon. Specs: 15′8″ × 5′9″ × 2′10″–6″. SA: 137, spinnaker, optional: 140. Hiking assists: straps. Hull: fiberglass. Spars: aluminum. Buoyancy: positive flotation. Kits, plans not available. Crew: 2. Area: 1–3, 5, 7, 11, 12. Number: U.S. 600; world 900. Rules: one-design. Price: $1,550. Designer: George McVey

Fennec. Specs: 11′6″ × 4′9″ × 3′–6″. SA: 92; no spinnaker. Hiking assists: straps. Hull: fiberglass. Spars: aluminum. Buoyancy: self-rescuing. Kits, plans not available. Crew: 2. Area: 1–3. Number: U.S. 30; world 2,200. Rules: one-design. Price: $840. Designer: Y. Mareschal

Fireball

Fireball. Specs: 16′2″ × 4′8½″ × 4′½″–6½″. SA: 123; spinnaker: 140. Hiking assists: straps, trapeze. Hull: wood or fiberglass. Spars: wood or aluminum. Buoyancy: self-rescuing. Kits, plans available. Crew: 2. Area: 2–5, 8, 10, 12, 13. Number: U.S. 400; world 6,000. Rules: one-design. Price: $1,295. Designer: Peter Milne

Firefly

Firefly. Specs: 12′ × 4′7″ × 4′–10″. SA: 100; spinnaker permitted. Hiking assists: straps. Hull: wood. Spars: aluminum. Buoyancy: self-rescuing. Kits available, plans not available. Crew: 2. Area: 1, 2, 5, 13. Number: U.S. 150; world 3,600. Rules: one-design. Price: $900. Designer: Uffa Fox

5-0-5. Specs: 16′6″ × 6′2″ × 3′9″–4″. SA: 172; spinnaker: 220. Hiking assists: straps, trapeze. Hull: any material. Spars: any material. Buoyancy: self-rescuing. Kits, plans available. Crew: 2. Area: 1–3, 7, 12. Number: U.S. 416; world 4,200. Rules: standing rigging open. Price: $1,750. Designer: John Westell

Flipper. Specs: 8′ × 3′11″ × 1′–3″. SA: 37; no spinnaker. Catboat. Hiking assists:

5-0-5

straps. Hull: fiberglass. Spars: fiberglass. Buoyancy: self-rescuing. Kits, plans not available. Crew: 1. Area: 2, 12, 13. Number: U.S. 1,000; world 1,100. Rules: one-design. Price: $400. Designer: Carter Pyle & Joe Quigg

Flying Fish. Specs: 14′ × 5′8″ × 2′8″–5″. SA: 120; no spinnaker. Catboat. Hiking assists: straps. Hull: wood. Spars: fiberglass and aluminum. Buoyancy: self-rescuing. Kits, plans not available. Crew: 1. Area: 1–4. Number: U.S. 450; world 500. Rules: one-design. Price: $1,100. Designer: Carter Pyle & Joe Quigg

Flying Junior. Specs: 13′3″ × 5′3″ × 2′6″–6″. SA: 100; spinnaker: 75. Hiking assists: straps. Hull: wood or fiberglass. Spars: wood or aluminum. Buoyancy: self-rescuing. Kits, plans not available. Crew: 2. Area: 1–15. Number: U.S. 3,000; world 9,000. Rules: one-design. Price: $975. Designer: Uffa van Essen

Flying Saucer. Specs: 15′ × 5′2″ × 3′3″–6″. SA: 115; no spinnaker. Hiking assists: straps. Hull: fiberglass. Spars: aluminum. Buoyancy: self-rescuing. Kits, plans not available. Crew: 2. Area: 1, 2. Number: U.S. 267. **Price:** $795. Designer: Andrew Kostanecki

Flying Scot. Specs: 19′ × 6′9″ × 4′–8″.

Flying Junior

Flying Scot

SA: 190; spinnaker: 200. Hiking assists: none. Hull: fiberglass. Spars: aluminum. Buoyancy: positive flotation. Kits, plans not available. Crew: 2. Area: 1–15. Number: U.S. 1,900. Rules: one-design. Price: $2,395. Designer: Gordon Douglass

Flying Tern

Flying Tern. Specs: 14′ × 5′3″ × 2′10″–6″. SA: 120; spinnaker: 168. Hiking assists: straps. Hull: fiberglass. Spars: wood or aluminum. Buoyancy: self-rescuing. Kits, plans not available. Crew: 2. Area: 1–5, 7, 12, 13. Number: U.S. 625; world 3,500. Rules: one-design. Price: $1,175. Designer: E. G. van der Stadt

420. Specs: 13′9″ × 5′5″ × 3′2″–6″. SA: 110; spinnaker: 95. Hiking assists: straps, trapeze for juniors. Hull: fiberglass. Spars: wood or aluminum. Buoyancy: self-rescuing. Kits, plans not available. Crew: 2 (sloop), 1 (cat). Area: 1–4, 7, 8, 12, 13. Number: U.S. 1,500; world 19,000. Rules: one-design. Price: $1,200. Designer: Christian Maury

470. Specs: 15′6″ × 5′6″ × 4′11″–6″. SA: 137; spinnaker: 150. Hiking assists: straps and trapeze. Hull: fiberglass. Spars: aluminum. Buoyancy: self-rescuing. Kits, plans not

420

Ghost 13

available. Crew: 2. Area: 1, 2, 4, 5, 7, 8, 11. Number: U.S. 200; world 9,000. Rules: one-design. Price: $1,500. Designer: Andre Cornu

Geary 18. Specs: 18′ × 5′2″ × 4′–8″. SA: 157; no spinnaker. Hiking assists: straps. Hull: wood or fiberglass. Spars: wood or aluminum. Buoyancy: self-rescuing. Kits, plans available. Crew: 2. Area: 8, 10–13. Number: U.S. 1,400. Rules: one-design. Price: $1,900. Designer: Ted Geary

Gemini. Specs: 16′1″ × 5′7″ × 3′4″–7″. SA: 140; no spinnaker. Hiking assists: straps. Hull: fiberglass. Spars: aluminum. Buoyancy: positive flotation. Kits, plans not available. Crew: 2. Area: 1–3. Number: U.S. 120. Rules: one-design. Price: $1,500. Designer: Sidney De W. Herreshoff

Ghost 13. Specs: 13′ × 5′ × 3′6″–6″. SA: 105; spinnaker permitted. Hiking assists: straps. Hull: fiberglass. Spars: aluminum. Buoyancy: self-rescuing. Kits, plans not available. Crew: 2. Area: 11, 13. Number: U.S. 141. Rules: standing rigging open. Price: $895. Designer: George Larsen

Goldfish. Specs: 13′9″ × 4′ × 2′3″–4″. SA: 80; no spinnaker. Catboat. Hiking assists: straps. Hull: fiberglass. Spars: aluminum. Buoyancy: self-rescuing. Kits available, plans not available. Crew: 1. Area: 1–13. Num-

ber: U.S. 605. Rules: standing rigging open. Price: $475. Designer: F. Gaines, Jr.

GP 14. Specs: 14′ × 5′ × 3′–7″. SA: 102; no spinnaker. Hiking assists: straps. Hull: wood. Spars: wood. Buoyancy: positive flotation. Kits, plans available. Crew: 2. Area: 1, 2. Number: U.S. 550; world 9,000. Rules: one-design. Price: $1,250. Designer: Jack Holt

Great Pelican. Specs: 15′9¾″ × 8′ × 4′–6″. SA: 188; no spinnaker. Catboat. Hiking assists: none. Hull: wood. Spars: wood. Buoyancy: positive flotation. Kits, plans available. Crew: 2. Area: 13. Number: U.S. 75. Rules: one-design. Price: $2,000. Designer: William H. Short

Grumman Flyer. Specs: 16′2″ × 6′8″ × 3′4″–7″. SA: 149; spinnaker: 200. Hiking assists: straps, trapeze. Hull: aluminum. Spars: aluminum. Buoyancy: self-rescuing. Kits, plans not available. Crew: 2. Area: 1, 2. Number: U.S. 125. Rules: one-design. Price: $1,649. Designer: William Shaw

Hampton. Specs: 18′ × 5′9½″ × 3′6″–7″.

Hampton

SA: 190; no spinnaker. Hiking assists: straps, trapeze. Hull: wood or fiberglass. Spars: wood or aluminum. Buoyancy: positive flotation. Kits, plans available. Crew: 2. Area: 3. Number: U.S. 680. Rules: standing rigging open. Price: $2,350. Designer: Vincent Serio

Heron. Specs: 11′3″ × 4′6″ × 2′10″–7″. SA: 70; no spinnaker. Hiking assists: straps. Hull: wood, fiberglass. Spars: wood. Buoyancy: self-rescuing. Kits, plans available. Crew: 2. Area: 2. Number: U.S. 80; world 8,300. Rules: one-design. Price: $430. Designer: Jack Holt

Highlander. Specs: 20′ × 6′8″ × 4′10″–8″. SA: 225; spinnaker: 250. Hiking assists: straps. Hull: wood or fiberglass. Spars: aluminum. Buoyancy: positive flotation. Kits, plans available. Crew: 3. Area: 1, 2, 5, 8. Number: U.S. 505. Rules: one-design. Price: $2,635. Designer: Gordon Douglass

Hustler. Specs: 18′ × 6′6″ × 4′5″–10″. SA: 180; no spinnaker. Catboat. Hiking assists: straps. Hull: wood or fiberglass. Spars: wood. Buoyancy: positive flotation. Kits not available, plans available. Crew: 2. Area: 1. Number: U.S. 159. Rules: one-design. Price: $1,500. Designer: Charles D. Mower

Indian. Specs: 21′ × 6′ × 4′–18″. SA: 240; spinnaker: 135. Hiking assists: none. Hull: wood. Spars: wood. Buoyancy: none added. Kits not available, plans available. Crew: 3. Area: 1, 2. Number: U.S. 108. Rules: one-design. Price: $2,000. Designer: John Alden

Interclub. Specs: 11′6″ × 4′7″ × 3′–5″. SA: 72; no spinnaker. Catboat. Hiking assists: straps. Hull: fiberglass. Spars: aluminum. Buoyancy: positive flotation. Kits, plans not available. Crew: 2. Area: 1, 2. Number: U.S. 453. Rules: one-design. Price: $775. Designer: Sparkman & Stephens

Interlake

Interlake. Specs: 18′ × 6′3″ × 4′8″–8″. SA: 175; spinnaker: 175. Hiking assists: straps. Hull: fiberglass. Spars: aluminum. Buoyancy: positive flotation. Kits not available, plans available. Crew: 2. Area: 1, 5, 7, 8, 10. Number: U.S. 850; world 856. Rules: one-design. Price: $2,100. Designer: Francis Sweisguth

International Canoe. Specs: (16′ to 17′) × (3′1″ to 3′7″) × 3′7″–4″. SA: 107.64 (sloop).

Hiking assists: sliding seat. Hull: any material. Spars: any material. Buoyancy: self-rescuing. Kits, plans available. Crew: 1. Area: 2, 4, 12. Number: U.S. 107; world 300. Rules: hull shape open, standing rigging open, sail plan open. Price: $1,200–$1,700. Designer: open

International 14. Specs: 14′ × 4′8″ to 5′6″ × 4′–6″. SA: 165; spinnaker: 160 to 200. Hiking assists: straps, trapeze. Hull: any material. Spars: any material. Buoyancy: self-rescuing. Kits, plans available. Crew: 2. Area: 1–4, 7, 11–13. Rules: hull shape open, standing rigging open, sail plan open. Price: $1,700. Designer: open

Javelin. Specs: 14′ × 5′8″ × 3′10″–6″. SA: 125; no spinnaker. Hiking assists: straps. Hull: fiberglass. Spars: aluminum. Buoyancy: positive flotation. Kits, plans not available. Crew: 2. Area: 1, 2. Number: U.S. 1,261. Rules: one-design. Price: $1,395. Designer: Uffa Fox

Jet 14. Specs: 14′ × 4′8″ × 4′2″–6″. SA: 113; no spinnaker. Hiking assists: straps. Hull: fiberglass. Spars: aluminum. Buoyancy: self-rescuing. Kits not available, plans available. Crew: 2. Area: 2, 3, 5. Number: U.S. 1,000. Rules: one-design. Price: $1,200. Designer: Howard Siddons

Jollyboat. Specs: 18′ × 5′2″ × 4′9″–8″. SA: 160; spinnaker permitted. Hiking assists: straps, trapeze. Hull: wood or fiberglass. Spars: wood or aluminum. Buoyancy: self-rescuing. Kits not available, plans available. Crew: 2. Area: 1–3, 5. Number: U.S. 160; world 350. Rules: one-design. Price: $1,900. Designer: Uffa Fox

Jolly Boat Dinghy. Specs: 8′4″ × 4′2″ × 1′9″–4″. SA: 56; no spinnaker. Catboat. Hiking assists: none. Hull: fiberglass. Spars: aluminum. Buoyancy: positive flotation. Kits, plans not available. Crew: 1. Area: 1–4. Number: U.S. 375. Rules: one-design. Price: $560. Designer: Seek Brandon

Jolly Roger. Specs: 8′4″ × 4′1″ × 3′6″–18″. SA: 40; no spinnaker. Hiking assists: none. Hull: fiberglass. Spars: aluminum. Buoyancy: self-rescuing. Kits, plans not available. Crew: 2. Area: 1, 2. Number: U.S. 475. Rules: one-design. Price: $389. Designer: Wes Lazott

Jolly Yare. Specs: 12′8″ × 5′2″ × 3′3″–6″. SA: 101; no spinnaker. Hiking assists: none.

Hull: fiberglass. Spars: aluminum. Buoyancy: positive flotation. Kits, plans not available. Crew: 2. Area: 4. Number: U.S. 100; world 125. Rules: one-design. Price: $970. Designer: Seek Brandon

Kestrel

Kestrel. Specs: 15′7″ × 5′4″ × 4′1″–7″. SA: 136; spinnaker: 165. Hiking assists: straps. Hull: fiberglass. Spars: aluminum. Buoyancy: self-rescuing. Kits, plans not available. Crew: 2. Area: 3, 5, 6, 8, 12. Number: U.S. 125; world 625. Rules: one-design. Price: $1,200. Designer: Ian Proctor

Kingfisher. Specs: 9′6″ × 4′8″ × 3′4″–6″. SA: 80; no spinnaker. Hiking assists: none. Hull: fiberglass. Spars: aluminum. Buoyancy: self-rescuing. Kits, plans not available. Crew: 2. Area: 2–10. Number: U.S. 900; world 1,100. Rules: one-design. Price: $795. Designer: Philip Rhodes

Kingfisher III. Specs: 11′9″ × 4′8″ × 3′1″–8″. SA: 77; no spinnaker. Hiking assists:

Kite

none. Hull: fiberglass. Spars: aluminum. Buoyancy: self-rescuing. Kits, plans not available. Crew: 2–4. Area: 2–5. Number: U.S. 1,200. Rules: one-design. Price: $849. Designer: Philip Rhodes

Kite. Specs: 11′7″ × 5′ × 3′–6″. SA: 78; no spinnaker. Catboat. Hiking assists: straps. Hull: fiberglass. Spars: wood. Buoyancy: self-rescuing. Kits, plans not available. Crew: 1. Area: 8, 10, 13, 15. Number: U.S. 1,000; world 1,500. Rules: one-design. Price: $945. Designer: Carter Pyle

Kohinoor. Specs: 15′3″ × 6′ × 4′9″–9″. SA: 145; no spinnaker. Hiking assists: none. Hull: wood. Spars: wood. Buoyancy: none added. Kits, plans not available. Crew: 2. Area: 5. Number: U.S. 300. Rules: one-design. Price: $1,500. Designer: Murray Wright

Koralle. Specs: 14′ × 4′8″ × 2′4″–4″. SA: 108; no spinnaker. Hiking assists: straps. Hull: wood and fiberglass. Spars: wood or aluminum. Buoyancy: self-rescuing. Kits,

plans not available. Crew: 2. Area: 12, 13. Number: U.S. 200; world 14,000. Rules: one-design. Price: $995. Designer: Atlanta Bootsbau

Korsar. Specs: 16′4″ × 5′7″ × 3′4″–4″. SA: 138; spinnaker: 150. Hiking assists: straps, trapeze. Hull: wood or fiberglass. Spars: wood or aluminum. Kits not available, plans available. Crew: 2. Area: 11, 12, 13. Number: U.S. 54; world 5,000. Rules: standing rigging open. Price: $1,485. Designer: Ernst Lehfeld

Lark. Specs: 13′4″ × 5′5½″ × 3′9″–4″. SA: 105; spinnaker: 80. Hiking assists: straps. Hull: fiberglass. Spars: aluminum. Buoyancy: self-rescuing. Kits, plans not available. Crew: 2. Area: 1, 2, 5. Number: U.S. 150; world 900. Rules: one-design. Price: $1,295. Designer: Michael Jackson

Laser. Specs: 13′10″ × 4′6″ × 2′6″–4″. SA: 76; no spinnaker. Catboat. Hiking assists: straps. Hull: fiberglass. Spars: aluminum. Buoyancy: self-rescuing. Kits, plans not available. Crew: 2. Area: 1–15. Number: U.S. 600; world 1,100. Rules: one-design. Price: $695. Designer: Bruce Kirby

Leader. Specs: 14′ × 5′5″ × 3′6″–5″. SA: 118; spinnaker permitted. Hiking assists: straps. Hull: wood. Spars: wood. Buoyancy: self-rescuing. Kits available, plans not available. Crew: 2. Area: 7, 5, 11. Number: U.S. 120; world 420. Rules: one-design. Price: $1,395. Designer: J. G. Polland

Lehman 12. Specs: 12′ × 4′6″ × 3′4″–4″. SA: 81; no spinnaker. Catboat. Hiking assists: none. Hull: fiberglass. Spars: aluminum. Buoyancy: positive flotation. Kits available, plans not available. Crew: 2. Area: 13. Number: U.S. 100. Rules: one-design. Price: $900. Designer: B. Lehman

Lido 14. Specs: 14′ × 6′ × 4′3″–6″. SA: 111; no spinnaker. Hiking assists: straps. Hull: fiberglass. Spars: aluminum. Buoyancy: positive flotation. Kits, plans not available. Crew: 2. Area: 6–15. Number: U.S. 2,500. Rules: one-design. Price: $1,800. Designer: W. D. Schock

Lightning. Specs: 19′ × 6′6″ × 4′11½″–1′5″. SA: 177; spinnaker: 300. Hiking assists: straps. Hull: wood or fiberglass. Spars: wood or aluminum. Buoyancy: positive flotation. Kits, plans available. Crew: 3. Area: 1–15. Number: U.S. 8,050; world 11,000. Rules:

Lightning

Mac Dinghy

one-design. Price: $2,700. Designer: Sparkman & Stephens

LS 13. Specs: 13′ × 5′ × 3′3″–5″. SA: 93; no spinnaker. Hiking assists: none. Hull: fiberglass. Spars: aluminum. Buoyancy: positive flotation. Kits, plans not available. Crew: 2. Area: 8, 10. Number: U.S. 1,800. Rules: one-design. Price: $1,095. Designer: Thomas Fall

LS 16. Specs: 16′ × 6′1″ × 2′10″–6″. SA: 160; spinnaker: 164. Hiking assists: straps. Hull: fiberglass. Spars: aluminum. Buoyancy: positive flotation. Kits, plans not available. Crew: 3. Area: 1–13. Number: U.S. 700. Rules: one-design. Price: $1,865. Designer: Thomas Fall

M-16. Specs: 16′ × 5′6″ × 2′6″–6″. SA: 150; no spinnaker. Hiking assists: straps. Hull: wood or fiberglass. Spars: wood. Buoyancy: self-rescuing. Kits, plans not available. Crew: 2. Area: 5. Number: U.S. 400. Rules: one-design. Price: $1,395. Designer: Harry Melges, Sr.

M-20. Specs: 20′ × 5′8″ × 3′6″–8″. SA:

167; spinnaker: 175. Hiking assists: straps. Hull: fiberglass. Spars: wood or aluminum. Buoyancy: self-rescuing. Kits, plans not available. Crew: 2. Area: 2–8. Number: U.S. 325. Rules: one-design. Price: $2,500. Designer: Harry Melges, Sr.

Mac Dinghy. Specs: 10′ × 4′1″ × 1′6″–4″. SA: 65; no spinnaker. Hiking assists: none. Hull: fiberglass. Spars: wood or aluminum. Buoyancy: self-rescuing. Kits, plans not available. Crew: 1. Area: 2, 5, 6. Number: U.S. 275; world 2,700. Rules: one-design. Price: $569. Designer: M. Dubdam

Mariner. Specs: 19′2″ × 7′ × 4′11″–10″ (× 3′3″ with keel). SA: 185. Spinnaker: 240. Hiking assists: none. Hull: fiberglass. Spars: aluminum. Buoyancy: positive flotation. (Also cabin with four berths, galley incl., head optional). Kits, plans not available. Crew: 2. Area: 1–15. Number: U.S. 2,000. Rules: one-design. Price: $2,765. Designer: O'Day Co.

Melody. Specs: 10′ × 3′3″ × 2′2″–3″. SA: 55; no spinnaker. Catboat. Hiking assists: straps. Hull: wood. Spars: wood. Buoyancy:

none added. Kits available, plans not available. Crew: 1. Area: 12. Number: U.S. 350. Rules: one-design. Price: $495. Designer: William Ashcraft

Minisail. Specs: 13′5″ × 3′7″ × 3′–6″. SA: 80; no spinnaker. Catboat. Hiking assists: straps. Hull: wood or fiberglass. Spars: aluminum. Buoyancy: self-rescuing. Kits available, plans not available. Crew: 1. Area: 7. Number: U.S. 1,000; world 5,000. Price: $249. Designer: Ian Proctor

Mirror Dinghy. Specs: 10′10″ × 4′7″ × 2′9″–4″. SA: 69; spinnaker permitted. Hiking assists: straps. Hull: wood. Spars: wood. Buoyancy: self-rescuing. Kits available, plans not available. Crew: 2. Area: 1–15. Number:

SA: 82; no spinnaker. Catboat. Hiking assists: straps. Hull: any material. Spars: any material. Buoyancy: optional. Kits, plans available. Crew: 1. Area: 1–3. Number: U.S. 585; world 5,200. Rules: hull shape, standing rigging open. Price: $700–$900. Designer: open

Naples Sabot. Specs: 7′10″ × 4′ × 2′–6″. SA: 36; no spinnaker. Catboat. Hiking assists: straps. Hull: wood or fiberglass. Spars: wood or aluminum. Buoyancy: positive flotation. Kits, plans available. Crew: 1. Area: 13. Number: U.S. 6,100. Rules: one-design. Price: $350. Designer: McCulloch

National One-Design. Specs: 17′ × 5′8″ × 3′6″–2′. SA: 137; no spinnaker. Hiking assists: straps. Hull: wood or fiberglass.

Mobjack

U.S. 400; world 22,000. Rules: one-design. Price: $500. Designer: Holt & Bucknell

Mobjack. Specs: 17′ × 6′6″ × 4′–9″. SA: 180; spinnaker: 165. Hiking assists: straps. Hull: fiberglass. Spars: aluminum. Buoyancy: positive flotation. Kits, plans not available. Crew: 2. Area: 1–3, 5. Number: U.S. 380. Rules: one-design. Price: $1,995. Designer: Roger Moorman

Moth. Specs: 11′ (beam and draft open).

National One-Design

Spars: wood or aluminum. Buoyancy: self-rescuing. Kits, plans available. Crew: 2. Area: 1, 2, 5–7, 11–13. Number: U.S. 700; world 750. Rules: one-design. Price: $1,400. Designer: William Crosby

Nipper. Specs: 12′ × 5′2″ × 2′8″–6″. SA: 100; no spinnaker. Hiking assists: straps. Hull: wood or fiberglass. Spars: wood or aluminum. Buoyancy: none added. Kits, plans not available. Crew: 2. Area: 1–15. Number: U.S. 3,200. Rules: one-design. Price: $850. Designer: Ray Greene

OK Dinghy. Specs: 13′1½″ × 4′8″ × 3′7″. SA: 90; no spinnaker. Catboat. Hiking assists: straps. Hull: wood or fiberglass. Spars: wood. Buoyancy: self-rescuing. Kits, plans available. Crew: 1. Area: 1–15. Number: U.S. 730; world 6,500. Rules: one-design. Price: $350–$900. Designer: Knud and Axel Olsen

Omega. Specs: 13′7″ × 5′4″ × 3′–4″. SA: 108; no spinnaker. Hiking assists: straps. Hull: fiberglass. Spars: aluminum. Buoyancy: positive flotation. Kits, plans not available. Crew: 2. Area: 5, 7, 8, 13. Number: U.S. 500. Rules: one-design. Price: $900. Designer: Ted Carpentier

Optimist Pram. Specs: 8′ × 3′6″ × 2′6″–6″. SA: 35; no spinnaker. Catboat. Hiking assists: straps. Hull: wood or fiberglass. Spars: wood. Buoyancy: positive flotation. Kits, plans available. Crew: 1. Area: 1–15. Number: U.S. 20,000; world 25,000. Rules: one-design. Price: $195. Designer: Clark Mills

Osprey. Specs: 17′6″ × 5′10″ × 4′–6″. SA: 150; spinnaker: 150. Hiking assists: straps, trapeze. Hull: wood or fiberglass. Spars: aluminum. Buoyancy: self-rescuing. Kits, plans available. Crew: 2. Area: 2–4. Number: U.S. 35; world 700. Rules: one-design. Price: $1,500. Designer: Ian Proctor

Peanut. Specs: 9′6″ × 4′ × 2′6″–4″. SA: 55; no spinnaker. Catboat. Hiking assists: straps. Hull: wood or fiberglass. Spars: wood or aluminum. Buoyancy: positive flotation. No kits, plans available. Crew: 1. Area: 2, 4, 7. Number: U.S. 325; world 375. Rules: one-design. Price: $565. Designer: Arnold Johnson

Pegasus. Specs: 14′6″ × 4′10″ × 4′3″–6″. SA: 137; spinnaker: 180. Hiking assists: straps, trapeze. Hull: fiberglass. Spars: wood or aluminum. Buoyancy: self-rescuing. Kits,

Penguin

plans available. Crew: 2. Area: 1,2. Number: U.S. 20; world 243. Rules: one-design. Price: $600. Designer: Uffa Fox

Penguin. Specs: 11′6″ × 4′6″ × 3′8″–4″. SA: 72; no spinnaker. Catboat. Hiking assists: straps. Hull: wood or fiberglass. Spars: aluminum. Buoyancy: required for fiberglass. Kits, plans available. Crew: 2. Area: 1–15. Number: U.S. 8,800; world 9,300. Rules: one-design. Price: $700. Designer: Philip L. Rhodes

Pintail. Specs: 14′ × 6′ × 4′–8″. SA: 122; spinnaker permitted. Hiking assists: none. Hull: fiberglass. Spars: aluminum. Buoyancy: positive flotation. Kits, plans not available. Crew: 2. Area: 1–5, 7. Number: U.S. 800. Rules: one-design. Price: $1,345. Designer: F. S. Ford, Jr.

Pioneer. Specs: 17′ × 6′4″ × 4′6″–10″. SA: 151; spinnaker: 100. Hiking assists: straps.

Hull: fiberglass. Spars: aluminum. Buoyancy: self-rescuing. Kits, plans not available. Crew: 2. Area: 1, 2. Numbers: U.S. 500. Rules: one-design. Price: $2,500. Designer: Talman Bigelow

Pirate Fish. Specs: 14'1" × 4'1" × 3'1"–7". SA: 75; no spinnaker. Catboat. Hiking assists: toe rail. Hull: fiberglass. Spars: aluminum. Buoyancy: self-rescuing. Kits, plans not available. Crew: 2. Area: 1, 2. Number: U.S. 220. Rules: one-design. Price: $530. Designer: William Bower

Rascal. Specs: 14' × 6' × 4'–6". SA: 127; spinnaker permitted. Hiking assists: straps. Hull: fiberglass. Spars: aluminum. Buoyancy: positive flotation. Kits, plans not available. Crew: 2. Area: 3, 5, 6. Number: U.S. 3400. Rules: one-design. Price: $1,395. Designer: Ray Greene

Raven. Specs: 24'2" × 7' × 5'4"–7". SA: 300; spinnaker permitted. Hiking assists: straps. Hull: wood or fiberglass. Spars: aluminum. Buoyancy: positive flotation. Crew: 3. Area: 2, 4, 5. Number: U.S. 320. Rules: one-

design. Price: $3,800. Designer: Roger McAleer

Rebel. Specs: 16' × 6'6" × 3'–7". SA: 166; no spinnaker. Hiking assists: straps. Hull: fiberglass. Spars: aluminum. Buoyancy: positive flotation. Kits, plans not available. Crew: 2. Area: 2, 5, 7, 8. Number: U.S. 3,200. Rules: one-design. Price: $2,000. Designer: Ray Greene

Rhodes Bantam. Specs: 14' × 5'6" × 4'6"–4". SA: 125; spinnaker: 144. Hiking assists: straps. Hull: wood or fiberglass. Spars: wood or aluminum. Buoyancy: self-rescuing. Kits, plans available. Crew: 2. Area: 4–8. Number: U.S. 1,800; world 1,900. Rules: one-design. Price: $1,100. Designer: Philip L. Rhodes

Rooster. Specs: 9'7" × 3'10" × 2'–5". SA: 37; no spinnaker. Catboat. Hiking assists: none. Hull: wood. Spars: wood. Buoyancy: positive flotation. Kits not available, plans available. Crew: 1. Area: 1, 2. Number: U.S. 300. Rules: one-design. Price: $250. Designer: Michael Smith

S-12. Specs: 12' × 4' × 2'3"–3". SA: 75;

Rebel

Scorpion

no spinnaker. Hiking assists: none. Hull: fiberglass. Spars: aluminum. Buoyancy: self-rescuing. Kits, plans not available. Crew: 1. Area: 1–9. Number: U.S. 2,500. Rules: one-design. Price: $459. Designer: Erich Swenson

Sailfish. Specs: 13'7" × 2'11" × 2"–5". SA: 75; no spinnaker. Catboat. Hiking assists: none. Hull: fiberglass. Spars: aluminum. Buoyancy: self-rescuing. Kits and plans not available. Crew: 1. Area: 1–15. Number: U.S. 40,000; world 50,000. Rules: one-design. Price: $394. Designer: AMF Alcort

San Francisco Pelican. Specs: 12'2½" × 6'2½" × 4'–4". SA: 105; no spinnaker. Hiking assists: none. Hull: wood or fiberglass. Spars: wood. Buoyancy: self-rescuing. Kits, plans available. Crew: 2. Area: 2, 5, 7, 11, 12. Number: U.S. 2,500; world 4,000. Rules: one-design. Price: $800. Designer: William Short

Scorpion. Specs: 13'9" × 4' × 2'4"–5½". SA: 75; no spinnaker. Catboat. Hiking assists: none. Hull: fiberglass. Spars: aluminum. Buoyancy: self-rescuing. Kits, plans not available. Crew: 1. Area: 1–8. Number: U.S. 2,000. Rules: standing rigging open. Price: $475. Designer: James Templeton

Super Porpoise. Specs: 14'8" × 3'2" × 2'6"–4". SA: 75; no spinnaker. Catboat. Hiking assists: none. Hull: fiberglass. Spars: aluminum. Buoyancy: self-rescuing. Kits, plans not available. Crew: 1. Area: 1–13. Number: U.S. 4,200; world 4,400. Rules: one-design. Price: $550. Designer: Molded Products Company

Scows

A-Scow. Specs: 38' × 8'6" × 5'3"–3". SA: 557; spinnaker permitted. Hiking assists: straps. Hull: wood. Spars: wood or aluminum. Buoyancy: positive. Kits, plans not available. Crew: 5. Area: 7. Number: U.S. 25. Rules: hull shape open, standing rigging open. Price: $9,000. Designer: John Johnson

C-Scow. Specs: 20' × 6'6" × 3'–6". SA: 215; no spinnaker. Catboat. Hiking assists: straps. Hull: wood or fiberglass. Spars: wood. Buoyancy: self-rescuing. Kits, plans not available. Crew: 2. Area: 1–12. Number: U.S. 1,000. Rules: one-design. Price: $2,250. Designer: Inland YA

Cub Scow. Specs: 12'3" × 4'6" × 2'6"–3". SA: 75; no spinnaker. Catboat. Hiking assists:

straps. Hull: fiberglass. Spars: aluminum. Buoyancy: positive. Kits, plans not available. Crew: 2. Area: 5, 7, 9. Number: U.S. 400. Rules: one-design. Price: $695. Designer: R. F. Holmgren

D-Scow. Specs: 20' × 6'6" × 3'3"–3". SA: 252; spinnaker permitted. Hiking assists: straps. Hull: wood. Spars: wood. Buoyancy: self-rescuing. Kits, plans not available. Crew: 2. Area: 5, 7. Number: U.S. 50. Rules: one-design. Price: $2,395. Designer: John Johnson

E-Scow. Specs: 28' × 6'9" × 4'9"–3". SA: 319; spinnaker: 400. Hiking assists: straps. Hull: wood or fiberglass. Spars: wood. Buoyancy: self-rescuing. Kits not available, plans available. Crew: 3. Area: 1–10. Number: U.S. 500. Rules: hull shape open, standing rigging open. Price: $2,995. Designer: Arnold Meyer

M-Scow. Specs: 16' × 5'8" × 2'8"–2". SA: 146; no spinnaker. Hiking assists: straps. Hull: wood or fiberglass. Spars: wood. Buoyancy: self-rescuing. Kits not available, plans available. Crew: 2. Area: 1–9. Number: U.S. 500. Rules: one-design. Price: $1,595. Designer: Harry Melges, Sr.

MC-Scow. Specs: 16' × 5'6" × 2'7"–2". SA: 135; no spinnaker. Catboat. Hiking assists: straps. Hull: fiberglass. Spars: wood.

E-Scow

Buoyancy: self-rescuing. Kits, plans not available. Crew: 1. Area: 7. Number: U.S. 50. Rules: one-design. Price: $950. Designer: Harry Melges, Sr.

W-Scow. Specs: 14′ × 4′4″ × 3′2″–3″. SA: 125; no spinnaker. Hiking assists: straps. Hull: wood. Spars: wood. Buoyancy: self-rescuing. Kits not available, plans available. Crew: 1. Area: 5. Number: U.S. 50. Rules: one-design. Price: $300 (home-built). Designer: C. J. Wagner

Sea Hawk. Specs: 14′ × 4′4″ × 2′8″–4″. SA: 90; no spinnaker. Hiking assists: straps, sliding seat. Hull: fiberglass. Spars: aluminum. Buoyancy: self-rescuing. Kits, plans not available. Crew: 1. Area: 2, 5, 8. Number: U.S. 125. Rules: one-design. Price: $695. Designer: Miguel Padilla

Seadog. Specs: 9′6″ × 4′1″ × 2′2″–4″. SA: 42; no spinnaker. Catboat. Hiking assists: straps. Hull: fiberglass. Spars: aluminum. Buoyancy: positive flotation. Kits, plans not available. Crew: 1. Area: 1, 2. Number: U.S. 600; world 650. Rules: one-design. Price: $500. Designer: Aero-Nautical, Inc.

Seagull. Specs: 14′6″ × 4′2″ × 2′8″–4″. SA: Lateen 85; sloop 102; no spinnaker. Hiking assists: straps. Hull: fiberglass. Spars: aluminum. Buoyancy: self-rescuing. Kits, plans not available. Crew: 1. Area: 1–5, 7. Number: U.S. 400; world 425. Rules: one-design. Price: Lateen $625; sloop $795. Designer: F. C. Gaines, Jr.

Seven/Eleven. Specs: 7′11″ × 4′2″ × 2′4″–4″. SA: 34; no spinnaker. Catboat. Hiking assists: none. Hull: fiberglass. Spars: aluminum. Buoyancy: positive flotation. Kits, plans not available. Crew: 1. Area: 1, 2, 5. Number: U.S. 917. Rules: one-design. Price: $425. Designer: Robert Baker

Signet. Specs: 12′5″ × 4′9″ × 3′4″–5″. SA: 88; spinnaker permitted. Hiking assists: straps. Hull: wood. Spars: wood or aluminum. Buoyancy: self-rescuing. Kits, plans available. Crew: 2. Area: 1, 2, 5. Number: U.S. 300; world 700. Rules: one-design. Price: $875. Designer: Ian Proctor

Skate. Specs: 10′2″ × 3′4″ × 2′1″–3½″. SA: 40; no spinnaker. Catboat. Hiking assists: none. Hull: fiberglass. Spars: aluminum. Buoyancy: self-rescuing. Kits, plans not available. Crew: 1. Area: 1–3. Number: U.S.

1,300. Rules: one-design. Price: $249. Designer: Wesley Lazott

Skipjack. Specs: 14′7″ × 5′3″ × 4′–9″. SA: 125; spinnaker: 150. Hiking assists: straps. Hull: fiberglass. Spars: aluminum. Buoyancy: self-rescuing. Kits, plans not available. Crew: 2. Area: 2, 3, 5, 11, 12. Number: U.S. 350. Rules: one-design. Price: $1,495. Designer: Sindle, Moorman, Pyle

Skunk. Specs: 11′1″ × 5′5″ × 2′6″–7″. SA: 70; no spinnaker. Hiking assists: none. Hull: fiberglass. Spars: aluminum. Buoyancy: positive flotation. Kits, plans not available. Crew: 2. Area: 1. Number: U.S. 100; world 280. Rules: one-design. Price: $749. Designer: Vandestadt & McGruer Ltd.

Skylark. Specs: 14′2″ × 4′8″ × 2′6″–6″. SA: 100; no spinnaker. Hiking assists: straps. Hull: fiberglass. Spars: aluminum. Buoyancy: self-rescuing. Kits, plans not available. Crew: 1. Area: 1–13. Number: U.S. 3,000. Rules: one-design. Price: $795. Designer: Stephen Taylor

Snipe. Specs: 15′6″ × 5′ × 3′3½″–6″. SA: 128; no spinnaker. Hiking assists: straps. Hull: wood or fiberglass. Spars: wood or aluminum. Buoyancy: positive flotation. Kits, plans available. Crew: 2. Area: 1–15. Number: U.S. 15,000; world 19,500. Rules: one-design. Price: $1,200. Designer: William Crosby

Snowbird. Specs: 12′ × 5′ × 2′7″–4″. SA: 102; no spinnaker. Catboat. Hiking assists: straps. Hull: wood or fiberglass. Spars: wood. Buoyancy: positive flotation. Kits, plans not available. Crew: 1. Area: 12, 13. Number: U.S. 500. Rules: one-design. Price: $850. Designer: W. D. Schock Company

Sparkler. Specs: 11′ × 4′6″ × 2′4″–3½″. SA: 79; no spinnaker. Hiking assists: straps. Hull: fiberglass. Spars: aluminum. Buoyancy: self-rescuing. Kits, plans not available. Crew: 1. Area: 4, 5. Number: U.S. 450. Rules: one-design. Price: $795. Designer: Bob Ellenbest

Sprite. Specs: 10′2″ × 4′9″ × 3′5″–3″. SA: 63; spinnaker: 38. Hiking assists: none. Hull: fiberglass. Spars: aluminum. Buoyancy: positive flotation. Kits, plans not available. Crew: 2. Area: 1–8. Number: U.S. 2,738. Rules: one-design. Price: $625. Designer: Robert Baker

Squall. Specs: 9′4″ × 4′5″ × 1′10½″–6″.

SA: 75; no spinnaker. Catboat. Hiking assists: none. Hull: fiberglass. Spars: aluminum. Buoyancy: self-rescuing. Kits, plans not available. Crew: 1. Area: 1–4. Number: U.S. 5,000. Rules: one-design. Price: $599. Designer: Howard Chappelle

SS. Specs: 16'6" × 4'9" × 2'10"–16". SA: 100; spinnaker: 35. Hiking assists: straps. Hull: wood or fiberglass. Spars: wood. Buoyancy: none added. Kits not available, plans available. Crew: 1. Area: 2. Number: U.S. 154. Rules: one-design. Price: $1,800. Designer: Benjamin Hallock

Starfish. Specs: 13'8" × 4' × 2'4"–4½". SA: 82; no spinnaker. Catboat. Hiking assists: none. Hull: fiberglass. Spars: aluminum. Buoyancy: self-rescuing. Kits, plans not available. Crew: 1. Area: 1–13. Number: U.S. 1,328. Rules: one-design. Price: $439. Designer: John Fillip

Stingray. Specs: 13'2" × 4'6" × 2'6"–1'4". SA: 95; no spinnaker. Catboat. Hiking assists: straps. Hull: fiberglass. Spars: aluminum. Buoyancy: self-rescuing. Kits, plans not available. Crew: 1. Area: 1, 2, 5. Number: U.S. 600. Rules: one-design. Price: $645. Designer: G. Linell

Sunfish. Specs: 13'10" × 4½" × 2'6"–4". SA: 75; no spinnaker. Catboat. Hiking assists: none. Hull: fiberglass. Spars: aluminum. Buoyancy: self-rescuing. Kits and plans not available. Crew: 1. Area: 1–15. Number: U.S. 59,000; world 75,000. Rules: one-design. Price: $537. Designer: AMF Alcort

Sunflower. Specs: 11' × 3'2" × 2'2"–4". SA: 45; no spinnaker. Catboat. Hiking assists: none. Hull: fiberglass. Spars: aluminum. Buoyancy: self-rescuing. Kits, plans not available. Crew: 1. Area: 1–15. Number: U.S. 5,000; world 5,500. Rules: one-design. Price: $200. Designer: Snark Products, Inc.

Super Satellite. Specs: 14' × 6' × 3'6"–4". SA: 130; no spinnaker. Hiking assists: straps. Hull: fiberglass. Spars: aluminum. Buoyancy: positive flotation. Kits, plans not available. Crew: 2. Area: 11–13. Number: U.S. 600. Rules: one-design. Price: $995. Designer: Ted Carpentier

Super Swift. Specs: 12'8" × 3'8" × 2'10"–4". SA: 80; no spinnaker. Catboat. Hiking assists: none. Hull: fiberglass. Spars: aluminum. Buoyancy: self-rescuing. Kits, plans not available. Crew: 1. Area: 1–15. Number: U.S. 950. Rules: one-design. Price: $520. Designer: O'Day Co.

Sweet Sixteen. Specs: 16' × 6' × 4'–4". SA: 127; spinnaker: 250. Hiking assists: straps. Hull: fiberglass. Spars: aluminum. Buoyancy: self-rescuing. Kits available; plans not available. Crew: 2. Area: 3, 6–8. Number: U.S. 262. Rules: one-design. Price: $1,445. Designer: Advance Sailboat Corp.

Swift. Specs: 10'4" × 3'2" × 2'6"–3". SA: 44; no spinnaker. Catboat. Hiking assists: none. Hull: fiberglass. Spars: aluminum. Buoyancy: self-rescuing. Kits, plans not available. Crew: 1. Area: 1–15. Number: U.S. 2,170. Rules: one-design. Price: $350. Designer: O'Day Co.

Tern. Specs: 12' × 4'6" × 3'4"–3". SA: 88; spinnaker: 70. Hiking assists: straps. Hull: wood or fiberglass. Spars: wood or aluminum. Buoyancy: self-rescuing. Kits not available, plans available. Crew: 1. Area: 4–10. Number: U.S. 225. Rules: one-design. Price: $350. Designer: C. Allen

Thistle. Specs: 17' × 6' × 4'6"–9". SA: 175; spinnaker: 225. Hiking assists: straps. Hull: wood or fiberglass. Spars: wood or aluminum. Buoyancy: self-rescuing. Kits, plans available. Crew: 2. Area: 1–15. Number: U.S. 2,900. Rules: one-design. Price: $2,070. Designer: Gordon Douglass

Thunderbird Pram. Specs: 7'7" × 3'10" × 2'6"–2½". SA: 35; no spinnaker. Catboat. Hiking assists: none. Hull: wood or fiberglass. Spars: wood. Buoyancy: self-rescuing. Kits available, plans not available. Crew: 1. Area: 1–8, 13. Number: U.S. 2,400. Rules: one-design. Price: $170. Designer: Ross Sackett

Turnabout. Specs: 9' × 5'3" × 2'–3". SA: 60; spinnaker: 30. Hiking assists: straps. Hull: wood or fiberglass. Spars: wood. Buoyancy: positive flotation. Kits available, plans not available. Crew: 2. Area: 1–3. Number: U.S. 2,300. Rules: one-design. Price: $450. Designer: Harold Turner

U.S. Monotype. Specs: 14'2" × 5'8" × 3'9"–6". SA: 95; no spinnaker. Catboat. Hiking assists: straps. Hull: wood or fiberglass. Spars: wood or aluminum. Buoyancy: self-rescuing. Kits, plans available. Crew: 1. Area: 4. Number: U.S. 119. Rules: one-design. Price: $1,050. Designer: H. Snyder

Turnabout

U.S. Monotype

Vauriens

Vaurien. Specs: 13′3″ × 4′9″ × 2′8″–3″. SA: 88; no spinnaker. Hiking assists: straps. Hull: wood. Spars: wood. Buoyancy: self-rescuing. Kits, plans available. Crew: 2. Area: 3. Number: U.S. 50; world 1,125. Rules: one-design. Price: $500. Designer: Jean-Jacques Herbulot

Viking 140. Specs: 14′ × 5′6″ × 3′–6″. SA: 113; no spinnaker in U.S. Hiking assists: none. Hull: fiberglass. Spars: wood or aluminum. Buoyancy: positive flotation. Kits, plans not available. Crew: 2. Area: 1, 2. Number: U.S. 160; world 4,500. Rules: one-design. Price: $1,095. Designer: Per Brohell

Wayfarer. Specs: 15′10″ × 6′1″ × 3′10″–8″. SA: 141; spinnaker permitted. Hiking assists: straps. Hull: wood or fiberglass. Spars: wood or aluminum. Buoyancy: self-rescuing. Kits available, plans not available. Crew: 2. Area: 5, 7, 12. Number: U.S. 400; world 1,160. Rules: one-design. Price: $1,695. Designer: Ian Proctor

Wianno Senior. Specs: 25′ × 8′ × 5′–2′6″.

SA: 366; spinnaker permitted. Hiking assists: none. Hull: wood. Spars: wood. Buoyancy: none added. Kits, plans not available. Crew: 4. Area: 1. Number: U.S. 150. Rules: one-design. Price: $6,400. Designer: H. Manley Crosby

Widgeon. Specs: 12′4″ × 5′ × 3′6″–5″. SA: 90; spinnaker permitted. Hiking assists: straps. Hull: fiberglass. Spars: aluminum. Buoyancy: positive flotation. Kits, plans not available. Crew: 2. Area: 1, 2, 5. Number: U.S. 1,950. Rules: one-design. Price: $875. Designer: Robert Baker

Winard Sabot. Specs: 7′10″ × 3′10″ ×2′1″– 3″. SA: 38; no spinnaker. Catboat. Hiking assists: none. Hull: wood or fiberglass. Spars: wood. Buoyancy: positive flotation. Kits, plans available. Crew: 1. Area: 3, 7, 10–13. Number: U.S. 1,800; world 2,000. Rules: one-design. Price: $350. Designer: Unknown

Windjammer. Specs: 16′9″ × 6′6″ × 4′–7″. SA: 158; no spinnaker. Hiking assists: straps. Hull: fiberglass. Spars: aluminum. Buoyancy: self-rescuing. Kits, plans not available. Crew: 2. Area: 1–3. Number: U.S. 220. Rules: one-design. Price: $1,348. Designer: Charles Wittholz

Windmill. Specs: 15′6″ × 4′8″ × 4′2″–6″. SA: 119; no spinnaker. Hiking assists: straps. Hull: wood or fiberglass. Spars: wood. Buoyancy: required for fiberglass, optional in wood. Kits, plans available. Crew: 2. Area: 1–13. Number: U.S. 3,000; world 3,700. Price: $1,000. Designer: Clark Mills

Wood-Pussy. Specs: 13′6″ × 6′ × 4′–6″. SA: 125; no spinnaker. Hiking assists: straps. Hull: wood or fiberglass. Spars: wood. Buoyancy: positive flotation. Kits not available; plans available. Crew: 1. Area: 2, 5, 12. Number: U.S. 1,500; world 1,600. Rules: one-design. Price: $1,250. Designer: Philip L. Rhodes

X-Boat. Specs: 16′ × 6′ × 2′7″–2″. SA: 110; no spinnaker. Hiking assists: straps. Hull: wood or fiberglass. Spars: wood. Buoyancy: self-rescuing. Kits, plans not available. Crew: 2. Area: 5, 7. Number: U.S. 700. Rules: one-design. Price: $1,300. Designer: Inland YA

Y-Flyer. Specs: 18′ × 5′8″ × 4′–6″. SA: 161; spinnaker not permitted in U.S. Hiking assists: straps. Hull: wood or fiberglass. Spars: wood or aluminum. Buoyancy: self-rescuing.

Wood-Pussy

Y-Flyer

Kits, plans available. Crew: 2. Area: 1–12. Number: U.S. 1,900; world 2,400. Rules: one-design. Price: $1,795. Designer: Alvin Youngquist

Other One-Design Class Sailboats

Class Name	Keel or Centerboard	Catboat or Sloop	Length Overall	Beam	Sail Area, Square Feet
A Class	K	S	27′9″	7′2″	368
A Class Dinghy	CB	C	11′6″	4′6″	72
Acadian	K	S	17′	6′	197
Adams Interclub	K	S	24′6″	6′	253
Advanced Trainer	K	S	28′	5′8″	250
Albatross	K/CB	S	20′	6′8″	225
Albatross	K	S	22′8″	5′10″	218
Albatross 15	CB		15′	5′4″	125
Alden O	CB	S	18′3″	6′2″	200
Alden 12	K	S	16′	5′9″	160
Alpha	CB	S	12′	5′	90
Annisquam Bird	CB	C	19′	6′	217
Annisquam Cat	CB	C	16′	7′6″	140
Annisquam Fish	CB	C	15′	6′6″	120
Aquilla	CB	S	14′	5′	120
Arrow	K	S	21′9″	6′	180
Atlantic City Cat	CB	C	15′	6′	170
Atlantic 404	CB	S	13′3″	5′3″	113
B Class	K	S	26′	6′6″	312
B Dinghy	CB	C	11′	4′6″	72
BB-11	K	S	20′2″	5′10″	119
BB Gull	CB	C	11′1″	4′8″	76
BB Sailer	CB	C	9′	4′6″	60
BB Swan	CB	C	12′8″	6′4″	90
Banshee	CB	C	13′	4′11″	88
Bar Harbor 17	K	S	21′	6′8″	200
Barracuda	CB	S	16′	5′3″	119
Barracuda	CB	C	13′3″	4′6″	95
Bay Bird	CB	S	18′	6′	135
Baymaster	CB	S	17′10″	6′11″	149
Beverly Dinghy	CB	C	11′6″	4′6″	66
Biddleford Pool 18	K	S	18′	6′	197
Black Rock	K	S	22′	6′9″	220
Blue Bird	CB	C	7′2″	3′6″	40
Blue Buoy	CB	S	13′6″	5′5″	108
B-O Dinghy	CB	C	11′6″	4′6″	72
Bobbin	CB	S	9′	4′2″	65
Bobcat	CB	C	9′	4′	60
Boothbay Harbor	K	S	21′	5′6″	200
Bosun	CB	S	14′	5′6″	115
Bristol (see Bull's Eye, page 108)					
Brutal Beast	CB	S	14′	6′	100
Buccaneer	CB	S	18′	6′	175
Buckeye	CB	S	12′8″	4′11″	101
Bull Dog	K	S	14′	5′4″	110
Bulter Cat	CB	C	18′	6′6″	170
Buster	CB	C	14′	6′	135
C Class	K	S	25′	6′6″	341
C-C	CB	S	18′	6′	170
Cactus	CB	S	10′	4′2″	52
Camal	K	S	18′	5′8″	150
Candy	CB	S	12′	4′	105

Class Name	Keel or Centerboard	Catboat or Sloop	Length Overall	Beam	Sail Area, Square Feet
Cape Cod Junior	CB	S	15′	5′	110
Cape Cod Nimblet	CB	S	15′	5′1″	136
Cardinal	CB	S	13′6″	5′9″	97
Catabout	CB	C	15′	5′8″	120
Catspaw	CB	C	16′	6′6″	140
Challenger 15	CB	S	15′	5′6″	139
Charles River Basin One-Design	K	S	15	5′5″	118
Chatauqua	CB		12′1″	4′9″	85
Chesapeake 20	CB	S	20′	6′7″	171
Chick	CB	C	10′11″	4′6″	60
CL 16	CB	S	16′	6′1″	141
Clamshell	CB	C	8′	3′6″	40
Class B	K	S	11′9″	4′6″	72
Clipper	K	S	17′	6′	150
Clipper	K	S	20′	5′6″	170
Clipperdink	CB	C	8′3″	3′6″	36
Coast 13	CB	S	13′5″	4′11″	104
Cold Spring Harbor One-Design	K	S	21′	5′6″	250
Columbia 21	K	S	21′8″	7′7″	234
Compass	CB	S	18′	6′	150
Conanicut 16	CB	S	22′	7′	230
Condor	K	S	18′	6′8″	180
Connecticut Moth	CB	C	11′	4′2″	67
Copperhead	CB	C	13′9″	4′5″	75
Corinthian	K	S	20′6″	6′4″	268
Corinthian One-Design	CB	S	23′9″	7′	225
Corsair	CB	S	20′	5′4″	135
Cottage Park 15	K	S	24′	5′	200
Cotuit Skiff	CB	C	14′5″	5′2″	115
Coypu	CB	S	11′6″	5′	86
Crescent	CB	S	13′6″	5′	95
Crescent	K	S	24′	7′	298
Cricket	CB	C	15′	5′	130
Crosby Cat	CB	C	14′	6′	100
Crosby 16	CB	S	15′8″	5′4″	133
Cub	CB	S	16′	6′	110
Cub	K	S	22′7″	6′6″	278
Cygnus	K/CB	S	20′	6′10″	180
D Class	CB	C	10′	4′3″	66
Daring	CB	S	14′3″	4′8″	150
Dark Harbor 17	K	S	25′10″	6′3″	311
Dee Cee	CB	S	9′6″	4′6″	
Defender	K	S	24′	6′	200
Delta	CB	C	12′	5′9″	75
Diamond	CB	C	12′6″	4′9″	65
Dolphin	CB	S	15′4″	6′	165
Dolphin	K	S	19′6″	6′3″	175
Dough Dish (see Bull's Eye, page 108)					
Down Easter	CB	C	9′3″	3′7″	31
Dublin Sloop	CB	S	13′6″	5′	100
Ducking	CB	S	9′4″	4′	40
Duo	CB	S	14′3″	6′1″	140
Dutch Pirate	K	S	21′6″	6′6″	183
Duxbury Duck	CB	S	18′	6′4″	210
Dyer Delta	CB	S	18′8″	6′1″	120
Dyer Dhow Midget	CB	C	7′11″	4′7″	35
Eagle	CB	S	19′	6′2″	159

Class Name	Keel or Centerboard	Catboat or Sloop	Length Overall	Beam	Sail Area, Square Feet
Edgartown Beach Boat	CB	S	13'10"	5'3"	100
Edgartown Dory	CB	S	17'	5'3"	160
Edgartown 15	CB	S	22'6"	6'6"	200
Edgartown Rover	CB	S	17'	6'	155
Edgartown Skiff	CB	C	12'6"	4'7"	80
Eighteen-Foot Knockabout	CB	S	18'	6'	185
Eka-L	CB	S	13'10"	5'	92
Eleven Plus	CB	S	11'	4'7"	70
Elvstrom Jr.	CB	C	11'2"	5'4"	70
Esquimo	CB	S	23'	6'6"	220
Fairey Falcon	CB	S	16'6"	5'11"	125
Falcon	K	S	22'6"	6'6"	256
Feather	CB	C	9'6"	4'2"	55
Fenwick Dory	CB	S	21'	6'3"	210
Firebird	CB	S	11'4"	4'10"	73
Fish	K	S	20'9"	7'1"	289
Fishers Island	K	S	25'8"	5'8"	200
Fleetwing Arrow	CB	S	15'10"	5'8"	113
Flibustier	CB	S	15'7"	5'5"	143
Flying Feather	CB	S	20'	6'	165
Ford 20	CB	S	20'	7'	190
4.45	CB	S	14'8"	5'9"	120
Frolic	CB	C	11'	4'5"	77
Frost 18	CB	S	18'	6'	185
Frostbite	CB	C	9'	4'1"	57
G Class	CB	S	18'	6'3"	200
Galaxy	K		14'	6'	110
Gannet	CB	S	14'	5'11"	125
Gazelle	CB	S	22'8"	6'7"	189
Gig	CB	C	9'3"	4'9"	56
Glastron Alpha	CB	C	15'	4'1"	98
Goldeneye	K	S	18'3"	6'4"	193
Goshawk	CB	C	11'6"	4'6"	72
Gosling	CB	S	11'6"	4'8"	98
Grand Duc	CB	S	15'7"	5'6"	145
Great Lakes 21 (same as International 21)					
Great South Bay One-Design	K/CB	S	24'	7'1"	280
Great South Bay Shore Bird	K	S	21'1"	6'4"	250
Grenadier	CB	S	11'6"	5'1"	85
Grumman Dinghy	CB	C	8'6"	4'2"	50
Grumman Sailing Canoe	CB	C	17'	3'	65
Gulf Fish	K	S	20'6"	6'8"	268
Gull	CB	C	11'	4'9"	70
H-14	CB	S	14'	4'6"	75
Harpoon	CB	S	18'	6'3"	177
Hawk	CB	S	14'8"	6'	123
Hellcat Mark IIIS	CB	C	25'	7'3"	300
Herreshoff 12	K	S	15'6"	6'	100
Herreshoff 15	CB	S	24'	5'9"	200
Herreshoff 16	K	S	20'9"	7'1"	280
Herreshoff 16	K	S	23'	6'3"	200
Hinckley Pilot 35	K	S	35'9"	9'6"	554
Hingham Dwarf	CB	C	10'	4'	52
Hodgdon 21	K	S	21'	5'10"	310
Holiday	K	S	19'1"	6'6"	173
Hornet	CB	S	16'	4'7"	121
Hull Seabird	CB	S	17'	6'3"	220
Hurricane	CB	S	19'	6'9"	176

Class Name	Keel or Centerboard	Catboat or Sloop	Length Overall	Beam	Sail Area, Square Feet
Hush Guppy	CB	C	12'	3'7"	72
Indian Harbor Pirate	K	S	18'	6'2"	193
Indian Landing 20	K	S	20'	6'4"	220
Indian River	CB	S	13'6"	5'10"	97
Indian Scout	CB	S	12'6"	4'8"	72
Inland Cat	CB	C	14'6"	5'4"	115
Intermountain One-Design	K	S	15'10"	6'	100
International One-Design 12-ft Dinghy	CB	S	12'	4'7"	95
International Skimmer	CB	S	16'	5'	190
International 12 Square Meter Sharpie	CB	S	19'6"	4'6"	130
Islander	K	S	21'4"	5'7"	175
Javelin	K	S	23'6"	5'	190
Jolly Yare Jr.	CB	S	10'2"	5'2"	89
Junior	CB	S	11'	3'10"	82
Junior Class	K	S	22'6"	5'10"	205
K Class	K/CB	C	22'	8'	270
Kadet	CB	C	11'2"	5'5"	75
Katama	K	S	25'3"	8'	270
Kayot Windward	CB	C	13'	4'6"	90
Kingfisher	CB	C	11'6"	4'8"	75
Kitten	CB	C	9'4"	3'10"	40
Kittiwake	K	S	17'9"	7'6"	248
Knickerbocker	K	S	26'3"	6'7"	306–339
Knockabout	CB	S	14'	5'3"	85
L Class	K/CB	S	28'	7'	325
L-16	K	S	26'	5'9"	260
L-18	K	S	22'10"	6'	195
Lancaster	CB	S	16'	5'6"	130
Lancer	CB	C	8'	4'	40
Lawley 15	K/CB	S	15'	5'	100
Lawley 110	K/CB	S	24'	6'6"	110
Lazy E	CB	S	15'	5'3"	136
Lehman Interclub	CB	C	10'6"	3'6"	67
Liberty	K	S	17'8"	5'4"	129
Lightning, Jr.	CB	S	13'10"	4'11"	92
Little Bear	CB	S	11'6"	4'6"	86
Loa 17	CB	S	17'	5'4"	125
Long Island	CB	S	16'	5'7"	125
Lowell 19	CB	S	19'	6'4"	200
M. B. Class	K	S	29'4"	6'6"	335
Mallard	CB	S	21'7"	7'6"	218
Man O' War	CB	C	15'	4'6"	85
Manchester 15	CB	S	18'	6'	125
Manhasset Bay One-Design	K	S	21'8"	5'2"	230
Maraudeur	K/CB	S	16'	5'9"	152
Marblehead T	K	S	22'2"	5'6"	218
Marblehead Trainer	CB	C	9'10"	4'2"	45
Mariner	CB	S	12'10"	6'4"	110
Mark	CB	C	12'	4'9"	80
Marshall Cat	CB	C	22'2"	10'2"	210
Massachusetts Bay 15	CB	S	25'	6'6"	250
Massachusetts Bay Indian	K	S	21'2"	6'5"	230
Mayfly	CB	S	12'9"	5'6"	90
Medalist 33	K	S	33'	10'	467
Menemshas	K	S	17'	6'	160
Merlin Rocket	CB	S	14'	5'	105

Class Name	Keel or Centerboard	Catboat or Sloop	Length Overall	Beam	Sail Area, Square Feet
Mermaid	K	S	23′	5′9″	194
Merry Mac	CB	C	13′6″	4′10″	95
Metcalf	CB	C	13′	4′6″	90
Meteor	K	S	16′	5′4″	134
Midshipmite	CB	C	14′6″	4′9″	120
Mighty Mite	CB	C	14′	6′6″	177
Minifish	CB	C	11′9″	3′9″	65
Minnow	CB	C	7′3″	4′	45
Mirror 16	CB	S	16′	6′	178
Missile	CB	S	14′	5′8″	124
MIT Dinghy	CB	C	12′	5′9″	75
Moffett	CB	S	19′	6′4″	153
Monomoy	CB	S	24′6″	7′2″	250
Monomoy Interclub	K	S	24′6″	6′	212
Montgomery 10	CB	C	10′	4′2″	62
Moon	CB	C	11′	4′3″	85
Moth Europa	CB	C	11′	4′9″	70
Mouette	CB	S	19′6″	6′11″	157
Mount Desert One-Design	K	S	21′	6′8″	260
Mustang	CB	S	17′	6′6″	120
Mystic Dinghy	CB	C	10′	4′5″	66
Nabob	CB	S	12′2″	5′11″	99
Nantucket Indian	CB	S	21′2″	6′3″	225
Nantucket Rainbow	CB	C	12′	5′	100
Narrasketuck	CB	S	20′	6′4″	230
Nassau Dinghy	K	S	13′10″	4′	115
National 19	CB	S	19′	6′6″	220
Naval Academy Knockabout	CB	S	26′	7′	338
Navigator	K	S	21′	6′4″	188
New Rochelle Rainbow	CB	S	16′	5′7″	125
Newport Dory	CB	S	16′	5′6″	120
Nod	CB	S	17′	5′8″	132
Nomolo	CB	C	10′	4′	44
Nord	CB	C	12′	4′6″	107
Nord Hawk	CB	C	12′	4′6″	75
North Shore One-Design	CB	S	15′6″	5′7″	122
North Star Doryette	CB	S	11′2″	5′2″	55
Nutshell	CB	C	10′	4′	45
O'Day 15	CB	S	14′11″	5′10″	105
OD 11	CB	C	11′	4′	56
OD 17	CB	S	16′5″	6′3″	155
Olso	CB	S	18′	5′	102
Olympic Monotype	CB	C	12′	5′	80
One-Design of Wales	CB	S	14′6″	4′10″	150
Ospray	CB	S	15′6″	6′	126
Oxford Sailer	CB	S	14′	4′8″	76
Oyster Harbor Cat	K/CB	C	14′	6′4″	133
Pacific 14	CB	S	14′	4′8″	120
Pacific 21	K	S	21′	5′	184
Patricia Skimmer	CB	C	16′	5′1″	185
Pelican	CB	C	11′2″	4′7″	62
Pennant 18	K	S	18′	6′2″	195
Pennant S	K	S	21′8″	6′6″	245
Pequot Indian	K	S	22′	6′11″	247
Peregrine 16	K	S	15′7″	6′	128
Pilot	K	S	16′6″	5′9″	165
Pine Tree	CB	S	19′	6′	175
Pinfin	CB	C	12′1″	4′8″	65
Piper One Design	K	S	24′5″	6′3″	220

Class Name	Keel or Centerboard	Catboat or Sloop	Length Overall	Beam	Sail Area, Square Feet
Piranha 9	CB	S	9'2"	4'	48
Piranha	CB	S	13'	4'7"	84
Pirate	K	S	19'	7'1"	247
Pirate Fish Jr.	CB	C	11'1"	2'10"	65
Porpoise	CB	C	13'10"	3'2"	75
Pow-Wow	CB	S	16'	5'6"	135
Privateer	K	S	26'	7'	275
Proctor 18	K	S	17'	6'5"	166
Puddle Duck	CB	C	7'10"	4'	36
Puffin	CB	S	14'	6'	102
Pup	K	S	20'4"	6'4"	231
Quincy Adams 17	K	S	26'6"	6'	253
Quincy Bantam	CB	S	18'	7'3"	200
Quincy Dolphin	CB	S	15'	6'	135
Quincy 15	CB	S	15'	7'9"	247
Quincy Pirate	CB	S	24'	6'	210
Raceabout	K	S	23'	5'8"	200
Radio	CB	S	16'6"	6'	142
Rainbow	CB	C	10'	4'4"	66
Rainbow	CB	C	12'	4'	70
Red Dragon	CB	S	12'6"	4'8"	78
Red Wing	K	S	15'9"	5'6"	150
Red Wing	K	S	17'5"	5'	125
Redhead	CB	S	17'3"	6'1"	170
Reliance	CB	S	21'4"	6'9"	182
Resolute	K	S	27'7"	6'4"	330
Robin	CB	S	17'6"	6'1"	180
Rocket	CB	S	18'	6'6"	180
Ross 13	CB	S	13'2"	4'7"	110
Royal Burnham One-Design	K	S	20'	6'7"	240
S-Class	K	S	27'6"	7'2"	425
S-14	CB	S	14'	5'1"	108
Sabot S	CB	S	8'	4'	45
Sabre	CB	S	16'	5'7"	120
Sabre Scow	CB	S	26'	6'6"	272
Sailoar	CB	C	10'	4'6"	65
Sakonnet Class	K	S	18'6"	6'6"	183
San Diego Sun	CB	S	22'	6'11"	205
Sandpiper	CB	S	12'6"	4'6"	94
Sandpiper	CB	S	16'9"	6'6"	161
Sandshark	CB	S	12'	4'6"	116
Sandusky 18	CB	S	18'	6'3"	175
Sandy Bay	CB	S	25'	7'	264
Saro Scimitar	K	S	20'3"	6'3"	193
Scamper 11			11'	3'	48
Scat	CB	S	13'	5'	90
Scat	CB	S/C	14'	5'1"	120
Scout	CB	S	16'	5'4"	140
Sea Bee	CB	S	15'6"	5'7"	125
Sea Bird	K	S	24'	5'9"	175
Sea Gull	CB	S	18'	6'2"	165
Sea Gull	CB	S	14'6"	4'2"	102
Sea Hawk II	CB	S	14'3"	4'4"	105
Sea Horse	CB	S	16'5"	5'5"	140
Sea Kettle	CB	S	16'	5'8"	110
Sea Scouter	CB	C	10'	4'2"	66
Sea Shell	CB	C	7'11"	4'	41
Sea Snark	CB	C	11'	3'2"	45
Sea Swinger	CB	C	12'	3'3"	50

Class Name	Keel or Centerboard	Catboat or Sloop	Length Overall	Beam	Sail Area, Square Feet
Seabright	CB	C	7′	3′8″	46
Seafarer Dinghy	CB	C	7′1″	4′	28
Seafly	CB	S	14′	5′8″	120
Seawanhaka 21	K	S	31′	6′6″	357
Seminole	CB	S	13′9″	4′7″	72
Senior B. K.	K/CB	S	23′	6′6″	215
Shamrock	K	S	25′	6′	215
Shark	K	S	22′	5′	210
Shinnecock	CB	S	24′	6′7″	300
Shore Bird	K/CB	S	21′	6′4″	249
Shrimp	CB	C	9′7″	4′10″	70
Shrimp Class	CB	S	12′	4′6″	90
Skim-Air	CB	C	9′	4′5″	47
Skipper	CB	S	14′	4′9″	83
Snow Flake	CB	C	9′4″	4′6″	50
Solitaire	CB	C	13′10″	5′4″	110
Sophomore	K	S	22′	5′9″	200
Sound Interclub	K	S	28′6″	7′9″	408
South Mass. 19	K	S	19′	5′10″	157
South Swansea Skiff	CB	C	12′	4′6″	87
Southeaster	CB	S	16′	4′6″	117
Spider	CB	S	18′	6′	125
Spindrift	CB	S	13′4″	5′2″	100
Splinter	CB	S	14′4″	5′2″	120
Squeegee	CB	C	17′6″	5′10″	200
Stage Harbor 18	CB	S	20′	6′	165
Stamford Bird	CB	S	18′	6′3″	162
Starlet	CB	S	16′	4′2″	130
Suicide	CB	S	22′	5′6″	125
Su-Mark	CB	C	8′2″	4′	36
Sun Boat	CB	S	15′3″	5′	122
Sundadee 18	K	S	24′8″	6′3″	230
Sunray Jr.	CB	S	13′9″	4′7″	100
Swallow	K	S	25′6″	5′8″	200
Swinger	CB	C	11′3″	4′2″	75
Swordfish	CB	S	16′	5′	130
T Class	K	S	22′2″	5′6″	218
Taft Cup Cat	CB	C	22′	8′	270
Tallstar	CB	S	14′	5′9″	121
Tanzer 14	CB	S	13′6″	5′6″	90
Tanzer 16	CB	S	16′4″	6′2″	145
Taurus	K	S	22′2″	5′6″	218
Taurus	CB	C	9′	4′	45
Teal	CB	S	15′6″	5′	122
Tech Dinghy	CB	C	12′	5′	72
Tech II	CB	C	12′6″	5′	108
Teddy Bear	CB	C	8′6″	4′4″	45
Telstar	CB	S	11′4″	4′5″	65
Ten-Square Meter Canoe	CB	C	17′9″	2′9″	108
Terrier	CB	S	12′	4′8″	96
Texas Long Horn	K	S	20′	6′	158
Thundercat	CB	C	13′2″	5′2″	110
Tiger	CB	C	11′6″	4′4″	84
Tinker Class	CB	C	14′	6′	100
Tomahawk	K	S	24′8″	7′4″	218
Top Ten	CB	C	10′	4′6″	55
Toppan Tot	CB	C	15′	6′6″	110
Tornado	CB	S	16′5″	5′7″	160
Totem 21	CB		21′	7′6″	270
Town	CB	S	16′6″	5′9″	152

Class Name	Keel or Centerboard	Catboat or Sloop	Length Overall	Beam	Sail Area, Square Feet
Toy	CB	S	15′	4′	90
Tradewind	CB	S	14′3″	4′4″	95
Tribe	K	S	15′8″	5′	111
Triss 14	CB	S	14′	5′	100
Tumlaren	K	S	27′8″	6′3″	220
Tutor Ten	CB	S	11′7″	4′3″	64
Twelve-foot International One-Design	CB	S	12′	4′8″	72
Udell	K	S	36′	6′6″	232
U.S. One-Design	K	S	37′8″	7′	378
Vagabond	CB	S	20′	6′6″	195
Valiant	CB	S	20′	6′6″	196
Vermilion 25	K	S	25′	7′2″	270
Viking	K	S	20′	6′	208
Viking	K	S	25′	7′6″	325
Viking 170	CB	S	16′10″	6′2″	159
Vineyard Haven 15	K	S	21′	6′	210
Vita Dinghy	CB	S	9′10″	5′	65
Vivacity	K	S	20′	7′	175
Vixen	CB	C	10′	4′6″	60
Wakefield Skimmer	CB	C	14′	5′	120
Warwick Necker	K	S	20′	6′7″	212
Warwick 16	K	S	21′	7′	220
Weasel	CB	C	11′4″	5′6″	90
Wee Scot	K	S	15′3″	5′3″	144
Wellfleet	CB	S	18′	6′9″	220
Wenaumet Kitten	CB	C	14′	6′	120
WeSorT	CB	S	11′11″	4′1″	72
Westport Dory	CB	C	12′2″	4′	85
Whaleboat	K/CB	S	14′8″	5′6″	80
White Cap	CB	S	13′	5′4″	90
Wianno Jr.	CB	S	16′6″	6′	139
Wildfire	K	S	16′9″	6′3″	165
Winabout 16	K/CB	S	16′	5′9″	152
Winabout 18	CB	S	18′6″	6′	210
Windsurfer	CB	C	12′	2′4″	56
Wineglass	CB	S	15′	5′10″	123
Winthrop 15	CB	S	22′	6′	210
Winthrop Hustler	CB	C	18′	6′	130
X Boat	CB	S	16′	6′	110
X Class One-Design	CB	C	11′6″	4′8″	72
X Scow	CB	S	16′	6′	110
Yankee Clipper	CB	S	13′6″	5′7″	100
Yankee Dory	CB	S	18′	5′7″	140
Zenith	CB	S	15′6″	6′3″	170
Zephyr	K/CB	S	24′	7′1″	280
Zest	K	S	30′2″	6′9″	313
Zip Class	CB	S	14′	5′	100

Meter Classes

Meter-class boats vary considerably in dimensions. That is, all boats in a meter class closely resemble one another, but they are not nearly as identical as one-designs. They differ in hull form and leading dimensions, thus keeping alive the art of the design; they all, however, fit within the closely knit framework of the International Class Meter Rule, and race together on level terms—without handicap. In other words, the boats are designed under strict formula—they are sometimes called "formula classes." The *approximate* dimensions of the leading meter classes are:

Class	Length Overall	Length at Waterline
12-Meter	70 feet	45 feet
10-Meter	60 feet	38 feet
8-Meter	50 feet	32 feet
6-Meter	40 feet	25 feet
5.5-Meter	35 feet	23 feet

These dimension figures, in addition to being approximate, are the so-called "classic" ones —that is, the dimensions established under the International Yacht Racing Union rule of 1920 and modified in detail on several occasions since then. In fact, since the 12-Meter class, for example, became active in the United States around 1930, the waterline lengths have increased from about 45 feet to almost 50 feet, while overall lengths have dropped from nearly 70 feet to around 63 feet. During the same period, sail area has been reduced from over 1,900 square feet to less than 1,750 square feet. Beam has been fairly stable just above the rule minimum, or around 12 feet. This same dimensional trend can be found in the design of other meter classes, too.

5.5 Meter

Restricted Classes

This group of racing sailboats is similar to the meter, or formula, classes. Actually, meter boats could be or should be considered members of the restricted classes. That is, boats in the restricted classes are built to certain restrictions, but the designers have certain leeway in living up to these rules. Thus, the restricted boats are permitted the employment of the designer's experience in an individual design to fulfill the given conditions of the class. This constructive competition among the designers produces a very healthy rivalry in all the popular restricted classes. Among these might be mentioned the O, P, Q, and R classes under the Universal Rule; and the 6-Meter and 12-Meter classes under the International Rule.

Boats of the restricted classes vary considerably in length, sail area, etc., but the following data are representative of the more popular classes:

Class	Overall Length	Waterline Length	Beam	Sail Area, Square Feet
O	59′9″	38′6″	12′	1,660
P	54′	33′	10′2″	1,450
Q	46′6″	26′	8′9″	930
R	38′	24′	7′8″	610

In some areas the racing fleets operate under restricted handicap classes such as Class A for all boats over 30 feet racing length, Class B for boats between 25 and 30 feet racing length, and Class C for craft between 20 and 25 feet racing length.

International Racing Classes

The meter classes and some one-design classes are built to the rules of the International Yacht Racing Union. This is the world authority controlling yacht racing, and the classes which it administers are known as International classes. The following are the classes recognized by the IYRU:

12-Meter	Fireball
5.5-Meter	Contender
Dragon	8-Meter
Tempest	30-Square Meter*
12-Square Meter Sharpie	Soling
Vaurien	Flying Dutchman

Lightning	22-Square Meter*
Cadet	Star
14-Foot Dinghy	5-0-5
(International 14)	Finn
Tornado	Snipe
6-Meter	Australis

* These classes are classified by their sail area. The Tumlaren class (The International Tumlaren Yacht Association) is a popular class based on the sail area in the United States. In the United States it is considered a member of the 20-Square Meter group, whereas those racing in Canadian waters are considered 25-Meter class.

When racing in foreign waters a letter or letters showing the nationality of the owner must be carried on the mainsail. The nationality code is given in IYRU racing rules, which appear in Section VI.

Multihull Classes

Multihull racing associations are on the increase. Many yacht clubs have added catamaran starts to their regatta schedule, and they have even been included in the big race weeks at Larchmont and Marblehead in the East and at San Francisco Bay in the West.

Where there is a variety of catamarans, and not enough for separate classes, they are usually raced in an open catamaran class with some type of handicap. The handicapping system employed by the race committee may vary greatly and all too often favors one class. Also, as noted previously, the larger boats will usually outperform the smaller ones even with well-formulated handicaps. For this reason, it is a good idea to have the catamarans grouped closely according to size, with at least two groups, starting at different times. Sixteen feet has been most widely accepted as the dividing point of sizes when handicapping.

At the present time there are three different organizations governing overall catamaran racing in North America. They are the Pacific Catamaran Association on the West Coast, the Eastern Multihull Sailing Association in the East, and the Canadian Catamaran Association in Canada. These three groups are working closely together and may soon merge into one group to control multihull racing in North America. The individual catamaran classes, of course, would each have their own association and control regulations for their own particular class.

The following are the specifications of the more common designs or classes that either have formed class associations or may do so in the near future:

Australis. Specs: 18' × 7'6" × 2'4"–3". SA: 145; no spinnaker. Hiking assists: straps, trapeze. Hull: wood or fiberglass. Spars: aluminum. Buoyancy: self-rescuing. Kits, plans not available. Crew: 1. Number: U.S. 20; world 100. Rules: one-design. Price: $1,600. Designer: Graham Johnson

Aqua Cat 12. Specs: 12'2" × 6'½" × 2'–6". SA: 90; no spinnaker. Hiking assists: none. Hull: fiberglass. Spars: aluminum. Buoyancy: positive flotation. Kits, plans not available. Crew: 1. Area: 1–12. Number: U.S. 8,300; world 9,000. Rules: one-design. Price: $895. Designer: American Fiberglass

Aqua Cat 18. Specs: 17'10" × 7'11" × 2'–7". SA: 180; no spinnaker. Hiking assists: none. Hull: fiberglass. Spars: aluminum. Buoyancy: positive flotation. Kits, plans not available. Crew: 2. Area: 2, 3. Number: U.S. 65. Rules: one-design. Price: $1,795. Designer: American Fiberglass

Aqua Cat 12s

A Lion. Specs: 18′ × 7′ × 2′2″–8″. SA: 150; no spinnaker. Hiking assists: straps, trapeze. Hull: fiberglass. Spars: aluminum. Buoyancy: positive flotation. Kits, plans not available. Crew: 1. Area: 2. Number: U.S. 60. Rules: one-design. Price: $1,795. Designer: Hubbard Brothers

B Lion. Specs: 20′ × 10′ × 2′–7″. SA: 235; no spinnaker. Hiking assists: straps, trapeze. Hull: fiberglass. Spars: aluminum. Buoyancy: positive flotation. Kits, plans available. Crew: 2. Area: 1, 2, 5. Number: U.S. 250; world 325. Rules: one-design. Price: $2,695. Designer: Hubbard Brothers

Cal Cat. Specs: 12′10 × 7′10″ × 2′–4″. SA: 100; no spinnaker. Hiking assists: straps. Hull: fiberglass. Spars: aluminum. Buoyancy: positive flotation. Kits, plans not available. Crew: 1. Area: 2, 3, 5, 13. Number: U.S. 550. Rules: one-design. Price: $1,195. Designer: Joe Quigg

Catfish. Specs: 13′2″ × 6′ × 2′–6″. SA: 105; no spinnaker. Hiking assists: none. Hull: fiberglass. Spars: aluminum. Buoyancy: posi-

tive flotation. Kits, plans not available. Crew: 1. Area: 2. Number: U.S. 1,300. Rules: one-design. Price: $986. Designer: George Patterson

Cheshire. Specs: 13′6″ × 6′ × 2′–6″. SA: 135; no spinnaker. Hiking assists: straps. Hull: fiberglass. Spars: aluminum. Buoyancy: positive flotation. Kits, plans not available. Crew: 1. Area: 3–5, 7. Number: U.S. 103. Rules: one-design. Price: $1,150. Designer: Frank Meldau

Cougar MK III. Specs: 18′9″ × 7′11½″ × 2′8″–5″. SA: 235; no spinnaker. Hiking assists: straps. Hull: fiberglass. Spars: aluminum. Buoyancy: positive flotation. Kits not available, plans available. Crew: 2. Area: 2–4, 6, 7, 9, 11. Number: U.S. 230; world 250. Rules: one-design. Price: $2,600. Designer: Prout Brothers

DC-14. Specs: 14′2″ × 7′ × 2′2″–6″. SA: 140; spinnaker not permitted. Hiking assists: straps. Hull: fiberglass. Spars: aluminum. Buoyancy: positive flotation. Kits, plans not available. Crew: 2. Area: 2, 5, 7. Number:

Cheshire

Cougar MK III

U.S. 195. Rules: standing rigging open. Price: $1,180. Designer: McLear & Harris

Hobie Cat 14. Specs: 14′ × 7′8″ × 8″. SA: 110; no spinnaker. Hiking assists: straps. Hull: fiberglass. Spars: aluminum. Buoyancy: self-rescuing. Kits, plans not available. Crew: 1. Area: 1–3, 5, 11–13, 15. Number: U.S. 1,500; world 3,600. Rules: one-design. Price: $1,195. Designer: Hobie Alter

Malibu Outrigger. Specs: 18′9″ × 11′8″ × 4′5″–8″. SA: 192; no spinnaker. Hiking assists: none. Hull: wood. Spars: wood. Buoyancy: positive flotation. Kits, plans available. Crew: 2. Area: 13. Number: U.S. 1,300. Rules: one-design. Price: $1,795. Designer: Warren Seaman

Pacific Cat. Specs: 18′9″ × 7′11″ × 2′11″– 7″. SA: 267; spinnaker: 370. Hiking assists: straps, trapeze. Hull: fiberglass. Spars: aluminum. Buoyancy: positive flotation. Kits, plans not available. Crew: 2. Area: 2, 5, 7, 8, 10, 13, 15. Number: U.S. 500. Rules: one-design. Price: $2,895. Designer: Carter Pyle

Phoenix. Specs: 18′ × 7′11″ × 2′8″–4″. SA: 204; no spinnaker. Hiking assists: straps, trapeze. Hull: fiberglass. Spars: aluminum. Buoyancy: positive flotation. Kits, plans not available. Crew: 2. Area: 1–5, 13. Number: U.S. 180; world 380. Rules: one-design. Price: $1,790. Designer: Rod MacAlpine-Downie

Quick Cat. Specs: 16′ × 6′4″ × 2′9″–4″. SA: 126; no spinnaker. Hiking assists: sliding seat. Hull: wood. Spars: wood or aluminum. Buoyancy: positive flotation. Kits, plans available. Crew: 1. Number: U.S. 35; world 1,700. Rules: one-design. Price: $1,700. Designer: Lindsay Cunningham

Shark. Specs: 20′ × 10′ × 3′3″–6″. SA: 272; no spinnaker. Hiking assists: straps, trapeze. Hull: fiberglass. Spars: aluminum. Buoyancy: positive flotation. Kits, plans not available. Crew: 2. Area: 4, 5, 7, 12, 13. Number: U.S. 290; world 350. Rules: one-design. Price: $2,600. Designer: Rod Mac-Alpine-Downie

Shearwater. Specs: 16′6″ × 7′6″ × 5′–11″. SA: 235; no spinnaker. Hiking assists: straps, trapeze. Hull: fiberglass. Spars: aluminum. Buoyancy: positive flotation. Kits, plans available. Crew: 2. Area: 1, 2. Number: U.S. 115; world 1,565. Rules: one-design. Price: $1,850. Designer: Prout Brothers

Tiger Cat. Specs: 17′ × 7′11½″ × 3′1″– 7½″. SA: 180; no spinnaker. Hiking assists: straps. Hull: fiberglass. Spars: aluminum. Buoyancy: positive flotation. Kits, plans not available. Crew: 2. Area: 1, 2, 5, 7. Number: U.S. 154. Rules: one-design. Designer: Robert Harris

Tornado

Tornado. Specs: 20′ × 10′ × 2′6″–7″. SA: 235; no spinnaker. Hiking assists: straps, trapeze. Hull: wood. Spars: aluminum. Buoyancy: self-rescuing. Kits, plans available. Crew: 2. Area: 1, 4, 5, 8, 12, 13, 15. Number: U.S. 200; world 1,000. Rules: one-design. Price: $1,600. Designer: Rodney Marsh

Triumph 24. Specs: 24′ × 14′ × 3′–1′6″. SA: 243; no spinnaker. Hiking assists: none. Hull: fiberglass. Spars: aluminum. Buoyancy: positive flotation. Kits available, plans not available. Crew: 2. Area: 12, 13. Number: U.S. 43. Rules: one-design. Price: $3,495. Designer: Lasco Marine

Yachting World Cat. Specs: 15′6″ × 7′ × 2′6″. SA: 175; no spinnaker. Hiking assists: straps, trapeze. Hull: wood or fiberglass. Spars: wood or aluminum. Buoyancy: positive flotation. Kits, plans available. Crew: 2. Area: 11, 13. Number: U.S. 50; world 220.

Rules: one-design. Price: $1,350. Designer: Rod MacAlpine-Downie

Other Multihull One-Design Classes

Class	Cat, Ketch, or Sloop Rig	Overall Length	Beam	Draft	Sail Area, Square Feet
Aero Cat	C	12′	7′7″	5½″	115
Barefoot 12	C	12′6″	7′11″	3″	100
Buccaneer	C	25′	19′	1′3″	402
Bunyip MK IV	S	20′	11′	1′	225
Car-Cat	S	11′3″	5′9″	8″	75
Catalina	S	16′	6′8″	3′2″†	234
Catalina Cat	S	17′1½″	7′11″	3′2″	234
Catoplane	S	12′	7′	3′6″	110
Cheetah	S	14′1″	7′11″	7½″	185
Corinthian 41*	Ke	41′	23′9″	26″	625
Cougar	S	17′9″	7′6″	2′8″†	155
Dingo	C	14′10″	7′2″	4″	125
Felix	C	14′2″	5′9″	2″	112
Fleetcat	S	18′	8′	8″	400
Flying Cat	S	16′	8′	7″	200
Flying Fox	S	14′	5′6″	11″	114
Frolic*	S	16′	8′	3′†	140
Gypsy	S	16′	8′	1′	175
Hellcat III S	S	25′	14′	18″	300
Isotope	S	16′	7′6″	8″	180
Jet Cat	C	17′	7′10″	2′8″†	235
Jumpahead	S	16′	7′6″	8″	167
Jungle Cat	C	14′2″	7′6″	2′6″	140
Junior Cat	S	12′6″	5′3″	6″	82
Kalua	S	16′	7′9″	7½″	160
Kangaroo	S	17′6″	11′	8″	235
Kimba Kat	C	12′	5′6″	6″	72
Manu Kai 23	S	23′	9′8″	1′2″	—
Medallion*	Ke	45′	24′	3′	830
Paper Tiger	C	14′	7′	6″	100
Polycat	S	18′	8′	1′	192
River Cat	S	12′	6′4″	8″	121
Scamper	C	12′	6′	7½″	85
Sea Spray	S	15′	6′5″	5″	135
Shark V	C	13′10″	9′	6″	115
Starlight	S	26′	13′8″	10″	383
Swift	S	14′6″	5′10″	2′10″†	120
Tiger Cub	C	10′	5′	4″	60
Tiki	S	12′1″	6′	4″	139
Tay Cat	C	12′	6′	22″	92
Thoi Mk IV	S	17′6″	8′6″	8″	216
Triad	S	19′	12′9″	10″	315
Trikini 13	C	13′	9′	7″	90
Trikini 17	S	16′9″	11′10″	7″	180
Trikini-D	S	34′	24′	10″	500
Trimar 24*	S	24′6″	12′2″	7″	200
Triumph Trimaran*	C	9′	5′	4″	60
Venture	S	15′1″	7′1″	9″	160
Vistress*	S	40′	22′	2′9″	446
Waverider	S	16′	8′	1′	160
Whisker	C	11′6″	5′9″	7″	87
Wild Cat	S	17′9″	7′11″	7″	176

* Trimaran-type multihull.
† Centerboard or boards down.

Class C catamarans as well as the Australis and Tornado one-design classes are recognized by the International Yacht Racing Union as International classes.

One-Design Class Associations

As stated earlier in this section, the more active one-designs have associations whose purpose is to police their class rules and promote well-run, well-organized racing. Some associations are informally run organizations handled completely by a devoted band of class owners, while others are large, formal affairs, administered by a paid executive secretary. The International Star Class Yacht Racing Association is a fine example of the latter, since it is one of few one-design classes with permanent offices and a secretarial staff.

The Star has been called the common ancestor of all one-design classes of small racing sailboats. As stated in Section I, it was the first. Because it is relatively expensive, it has been surpassed in numbers by some of its more prolific offspring, such as Snipes and Lightnings. It was May 30, 1911, that the first race for the class was held on Long Island Sound. The Harlem Yacht Club ran it, and there were five starters. The late George Corry, founder and first president of the association, was the winner. Over all these years, the lines of its hull have never been changed, nor has the sail area. The same cannot be said of the rig, which evolved from gaff to short Marconi, and then to tall Marconi, and developed along the way the flexible spars that have made and kept it a modern racing machine.

One reason, other than the boat itself, for the lasting success of the Star class is its organization. In 1922, when the International Star Class Yacht Racing Association was founded, no one knew how to run a one-design class because none existed. A few far-sighted individuals set up the new organization and nursed it through its formative years, producing eventually the smooth-running worldwide body which its members enjoy today. Many other classes have copied the Star Association's structure and methods, and it is only through the efficient functioning of racing organizations like the Star class that

small-boat yachting can be kept going on a large scale.

Let us look at how the Star class organization operates. The central authority and chief business head is its Executive President, who, assisted by a governing committee, handles the principal business of the class through the central office. Besides the executive officers there is a far-flung network of continental, district, and fleet officers, the key members of which are the fleet secretaries who run the local affairs of each fleet. The primary purpose of this worldwide organization is to provide the best and fairest possible racing on all levels. Each fleet holds local races, among them a series of eliminations, the winner of which is eligible to participate in the World's Championship, an annual affair. Besides this major series there are continental and district championships, for which all entries must also qualify through eliminations; and other important international and interfleet events open to all. For the less experienced, there are novice championships, which the experts may not enter. And in addition to all these special events, the local weekend or daily races of the home fleets continue throughout the sailing season.

To find out what an association does for you, let us suppose that you have just bought a new Star class boat. Through the former owner, or possibly through another Star sailor, all of whom keep in close touch with all Star activities, the central office in New York will receive word of your purchase. The office will notify the secretary of the Star fleet in whose area you sail, who will then get in touch with you personally and explain the membership idea. As soon as you join the class, by payment of the small annual dues (there is no initiation fee), you will receive a copy of the current yearbook containing the complete rules and regulations of the Star class, as well as *Starlights,* a monthly publication of news and information. You will be invited to attend meetings of the Star owners in your vicinity. You will be eligible to sail in all open races of the class, and to compete for the privilege of sailing in the championship series. Perhaps more important than any of these things will be the discovery that you have become a member of a worldwide club of friendly enthusiasts united by their common interest in Star boat racing.

Membership in a Yacht Club

As previously mentioned in Section II, if you plan to race, membership in a class association is a must. Since many of the classes are affiliated locally with yacht or sailing clubs, and because many of these organizations hold regattas, it is usually desirable to become a member of a club.

Racing Associations

In addition to class associations and yacht clubs, there are racing associations which are made up of class association and/or yacht-club members. The purpose of a racing association generally is to foster and develop the interests of one-design racing craft through the supervision of boat regattas for recognized one-design classes.

United States International Sailing Association

Another sailing organization you may wish to join is the United States International Sailing Association. In 1968 the U.S.I.S.A. paid all expenses of the United States Olympic sailing team. It plans to in the future too, and also plans to meet expenses of certain international competitions to our *best* sailors, not just to the more wealthy. The necessary funds come solely from membership dues and contributions. Dues range from $10 up depending on category and they are tax deductible. For further information, write U.S.I.S.A., 37 West 44th Street, New York, N.Y. 10036.

OFFSHORE RACING-CRUISING SAILBOAT CLASSES

This section is reserved for offshore racers only. We define an offshore sailboat as a sailboat with cruising accommodations for at least two, provisions for a head and galley, and a self-bailing cockpit which meets the requirements of either the CCA or MORC rules (pages 377–380) for maximum volume; also, it must be capable of racing with some reasonable expectation of winning. That is, now we are going to take a look at the more popular classes of boats used for distance and handicap racing as well as overnight or extended cruising. Also many of these sailboats are raced in one-design classes and have class associations the same as the craft mentioned earlier in this section.

The vast majority are designed for auxiliary power, either inboard or outboard. This type of sailboat represents a considerable investment of money. However, when purchasing a class boat such as described in this section, the investment is usually a good one since you also are making an investment in years of family fun.

In the field of offshore cruising-racing auxiliaries there is a very wide range of choice in the class, or "stock," models available. The reason for this is that skippers like designs that are custom-made to their needs. But there is no "planned obsolescence" in these boats. Model or classes do not change by the year, and only a few new ones are added. Once a design has been established, it is continued unchanged for as long as there is a public for it. As is the case with many racer–day sailers, many of the designs are perpetuated by associations formed by owners which establish rules for maintaining the one-design characteristics so that the boats can be raced without handicapping. This also protects used-boat values. The builder may define or modify certain features of the layout or equipment, but the basic design will remain the same year after year.

Of the vast catalog of stock auxiliaries, the following are the more popular over the years. They are generally available without too much of a wait for delivery from the manufacturer or local dealers. Prices given are approximate, as extra equipment and choice of power plant affect the total delivered price.

Specifications are given in the order: length overall × waterline length × beam × draft–draft with centerboard up. SA indicates the mainsail area plus 100 percent fore-triangle in square feet. Displacement and ballast are

Alacrity

Apache 37 MK II

given in pounds. Because ratings for a particular type of yacht vary with each individual measurement process, figures given for rating are approximate (see page 380). Cruising equipment (galley, head) is listed as either optional or incl (included). Price lists only new price (without sails) except when the yacht is no longer in production.

Alacrity. Specs: 18′6″ × 17′ × 6′11″ × 2′. SA: 150, sloop. Disp: 1,450. Ballast: 540, iron. Rating: 14.0 MORC. Hull and deck: fiberglass. Spars: aluminum. Cabins: 1; berths: 3; galley and head: optional. Aux power: optional. Price: $2,995. Designer: Peter Stephenson

Alberg 35. Specs: 34′9″ × 24′ × 9′8″ × 5′2″. SA: 545, sloop; 583, yawl. Disp: 12,600. Ballast: 5,300, lead. Rating: 26.6 CCA. Hull and deck: fiberglass. Spars: aluminum. Cabins: 2; berths: 6; galley and head: incl. Aux power: 30 hp incl. Price: $19,995. Designer: Carl Alberg

Alberg 37. Specs: 37′2″ × 26′6″ × 10′2″ × 5′6″. SA: 646, sloop. Disp: 16,800. Ballast: 6,500, lead. Rating: 29.4 CCA. Hull and deck: fiberglass. Spars: aluminum. Cabins: 2; berths: 6; galley and head: incl. Aux

power: 30 hp incl. Price: $25,800. Designer: Carl Alberg

Amphibi-Con. Specs: 25′5″ × 21′8″ × 7′9″ × 5′9″–2′5″. SA: 266, sloop. Disp: 3,900. Ballast: 1,100, iron. Hull: fiberglass. Deck: wood. Spars: aluminum. Cabins: 2; berths: 4; galley and head: optional. Aux power: optional. Price: $8,000. Designer: Mount Desert Yachts

Apache 37 MK II. Specs: 37′ × 26′3″ × 10′2½″ × 5′9″. SA: 606, sloop. Disp: 14,280. Ballast: 5,700, iron. Rating: 30.7 CCA. Hull and deck: fiberglass. Spars: aluminum. Cabins: 2; berths: 6; galley and head: incl. Aux power: 30 hp incl. Price: $22,880. Designer: Sparkman & Stephens

Bermuda 40. Specs: 40′9″ × 27′10″ × 11′9″ × 8′7″–4′1″. SA: 725, yawl. Disp: 19,000. Ballast: 5,500, lead. Rating: 28.4. CCA. Hull and deck: fiberglass. Spars: aluminum. Cabins: 2; berths: 6; galley and head: incl. Aux power: 35 hp incl. Price: $55,500. Designer: William H. Tripp, Jr.

Blue Jacket. Specs: 22′10″ × 17′6″ × 7′0″ × 3′9″. SA: 200, sloop. Disp: 2,000. Ballast: 900, iron. Rating: 21 MORC. Hull and deck: fiberglass. Spars: aluminum. Cabins: 1;

Bristol 29

Cal 20

berths: 2; galley: incl; head: optional. Aux power: 6 hp optional. Price: $4,495. Designer: Cuthbertson & Cassian

Bristol 29. Specs: 29'1½" × 22'8" × 9'2" × 4'6" (keel), 3'4" (centerboard, board up). SA: 402, sloop. Disp: 8,400. Ballast: 3,450, lead. Rating: 24.4 CCA. Hull and deck: fiberglass. Spars: aluminum. Cabins: 2; berths: 5; galley and head: incl. Aux power: 30 hp incl. Price: $12,350. Designer: Halsey Herreshoff

Bristol 33. Specs: 33'7" × 25'9" × 10'3" × 5'6". SA: 486, sloop. Disp: 11,500. Rating: 28.0 CCA. Hull and deck: fiberglass. Spars: aluminum. Ballast: 5,000, lead. Cabins: 2; berths: 7; galley and head: incl. Aux power: 30 hp incl. Price: $17,995. Designer: Halsey Herreshoff

Bristol 35. Specs: 34'8" × 23'9" × 10' × 5'. SA: 531, sloop. Disp: 12,500. Rating: 24.9 CCA. Hull and deck: fiberglass. Spars: aluminum. Ballast: 5,980, lead. Cabins: 2; berths: 6; galley and head: incl. Aux power: 30 hp incl. Price: $20,900. Designer: John G. Alden

Bristol 39. Specs: 39'2½" × 27'6½" × 10'9" × 5' (keel) 4' (centerboard, board up). SA: 694, sloop. Disp: 17,580. Rating: 28.0 CCA. Hull and deck: fiberglass. Spars: aluminum. Ballast: 9,500, lead. Cabins: 2; berths:

6; galley and head: incl. Aux power: 30 hp incl. Price: $29,900. Designer: Ted Hood

Cal 20. Specs: 20' × 18' × 7' × 3'4". SA: 196, sloop. Disp: 1,950. Ballast: 900, iron. Hull and deck: fiberglass. Spars: aluminum. Cabins: 2; berths: 4; galley and head: optional. Aux power: optional. Price: $3,670. Designer: C. William Lapworth

Cal 21. Specs: 20'6" × 16'8" × 6'8" × 4'3". SA: 196, sloop. Disp: 1,100. Ballast: 360, iron. Hull and deck: fiberglass. Spars: aluminum. Cabins: 2; berths: 4; galley and head: optional. Aux power: optional. Price: $2,650. Designer: C. William Lapworth

Cal 2-24. Specs: 24' × 19'2" × 7'9" × 4'. SA: 274, sloop. Disp: 3,700. Ballast: 1,400, iron. Hull and deck: fiberglass. Spars: aluminum. Cabins: 2; berths: 4; galley: optional; head: incl. Aux power: optional. Price: $5,400. Designer: C. William Lapworth

Cal 25. Specs: 25' × 20' × 8' × 4'. SA: 286, sloop. Disp: 4,000. Ballast: 1,700, lead. Rating: 22.6 CCA. Hull and deck: fiberglass. Spars: aluminum. Cabins: 2; berths: 4; galley: optional; head: incl. Aux power: optional. Price: $6,300. Designer: C. William Lapworth

Cal 29. Specs: 29' × 24' × 9'3" × 4'6".

SA: 434, sloop. Disp: 8,000. Ballast: 3,350, lead. Rating: 27.3 CCA. Hull and deck: fiberglass. Spars: aluminum. Cabins: 2; berths: 4; galley and head: incl. Aux power: 30 hp incl. Price: $12,392. Designer: C. William Lapworth

Cal 34. Specs: 33'3" × 26' × 10' × 5'. SA: 515, sloop. Disp: 9,500. Ballast: 3,750, lead. Rating: 29.5 CCA. Hull and deck: fiberglass. Spars: aluminum. Cabins: 2; berths: 6; galley and head: incl. Aux power: 30 hp incl. Price: $19,277. Designer: C. William Lapworth

Cal 40. Specs: 39'4" × 30'4" × 11' × 5'7". SA: 700, sloop. Disp: 15,000. Ballast: 6,000, lead. Rating: 36.1 CCA. Hull and deck: fiberglass. Spars: aluminum. Cabins: 2; berths: 8; galley and head: incl. Aux power: 30 hp incl. Price: $33,850. Designer: C. William Lapworth

Cal 43. Specs: 42'8" × 32'6" × 11'6" × 6'6". SA: 832, sloop. Disp: 20,000. Ballast: 8,000, lead. Hull and deck: fiberglass. Spars: aluminum. Cabins: 3; berths: 8; galley and head: incl. Aux power: 40 hp incl. Price: $38,250. Designer: C. William Lapworth

Caravel. Specs: 22' × 19'6" × 7'9" × 3'6". SA: 206, sloop. Disp: 2,850. Ballast: 1,150, lead. Hull and deck: fiberglass. Spars: aluminum. Cabins: 2; berths: 5; galley: incl; head: optional. Aux power: optional. Price: $3,995. Designer: Halsey C. Herreshoff

Catalina 22. Specs: 21'6" × 19'4" × 7'8" × 5'–20". SA: 212, sloop. Disp: 1,800. Ballast: 500, iron. Rating: 19 MORF. Hull and deck: fiberglass. Spars: aluminum. Cabins: 2; berths: 5; galley and head: optional. Aux power: 10 hp optional. Price: $2,595. Designer: Butler & Finch

Columbia 22. Specs: 22' × 20'1" × 7'9" × 3'2". SA: 232, sloop. Disp: 2,300. Ballast: 1,000, lead. Rating: 18.7 CCA. Hull and deck: fiberglass. Spars: aluminum. Cabins: 2; berths: 4; galley and head: optional. Aux power: optional. Price: $3,995. Designer: William Crealock

Columbia 26 Mark II. Specs: 26' × 19' × 8' × 3'5". SA: 321, sloop. Disp: 5,200. Ballast: 2,300, lead. Rating: 20.5 CCA. Hull and deck: fiberglass. Spars: aluminum. Cabins: 2; berths: 4; galley and head: incl. Aux power: optional. Price: $6,950. Designer: William H. Tripp, Jr.

Columbia 28. Specs: 27'7" × 21'8" × 8'6"

Columbia 22

× 4'4". SA: 343, sloop. Disp. 5,800. Ballast: 2,600, lead. Rating: 24 CCA. Hull: fiberglass. Deck: aluminum. Spars: aluminum. Cabins: 2; berths: 6; galley and head: incl. Aux power: optional. Price: $9,995. Designer: William Crealock

Columbia 36. Specs: 35'9" × 28'3" × 10'6" × 5'5". SA: 557. Sloop or yawl. Disp: 12,000. Ballast: 5,000, lead. Rating: 32.7 CCA. Hull and deck: fiberglass. Spars: aluminum. Cabins: 2; berths: 6; galley and head: incl. Aux power: incl. Price: $27,750. Designer: William Crealock

Columbia 43. Specs: 43'3" × 32' × 12'4" × 6'11". SA: 805, sloop. Disp: 19,000. Ballast: 10,300, iron. Hull and deck: fiberglass. Spars: aluminum. Cabins: 2/3; berths: 8/9; galley and head: incl. Aux power: incl. Price: $32,995. Designer: William H. Tripp, Jr.

Columbia 50. Specs: 50' × 33'3" × 12½" × 6'7". SA: 977, sloop or yawl. Disp: 32,000. Ballast: 13,100, lead. Rating: 39 CCA. Hull and deck: fiberglass. Spars: aluminum. Cabins: 3; berths: 7; galley and head: incl. Aux power: 70 hp incl. Price: $55,000. Designer: William H. Tripp, Jr.

Columbia 57. Specs: 56'8" × 40' × 13' ×

8'. SA: 1,293, sloop. Disp: 42,000. Ballast: 22,000, lead. Hull and deck: fiberglass. Spars: aluminum. Cabins: 3; berths: 9; galley and head: incl. Aux power: 85 hp diesel incl. Price: $110,000. Designer: William H. Tripp, Jr.

Constellation. Specs: 29'8" × 21'8" × 8' × 4'8". SA: 390, sloop. Disp: 6,000. Ballast: 2,750, lead. Rating: 23.9 CCA, 28 MORC. Hull: fiberglass. Deck: plywood. Spars: aluminum. Cabins: 2; berths: 4; galley and head: optional. Aux power: optional. Price: $7,990. Designer: E. S. Graves, Jr.

Corinthian 28. Specs: 27'9" × 21'3" × 8'8" × 3'9". SA: 348, sloop. Disp: 6,860. Ballast: 2,400, lead. Hull and deck: fiberglass. Spars: aluminum. Cabins: 2; berths: 5; galley and head: incl. Aux power: 30 hp incl. Price: $11,000. Designer: C. Martzoucos

Coronado 23. Specs: 22'7" × 20'1" × 7'9" × 3'2". SA: 232, sloop. Disp: 2,200. Ballast: 1,100, lead keel/CB. Hull and deck: fiberglass. Spars: aluminum. Cabins: 2; berths: 4; galley and head: optional. Aux power: optional. Price: $3,995. Designer: Coronado Yachts

Coronado 25. Specs: 25' × 20' × 8' × 3'8". SA: 299, sloop. Disp: 4,300. Ballast: 2,150, lead. Rating: 22.8 CCA. Hull and deck: fiberglass. Spars: aluminum. Cabins: 2; berths: 5; galley: optional; head: incl. Aux power: optional. Price: $6,500. Designer: Ed Edgar

Coronado 30. Specs: 30' × 24' × 10'1" × 5'2". SA: 419, sloop. Disp: 7,700. Ballast: 2,700, lead. Hull and deck: fiberglass. Spars: aluminum. Cabins: 2; berths: 5; galley and head: incl. Aux power: 35 hp incl. Price: $13,995. Designer: Finch & Butler

Corvette. Specs: 31'2½" × 22'6" × 9'1" × 7'–3'3". SA: 444, sloop. Disp: 8,545. Ballast: 3,990, lead. Rating: 24.9 CCA. Hull and deck: fiberglass. Spars: aluminum. Cabins: 2; berths: 4; galley and head: incl. Aux power: 30 hp incl. Price: $16,500. Designer: Cuthbertson & Cassian

Countess 44. Specs: 44'6" × 30'6" × 12' × 5'4". SA: 856, ketch. Disp: 28,000. Ballast: 8,000, lead. Hull and deck: fiberglass. Spars: aluminum. Cabins: 3; berths: 6; galley and head: incl. Aux·power: 110 hp incl. Price: $53,600. Designer: John Alden & Co.

Douglas 32. Specs: 31'3" × 22'8" × 9'3" × 4'8". SA: 450, sloop. Disp: 9,500. Ballast: 3,500, lead. Rating: 23.9 CCA. Hull and

Ericson 32

deck: fiberglass. Spars: aluminum. Cabins: 2; berths: 4–5; galley and head: incl. Aux power: 22 hp incl. Price: $15,500. Designer: Edward S. Brewer

Ericson 23. Specs: 22'7" × 19'2" × 7'6" × 3'6". SA: 225, sloop. Disp: 2,700. Ballast: 1,300, iron. Rating: 20.6 CCA. Hull and deck: fiberglass. Spars: aluminum. Cabins: 2; berths: 4; galley: incl; head: optional. Aux power: optional, up to 10 hp outboard. Price: $4,250. Designer: Bruce King

Ericson 30. Specs: 30'3" × 23'4" × 9'6" × 4'10". SA: 425, sloop. Disp: 7,800. Ballast: 3,000, lead. Rating: 27.0 CCA. Hull and deck: fiberglass. Spars: aluminum. Cabins: 3; berths: 6; galley and head: incl. Aux power: 30 hp incl. Price: $14,395. Designer: Bruce King

Ericson 32. Specs: 31'7" × 24' × 9'8" × 4'11". SA: 425, sloop. Disp: 8,800. Ballast: 4,000, lead. Rating: 27.7 CCA. Hull and deck: fiberglass. Spars: aluminum. Cabins: 3; berths: 6; galley and head: incl. Aux power: 30 hp incl. Price: $15,850. Designer: Bruce King

Ericson 35. Specs: 34′8″ × 25′10″ × 10′ × 4′11″. SA: 533, sloop. Disp: 11,600. Ballast: 5,000, lead. Rating: 29.3 CCA. Hull and deck: fiberglass. Spars: aluminum. Cabins: 3; berths: 6; galley and head: incl. Aux power: 30 hp incl. Price: $19,500. Designer: Bruce King

Ericson 41. Specs: 41′4″ × 29′2″ × 10′8″ × 5′11″. SA: 715, sloop. Disp. 17,800. Ballast: 8,200, lead. Rating: 33.8 CCA. Hull and deck: fiberglass. Spars: aluminum. Cabins: 2; berths: 7; galley and head: incl. Aux power: 30 hp incl. Price: $29,950. Designer: Bruce King

Fastnet 45. Specs: 44′10″ × 32′ × 12′3″ × 6′9″. SA: 878.5, sloop. Disp: 24,000. Ballast: 10,000, lead. Hull and deck: fiberglass. Spars: aluminum. Cabins: 3; berths: 8; galley and head: incl. Aux power: 46 hp diesel incl. Price: $55,900. Designer: A. E. Luders, Jr.

Folkdancer. Specs. 27′ × 19′8″ × 7′6″ × 4′. SA: 296, sloop. Disp: 5,040. Ballast: 2,500, iron. Hull and deck: fiberglass. Spars: aluminum. Cabins: 2; berths: 6; galley and head: incl. Aux power: 5 hp incl. Price: $8,995. Designer: F. R. Parker

Frigate. Specs: 35′8″ × 24′5″ × 10′2½″ × 7′2″–3′7″. SA: 550, sloop. Disp: 11,575. Ballast: 5,400, lead. Rating: 28.8 CCA. Hull and deck: fiberglass. Spars: aluminum. Cabins: 2; berths: 4/6; galley and head: incl. Aux power: 30 hp incl. Price: $26,450. Designer: Cuthbertson & Cassian

Galion. Specs: 22′ × 20′ × 7′3″ × 3′3″. SA: 207, sloop. Disp: 3,400. Ballast: 1,700, iron. Rating: 17.6 CCA. Hull and deck: fiberglass. Spars: aluminum. Cabins: 2; berths: 4; galley and head: optional. Aux power: 6 hp optional. Price: $5,900. Designer: Ian Hannay

Greenwich 24. Specs: 24′3″ × 17′5″ × 7′3″ × 3′. SA: 225, sloop. Disp: 3,825. Ballast: 1,500, lead. Hull and deck: fiberglass. Spars: aluminum. Cabins: 2; berths: 5; galley and head: incl. Aux power: optional. Price: $5,250. Designer: George Stadel

Haida 26. Specs: 25′9″ × 21′ × 8′3″ × 4′6″. SA: 330, sloop. Disp: 4,700. Ballast: 1,800, iron. Rating: 22.4 CCA. Hull: fiberglass. Deck: plywood. Spars: aluminum. Cabins: 2; berths: 4; galley and head: incl. Aux power: optional. Price: $7,400. Designer: Raymond Richards

Halcyon 23. Specs: 22′9″ × 18′8″ × 7′6″ × 3′6″. SA: 225, sloop. Disp: 3,000. Ballast:

1,100, iron. Hull and deck: fiberglass. Spars: aluminum. Cabins: 2; berths: 4; galley and head: incl. Aux power: 5 hp incl. Price: $5,980. Designer: Alan Buchanan

Hinckley 48. Specs: 48′5″ × 34′6″ × 13′ × 11′10″–5′3″. SA: 1000, sloop. Disp: 35,000. Ballast: 10,600, lead. Rating: 36.9 CCA. Hull and deck: fiberglass. Spars: aluminum. Cabins: 3; berths: 8; galley and head: 2 incl. Aux power: 35 hp incl. Price: $99,000. Designer: Henry R. Hinckley

HR-25. Specs: 25′1″ × 19′10″ × 8′ × 4′. SA: 245, sloop. Disp: 3,200. Ballast: 1,100, iron. Rating: 21.6 CCA. Hull and deck: fiberglass. Spars: aluminum. Cabins: 2; berths: 5; galley and head: incl. Aux power: 6 hp incl. Price: $7,500. Designer: George Hinterhoeller

Irwin 25. Specs: 25′3″ × 20′6″ × 8′ × 4′–2′8″. SA: 315, sloop. Ballast: 2,200, lead keel/CB. Disp: 5,400. Hull and deck: fiberglass. Spars: aluminum. Cabins: 2; berths: 6; galley and head: incl. Aux power: optional. Price: $6,250. Designer: Ted Irwin

Irwin 38. Specs: 37′10″ × 27′6″ × 10′6″ × 5′9″–3′9″. SA: 617, sloop. Disp: 15,400. Ballast: 6,500, lead keel/CB. Rating: 30 CCA. Hull and deck: fiberglass. Spars: aluminum. Cabins: 2; berths: 7; galley and head: incl. Aux power: 30 hp incl. Price: $22,995. Designer: Ted Irwin

Kettenburg 41. Specs: 41′ × 27′5″ × 10′4″ × 5′6″. SA: 626, sloop. Disp: 14,000. Ballast: 5,000, lead. Hull and deck: fiberglass. Spars: wood. Cabins: 1; berths: 6; galley and head: incl. Aux power: incl. Price: $32,975. Designer: Kettenburg Marine

Luders 33. Specs: 33′ × 24′ × 10′ × 5′. SA: 529, sloop. Disp: 12,800. Ballast: 4,500, lead. Rating: 26.0 CCA. Hull and deck: fiberglass. Spars: aluminum. Cabins: 2; berths: 6; galley and head: incl. Aux power: 22 hp incl. Price: $26,500. Designer: A. E. Luders, Jr.

Medalist. Specs: 33′ × 24′ × 10′ × 5′3″. SA: 467, sloop. Disp: 10,000. Ballast: 4,000, lead. Hull and deck: fiberglass. Spars: aluminum. Cabins: 2; berths: 6; galley and head: incl. Aux power: 30 hp incl. Price: $24,750. Designer: William H. Tripp, Jr.

Mercer 44. Specs: 44′ × 30′ × 11′9″ × 4′3″. SA: 885, sloop; 902, yawl. Disp: 27,000. Ballast: 8,600, lead. Hull and deck: fiberglass. Spars: aluminum. Cabins: 2; berths: 7; galley and head: incl. Aux power: 60 hp incl. Price:

Irwin 38

$61,500 sloop; $64,600 yawl. Designer: William H. Tripp, Jr.

Morgan 22. Specs: 22'6" × 20' × 8' × 4'11"–1'10". SA: 238, sloop. Disp: 2,700. Ballast: 1,400, lead. Rating: 18.0 MORC. Hull and deck: fiberglass. Spars: aluminum. Cabins: 2; berths: 4; galley: incl; head: optional. Aux power: 10 hp optional. Price: $4,995. Designer: Charles E. Morgan, Jr.

Morgan 24. Specs: 24'11½" × 21'6" × 8' × 6'4"–2'9". SA: 310, sloop. Disp: 4,900. Ballast: 1,900, lead. Rating: 21.8 CCA, 20.8 MORC. Hull and deck: fiberglass. Spars: aluminum. Cabins: 2; berths: 4; head: optional; galley: incl. Aux power: optional. Price: $7,500. Designer: Charles E. Morgan, Jr.

Morgan 28. Specs: 28' × 23'9" × 9' × 6'8"–3'. SA: 405, sloop. Disp: 7,600. Ballast: 3,000, lead. Rating: 24.1 CCA. Hull and deck: fiberglass. Spars: aluminum. Cabins: 2; berths: 5; galley and head: incl. Aux power: 22 hp incl. Price: $12,495. Designer: Charles E. Morgan, Jr.

Morgan 30. Specs: 29'11" × 24'6" × 9'3" × 7'2½"–3'8". SA: 466, sloop. Disp: 10,500. Ballast: 4,500, lead keel/CB. Rating: 25.2 CCA. Hull and deck: fiberglass. Spars: aluminum. Cabins: 2; berths: 6; galley and head: incl. Aux power: optional (inboard or outboard). Price: $13,995. Designer: Charles E. Morgan, Jr.

Morgan 33. Specs: 32'6" × 24' × 9'4" × 5'. SA: 500, sloop. Disp: 11,000. Ballast: 5,500, lead. Rating: 26.5 CCA. Hull and deck: fiberglass. Spars: aluminum. Cabins: 2; berths: 6; galley and head: incl. Aux power: 22 hp incl. Price: $14,995. Designer: Charles E. Morgan, Jr.

Mustang. Specs: 22' × 17'10" × 7' × 5'3"–2'4". SA: 247, sloop. Disp: 2,000. Ballast: 800, iron. Rating: 19 MORC. Hull and deck: fiberglass. Spars: aluminum. Cabins: 1; berths: 4; galley and head: optional. Aux power: optional. Price: $3,995. Designer: Martin Bludworth

Newell Cadet. Specs: 26'5" × 18'9" × 7'8½" × 4'4". SA: 323, sloop. Disp: 6,700. Ballast: 2,700, iron. Hull and deck: fiberglass. Spars: spruce. Cabins: 2; berths: 4; galley: incl. Aux power: 8 hp diesel incl. Price: $9,950. Designer: Taylor Newell

Newport 27. Specs: 27' × 12'6" × 9'1½" × 4'3". SA: 350, sloop. Disp: 5,000. Ballast: 2,400, lead. Rating: 25.3 CCA. Hull and deck: fiberglass. Spars: aluminum. Cabins: 2; berths: 5; galley and head: incl. Aux power: 25 hp incl. Price: $9,995. Designer: Cuthbertson & Cassian

Newport 30. Specs: 30' × 25' × 10'6" × 4'9". SA: 409, sloop. Disp: 7,500. Ballast: 2,500, lead. Rating: 28.5 CCA. Hull and deck: fiberglass. Spars: aluminum. Cabins: 2; berths: 7; galley and head: incl. Aux power: 30 hp incl. Price: $13,950. Designer: Gary Mull

Newport 41. Specs: 40'9" × 30' × 11'2" × 6'3". SA: 741, sloop. Disp: 18,000. Ballast: 8,215, lead. Rating: 36.0 CCA. Hull and deck: fiberglass. Spars: aluminum. Cabins: 2; berths: 7; galley and head: incl. Aux power: 30 hp incl. Price: $29,995. Designer: Cuthbertson & Cassian

Northeast 38. Specs: 38'2" × 26'8" × 10'10" × 5'4". SA: 596, sloop. Disp: 17,000. Ballast: 5,260, lead. Hull and deck: fiberglass. Spars: aluminum. Cabins: 2; berths: 7; gal-

Northwind

ley and head: incl. Aux power: 30 hp incl. Price: $35,910. Designer: William H. Tripp, Jr.

Northwind 29. Specs: 28'9½" × 22' × 9'2" × 6'9"–3'1". SA: 374, sloop. Disp: 6,193. Ballast: 3,000, lead. Rating: 25.3 CCA. Hull and deck: fiberglass. Spars: aluminum. Cabins: 2; berths: 5; galley and head: incl. Aux power: 30 hp optional. Price: $11,800. Designer: Cuthbertson & Cassian

Olympic Princess. Specs: 30'4" × 22'4" × 9'6" × 4'2". SA: 421, sloop. Disp: 9,185. Ballast: 4,250, lead. Rating: 21.2 MORC. Hull and deck: fiberglass. Spars: aluminum. Cabins: 2; berths: 4–6; galley and head: incl. Aux power: 30 hp incl. Price: $15,500. Designer: C. Martzoucos

Olympic Star. Specs: 23'4" × 17'7" × 7'5" × 2'11". SA: 255, sloop. Disp: 3,850. Ballast: 1,500, lead. Rating: 18.7 MORC. Hull and deck: fiberglass. Spars: aluminum. Cabins: 2; berths: 4; galley and head: incl. Aux power: 9 hp optional. Price: $5,690. Designer: C. Martzoucos

Palmer Johnson 34. Specs: 33'7" × 24'2" × 10'1" × 5'11". SA: 483, sloop. Disp: 9,195. Ballast: 4,800, lead. Rating: 28.4 CCA.

Hull and deck: fiberglass. Spars: aluminum. Cabins: 2; berths: 7; galley and head: incl. Aux power: 16.5 hp incl. Price: $26,950. Designer: Sparkman & Stephens

Palmer Johnson 36. Specs: 36' × 25'10" × 9'8" × 6'. SA: 545, sloop. Disp: 14,300. Ballast: 8,000, lead. Rating: 30.4 CCA. Hull and deck: fiberglass. Spars: aluminum. Cabins: 2; berths: 7; galley and head: incl. Aux power: 16.5 hp incl. Price: $32,500. Designer: Sparkman & Stephens

Palmer Johnson 43. Specs: 43' × 31' × 11'8" × 6'11½". SA: 818, sloop. Disp: 19,850. Ballast: 9,000, lead. Rating: 38.2 CCA. Hull: fiberglass. Deck: teak over fiberglass. Spars: aluminum. Cabins: 3; berths: 8; galley and head: incl. Aux power: 37 hp incl. Price: $69,500. Designer: Sparkman & Stephens

Pawnee 26. Specs: 26'2" × 20' × 8' × 4'. SA: 340, sloop. Disp: 4,074. Ballast: 1,900, lead. Hull and deck: fiberglass. Spars: aluminum. Cabins: 1; berths: 5; galley and head: incl. Aux power: optional. Price: $5,995. Designer: Sparkman & Stephens

Pearson 22. Specs: 22'3" × 18'5" × 7'7" × 3'5". SA: 217, sloop. Disp: 2,600. Ballast: 1,000, iron. Hull and deck: fiberglass. Spars: aluminum. Cabins: 2; berths: 4; galley: incl; head: optional. Aux power: optional outboard. Price: $3,995. Designer: W. H. Shaw

Pearson 35. Specs: 35' × 25' × 10' × 7'6"– 3'9". SA: 550, sloop or yawl. Disp: 13,000. Ballast: 4,700, lead. Hull and deck: fiberglass. Spars: aluminum. Cabins: 2; berths: 6; galley and head: incl. Aux power: 30 hp incl. Price: $21,500. Designer: W. H. Shaw

Pearson 43. Specs: 42'9" × 31'3" × 11'9" × 6'3". SA: 825, sloop or yawl. Disp: 21,796. Ballast: 9,152, lead. Hull and deck: fiberglass. Spars: aluminum. Cabins: 3; berths: 8; galley and head: incl. Aux power: 30 hp incl. Price: $43,895. Designer: W. H. Shaw

Redline 41. Specs: 41'5" × 30' × 11'3" × 6'4". SA: 775, sloop. Disp: 19,475. Ballast: 9,500, lead. Rating: 35.7 CCA. Hull and deck: fiberglass. Spars: aluminum. Cabins: 3; berths: 7; galley and head: incl. Aux power: 30 hp incl. Price: $43,000. Designer: Cuthbertson & Cassian

Redwing 30. Specs: 30'3½" × 21'9" × 8'9½" × 4'6". SA: 403, sloop. Disp: 7,650. Ballast: 3,600, lead. Rating: 24.4 CCA. Hull

Pearson 35

Santana 22

and deck: fiberglass. Spars: aluminum. Cabins: 2; berths: 5; galley and head: incl. Aux power: 35 hp incl. Price: $12,950. Designer: Cuthbertson & Cassian

S-31. Specs: 31′ × 24′ × 9′2″ × 5′. SA: 450, sloop. Disp: 9,000. Ballast: 3,100, lead. Rating: 26.8 CCA. Hull and deck: fiberglass. Spars: aluminum. Cabins: 1; berths: 6; galley and head: incl. Aux power: 22 hp incl. Price: $18,500. Designer: John Brandlmayr

S-35. Specs: 35′ × 25′ × 9′6″ × 5′3″. SA: 527, sloop. Disp: 12,000. Ballast: 4,200, lead. Rating: 25.0 CCA. Hull and deck: fiberglass. Spars: aluminum. Cabins: 1; berths: 5; galley and head: incl. Aux power: 30 hp incl. Price: $24,550. Designer: John Brandlmayr Ltd.

Santana 22. Specs: 22′ × 18′9″ × 7′10″ × 3′6″–2′6″. SA: 217, sloop. Disp: 2,600. Ballast: 1,200, iron keel/CB. Hull and deck: fiberglass. Spars: aluminum. Cabins: 1; berths: 4; galley: incl; head: optional. Aux power: optional. Price: $4,325. Designer: Gary Mull

Santana 27. Specs: 27½″ × 22′6″ × 9′ × 4′3″. SA: 348, sloop. Disp: 5,000. Ballast: 2,300, iron. Rating: 21.9 CCA. Hull and deck: fiberglass. Spars: aluminum. Cabins: 2; berths: 6; galley and head: optional. Aux

power: optional. Price: $10,625. Designer: Gary Mull

Santana 37. Specs: 37′8″ × 30′ × 11′8″ × 5′7″. SA: 627, sloop. Disp: 15,000. Ballast: 6,600, iron. Hull and deck: fiberglass. Spars: aluminum. Cabins: 2; berths: 8; galley: incl; head: incl. Aux power: 30 hp incl. Price: $29,500. Designer: Gary Mull

Seabreeze 35. Specs: 34′6″ × 24′ × 10′3″ × 3′10″ (board up). SA: 550, sloop. Disp: 13,600. Ballast: 4,000, lead keel/CB. Rating: 26.5 CCA. Hull and deck: fiberglass. Spars: aluminum. Cabins: 2; berths: 6; galley and head: incl. Aux power: 22 hp incl. Price: $29,000. Designer: Thomas Gilmer

Seafarer 23. Specs: 23′1″ × 16′9″ × 7′2″ × 2′4″ (board up). SA: 229, sloop. Disp: 3,400. Ballast: 1,400, lead keel/CB. Rating: 16.5 CCA. Hull and deck: fiberglass. Spars: aluminum. Cabins: 2; berths: 4; galley and head: optional. Aux power: optional outboard. Price: $3,800. Designer: Sparkman & Stephens

Seafarer 26. Specs: 25′7″ × 17′9″ × 7′3″ × 3′7″. SA: 300, sloop. Disp: 4,960. Ballast: 1,400, lead. Rating: 18.0 MORC. Hull and deck: fiberglass. Spars: aluminum. Cabins: 2; berths: 4; galley: incl; head: optional. Aux power: optional outboard. Price: $4,500. Designer: Philip L. Rhodes

Seafarer 31. Specs: 31′ × 21′ × 8′9″ × 4′7″. SA: 413, sloop. Disp: 8,800. Ballast: 3,360, lead. Rating: 20.0 CCA. Hull and deck: fiberglass. Spars: aluminum. Cabins: 2; berths: 6; galley and head: incl. Aux power: optional. Price: $9,990. Designer: William H. Tripp, Jr.

Seafarer 34. Specs: 34′ × 23′6″ × 10′ × 3′6″. SA: 511, sloop. Disp: 11,000. Ballast: 4,800, lead. Rating: 22.5 CCA. Hull and deck: fiberglass. Spars: aluminum. Cabins: 2; berths: 7; galley and head: incl. Aux power: 30 hp incl. Price: $18,950. Designer: McCurdy & Rhodes

Seafarer 39. Specs: 39′3″ × 26′ × 10′ × 5′5″. SA: 633, sloop or yawl. Disp: 17,500. Ballast: 6,500, lead. Hull and deck: fiberglass. Spars: aluminum. Cabins: 2; berths: 7; galley and head: incl. Aux power: 30 hp incl. Price: $25,750. Designer: William H. Tripp, Jr.

Seafarer 48. Specs: 48′2″ × 33′ × 11′10″ × 6′9″. SA: 1,047, sloop. Disp: 30,100. Ballast: 14,000, lead. Rating: 33.0 CCA. Hull and deck: fiberglass. Spars: aluminum. Cabins: 3; berths: 9; galley and head: incl. Aux power: 70 hp incl. Price: $49,500. Designer: Sparkman & Stephens

Seawind. Specs: 30′6″ × 24′ × 9′3″ × 4′4″. SA: 400, sloop. Disp: 12,080. Ballast: 4,200, lead. Rating: 23.5 CCA. Hull and deck: fiberglass. Spars: aluminum. Cabins: 2; berths: 5; galley and head: incl. Aux power: 20 hp diesel incl. Price: $22,000. Designer: Thomas Gilmer

Shark. Specs: 24′ × 20′ × 6′11″ × 3′. SA: 190, sloop. Disp: 2,200. Ballast: 675, iron. Rating: 20.0 MORC. Hull and deck: fiberglass. Spars: aluminum. Cabins: 1; berths: 4; galley: incl; head: optional. Aux power: optional. Price: $4,800. Designer: George Hinterhoeller

Snapdragon 26. Specs: 26′ × 21′8″ × 8′6″ × 2′6″. SA: 285, sloop. Disp: 4,500. Ballast: 2,000, iron. Hull and deck: fiberglass. Spars: aluminum. Cabins: 1; berths: 5; galley and head: incl. Aux power: optional outboard. Price: $7,750. Designer: Len Wakefield

Snapdragon 29. Specs: 29′ × 24′ × 9′6″ × 3′3″. SA: 376, sloop. Disp: 7,500. Ballast: 3,000, iron. Hull and deck: fiberglass. Spars: aluminum. Cabins: 2; berths: 6; galley and head: incl. Aux power: incl. Price: $13,995. Designer: Len Wakefield

Tartan 27

Soverel 30. Specs: 30′ × 26′ × 8′4″ × 4′. SA: 442, sloop. Disp: 9,000. Ballast: 4,100, lead. Rating: 27.3 CCA and 23 MORC. Hull and deck: fiberglass. Spars: aluminum. Cabins: 2; berths: 5; galley and head: incl. Aux power: 30 hp incl. Price: $16,250. Designer: Bill Soverel and Walt Walters

Tartan 27. Specs: 27′ × 21′5″ × 8′7½″ × 6′4″–3′2″. SA: 372, sloop. Disp: 6,875. Ballast: 2,000, lead. Rating: 20.2 CCA. Hull and deck: fiberglass. Spars: aluminum. Cabins: 2; berths: 5; galley and head: incl. Aux power: 30 hp incl. Price: $12,800. Designer: Sparkman & Stephens

Tartan 34. Specs: 34′5″ × 25′ × 10′2″ × 8′4″–3′11″. SA: 515, sloop or yawl. Disp: 11,200. Ballast: 4,400, lead. Rating: 27.5 CCA. Hull and deck: fiberglass. Spars: aluminum. Cabins: 2; berths: 6; galley and head: incl. Aux power: 30 hp incl. Price: $21,800. Designer: Sparkman & Stephens

Tartan 37. Specs: 37′ × 25′6″ × 10′6″ × 9′4″–3′10″. SA: 618, sloop or yawl. Disp: 15,700. Ballast: 4,600, lead. Rating: 28.5 CCA. Hull and deck: fiberglass. Spars: aluminum. Cabins: 2; berths: 6; galley and head: incl. Aux power: 30 hp incl. Price: $27,700. Designer: Ted Hood

Tempest. Specs: 23′2″ × 17′ × 7′8″ × 3′9″. SA: 211, sloop. Disp: 3,000. Ballast:

1,250, iron. Rating: 21 CCA. Hull and deck: fiberglass. Spars: aluminum. Cabins: 1; berths: 2; galley: incl; head: optional. Aux power: optional. Price: $3,950. Designer: Philip L. Rhodes

Thunderbird. Specs: 26′ × 19′ × 10′ × 5′. SA: 364, sloop. Disp: 3,900. Ballast: 1,500, iron. Rating: 25.0 CCA. Hull and deck: plywood & glass. Spars: wood. Cabins: 1; berths: 4; galley and head: incl. Aux power: 9 hp incl. Price: $6,000. Designer: Ben Seaborn

Trintella 1. Specs: 28′11″ × 21′4″ × 8′3″ × 4′4″. SA: 396, sloop. Disp: 8,400. Ballast: 3,850, iron. Rating: 20.8 MORC. Hull and deck: fiberglass. Spars: aluminum. Cabins: 2; berths: 5; galley and head: incl. Aux power: 12 hp incl. Price: $12,990. Designer: E. G. van de Stadt

Triton. Specs: 28′6″ × 20′6″ × 8′3″ × 4′. SA: 362, sloop; 400, yawl. Disp: 8,400. Ballast: 3,019, lead. Rating: 20.6 CCA, sloop; 20.9 CCA, yawl. Hull and deck: fiberglass. Spars: aluminum. Cabins: 2; berths: 4; galley and head: incl. Aux power: 30 hp incl. Price: $11,995. Designer: Carl Alberg

Tylercraft 24. Specs: 24′ × 20′ × 7′5″ × 2′. SA: 243, sloop. Disp: 4,000. Ballast: 1,450, iron. Hull and deck: fiberglass. Spars: aluminum. Cabins: 2; berths: 4; galley and head: optional. Aux power: optional. Price: $4,995. Designer: Ted Tyler

Vega. Specs: 27′1″ × 23′ × 8′ × 3′10″. SA: 295, sloop. Disp: 5,070. Ballast: 2,020, iron and lead. Hull and deck: fiberglass. Spars: aluminum. Cabins: 2; berths: 4; galley and head: incl. Aux power: 12 hp incl. Price: $11,300. Designer: Per Brohall

Venture 17. Specs: 17′4″ × 15′3″ × 6′4″ × 4′6″. SA: 93, sloop. Disp: 800. Ballast: 250, lead. Hull and deck: fiberglass. Spars: aluminum. Cabins: 1; berths: 4; galley and head: optional. Aux power: 10 hp optional. Price: $1,595. Designer: Roger MacGregor

Venture 21. Specs: 21′ × 18′6″ × 6′10″ × 5′6″–1′6″. SA: 265, sloop. Disp: 1,200. Ballast: 400, lead. Rating: 23.1 CCA. Hull and deck: fiberglass. Spars: aluminum. Cabins: 1; berths: 4; galley and head: optional. Aux power: optional. Price: $1,995. Designer: Roger MacGregor

Venture 22. Specs: 22′ × 18′2″ × 7′4″ × 4′6″. SA: 110, sloop. Disp: 1,600. Ballast: 475, lead. Rating: 22.6 CCA. Hull and deck:

fiberglass. Spars: aluminum. Cabins: 1; berths: 4; galley and head: optional. Aux power: 20 hp incl. Price: $2,395. Designer: Roger MacGregor

Venture 24. Specs: 24′7″ × 21′6″ × 7′11″ × 4′6″. SA: 231, sloop. Disp: 2,000. Ballast: 500, lead. Rating: 24.0 MORC/CCA. Hull and deck: fiberglass. Spars: aluminum. Cabins: 2; berths: 5; galley and head: optional. Aux power: optional. Price: $2,995. Designer: Roger MacGregor

Vivacity 20. Specs: 20′ × 17′6″ × 7′ × 2′4″. SA: 175, sloop. Disp: 1,800. Ballast: 775, iron. Rating: 15 MORC. Hull and deck: fiberglass. Spars: aluminum. Cabins: 1; berths: 4; galley: incl; head: optional. Aux power: optional. Price: $3,595. Designer: Peter Stephenson

Wanderer. Specs: 30′3″ × 23′4″ × 9′4″ × 6′9″–3′6″. SA: 421, sloop. Disp: 9,800. Ballast: 3,800, lead. Rating: 21.8 CCA. Hull and deck: fiberglass. Spars: aluminum. Cab-

Westerly Nomad

ins: 2; berths: 6; galley and head: incl. Aux power: 30 hp incl. Price: $14,600. Designer: W. H. Shaw

Westerly Centaur. Specs: 26′ × 21′4″ × 8′5″ × 3′. SA: 294, sloop. Disp: 4,800. Ballast: 2,800, iron. Hull and deck: fiberglass. Spars: aluminum. Cabins: 2; berths: 6; galley and head: incl. Aux power: optional. Price: $7,980. Designer: Laurent Giles

Westerly Cirrus. Specs: 21′ × 19′ × 8′ × 3′6″. SA: 214, sloop. Disp: 3,240. Ballast: 1,460, iron. Hull and deck: fiberglass. Spars: aluminum. Cabins: 1; berths: 6; galley and head: incl. Aux power: optional. Price: $5,750. Designer: John A. Butler

Westerly Jouster. Specs: 21′ × 18′3″ × 7′6″ × 3′6″. SA: 197, sloop. Disp: 3,500. Ballast: 1,500, iron. Hull and deck: fiberglass. Spars: aluminum. Cabins: 2; berths: 4; galley and head: incl. Aux power: 9 hp optional. Price: $4,350. Designer: Laurent Giles

Westerly Nomad. Specs: 22′3″ × 18′4″ × 7′5″ × 2′3″. SA: 232, sloop. Disp: 3,300. Ballast: 1,050, iron. Hull and deck: fiberglass. Spars: wood or aluminum. Cabins: 2; berths: 4; galley and head: incl. Aux power: optional. Price: $6,330. Designer: Denys Rayner

Westerly Pageant. Specs: 23′1″ × 19′ × 8′ × 2′10″. SA: 236, sloop. Disp: 4,300. Ballast: 2,100, iron. Hull and deck: fiberglass. Spars: aluminum. Cabins: 2; berths: 4; galley and head: incl. Aux power: 7 hp optional. Price: $6,650. Designer: Laurent Giles

Westerly Tiger. Specs: 25′1″ × 21′10″ × 8′9″ × 4′3″. SA: 311, sloop. Disp: 5,264. Ballast: 2,240, iron. Rating: 19.5 MORC. Hull and deck: fiberglass. Spars: aluminum. Cabins: 2; berths: 6; galley and head: incl. Aux power: 7 or 15 diesel optional. Price: $7,900. Designer: John A. Butler

Westwind. Specs: 23′11″ × 18′1½″ × 8′ × 5′6″–2′1″. SA: 304, sloop. Disp: 4,670. Ballast: 2,370, iron. Rating: 18.4 CCA, 21 MORC. Hull and deck: fiberglass. Spars: aluminum. Cabins: 2; berths: 4; galley and head: incl. Aux power: optional. Price: $5,795. Designer: Ted Hood

XL-2. Specs: 41′6″ × 28′6″ × 11′6″ × 8′4″–4′2″. SA: 762, sloop. Disp: 17,220. Ballast: 7,000, lead. Rating: 32.0 CCA. Hull and deck: fiberglass. Spars: aluminum. Cabins: 2; berths: 4; galley and head: incl. Aux power: 45 hp diesel incl. Price: $51,700. Designer: Sparkman & Stephens

Other One-Design Class Sailboats

Name	Keel or Centerboard	Type	Length Overall	Beam	Draft	Sail Area, Square Feet
Adventurer	K	S	24′	7′6″	4′3″	244
Allegro	CB	S	20′9″	7′	3′9″	199
Alongshore	K	Cu	28′9″	8′2″	4′8″	380
Alpha	K	S	28′	8′10″	4′	400
Amethyst	K	S	28′6″	8′2″	5′2″	405
Apache	K	S	28′6″	8′9″	4′3″	214
Arcoa 520	K	S	17′1″	7′3″	1′6″	151
Atalanta	K	S	26′	7′9″	1′6″	240
Bahama	K	S	35′	10′6″	4′6″	484
Barnacle	K	S	34′	8′6″	5′4″	531
Barnegat Bay Catboat	CB	Ca	23′10″	10′	2′	470
Barnegat 20	K	S	20′1″	7′	3′9″	175
Bay Bird	K	S	30′	6′	5′	397
Bermuda One-Design	K	S	29′	6′1″	5′	396
Bermuda 30	K	S	29′7″	8′9″	3′8″	383
Blue Quill	K	S	24′	8′7″	4′1″	276
Bon Voyager	K	S	27′	8′10″	4′4″	445

Key:
K—keel
CB—centerboard
Ca—catboat
S—sloop
Y—yawl

Ke—ketch
Cu—cutter
Sc—schooner
K/CB—combination keel and centerboard
* Centerboard up
† For sloop

Name	Keel or Centerboard	Type	Length Overall	Beam	Draft	Sail Area, Square Feet
Bonito	K	S or Y	34'9"	9'7"	4'8"	510
Bounty	K	S	38'9"	9'8"	5'8"	635
Bowstring	K	S or Y	42'9"	10'	6'25"	718
Brabant	K	S	30'6"	8'11"	4'7"	400
Bristol 27	K	S	27'2"	8'	4'	340
Brewer 32	K	S	32'	9'11"	5'3"	486
Brunswick Mariner 22	K	S	31'1"	7'6"	5'6"	470
Buccaneer	K	S	23'2"	7'6"	3'9"	236
Buzzards Bay M-B	K	S	29'3"	6'6"	4'4"	400
Buzzards Bay 30 Square Meter	K	S	39'	6'10"	4'6"	322
C-30	K	S or Y	30'6"	8'	4'	400
C. C. C.	K	S	25'	8'7"	4'6"	320
California Cruising Club	K	S	25'	8'6"	4'	350
Calkins Forty	K	S	39'10"	10'5"	6'	927
Calkins Fifty	K	S	49'11"	11'11"	7'6"	1,034
Caller	K	S	27'6"	8'6"	4'6"	365
Calliope X	K	Y	30'	10'	5'9"	560
Calypso	CB	Ke	44'8"	12'6"	4'3"	673
Cambridge Cadet	K	S	28'7"	8'7"	4'10"	405
Cape Cod Catboat (*see* Sea Cat)						
Cape Cod 30	K	S	29'10"	9'6"	4'3"	465
Cape Horn (*see* Le Cape Horn)						
Caravel	K	S	22'10"	7'5"	3'	228
Caravel Mark II	K	S	24'6"	8'	3'8"	267
Carlson 29	K	S	29'1"	8'11"	4'10"	336
Casey 31	K	S	31'	8'6"	4'	405
Casey 36	K	S	36'	9'6"	6'	510
Casey 40	K	S	39'10"	10'	6'	610
Challenger	K	S	29'	9'4"	6'	365
Champion	K	S	21'	7'6"	3'3"	232
Chesapeake One-Design	K	S	34'	7'9"	5'3"	444
Chris Craft 35	K	S	35'	11'	4'8"	563
Cinder	K/CB	S	21'6"	7'	3'3"	223
Cinderella	CB	Y	38'6"	11'	4'*	670
Classic	K	S	19'	7'2"	2'6"	140
Clipper	K	S	32'	10'6"	4'6"	464
Coast Cruiser	K	S	25'	8'	3'2"	295
Coast Knockabout	K	S	26'	6'6"	4'	286
Coastal Cruiser	K	Cu	36'6"	6'6"	4'9"	536
Coaster 25	K	S	25'	7'6"	4'1"	281
Coaster 32	K	S	32'	7'7"	5'1"	294
Coastwise Cruiser	K	S	36'6"	9'9"	5'2"	585
Cohasset 21	K	S	32'	8'	5'6"	300
Coleman Bounty	K	S	38'9"	9'8"	5'10"	638
Columbia	K	S	28'6"	8'	4'	400
Columbia Challenger	K	S	24'4"	8'	3'4"	306
Columbia Contender	K	S	24'	7'10"	3'3"	283
Columbia Defender	K	S	28'6"	8'	4'	381
Columbia Sabre	K	S	32'5"	6'3"	4'4"	347
Concordia 25	K	S	31'3"	9'4"	5'	538
Concordia 41	K	S	41'	10'3"	5'10"	710
Concordia Yawl	K	Y	39'10"	10'3"	5'8"	650
Controversy 26	K/CB	S	25'11"	8'3"	2'6"	292
Controversy 27	K/CB	S	27'2"	7'11"	2'10"	316
Controversy 28	K/CB	S	28'5"	8'6"	3'4"	330
Controversy 30	K	S	31'2"	8'5"	3'4"	374
Controversy 36	K	Y	37'1"	10'1"	5'4"	520
Coquette	K	S	25'5"	7'	3'11"	290

Name	Keel or Centerboard	Type	Length Overall	Beam	Draft	Sail Area, Square Feet
Corinthian	K	Y	39′6″	9′9″	5′9″	675
Corsair Jr.	K	S	22′	7′3″	3′7″	327
Corsair Sr.	K	S	28′	9′	4′7″	400
Corsair 32	CB	S	32′	9′6″	4′2″	550
Corsair 35	K	Y	35′	10′	5′2″	650
Creekmore 36	K	S	36′	6′2″	5′1″	580
Crescent	K	S	24′	7′	4′1″	298
Crod	K	S	28′	8′9″	2′4″	344
Cruisken	K	S	29′8″	8′9″	3′9″	296
Crusader Mark II	K	S	27′3″	8′2″	4′3″	305
Crusailer	K	S	41′	11′7″	5′	713
Crystal	K	S	22′4″	7′6″	3′6″	225
Dark Harbor	K	S	30′	6′6″	4′2″	340
Dasher	K	S	31′6″	8′9″	5′6″	475
Dater	K	S	20′6″	7′6″	3′8″	222
Debutante	K	S	26′6″	7′2″	3′10″	240
Del Rey 24	K	S	24′	7′10″	3′8″	272
Delta	K	S	25′6″	7′10″	3′7″	253
Diamond Mark II	K	S	26′8″	7′7″	4′1″	289
Dickerson	K	S	26′6″	8′6″	3′	346
Dobson 25	CB	S	25′	4′6″	3′4″	310
Dragonfly	K	S	18′1″	6′11″	2′9″	120
Duchess	K	S	26′	6′8″	—	333
Dutch Main	K	S	30′	8′7″	4′4″	295
Dutchy	K	S	27′9″	8′7″	3′8″	285
Duxbury	K	S	29′2″	8′3″	3′6″	391
Duxbury One-Design	K/CB	S	26′9″	7′	3′	360
Eagle	K	S	29′1″	6′8″	4′8″	439
Eagle 27	K	S	27′	8′5″	3′9″	335
Eastern Interclub	K	S	35′	7′2″	5′	450
Eastward Ho Jr.	K	S	23′5″	8′8″	3′10″	250
Eastward Ho Sr.	K	S	30′	9′1″	3′6″	404
Elizabeth 29	K	S or Y	29′	7′6″	4′2″	320
Excalibur	K	S	36′1″	10′	5′11″	644
Explorer	CB	S	26′	9′	5′*	317
Explorer	K	Cu	37′5″	10′11″	3′8″	614
Explorer	K/CB	Ke	40′	11′2″	2′8″*	615
Falcon	K	S	33′	8′8″	4′10″	462
Felicity	K	S	20′	7′1″	3′1″	185
Feria	K	S	28′	27′11″	4′11″	333
Fifty-Fifty 32	K	S	32′	10′	3′8″	450
Fifty-Fifty 38	K	S	38′	12′	4′2″	550
Finnish Class	K	S	31′5″	6′5″	3′8″	310
Fishers Island 31	K	S	43′6″	10′9″	6′	950
510	K	S	44′8″	6′7″	6′	519
Flyer	K	S	25′1″	7′3″	3′11″	304
Folkboat	K	S	25′1″	7′2″	3′11″	269
Four-sum	K	S	28′	8′6″	4′6″	378
Fox	K	S	39′	9′	5′	600
Gallant	K	S	23′6″	7′	2′9″	180
Georgetown 25	K	S	25′	7′2″	3′11″	295
Georgetown 30	K	S	30′	8′2″	4′3″	395
Glass Slipper	K	S or Y	48′9″	12′9″	6′2″	937
Goldeneye	K	S	18′3″	6′4″	3′	193
Great Dane	K	S	25′1″	7′2″	3′10″	230
Great Dane Jr.	K	S	18′7″	5′8″	2′10″	162
Great Lakes 30	K	S	43′	9′	6′3″	600
Greenwich Bay Cutter	K	Cu	28′	9′6″	4′9″	512
Gulf Coast 40	CB	Y	40′	10′6″	5′6″	614

Name	Keel or Centerboard	Type	Length Overall	Beam	Draft	Sail Area, Square Feet
Gulf Stream 36	K	S	37′	10′	4′7″	599
Gulf Stream 38	CB	S	38′6″	11′3″	3′8″	713
Gulf Stream 42	K	Y	41′6″	11′	6′3″	784
Gypsy	CB	S	19′3″	6′6″	3′10″	173
H-28	K	Ke	28′	8′9″	3′6″	343
Halfhander	CB	S	23′	7′2″	3′10″	212
Hankosloop	K	S	36′	9′6″	5′5″	550
Herreshoff Double Ender	K	Ke	30′9″	8′	4′6″	333
Herreshoff Meadow Lark	CB	Ke	33′	8′	1′6″	475
Herreshoff 23	K	S	33′	7′	4′6″	350
Herreshoff 28	K	S or Ke	28′	9′	3′6″	400
Herreshoff 31	K	S	43′6″	8′9″	6′6″	1,100
Hillyard 2½ Tonner	K	S	18′	6′6″	3′6″	170
Hinckley 21	K	S	28′6″	8′	4′7″	340
Hinckley 28	K	S or Y	40′9″	10′	5′8″	682
Hinckley 32	K	S or Y	45′9″	11′2″	6′8″	715
Hinckley 36	K	S or Y	36′	9′4″	5′1″	524†
Holiday	K	S	31′	7′10″	4′8″	330
Holland 25	K	S	24′9″	7′3″	3′6″	218
Holman	K	S	40′	10′4″	6′	780
Honeymoon	K	S	23′10″	6′5″	3′7″	220
Huntress	K	S	37′4″	6′3″	4′6″	360
International 600	K	S or Y	36′	10′	5′	641
Invicta	K/CB	S or Y	37′8″	10′8″	4′6″	614
Island Clipper	K	S	44′3″	9′6″	6′6″	715
Island Creek 25	CB	S	25′	7′9″	3′3″	250
Islander 24	K	S	24′	7′10″	3′10″	294
Islander 30	K	S	30′	9′	4′3″	420
Islander 34	K	S	34′6″	10′7″	5′2″	599
Islesboro	K	S	30′	6′8″	4′2″	350
Jr. Clipper	K	S	25′9″	7′4″	4′9″	245
K-25	K	S	25′4″	8′	3′8″	327
K-35	K	S	35′	9′10″	5′	610
K-37	K	S	37′	8′4″	5′3″	479
K-38	K	S	38′	8′	5′2″	538
Kappa Class	K	Y	35′	10′	4′9″	590
Kreuter Class	K	S	30′	8′2″	4′4″	434
L-24	K	S	38′3″	6′3″	4′10″	400
L-36	K	S	36′	9′	5′3″	590
L-40	K	S	39′11″	10′6″	5′6″	690
Lake One-Design	K	S	34′	7′9″	5′3″	444
Lapworth 24	K	S	24′	7′6″	4′	300
Larchmont "O"	K	S	59′10″	12′	7′10″	1,704
Larsen Jr.	K	S	22′	7′	3′7″	247
Larsen Sr.	K	S	28′	8′10″	4′7″	387
Larsen 32	K	S	32′	9′10″	5′	500
Larsen 36	K	S	36′1″	10′6″	5′2″	600
Laurel	K	S	39′10″	8′9″	6′	520
Le Cape Horn	CB	S	21′4″	7′1″	2′2″	254
Leeward	CB	S	19′	7′	1′8″	160
Lion	K	S	35′2″	8′10″	5′6″	587
Little Sister	K	S	27′2″	8′2″	4′2″	349
Mackinac	K	S	40′	10′	5′11″	690
Maine Coast 36	K	Y	37′	9′8″	6′2″	670
Malabar Jr.	K	S	32′3″	8′8″	4′11″	476
Malabar 36	K	S or Y	36′	9′9″	5′	571
Manchester 18	K	S	31′	6′	4′6″	520
Marco Polo	K	Sc	55′	10′	5′6″	819
Mariner	K	S	36′	9′3″	5′3″	620

Name	Keel or Centerboard	Type	Length Overall	Beam	Draft	Sail Area, Square Feet
Marlin			23′	7′2″	3′2″	245
Marshall 22	CB	C	22′2″	10′2″	2′	404
Melody 34G	K	S or Y	34′	11′	4′6″	467
Melody 40	K	Y	40′	10′9″	5′	550
Mercer	CB	S	44′	11′9″	4′3″*	884
Meridian	K	S	24′9″	7′	3′3″	274
Merryboat	K	S	19′2″	7′	2′10″	164
Mills 24	CB	S	24′	7′6″	2′9″	250
Minneford 23	CB	S	23′	7′	4′9″*	261
Mistral	K	S	36′4″	10′6″	5′	596
Musketeer	K	S or Y	40′8″	9′11″	5′11″	709
Navara	K	Y	34′4″	8′5″	5′6″	640
New Bedford 29	K	S	29′	8′	4′7″	386
New Bedford 35	K	S	35′	9′6″	5′6″	569
New Campaigner	K	S	30′6″	9′6″	5′2″	420
New Weekender	K	S	39′	9′9″	5′10″	660
New York 30	K	S	43′7″	8′9″	6′5″	1,100
New York 32	K	S	45′4″	10′7″	6′6″	950
Nicholson 36	K	S	36′3″	9′6″	5′11″	670
Nimrod	K	S	45′	11′1″	6′8″	1,137
Nomad	CB	S	22′7″	7′6″	8″	285
Norge	K	S	22′	7′3″	3′7″	247
Norsaga	K	S	32′5″	8′6″	4′8″	485
Norseman	K	S	30′4″	7′9″	4′4″	435
North East Harbor (Class A)	K	S	27′9″	7′3″	4′6″	380
North East Harbor (Class E)	K	S	26′	6′6″	4′6″	232
North Sea 24	K	S	30′11″	9′	5′6″	581
Northporter	K	S	23′	8′6″	3′6″	275
Norvega	K	S	27′6″	7′6″	4′3″	300
Nutmeg	CB	S	24′6″	7′7″	2′9″	268
Off Sounding Class	K	Y	42′2″	10′6″	5′10″	903
Offshore	K	S	25′	9′2″	3′	339
Ohlson 26	K	S	26′	8′	4′1″	359
Over-Nite	K	S	30′	8′6″	4′6″	420
Owens Cutter	K	Cu	40′6″	10′6″	5′10″	862
Oxford 400	K	S	29′	8′4″	4′6″	400
P 28	K	S	28′3″	7′8″	4′2″	491
Pacific 22 Square Meter	K	S	36′	6′	4′4″	500
Pennant 24	K	S	24′	7′	3′1″	290
Pennant 25	K	S	25′	7′10″	3′5″	320
Picnic	CB	S	17′3″	6′8″	1′	187
Pied Piper	K/CB	S	26′8″	8′8″	2′11″	311
Pilot	K	S	33′	9′6″	4′9″	495
Pioneer	K	S	30′	8′	4′8″	451
Priscilla	K	S	30′	8′6″	4′3″	391
Privateer	K	S	35′	8′10″	5′3″	522
Prudence	K	S	23′	8′	3′	293
Q Class	K	S	53′	8′9″	6′9″	890
Quadrant	K	S	25′7″	8′6″	3′9″	300
Quicksilver	CB	S	42′	11′	3′	600
R Class	K	S	38′	7′	5′9″	590
Raider	K	S	42′	11′9″	6′	726
Ranger	K	S	38′6″	10′6″	3′10″	655
Ranger 11	K	S	28′6″	8′	4′	334
Rhodes Reliant	K	S or Y	40′9″	10′9″	5′9″	686
Rhodes 27	K	S	39′2″	9′9″	5′9″	635
Rhodes 33	K	S	33′8″	6′10″	5′	272

Name	Keel or Centerboard	Type	Length Overall	Beam	Draft	Sail Area, Square Feet
Robb 35	K/CB	S or Y	35′6″	10′	4′7″	587
Robinhood	K	Ke	42′	13′	5′6″*	851
Rocket	C	S	23′	7′	1′6″*	529
Roué	K	S	20′	8′6″	5′	480
Royal 30	K	S	30′4″	8′7″	4′4″	340
S-28	K	S	28′	7′	4′4″	329
Sagitta	K	S	30′	9′	4′9″	430
Sanderling	CB	C	18′2″	8′6″	1′7″	255
Sea Cat	CB	C	18′9″	8′9″	2′*	165
Sea Dream	K	S	25′	8′6″	4′6″	375
Sea Rover	K	S	30′	10′	5′4″	420
Sea Spray	K	S	21′	6′2″	3′8″	225
Seafarer	K	S	25′	7′9″	4′	344
Seagoer	K	Ke	44′	11′4″	5′1″	777
Seagull	CB	S	18′6″	6′9″	1′5″*	825
Seaman 27	K	S	27′	8′6″	4′3″	360
Seaman 30	K	S	30′	8′6″	4′3″	424
Seamew	K	S	22′	7′4″	1′9″	202
Searider 25	CB	S	25′	7′9″	2′11″	280
Seawanhaka Schooner	K	Sc	58′6″	12′	7′6″	1,413
Seawind	K	Ke	30′6″	9′3″	4′4″	410
Seawind 30	K	S or Ke	30′6″	9′3″	4′4″	400†
Sharpie	K	Ke	25′	7′	4′6″	380
Shelter Island 26	K	S	26′	6′10″	4′	330
Shelter Island 31	K	S	31′	11′	3′	425
Shock-22	CB	S	22′	7′6″	2′2″	241
Signet 20	K	S	19′10″	6′8″	2′	192
Silhouette Mark II	K	S	17′8″	6′7″	1′8″	140
Silver Spray	K	S	23′5″	8′8″	3′10″	250
Single-Hander	K	S	35′	8′6″	5′3″	480
Siren	K	S	30′	9′	3′	350
Sisu	K	S	24′7″	7′7″	4′3″	330
Skylark	K	Y	22′1″	7′6″	3′	312
Snapdragon	CB	S	23′	7′8″	1′6″	215
Sojourner	K	S	32′10″	10′3″	4′6″	499
Sound Clipper	K	S	24′	8′1″	3′2″	335
Sound Interclub	K	S	28′6″	7′9″	4′7″	408
South Coast 21	K	S	21′4″	6′11″	3′	191
South Coast 23	K	S	23′	7′3″	2′10″	246
South Coast 25	K	S	25′6″	8′	3′6″	310
Southern California	K	S	30′1″	7′8″	5′2″	370
Sou'wester Sr.	K	S	38′	10′3″	5′	654
Sou'wester 30	K	S	30′5″	8′10″	4′6″	405
Soverel 36	K	S or Y	36′7″	11′	4′6″	837
Spurn	K	S	21′4″	7′1″	3′1″	191
Squarehead	K	S	20′6″	7′9″	3′	175
Stadel 24	K	S	24′4″	8′1″	3′7″	280
Starflame	K	S	27′10″	8′6″	4′6″	390
Stella	K	S	25″9″	7′6″	3′10″	278
Stone Horse Junior	K	S	22′8″	7′	2′6″	243
Stone Horse Senior	K	S	33′	10′2″	4′	537
Stout Fella Junior	K	S	23′4″	7′4″	3′6″	247
Stout Fella Senior	K	S	26′8″	7′4″	3′10″	301
Stout Fella 33	K	S or Y	33′	8′6″	4′6″	455†
Summercraft 31	K	S	31′	10′2″	3′1″	380
Sunset	K	S	34′	8′	5′3″	407
Swallow	K	S	23′	6′4″	3′8″	233
T-21	K	S	20′4″	6′9″	3′6″	180
Temperance	K	S	33′3″	10′	5′	503

Name	Keel or Centerboard	Type	Length Overall	Beam	Draft	Sail Area, Square Feet
Tempest 21	K	S	21′	7′2″	4′	232
Temple	K/CB	S or Y	38′8″	11′4″	3′10″	675
Ten-ten	K	S	32′2″	10′	4′7″	342
Three Sisters	K	S	26′6″	9′2″	5′	448
Tiger V	K	S	23′	7′	4′	214
Timber Point	K	S	22′4″	7′6″	3′	247
Tom Cod	K	S	20′	7′4″	3′2″	200
Topaz	K	S	29′	8′2″	5′2″	470
Toppan Twosome	K	S	23′3″	7′6″	3′6″	281
Traveler 22	K/CB	S	22′3″	7′1″	2′10″	228
Triangle	K	S	28′6″	7′6″	4′9″	410
Triangle 20	CB	S	20′6″	7′1″	2′2″	205
Triangle 32	K	Ke	32′	10′	3′5″	480
Trotter 21 Mark II	K/CB	S	21′6″	7′	3′9″	240
Truant	K	S	30′4″	8′10″	4′9″	424
24-Foot Sloop	K	S	24′	7′3″	3′3″	209
U.S. 41	CB	Y	41′11″	12′	4′11″	813
Vagabond	K/CB	S	21′	7′6″	4′	243
Valencia	K	S	39′6″	11′2″	5′10″	722
Valkyrie	CB	S	29′6″	10′	2′3″	415
Vedette	K/CB	S or Y	23′11″	7′9″	4′6″	276
Venture	K	S	25′3″	7′2″	4′6″	290
Venturer	K/CB	Ke	38′	11′	2′8″	635
Victory	K/CB	S or Y	37′6″	10′9″	4′6″	660
Victory Class	K	S	31′	7′	4′9″	450
Viking Class	K	S	23′4″	7′	3′6″	284
Viking 23	CB	S	24′4″	7′10″	1′10″	258
Viking 28	CB	S	29′	9′7″	2′1″	325
Vineyard Sound Interclub	K	S	28′3″	7′4″	4′6″	391
Visitor	K	S	29′	8′	4′6″	372
Vitesse 40	CB	Y	40′8″	11′9″	4′	778
Vixen	K	S	32′3″	8′6″	5′6″	486
Voyager	K	S	44′3″	10′7″	6′3″	880
Wayward Wind	CB	S	22′6″	7′8″	2′8″	233
Weekender	K	S	35′	9′6″	5′6″	562
Weekender 20	CB	S	20′6″	7′	1′4″*	165
West Solent	K	S	24′6″	7′6″	5′	567
Westcoaster	K	S	20′	6′11″	2′	216
Westerly 25	K	S	25′1″	7′5″	2′6″	276
Whistler	CB	S	23′	7′6″	3′7″	235
Winter Harbor 21	K	S	31′	7′	5′6″	516
X-Touché	K/CB	S	48′	13′6″	4′7″	1,068
Yankee One-Design	K	S	30′6″	6′6″	4′6″	312
Zeeland	K	Y	37′	9′9″	4′6″	500
Zenith Clipper	CB	S	32′	10′6″	3′9″	464
Zephyr	CB	S	36′	10′6″	4′	552

International Cruiser-Racer Classes

These are meter boats which have accommodations to live aboard. They differ from the first-described offshore racing yachts whose performance is leveled out by a system of handicaps (see page 375), as they race level without time allowances and the equality in performance is arrived at by means of an International Rule (similar to the one given on page 379) governing the dimensions and sail areas within certain limits.

The rule applies to seven classes of these meter cruiser-racers, which are of the following *approximate* dimensions:

Class	Length Overall	Length at Waterline
7-Meter	33 feet	23 to 24 feet
8-Meter	40 feet	26 to 27 feet
9-Meter	46 feet	29 to 31 feet
10.5-Meter	51 feet	34 to 36 feet
12-Meter	62 feet	39 to 41 feet
13.5-Meter	74 feet	47 to 49 feet
15-Meter	86 feet	54 to 57 feet

These seven classes are recognized by the International Yacht Racing Union as International classes. Information on CCA (Cruising Club of America), MORC (Midget Ocean Racing Club), and RORC (Royal Ocean Racing Club) racing classes may be found in Sections VI and VII.

SECTION IV

The Art of Sailing

There is a great deal of meaning in the word "seamanship." Think of it: *sea–man–ship*. A blending of three very different things, each of which covers a variety of interests. Little of it can be taught, but it may be learned, and in one way only—by experience. So, if you should ask us how to discover the best way of handling your sailboat, how to know what to do and how to do it, there is only one honest reply that we can make—take your boat out on the water and find out for yourself. But we would advise you to read all you can about sailing, to study the various sailing books and the yachting magazines; then you will learn more quickly. Do not, however, rely upon reading to teach you seamanship. Books can and do explain the theory and the reason; they can also make you think. But to learn to handle your sailboat under all conditions of wind and weather, you must serve your time out on the water. For the time being, however, the beginner can hasten his learning and avoid many pitfalls by a little preliminary book study.

THEORY OF SAILING

Since the wind is the "power," a sailor must learn how to make the best use of it. When wind fills a sail, it not only pushes the boat, but reduces the pressure on the sail's other side, which pulls the hull along. The direction of the wind is up to Nature, so the sailor must be able to reach his destination regardless of which way it is blowing.

Points of Sailing

A sailboat's directional heading with respect to wind is called her point of sailing. Actually, there are five basic points of sailing: running, beating, close reaching, beam reaching, and broad reaching. For instance, running, or wind aft, is sailing in the same direction in which the wind is blowing, or nearly so. The wind comes from astern or slightly on the quarter. When the average boat sails with the wind broad on her bow, she is beating. As the wind comes from farther ahead, the sails begin to flap or luff, and they become increasingly ineffectual until the boat is on the wind, or head to wind (headed directly into the wind), at which time they are totally ineffectual. A sail that is not luffing is said to be full (full of wind). The terms luffing and full can be applied to the boat herself, as well as to individual sails.

Close reach, beam reach, and broad reach are all intermediate points of sailing between

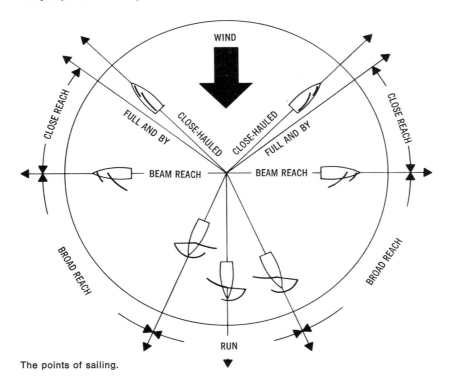

The points of sailing.

that of on the wind and running. That is, when wind comes from a point directly abeam, the boat is on a beam reach. When wind comes from directions between that of a beam reach and a beat, the craft is close reaching. A boat is said to be sailing a broad reach when wind comes from directions between that of a run and a beam reach.

Sail positions are governed by wind and are achieved by adjusting the sheets, which pull the sails in toward the boat's centerline or allow them to swing out to a more athwartships position. When the sheets are pulled in, the sails are said to be trimmed, but when the sheets are let out they are said to be cracked, started, eased, or slacked, to use the terms in increasing order. The word trim is also used to indicate whether or not a boat's sails are in exactly the right position for a given point of sailing, a vital factor for speed, as for example, "Her sails are well trimmed," or "She is trimmed too flat."

When running, a boat is often said to be sailing before the wind, off the wind (also applied to reaching), sailing free (with sheets eased), or sailing with a fair wind. Frequently,

when running, a boat's jib will go limp because the wind is from nearly dead astern, and the mainsail is blanketing the jib or blocking off its wind. The jib might be made to draw (fill with wind) if it were wung out, or pushed out on the opposite side from the mainsail. The boat then would be said to be sailing wing and wing. When running, the main boom (mainsail's boom) is let out so that it is almost athwartships. When a boat is running with the wind nearly dead astern, her boom is let out as far as it will go without chafing against the aftermost shroud. As the boat is gradually turned toward the wind, her sheets are slowly trimmed until, when beam reaching, her jib and main boom are about halfway in, roughly 135 degrees to the wind or 45 degrees to the boat's centerline. When close reaching, the sheets are trimmed still closer, somewhere between the beam reaching position and about 10 degrees from the boat's centerline.

On various points of reaching, especially when beam reaching or sailing slightly further away from the wind, boats usually achieve their highest sailing speeds. As mentioned in

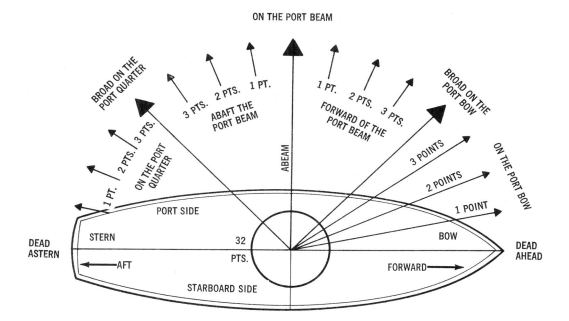

Directional terms. Note the same system is used on starboard side.

Section II, some boats having planing hulls—lightweight, and with flattish bottoms—will gain considerable speed by planing, or lifting up on their bow waves and skimming over the top of the water rather than plowing through the water like a boat with a displacement hull. At most times when boats are traveling at their highest speeds, sails must be trimmed a little flatter than normal. This is due to the apparent wind, or the direction from which the wind appears to blow, when aboard a boat in motion. As shown in the diagram here, the boat moving ahead at 4 knots causes a 4-knot wind from directly ahead. The true, or actual, wind is 9 knots from slightly forward of the beam; thus the apparent wind is a resultant of these two forces (boat-speed wind and true wind), which in this case is blowing at 11 knots from broad on the bow. Sails should always be trimmed to the apparent wind. To put it very simply, the faster a boat travels (unless dead before the wind), the closer her sheets are trimmed. This becomes evident especially when the true wind is nearly on the beam.

When beating, a boat's sails are trimmed

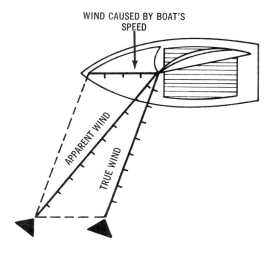

Apparent wind. It is important to note that any mention in this book of wind refers to true wind unless specifically called apparent wind.

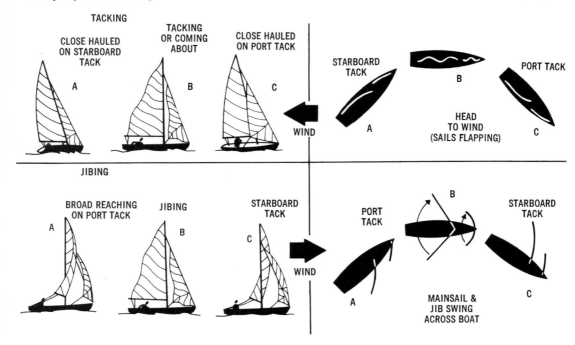

TACKING

CLOSE HAULED ON STARBOARD TACK
A

TACKING OR COMING ABOUT
B

CLOSE HAULED ON PORT TACK
C

WIND

STARBOARD TACK
A

HEAD TO WIND (SAILS FLAPPING)
B

PORT TACK
C

JIBING

BROAD REACHING ON PORT TACK
A

JIBING
B

STARBOARD TACK
C

WIND

PORT TACK
A

MAINSAIL & JIB SWING ACROSS BOAT
B

STARBOARD TACK
C

quite flat. Very generally speaking, this is to within about 10 degrees or less of the boat's centerline. The average modern boat intended for day sailing or cruising-racing can be made to sail to within about 45 degrees of the wind. Strictly cruising types will not sail quite this close, but some racers will sail closer than this. Progress directly to windward (upwind) is accomplished by making a series of tacks, or zigzag courses, toward the windward destination. On the zig course, the sails lie to one side of the boat, and on the zag course, they are held by the wind to the boat's opposite side. With the sails on the starboard side and the wind blowing from the port side, the craft is said to be on the port tack, but she is on the starboard tack when the wind comes from the starboard side and the sails lie to port. Obviously, with an average boat that can point or head up to within 45 degrees of the wind, the highest heading on the starboard tack will be at right angles to the highest heading on the port tack. Other terms for beating are sailing close-hauled, sailing to windward, tacking, on the wind or hard on the wind, and by the wind. Full and by means beating, with the emphasis on keeping the sails full rather than on heading as close to the wind as possible.

There are two ways a boat can turn from one tack to the other. First, she may luff, or head up into the wind, and continue turning through the eye of the wind until her sails fill on the other tack. This is called coming about, or tacking. Second, she may bear off, or head away from the wind, until the wind is dead astern and then continue turning until the wind suddenly swings her sails across to the boat's opposite side. This is called jibing, or wearing ship. To put it simply, a tack is an upwind turn with the bow swinging across the wind, causing the sails to flap; but a jibe is a downwind turn with the stern crossing the wind and the sails suddenly filling on their opposite sides and swinging across the boat.

Prior to making the final tack when beating toward a windward destination, there arises the question of exactly when to tack in order to arrive at the mark in the quickest time without sailing any extra distance or having to make additional tacks. If the boat can be brought about at the proper moment so that she is pointed directly at the windward mark on her final tack, she is said to be fetching, or laying, the mark. This final approach tack which brings the close-hauled boat directly to the mark lies on an imaginary line called the fetch line, or lay line. If the helmsman

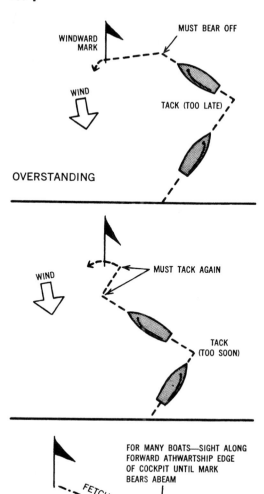

OVERSTANDING

FETCHING

Fetching the windward mark. Remember that a boat pointed and fetching a mark is on her fetch, or lay, line. To take advantage of wind shifts, do not sail up to the fetch line until fairly close to mark.

tacks his boat too soon, before reaching the fetch line, then he has understood the mark (he is heading below it). On the other hand, if he waits too long before tacking or sails beyond the fetch line, he has wasted time and distance. In this case he has overstood the

mark (he can head above it). Assuming that the boat can sail to within 45 degrees of the wind, then the proper time to tack is when the mark bears abeam, or lies at right angles to the boat's centerline, if there is no current (flow of water). The foregoing points have been concerned with only the final windward tack when approaching a mark. Planning windward courses and the general strategy of beating will be discussed in Section VI.

Aerodynamics of Sailing

What makes a sailboat sail? There are two simple laws of physics which you learned years ago in class and promptly forgot. The first law, translated into sailing terms, says that if a boat is sailing downwind, or running, the wind, being behind, simply pushes it along. To take advantage of this, the sail is positioned, or trimmed, so as to present its maximum resistance to the wind. Thus the sail should be roughly at right angles to the direction of the wind, no matter in what direction the boat itself is going.

The second law comes into effect when the boat is sailing against the wind. The sail now becomes an airfoil, just like the wing of an airplane. The wind exerts pushing pressure on the windward side, and pulls on the downwind side because of the vacuum thus created. The correct sail angle is approximately 45 degrees from the wind to take best advantage of this point of sailing. When a boat is on a reach, sailing across the wind, both pressures are at work at once and the boat goes fastest of all.

All possible points of sailing are thus covered. No boat will sail directly into the wind; most boats will not sail into the wind, or point, higher than about 45 degrees either side of the wind direction. A boat will sail, however, anywhere else in the other 270-degree area.

Now we come back to the hull of the boat. This hull floats in the water, displacing its own weight. Therefore, there is a certain amount of resistance which must be overcome before the hull will come in motion. When wind pressure is sufficient to overcome this drag, you sail. However, except when running directly before the wind, a third set of forces come into play. It is obvious that when the wind pushes on the sail it also pushes on the rest of the boat. Therefore, except when run-

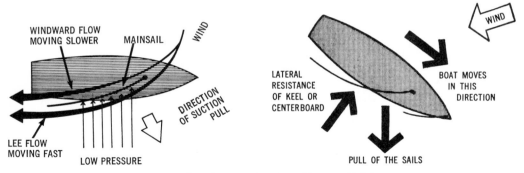

How the lee-side suction is obtained (left), and what makes the sailboat go (right).

ning, there will always be a sideways pressure on the hull. To overcome this, it is necessary to present enough counterbalancing force so that the boat will not sail sideways. The means of achieving this is accomplished by adding a keel, a centerboard, or a combination of the two to the underbody of the hull.

It is another simple physical law that wherever your stress is greatest, there you will need the greatest resistance to that stress. There is one point on the surface of your sail or sails where the force of the wind is centered. (This point is known as the center of effort of the sail plan.) Or, it may be stated to be the point where the force of the wind aft of the center of effort is equal to the force of the wind forward of that point. There is likewise a center of lateral resistance on keel or centerboard, and the position of these two points in relation to one another is most important in the design of a boat. (If this underwater extension is fixed, as was described in Section II, it is called a keel; if adjustable, so that it can be lowered or raised, it is known as a centerboard.) For instance, if the center of lateral resistance were near the middle of the boat, and the center of effort of the sail plan were toward the bow, the latter's tendency would be to rotate the bow away from the wind, the center of lateral resistance simply acting as an axis. (Such a boat is said to have a *lee helm*.) On the other hand, if the center of effort is behind the center of lateral resistance, the stern will go to leeward (away from the wind), and simultaneously bring the bow into the wind. (Such a boat is said to have a *weather helm*.) While theoretically any rotary motion could be prevented by having

the two centers directly beneath or above one another, actually most boats are designed with a slight weather helm. Thus, if you let the helm go for any reason, the boat sails gently and quietly up into the wind for safety.

The rudder is a flat perpendicular plane which is essentially a continuation of the keel. When it is directly in line with the keel, it contributes to the resistance to leeway and allows the craft to progress on her course. (The pressure on both sides of the rudder, caused by water flowing past the keel or hull, is equal.) When it is swung to one side or another by either tiller or wheel, one side of the rudder is more exposed to the force of the flowing water than the other, and an unequal or unbalanced effect is produced which pushes the stern around, thus causing the boat to swing from her original course and turn on its center of rotation. It is important to remember that there is a difference in steering with a tiller and with a wheel. A tiller is always pushed opposite to the direction the boat is to head. If you want to go to the port (left), you push to starboard (right) side; and vice versa. A wheel, used on larger craft, is turned in the direction you want to go. Turn it to the left and the boat steers to the port. Turn to the right and the craft steers to the starboard, like an automobile.

While the fundamental task of the keel or centerboard is to reduce the boat's chance of moving to leeward, and keep her moving forward, it has the additional important function of helping maintain the boat in an upright position when the wind, striking sidewise on the sail, might overturn it. Any sailboat, when pointing into the wind, has a natural tendency to heel, or lean to leeward. Since the lateral force of the wind is resisted below the water-line, this force acts on the sails, above the waterline, where some yielding to this force may be essential as a safety valve. But, too much heel to leeward is dangerous—and inefficient. By this we mean that the greater the angle of heel, the less sail area exposed to the wind. This is a safety factor because as a boat heels, it tends to spill the wind over the top of the sails—just as water would spill over a dam, if you tilted the dam. Usually before a boat heels far enough to overturn it will be spilling enough of the wind to keep from capsizing. However, too much heel cuts down on the effective drive of the sails. Hiking—crew leaning out on windward side of the boat—to the high side of the craft when it heels in strong winds not only keeps her more upright but keeps more sail in the wind for driving purposes.

While the hull shape, the rudder, and the keel all contribute to the necessary forward drive, the action of the wind on the sail or sails is the major factor. When properly drawing in the wind, a sail has a gently varying curve over its whole area. (This curve is called the *airfoil*.) The side facing the wind will take a concave form; the side away from the wind is convex, which permits the flowing wind to pass over this side of the sail quicker than it can on the windward side. As the wind strikes the sail, it divides and is caused to change direction. Thus, on the windward side we have an increased pressure and on the leeward side a decreased pressure. This difference in pressures on opposite sides of the sail creates forces that move the boat upwind; the force on the windward side pushing against a lesser or negative force contributes as much as 75 percent of the driving force when sailing as close to the wind as possible. In other words, only approximately 25 percent of the actual force of the wind is utilized in driving the craft forward, and of this, only a very small proportion is actual forward-driving force. Careful experiments in wind tunnels have shown that 75 percent of the pulling force driving a boat is derived from the suction, or negative pressure, on the lee-ward side of the sails. The combination of these two is what gets the boat to windward.

No craft will sail directly against the wind; the nearness with which it will sail against the wind is determined by a number of factors of hull and sail design. Most boats will sail about 4 points off the wind or at roughly a 45-degree angle to the wind's direction. It will be seen therefore that to sail a course against the wind, you must sail at a 45-degree angle from it, first in one direction and then in the other.

Jib Slot Effect. As stated in Section II, the sloop with the jib sail is the most popular type of sailboat afloat today. Besides furnishing some additional drive in itself, the principal function of the jib when sailing close to the wind is to guide the wind around the leeward side of the mainsail. If the wind were not so guided it would not flow evenly around the mainsail, and eddies, or "turbulence," would form on the leeward side. It is interesting to note that the slots on the wings of certain types of aircraft perform much the same function as the jib of a boat. This turbulence on the leeward, after side of a sail is indicated by the flapping of the sail. It may be caused by a badly setting sail—one that has perhaps stretched out of shape—or by a badly trimmed jib. Thus the jib performs the function of a slot and, in addition, by blanketing the mast (which always causes back eddies of wind), it improves very greatly the efficiency of the sail; this is because the thin forward edge (luff) of the jib makes a good "entry" into the wind, causing little or no back eddies. This guidance of the wind is called the "slot effect," and greatly improves the performance of the boat by directing the wind into the area behind the mainsail, thus increasing the suction, or pulling, effect.

As stated earlier in this section, when a boat moves ahead faster and faster, the wind will appear to draw more and more ahead, and it will be under the influence of this apparent wind that any forward movement will continue. The apparent wind, whose direction is most important to the sailor when handling his boat, will continue to draw ahead until the water resistance set up by the hull form of the boat to any forward movement exactly balances the forward-acting force. When this point is reached the only way in which an increase of speed can be obtained is by increasing the amount of sail carried (assuming that

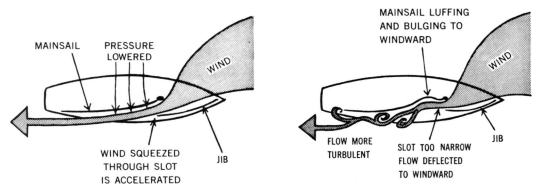

How the jib affects the slot action and what jib backwind causes.

the wind remains constant) and so pushing back the point of balance between the drive of the wind and the resistance of the water. Your wind pennant or telltales show the true wind when your craft is stationary. But, when she is moving, the pennant indicates the apparent wind.

The man at the tiller or wheel must not only keep an eye on the wind but must also watch the water. Very rarely do the wind and the waves come from exactly the same direction. Generally steering is easier, and the helmsman will have far greater control, when the waves are running toward the boat and she takes them on the bow.

In addition to the waves, you must consider the effect of tide and current. Rivers flow in only one direction, but in salt water, tide and current flow in one way for a certain number of hours and in the next period they flow in the opposite direction. You should know which way the tide and current are going so that you can use them to your advantage. For instance, when starting a brief sail it is generally wise to sail against the tide so that when you are heading back you will be moving with the tide and will get a lift from it. Tides and currents will be covered more thoroughly in Section V.

TRIMMING, BENDING, AND HOISTING SAILS

A sail is trimmed with its sheet. Let us review briefly the general sail positions for each point of sailing. When running, a sail is let all the way out; when beam reaching, it is about halfway out or somewhat closer; when broad reaching, the sail should lie somewhere between the running and beam-reaching positions; when close reaching, it should lie between the beam-reaching position and its closest point of trim; and when beating, the sail should be trimmed in almost as far as it will come. These are only approximate positions. Exact positions will depend on the strength of the breeze, the design of the boat, the cut of her sails, the boat speed, and the size of the seas.

How to Trim Properly. As said earlier in the section, sails are always trimmed to the apparent wind. The faster a boat travels, espe-

cially when she is beam reaching, the closer her sheets must be trimmed. When she is beating, the difference between the true and apparent wind will not be very great in either direction, but there will be a great difference in velocity. On this point of sailing the boat speed wind is added to true wind, which increases the apparent wind speed. When running, however, the boat speed wind is subtracted from the true wind to give a decreased apparent wind. There is no directional change in the apparent wind when a boat runs dead before the wind; therefore in all breezes on this point of sailing the mainsail should be let out until the boom almost touches the after shroud. When trimming sails, always refer to the telltales or wind indicator, because these give the apparent wind direction.

The simplest way to obtain proper trim on

a reach is to slack the sheets until the sail begins to luff, then the sheet is pulled in until the sail stops luffing. It is usually better to err on the side of trimming the sails too far out than too far in. A sail that is trimmed too far in will stall (lose sail effectiveness) and, in addition, causes extra heeling. A sail that is trimmed too far out, although not correct, at least will be in such a position that the suction pull, on the sail's leeward side, has a more favorable angle with the boat's centerline to pull her ahead instead of sideways. It is usually advantageous to keep the sail on edge, so that it is just on the verge of luffing. This is when the sail is most effective. In order to do this while holding a straight course on a reach, the sheets must be tended constantly. Especially when racing, the sheets should be played or adjusted for every wind shift and every puff or lull.

On the beat, sail trim is not changed so often as when reaching. This is because the helmsman changes his course more often to conform with changes of wind direction and velocity. However, when there are great variations in wind speed, sheets should be slacked slightly during the lulls and tightened during puffs. There are two exceptions to this rule. In heavy breezes when the boat is overburdened (carrying too much sail), the mainsheet should be eased so that it carries a slight luff. The other exception is that when sailing into a rough sea which tends to slow the boat, sheets should be started, and the helmsman should bear off slightly to keep the boat moving at fairly good speed.

When we consider sail trim, as previously stated in Section II, the location of the sheet's lead must also be considered as well as its in-and-out adjustment. Most leads are mounted in such a way that their location (fore and aft and/or athwartships) can be changed slightly to give the sheet the most favorable angle of trim for various sailing conditions. For instance, the correct lead for the working jib in the fore-and-aft location should be at a point where neither the foot nor the leech is stretched excessively tight. A tight leech, caused by a lead which is too far forward, almost closes the upper part of the slot, or space, between the jib and the mainsail, thereby restricting the air flow, and the leech deflects the flow into the lee side of the main-

sail producing harmful backwind. A loose leech, on the other hand, opens the slot aloft too much, so that the space between the jib's leech and the mainsail's luff is too wide, thereby harming the efficiency of the wind's driving effect. A correct jib lead is placed so that neither the jib's leech nor the foot is stretched excessively tight when the sail is trimmed in flat. It is often very helpful to gauge the fore-and-aft lead position by its relationship to a projection of the jib's miter seam. The correct lead position for most working jibs lies slightly forward of the point where the miter seam projection strikes the deck. When the sheet of the average close-hauled jib is properly led, the sail will first begin to luff along the general area just above the miter seam. If the jib's luff begins to shake below the miter seam, the lead is usually too far forward; but if the luff shakes aloft near the sail's head, the lead is too far aft. When reaching, with the mainsheet slacked off, it sometimes pays to move the jib lead slightly farther aft than its normal position for beating. This is done to help prevent the upper mainsail from being backwinded by the jib. In addition to the fore-and-aft sheet lead, we must consider the athwartships position, or how far inboard or outboard the lead is located. On many fast, narrow racing boats the jib lead should be placed on an imaginary line from the bow that forms an angle of about 10 degrees with the boat's centerline, but for the average day sailer with moderate beam, 12 degrees is a more realistic angle. Actually, this angular measurement should be used only as a guide. The exact athwartships point of trim should be decided upon only after experimentation. It should be located as far inboard as possible without causing the jib to backwind the mainsail when the sails are trimmed in flat for beating.

Genoa-Jib Trim. The genoa jib is nearly always led from an adjustable slide on a track which is mounted on the boat's rail; thus there is no athwartships adjustment but only a fore-and-aft choice for the lead position. This jib lies outside the shrouds; when the average genoa is trimmed in flat for beating, its foot lies snugly against the shrouds while its upper leech lies an inch or less from the end of the spreaders (the struts which hold the shrouds away from the mast). Of course, the genoa

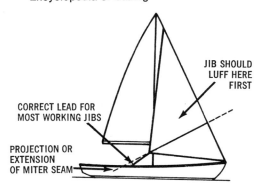

CORRECT LEAD FOR
MOST WORKING JIBS

JIB SHOULD
LUFF HERE
FIRST

PROJECTION OR
EXTENSION
OF MITER SEAM

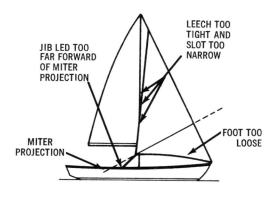

JIB LED TOO
FAR FORWARD
OF MITER
PROJECTION

LEECH TOO
TIGHT AND
SLOT TOO
NARROW

FOOT TOO
LOOSE

MITER
PROJECTION

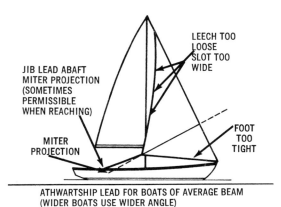

JIB LEAD ABAFT
MITER PROJECTION
(SOMETIMES
PERMISSIBLE
WHEN REACHING)

LEECH TOO
LOOSE
SLOT TOO
WIDE

FOOT
TOO
TIGHT

MITER
PROJECTION

ATHWARTSHIP LEAD FOR BOATS OF AVERAGE BEAM
(WIDER BOATS USE WIDER ANGLE)

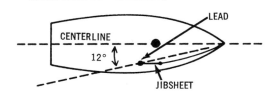

LEAD

CENTERLINE

12°

JIBSHEET

Jibsheet leads.

lead position will vary according to the size and shape of the particular jib, the position of the shrouds, the length of the spreaders, and the position of the lifelines around the boat. Most authorities say that the lead should be located slightly abaft the miter projection; however, some genoas are more effective when the lead lies at the point where the projection strikes the rail or even slightly forward of this point. As previously said, a little more backwind can be expected from a genoa than from a working jib, therefore, with a genoa, it is not usually harmful to carry a very slight shake in the lower luff of the mainsail, especially in a fresh breeze.

As with a working jib, the genoa's leech becomes tight when its lead is too far forward; but when the lead is too far aft, the leech becomes loose. It is usually better to favor the loose leech, because the tight leech will cause excessive backwind. However, a leech which is too loose will often develop an annoying flutter. Some authorities say that a leech flutter does no real harm; nevertheless, it should be minimized or stopped if possible. Sliding the lead forward slightly will help. If your genoa has a leech line (a light adjustable line sewn into the leech), this can be tightened slightly to help eliminate the flutter. However, great care should be taken not to overtighten the leech line, as this can cause a tight, curling leech which can be very harmful aerodynamically.

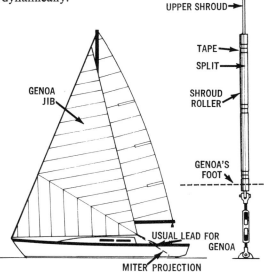

UPPER SHROUD

TAPE
SPLIT

SHROUD
ROLLER

GENOA
JIB

GENOA'S
FOOT

USUAL LEAD FOR
GENOA

MITER PROJECTION

Genoa-jib lead and shroud roller.

Quite often chafing problems arise from constant sailing with a genoa. If the spreader ends touch the sail, it should have a reinforcing patch (an extra piece of cloth) sewn over the weak or rubbed area. This is especially true if the spreaders touch a sail seam because the stitching will soon chafe through. Also the spreader ends should be wrapped with felt or some soft material. The genoa foot will usually rub on the shrouds, therefore the outboard and forward shrouds should be equipped with shroud rollers. These are split tubes of wood or plastic which are taped closed on the shrouds so that the tubes can roll and minimize chafe to the jibs or sheets. Rollers will also speed up tacking because there is less friction when the jib wipes across the shrouds as the boat turns through the eye of the wind.

Mainsheet leads can only be adjusted athwartships because this sail is attached to a boom, and so there would be little point in having a fore-and-aft adjustment. When beating in light airs the mainsheet lead should be kept near the centerline of the boat. This will permit the boom to lift a little which will give the sail maximum draft. At the same time, of course, the sheet should be eased. When beating in a fresh breeze, the mainsheet should be moved to a position farther outboard where the sheet can pull the sail down as well as in. This will tend to flatten the sail and give it a more desirable draft for a good breeze. One word of caution, however: do not lead the mainsheet very far outboard when carrying a genoa, because this will tend to close the slot and increase jib backwind.

Bending Sails Properly. Although sail construction and fitting details often vary with different boats, the procedure for bending sails (putting them on) is basically the same for all boats. When bending on a jib or staysail, we start with the tack, which is fastened to the stem-head fitting (a metal fitting with eyes at the top of the seam) or some other eye fitting at the lower end of the jibstay. The tack is secured with a shackle (a U-shaped fastener), which is usually closed with a screw or twist pin or spring-loaded piston. The jib is usually hooked to its stay with piston hanks or snap hooks unless it is set flying (set without being hooked to a stay). When snapping on the hanks or hooks, we start at the sail's

tack and work toward the head, being sure that the hanks all face the same way so that they are not twisted. Then we shackle on the halyard to the head and attach the sheets to the clew. After the sheets are run through their lead blocks, figure-eight knots should be tied in the very ends of the lines to prevent them from accidentally being pulled back through the blocks.

On most boats the mainsail is held to the mast and boom by one of two means: slides on a track, or with grooved spars. When the spars are grooved, the sail's bolt rope (a rope sewn to the edge of the luff and foot) is fed into the boom groove as the clew is pulled aft, and then the bolt rope is fed into the mast groove as the sail is hoisted. In some cases, small plastic cylinders are fastened to a sail's luff or foot and these are fed into the grooves. In any event, in bending on the luff of a mainsail, it is obviously necessary to start with the head and work down toward the tack. Also it is necessary to work from clew to tack when bending on the foot. The second edge of the sail (luff or foot) to be bent should be run through the hands to see that the sail is not twisted before the bending is completed. Next the battens should be inserted. They should be shorter than their batten pockets by an inch or more. A sail equipped with batten pockets should not be used without the battens being inserted.

When bending on the mainsail, make certain that the pins in the tack and clew fittings are so placed that they hold the foot of the sail in a straight line on the boom. The sail was built to be set in this way and is bound to be less than perfect if it angles up or down at the tack or clew. Before hoisting, take up on the topping lift so that it will bear the weight of the boom; in a small boat that is not equipped with a topping lift, have someone hold up the boom. Failure to do this results in an unnecessary strain on the sail.

Checking Your Sails. When most sailmakers go aboard to check the fit of sails, the first observation they usually make is to squint up the mast track to make sure the spar is straight. If it is not, the sail cannot set correctly. Most sailors check their masts from time to time but comparatively few pay the same attention to the boom. Yet the boom is of equal importance to the set of the sail.

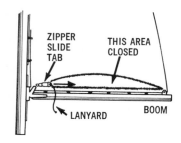

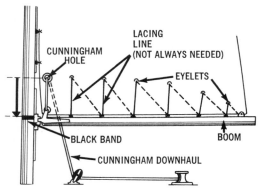

Two methods of improving sail draft. The Cunningham cringle, or hole, method is popular with racing skippers.

While someone is sailing your boat to windward, go forward and sight along the top of the boom, using the gooseneck much as you would a rifle sight. A curve in the boom may be eliminated merely by a change in the lead of the mainsail sheet, but sometimes it may be necessary to replace the boom with a heavier or less rubbery one. Unless you feel qualified to cope with the problem, get an expert's advice.

Battens are a nuisance at best, but they do help to make a well-fitting sail; and they permit the sailmaker to put roach into the leech, which gives a sail a little greater area than it otherwise would have. Before the advent of crosscut sails, when the seams ran parallel to the leech, battens were used only in exceptional cases. Even today a nonbattened sail has its points for cruising, but such sails are not often seen. Many substitutes for the good old ash batten now are used including aluminum, pressed wood, plastic, and fiberglass.

Battens should be an inch or more short of the full length of the pocket and should be an easy, not a tight, fit. They should taper fore and aft; the thinner, more flexible part is the leading end. Well-made battens should have all edges and corners carefully rounded and sanded smooth and should be either varnished or treated with linseed oil. (The oil treatment must be applied months before the batten is to be used, for oil dries slowly and undried oil may stain the sails.) When batten pockets are provided with small lanyards, these should be passed through the hole in the end of the batten, through the grommet in the opposite side of the pocket, and securely tied into a multiple square knot (not a bow). Tie it four, five, or six times to minimize the possibility that the lanyard will work loose when you bring the boat about or when she lies head to the wind. Dot fasteners have been tried as substitutes for batten ties or lanyards, but they are not in general use. Many modern sails are made with pockets which need no tying, hold the batten in place, yet are so constructed that battens can easily be slipped in or out. This sounds paradoxical but it works well. The pocket at the leech end is curved upward and left open for a short distance so the batten can be inserted or removed by flexing the sail and sliding the batten in or out over the top of the stitched part. This is a really improved pocket and takes a lot of the curse out of the use of battens.

As previously stated, the jib should aid and not destroy the forces creating drive. A jib that sets well always helps the performance of a mainsail. It increases the wind speed and smooths out the wind flow on the leeward side of the larger mainsail, thereby increasing the speed of the boat. When the jib is raised the halyard must be snugged up tight so no wrinkles or loops form in the luff. This leading edge, the first to strike the wind when under way, must always be kept taut. Should the luff hang loose, the shape of the sail is detroyed. It will lose much of its driving power, especially when sailing into the wind. It is most important that the jib be set up correctly, not only for the greater efficiency derived but because most skippers sail by the actions of a taut luff. From its actions, whether shivering, violently shaking, or quietly full, they can tell whether they are sailing correctly.

It is a good idea to mark, as a frame of reference, all the sheets and other adjustable rigging and hardware at appropriate spots so that you will have a continuing frame of reference every time you set or trim a sail. If your boat moved well with the sails set to certain marks, you can easily duplicate the settings on a similar day.

Balance and How to Improve It

As previously mentioned, helm balance has to do with the ability of a boat to hold a straight course when her helm is left alone. If she tends to head up into the wind, she has a weather helm; but if she heads away from the wind, she has a lee helm. Every boat should be designed or tuned (properly adjusted) to carry a slight weather helm in all but the lightest breezes. A slight weather helm makes it easier for the helmsman to feel his boat, and also it is a built-in safety device; because, if the helmsman should happen to leave or lose his grip on the helm, the boat will automatically round up into the wind where she will lose headway and gain stability.

Furthermore, it has been found that a slight weather helm when beating actually boosts a boat to windward. If a rudder which is attached to the trailing edge of a keel is held at a yaw angle of from 3 to 6 degrees from the boat's centerline, depending on the design, the keel-rudder combination will act as a hydrofoil and create a lateral lifting force. Of course, too much weather helm can be very harmful because a rudder which is held over too far will partially stall and create a great amount of drag. When this happens the rudder acts as a brake.

Improper balance is seldom extreme in a one-design class boat or boats designed by rec-ognized naval architects, but many individual boats have minor helm faults which can be corrected by various minor adjustments. Most of these adjustments—raking the mast, raising or lowering the centerboard, moving crew weight, and setting larger or smaller sails forward or aft—will change the boat's balance sufficiently.

There is a possibility, however, that one or two of these adjustments may be harmful to the boat's speed even though her helm is improved. For example, setting a smaller jib in light air to help correct a lee helm might cause a loss of speed. Therefore, care should be taken to see that helm balance is not improved at the expense of overall performance. The first correction to be made when a boat is improperly balanced is to change the angle of heel. The severe weather helm often experienced when sailing in a blow is due mainly to an extreme angle of heel. This can be lessened by hiking or putting the crew as far as possible to windward and also by carrying a slight luff in the mainsail while the jib is trimmed flat.

The ballast of your boat can have an effect on the helm. In most keel boats the ballast is usually sealed inside the shell of the hull, and, unless the boat is being raced, the live ballast (your crew) and gear on board are usually of little concern. But, in the smaller day sailer and sailing dinghy, you must make sure that her fore-and-aft trim is correct. A modern day sailer is designed so that the crew members may be in their normal sailing positions and maintain the trim, but there has to be some adjustment for the conditions and for the relative weight of helmsman and crew. A properly trimmed craft should have a clean wake, her transom just dipping below the surface of the water, and the wake streaming away smoothly without eddies or bubbling.

Tuning the Rigging

Tuning the standing rigging can be a complicated and sometimes controversial procedure. A detailed study will not be attempted here but simply an introduction to the generally accepted rules. A common-sense rule is to adjust the shrouds so that the mast is held up vertically, at right angles to the deck near the partners, when the boat is viewed from

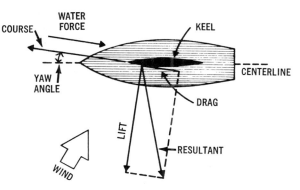

Yaw angle and its resultant forces.

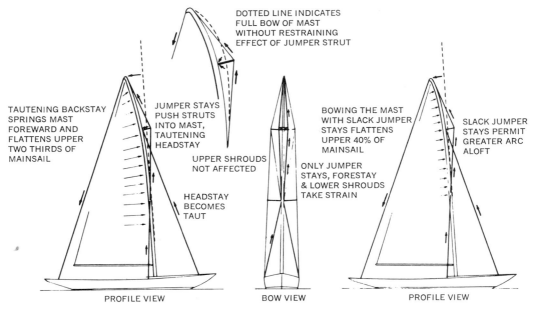

DOTTED LINE INDICATES
FULL BOW OF MAST
WITHOUT RESTRAINING
EFFECT OF JUMPER STRUT

TAUTENING BACKSTAY
SPRINGS MAST
FOREWARD AND
FLATTENS UPPER
TWO THIRDS OF
MAINSAIL

JUMPER STAYS
PUSH STRUTS
INTO MAST,
TAUTENING
HEADSTAY

UPPER SHROUDS
NOT AFFECTED

HEADSTAY
BECOMES
TAUT

BOWING THE MAST
WITH SLACK JUMPER
STAYS FLATTENS
UPPER 40% OF
MAINSAIL

ONLY JUMPER
STAYS, FORESTAY
& LOWER SHROUDS
TAKE STRAIN

SLACK JUMPER
STAYS PERMIT
GREATER ARC
ALOFT

PROFILE VIEW   BOW VIEW   PROFILE VIEW

Bending the mast.

her bow or stern. When the boat heels, of course, the mast will be supported by the windward shrouds only, and they will tighten, which will cause the leeward shrouds to slacken considerably. In this case, the mast will not be exactly at right angles to the deck, but it should be nearly so. From this same view (from the bow or stern), the mast should be kept straight. This requires that the lower shrouds be kept slightly more slack than the upper shrouds, because the latter are longer, pass over a spreader, and therefore have more stretch when the boat heels. Lateral bends and S curves in a mast can be very harmful to the set of its sail.

Another fundamental of tuning is to keep the jibstay or headstay taut. This is essential to good windward performance. In order to keep these forward stays taut, naturally the permanent backstay must be kept taut to counteract the pull of the forward stays; and if the boat has running backstays, which pull directly behind the jibstay, these must be kept taut alternately when beating. Jumper stays on a seven-eighths rig should be kept taut if it is desired that the mast be kept straight when it is viewed from the side.

Mast Bending. It has already been mentioned that there are certain occasions when masts are intentionally bent aft in order to alter draft. This is common practice with certain small-boat classes. Actually when a mast is bent so that its top leans aft and its lower portion, below the jibstay point of attachment, bows forward, then the sail is stretched fore and aft abaft the luff, and this flattens the draft. Boats with "bendy" rigs carry very full mainsails on straight spars in light airs or rough seas, but sail with bent spars in a good breeze to reduce the draft. If the boat is equipped with jumper stays and a permanent backstay, the former can be slacked while the latter is tightened to achieve a bend. In some very small boats with limber masts and few stays, bending the mast may be accomplished simply by tightening the boom vang or sheet.

Mast bending works very well in many cases, but there should be a few words of warning. Sails must be specially cut for flexible spars. If the sail is cut for a straight mast, it will often be badly distorted if carried on a bent mast. A mast should rarely be bent in light airs as this is when full draft is needed. Also, it is usually not wise to attempt bending a mast which has a headstay to the masthead because of difficulties in pulling the masthead aft without putting a compression bend in the mast, changing the normal set of the jib, and having a slack headstay and upper shrouds because the top of the mast will be lower when it is bent. As a general rule, it is wise not to attempt bending the spars of any large cruising-racing yacht. The result could be the loss of a mast.

Standing-rigging Adjustment. Standing rigging is adjusted with turnbuckles. Once the shrouds are adjusted correctly, they should be left alone for most of the sailing season with only an occasional tightening if the rigging stretches; therefore shroud turnbuckles should be locked with cotter pins. Do not forget to wrap the cotter pins with tape. Stay turnbuckles, however, might need more frequent adjustment; therefore it is often wise to use lock nuts at the top and bottom of the turnbuckle barrels to prevent them from becoming unscrewed accidentally. Headstays and jibstays often have a lot of lateral movement due to the side pressure of a jib or staysail; thus it is important that, on large boats at least, these stays be fitted with toggles. A toggle is a small fitting with a pin which makes a movable joint between the bottom of the turnbuckle and its eye, stem-head fitting, or other point of attachment. Without a toggle, the lower jaws of a turnbuckle are subject to breakage through metal fatigue.

The question of how tight to set up the rigging is an often debated one. Rigging that is too loose allows the mast to jump around and move too much in a seaway, but on the other hand, rigging that is too tight often seems to kill a boat's speed, and it puts unnecessary strain and stress on the hull. Almost everyone agrees that the jibstay or headstay should be taut for windward sailing, but these should not be so taut that they put great strain on the stem or that they put compression bends in the mast. When tightening up the headstay, sight up the mast track, on the after side of the mast, to see that no bend is developing. Sight from aft forward and also from the side.

For most boats, shrouds should not be any tighter than they have to be to hold the mast nearly at right angles to the deck (when viewed from the bow or stern) when the boat is heeled. In other words, the mast should not be allowed to lean too far to leeward. As for the amount of rake in a mast (the amount it leans fore and aft when viewed from the side), most boats are designed to carry a slight rake aft. This usually makes the mainsail hang better (provided the after end of her boom is not too low) and it also causes the jibstay to stand better, allowing a minimum of sag. The question of rake, however, will depend primarily on the balance of the boat as mentioned in the last section. If the boat has too little weather helm or a lee helm, her mast should be raked fairly far aft; but with too much weather helm, the mast should be almost vertical and in some rare cases, raked slightly forward of the vertical.

A few last words of advice about rigging: a spreader should be adjusted so that the angles between the shroud and spreader above and below are exactly equal. Failure to do this can cause the spreader to slip, which could result in the loss of the mast. Get in the habit of checking fittings for cracks, wear, or fatigue. Particularly, check lock nuts which often seem to come loose. Avoid or at least be very cautious about making rigging adjustments while under way. Rigging on the leeward side is normally quite slack when a boat is heeled, and it is easy to adjust it too tight, which can destroy the proper tune and put a great strain on the boat.

GETTING UNDER WAY

Leaving the Mooring

To get to your boat on a mooring or at anchor, of course you can use a tender or dinghy. Generally it is rowed, or powered by a small outboard motor. Upon leaving the dock, aim your tender to pass other boats just astern rather than to cut close across their bows. Look out for mooring lines, which may hold you up. To make a direct crossing of an anchorage with a strong tide running, it may be necessary to point the boat obliquely up tide, that is, into the tide, for the crossing.

Unless there is an adverse stronger tide to contend with, the sailboat will always be facing into the wind while at her mooring. Thus, if you approach the moored craft from aft you will also be pointing into the wind (or tide), which will act as a brake. When coming alongside, ship one oar and make your dinghy's painter (a short line attached to the tender's stem) fast to a cleat on the deck. Be sure to make fast as soon as possible and put out fenders from your dinghy. The dinghy may be towed or may be secured to the sailboat's mooring; it will probably be used to get back ashore.

On arriving at your moored boat, check to see that the tiller is firmly in place, the centerboard (if you have one) lowered to its desired sailing position, and all sheets coiled so that they will run freely through the blocks. If there is a topping lift, take up on it until the boom has lifted from its crotch (if it has one). Remove the crotch and stow it where you will not fall over it while out on the water. Also be sure to stow it where none of the running rigging can get tangled about it. Then bend on the mainsail or remove the sail covers.

When you are leaving your mooring, it is well to plan in advance in which direction you intend to sail. Let us say that there are several boats close to your port side, so you decide to go off to starboard—in other words, on a port tack. With both sails hoisted, haul in the starboard jibsheet, taking up all the slack. Push the clew of the jib to port; the wind will fill the sail and force the bow of the boat to starboard. Untie your mooring line; but before casting off, walk back with it along the port deck. This will throw the boat's bow to starboard and bring the wind over the port side. As soon as the boat begins to swing around, let go of the mooring line. Swing the tiller to port; this will help push the nose of the boat to starboard. Then trim the mainsail by taking in the mainsheet until the sail is fairly flat. As the jib pushes the boat around, the mainsail will fill and the boat will move forward. As your boat begins to make headway, bring the tiller back to starboard, so that the craft doesn't fall off too much. When the boat is on the desired course, bring the tiller amidships (to the center).

In casting off the mooring line make certain that everything is clear. In the above example, let us assume you go out to your mooring in a dinghy. Your mooring line should be over the starboard bow and your dinghy's painter taken aft and brought around forward

on the port side outside all shrouds and stays. Then pass it around the bow to the starboard side and secure it to the mooring line. By following this procedure you will not have any fouling of lines when casting off. To help in all this sort of close-quarters work, the rudder may or may not be of much use. Bear in mind that a rudder is of little value unless the boat is either moving through the water at an appreciable speed or (and this is a point too often ignored) fast to her mooring with a current flowing by her.

If the wind is light, the current sometimes may have more effect on a boat lying to a mooring than the wind, and, instead of finding the boat lying head to wind when you board her, you may find her heading into the current with her stern to the wind, or tailing to the wind, or "tide rode," as it is called. In other words, the current and wind are in opposite directions from each other. In such a situation, it is best to leave the mooring under the jib alone. But you should get the gaskets or stops off the mainsail to be ready to hoist it promptly, then set the jib, sheet it on the side opposite to which you intend to sail out, cast off the mooring, and, under jib alone, sail before the wind or with the wind on the quarter until you have gotten into clear water. Then, when there are no boats or other obstructions to interfere with the maneuver, hoist the mainsail as quickly as possible, first putting the boat's head as much into the wind as it will go by shoving the tiller down and letting go the jibsheet. When the mainsail is set, both sails can be sheeted in and the boat will gather headway immediately. Remember, however, that the boat will drift some, and the tide may turn you, so allow sea room. Put the jib aback so that the bow falls off. Now, with all the sail up, sail on a reach to again pick up momentum. A yawl is perfect in this respect. With everything furled but the mizzen, such a boat will head up and, if moored, lie more or less quietly awaiting your next move. If she is adrift, she will still lie up into the wind and drift astern. If there are exceptions to this rule, they will occur when the wind is light and the current strong.

If the wind is across the tide you can adopt either of the two previously mentioned methods. You will usually be able to hoist the mainsail, but you will have to let the sheet well out, to prevent the sail's filling before you are ready to move. All you have to do to get under way is to cast off the mooring and at the same time haul in your sheets.

Getting away from a mooring at a crowded anchorage can sometimes become a ticklish undertaking. Before attaining proper sea room and speed, the question frequently arises whether to attempt to pass ahead or astern of other craft at anchor or moored. It is always safer to pass astern under crowded conditions, as wind and current leeway could readily set you back to foul mooring buoys and lines, or even the boat itself, if you attempt to pass ahead of other boats with insufficient clearance. When maneuvering in a crowded anchorage remember that you must be on constant alert. Winds may quickly go flat and fail, leaving the boat to drift. While the speed of drift will be low, the boat may collide with others, and the crew can do little to prevent contact. The simplest scheme is to hold the boats apart by hands and feet, boat hook, and fenders as they pass and secure a bow line to the moored craft as you go by. This will serve to check the drifting and hold you safely astern of the other boat until the wind freshens and you can again make headway and get clear. If there should be no moored vessel in reach there is of course no danger of contact; then it might be practical to grab a mooring and hold on until again able to proceed.

None of the remarks about the difficulty of getting under way in a crowded anchorage or from a wind-stoppered bottleneck apply if you have auxiliary power on board. You then start the engine, motor out to a less crowded area, and get up your sails in a leisurely manner. Details on auxiliary operation are given later in this section.

Sailing Away from a Dock

It is usually more difficult to cast off from a dock than to clear a mooring mainly due to the fact that there are generally more boats close at hand. Actually it is not too hard to leave a dock when the craft is to leeward or when she is headed to the wind. In these cases, cast off her stern line and springs so she can swing into the wind. After the sails are hoisted and the boat is ready to leave, she is shoved straight back with the rudder amid-

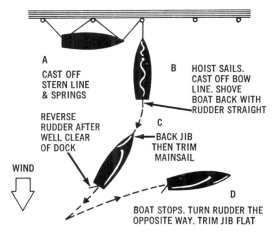

A
CAST OFF
STERN LINE
& SPRINGS

REVERSE
RUDDER AFTER
WELL CLEAR
OF DOCK

WIND

B   HOIST SAILS.
CAST OFF BOW
LINE. SHOVE
BOAT BACK WITH
RUDDER STRAIGHT

C
BACK JIB
THEN TRIM
MAINSAIL

D
BOAT STOPS. TURN RUDDER THE
OPPOSITE WAY. TRIM JIB FLAT

Leaving a dock.

ships (held straight or on dead center). When she is well clear of the dock, the rudder is put over to the right or left to swing the bow in the opposite direction (since the boat has sternway). The sails will begin to draw because the boat will turn so that the wind is broad on the bow. Putting the helm over too soon will result in the boat gaining headway too soon, which might cause her to strike the dock before she can be turned away from it. After the boat has stopped drifting backward, the helm is turned the opposite way because the boat will begin to move ahead as her sails fill. The jib should be backed or pulled in by its windward sheet so that it is trimmed from the wrong side. This will cause the bow to fall off, away from the wind, very rapidly. When the boat has gained headway and if she is clear of the dock, the windward jibsheet is released and the jib is trimmed on the boat's proper side.

There are just a few times when it might be advisable to hoist sail downwind instead of when head to wind. These might occur in a very constricted docking area. In these cases it is often best to drift with the wind or current or sail away under jib alone until the boat is clear of docks and obstructions, and then head as close to the wind as possible before hoisting the mainsail.

Leaving the windward side of a dock under sail presents a problem usually. The boat must be moved so that she is headed into the wind when sails are hoisted. She might be moved by warping (moving her with lines) or kedging with the anchor, or by paddling if the boat is small and the wind is light. No matter how she is moved, her bow should be fairly near the wind. If she cannot be brought directly head to wind, great care should be taken to see that booms do not strike anything on the dock and that sheets do not catch on dock pilings (posts) or cleats.

Sailing off the Beach

Sailing off the beach is becoming very popular in many sections of the United States, thanks to better designed trailers for sailboats. But, getting your boat afloat and away from the beach or launching ramp is far tougher than sailing away from a dock or buoy. Most important is teamwork of crew and skipper; split-second timing means the difference between getting away from the shoal water smoothly or chaotically racking your boat up on the beach, especially if there is any kind of sea.

Recognizing the initial problems comes first. The rudder cannot be shipped (unless it is the flip-up type) and the centerboard cannot be dropped in shoal water. This lack of steering and leeway control is compounded by an initial lack of speed—especially in a rolling surf. Also, unless there is a following, or at least a beam wind, the absence of centerboard and rudder will make itself felt acutely. Then there is the problem of getting aboard; wet pants are no fun. But, again, a little sense solves a lot of problems.

Look around—maybe there is an alternative to where you are standing. It is easier to get off if there is a beam wind; an inlet, promontory, or creek on the beach might permit a beam-wind takeoff if the wind is blowing onto the beach. And remember these axioms: the boat will be hard to steer in the first few moments; get up speed as soon as possible; and do not sheet in hard on the sails. Use your sails for driving and steering. If your boat's light enough, carry it bows first instead of dragging it if you have no dolly, if the wind's on the beach. With a stern wind, roll or carry it in backward. A beam wind calls for turning the boat parallel to the shoreline once it is in the water.

Now the teamwork becomes important. Generally, the skipper should hold the boat head to wind, by the stern, if the wind's on the beach. The crew should hop aboard first, clear the centerboard for dropping, and hoist the sails, while making that last-minute check of the equipment. The skipper should ship the rudder if it has a flip-up blade and then push the boat off, hopping in as he does so. Steering and picking up speed are crucial at this point. Use the jib for drive, the mainsail for steering. Without a centerboard, control of heeling is important. Crew and skipper placement is vital here: the crew should be amidships, feet spread wide and body bent to dodge the boom, the skipper aft in the same position. At this point the crew should be ready to alter the heeling angle by judicious weight-shifting, and be ready to jump overside before the boat should go aground. The helmsman *could* use a paddle to steer, but the sails must be looked to.

Sail-steering is simpler than it sounds. Sheeting in the jib will make the boat bear down, while sheeting in the main and letting off the jib will make her luff up. Heeling to windward will make her bear down; heeling to leeward will make her luff. Never use a paddle to pick up speed; use the jib. Even with a couple of stalwarts paddling up a gale, speed reached with paddles is never enough, except when the water is glassy calm, to get into deeper water where the board and rudder can be used.

Getting off with the wind abeam is a rather simple matter; it is easy to pick up speed, and your boat will make little leeway. First, once the crew and skipper are aboard, the sheets loose and the boat parallel to the shore, sheet the jib normally, just enough to prevent luffing, with the mainsail well out and luffing. The boat will try to pay off under the jib to a broad reach, then the main will fill and speed up the boat, making her luff to the lifting point. Then start the cycle over again, repeating it until deep enough water is reached to ship the rudder and drop the centerboard. During the cycle, the boat should be heeled only slightly to leeward to keep from turning into the wind. Too much speed induces weather helm, and without rudder the boat might drop into irons; so sheet the sails judiciously.

With the wind astern, the prime difficulty in escaping the beach is going slowly enough.

The boat should be run in stern first, then the crew hops aboard and hoists the sails while the helmsman pushes her out. After the boat is out far enough, the skipper should work the boat around by pulling her in and pivoting her by the stern, then hop in over the transom. The sheets should be let out on the run (remember, the wind will pick up the farther you get away from the shore); then, on a bit of offing, luff up gently while sheeting the mainsail well in. With the wind then abeam or full and by, the helmsman should kneel facing aft and ship the rudder, while the crew looks to the sheet-steering.

Getting off into the wind is tougher. Common sense, again, dictates that the skipper and crew find, if possible, a point on the beach to enable the boat, hopefully, to leave on a close reach and be able to get off on a broad reach to pick up speed and luff again, all the time edging out to a point beyond the surf which will give the skipper and crew a chance to get the board and rudder down pronto. Make up your mind on which tack to go out. One is usually better than the other, since the wind is rarely perfectly perpendicular to the beach, and the best position is to the windward in order to benefit from a beam wind—or as close to it as possible. If the shore is not a straight line, of course the best places to launch would be where the wind is as close to abeam as possible. But if the wind *is* at right angles to a straight beach, the problems are greatest. In either case, try to get off from a place where the rollers are smallest, such as near a promontory or jetty. Deeper water throws smaller rollers, especially where sandbars lie offshore. Smaller rollers usually mean lessened wind as well.

The boat should be launched bows first as the crew readies the centerboard and hoists the sails, while the skipper stands in the water to windward holding the boat abreast the mast, grasping a shroud. Then the skipper should wade out, pulling the boat with him. At this point, the crew should ease down the centerboard, hand the mainsheet to the skipper and sheet in the jib as the latter gives the boat a healthy shove and jumps in over her counter as she goes by. The boat will then pay off, and the mainsail must be sheeted in. Run parallel to the beach to pick up speed, then luff gradually, dropping the centerboard as

deeper water is reached. Do not point up too high too soon before the board is down, or the boat will go into irons and get tossed up on the beach. During this time give the boat all possible speed, running with the sheets as free as possible, but not luffing; this way, you will get maximum drive and minimum drift until rudder and board are down.

Getting back onto the beach is easier than getting out, but if any kind of a surf is running, extreme care is required. With a moderate wind, it is simpler. Sailing in under a minimum of speed, when the wind's on shore, does not offer too much of a problem. But the danger is in coming in too fast, especially when the surf's running. A skillful sailor can come in and turn head to wind a few yards off the beach and sail in astern. But generally the sailor should come in under jib alone, dropping his mainsail a few yards off as the boat is full and bye, then pay off and beach her under the jib—unshipping his rudder and raising the centerboard at the last moment in order to have steerageway as long as possible. Under a good surf, put the weight of the crew and skipper forward. As the beach is neared,

A Hobie Cat 14 riding the surf.

the crew should jump out first, lightening the boat and making it easier to stop. Once the bow has grounded, use the boat's inertial speed to get it up (the skipper's weight should now be in the stern) a few yards out of the reach of the surf.

Surf Sailing. Surf sailing is popular on the West Coast, but it also can be one of the most hair-raising experiences a sailor can have, especially if he has never before done it. Since not all waves are the same, and there is always a "shoulder" to every breaker, the skipper selects the part of the beach he is going out on, and which wave he is going out on. It is essential, before the big roughs start running with the sailor and his boat on their shoulders, that they are close enough to the broken spume of the last wave so that when they "throw" him out there, momentum will carry the boat over the crest of the next wave before its face turns concave and curls. Generally, the breaker line of each wave is readily

predictable at a glance by anyone experienced in either beach launching or surfing.

Regulating the boat's speed and keeping its distance in relation either to the crest in front or behind is most critical and is done almost entirely with sails. One could never paddle fast enough. Paddles and legs in the water are effectively used to slow the boat up when it becomes apparent that one has come in too fast and has to wait for the wave ahead to break. To keep proper speed up, one then has to paddle as a last resort.

A centerboarder will seldom be destroyed in the surf, or even seriously damaged. But if one capsizes or broaches, the rig is almost guaranteed to go. Probably the best type of centerboarder to launch through the surf is one with a double bottom that will allow the water to drain out between waves. The drainage ports must be large, though, so that any water aboard can be relieved before the next wave comes.

HELMSMANSHIP AND MANEUVERING UNDER SAIL

The fine points of sailing should be tried and practiced in open water, where there is sea room (ample room for maneuvering) for holding a fairly long board (tack or leg to windward). Before going into the techniques of the various sailing points, it may be wise to say a word about helmsmanship.

Helmsmanship is usually the responsibility of the skipper. As was stated in Section II, small boats are generally equipped with tillers for steering and large boats have steering wheels. A tiller usually turns the rudder directly, its length providing leverage, while a wheel often has a worm gear or is rigged in some other way to give the helmsman (steersman) a mechanical advantage. As a rule, tillers are quicker and more sensitive, while wheels are more powerful and require more movement to make the boat respond. The illustration here shows how the turning of the helm (wheel or tiller) affects the turning direction of the boat. A helmsman turns his wheel in the direction he wants his boat's bow to turn when moving ahead. This is similar to steering an automobile. But with a tiller the reverse is true. The helmsman pushes the tiller in the opposite direction from that

in which he wants his bow to turn. When moving backward the stern follows the direction in which the rudder is turned. An important point the helmsman should always keep in mind is that the rudder is effective in turning the boat only so long as the boat is moving ahead or backward. The more way she carries, or the faster she moves, the more effective is the rudder.

Wind Indicators. To control a boat's headings, the helmsman must also know from what precise direction the wind is blowing. Fortunately, wind direction can be detected by careful observation of the water's surface. Small ripples will move in the direction the wind is blowing. However, do not be misled by the movements of larger waves. Quite often the larger waves are controlled by a previous wind, and their movement does not indicate the direction of a new wind which has recently shifted or changed its direction. The present wind must be determined by watching the movement of the smallest ripples. Other signs of wind direction are flags flying; smoke from ships, chimneys, or cigarettes; and the heeling as well as the sail trim of other boats. If anchored by the bow, boats

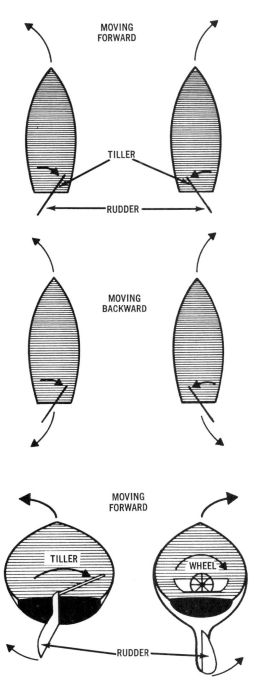

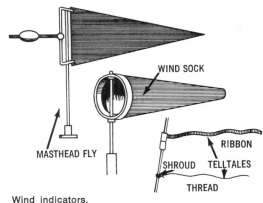

Wind indicators.

The helm (tiller or wheel) and how it controls direction.

and ships will lie with their bows pointed directly into the wind unless their heading is controlled by a strong current. The most effective means of determining wind direction and observing momentary shifts is by making use of wind indicators. The masthead fly and wind sock illustrated are carried at the top of the mast, where they are either permanently secured or hoisted into position when needed with a flag halyard. Telltales are short pieces of yarn, thread, or ribbon tied to the shrouds about 7 feet above the deck. These are easy to watch and respond instantly to even the lightest breeze. It must be borne in mind, however, that wind indicators on a moving boat do not show the true wind, but only the apparent wind.

Sight is not the only means of determining wind direction. Most experienced sailors develop a sensitivity to the feel of the wind. They can detect slight shifts and velocity changes by feeling the breeze on their cheeks, necks, arms, or hands. Of course, this method is particularly valuable when sailing at night. But for now, let us take a look at the fine points of helmsmanship.

Sailing to Windward

Sailing to windward is usually the wettest, the most challenging, and the most enjoyable part of sailing. As previously stated, a boat cannot be sailed *directly* into the wind. Thus, when sailing to windward, we are concerned with sailing the boat as close to the wind as possible but at her best possible speed on this point of sailing. If we sail her too close, her sails will begin to shake at the luffs, and we will feel her begin to slow down. On the other hand, if we bear off too far, the boat will pick up speed, but we will not gain as much distance to windward as she could. Beating is always a delicate balancing of these two factors, pointing (heading as close as possible to the windward objective) and footing (sailing through the water as fast as possible). When we sail too high so that we accentuate the gain to windward at a sacrifice of speed, we are said to pinch, but when sailing too low, at a good speed but at a sacrifice to windward gain, we sail too full. Usually, under normal conditions, the best windward course lies somewhere between pinching and sailing too full. Making a boat do her best to windward is always an interesting challenge. Some sailboats cannot sail any closer than 45 degrees to the true wind direction, while others can sail closer to the wind.

The best way to determine if you are sailing as close into the wind as possible is to turn the boat gradually up into the wind until the outer edge of the sail begins to shiver and shake. The jib is generally the first to show signs of pinching; it will flutter at the luff. Then the mainsail will begin to shake at the luff. This indicates, as just mentioned, that you have sailed too far into the wind, so that the wind is now blowing on both sides of the sails. When this occurs, move the tiller away from the sails so that the boat will head farther from the wind. Since the wind is almost continually changing in strength and slightly in direction, it is a good idea to test frequently by pushing the tiller toward the sails and pointing up to make sure you are sailing as close to the wind as possible. When you see that the telltales or burgee are making a broader angle with the boat than the sail, this is your warning that you are not pointing high enough. You must then put the helm "down" (away from the wind) and bring the bow up into the wind until the luff starts to shake, then bear away just enough to put the luff to sleep again. By experimenting several times, you will soon know how far you can point up before the sails begin to flutter or luff.

On boats with fixed keels, nothing further in the form of adjustments is required to sail into the wind. In a centerboard boat the board as well as the sheets must be adjusted for the different points of sailing. When going to windward, the centerboard should be lowered all the way to prevent the boat from sliding to leeward.

When sailing close-hauled, there is certain to be some leeway being made, and you should, if possible, take advantage of every little strong puff of the wind to get back a little to windward. While some winds are relatively steady, most winds constantly vary in direction and velocity. A temporary increase in velocity over a limited area is known as a puff, and it can be seen as a dark patch of ripples darting across the water's surface. Most puffs allow a boat to point higher because they cause the apparent wind to blow from more off the beam. Some puffs are the radiating type, often called catspaws. This type will force the helmsman to bear off when he first feels the puff, but then he is let up, or allowed, to point increasingly higher as he sails through the puff.

When the breeze shifts and blows from farther ahead (more from the bow) and forces the helmsman to bear off, this change in wind direction is called a header, but when it blows from farther aft (more on the beam), enabling the helmsman to point higher, it is called a lift. Fluctuations in direction can be detected immediately by watching the masthead wind indicator and particularly the telltales on the windward shrouds. When they swing more abeam the helmsman should point up, but when they swing more ahead he must bear off.

The skilled, experienced helmsman uses all of his senses when sailing a boat to windward. In addition to watching the telltales, he watches the luffs of his sails. When they begin to flutter or luff in normal winds or sailing conditions, he is generally sailing too high and must bear off. The experienced helmsman also watches for puffs on the water on his windward bow. If the water darkens with ripples from a puff, he is ready to head up when the boat first feels its effect. The sense of hearing is used by listening to the sound of the bow wave. A clearly audible bow wave indicates that the boat is moving at her best speed, while only a slight murmur of the wave suggests that perhaps the helmsman is pinching slightly or perhaps the sheets could be better trimmed for more speed. A good helms-

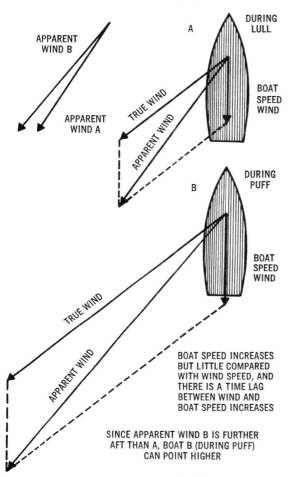

DURING
LULL

A

APPARENT
WIND B

BOAT
SPEED
WIND

APPARENT
WIND A

TRUE WIND

APPARENT WIND

DURING
PUFF

B

BOAT
SPEED
WIND

TRUE WIND

APPARENT WIND

BOAT SPEED INCREASES
BUT LITTLE COMPARED
WITH WIND SPEED, AND
THERE IS A TIME LAG
BETWEEN WIND AND
BOAT SPEED INCREASES

SINCE APPARENT WIND B IS FURTHER
AFT THAN A, BOAT B (DURING PUFF)
CAN POINT HIGHER

The effects and actions of wind puffs.

man also uses his sense of balance as well as his vision to detect a change in the boat's angle of heel. When beating, a boat should be heeled to leeward at least slightly, but the heel should not be excessive. For the average boat, if the lee rail begins to bury (dip in the water), the boat is being heeled too far. This can result in loss of speed and even a capsize in a centerboard boat. Excessive heeling can be controlled in two ways, by heading up or pointing higher, or, as a last resort, by slacking the mainsheet so that the mainsail begins to luff.

Perhaps the most important sense used by the skilled helmsman is the sense of feel or touch, often called the tiller touch, though,

of course, it applies to steering with a wheel also. This is sailing "by the seat of the pants," or sensing when the boat is going to windward at maximum efficiency. Of course, such a sense can be acquired only after a good deal of practice. The average, properly balanced boat will have a slight weather helm or tendency to turn into the wind in moderate breezes. The weather helm will exert a light pull or pressure against the helmsman's hand. This pressure will increase as the wind freshens and heels the boat, or it will decrease when the wind slackens and causes a smaller angle of heel. In the former case, the helmsman should relax his pressure on the helm and let the boat point up until he senses that she is beginning to lose speed or when her sails start to luff. In the latter case, however, when the helm pressure slackens, he should bear off slightly to see if the boat will pick up a little speed.

Sailing in Rough Waters. Good helmsmanship to windward is really a matter of experimentation. The helmsman should alternately point up, or prod the wind, to see if she will not sail just a little higher without slowing down, and then, as soon as she shows signs of slowing down, bear off a little to see if she won't sail a little faster. Remember that a helmsman should use all his senses when beating to windward. One useful visual sign which has not been discussed is the sagging of the jibstay. Ordinarily the jibstay should be set up tight for best efficiency to windward, but it will always sag off to leeward slightly. When the boat is sailing full and by, the sag will be most pronounced, but when she is being pinched the stay will be almost straight. Thus if there is considerable sag the helmsman should point up somewhat, but with little or no sag he should fall off a little. This aid to helmsmanship should not be relied on in rough water because as the boat pitches (rocks fore and aft), the mast will move forward and aft somewhat, causing the jibstay to slacken and tighten correspondingly.

When sailing into a chop (a short, steep sea) the helmsman should sail his boat full and by, because wave action tends to kill headway. The boat must be given enough power to drive through the waves. Likewise, in very light airs, the boat should not be sailed extremely close to the wind. She should be kept footing to minimize leeway and to take advantage of a stronger apparent wind. In a moderate breeze, however, most boats can be sailed fine, or quite close to the wind. Rudder action in light airs should be slow and gentle, but in moderate breezes the helm of a small boat can be turned quite rapidly to respond to lifts and headers. With large, heavy boats a slower action must be used. Remember that excessive rudder angles have a braking effect.

Sailing in Puffy Breezes. In a strong or puffy breeze, the helmsman should be ready to release his mainsheet at a moment's notice. In a small, capsizable centerboarder, the mainsheet should be held in hand. If its pull is too great, a turn may be taken around a cleat. On larger boats jam cleats may be used. It is perfectly permissible to cleat the mainsheet on a large keel boat which will not capsize, but it is dangerous practice to hitch the mainsheet on a cleat, unless a slippery hitch is used. As previously mentioned, wind may be spilled from the sails by luffing up, and naturally this method of righting an excessively heeled boat should be used before the mainsheet is released so that distance can be gained to windward. Sheets should be slacked only as a last resort. Keeping a boat on her feet (as upright as possible) by luffing up sharply in the

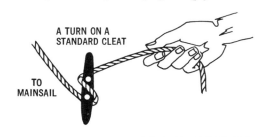

A TURN ON A
STANDARD CLEAT

TO
MAINSAIL

JAM CLEATS

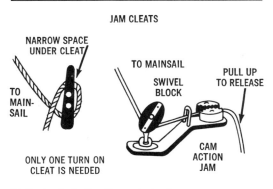

NARROW SPACE
UNDER CLEAT

TO
MAIN-
SAIL

ONLY ONE TURN ON
CLEAT IS NEEDED

TO MAINSAIL

SWIVEL
BLOCK

PULL UP
TO RELEASE

CAM
ACTION
JAM

Methods of cleating the mainsheet.

puffs is known as feathering. By using this technique, a skillful small-boat sailor can gain a much greater distance to windward than can a sailor who merely slacks his sheets to keep upright. That is, as soon as the puff comes and the boat heels to it, ease the helm down very gently and let the craft sail closer to the wind; as the puff dies down, the luff of the mainsail and the back of the jib will begin to quiver and lift and you will have to bear away again. By following such a procedure you will cancel or help to cancel out your leeway and will save a surprising amount of ground.

Positioning Your Crew. How the crew is seated can have an effect on your leeway since it helps to control the heel of the craft. Human weight on the high-side rail will counteract excessive heel. Every boat, of course, has her best position with regard to heel and weight distribution. This can be learned only by experimentation and feel. But always remember that a boat always heels more sharply when sailing to windward. It has one great advantage: you can always point the boat's bow up into the wind (luff up) by a quick movement of the tiller downwind. This lets the wind blow on both sides of the sail at the same time; the sails flutter out, doing no work, and the boat cannot be knocked down. When running and reaching, the sheets are your safety valve. You can let them fly if a squall should make it necessary. When close-hauled, the best safety valve is to luff up. In very squally weather the puffs of wind may strike you so suddenly that the boat will not respond quickly enough to be safe; in this event your best safety valve would be the mainsheet. Starting the sheet, as it is called, is of course a much quicker safety valve than luffing up. Its effect is immediate; whereas when luffing, the boat takes a second or two to respond to the helm. It is better to luff than to start the sheet, as by luffing up and bearing away again you can keep the boat moving. You should always keep way on a boat. A boat that is moving is under control. When she is stopped she is at the mercy of the elements. Every time you luff you kill the craft's headway, and you must be careful to sail away from the wind again before headway is lost. In the same way, starting the sheet immediately kills the boat's headway and you must trim the sheet in

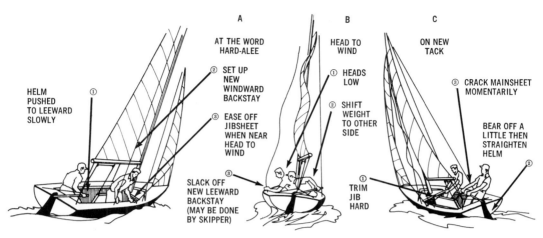

Tacking procedure.

again quickly before you lose steerage way. Thus, when sailing into the wind you must do a great deal of experimentation to find out just how your boat will handle.

Tacking. As was stated previously in this section, a boat can arrive at a point directly upwind only by making a series of diagonal slants, or tacks, first one way, then the other. This operation can be compared to a skier climbing a slope on skis. As we know, a skier does this by using the so-called "herringbone" technique—alternately placing one ski before the other at an angle of about 45 degrees to the direction in which he wishes to go. If we consider the wind as being represented as the slope, and flowing downhill, the boat follows the same technique as does the skier to go upwind.

Changing a sailboat's course so that the bow swings past the eye of the wind and pays off on the other tack is called coming about. If we assume you are sailing on a port tack, swing the tiller sharply to starboard (leeward side) or toward the sail, thus causing the bow to turn to port. At the same time, release the jibsheet (the starboard or leeward sheet) so that the jib will not present any resistance to the wind as the bow swings into the eye of the wind. Be careful to ease the mainsail sheet loose so that you do not heel too suddenly. For an instant the boat will be pointed directly into the wind, with the sails shaking violently. As the boat continues to

swing around, the wind will strike the sail more fully and the jib must be trimmed. It will fill and push the bow of the boat around to the starboard tack. Midship the rudder as you approach the new heading (a starboard tack), and when straightaway, trim the sails again. The reverse procedure is followed when swinging from a starboard tack to a port tack.

Be careful when coming about. The boom swings from one side of the boat to the other. If you are not watching, it can strike you or one of your crew members on the head or even knock someone right out of the boat. Actually, in any boat which carries a crew, certain commands should be given by the helmsman so that the crew can know what to expect and can carry out his or their duties at the proper moment. The first command should be "Stand by to come about." This is especially important in a large boat because it alerts the crew and gives them time to get to their proper stations. The next command is "Ready about," and this is promptly followed by "Hard-alee," or "Helm's-alee." The latter expression is said when the helm is actually moved. The tiller is pushed to leeward, or alee (a wheel, of course, is turned to windward), and this naturally turns the bow into the wind. When the boat is head to wind, all crew members should keep their heads low and watch out for booms or flogging fittings (boat hardware) that could hit

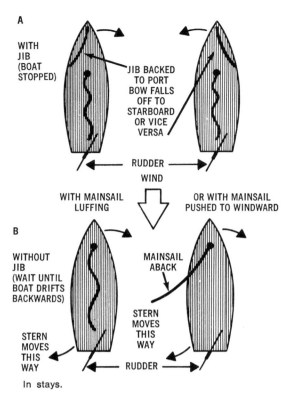

A

WITH
JIB
(BOAT
STOPPED)

JIB BACKED
TO PORT
BOW FALLS
OFF TO
STARBOARD
OR VICE
VERSA

RUDDER

WIND

WITH MAINSAIL
LUFFING

OR WITH MAINSAIL
PUSHED TO WINDWARD

B

WITHOUT
JIB
(WAIT UNTIL
BOAT DRIFTS
BACKWARDS)

MAINSAIL
ABACK

STERN
MOVES
THIS
WAY

STERN
MOVES
THIS
WAY

RUDDER

In stays.

someone. Crew weight is usually shifted to the new windward side unless there is very light air. In addition, the leeward jibsheet is not released until the boat is almost head to wind. It is a very common mistake to release the jibsheet too soon. This results in loss of boat speed and less distance gained to windward when making the turn.

After the boat turns through the eye of the wind, the jib should be trimmed immediately for two reasons. First, it is easier to trim before it completely fills with wind, and second, the trimmed jib will help pull the bow around onto the new tack. After the tack has been completed, the boat will have lost some way, therefore the helmsman should bear off to slightly below his normal windward course in order to get her moving again. It often helps to crack or slightly slack the mainsheet momentarily until speed is regained. As the boat picks up speed, the helmsman can begin to head up and trim the mainsail.

Immediately prior to tacking, the helmsman should see that his boat is moving at her best close-hauled speed, for if the boat is

tacked without sufficient way, she is liable to get in stays, or in irons. This means that so much way is lost when the boat is head to wind that she is unable to complete the tack. In such a predicament, the boat drifts helplessly backward with her sails flapping. In order to get way on again, haul the headsheets to windward, which we will suppose is the port side. Put the tiller to starboard. As the vessel is going astern, the rudder will now produce the reverse effect of what it would were the boat going ahead; so putting the tiller to starboard turns the craft's head to starboard. To assist her still further in paying off, slack out main and jibsheets; these sails have a tendency to keep her up into the wind. When she has paid off sufficiently, trim the sheets, and she will soon gather way on the port tack. If you are aboard a cat-rigged boat and caught in stays, the helmsman must wait until the boat gains sufficient stern way so that the rudder may be used. The mainsail may be pushed to windward to accelerate the backward speed. Of course, the stern will follow the direction of the rudder when moving backward.

Proper rudder action is important to avoid getting in stays. If the rudder is jammed hard over, it will act as a brake and kill headway. On the other hand, if the rudder is turned too slowly, the boat may not have enough momentum to carry her through the resulting long, slow turn. As said before, have ample way on your boat before bringing her about. When tacking in a rough sea, wait for a relatively smooth spot before tacking, and be sure to trim the jib flat after passing through the eye of the wind.

When coming about in a boat with a genoa jib, the clew of this big sail must move itself forward, past the shrouds, and around the mast. For this to occur smoothly, the genoa's sheet must be released in sufficient time for the sail to swing in its path, and the craft must be brought about more slowly than when using a working jib. Sometimes the sheet or the big sail itself will catch on a projection, such as a winch or cleat on the mast, as it flaps its way from one side of the craft to the other. To prevent this, a crew member often takes the genoa's clew forward, and leads it around the shrouds and mast to the other side. While carrying out this operation, do not permit the boat to go into irons. That is, aboard a big boat such as a yawl, the skipper alerts his crew to stand by to come about. The crew take their stations. If the genoa is set, a tall man takes his position as far forward as possible on the bow where he straddles the headstay. One or two men should take a position along the foot of the sail to run the foot forward during the tack. A man stands by to release the jibsheet and set up the running backstay if it is in use. Two men stand by the windward genoa sheet winch that will be used to bring the jib in on the new tack. Another man stands by to pull back on the jib's clew when it is first being trimmed in, and this same man can then release the leeward running backstay if it is set up. Be sure that every man has a station and knows his job.

At the command hard-alee, the helm is put over. The jibsheet is slacked when almost head to wind, and it is eased off. It is not suddenly released, because this will noticeably slow the boat and kill her momentum. The skipper often tells the man on the sheet when to release it. If the runners are being used, the man who releases the sheet can set up the new windward backstay. Some authorities advise setting up the runner before the jibsheet is released, because at this time it is often possible to get the stay very taut. The men stationed at the foot of the genoa carry it forward while the bowman gathers in the slack. If the forestay is set up, the jib must be fed through the space between the forestay and headstay. When the boat swings past the head-to-wind position onto the new tack, the jib will be blown through the space between

the stays. The helmsman luffs his boat slowly until head to wind, and then he momentarily turns sharply in the same direction, so that the jib will quickly blow through the space. After this, the helm is again turned slowly to give the sheet trimmers maximum help in winching in the jib. Of course, if the backstays are not in use, and especially if the forestay is not set up, tacking is a much simpler job.

When tacking to windward, the duration of tacks may not be all the same. Obstructions, channels, sand bars, and the like make each tack of different length. (In sailor parlance, a short tack is called a short board, or short hitch, and a long tack a long board, or long hitch.) All the words in the world could not describe the correct length of each tack, for every different condition of the water, the wind, and the ability of the boat to sail close to the eye of the wind will enter into the problem. On long trips in open water, the tacks might be several hours in length. A small boat sailed in restricted waters may have to come about on another tack at intervals of a few minutes. The only rule is to keep a tack as long as possible, for each time you come about reduces the speed of the boat, demands adjusting of sails, and, in small boats, causes the crew to shift from side to side.

Hiking. Hiking aids are essential, for hike we must. The tiller extension must be long enough for the skipper to get out and do his share. Hiking straps are a help but if you sail in crowded waters requiring quick tacking, make sure you do not get your feet tangled up. Instead the crew may favor a

The hiking strap (left) and hiking board (right).

"ladies aid," which is a 5-foot length of ½-inch Dacron line tied around the thwart in the center of the boat where it crosses the centerboard trunk. When hiking out the crew grips the line by a couple of large knots spaced near the outboard end. It helps.

When hiking, the skipper is always in front of the tiller and on the weather side. In this position his body does not restrict the movement of the tiller and he can hike quickly if necessary. This is a critical and oft-violated maxim. In light air the crew starts out sitting to leeward and on the floor to offset the weight of the skipper to weather. As the breeze picks up, the crew shifts to the floor on the weather side and from there to the rail. In general, the harder it blows, the flatter the boat should be. In light air a slight heel keeps the sail set, provides enough weather helm to sail the boat, and reduces wetted surface.

The trapeze is well established as a hiking device and will be used more, not less, in the future. In the United States only a few classes are equipped with this instrument of all-out war, but in Australia only a few are not. And the worldwide trend in newer small-boat designs as well as in most of the growing catamaran classes is to include the trapeze.

The reason is not hard to find: as boat weight has been forced downward in the quest for liveliness and speed, the proportion of human weight to total weight has gone up. The effect of getting live weight outboard is therefore all the greater. Getting a man over the side on a heavy centerboarder or keel boat made a difference before, but with the new boats the difference is so fantastic that it can-

Out on a trapeze.

not be ignored or dismissed for the sake of avoiding physical pain. So, all forms of hiking are now "in."

Which underscores an important point: trapezing is only one form of getting human weight away from the center of buoyancy, and although it is physically demanding in its own way, it is by no means any more demanding than most other forms of hiking. We would much rather lie comfortably in a well-designed trapeze belt for a long weather leg than hang in hiking straps (especially in a boat like the Lightning, with its cockpit coaming and rubrail designed originally with nonhiking in mind). Others might prefer lying vertically along Star topsides, riding bilge boards, or using hiking straps with a hull designed for them (e.g., the Finn). None of these requires a superman, and each has its own special kind of hurt that can be accepted. The beauty of the trapeze, of course, is that it gets the crew further outboard than any other method, with the possible exception of the sliding seat. Mastering it includes learning how to get in and out, knowing when to move in or out, being in reasonable physical condition, and having equipment properly designed and maintained.

Getting out is difficult at the beginning. You tend to distrust the wire and its hookup, and therefore at first you probably will try to stand up holding the wire by hand, gently and gingerly lowering yourself over and out. This is all wrong. You must simply slide out over the rail, putting your full weight on the wire as soon as possible, and definitely before moving away from the hull. At this point you are a pendulum. Then you push off with both feet and your free hand. After you have convinced yourself the wire really is safe, the operation will become second nature.

Getting in takes two forms; the quickest is to lift both feet off the rail, swing in until you hit the side of the boat, and keep on moving. This is fine when there is enough wind that catlike movements are not so necessary, and speed is more important. (The Flying Dutchman and 5-0-5, for example, are both so light that they need to be tacked quickly, and the only limit on tacking speed is the time it takes the crew to get through the whole cycle of swinging in, trimming the new jibsheet, and swinging out on the other side.)

The other way is by reversing the procedure used in getting out: bend your knees, use the free hand to ease in further after you have put one leg inside, sit on the deck and unhook. Do this in light air, any time you find your weight is overpowering the hull, or when smoothness is more important than speed. Using handles is handy in some situations and changes some of the procedure already described. The handle is located just within reach higher up on the wire and is great for quick tacks in medium weather. When finishing a tack, instead of hooking up on the new wire, grab the new handle with one hand and the jibsheet with the other, and swing on out, trimming the jib as you go. By now the skipper has cleated the mainsheet, and will temporarily hold the jibsheet (which you keep hanging over one wrist) while you hook up. The whole operation gets the weight out sooner, but can be rather exhausting in really heavy air when wearing several soaked sweatshirts. The handle can be used most of the time in swinging inboard; you swing farther in by keeping your weight above the gunwale as you swing.

Knowing when to move in or out is normally not difficult to feel; going upwind the question simply does not arise in medium and over winds. Stay out, period. And in light air, it is best for skipper and crew to lean out in hiking straps together for the occasional puff, rather than the crew trying to stay half in and half out. But there will be times when the crew needs to move continually, adjusting his position with changes in the wind velocity.

Sailing Before the Wind

Sailing or running in the same direction as the wind is blowing—or in nearly the same direction—is rather tricky. Contrary to what you might think, it calls for better seamanship than close-hauling, or tacking against the wind. It is probably the least exciting point of sailing, since the boat's speed is usually reduced and the apparent wind is much lighter. Also, the sense of control and response which the helmsman feels when the craft is close-hauled is diminished to a great degree. That is, the boat moves less easily, responds less surely to the helm.

In order to obtain maximum power from the wind, the mainsail is set by letting out its sheet until it is approximately 90 degrees (at right angles) to the centerline of the boat. (Note that we said the *mainsail* should be at 90 degrees, not the boom.) This is done to obtain full pressure of the wind against the greatest possible sail area. If you are sailing dead before the wind, the mainsail may be paid out either to starboard or port; if the wind should be coming from one quarter or the other, the mainsail should be out on the opposite side. After setting the mainsail, the jibsheet should be trimmed so that the jib will be nearly at right angles to the fore-and-aft line of the boat. However, you will probably find, when running before the wind, that the jib will be completely blanketed by the mainsail and will just flap idly. After you have gained some experience and have become fairly adept at running, you can spread the jib out on the opposite side of the craft to the mainsail (commonly called sailing wing and wing) by using a whisker pole, or in some cases a boat hook. A whisker pole is a light spar with jaws on one end like a gaff and a spike on the other end. The spike is pushed through the clew of the jib, and the jaws rest against the mast. The whisker pole holds the jib out at more or less a right angle to the boat. The jib is most effective used this way. To make the whisker pole stay in place, it is necessary to trim the jibsheet to put a strain on the spar, and thus hold it against the mast. As explained later in this section, you may wish to substitute a spinnaker for the jib.

In the case of centerboard craft, the centerboard should be raised. Most boats will sail at their fastest (when running) with the centerboard raised entirely, but if she shows a tendency to yaw or swing off her course in either direction, it is wise to lower the board a quarter of its full depth.

Rudder action is also important when sailing before the wind. In fact, it might be said that sailing downwind requires rudder action which is almost directly opposite to that used when sailing to windward. The windward helmsman bears off in the lulls and heads up in the puffs, but the downwind helmsman bears off in the puffs and heads up in the lulls. That is, during a lull, the helmsman heads up from a running course to a broad reaching course in order to keep his boat moving

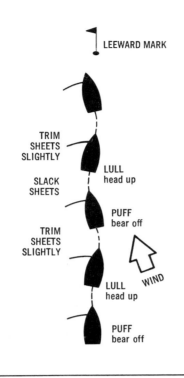

TRIM
SHEETS
SLIGHTLY

SLACK
SHEETS

TRIM
SHEETS
SLIGHTLY

LEEWARD MARK

LULL
head up

PUFF
bear off

LULL
head up

PUFF
bear off

WIND

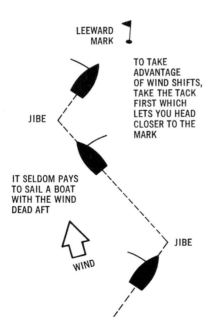

LEEWARD
MARK

JIBE

IT SELDOM PAYS
TO SAIL A BOAT
WITH THE WIND
DEAD AFT

TO TAKE
ADVANTAGE
OF WIND SHIFTS,
TAKE THE TACK
FIRST WHICH
LETS YOU HEAD
CLOSER TO THE
MARK

JIBE

WIND

despite the decrease in wind. During the puffs, he bears off to almost a dead run because he has sufficient power from the puff to retain his speed. Also his boat will be less subject to speed-retarding heeling forces when the wind is from nearly dead astern. Furthermore, by heading far off during the puffs, the helmsman sails slightly below his course for the leeward destination and so compensates for the high heading he sailed during the previous lull.

Working to leeward is a constant weaving back and forth during the puffs and lulls to maintain boat speed. This principle applies when sailing slightly below a beam-reaching course, because as we approach a beam reach, the boat speed increases. In moderate to heavy winds when we sail higher than a beam reach, speed begins to decrease. In light airs the best speed often occurs near the close-reaching point of sailing. Thus it should be kept in mind that when sailing lower than a beam reach in moderate to heavy breezes or lower than a close reach in light airs, the helmsman bears off in the puffs and heads up in the lulls.

Sailing for longer than very brief periods with the wind from dead astern should be avoided if possible. As previously said, a dead run is a slow point of sailing, and when the wind is dead astern, the after sails will have a blanketing effect on the forward sails causing a definite reduction in boat speed. A means of avoiding this predicament is to use the procedure called tacking downwind. That is, instead of running directly for the leeward mark, you sail a broad reach toward the mark on one tack and then jibe over and broad reach toward the mark on the other tack. Quite often the extra distance sailed to reach a destination is more than compensated for by additional speed gained in broad reaching. It is easy to overdo this strategy, however, and to sail too high so that the extra speed does not make up for the extra distance sailed. Generally, a safe rule to follow is to sail as far off as possible yet still keep the forward sails drawing or filled with wind. In puffy weather, of course, this strategy should be used with the previously mentioned working-to-leeward technique. Quite often, when tacking downwind, the boat can be headed (with her forward sails drawing well) closer to her desired course on one tack than on the other tack. In such a case, the helmsman should first take the tack which allows him to head closer to his destination.

Aside from the consideration of boat speed, there is another reason to avoid running with the wind flat aft, or from dead astern. Since the wind is usually shifty or slightly oscillating in direction, a boat sailing dead before the wind is subject to a shift from the "wrong side," or a shift which blows from the leeward side instead of the windward side. When this happens the boat is said to be running by the lee. To put it another way, when a boat, sailing with the wind flat aft, turns to leeward as though to jibe but does not jibe, she is sailing by the lee. Of course, she can only turn to leeward a limited extent before she is forced to jibe, but from a dead run to the point where her sails go aback and force her to jibe, she is by the lee. This is a dangerous point of sailing because, since the boat is on the verge of jibing, there is a possibility she might have an accidental or unintentional jibe. Actually, when running before the wind in this fashion, there are three things you must guard against: an accidental jibe, a goosewing jibe, and a broaching jibe. All can cause serious bodily injury as well as damage to the craft.

Controlled Jibe. As opposed to the three just mentioned jibes, the "controlled jibe" is a much-used maneuver and it is essential to sailing. It is generally employed when sailing before the wind and when you have to round a buoy or breakwater where there is limited space; when the wind has shifted and you wish to avoid sailing by the lee; or when you wish to change your course without coming about. Actually, you could say that jibing (sometimes called "wearing") is the opposite of coming about. In both maneuvers the sail shifts, catching the wind on its other side. The difference is that you come about when you are sailing into the wind, and you jibe when you are sailing with the wind. In other words, as previously stated, a controlled jibe is a downwind turn from one tack to the other. When the sails cross from one side of the boat to the other, they do not flap as when tacking, but they fill from the lee side and swing over rapidly. When it is blowing so hard that a jibe would be dangerous, an alternative method of getting the boat on the other tack is to bring her up close-hauled, tack, and then head off to the desired course.

As with tacking, certain commands should be given prior to jibing in order to alert the crew. The helmsman first calls out "Stand by to jibe." At this warning the crew get to their proper stations and prepare to duck their heads to avoid being struck by the boom. The helmsman steers off dead before the wind. The sheets may have to be slacked to effect this maneuvering, especially if the wind is blowing hard and the boat is reaching. Once dead before the wind, he or a crew member begins

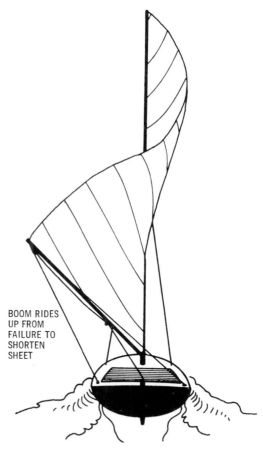

BOOM RIDES UP FROM FAILURE TO SHORTEN SHEET

Goosewing jibe is more likely to occur on gaff-rigged boats, but to recover, jibe back to original tack. Note: If rolling severely while running, a boat with low freeboard and long boom might need her boom's end slightly lifted with topping lift to prevent dipping boom in water. This may increase tendency to goosewing.

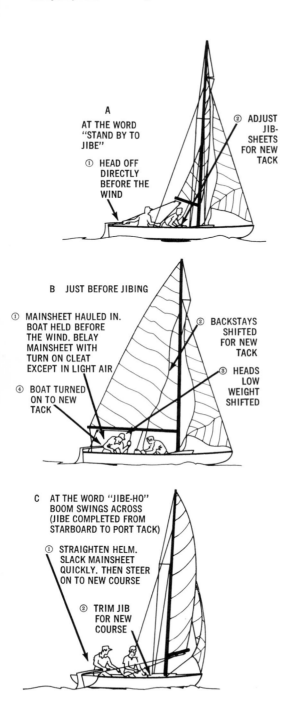

A
AT THE WORD "STAND BY TO JIBE"

① HEAD OFF DIRECTLY BEFORE THE WIND

② ADJUST JIB-SHEETS FOR NEW TACK

B   JUST BEFORE JIBING

① MAINSHEET HAULED IN. BOAT HELD BEFORE THE WIND. BELAY MAINSHEET WITH TURN ON CLEAT EXCEPT IN LIGHT AIR

④ BOAT TURNED ON TO NEW TACK

② BACKSTAYS SHIFTED FOR NEW TACK

③ HEADS LOW WEIGHT SHIFTED

C   AT THE WORD "JIBE-HO"
BOOM SWINGS ACROSS (JIBE COMPLETED FROM STARBOARD TO PORT TACK)

① STRAIGHTEN HELM. SLACK MAINSHEET QUICKLY. THEN STEER ON TO NEW COURSE

② TRIM JIB FOR NEW COURSE

Controlled-jibing procedure.

to haul the mainsail in by its sheet. It is important that the sheet is pulled in as far as it will come before the boat is turned onto the new tack. A crew member changes the jib-sheets, casting off the cleated sheet and cleating the windward sheet which will be on the leeward side after the jibe has been completed. If the wind has much strength, it is necessary to avoid having both jibsheets cast off simultaneously, even for an instant, or the jib may blow out ahead and its flogging may quickly snarl the sheets. If the boat has running backstays, of course these must be changed so that the leeward stay on the new tack will be slack. When the helmsman is ready to turn onto the new tack, he calls out "Jibe-ho." This warns the crew that he is jibing at that moment. The crew duck their heads and shift their weight to the new windward side if the boat is a small one, while the helmsman steers slowly off to leeward until the main boom swings over. At this point the helmsman should straighten up his helm or steer almost dead before the wind until the mainsail is slacked off rapidly to the position in which it should be for running.

It is a common mistake, when it is blowing, to round up into the wind too quickly after jibing. This has led to the capsizing of many centerboarders. In a fresh breeze the mainsail must be slacked all the way off before rounding up. Unless this is done, the boat is exposing her beam to the wind with flattened sheets which will cause extreme heeling, and furthermore she is heeled by the centrifugal force of her turn toward the wind. Immediately after jibing, most boats will have a natural tendency to turn into the wind. The helmsman must counteract this tendency by straightening his helm or even reversing it momentarily in order to hold his boat before the wind until the sheets are slacked.

When aboard a big yacht, such as a yawl, jibing involves essentially the same crew activity as tacking, except that not as many men are needed to handle the jib and two men are needed to tend the mizzen and mainsheets. The man on the mainsheet has an especially important job because the mainsail is quite large and its boom has considerable weight. He must be sure that, in a breeze, the sheet is pulled all the way in when the boom crosses over the boat's centerline, and he must never ease the sheet until the new leeward running backstay has been slacked. The helmsman does not actually turn onto the new tack until the mainsheet tender is ready and has the main boom amidships. At the word jibe-ho, the helmsman turns the bow to leeward so that the boom swings across onto the new tack.

Virtually all modern small boats have a boom vang, which is a tackle that holds the boom down to increase the efficiency of the mainsail when reaching and to control the boom when jibing. It is not necessary to pull in the mainsheet when jibing a boat with a boom vang. In fact in strong winds it is very difficult, when jibing, to trim in the mainsail to the center of the boat without causing a capsize. The proper method is to lay the boat off away from the wind, watching the leech of the sail to see when it is about to catch the wind on the other side. Then the helmsman should shout "jibe-ho" as the sail swings across, and the crew should duck low to avoid the boom. As the boom is crossing the centerline of the boat the helmsman should make a small adjustment with the tiller to check the boat's turn and keep it heading straight downwind. This is to keep the boat from heeling over suddenly as the sail slams across by interrupting the centrifugal force set up by the turn. When he is sure normal balance has been achieved on the new tack the helmsman can steer the planned course.

In moderate weather jibing a boat with a boom vang is very simple. The helmsman should warn the crew with the usual orders of "stand by to jibe" followed by "jibe-ho" and then just turn the boat to the desired new course, letting the boom swing across freely. The boom vang has taken much of the mystery and dread out of jibing small boats.

Reaching

As we said earlier, when a sailboat is under way and is neither sailing to windward nor before the wind, it is said to be reaching. In other words, the craft sails more or less across the wind. When sailing in this manner, your boat is able to sail from one point to another and return with no complicated maneuvering. To trim the sails correctly for a reach, as soon as the vessel is on her correct course, ease out the mainsheet and headsheets until the

luffs of the sails are beginning to shake. Then haul in on the sheets until they cease to shake, and then haul in a little more to get the best trim. Now make fast the sheets. You will be able to tell if the wind draws ahead or aft by watching the wind pennant, the sails, the direction of the waves, and by the feel of your boat when you have had more experience. To get the best out of your craft you should always study the wind's direction and trim your sheets accordingly. For example, if the wind draws ahead, the luffs of the sails will start to shake, and in order to trim the sheets correctly for the course you are sailing, you should haul them in until the luffs cease to shake. If, on the other hand, the wind draws further aft, the boat will be heeled over, but you will lose speed; the burgee or telltale will point further ahead and the feel of the wind on your face will be less. To trim the sheets correctly, ease them until the sail is making roughly the same angle with the craft's centerline as the wind pennant. The pennant is always a good guide to the trim of the sails when reaching or sailing close-hauled.

To change from sailing close-hauled to close reaching, move the tiller up (toward the wind). Then, as the boat's head falls off to leeward, set the sails until both the jib and mainsail start to flutter along the luff. Both sheets are then hauled in until the fluttering stops. The sails should be trimmed in a nearly parallel position to the centerline of the craft. The boat will move faster and have less heel than when sailing to windward close-hauled.

When on a broad reach, the same procedure is followed after the craft has been put on her desired course. The sheets are hauled in just enough to stop fluttering of the sails. The boom is usually kept at an angle halfway between the centerline of the craft and the direction the burgee or telltale is pointing. Broad reaching is possibly the easiest maneuver in sailing, since the boat then has its best balance, though some care should be taken to keep the sails at their full drawing angle to the wind. When sailing on a beam reach, you handle the sails in the same way as when sailing on a broad or a close reach. In the case of centerboard craft on a beam reach, the board should be about halfway down; on a close reach it should be about three-quarters down; and for broad reaching about one-quarter down.

When you are on a reach course, it generally is a good idea to choose some landmark, or if none is in sight, to sail by compass bearing, so that you keep the craft going in the desired direction. You will find that it is rather difficult to keep any small sailing vessel on an exact course, especially if there is a heavy sea running.

The only concern, when reaching, is from a beam sea, since it may cause the craft to roll slightly and may slop over the windward side. But serious rolling seldom occurs except when the seas are very high, because in this sailing position the sails have an excellent steadying influence.

Use of a Spinnaker

The spinnaker can be effectively employed when sailing before the wind and when broad or beam reaching. It is effective in very light airs, where it does more to keep a boat moving than the mainsail. In strong winds it "pulls like a mule" and care must be taken in its handling. Interestingly, the spinnaker is said to have derived its name from the fact that an early version of the sail was first carried by the British yacht *Sphinx*. It is said that rival crews called the sail a "Sphinxer" and sometimes referred to it as "Sphinx's Acre." These

names soon evolved into our present term for the sail.

The spinnaker carried on most racing craft can properly be termed a parachute spinnaker. It is shaped like a ballooned isosceles triangle, the upper corner of which is called the head, and the lower corners both of which are called clews. When set, the sail is supported at these three corners only. Either clew may be fastened to the end of a boom called the spinnaker pole, which is carried on the side of the boat opposite to the main boom, and the clew on the pole would then actually be called the tack. The clews are interchangeable, that is, either may be used as the tack, depending on whether the sail is set to port or to starboard. The line attached to the tack and pole is called the after guy (or often just guy), while the line attached to the clew is the sheet. Of course, the head is supported by the halyard. Another line is attached to the pole to hold it down and forward, and this line is called the pole downhaul, or foreguy. Still another line is the pole topping lift, or simply lift, and this holds the pole up.

At its inboard end the pole is attached to a slide on a track that is fastened to the fore side of the mast. The outboard end of the pole may swing forward until it touches the headstay or aft until it touches the forward shroud. The after guy controls the pole's fore-and-aft position. When beam reaching, the

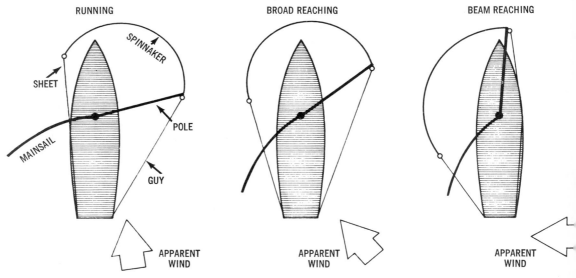

Fore-and-aft spinnaker-pole position.

pole is carried all the way forward; when running, the pole is all the way aft; but when broad reaching, the pole is about halfway between the running and beam-reaching positions. Remember that most spinnakers cannot be carried effectively when the true wind comes from forward of the beam or when the boat is on a point of sailing that is slightly higher than a beam reach.

The pole may be raised or lowered at either end. The height of the outboard end is controlled with the lift, and the inboard end is controlled with the adjustable slide on the mast track. Given a good breeze, a well-designed parachute spinnaker will lift, and it should be encouraged to do so. The pole should be carried as high as possible when the 'chute is lifting, but the tack should not be allowed to lift much higher than the clew. In other words, the tack and clew should be kept at about the same level, almost parallel to the deck or horizontal when the boat is unheeled. Then also, the pole should not be cocked up very much with its outboard end a great deal higher than its inboard end.

In a light breeze the pole should make an approximate right angle with the mast with the inboard end at the highest position that will keep the tack level with the clew. In very light airs the clew will not lift; therefore, the inboard pole end must be kept low. As the breeze freshens, the inboard end can be pushed higher up the mast until, in a moderate breeze, the pole is at the top of its track.

When the wind is aft the pole should be kept low, and if necessary the sheet should be held down amidships by a block or open hook so that the clew does not lift above the tack. As the wind comes further forward—to a broad reach—the sheet should lead straight from its normal lead near the stern and the pole should be raised slightly to keep the spinnaker clew and tack level. On a beam reach the spinnaker should be encouraged to lift at both clew and tack as this flattens the spinnaker in the fore-and-aft plane, making it more suitable for sailing closer to the wind.

Setting the Spinnaker. It is generally considered that there are three ways to set a spinnaker: by stopping it, setting it from a turtle, or setting it from its bag. Actually, however, the latter two methods are practically the same. The turtle is a special container which holds the folded or bundled spinnaker on deck prior to hoisting. These containers are often quite varied in design, depending on the fancy of each particular skipper or foredeck captain. With each, however, the three corners are rigged to their proper lines: the head to the halyard, the guy to the tack, and the sheet to the clew. With this arrangement, rigging the pole on the guy (as illustrated) is perhaps preferable for short races in sheltered waters, but snapping the pole on the ring at

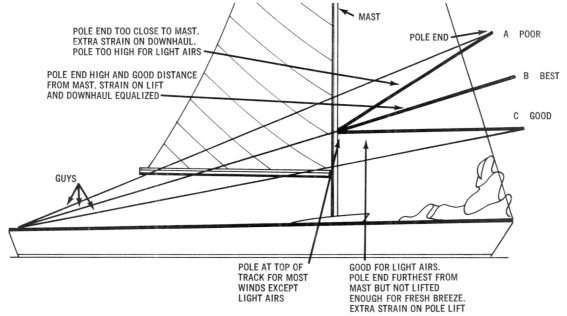

Spinnaker-pole lift adjustment. Note that tack should not be lifted above the height of the clew. The spinnaker's foot should be kept horizontal.

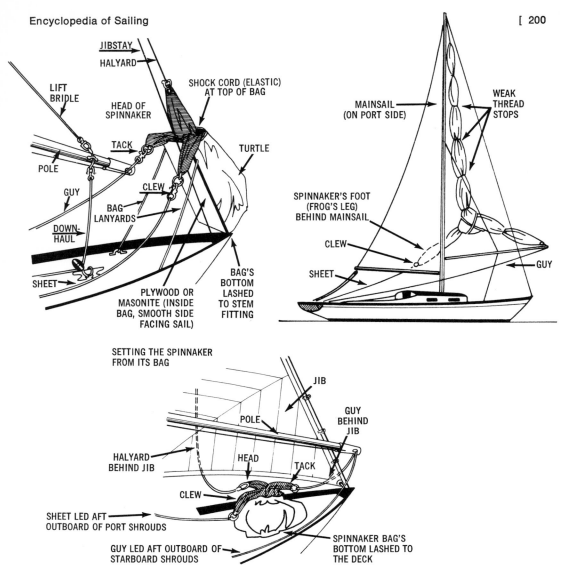

Setting a spinnaker from a turtle, bag, or stopped position.

the spinnaker's tack is better for distance and offshore sailing because there is less chafe.

When setting the 'chute from its bag, the bag becomes a simplified turtle. About the only difference between the bag and the turtle is that the latter is more elaborate, and it is usually (though not always) designed to be secured forward of the headstay or jibstay. Sometimes the turtle is equipped with snap hooks which snap on to the bow pulpit if the boat has one. When the spinnaker is set from its bag, however, it is usually secured to the foredeck abaft the headstay. The bag must have a lanyard at its bottom so that it can be lashed to the bow cleat or some other fitting on the foredeck. The sail's three corners hang out of the bag's top, which is closed with the bag's draw string and tied with a slip knot. Immediately prior to hoisting the spinnaker, the slip knot is pulled to release the sail. Usually, the jib is not lowered until after the spinnaker has been hoisted, at which time the jib is quickly dropped, so it will not blanket the spinnaker.

Remember that part of the halyard which fastens to the sail's head must lie to leeward of the jib. The hoisting part of the halyard is, of course, to windward of the jib, next to the mast. The halyard's end that snaps on the head must be put to leeward of the jib by running it aft, outside the shrouds, to the sail's leech. Then the halyard is put behind the leech and the halyard's end is worked forward under the foot of the jib until it is opposite the spinnaker bag, where the end can be snapped onto the sail's head. Putting the halyard to leeward of the jib by running the line forward and around the headstay will often cause the halyard to make a wrap around the stay. More will be said about this later when we discuss spinnaker problems. Always look aloft to see that all is clear before hoisting the spinnaker. It should be noted that the after guy runs around the headstay and to leeward of the jib tack, where it is fastened to the spinnaker's tack. If it is desired that the pole be snapped to the guy's shackle ring, then the spinnaker's tack corner must be carried to leeward of the jib and around the headstay to where the ring can be fastened to the pole's outboard end, which is resting up against the headstay. The sheet leads outboard of the lee shrouds and snaps into the clew.

On large boats with lifelines (lines forming a safety railing around the outboard edge of the deck), it is especially important to check the sheet, guy, and halyard to make sure they are not fouled in the lifelines. The spinnaker sheet, guy, and halyard are always led over, and never through, the lifelines.

It is very important that the spinnaker be "made up," or properly prepared, before it is stuffed into its turtle or bag prior to hoisting. This preparation consists of folding the two spinnaker leeches together before the sail is bagged so that the sail will not become twisted when it is hoisted. A simple method is to dump the loose sail on the cabin sole where it is protected from the wind; then starting at the head, each leech is located and folded one against the other. The man doing this works his way down toward the sail's foot, flaking down, or folding, the sail accordion style with the leeches together. When almost at the foot, the two clews are separated and pulled out in opposite directions. The loose bulk of the sail is stuffed into the bag followed by the folded leeches. The

head and the two clews are left hanging out of the bag or the turtle's top with the head in the middle between the two clews. On large boats when the spinnaker is being hoisted, a man should "see" it out of the bag or turtle. He should let the spinnaker run through his hands or arms while looking aloft to see that the sail does not foul on a stay or spreader and that it does not become twisted.

The other method of setting a spinnaker is to hoist the sail while it is rolled up and tied with light stops. After the sail is hoisted, the stops are then broken. In former days, before the advent of the turtle, stopping a spinnaker was the usual practice, but now this is not often done except on a big boat in a strong wind. In most instances, using a turtle or bag is simpler and quicker. When a spinnaker is stopped, its leeches are put together in much the same manner as when preparing the sail for a turtle. The sail should be stretched tight between its head and foot, and then the loose part of the sail between the leeches is rolled or bunched up so that it makes the appearance of a long, thin, sausage. A rolled sail is usually more difficult to break out than one that is bunched. The sail is then stopped tightly at about every 2 or 3 feet with rotten twine or light cotton thread which may be broken very easily. The tighter the twine is tied the easier it may be broken. It is usually a good practice to make "frog's legs" at the foot. That is, the lowest stops are not put around the two leeches but around the foot and leech so that each clew forms the end of a leg. It is important that the upper stop not be tied too close to the spinnaker's head because this stop is often difficult to break. Upper stops are usually tied with one turn, while lower stops may have two. The lower the stop, the more force can be applied to it by a pull on the sheet. Occasionally a special line is tied under the stops in such a way that the line may be pulled from the deck after the sail is hoisted to facilitate breaking the stops. Usually, however, a breaking line is not necessary. The leg stops can be reached and broken by hand, and a hard pull aft on the sheet will break the higher stops. When the stops begin to break, the wind will fill out the lower portion of the sail and help break the upper stops.

The important thing in preparing a spinnaker for hoisting (whether it be in a bag, turtle, or stops) is to have the leeches running continuously together in order that the sail will not become twisted. After the sail is hoisted, in a moderate or stronger breeze, ease the halyard slightly (about 12 to 18 inches) so that the head is blown slightly out and away from the mast. In light airs, however, the head should be as high as it can be hoisted.

Spinnaker Helmsmanship. One of two or a combination of two methods are used to sail with the spinnaker set. The first method is to trim the sail properly and leave it alone while the helmsman changes course to conform with changes in the velocity and direction of the wind. The second method is for the helmsman to hold a steady course while the spinnaker's trim is changed to match every change in the wind. On most top racing boats, however, a combination of these two methods is used.

When the first technique of sailing with a spinnaker is used, the helmsman must be able to watch the spinnaker's luff (the forward edge from masthead to the outboard end of the pole). When the sail begins to collapse, he must quickly alter course. When sailing between a beam-reaching and broad-reaching course, the helmsman bears off if the spinnaker starts to break (to luff, beginning to collapse). But if the boat is running and the spinnaker begins to collapse, it is often diffi-

cult for the helmsman to know which way to turn. The sail could be luffing on account of a wind shift that is more on the beam, or the sail might be blanketed by the mainsail because of a shift which comes from astern and puts the boat by the lee. This can become a real problem even for an experienced sailor in a rapidly shifting wind. The best way to overcome the problem is to look at the windward telltales or a masthead wind indicator. These will tell which way the wind is shifting. The helmsman should remember that the pole should be kept at right angles to the apparent wind. Of course, the wind indicators will give the apparent wind direction; thus when an indicator makes an acute angle (less than 90 degrees) with the pole, the helmsman should head up to make the angle 90 degrees, but when the indicator makes an obtuse angle (more than 90 degrees) with the pole, he should bear off to make the angle 90 degrees.

The second method of sailing with the spinnaker (changing the sail's trim for shifts while the helmsman holds a straight course) requires a lot of action and coordination on the crew's part, because the guy as well as the sheet must be constantly tended. The responsibility for preventing a spinnaker collapse lies primarily with the sheet tender instead of the helmsman. This method is rarely used unless the boat is being steered on a compass course at night or in a fog or if it is fairly

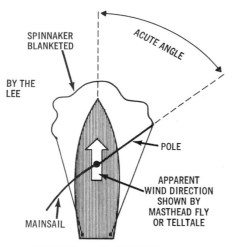

HEAD UP (TURN TO STARBOARD)

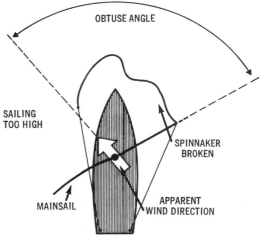

BEAR OFF (TURN TO PORT)

Spinnaker helmsmanship.

certain that the course is the fastest one and the breeze is almost steady.

At most times it is best to use a combination of the two methods discussed, whereby the helmsman alters course to keep on the fastest point of sailing while a man stands by the sheet to prevent a collapse in the event of a sudden wind shift. With this technique, the fore-and-aft pole position is not often changed. The most frequent adjustments are with the helm and sheet. The helmsman should sail according to the principles discussed earlier in this section. He should bear off in the puffs and head up in the lulls; and unless there is a good reason for not doing so, he should moderately tack downwind. It is nearly always harmful to run dead before the wind with the spinnaker set, because this is a slower point of sailing and there is the danger of the spinnaker collapsing from being by the lee. Of course, the helmsman should steer as low as possible but with the sails, especially the spinnaker, drawing at maximum efficiency.

On a yawl, the mizzen staysail can be an effective guide to the helmsman. If he steers too low, this sail will collapse because of being blanketed by the mizzen. A simple rule of thumb for sailing a yawl downwind is to sail as low as possible without collapsing the mizzen staysail.

Trimming a Spinnaker. Principles for trimming the spinnaker sheet are essentially the same as for any other downwind sail. The sheet should be eased as far as possible without the sail beginning to bulge in at the luff. The sail should actually be carried "on edge," with the luff just beginning to curl. The man who tends the sheet is the key to successful spinnaker sailing. Since the wind and the boat's heading change almost continuously, he must follow with almost continuous experiments to try to ease the sheet more and more until the luff curls too much, then quickly trim in just enough to straighten the curl, then try to ease it out again, and keep on repeating this cycle. He must be stationed far enough forward so that he can always watch the luff of the sail. At times he may be able to put several turns around the winch with the sheet and then lead it forward to a position just forward of the main boom. At other times, on a large boat, he may stand at the shrouds and reach outboard to the sheet to give it frequent inward tugs while another sheet trimmer backs him up aft at the winch. If the man at the shrouds cannot reach the sheet with his hand, he may use a short piece of line looped over the sheet. This short line is sometimes called a snatch line, or jerking line. The man at the shrouds should watch the luff continuously and give the sheet a jerk when the luff edge begins to curl too much. In light airs, light sheets with lightweight shackles (or no shackle at all) should be used so that the clew will lift as high as possible. This sheet should be played by hand every moment.

The spinnaker sheet should be led as far aft as possible where it is a maximum distance outboard. On many boats this lead point is at the top corners of the transom, but on some cruiser-racers the lead blocks are somewhat farther forward because these boats have such narrow sterns. When reaching, it sometimes pays to lead the spinnaker sheet through a block at the end of the main boom in order to move the lead outboard.

Handling or taking in the spinnaker is not often difficult if the job is done properly and carefully, but poor helmsmanship and sail-handling during the lowering operation can mean trouble aplenty. In nearly all cases, the genoa or some other jib is set before the spinnaker is taken down. This will provide continual sail power during a race, and the jib will help blanket the spinnaker and thereby make it easier to handle when it is being lowered. After the jib is hoisted, the guy is slacked all the way forward until the pole lies against the headstay or jibstay. Then the spinnaker's tack is released from the guy snap shackle so that the sail's luff flies free.

It is preferable that the boat be headed nearly dead before the wind when the tack is released in order that the spinnaker is blanketed to the greatest extent. At this point in the operation, a man or two is standing by the 'chute's clew and sheet. It is very important that the sheet's end is knotted so that it cannot run through its lead block in the event that the sail should get away from its sheet handler in a fresh breeze. In the event of a sudden knockdown to leeward, the spinnaker

Two major spinnaker problems: hourglassing and knockdown. A crew member of the lead Raven Class boat (left) is attempting to make the swivel at the sail's head turn. However, the twist is so low it is doubtful that this attempt will succeed. The sail will probably have to be lowered to clear it, or if the breeze is light, the tack and clew could be detached and the lower half of the sail untwisted. The 5.5-Meter boat (right) has heeled too far, thus causing spinnaker knockdown. This is similar to a broaching jibe.

sheet should be released so that the sail spills its wind. Be sure the sheet is of sufficient length (twice the boat's overall length is the rule of thumb) in order that the sail will completely spill when the knot at the sheet's end jams in the lead block. When the men on the sheet are ready, a man on the halyard slowly lowers the sail. The sheet tenders, who are usually stationed abaft the main shrouds, pull in on the sheet and gather in the sail as it is lowered, either smothering the sail to keep it from blowing overboard or stuffing it out of the way. The halyard man must be sure he does not lower the spinnaker faster than it can be taken in; otherwise the sail will blow overboard and possibly scoop up water which could tear the sail and make it very difficult to haul it back aboard. In the rare instance that no jib is hoisted, the boat should be headed dead before the wind so that the spinnaker can be lowered in the lee of the mainsail.

A frequently encountered spinnaker-lowering situation occurs when approaching a leeward turning mark during a race, when the next leg of the course is closer than a beam reach. The 'chute should be lowered in advance of reaching the mark. Unless sailing with an experienced crew who have worked together, it is far better to be too soon than

too late getting the spinnaker off. If the mark can be approached on a broad reach, the genoa can be hoisted early to substitute for the 'chute, and not a great deal of speed will be lost if the jib is not blanketed by the mainsail. When jibing around the mark, try to jibe early or else hoist the jib, lower the spinnaker, and then jibe. If the mark is rounded sharply and the boat heads onto a close reach before the spinnaker has been lowered, the sail will blow quite far aft when its tack is released from the guy, and the dousing operation may be difficult because the 'chute will be partly out of the mainsail's wind shadow. In this case the 'chute must be brought in under the after end of the main boom. On a yawl great care must be taken to see that the sail does not foul the mizzenmast or its rigging. This has happened. When the 'chute is being lowered, it should be gathered in by the clew edge of the sail. Work only one leech at a time. If both leeches are pulled on, the sail will fill with wind and become very difficult to handle. The man lowering the spinnaker should always keep a turn of the halyard on its cleat or winch to be sure the sail will not get away from him.

The Rules of the Road are the regulations governing water traffic, and they are the basis upon which maritime law is maintained. They

SAILING RULES OF THE ROAD

cover all crossings, convergings, and meetings, and they establish which vessel is responsible for keeping clear of another.

According to the Rules of the Road, sailboats always have the right of way over powerboats, except in the not very likely possibility of a boat under sail overtaking one under power. In this case the motorboat would have the right of way. As a matter of fact, *every* vessel overtaking any other vessel must keep out of the way of the overtaken one. Also, remember that *all* vessels must keep out of the way of any vessels fishing with nets or lines or trawls. However, even if you have the right of way, do not press your advantage. It can be dangerous. Do not expect all motorboaters to understand your intentions, such as when jibing or coming about in

tight areas. In such cases, keep in mind that the only purpose of the Rules of the Road is to prevent collisions. A large helping of common sense and courtesy, along with observance of the Rules of the Road, should help the sailor avoid collisions.

The rules of right of way for sailing craft are determined by direction of the wind and sailing directions of the boats at their time of meeting. The following are the most common situations you will encounter during normal sailing:

1. A vessel which is running free shall keep out of the way of a vessel which is close-hauled.

2. A vessel which is close-hauled on the port tack shall keep out of the way of a vessel which is close-hauled on the starboard tack.

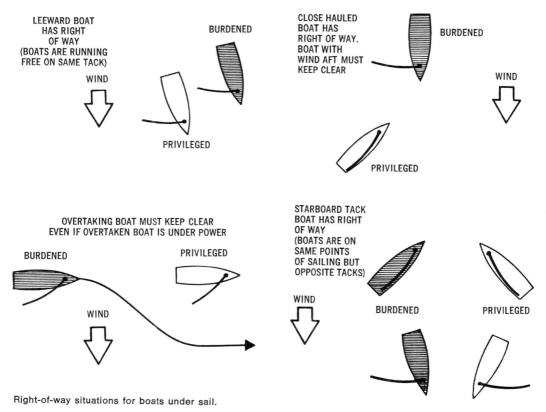

Right-of-way situations for boats under sail.

3. When both are running free, with the wind on different sides, the vessel which has the wind on the port side shall keep out of the way of the other.

4. When both are running free, with the wind on the same side, the vessel which is to the windward shall keep out of the way of the vessel which is to the leeward.

5. A vessel which has the wind aft shall keep out of the way of the other vessel.

Another situation not covered under the preceding rules would arise if a sailboat overtakes another sailboat on the same tack and the same point of sailing when neither is to windward of the other. In this case, the overtaken boat is privileged or has the right of way. The overtaking boat is burdened and must keep clear. In any converging situation the privileged boat must hold her course until there is no longer any danger of collision. If a sailboat is equipped with an auxiliary engine, the only time she is considered a sailboat is when she is propelled by sail alone. When under auxiliary power, the boat *must* follow the motorboat's Rules of the Road, which are explained later in this section.

Common sense and courtesy should be exercised at all times on the water. A sailboat skipper should, as previously stated, never demand his right of way when converging with a large ship in constricted waters. In fact, International Rules and Inland Rules strictly forbid sailboats to hamper large power vessels in a narrow channel. Boats which are not racing should attempt to stay out of the way of boats which are racing, even though the former have the right of way. Rules for racing are quite different from the present Inland Rules of the Road. Racing rules apply only to boats racing among themselves. Obviously, these rules do not apply to boats not racing. Racing rules are taken up in Section VI.

ANCHORING AND LEAVING AN ANCHORAGE

There are many considerations in anchoring safely. The following points are well worth noting:

1. Know the type of bottom. Hard sand holds anchors best; soft sand, next: then soft mud, coral, and rock. Nautical charts usually show bottom conditions you may encounter. If not, heave a lead with tallow on it to pick up bottom specimen. Also, do not pick an anchoring spot so shallow that you may be aground at low tide; or one that is a hundred feet deep when there is one 20 feet deep a little farther away. A chart or lead line will give you the answer.

2. When selecting an anchorage, do not pick a spot too close to other boats. You may swing down onto them if the wind shifts or the tide turns. Actually, shelter from wind is an important consideration. The wind often changes in the night, so make sure you have enough room to swing in a full circle without knocking into other boats, piers, or the beach. Avoid anchoring in or near busy channels where the traffic and the wash from other boats might keep you awake all night.

3. Do not throw the anchor. This will avoid fouling the line and will help "set" the anchor. Never, under any conditions, should you toss out the anchor like a shot-putter trying for an Olympic record. If you do not end up in the drink with the anchor you will be lucky, and a stumble can cause the anchor to gouge the bow. Also, feed the anchor line out by hand so it does not touch the side of your yacht.

4. Sufficient scope is important for holding power because when the line makes a small angle to the bottom (when it is nearly parallel to the bottom), this causes the anchor to dig in. However, in many of today's crowded harbors, it is not always possible to let out all the scope one might desire. It is of the utmost importance to have swinging room, or room to clear other anchored boats no matter what direction the boats are swung by the current or wind. Small boats should be anchored in shallow water so that they will need relatively little scope to achieve the ideal (6 or 7 to 1) scope to depth of water ratio (see p. 91). If large boats cannot veer sufficient scope due to crowded conditions, a heavy anchor should be used. When veering scope be sure to take into consideration and allow for the

rise or fall of the tide. After anchoring, take bearings on various stationary objects so that these may be checked later to see if the anchor is holding.

5. Your boat will be most secure if the "pull" on the anchor is as nearly horizontal as possible. This way the stock can position the flukes properly so the anchor can "dig in." Should you want to make certain how much line you are putting out, paint the anchor line every 10 feet, or tie on markers of light line that you can see by day and feel by dark. Count these markers as the anchor settles straight down and strikes bottom.

6. If you are anchoring in company with other craft, watch the radius and direction of their swing and place yourself accordingly. Be careful of fouling someone else's line, and allow for a sudden wind shift that might cause a collision or beaching. One hint, when anchoring in a fleet, that might help you avoid midnight fending parties is to anchor, if possible, with a group of boats that are similar in size and type to yours. When doing this, locate your boat at least three or four boat lengths away from the nearest boat, whether that boat is ahead, astern, or on either beam. If you anchor among larger boats, allowances must be made for their greater swinging radius.

7. If the anchor line is too short or if you must anchor in a confined area (such as close to other boats) to allow enough scope to hold the boat in heavy seas, add a second anchor to the line, tied about one-third to one-half the distance from the terminal anchor. The second does not need to be as heavy as the lower one. This will increase the scope of the lower end of the anchor line from 50 to 90 percent, by decreasing the lift of the line. In other words, the line between the two anchors will remain nearly horizontal, depending upon the weight of the upper anchor and the size of the waves lifting the boat. This will cause the lower anchor to bite deeper in the bottom instead of lifting or dragging. The upper anchor has almost no bite into the bottom and acts as a shock absorber. Instead of the boat coming up short against the heavy anchor, the boat will have to lift the upper anchor before it can pull against the lower one. This will eliminate any sudden jerks against the mooring bitt.

8. In crowded areas, it may be necessary to use a stern anchor to prevent your yacht from swinging into a nearby boat. But this should be done only where there is very little likelihood of strong cross currents or winds, since a strong push from the side would exert tremendous pull on the two anchors, possibly causing one or both of them to drag.

9. If you know you are anchoring in rocky or snag-strewn waters, attach the end of your line to the anchor's crown, then lead it past but not through the ring. Bind the line to the ring with two turns of twine. Then run the line to the boat. When you anchor, the hook will act the same as if it were conventionally fastened to the line. But should your anchor foul under a rock or snag and refuse to break out, haul up on the line until it is straight up and down. Jerk repeatedly as you run your boat slowly ahead until the binding breaks and the pull is transferred to the anchor's crown. It should then back out from whatever has fouled it.

10. With the anchor and line set, it may be desirable, particularly during heavy weather, to install chafing gear to protect the anchor line. The chafing gear might be split hose or canvas wrapped around the anchor cable where it would rub.

11. After anchoring, in most places it is good practice to set an anchor light before dark. Usually this is located on, or suspended from, the forestay. Also before darkness sets in, take cross bearings on your anchorage; or better still, note ranges by two prominent objects in line on shore. These ranges should preferably be at right angles to one another, and they should be of such a nature that you can recognize them in the dark. You can easily determine whether or not you are dragging by subsequently noting these ranges.

12. When raising, or weighing, the anchor, pull in on the line until it lies straight up and down. At this time, there is a minimum of scope and the anchor has little if any holding power. Then a hard tug up on the line will pull the anchor's head up and break the flukes out of the bottom. If the anchor is difficult to break out, additional force may be applied to the line, once it is straight up and down, by taking a turn or two on the cleat and swaying on the line. Taking a turn and swaying on the last few inches of line to

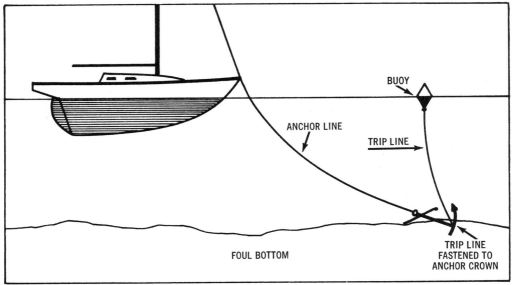

BUOY

ANCHOR LINE

TRIP LINE

FOUL BOTTOM

TRIP LINE
FASTENED TO
ANCHOR CROWN

Using a trip anchor line.

bring it truly up and down is a most per-suasive technique against a recalcitrant an-chor. Or the anchor may be sailed out by heaving in to up-and-down, belaying, and set-ting a headsail and backing it to blow the bow off. With the anchor line straight up and down, any motion of the boat applies tre-mendous force to the line.

Anchoring Situations. There are three situa-tions you may be faced with when anchoring:

1. *When close-hauled, and wind and tide are in the same direction:* Luff or swing up-wind; lower jib; wait until the boat gathers sternway; and then let go the anchor. This technique is also used where there is no tide or where it is negligible.

2. *When running, and the wind is against the tide:* Lower mainsail and approach under jib only; just before reaching desired anchor-age spot, lower jib; wait until boat gathers sternway, and then let go the anchor.

3. *When running, and wind and tide are in the same direction:* Lower mainsail and ap-proach under jib only; lower jib a little way from the chosen location; let go the anchor; and then snub (stop the running out of) the

anchor line and allow the boat to swing to the tide.

Except in the latter case, it is usually wise not to let go of the anchor until the boat has stopped forereaching and has begun to gather sternway. Make sure that the anchor rode is laid out along the deck or coiled down care-fully so that it will run free. Do not stand in the coils, and make sure that they cannot take a turn around your legs or around any other object on board. Then lower the anchor until you feel it strike bottom, and as your boat gathers sternway, pay out the amount of rode necessary for the desired ratio of scope to depth. (If you have an engine, it is not a bad idea to start it and back away from the an-chor.) When the anchor is set and scope ad-justed, make your anchor rode or cable fast.

When you are ready to weigh anchor, fol-low much the same procedure as when leav-ing a mooring, except that the anchor and anchor line must be contended with. Recov-ering the anchor itself is best accomplished by moving up to a position over the anchor under power (or if necessary, under sail in short tacks), taking in the slack until the shank of the anchor lifts from the bottom.

HEAVING TO

While sailing, there are often times you wish to "heave to," or "lay to"—to stop the boat and maintain its approximate position without the use of an anchor. As was already explained, a boat can be stopped from going ahead by pointing it into the wind. But as you will remember, in this position the boat will begin to drift backward until it falls off the wind and fills away, at which point it will start sailing again. If you wish the boat not to fall away, you can arrange the tiller to the leeward side of the boat and trim the sheets to the point where the craft will not sail. The exact position of tiller and the trim of sheets varies from boat to boat, and only by practice can you determine the proper positions for laying to. But, as the size of the boat increases, the harder it is to make her lay to.

APPROACHING AND PICKING UP A MOORING

The easiest way to pick up a buoy is to pass to its lee and then "shoot" up into the wind with sufficient way to carry the boat up to the buoy. The object is to come dead in the water as the bow is laid alongside the buoy. To accomplish this, as you approach the spot where the buoy is located, the momentum of the boat should be checked by letting go the jib halyard and taking in the jib. This should slow the boat up, if sailing close-hauled or on a reach, and will leave the forward part of the boat clear for you to handle the mooring line. If the boat is still going too fast, the main sheet can be slacked a bit until the sail shivers along its luff. When directly to leeward of the buoy, shove the tiller or wheel hard down (to leeward) and the boat will spin around head to wind while the momentum will make her forereach, with the mainsail fluttering, as she glides up to the mooring buoy under control of the rudder. If the main boom has been well off, the sheet can be trimmed in a little as the tiller is shoved down, and this will accelerate the turn. Care must be taken to make sure that the sail does not fill from one side or the other as the boat shoots for the mooring. Filling will add to the boat's headway and may make her overshoot the buoy, so the sheet should be left with plenty of slack after the boat has come head to the wind. The boat will coast toward the mooring. Your crewman should be ready at the bow to pick up the buoy and make the mooring line fast to the cleat in the bow. A boat hook will help in the picking-up operation.

Helm control is very important when shooting for a mooring. If the wheel or tiller is turned suddenly and to its full extent, the boat's way or momentum is partially killed because a rudder rapidly jammed to one side acts somewhat like a brake. If it is desired to make a long shoot, the helm is eased over slowly, and the boat carries a lot of way or coasts a long distance before coming to a stop. A boat's weight or displacement will have a great bearing on how much way she carries also. A heavy boat will carry way for a very long distance compared to a light boat. The exact distance a given boat will shoot under any given conditions will vary greatly and can only be determined by experience. A boat's momentum also depends on how fast she is moving and on conditions of wind and water. In a strong wind and rough water, a boat will carry less way. Strength and direction of current must be noted, because naturally this will affect the boat's speed greatly. Since the latter part of a "shoot" will be at very slow speeds, any current will affect the maneuver out of all normal proportion. A boat with a favorable current under her seems to shoot forever. Many an otherwise well-planned maneuver has been spoiled because it was only when the boat slowed down in a shoot that a small but significant current announced its presence to a surprised skipper by taking over the situation. Even the best of sailors sometimes misjudge a boat's shooting speed and distance. When this happens, if the boat is carrying too much way, do not attempt to pick up the mooring, but bear off, sail away, and try the approach again.

Steps in picking up a mooring.

There is another basic method of slowing a boat down to pick up a mooring besides shooting into the wind. This is to slack the sheets while on some point of sailing between close-hauled and a beam reach. A close reach is the optimum. With sheets slacked and sails luffing all over on a close reach, no power is being applied to the boat, and she will lose headway. If more headway is desired during such a maneuver, the sheets need simply be trimmed back in. The amount they are trimmed back in will correspond to the amount of power applied to the boat. By alternately trimming in and slacking out the sheets to achieve the desired amount of luff, precise speed control can be attained, and the boat can be eased slowly up to a mooring buoy.

The reason why a close reach is the optimum heading for this maneuver is that wind shifts can then be responded to merely by adjusting the trim of the sails, while maintaining the same heading. By contrast, if the boat were luffing along close-hauled, and the wind shifted more ahead during the maneuver, the option of trimming in for more power would be lost, and the only way to gain headway would be to head off, which would take the boat away from the course desired to her buoy. If, on the other hand, the boat were luffing along on a beam reach, and the wind shifted aft more, then the option of continuing to luff the sails would be lost, and the only way to slow down would be to head up, again heading the boat away from her desired maneuvering course. Significant wind shifts are common in harbors, where this kind of maneuvering is likely to be done.

Checking Your Mooring. Before leaving the subject of permanent moorings, here is a very important fact to remember: Just because you have a good mooring firmly set in a safe place, do not assume all will be well forever. Moorings get dragged out of position. Rust, chafe, and rot are constant enemies and so, especially in salt water, is that insidious malady electrolysis, caused by proximity of dissimilar metals. Here are some things to do:

1. Several times a season, especially after a blow, check the position by taking bearings on fixed shore points, which you should have done when you dropped the anchor. Even swinging at the end of a long mooring cable, the bearings will not change much unless the anchor has dragged.

2. Some moorings are pulled every autumn and stored ashore until the following season. More are lifted and inspected every two or three years. But it is best to lift and inspect them at the beginning of each season, except for the rope pendant, which comes off at the end of each season to be replaced with a "winter stick." (Follow local practice on this.) This annual inspection is particularly important where underwater chemical or electrical conditions accelerate corrosion of the anchor and lower chain. Such conditions may differ in various parts of the same harbor.

3. An anchor that spends practically all its time in the mud will rust less than one that is hauled and left out in the weather all winter. But they will rust, and the shackle especially should be inspected for rust, corrosion, or erosion from friction with sand. The eye that holds the shackle in the end of the shank is also sensitive to these troubles, and swivels often have to be examined and replaced.

4. All shackles and pins should be checked, pins set up if at all slack, and rewired.

5. If the chain, shackles, or any parts look badly rusted, knock and scrape the rust away. Get down to bright metal wherever you suspect weakness, and if a noticeable amount

of solid metal is gone, junk the item. That old saw about a chain being as strong as its weakest link applies literally to moorings.

6. The upper end of a chain—the fathom or two nearest the surface—seems to wear or corrode out faster than the lower part. Even if you don't inspect your whole mooring every year, pull up as much of the chain by hand as you can. Look it over carefully to see if the top few feet need replacing.

7. Various schools of thought as to mooring pendants all agree that no mooring pendant can be too strong. One school, while admitting the strength and durability of the synthetics preferred by many, points out that good manila is plenty strong in its first season and is enough cheaper so they can afford to throw away the old pendant and rig a new one each year. Most new pendants are rigged at the beginning of the season, but some people along the East Coast put on their new pendants around midsummer when the hurricane season is imminent.

Another important point is a word about guest moorings: Check them carefully. Certainly all of us who cruise appreciate the courtesy of guest moorings offered by a yacht club or town in the ports we visit. But never blindly assume that the moorings offered will hold your boat. When you pick up such a mooring, haul up the pendant and some of the top chain and satisfy yourself that it is of a size and condition to hold your boat. Check with the yacht-club launchman or someone else in a position to know what, and how much of it, is on the bottom of that chain. You might find that you're safer on your own anchor.

RAFTING

A popular form of mooring several boats at a club rendezvous or similar social gathering is to tie up or raft alongside a friendly earlier arrival. This is sociable, for it is possible for people to visit back and forth between the boats. Generally, such tie-ups are of short duration and the visitor does not drop his own anchor. He merely ties up to the first boat, using bow and stern lines with fenders

between to protect both craft. Often a spring line is required to prevent movement fore and aft. If there is dragging of the one anchor, or should the group wish to raft overnight, other anchors should be properly lowered. When rafting, follow the same general sailing procedure you would follow in picking up a mooring.

When you want to leave a rafting situation,

A fore view of how boats can be rafted together.

walk your boat astern by the use of light lines. This will permit her to be under complete control at all times, and with a couple of fenders between the hulls no harm can result. The boat should be carried far enough along so that she can hang to the stern of the anchored craft by a bow line while the sails are being hoisted. When all is ready the bow line is cast off exactly as when leaving a mooring and your boat can then proceed on your chosen tack. The chosen tack should be one which will allow the greatest freedom of movement, as well as being the most expeditious from the standpoint of getting way on and retaining full control of the craft. Generally winds would be light, for boats should not tie up alongside in heavy weather, so ease the sheets and get moving as quickly as possible so that the boat will respond to her rudder and be under control.

DOCKING PROCEDURE

In coming alongside a dock or another boat, under sail, follow the same general procedure as when picking up a mooring. Approaching a dock from leeward or windward is simple. If it is leeward, head-reach up to the dock with the sheets loose and attach the mooring lines to the dock. A member of the crew should be up forward to see that the bow of the boat does not ram the dock. Landing on the windward side, sail downwind until you are beam-on to the dock. Put out the fenders, break out docking lines, and make ready the boat hook. Push the tiller hard over so that the boat swings around into the wind. The hard-over rudder acts as a brake and the vessel will be almost dead in the water about a boat length away from the dock. The craft will drift broadside against the dock. Tie up, and the job is done.

If you are coming in too fast to a dock, you can hold or fend a small sailboat off with a boat hook, or one of your crew members can do it with his feet. But when a crewman fends off a boat with his feet, be sure he sits down on the bow and holds both his feet straight out, balancing himself with his hands on the jibstay. In this way his legs will better take the shock of fending off the boat and yet he will not be pushed overboard. If you do

not have quite enough speed to make a dock, a light line can be heaved to someone on the dock. But be sure that one end of the line is made fast to your boat. If your heaving line misses the dock and you start drifting backward, you can follow the same procedure as when caught in stays or in irons. However, the action of the tiller is reversed. Usually you can get enough momentum to get to the dock; if not, you will have to catch the wind and make a fresh attempt to dock your boat.

Should you run into a situation where there is simply not enough room to come about and approach a dock into the wind, it might be expedient to drop an anchor out from the dock and then allow the boat to drift back under check from the anchor until close enough to reach the dock from the stern of the boat. It is generally the best practice to lower all sails when at a dock so that the boat will lie quietly without the possibility of stray gusts of wind surging it ahead or sideways into possible trouble with neighboring craft. Fenders, where used, should be employed with intelligence. If they are secured to the boat, as is the normal practice, there is always the chance that the vessel will move along the dock and the fender slip into a void, leaving her unprotected. If the fend-

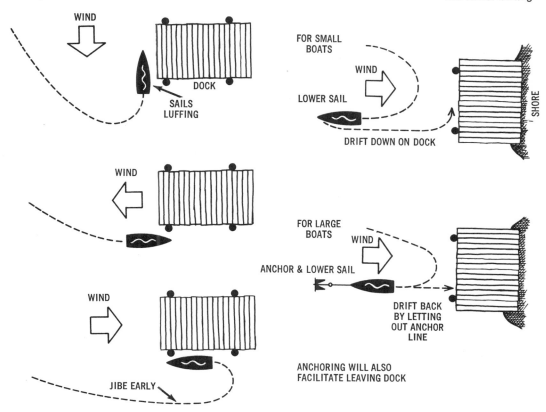

Methods of approaching a dock.

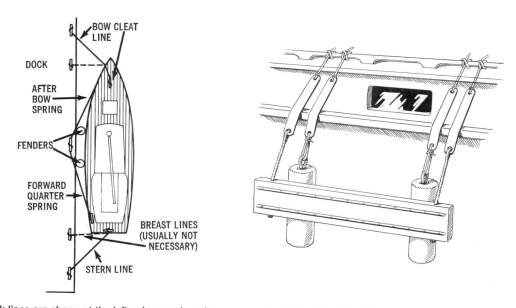

Dock lines are shown at the left; a bumper-board arrangement is illustrated at the right.

ers are made fast to the dock the protection is better, but there is the possibility of sailing away, leaving the fenders behind.

Occasionally it is necessary to make a direct right-angle approach in the dock's middle so that the landing must be made bow first. This can be very dangerous in a large, heavy boat, and it should be avoided if possible. If unavoidable, however, a very slow approach should be made. It is better to have the boat stop short than carry too much way. If she stops short without quite reaching the dock, a crewman stationed on the bow might be able to throw a line to someone standing on the dock. In a small, light boat a fast landing, with too much way, is not quite as serious, though it is certainly most unseamanlike. A crewman can sit on the foremost part of the bow facing forward with a leg on each side of the jibstay so that he can fend off with his feet just before the bow makes contact with the dock. Falling short and having to make another try is far preferable to risking damage to the boat and injury to the crew.

Docking Lines. Three lines are vital for tying up a larger boat—bow, stern, and spring. The spring line is fastened to the stern cleat and is brought amidships and fastened to a dock cleat. This third line keeps the boat parallel to the dock and prevents the boat from swinging and banging against the dock. It also provides enough slack on bow and stern lines to allow for the rise and fall of the tide.

LEAVING HER SHIPSHAPE

When you have secured to a mooring or tied up at a dock, you should then "stow ship." While every skipper has his own ideas about how to leave his boat after a sail, there are certain things that must be done. If you have a boom crutch, for example, ease down the boom on the topping lift until it rests in its crutch. Haul in the mainsheet to keep the boom and crutch in a secure position. We now come to the subject of stowing and furling the sails. Methods vary for the small-boat owner and the cruiser-racer skipper.

Stowing and Furling Sails. When small-boat sails arrive from the sailmaker they will probably come in a small box. This is done from a combination of habit and the need to conserve space and minimize shipping charges. Leave the spinnaker as is for the present, but unpack the main and jib and fold them in a flaking manner along the foot. The theory is that the sailmaker has gone to a lot of trouble to develop a fabric with an extra-smooth finish—and it should be kept that way. The fewer creases the better, and those that are necessary should run fore and aft. Some sailmakers also have recommended rolling sails entirely. Sails should be kept in sail bags.

As mentioned before, the cruising and distance-racing enthusiasts have gained most from the development of nylon and Dacron. Where sails must be furled on spars or stowed below, synthetics have reduced to a fraction the time needed for drying and airing compared to cotton. However, certain precautions should be taken. Sail covers are a must. A light Dacron cover that will stow away easily is adequate, as its prime function is to keep out the sun and dirt. There have been cases where gases from factories have done serious damage to synthetic sails; and soot itself, while possibly not harmful, seems to adhere to Dacron and is difficult to wash off.

There are two ways to start a furl of the mainsail. One is to roll the bunt up on the boom in a neat roll. The other is to flake or fake the sail down in folds on the boom as it is lowered. It is easier to fake down a large sail than to roll it up. Before lowering away, if the boom is not grooved, it is good practice to rig the stops (strips of material or lines) between the boom and the foot rope ready for instant use when the sail is down. The battens should be removed before the sail is faked down; once the sail is faked, install the sail cover.

The next thing to do is to fold and put the jib or jibs into their respective sail bags after the battens have been removed. Put the head of the sail in the bag first—the foot last. But the cruising-boat owner should be sure his sail lockers are ventilated. Nylon spinnakers should be given special care as the fabric will weaken and colors may bleed if wet or salty (attracting more moisture) when put away. It is still a good idea to dry sails whenever possible, and synthetics dry faster than natural fibers.

Other Tasks. Having finished with the sails, belay all halyards around their proper cleats and coil down the ends. Then, to prevent their beating a tattoo on the mast when it blows, either secure them to the main shrouds with thin line, or twist one of them, say the main halyard, around the mast and then belay it to its cleat. Coil and make fast all other cordage. Collect all the life preservers and other gear; either stow them in compartments on the boat or take them ashore. Make fast all loose gear.

In centerboard craft, be sure to raise the board and leave it secured with the pin provided for that purpose. The board should always be left in the full-up position; for if left down, it may work back and forth, causing serious wear of the bearings or strain on the centerboard well. On some small boats, it is good practice also to unship the rudder and stow it. If the rudder is left shipped (on any boat), the tiller should be lashed to prevent excessive movement of the rudder as the boat rides at her moorings.

Check your boat very carefully and make note of anything and everything that should be done before your next outing. It is far better to do any repairs now while they are fresh in your mind than to wait until a later time.

It is well too to break out a sponge, and swab, and tidy up the sides and deck. Scum and dirt is far easier to remove while it is still wet than later, when it has dried and hardened. Also make sure that the cabin area is clean and straightened up. Check your plumbing closing and engine (if used) closing schedule as recommended in the boat's instruction manual. This usually includes closing certain sea cocks, opening the main battery switch, and shutting off the gasoline supply line. Turn ventilators against the chance of rain; close and lock all hatches. Some sailboats have cockpit covers. These are canvas coverings that fit over the cockpit, enclosing it completely. If you have one, unroll the cockpit cover and lash it in place securely.

Finally, check the mooring line very carefully. Be sure that it runs from mooring cleat through the bow chock and then to the mooring. If you are tying up at a dock, be sure your boat fenders are down to prevent any damage to the hull. When all these tasks have been accomplished, you are ready to go ashore.

SAILING A CATAMARAN

A catamaran has no major differences in sailing principle and basic technique from a monohull. But there are some things about sailing techniques that do require understanding.

To Windward. It has been said often that it is difficult to go about in a catamaran, but this is not correct. Here is a detailed description to show newcomers to catamarans that there is nothing difficult involved.

It is necessary to sail the boat around in a smooth arc and to keep it moving fast all the time. This is satisfactory in most weather, but in heavy weather the skipper will have to put the boat round as it comes down the back of a wave. The next wave will help to push the bow round on to the new heading. The jib should be kept sheeted as the helm is put down and the boat luffs. This will keep the boat driving until it comes slightly past head to wind and falls on to the other tack. When the wind is coming over the bow at about 25 degrees on the new heading, the jib is released and the crew moves across. The for'ard hand should snap the jib on while the skipper checks that the mainsheet traveler has gone across. The jib should always be sheeted in before the mainsail. The boat should now be driving off again on the other tack, but it is still a good idea to drop about a point below the best heading so the power is delivered more quickly. The amount the boat is allowed to fall away can be reduced as you get more expert. When she picks up speed, the boat should be brought slowly back to the proper heading. If a catamaran does get in irons the correct way out is to release the mainsheet and allow the boat to drift astern.

When going astern the rudders must be reversed. If you want to sail off on the starboard tack the tiller is held over to port, putting the rudders to starboard. As the boat drifts astern, the stern moves to starboard and the bow falls off to port. When the boat is at 45 degrees to the wind, the sheets are pulled on again and the boat will then have enough power to sail off on starboard tack. The reverse applies to port tack.

In sailing to windward, a catamaran needs slightly flatter sails than a single-hulled boat because of its greater speed and therefore higher apparent wind speed. The angle at which boats sail to windward varies among classes, and even between different boats of the same class, but reaching to windward, which is calamitous in single-hulled boats, is not as unprofitable in catamarans. However, as it is still not as good as pointing close, have your sails cut for good windward work and sail the boat as close to the wind as is consistent with speed. In general the only way to find the best angle to sail to windward is to do a lot of sailing in all conditions, but to learn all the lessons this will give you, it is vital to have some way of telling at what angle of attack you are sailing.

One device to give you the angle of attack is a combination of fixed and movable wind indicators. The fixed indicator is set at the average of the angles your boat makes to the wind when sailing to weather in varying conditions. The best thing to use is a small metal tag attached to the shrouds about 6 feet above the deck. Just below each of these tags are the movable indicators, made of anything which will follow wind variations without tangling. When you are on the wind, provided your sails are set at their best, sail at such an angle that the movable indicator is close to the fixed indicator; but remember that you can sail higher in heavy weather than in light weather. This means that in heavy going, you will have to sail high of the fixed indicator, and in light weather, low of it. The sails themselves must be adjustable for various conditions—the jib and main being moved out on the travelers as the wind freshens to widen the slot between the two sails, thus giving more drive with less heeling moment. With high-aspect mainsails, it is necessary to keep the leech tight and keep the twist out of the sails.

The mast is bent to flatten the sail as the wind freshens, and in lower-aspect sails, the boom can be bent to advantage by leading most of the mainsheet purchases from the middle of the boom. The tension on the boom outhaul should be easily adjustable, and needs to be used continually to vary the fullness of the sail over a wide range. This is particularly convenient as it can make it possible to have the same set of battens for all weathers. The battens are shaped to have the maximum fullness near the mast with a very straight run to the leech.

Going to weather in seas makes any boat pitch and therefore the top of the sail travels at varying speeds. It is more efficient if the angle of attack of the wind on the sail can be kept constant, and to do this, the boat should be pulled away going down the seas and pointed high going into them. In light weather both plates (daggerboards) need to be down. In heavier weather less plate is necessary and by not putting the plates down so far, the heeling movement is reduced. The crew and skipper should both be as far forward as possible (the for'ard hand forward of the mast) and the boat should be kept as flat as possible to keep the sails operating properly. It is permissible to sail on one hull provided the angle of heel is not excessive.

Coming About. The fastest come-abouts are made by helmsmen who practice the principle of steering with their sails. Here is how:

1. Be sure you are really close-hauled—not the wider angle of close reaching. A cat will not come about from a reach.

2. Do not push your tillers over all at once. At the beginning of your turn, apply only a small angle to your rudders then add angle progressively as your turning speed increases. (Water should flow along both sides of your rudder blades to develop "lift" in the direction you want the sterns to swing.) If you apply too much angle too quickly your rudder blades will "stall out" and produce drag instead of turn.

3. At the point when you are head-to-wind let your mainsheet run about a foot. (If kept cleated the boat might "weather cock" and go into irons.)

4. As soon as you are on your proper course in the new direction and moving, retrim your sail and begin pointing her to best advantage.

Three positions of catamaran sailing: (left) beam reaching; (center) close-hauled; and (right) running.

5. The maneuver should be accomplished with a smooth, unhesitating motion throughout. You will soon discover the proper speed necessary.

6. In a rough sea, pick a relatively smooth spot in which to come about. If a sea "busts" the boat she will stop dead and go into irons. Be sure to move your weight a bit forward during the maneuver (this gets your sterns out of the water and enables them to swing).

Getting Out of Irons. The sailing-backward technique is the quickest way to get out of irons. Push your tillers (about 45 degrees) and the boom to the same side of the boat and hold them there. When you stop going backward, pull your tillers to windward. As soon as the boat begins to move forward, trim in your mainsail and steer your proper course.

Jibing. One of the easiest maneuvers in a catamaran is to jibe. Apply a slow steady turn toward your new course and when the sail is by the lee, take hold of the mainsheet above the stern bridle and pull it around by hand with one quick motion. *Do not* round up but assume your new course quickly and firmly. A catamaran does not gyrate on a jibe like a monohull.

Reaching. Wide hawses are advantageous on the reach because, by keeping the twist out of the sail, they ensure that the whole height of the sail is working effectively. Here again the wind indicators are invaluable. They should be used to set the sails so the wind flows on to their leading edges smoothly, i.e., so the leading edge of the sail is approximately tangential to the apparent wind. The aim is to divert as much wind as possible directly astern of the boat. In hard weather on reaching legs, it is necessary to keep the crew's weight as far aft as possible and to keep him steady. This is done by a lanyard attached to the stern which is hooked onto the crew's trapeze wire. The trapeze wire should be long enough for the crew to move well aft, and should have three rings attached to it, each about 6 to 8 inches apart. The bottom one is used for reaches.

There is an advantage in having the trapeze hand "fixed" in position this way. If the boat becomes overpowered, the for'ard hand does not move—because he already is as far aft as he can go—the skipper then knows he must overcome the puff through easing the main. In this way, there will be no ghastly misunderstanding where both skipper and crew try to fix the trouble, and end up by causing more.

At very high speed on a beam reach, the jib often impedes the flow around the leeward side of the mainsail. This will happen unless you have a full-width jib hawse, so the jib can lead further outboard to match the reaching setting of the main, thus giving you the wider, more effective slot.

As with windward work, the seas have to be negotiated properly. If there is any danger of burying the lee bow in a sea, it is better to sail slightly higher and angle over the wave rather than ease the main which will reduce the drive but not alter the course. This is particularly true when the waves are on the quarter. The safest spot is going along the waves (on a beam reach). In addition it is generally best to keep the same course and ease through the puffs. Changing course would only reduce speed. Like single-hulled planing boats, the cat exceeds the speed of the waves and has to sail up and over them.

As a general rule, it is advisable to ease the sheets as little as possible and keep going straight for the mark. At the very high speeds a cat can travel, it does not pay to go too far off the course. On the reach, the leeward plate is kept right up, with the windward plate only as far down as is necessary to stop excessive leeway—say about a third of its depth—and raked as far aft as possible to reduce drag.

Running. A catamaran runs dead downwind the same as any conventional sailboat. This is her slowest point of sailing but you will notice that she is a much more steady platform and will not roll, yaw, and pitch like a monohull.

A SAILBOAT UNDER POWER

As previously stated, all sailboats equipped with inboard propulsion engines are referred to as auxiliaries. But sailing an auxiliary adds an entirely new dimension to the responsibilities of the skipper. He must be able to handle the boat under power as well as under sail. He must know how to operate the power plant and all its associated electrical circuits and piping systems, be conversant with the minimum daily maintenance needs of the engine, and have a knowledge of basic troubleshooting procedures. He has to be aware of all safety precautions. Remember that if a skipper does not really know his sailboat engine, it becomes a liability, because of the inherent dangers that exist when adequate safety precautions are not followed, or when the engine is not kept in good running order. An unreliable engine is worse than none at all, for it leads to a false sense of security, and the skipper can count on neither a reliable engine, nor the absolute certainty that all his maneuvers must be carried out under sail.

In handling a sailboat under power, many of the principles learned about handling her under sail can be put to good use. In particular, the effects of wind and tide on the hull, the speed required for adequate steerage way, and an appreciation for the amount the boat will forereach under varying conditions are important. There are, however, forces that affect a sailboat only when she is under power. The effects of these forces must be understood in order to handle the boat properly. Most important is the force of ahead *propeller wash,* water forced astern when the engine is going ahead. This wash, when deflected by the rudder, will move the stern of the boat in the opposite direction to that of the rudder. Astern propeller wash has much less maneuvering potential, since it is not deflected by the rudder.

This lateral force created by ahead propeller wash against the rudder can be used to pivot a sailboat in restricted waters. This maneuver is accomplished by rapidly shifting the engine from ahead to reverse, so that the boat gains very little headway or sternway. In a turn to starboard, each time the engine is put ahead, right rudder is used; the surge of water from the propeller forces the stern to port, and consequently the bow to starboard. Before the boat gathers much headway, the engine is reversed and the rudder is shifted. This operation is repeated until the boat is headed in the direction desired. A turn in like manner to port necessitates just the opposite rudder action. The same force is also used to good advantage to spring away from the windward side of a dock, as will be explained in detail later.

A second force that affects a sailboat under power is that of *torque.* Briefly, it is a force that tends to *walk* (move slowly sideways) the stern of a boat in the direction toward which the propeller is turning. As most propellers rotate clockwise (when viewed from astern) when going ahead and counterclockwise when going astern, torque forces the stern to starboard when going ahead and to port when going astern. Propeller torque has more effect on shallow-draft boats than on those with deep draft, because of the greater lateral resistance of the latter's underwater body. With ample steerage way, torque is of little importance, except that, when going ahead, the boat will tend to steer to port with the rudder amidships. With little or no way on, however, the rudder has very little effect when the engine is first put in reverse and the torque cannot be counteracted. With no wind, the stern will back to port with the rudder amidships, but a moderate, or stronger, breeze adds another factor. A sailboat nearly always will back into the wind. The reasons for this are that the center of effort of the spars and rigging is located forward of the center of lateral resistance and that the underwater shape is more cut away forward than aft, and consequently the bow falls off to leeward. In a light breeze the rudder can be used to counteract this tendency, but with more breeze the bow will fall off faster than the stern can be turned and the boat will almost *always* end up stern to the wind.

Docking Under Power. When docking under power, some basic rules must be taken into consideration. Maneuver the boat slowly, surely, and with minimum risk of damage; speed is not a seamanlike objective in handling a boat alongside a dock or another boat. Always know the precise direction and strength of the wind and the current. Knowing these, when possible choose the most advantageous docking situation, that is, moving into the wind and current. Wind and current often will not be from the same direction, and in such cases it is best to dock *into* the dominating force. For example, in a 10-knot breeze, you should dock into a 2-knot current, and conversely, in a 25-knot breeze with a slight current of 1 knot or less, the docking should be made into the wind, if possible. The reason for docking into the forces affecting the boat whenever possible is that a sailboat is very hard to stop when under power due to her large forward momentum and the inefficiency of her propeller. Most sailboats use propellers with minimum drag when stopped, so that the propeller slows the boat down as little as possible when she is under sail. These propellers, usually two-bladed or *feathering* (with blades that turn to a vertical position for minimum drag), are not very efficient for backing down. Also, with a heavy current, steerage way is maintained to the end of the maneuver, while with a fair current steerage is lost while the boat is still making way over the bottom.

When the wind and current are perpendicular to the pier, instead of parallel to it, another choice presents itself. The maneuver is more difficult when the approach is made on the side of the pier toward which the stronger force is moving. In this case, the wind or current (or both, if they have the same direction) will set the boat against the dock, and the danger is that of not allowing enough room for leeway when making the initial approach, with the result that the boat may be set against the dock hard enough to damage her. With strong forces setting onto the only available pier, it may be necessary to drop an anchor to control the boat's motion toward the pier. If the water is rough alongside the pier, such an anchor can also be used to hold the boat off the pier after the landing, so that she will not be damaged.

Experienced sailors prefer the leeward or into-the-current approach. This maneuver has the advantage that, during the approach and once alongside, wind or current tend to keep the boat away from the pier. An approach to the leeward side of a pier should be made with decisiveness and adequate steerage way. The boat should be brought into the pier at a slight angle, so that the leeward setting effects of the wind and current can be compensated for. The stronger the leeward set, the faster the approach should be. At very nearly the last moment, the boat is swung parallel to the pier and the engine is reversed smartly to kill headway. The first line over should be the bow spring line (a line leading from the bow to a point well aft on the pier), which can be used both to check forward motion and to spring the boat in to the pier. The second and third lines over should be the bow line (a line leading from the bow forward to the pier) and stern line (a line leading from the stern aft to the pier); lastly, the quarter spring line (a line leading from the quarter to a point well forward on the pier) may be made up.

Landing in all possible combinations of

wind and current cannot be explained within the confines of a book. If the beginner remembers that the deeper the draft of the boat, the more current affects the hull in relation to wind, he has the basic principle on which to decide the approach in each situation. He should also remember that it is easy to overestimate the effect of wind and to underestimate the effect of current, perhaps because wind strength is much easier to sense than is current strength. It is recommended that docking evolutions be practiced often under varying conditions, not just when you need to dock.

In preparation for docking maneuver, it is important that the entire evolution be worked out in your own mind ahead of time, including an alternative plan to be used if the initial approach fails at any point in its execution. The experienced sailor tries never to get himself into a situation from which he cannot recover. He makes elaborate preparations even for a simple maneuver. An anchor should always be ready for use in any situation where engine failure would endanger or embarrass the boat. Under some circumstances, a ready stern anchor may also be necessary. In every case, dock lines should be ready and led. Fenders should be out, but preferably not over the side until near the pier. Most important, the crew should be briefed on the skipper's plan and exactly what their individual jobs will be. Confusion at the last minute is the cause of most unseamanlike docking maneuvers. The crew, once briefed, should keep out of the skipper's way, and out of his line of vision.

Getting Under Way. When getting under way, the same detailed preparations should be made. It is worth emphasizing again that it is care in preparation that separates the seaman from the landlubber. If the boat is on the leeward side of the pier, the maneuver is relatively simple. (This is another reason for landing on the lee side of a dock.) Spring lines are taken in, coiled, and stowed. Then bow and stern lines are taken in together. Remember that the bow will swing faster than the stern and a strong breeze could cause the stern to walk toward the pier before clearing. For this reason, it is best to cast off the stern line first in a strong breeze, then cast off the bow line, and then go ahead when clear.

When leaving the windward side of the pier, the maneuver is more complex. If the wind or current is very strong, the only solution is to row out an anchor to weather (if one was not dropped during the landing) and warp the boat around head to wind or current. If, however, the forces setting onto the pier are not too strong, the boat may be gotten under way under power alone. This is accomplished by springing the stern away from the pier. First, the bow line, stern line, and quarter spring are taken in, then a fender is positioned forward and a crewman is stationed forward to fend off the bow. The engine is put ahead slowly and the rudder put over toward the pier. The boat pivots slowly against the bow spring. Power is kept on until the bow comes in against the forward fender and the stern swings away from the pier. When the stern is well away from the pier, the engine is reversed smartly, the rudder is shifted, and the bow spring is taken in. If the wind is not too strong, the boat can be backed rapidly away from the pier. When the wind is strong, there is the danger that the bow will scrape along the pier before the boat can be backed clear. If this is the case, the rudder should *not* be shifted immediately, allowing the boat to back in a direction more parallel to the pier until the bow is well clear. In this maneuver, it should be remembered that torque effect tends to walk the stern to port. In *all* cases the boat should be backed clear smartly to avoid being blown back against the pier. Again, practice is essential.

Mooring or Anchoring Under Power. When mooring to a buoy or anchoring, it is most important to determine whether the wind or the current will have the greater effect on the boat's heading, once she is stopped. Simply, after anchoring or mooring, will the boat lie head to wind or head to current? Observation of other craft in the anchorage is a good indication. Beware, however, of using power boats as a guide, because their large windage and shallow draft tend to make them lie head to wind when a deep-draft sailboat with opposite characteristics may lie head to current. Once this determination has been made, the approach should be in the direction that the boat will assume when stopped. Care should be taken when picking up a mooring to retain at least bare steerage way until just before the mooring line is picked up. If this is not done, the bow may blow off before the mooring line can be taken on board. When anchoring, care should be taken to ensure that *all* forward way is off the boat before the anchor is let go. If the boat overrides her anchor, the line may foul the anchor or even foul the propeller. Once the anchor is down and has been given adequate scope, it should be *set* (dug into the bottom) by reversing the engine while the anchor line is *snubbed* (held taut). This procedure is especially important when using the Danforth anchor.

When weighing anchor under power, heave in to straight up and down, belay, and ease ahead on the engine to break out the anchor. Then stop the boat until the anchor has been brought aboard.

In coming alongside an anchored or moored boat, the problem is simplified in one respect in that the direction of approach is dictated. When possible, one should come alongside to starboard of the moored boat. The point where the bow will lie when secured alongside should be determined. Then an angled approach toward the point is

made. The bow spring and bow line are put over. With the engine reversed, the torque effect will tend to bring the stern to port, parallel to the anchored boat. Of course, fenders should be rigged on both boats before the maneuver is begun. Remember to look aloft when going alongside another sailboat. It is distressing to have a nice landing spoiled by the sound from aloft of spreader crunching against spreader.

Powerboat Rules of the Road. When operating under power, whether or not sails are set, a sailboat must comply with those regulations governing motor vessels. She is no longer a sailboat and the International Rules of the Road and Inland Rules of the Road apply. In addition to knowing which boat has the right of way in meeting, overtaking, and crossing situations, the skipper of a sailboat under power must be familiar with the maneuvering whistle signals prescribed by International and Inland rules.

In the illustration the diagrams *A* to *F* illustrate the six basic situations encountered by vessels under power under Inland Rules. The proper reaction to each situation should

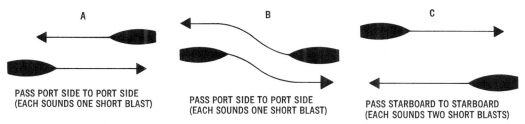

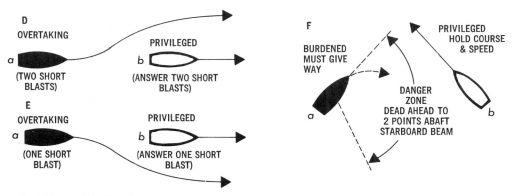

Powerboat Rules of the Road.

be, or become, instinctive to the skipper. In diagram *A*, both vessels are evidently passing to port of each other, which is preferable in this situation. Each had signified his intent by one short blast of the whistle. Both are burdened, while neither is obliged to change course. At night the masthead light and red (port) side light would be visible to each.

In diagram *B*, both vessels were headed directly toward each other. In this situation the rule is that each shall turn to starboard and pass on the port side of the other. Each has signified his intent to do so by one short blast of the whistle. Both are burdened and both are obliged to alter course. At night, both side lights (red and green) and the masthead light would be visible to each before altering course, and the red side light and masthead light would remain visible after the vessels had altered course.

In diagram *C*, the vessels are going to pass to starboard of each other. Each has signified this to be his intent by two short blasts of the whistle. Both are burdened, but neither has to alter course. At night, the masthead light and green (starboard) side light would be visible to each.

Diagrams *D* and *E* illustrate overtaking situations. (To be considered an overtaking rather than a crossing situation, the overtaking vessel must be at least two points or more abaft the beam of the overtaken vessel.) In both cases the overtaken vessel (*b*) is privileged and must maintain course and speed, while the overtaking vessel (*a*) is burdened and must alter course. In diagram *D*, vessel *a* should signify intent to pass to port of vessel *b* by sounding two short blasts. If such a passage is clear, and acceptable to vessel *b*, she should answer two short blasts, and the passing will be effected. In diagram *E*, vessel *a* should signify intent to pass to starboard of vessel *b* by sounding one short blast. If the passage is clear and acceptable to vessel *b*, she should answer with one short blast. If, in either case, the initially proposed passage is dangerous, vessel *b* would sound the Inland Rules danger signal of four or more short blasts. After the passage is clear, vessel *b* would sound the proper answering signal.

In the crossing situation, diagrammed in *F*, two vessels are approaching each other at right angles or obliquely in such a manner that there is a risk of collision. Vessel *a*, which holds the other to starboard, is burdened and should maneuver to keep clear either by altering course to starboard, by slowing, or both. She may signify this to be her intent by sounding one short blast. Vessel *b*, which holds the other to port, is the privileged vessel and is obliged to maintain course and speed. This intent should be signified by one short blast. Whistle signals are not mandatory, however, in the crossing situation under Inland Rules. At night, vessel *a* would see the masthead light and red (port) side light of vessel *b*, while *b* would see the masthead light and green (starboard) side light of *a*.

Navigational Lights Under Power. The navigational lights required by both International and Inland rules for a sailboat under sail were described in Section II. When under power, sailboats are required to carry the same lights, plus a single, white, twenty-point masthead light at least 3 feet above the side lights on the forward mast. This light should be visible for a distance of at least 2 miles on a clear, dark night.

(Information on the care and repair of an auxiliary's inboard engine can be found in Section V.)

MARLINSPIKE SEAMANSHIP

Associated with seamanship is a branch of the art called *marlinspike seamanship*. This involves the ability to tie knots properly and to use the knot best suited to any one application. How long has man been tying knots? A lot longer than he has been keeping records, so we do not know just when the first simple overhand knot lashed an axhead to its handle. Nor do we know when rope, twisted or braided from fibers, replaced jungle vines and leather thongs. But we do know that more than 5,000 years ago, at opposite ends of the earth, Chinese boatmen on the Yangtze and Egyptian sailors on the Nile expertly spliced and braided rope and made fast lines with the same knots American yachtsmen are using today. With the same basic materials, rope twisted of cotton or hemp, the ancient Greeks, Romans, Incas, and American Indians all tied square knots, figure-eights, overhands, and clove hitches. Until recently, neither knots nor the ropes they were tied of had changed substantially since those times.

Knots and How to Tie Them. Many different kinds of knots may be employed in working with line; only those knots, bends, and hitches that are necessary for the proper and efficient working of lines aboard a vessel will be discussed in this sailing book. It is customary to speak of different parts of the line as follows: the *bitter end* is the very end of the rope; the *bight* is a loop formed by turning the rope back on itself; the *standing part* is the long, unused portion of the rope.

Whenever two sections of rope cross, one section must go *over* and the other *under*. The over and under arrangement for each knot must be followed exactly; if an overhand loop is called for, an underhand loop will not work. The wrong knot for the job—or no knot at all—will result. The popular sailing knots are illustrated here.

Figure Eight Knot: Can be tied simply and quickly. Used in the end of a rope to temporarily prevent the strands from unlaying. Does not jam as easily as the overhand knot and is therefore useful to prevent the end of a rope slipping through a block or an eye.

Reef Knot: Probably the most useful and popular of all knots, also known as the Square Knot. Used to join two ropes or lines of the same size. Holds firmly and is easily untied.

Surgeon's Knot: Usually tied with twine. This is a modified form of the Reef Knot and the extra turn taken in the first tie prevents slipping before knot is completed.

Fisherman's Knot: Probably the strongest known method of joining fine lines such as fishing lines. Simple to tie and untie.

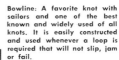

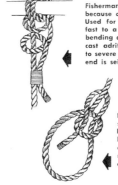

Fisherman's Bend: An important knot because of its strength and simplicity. Used for making the end of a rope fast to a ring, spar or anchor, or for bending a line to a bucket. It is easily cast adrift, even after being subject to severe strain. More secure when the end is seized as shown.

Bowline: A favorite knot with sailors and one of the best known and widely used of all knots. It is easily constructed and used whenever a loop is required that will not slip, jam or fail.

Running Bowline: This is merely a Bowline Knot made around the standing part of a rope to form a running noose or slip knot. Very reliable. Runs freely on the standing part and is easily untied.

Bowline on a Bight: Used to form a loop which will not pull tight. Particularly useful for making a seat to lower or hoist a man.

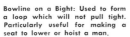

Sheepshank: Used for shortening a rope. The method shown is especially useful where the ends of the rope are not free as it can be employed in the center of a tied rope. Another use is for taking the strain off a damaged piece of rope when there is not time to immediately replace with sound rope. More secure when seized as shown.

Blackwall Hitch: Handy to secure a rope temporarily to a hook for hoisting. Used exclusively for light loads and safe only when the tension is not allowed to slacken.

Timber Hitch: Very useful for hoisting spars, boards or logs. Also handy for making a towline fast to a wet spar or timber. Holds without slipping and does not jam.

Catspaw: Useful to secure the middle of a rope to a hook. To make, take two bights (loops) in the rope and twist in opposite directions. Then bring the loops together and pass over hook.

Clove Hitch: Also known as Builder's Hitch because of .its wide use by builders in fastening staging to upright posts. Another common use is for making a line fast to a wet spar.

Carrick Bend: This knot is used for joining large hawsers together and is easier to untie than most knots after being subjected to strain.

Sheet Bend (Weaver's Knot): Regularly used aboard ship for joining small or medium sized ropes. Sometimes used for attaching the end of a rope to an eye splice. Popular in textile mills for joining threads or yarns.

Round Turn and two Half Hitches: Used to secure a rope to a bollard or stake. Easily tied and does not jam. Will stand heavy strain without slipping.

SHORT SPLICE

Used where it is not necessary for the spliced rope to pass through a pulley block, the Short Splice provides maximum strength since it is nearly as strong as the rope. The diameter of the rope is almost doubled at the point of joining, making this splice too bulky for pulley work.

1. To make a Short Splice, the first step is to unlay the strands at one end of each rope for 6 or 8 turns. The ends of the strands should be whipped to prevent their untwisting and brought together so that each strand of one rope alternates with a strand of the other rope. This can be seen .in Fig. 1.

2. Now bring the ends tightly together and apply a temporary seizing where they join, as shown in Fig. 2.

3. Next, take any one strand and begin tucking, the sequence being over one and under one. Fig. 3 shows how Strand A is passed over the strand nearest to it, which is Strand D, and then under the next strand, Strand E.

4. Rotate the splice away from you one-third of a turn and make the second tuck, shown in Fig. 4. Strand B is passed over Strand E and then under Strand F.

5. Before making the third tuck, rotate the splice again one-third of a turn away from you. Strand C is then passed over Strand F and under the next one, Strand D. The splice now appears as in Fig. 5.

6. This completes the first round of tucks in the left hand half of the splice. Each strand should now be tucked at least twice more, always over one and under one as before, making sure that each strand lies snug and with no kinks.

7. To finish the splice, reverse the rope end for end so that strands D, E and F are now at the left instead of the right (in the same position of strands A, B and C in the illustrations) and repeat the tucking operation on their side of the rope. Each of the six strands will now have had at least three tucks. A tapered splice is made by taking two more tucks with each strand, cutting away some of the threads from each strand before each extra tuck.

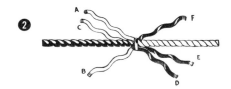

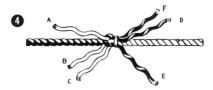

8. When tucking is finished, remove the center seizing and cut off the ends of all strands, leaving at least ¾" on each end. To give a smooth appearance, roll the splice back and forth, either under your foot or between two boards. The completed Short Splice should look something like Fig. 6.

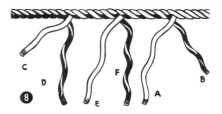

How to make a...
LONG SPLICE

The Long Splice is used for pulley work since it permits the ropes that have been spliced to be run through sheave blocks without jamming or chafing. Unlike the Short Splice, the diameter of the spliced rope is increased very slightly.

1. To make this splice, begin by unlaying one strand of each rope for 10 or 15 turns, and whip the ends of each strand to prevent untwisting. Then splice two ropes together by alternating the strands from each end, as shown in Fig. 7.

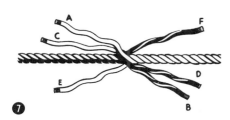

2. Starting at one end, take an opposite pair of strands, A and B, and unlay Strand A. Follow it with Strand B, turn by turn, continuing until only a foot or less of Strand B remains. Keep Strand B tight during this step and pull it down firmly into Strand A's former place. Repeat this operation with strands C and D. Strand D is unlaid and Strand C is laid in its place. Fig. 8 shows the splice at this stage.

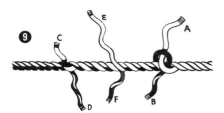

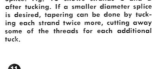

4. Each strand is now tucked twice, over and under, as done in making the Short Splice. Fig. 10 shows strands C and D after tucking. If a smaller diameter splice is desired, tapering can be done by tucking each strand twice more, cutting away some of the threads for each additional tuck.

3. Now each pair of strands is tied loosely together with a simple overhand knot, as indicated by strands A and B in Fig. 9. Each knot is then pulled down into the rope like strands C and D.

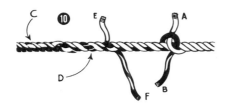

5. When tucking is finished, cut all strands off close to the rope and roll the splice on the floor under your foot to smooth it out. The completed Long Splice is shown in Fig. 11.

The **EYE** or **SIDE SPLICE**

The Side Splice is also called the Eye Splice because it is used to form an eye or loop in the end of a rope by splicing the end back into its own side. This splice is made like the Short Splice except that only one rope is used.

1. Start by seizing the working end of the rope. Unlay the three strands, A, B and C, to the seizing and whip the end of each strand. Then twist the rope slightly to open up strands D, E and F of the standing part of the rope, as indicated in Fig. 12.

2. The first tuck is shown in Fig. 13. The middle strand is always tucked first, so Strand B is tucked under Strand E, the middle strand of the standing part.

3. The second tuck is now made, as shown in Fig. 14. Left Strand A of the working end is tucked under Strand D, passing over Strand E.

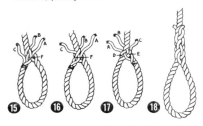

4. Fig. 15 shows how the third tuck is made. In order to make Strand F easy to get at, the rope is turned over. Strand C now appears on the left side.

5. Strand C is then passed to the right of and tucked under Strand F, as shown in Fig. 16. This completes the first round of tucks.

6. Fig. 17 shows the second round of tucks started, with the rope reversed again for ease in handling. Strand B is passed over Strand D and tucked under the next strand to the left. Continue with strands A and C, tucking over one strand and then under one to the left. To complete the splice, tuck each strand once more.

7. The finished Eye Splice is shown in Fig. 18. Remove the temporary seizing and cut off the strand ends, leaving at least ½" on each end. Roll the splice back and forth under your foot to even up and smooth out the strands.

How to put a **WHIPPING** on a Rope

The end of a rope should always be bound or whipped to prevent it from fraying or becoming unlaid. Whippings are usually made with a strong twine and the length should be approximately equal to the diameter of the rope on which it is used.

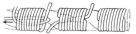

The above illustration shows a simple method of whipping a rope. It is made by laying a loop along the rope and then taking a series of turns over the loop. The working end is finally brought up through this loop and hauled out of sight by pulling on the other end. Both ends are then trimmed.

is shown above. Lay one end of the twine on the rope and take several turns over it, then pull taut. Take the other end of the twine, lay it on the rope as shown and take several additional turns over it with the loop that is formed. Now pull the end tight. To finish it off, the ends can be trimmed close to the whipping or tied together with a Reef Knot.

How to Make Fast. The following is an easy but effective method of making fast: Loop the running part of the rope around the cleat's far side, away from the direction of the strain. Then take a turn around the stem with the running part and up and over the center (additional turns would jam the line). Add several more figure-eights or slip a half hitch over a horn of the cleat immediately if there is little strain. Your line is now made fast, yet ready for prompt castoff with no part under tension binding loops.

This method makes it easy to cast off without having to take up the slack in the standing part and ensures against accidents that occur when lines cannot be freed quickly.

Care of Fiber Lines. Another part of the ways of good marlinspike seamanship is to know the proper care of your boat's line. Here are some tips:

1. *Avoid kinks.* Kinks cause overstress at the sharp bend, weakening fibers inside the strands. Because of this, always coil a line when you have finished using it. The correct method is to coil a line with the sun, that is clockwise, to the right. This is because of the twist imparted to the rope in manufacture. However, if the rope tends to kink when coiling this way, it is because a reverse twist has been imparted to the rope in use, and to take out this twist the line must be coiled counterclockwise.

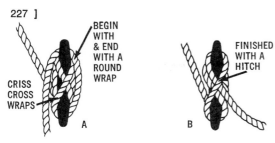

CRISS CROSS WRAPS

BEGIN WITH & END WITH A ROUND WRAP

A

FINISHED WITH A HITCH

B

METHOD B MAY BE USED ON A HALYARD
BUT A SHEET SHOULD NEVER BE HITCHED
UNLESS A SLIPPERY HITCH IS USED

TO MAINSAIL

SLIPPERY HITCH

PULL TO UNTIE

Belaying a line.

2. *Heaving a line.* To throw a line to another vessel or to a shore installation, make up the heaving line into two coils—about two-thirds of the rope held in the left hand, about one-third in the right hand for throwing, and the whole ready to run out easily. The end of the left-hand coil should be made fast. The right-hand coil is thrown by swinging the arm and body.

3. *Keep lines clean.* To clean, drape in loops over the rail and hose down gently, with fresh water if possible. A high-pressure stream will only force grit and grime deeper into a rope's fibers.

4. *Stow carefully.* Dry lines thoroughly before stowing. Rot fungus and mildew will grow on a stored wet line and could destroy it. If possible, stow by hanging from pegs rather than on a deck so air will circulate around it. Never use a line that has been frozen without allowing it to thaw out and dry.

5. *Prevent chafe and abrasion.* Never allow a line to rub on sharp edges, or one rope to chafe against another. When riding at anchor for long periods, it is well to "freshen the nip" by playing out the line slightly so wear is not centralized on one spot.

6. *Do not lubricate the line itself.* Manufacturers treat rope with an oil or solution which preserves and lubricates internal fibers.

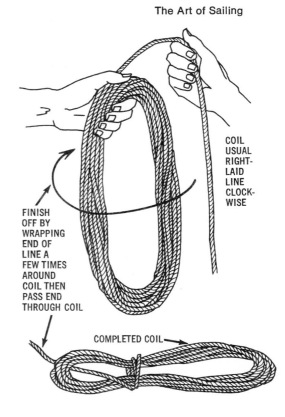

COIL USUAL RIGHT-LAID LINE CLOCKWISE

FINISH OFF BY WRAPPING END OF LINE A FEW TIMES AROUND COIL THEN PASS END THROUGH COIL

COMPLETED COIL

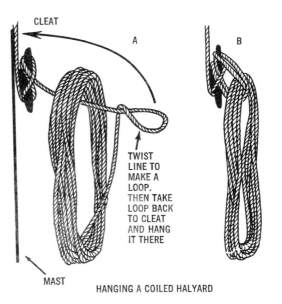

CLEAT

MAST

A

TWIST LINE TO MAKE A LOOP. THEN TAKE LOOP BACK TO CLEAT AND HANG IT THERE

B

HANGING A COILED HALYARD

Coiling a line.

Users are cautioned against trying to improve on the manufacturer's protection.

7. *Beware of chemicals.* Acids and alkalis attack rope. They burn the fibers and make them brittle. Rust, too, is bad for rope. Spots of discoloration are a danger sign showing when fibers have broken down.

8. *Never overload.* The safety factor allowed in determining the load on a rope is commonly taken as 5 to 1. That is, if a rope must lift 500 pounds, select one of sufficient tensile strength to handle 2,500 pounds. If the load ever exceeds 75 per cent of the rope's breaking strength, chances are it will be permanently injured.

9. *Check lines during sailing season.* To make sure the line is serviceable during a season's usage, it should be inspected inside and out. On the outside, you should look for signs of abrasion and broken fibers.

Care of Wire Rope. Wire rope needs better care than fiber rope and far better care than it generally receives. For instance, when being wound on the drum of a winch, the turns of wire rope must never be overlapped. A single kink in the finest wire rope will ruin it. The rope must be kept on a reel or drum when not actually in use.

Wire hawsers should be thoroughly coated with linseed oil or other preservative monthly. When the hawser is not to be used for some time, it should be coated with a heavy petroleum lubricating oil to which graphite has been added. It is important to remember that whatever kind of lubricant is used, it must be thin enough to penetrate through the wires to the core of the rope and thick enough to adhere to the wire for a reasonable length of time.

All personnel using rope must inspect it continually. A broken wire can cut a crewman's hand or arm seriously. Wear should be measured frequently when ropes are in constant use. Rope must be discarded when the outside wires are worn down to half their original diameter or when it is apparent that the rope has been severely damaged by kinking or excessive strain.

When cutting wire rope, a whipping of soft iron wire should be made on each side of the point where the cut is to be made to prevent the rope from unlaying. If wire is not readily available, fairly heavy seizing stuff may be used—the turns being passed

THIMBLE EYE, SPLICED AND SERVED

THIMBLE EYE WITH ROPE CLIPS

OPEN END SOCKET   CLOSED END SOCKET

SHACKLE   HOOK AND THIMBLE

TURNBUCKLE

JOINING THE ENDS OF ROPE

Fittings used with wire rope.

very tautly. Wire splicing work usually requires the services of a professional rigger.

Wire-rope Fittings. Most of the fittings used with wire rope are designed to provide an eye in the end of the rope. This affords a convenient means of connecting two ropes or otherwise securing a rope.

U-bolt clamps or rope clips can be applied in a few minutes, whereas a splice takes many hours. It should be noted that the U of the clamp is always applied to the bitter end of the rope. For rope sizes from ¾ to 1⅛ inches, five clamps should be used to make the fastening. For smaller sizes, at least four clamps should be used. On 1¼-inch rope, use six clamps. On larger sizes it is preferable to socket the rope and avoid the use of clamps.

Sockets are devices secured to the end of wire ropes to provide a quick, convenient means of bending two ropes together or attaching a load. Sockets, classed as open or closed, are illustrated above.

SECTION V

Sailing Is Fun

True, all sailing is fun. Actually everything about a sailboat—even the required maintenance—is fun. In this section and in Section VI we have divided the two major fun categories—cruising and racing. In this section we will cover the aspects of cruising.

By cruising, we mean getting from one place to another. We also mean just going out for a sail on a body of water with nothing but *fun* on the mind of the sailor.

GETTING WHERE YOU WANT TO GO

When you cast off from your mooring, or from a dock, you are under way—going somewhere—and the task of navigating your sailing craft begins. As we know, navigation is the art of getting your yacht where you want her. It does not make any difference if your "yacht" is an 8-foot dinghy or a 90-foot schooner. Furthermore, it is not important what kind of boat you are the skipper of; but it is important that you are able to navigate her safely and efficiently, according to her ability and according to the waters you are sailing on. This calls for a certain degree of learning; and it also calls for proper gear.

Coastwise Navigation. There are two basic types of navigation: coastwise navigation, or piloting, and offshore navigation. The former is the act of navigating a boat by means of sight and hearing, while in offshore navigating you do not use these faculties in the normal manner. In other words, while the pilot can actually see the shore and lighthouses, ranges, and buoys, read the depth under him, and listen to foghorns and bells, offshore navigation must proceed without these aids.

Celestial Navigation. At one time, celestial navigation, which involves determination of a vessel's position from observation of known heavenly bodies, was the only form of offshore navigation. Since World War II celestial navigation, once so much black magic except to the initiated, has been simplified to a degree where anyone wishing to give the time necessary to learn it can do so. Unfortunately, however, these new teaching techniques of the old science came a little late for the average offshore sailor, since electronic aids to a great extent supersede celestial navigation in all but some ocean-racing events. Actually, the electronic form of offshore navigation—mentioned in Section II and described later in this section—requires, in general, little or no skill or mathematics to work out a position.

Celestial navigation, of course, can provide information of utmost importance should the so-called artificial aids (the name given electronic devices by old-time deep-water yachtsmen) fail or become unavailable. But, because the subject of celestial navigation to be *properly* explained would require more space than we could possibly allot to it, we suggest reading Benjamin Dutton's *Navigation and Piloting,* edited by John C. Hill and others, or the *Primer of Navigation* by George W. Mixter.

Another way to learn celestial navigation is to attend courses given on the subject by the various sailing schools throughout the United States. Incidentally, these schools are an excellent way to learn sailing—from beginning techniques to graduate racing procedures. Some schools even offer vacation cruise courses where the entire family may attend classes while taking an interesting cruise.

Aids to Coastwise Navigation

It would be difficult to drive cross-country without road signs to point the way. It would be even more difficult on the waterways of North America if it were not for the various aids to navigation. These aids include buoys, day beacons, range lights, lightships, lighthouses, etc., and they help a skipper to get where he wants.

Buoys and Waterway Markers. A buoy is nothing more than a visual warning device used as a navigation aid for signaling danger, obstructions, or changes in the contours of the sea bottom, and designed to set forth a safe course for yachtsmen. The coloring and numbering of buoys is determined by their position with respect to the channel as entered from seaward and followed toward the head of navigation. The expression "red light returning" has long been used by the seafaring man to remind him that red buoys are passed on his starboard side when proceeding from the open sea into port (upstream). Likewise black buoys are left to port. Conversely, when proceeding toward the sea or leaving port, red buoys are left to port, and black buoys to starboard.

In addition to several special-purpose buoys, having no lateral significance, and used

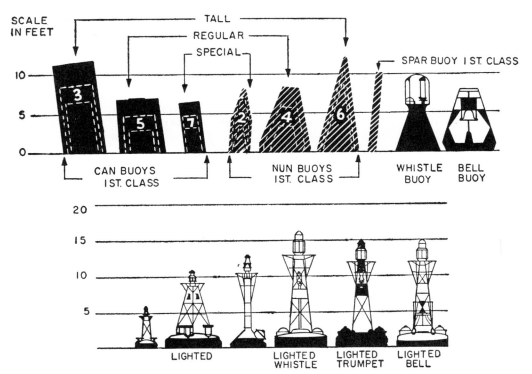

The United States buoyage system.

to mark such things as dredging areas, fish nets, quarantine anchorage, etc., the yachtsman can expect to encounter eight different types of buoys marking the nation's waterways. Each kind is marked, shaped, and designed to serve under definite marine conditions. Some are equipped with lights for night navigation, others have sounding devices for fog and darkness. The buoyage system of the United States (and Canada, too) is illustrated here.

All solid-colored red or black buoys (except those in the Mississippi River System) are given numbers or combinations of numbers and letters. Others may be given letters. Odd numbers are used only on solid-black buoys, even numbers are used only on solid-red buoys. Numbers followed by letters are used on solid-colored red or black buoys when a letter is required, or on buoys marking isolated offshore dangers. Number followed by letter, such as 10A, 10B, 10C, usually indicates that buoys have been added to a channel and the series not at once renumbered. Letters without numbers are sometimes applied to black and white vertically striped buoys; red and black horizontally banded buoys; solid-yellow buoys; and other buoys not in solid red or black colors.

Lights on buoys are either red, green, or white. Red lights serve to identify red buoys and are found on red or banded buoys with topmost band of red. Green lights mark only black buoys. Thus entering a channel, red lights mark the starboard buoys; green marks the port buoys. White lights on buoys have no special color significance.

Since all channels do not lead from seaward, arbitrary assumptions must at times be made in order that the system may be consistently applied. Proceeding from seaward is considered in a southerly direction along the Atlantic Coast, in a westerly and northerly direction along the Gulf Coast, and in a northerly direction on the Pacific Coast. On the Great Lakes proceeding in a westerly and northerly direction is proceeding from seaward; and on the Intracoastal Waterway, proceeding generally southerly along the Atlantic Coast, and in a generally westerly direction along the Gulf Coast is considered proceeding from seaward. The characteristics of aids to navigation on the Mississippi and Ohio rivers and their tributaries follow the basic assumption that proceeding from the sea toward the head of navigation will find red on starboard (right side).

Buoys can be carried away, shifted, capsized, or sunk as the result of storms, ice conditions, collisions, or other accidents. Lighted buoys may become extinguished or their lighting apparatus broken or deranged, causing them to show improper light colors or light-phase characteristics. Buoys are moored to chains of various lengths, and in some cases, several times the depth of the water in which they are located. The radius of the swing should be considered. The buoy does not maintain position directly over its sinker. Buoys usually yaw about under the influence of the wind and current, and a boat attempting to pass too close risks collision. Buoys should always be regarded as warnings or guides, rather than infallible navigation marks. Whenever possible, navigate by bearings or angles on fixed objects on shore and by soundings rather than by reliance on buoys.

Local or private channel markers put out by fishermen and local yachtsmen usually are wooden stakes, stone monuments, cage structures of wood or metal, reinforced concrete tripods, or even small trees with the leaves still rattling in the breeze. As a rule, unless you know the local waters, it is risky to pass through such a channel. Sometimes the markers are not channel markers at all but indicate fish traps, nets, or setlines. There is no way of telling, so it is best to keep clear.

Day Beacons. These are aids to navigation in the form of unlighted structures. Design and construction vary. A day beacon may simply consist of a single pile with a day mark on the top. They are colored to distinguish them from their surroundings and to provide a means of identification. Where they mark the sides of channels, coloring follows the standard color scheme of the United States system of buoyage, i.e., red indicating the right side entering and black the left side entering. Many day beacons are fitted with reflectors to facilitate locating them at night by means of a searchlight.

Intracoastal Waterway Buoys. The Intracoastal Waterway runs parallel to the Atlantic and Gulf coasts from Manasquan Inlet on the New Jersey shore to the Mexican border. Aids marking these waters have some portions of them painted yellow. Buoys have a band of yellow at the top, day beacons have a band or border of yellow, light structures are similarly painted. The coloring and numbering of buoys and day beacons and the color of lights follow the same system as that in other United States waterways. In order that vessels may readily follow this route where it coincides with another waterway such as an important river marked on the seacoast system, special markings are employed. These special marks consist of a yellow square or a yellow triangle painted on the dual purpose aid. The yellow triangle has the same meaning as a nun and indicates the aid should be passed on the starboard side when proceeding in a direction from Chesapeake Bay toward Mexico. The yellow square has the same meaning as a can; in the above direction of travel it would be passed on the port side.

Buoyage System for State Waterways. On water completely within state boundaries (not navigable to the sea), many states have adopted a uniform system of waterway markers. Just as the Intracoastal Waterways markers are distinguished by a special yellow shape, orange and white identify state regulatory markers. On buoys, a 3-inch orange band is *usually* used at the top and bottom, and on the white area between bands a geometric shape appears, also in orange. A diamond shape indicates danger. A diamond with a cross signifies a prohibited area. A circle denotes zoning or control. A square or rectangle conveys other information. On shore structures, the orange bands are optional.

Lighthouses. Lighthouses are found on the coasts of the United States and along some of the interior waterways. They are placed where they will be of most use, on prominent headlands, at entrances, on isolated dangers, or at other points where it is necessary to warn or guide the navigator. Each lighthouse has its own distinctive paint job—some are white all over, others are striped in different colors, and still others are spirally painted like a barber's pole. This is done for day identification. At night these lights flash their warnings in set patterns. With a government publication called *Light Lists,* you can identify each light by its characteristic flash. Some lights show green and some show white. Red,

unless specifically stated otherwise in *Light Lists,* denotes danger area. You may approach a light at night and see it flashing white or green, then suddenly see it turn red. Look at the chart at once, because when you get into the red sector of a light, you are heading for trouble. A lighthouse may have manned or automatically operated lights. In addition to the visual kind, lighthouses are usually equipped with fog and radio-beacon signals.

Lightships. Lightships are placed in exposed locations where it is impractical to construct fixed aids to navigation. They provide light, fog, and radio-beacon signals and are distinguished from each other by the characteristics of their signals. Lights are displayed from one hour before sunset until one hour after sunrise and at all times when the sound signal is operating. By day, lightships, especially relief lightships, display the International Code signal of the station when a vessel is approaching or is in the vicinity, when there are indications that a vessel is in strange waters or fails to recognize the station, or when a vessel asks for information. The code signal for each lightship station is stated in the *Light Lists.* In addition, the hulls of all lightships, with the exception of the Lake Huron lightship, which is painted black, are painted red with the name of the station in white on both sides. The word RELIEF is painted on relief lightships instead of the name of the station.

A lightship under way, or off station, will fly the International Code signal flags "PC." This signal indicates that the lightship is not at anchor or on her station. While under way she will not show or sound any of the signals of a lightship, but will display the lights prescribed by the Rules of the Road. In the last few years, Texas-tower lighthouses are replacing lightships at most offshore light stations.

Minor Lights. These light structures may be painted similarly to lighthouses. Sometimes, however, they are painted black or red, to indicate the sides of the channel which they mark, following the color scheme of the United States system of buoyage. Minor lights are given distinctive light characteristics for purposes of identification. These lights are occasionally fitted with fog signals and may also be equipped with low-powered, continuously operating radio beacons.

Range Markers. Ranges are two objects—whether they be range lights, day beacons, lighthouses, minor lights, or one day beacon and a lighthouse—or two of anything identified on the chart as a range. Similar to the principle of rifle sighting, one of these objects or markers is always nearer to you than the other, and the one closer to you is lower than the one further back. When these markers are in line—one over the other—they indicate to the yachtsman that he is on a safe course within the confines of the channel. If the closer marker of the range begins to shift to the left, you will know that your boat is going too far to the right. Correct this with left rudder immediately, and keep the range markers lined up. If the closer marker moves to the right, you are too far to the left, and you must correct it with right rudder. To be valuable in piloting, ranges need not always be established navigational marks; they may be natural ranges, such as a church steeple and a water tower, a tree stump and a fence post, or two hills or mountains. Within harbors, fixed ranges enable small boats to maintain prearranged courses without recourse to navigational aids.

Day Marks. The distinctive painted pattern on a lighthouse serves to identify the light during daylight. For minor lights and day beacons, it may be merely a lantern on a single pile dolphin. The day mark, in any case, serves to make the aid readily visible and easily identified against background conditions. It conveys to the mariner the significance which the light does at night. Square day marks either black or white with green reflective borders are used on lights marking the "black," or "odd-numbered," side of the channel. Triangular day marks either red or red-fluorescent with red reflective borders are used on lights marking the "red," or "even-numbered," side of the channel. On Intracoastal Waterway day marks yellow reflective borders are used instead of green or red. Day marks can also be used on structures without lights. Such aids are called day beacons. In addition to channel day marks the mariner should recognize special-purpose day marks such as those on ranges.

Range Lights. Range lights are the principal night markers of the range system, and

they usually are small or skeleton-type structures which when in line (i.e., one over the other) indicate to the boatman that he is on a safe course. Generally they are visible in one direction only. By steering a course which keeps these lights in line (range-up) the sailor will remain within the confines of the channel. Remember that quite a few range lights are on shore and that is where you will be if you do not consult your chart as to where to change course. The range lights may be white, red, or green and may also be fixed or flashing.

Visibility of Lights. The visibility of the lights given on nautical charts is at 15 feet above sea level—the assumed height of the observer's eye. This visibility must be modified proportionately for any other height. For example, when the observer is 10 feet above sea level and the observed light is known to be 50 feet above sea level (given on the chart), the distance from the light, using the table given here, is:

	Height in Feet	Visibility in Nautical Miles
Observer	10	
Observer's range of vision		3.6
Light	50	
Arc of illumination (light)		8.1
Distance of observer from light		11.7

It must be remembered that atmospheric and other conditions affect visibility appreciably; therefore, it must not be assumed on sighting a light, even in perfectly clear weather, that a vessel's distance from the light is equal to the range of visibility. The range of visibility may be slightly greater or less than it appears because of the refraction of the light rays near the horizon.

Distance by Visibility

Height in Feet	Distance in Nautical Miles	Height in Feet	Distance in Nautical Miles
1	1.1	9	3.5
2	1.6	10	3.6
3	2.0	12	4.0
4	2.3	14	4.3
5	2.6	16	4.6
6	2.8	18	4.9
7	3.0	20	5.1
8	3.1	30	6.3

Height in Feet	Distance in Nautical Miles	Height in Feet	Distance in Nautical Miles
40	7,2	150	14.6
50	8.1	200	16.2
60	8.9	250	18.2
70	9.6	300	19.9
80	10.3	400	22.9
90	10.9	500	25.6
100	11.5	1,000	36.1

Reduced-visibility Audio Aids. Fog signals warn of danger when visibility is limited by fog, rain, or thick weather. They also provide a means of determining position when such conditions exist. The devices used for this purpose, generally termed reduced-visibility audio aids, are as follows:

1. Diaphones are devices that produce sounds by means of a slotted reciprocating piston actuated by compressed air. Blasts may be of one or two tones; if two tones are employed, the second tone is lower than the first.

2. Diaphragm horns which produce sound by means of a diaphragm vibrated by compressed air, steam, or electricity. Duplex or triplex horns of different pitch produce a chime signal.

3. Reed horns which produce sound by means of a steel reed vibrated by compressed air.

4. Sirens operated by compressed air.

5. Whistles.

6. Bells.

Fog signals on fixed stations and lightships produce, each minute, a specific number of blasts which are interspersed with periods of silence to provide positive identification. The *Light Lists* describe the characteristics of the fog signals.

Radio Beacons. There are several classes of radio stations that can be used in electronic navigation as beacons. Marine radio beacons operated by the U.S. Coast Guard, standard broadcast stations, and aircraft beacons are the most popular stations used in conjunction with radio direction finders by yachtsmen.

Basic Navigation Gear

The following are considered basic navigation gear that you should have aboard any cruising yacht:

1. Charts covering in detail all the waters on which you expect to cruise should be aboard—charts made by the National Ocean Survey, U.S. Navy Hydrographic Office, or Lake Survey, depending on where you are going. Charts should be renewed each year or kept up to date by use of the *Notices to Mariners*.

2. A compass—a marine type which, in any but the *smallest* boats, should be set in a permanent binnacle in front of the helmsman at a level convenient to his eye.

3. Tools for chart work including, at least, parallel rules or one of the various types of course protractors; dividers for measuring distance; sharp pencils.

4. In the book line, you will want *Tide Tables* and *Current Tables* (if on salt water); the *Coast Pilot* for your area; a *Light List*, which is mentioned later in this section.

5. If you have a radio direction finder you need RDF beacon charts giving location, frequency, signal, and on-the-air time of each station (mentioned later in this section).

6. An electronic depth sounder is a handy gadget, but even if you have one, carry a marked leadline aboard and, if you poke around really shallow water, a long sounding pole marked in feet.

Nautical Charts. To meet our country's need for nautical charts, the United States Coast Survey was organized in 1807, during the administration of President Thomas Jefferson. The nautical charts published by the National Oceanic and Atmospheric Administration (formerly the U.S. Coast and Geodetic Survey), together with related publications, furnish information necessary for safe navigation. The charts show bottom depths and characteristics, dangers, channels, landmarks, aids to navigation, fish-trap limits, anchorage, restricted and prohibited areas, cable and pipeline areas, wharves, cities, etc. Loran lines of position are shown on some nautical charts. Nautical charts vary in scales with the importance of the area, purpose for which the chart is designed, and necessity for showing clearly all the dangers within that area.

There are two basic types of charts; the so-called conventional charts, and small-craft charts. The latter are accordion folded ones, which contrast sharply with the conventional charts that were designed for use by large commercial vessels. The small-craft charts emphasize additional navigational information for recreational boating such as large-scale insets of small-boat harbors, blue tint to the 6-foot or critical depth curve, facilities and supplies available to small craft, weather, tides, currents, magnetic courses and distances between points of interest, symbols and abbreviations, whistle signals, and a wealth of other references. Many a novice skipper is accepting the compact charts with confidence, whereas in the past he had been intimidated by those 3 by 4-foot unwieldy conventional charts which more rightly belong in seagoing vessels.

Both types of charts are not the same as maps. They need study. A look at a National Ocean Survey chart shows that it has a gridwork of vertical and horizontal lines over the surface of the chart. The vertical lines are the meridians of longitude, and the horizontal lines are the parallels of the latitude. These lines run true north and south, and true east and west. Longitude is marked off in degrees, minutes, and tenths of minutes in the top and bottom margins of the chart. Of much more importance to the navigator are the scales of latitude found in the left and right margins of the chart, marked in degrees, minutes, and tenths of minutes. Each minute of latitude is equal to one nautical mile, thus the scale can be used to measure distance. Just be sure you do not use the scales at the top and bottom (horizontal scale—longitude) for this purpose, as it will not give an accurate reading (except at the equator) because of the way the charts are made.

Other Government Publications. The yachtsman is dependent upon accurate charts in navigating unfamiliar waters. However, to supplement this information, he has recourse to a number of other publications issued by the government. These include *Tide Tables, Tidal Current Tables, Tidal Current Charts, Coast Pilots, Notices to Mariners,* and *Light Lists.* These should be aboard every cruising sailboat.

The first five publications are available through the National Oceanic and Atmospheric Administration, and information about them, as well as nautical charts, may be obtained from the director of that branch of the Department of Commerce. *Light Lists* are published by the U.S. Coast Guard.

Marine Compass

History has revealed that the property of a loadstone to align itself in a north-south direction was observed over 2,000 years ago in the Near East and perhaps 1,000 years earlier in China. However, the practical application of this property as a direction-indicating source at sea was not observed until about the thirteenth or fourteenth century. Today, of course, a magnetic compass is an important fixture aboard any seagoing cruising yacht; and like anything aboard a boat, it helps to know how as well as why it functions as it does.

The modern marine compass's operation is based on the fact that a magnetic needle, freely suspended, will align itself parallel to the lines of the magnetic force of the earth itself—a stable, continuous, and predictable source of power. Modern compasses generally use two magnets, which are suspended from the compass card and fixed parallel to its north and south markings. A pivotal and synthetic sapphire provide virtually frictionless support, thus permitting the card to rotate freely. To dampen the motion of the card, the compass bowl is filled either with an alcohol and water mixture, or more commonly today, a fine oil. Expansion and contraction of the liquid is compensated for by an expansion chamber in the bowl. The bowl is enclosed at the top with a flat glass in the older-type compasses, through which the compass heading may be read. Modern compasses have a ground, polished glass dome which gives the compass much greater freedom of movement as well as magnifying the card, and beyond this the quality of greater steadiness. In the past, this bowl was gimbaled externally against the rolling of the boat, but the modern compasses are internally gimbaled to keep them level regardless of the motion of the craft. Every marine compass has a lubber line marked on its case or mounting. This is a fixed reference line set on, or placed parallel to, the centerline of the vessel and indicating the heading of the ship with reference to the compass card. The compass card is marked by degrees in a 360-

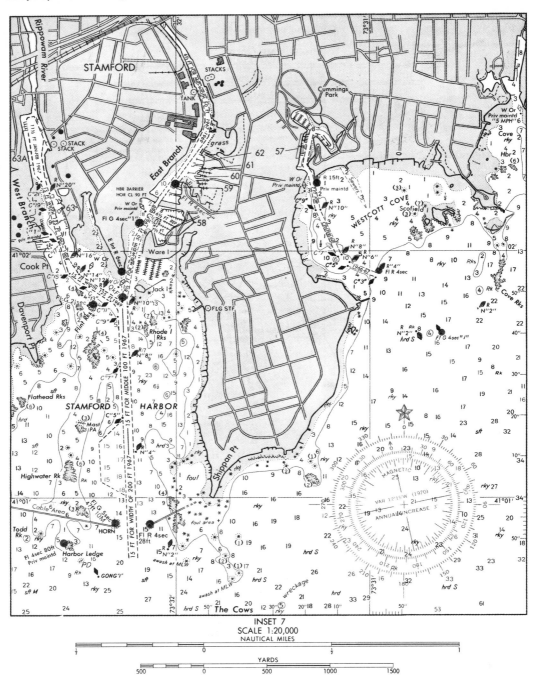

INSET 7
SCALE 1:20,000
NAUTICAL MILES

YARDS

A typical National Ocean Survey chart.

degree circle with north as 000. Some compass cards may also be marked in cardinal and intercardinal points such as N, NE, S, SE, W, SW, and so forth.

The compass should never be located in close proximity to masses of iron or steel. Keep it away from instrument panels, steel steering wheels (they may be steel even if coated with a plastic), and in general from all circuits carrying heavy amperage such as ammeters, etc. The lubber line must be properly aligned parallel with the fore-and-aft line of the ship. Generally, it should be located at an angle of about 25 degrees below the helmsman's eye level.

A marine compass is subject to two influences, or errors, which prevent it from pointing to the geographic North Pole; these must be considered when navigating. One of these errors, called *variation,* is primarily caused by the earth's magnetic poles not being located in the same places as the geographic poles. The housing of the magnetic compass, called a binnacle, is made of nonmagnetic material, usually wood and/or brass, and contains features for compass correction and illumination. (The light bulb for after-dark use should be red—as red interferes least with night vision.) The other error in the magnetic compass, called *deviation,* is caused by magnetic influences of metal in the ship itself. Normally this error changes with every different heading of the ship and is seldom the same for any two headings.

Compass Variation. Variation is the difference in direction between the geographic North Pole and the magnetic north. The amount can vary depending upon where you are located and also may change slightly from year to year in some localities. The variation error of the compass is taken care of with one of the compass roses on your chart —the one nearest to your location. The star at the top of the outer circle of the compass rose points to the true north. The difference between the star and arrow is the amount of variation in the vicinity of this particular compass rose on the chart. To make it easy, the specific data on variation is printed in the center of the compass rose: "Variation 12° 15′ West (1970)." Remember that variation changes and is normally not constant for any given location. Therefore all compass readings must be corrected for variation unless a yacht happens to be in an area of no variation. Variation, when present, is either easterly or westerly, depending on the location of the compass on the earth. If the magnetic pole is to the west of geographic north at the location, variation is west; if the magnetic pole lies to the east at the location, variation is east. For example, the variation at Stamford, Connecticut, shown in the chart here, is 12 degrees 15 minutes westerly. This means the compass needle while pointing to magnetic north is actually pointing 12 degrees 15 minutes west of true north, or 347¾ degrees. If a ship were steering a course of 360 degrees by the magnetic compass (no deviation considered), the true course would be 12¼ degrees less than 360 or 347¾ degrees. When variation is west, the amount of variation should be subtracted from the magnetic course to find the true course. When variation is east, the amount should be added to the magnetic north to find the true course.

Compass Deviation. Variation is a constant error in all magnetic compasses. This is not the case with deviation, which is an error caused by the magnetic effect on your compass of anything in your boat that is made of iron or steel. Deviation varies with different boats and also with different directions in which a boat may be headed. For example, a compass may show a deviation of 5 degrees to the west when the boat is headed one way, and a deviation of 2 degrees to the east when headed in the opposite direction. Your compass can be compensated for deviation. It is best to employ a professional to do this for you, and at the same time have a deviation card made up. This card will show how far off your compass is in degrees, and you then can correct easily for your true course. If your boat is an auxiliary, you should have two deviation cards, one made with the power off and one with it on.

Deviation is not a fixed figure; it may change when the yacht changes course. Compass-deviation cards or Napier diagrams show the deviation for various ship headings. Variation and deviation usually are handled together, their sum comprising the *total compass error.* This error, when correctly applied to the compass course in accordance with the directional symbol of E (east) or W (west), gives the true course. The mariner's rule is: "East, you add; west, you subtract when correcting." This is the method used to convert a compass course to a true course.

The procedure is reversed to convert a true course to a compass course. That is, to find a compass course from a true course, add westerly errors, subtract easterly errors.

Compass Course to True Course

Compass course	= 231°		Compass course	= 169°	
Dev. W = −4			Dev. W = −7		
Var. E = +7			Var. W = −3		
Error = +3	+3		Error = −10	−10	
True course	= 234°		True course	= 159°	

True Course to Compass Course

True course	= 282°		True course	= 137°	
Dev. W = +4			Dev. W = +2		
Var. E = −9			Var. W = +7		
Error = −5	−5		Error = +9	+9	
Compass course	= 277°		Compass course	= 146°	

Heeling Error. With many keel-type sailboats there is sometimes a slightly different compass deviation error when she is heeled over. This so-called *heeling error* is probably most easily determined by running between known objects such as buoys or other aids to navigation on a given course on various tacks and heel angles. While this error is slight in many cases and ignored in others, it can be corrected, if desired. It is a task, however, for a professional compass adjuster. Before leaving the subject of the compass itself, remember that a compass calibration and correction will not stay accurate forever, since the deviation may change from time to time during the sailing season. For this reason, it is wise to check your compass frequently against a known bearing.

The Pelorus

This is a navigating instrument that is seldom used by amateur sailors, but is highly regarded by professionals. Actually, the pelorus is only a dummy compass fitted with sight vanes for taking bearings of celestial or terrestrial objects. It is generally made of brass. It is without magnets and wholly nonmagnetic. The dial, or card, has a compass rose painted or engraved upon it and is divided into 360 degrees. The card and the sight vanes revolve, independently of each other, upon a pivot. Two clamps, one above the other on the top of the pivot, permit the card and the sight vanes to be set in any desired position. One clamp is used to set the card, the other to set the sight vanes. Because of the lack of space on board, some smaller boats use a portable pelorus and find it more practical than the one just described. The portable type can be set up when needed on the cabin top or in the cockpit.

A bearing is taken on an object by first aligning the pelorus card with the compass card and clamping it in position. The lubber line must be aligned with the boat's keel. The sighting vanes of the pelorus are then aligned on the object of the bearing and are clamped in position. The bearing is read from the pelorus dial. For the bearing to be accurate, the craft must be kept exactly on the course on which the pelorus dial is clamped. Because of currents, wind, and seas, it is sometimes difficult to hold course; therefore, the helmsman must call out "Mark" when the vessel is on course. The crewman who takes the bearing clamps the sighting vane in position at this instant, and an accurate bearing is obtained.

The bearing thus taken from a pelorus is a compass bearing and must be corrected in the same manner as a compass reading. The pelorus is also used to obtain relative bearings. In obtaining a bearing of this kind the pelorus dial is clamped in position with 000 (zero) on the lubber line. After the lubber line is aligned with the boat's keel, a bearing can be taken, the sighting vanes clamped in position, and the bearing read. This bearing is relative to the vessel's heading at the time the bearing is taken and must be added to the boat's heading to obtain the compass bearing of the object.

Plotting a Course

Plotting involves the measuring and laying out of direction angles, distances, recording and projection of time, applying corrections for total compass error, and the effect of current. You need three simple instruments to do the job: parallel rulers (to lay out directions on the chart), a pair of dividers (for measuring distances), and a course protractor with a straight edge (to take a bearing from one object to another). These items can be purchased at almost any marine supply store.

Let us start with the simplest of courses; that is, one between two points such as buoys, docks, or other fixed and recognizable objects. (The object you leave from is the "point of departure," while the point of arrival is known as the "destination.") To determine the course between the two points, place the centerline of the protractor or the parallel rulers on your point of departure and align it with the destination. The true course to be steered can be read directly from the protractor or obtained by transferring the line with the parallel rulers to the nearest compass rose. (If your parallel rulers will not reach from the course you want to sail to the compass rose, you can "walk" them across the face of the chart by (1) placing one ruler along the course you want to sail, (2) moving the second ruler as far toward the compass rose as it will go, (3) holding the second ruler firmly in position, and moving the first up against it, (4) repeating this proc-

ess till your second ruler reaches the center of the compass rose.) A correction should, of course, be made for both variation and deviation while steering in this direction. Once you have obtained the total compass error, you can determine the exact compass course to be steered.

It is generally a good idea to lay off a series of short courses, or legs, rather than one long one. Locate several intermediate checkpoints, such as navigational buoys or other similar aids, and use these as points of destinations or points of turning. It is much easier to maintain an accurate course with short legs because you can correct your position automatically at each intermediate checkpoint. When a course changes direction, the turning point of the new course is laid out in the same manner as previously described, using the turning place as the new point of departure. The distance of the legs of a course can be determined by drawing the compass course lightly on the chart in pencil. Then set the arms of your pair of dividers on your points of departure and destination, or turning point. These distances can be measured off on the chart's nautical-miles scale.

It is usually possible, by estimating how many knots you are making, to give a fairly reasonable guess as to how far you have proceeded along your selected compass course. You can check your speed over the course continuously by timing yourself between buoys or other known objects, measuring the distance between them on your chart with your dividers, and transferring this to your nautical-miles scale. If your course is such that you have to tack to windward, by applying the same procedure you should be able to locate yourself at any time. Naturally, if you can hold to a given tack for the same length of time whenever you tack, your calculation will be simpler. If you can time yourself for a mile, you can estimate your speed by using the table below:

Time for 1 Nautical Mile in Minutes	Boat's Speed in Knots	Time for 1 Nautical Mile in Minutes	Boat's Speed in Knots
60	1	10	6
30	2	8½	7
20	3	7½	8
15	4	6½	9
12	5	6	10

Time for 1 Nautical Mile in Minutes	Boat's Speed in Knots	Time for 1 Nautical Mile in Minutes	Boat's Speed in Knots
5½	11	3¾	16
5	12	3½	17
4½	13	3¼	18
4¼	14	3⅛	19
4	15	3	20

On a well-equipped cruising sailboat, guess-work will be reduced by trailing a taffrail log, which will give you the distance traveled through the water. Timing this, of course, allows you to compute your speed.

There are two other factors that must be taken into consideration when plotting a course. One is the allowance for leeway and the other is direction of the current or tidal current. An easy way to determine your leeway is to sail the compass course for a short distance and then look back at your wake. Estimate the angle that the wake makes with the craft's course, and this will show you how much you should allow for leeway. If your leeway shows you are being set half a point down to leeward, you will have to steer half a point to windward to compensate for it. Actually, the amount of leeway your own boat makes can only be judged accurately by experience. But the average well-built cruising craft only makes appreciable leeway when close-hauled, and in good weather does not make very much then. If there is much sea running, you will find it very difficult to judge the angle of the wake owing to the broken water. Making an accurate leeway allowance is, in point of fact, dependent on knowing your own particular craft.

Correcting courses for tidal current is fairly easy for a powerboat man, but fairly difficult for the sailor. When you find it necessary to compensate for the current, use the current tables for times of slacks, and times and velocities of strengths. Tidal-current charts will show you hourly velocities and directions. The direction is equally important because this will greatly affect the course you make. Technically speaking, current velocities are directly added to or subtracted from a boat's speed when the boat's course is directly in line with the current. It should be understood that if the current is "fair," that is, running in the same direction as you wish to sail, it will increase your speed. If it is "foul," that is,

against you, it will have the opposite effect. It is when the current is setting across your course, pushing you to one side or the other of your destination, that you will have to allow for it by steering an equal amount in the opposite direction to which it is setting.

Piloting Techniques

There are several different piloting methods for finding a yacht's position, depending upon the number of objects in sight, their bearing relative to the heading of the craft, and the character of the sailing area.

In order that the information plotted on a chart may be of value to the navigator and to other people who are required to interpret correctly what has been drawn, a system of marking, or labeling, is required. All lines of position (bearings) and courses should be true (referring to direction). The alternate and intermingling use of magnetic bearings and true bearings can result in costly errors. Lines of position and course lines are each drawn distinctly. Care should be taken not to draw heavy lines on the chart which may damage the chart or mislead the navigator when the chart is used again. Course lines should be labeled on the upper side of the line by writing *C* (course) followed by the true course in three figures. On the lower side of the line, under the course label, *S* (speed) and numerals indicating the speed in knots should be written. Over the lines of position (bearing lines) the time of observation should be written in four figures; the three figures denoting the true bearing should be written beneath the time figure. The label now contains both a time notation and an abbreviation for the type of point identified. Identification points are normally written to one side of the points they identify and at an angle to the course line or the lines on which they lie.

The Cross Bearing. To get a cross bearing,

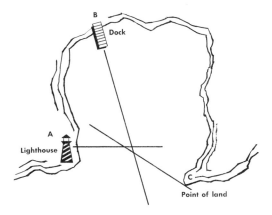

The cross-bearing method of finding your position.

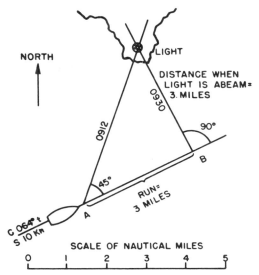

The bow-and-beam method of finding your position.

take bearings with your pelorus or compass sight vanes on two or more charted objects: buoys, lighthouses, lightships, church steeples, etc. Apply error and convert to magnetic or true bearings, then lay them on the chart by using a course protractor or by extending the bearing from the compass rose on the chart with your parallel rules. Your "fix" is where the lines converge.

The cross-bearing method of obtaining a fix affords a high degree of accuracy, especially when three bearings can be used for lines of position. The most accurate fixes are those obtained from lines of position that are at a 60 to 90 degree angle from each other and are made from established navigational marks. It is well to remember that whenever possible the navigational mark should be a landmark or a lightship. Buoys may shift position and are relatively hard to locate and identify from small boats. It is most important to be sure that the mark being used for a bearing has been properly identified.

The Bow-and-Beam Method. In coastwise navigation it is not always possible to see more than one established navigational mark. One method under this circumstance is the bow-and-beam method illustrated below. The bearings used in this method of obtaining a fix are "relative bearings." The term means that the bearing is in relation to the center-line or keel of the ship. The bow of the vessel, therefore, is considered as being 000 (zero) degrees, whereas the stern is considered as being 180 degrees. Two relative bearings are used in this method, 45 degrees

and 90 degrees. It makes no difference whether these bearings are taken to the left or right of the bow. The vessel in the illustration has noted the exact time the light bore 45 degrees to port. The time is again noted when the light bears exactly abeam, or at 90 degrees, as at B. The run between points A and B is estimated, and this distance run is equal to the distance the vessel is off the light when the vessel reaches point B. This holds true only if the vessel maintains the same course throughout the run. A fix can be plotted on the chart with this method by noting that the ship's heading during the run was 064 degrees true. At B, the angle of the bearing was 090 degrees. The line of position then, from B to the light, must be 064 degrees less 090 degrees. In this case, 090 degrees cannot be subtracted from 064 degrees, therefore, add 360 degrees to 064 degrees and then subtract, giving a *true* bearing from the ship to the light of 334 degrees *true*. This line of position is drawn on the chart, then, with a pair of dividers, the distance run along this line is measured from the light to the ship, and a fix is obtained.

The Seven-tenths Rule. This method makes use of two angles, 22½ and 45 degrees. Here, the time is first noted when the navigational mark bears 22½ degrees off the bow. The time is again noted when the mark bears 45 degrees off the bow. Again, the distance off

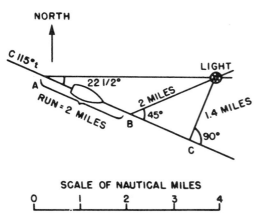

The seven-tenths method of finding your position.

is equal to the run between bearings. If the vessel maintains course until the mark is directly abeam, the distance off will be seven-tenths the distance run between the first and second bearings. The seven-tenths rule and bow-and-beam bearings are two of the most valuable methods of determining position that are available to the navigator in coastwise navigation. For small boats not equipped with a pelorus, satisfactory results can be obtained if the 22½-degree, 45-degree, and 90-degree points are marked in some manner, both port and starboard. Thumbtacks in the railing, precisely placed, can be used. It is not absolutely necessary to plot the estimated positions.

Danger Bearing. The danger-angle method is used to avoid sunken rocks or shoals or other dangers marked on the chart. There are two kinds of danger angles: the horizontal

and the vertical. The former requires two well-marked objects indicated on the chart and the latter requires an object of known height. As shown here, the desired course line is CD. A and B are two prominent objects shown on the chart and S and S' are the danger points through which the ship wishes to pass. Inscribe a circle around the danger nearest the beach, well clear of the danger. From E, the outermost tangent of this circle, draw lines AE and BE to the objects ashore. The angle AEB is the greatest angle which can safely be reached in making the pass. Describe a similar circle around the outlying shoal. Lines GB and GA are joined, forming AGB, which becomes the minimum angle that can be attained to safely pass the outlying shoal or danger.

The same rule is used in the vertical danger-angle method as in the horizontal danger-angle one, except that an object of known height and distance, such as a lighthouse, is used. Lighthouses are measured from mean high water to center of the light. Allow for the stage of the tide if there is much range.

Dead Reckoning. For the sailboat enthusiast, the least accurate, and possibly the most difficult, method of determining your position is by a procedure known as dead reckoning. Here, knowing that you have started from a given point of departure and have traveled in a specific direction for a given length of time at a certain speed, you can lay off a line on the chart from the point of your departure, in the proper direction, for a distance which is supplied through calculation of the speed and the time on your course.

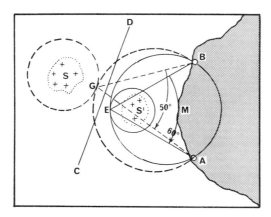
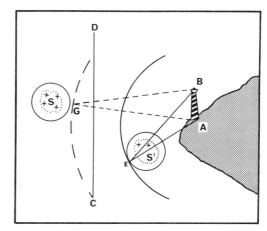

The horizontal (left) and vertical (right) danger angles.

Electronic Navigation

As said earlier in this section, electronic navigation has replaced the more complicated forms of offshore navigation. It has made offshore sailing available to the average sailor.

Radio Direction Finder. Possibly the most valuable aid to foul-weather navigation is the radio direction finder. This electronic device obtains its bearings in a manner similar to a pelorus, and the bearing lines found by operating the RDF are laid out on the chart in the same way as bearing lines determined by eye. Bearings taken with an RDF may be *relative, magnetic,* or *true.* Which you elect to use will depend on which is most desirable for your particular situation. Whether you read relative, magnetic, or true bearings will depend on how you set the azimuth scale on the RDF. The azimuth scale is the plastic ring on top of the unit immediately beneath the antenna. It is calibrated from 0 to 360 degrees and is rotatable so that you may set your own boat's course opposite the lubber line.

First the RDF should be so positioned that the two lubber lines are lined up parallel with the ship's keel. To take relative bearings, set the azimuth scale with zero opposite the forward lubber line. Read the bearing opposite the line on the end of the antenna. One end of the antenna will indicate bearing to the station, the other end will indicate bearing away from the station. These bearings are *relative* to your own ship's heading.

To take magnetic bearings, set your ship's compass course opposite the forward lubber line. If your ship's compass has deviation on the particular heading, add or subtract the correction and set the corrected magnetic bearing on the azimuth scale. Read the indicated bearing from the mark on the end of the antenna as for relative bearings described above. The indicated bearing will be *magnetic,* and can be plotted directly on the chart using the magnetic compass rose on the chart.

To take true bearings, proceed the same as for magnetic bearings except correct the compass course for deviation and variation, and set your true course on the azimuth scale. Bearings read opposite the end of the antenna will be *true* and can be plotted directly on the true-bearing compass rose found on all navigation charts. Regardless of whether you take relative, true, or magnetic bearings with your set, bearings on the navigational chart must be plotted in true or in magnetic. Also, the bearings that you take are the bearings of the station *from* you and must be reversed to be plotted. Finally, all bearings must be corrected for the error of the compass on the ship's heading on which the bearing is taken. Regardless of the method used, exercise care in correcting. This is most important.

A radio direction finder can be used in much the same way a pelorus is used for taking cross bearings. Just like the visual line of position obtained with the pelorus, the radio bearing obtained with the direction finder is plotted on the chart and, when crossed with a second radio bearing, will give a radio fix. The sequencing of Coast Guard radio beacons should be very helpful when taking cross bearings. Very often two beacons which lend themselves to cross bearings will both be found on the same frequency. When possible it is always better to take bearings on three stations. All three lines will not always cross at a point, but will form a small triangle. The center of the triangle should be assumed to be your probable position.

An RDF may also be used in connection with such visual piloting techniques as **bow-and-beam** bearings, doubling the angle on the bow, danger bearings, etc. The data may be determined by radio rather than eye, but the navigational procedures are the same.

An extremely valuable part of radio navigation is homing, whereby the boat's head is swung so that the null point of a beacon is just over the bow. If the craft wanders off course, the radio signal will pick up in strength, and the boat must be turned to restore the signal to the null point. By repeating the bearing every time the beacon is transmitting, it is easy to run up the beam to the beacon. Actually this system is so accurate that lightships with beacon-transmitting equipment on board have been rammed by vessels homing on them.

Radio beacons, maintained by the government at frequent intervals all along both coasts and throughout the Great Lakes, operate, in general, for two 10-minute intervals every hour during clear weather and continuously during fog. Operating schedules, wave lengths, and signals are listed in the United States *Light Lists,* and special charts showing their locations are issued by the Coast Guard. No knowledge of code is necessary to use the radio beacons, as the signals are easy to distinguish. But, remember that a radio-beacon signal travels a great-circle track and a correction must be applied when 50 miles or more from the station. A table for correcting these bearings is found in H.O. #117, *Radio Aids to Navigation,* and in the *Coast Pilot* books. Sunrise-sunset effect is the distortion of a radio signal caused by the rising or lowering of the Heaviside layer in the atmosphere at this time. This causes the intensity of the signal to vary from time to time and will upset a null.

Before relying on RDF bearings for navigation during poor visibility, it is recommended you practice with it under conditions of good visibility. It is also recommended you make up a calibration curve or table showing deviation for each heading. This can be done very simply by taking visual bearings on a known transmitting tower and at the same time taking radio bearings on the station. Bearing should be taken with boat's heading on various courses from zero to 360 degrees at about 20-degree intervals. The results should be tabulated for future reference. The deviation should be marked plus if it has to be added to the radio bearing to agree with visual bearing, and minus if it has to be subtracted from the radio bearing to agree with the visual bearing. As you become familiar with your set you may use any of the equally valuable visual methods to obtain a fix. Cross your beacon bearing with a visual bearing, or with a sounding from your depth sounder. Or, if the beacon station has synchronized signals for distance finding, take your stop watch and measure the time interval in seconds between the radio and sound signals and divide by five to find your distance off in nautical miles. In short, use all your navigational aids for the purpose for which they were designed and in an intelligent and efficient manner for your own safety and protection.

As mentioned in Section II, there are four other pieces of gear that often are used in electronic navigation, especially on ocean-going sailing vessels. They are loran, consolan, radar, and the depth finder. In some sailing

circles, there is a deplorable insistence on barring electronic equipment—except radio receivers, direction finders, and depth finders—in ocean racing. But for ocean cruising there is no reason why these aids to navigation (loran and radar) should not be employed to their fullest advantage. It is a great deal easier than celestial navigation.

Loran. A loran chain consists of two or three radio stations, a "master" and one or two "slaves." These transmitters are located from 200 to 400 miles apart and transmit short pulses simultaneously or offset by a precise time interval. The pulses are repeated between 25 and 35 times per second. The difference in arrival time of signals from a group of loran stations is measured by a loran unit aboard ship. To get a "fix," it is necessary to take readings on two pairs of loran stations or a single three-station loran chain. The ship is located at the point where the hyperbolic curves or distance lines on the loran chart intersect. The daytime range of loran is around 700 miles over water; at night the effective range is about 450 miles, using the direct ground wave from the loran stations. At night the reflected sky wave permits use at distances up to 1,400 miles, but the results are less accurate.

Consolan. The newest long-range radio navigational aid is consolan, known as "the poor man's loran." Unlike loran, it requires no expensive equipment; unlike RDF it provides a bearing accurate to from 0.3 to 0.7 degrees and has an effective range of 800 miles. (It is not usable within 50 miles.) There are at present only a few stations (Miami, San Francisco, Atlantic City, and Nantucket Island) in or near operational status. In operation, for example, is Nantucket Island, which provides an excellent single bearing source from Nova Scotia to Delaware (and is particularly helpful in the Bermuda race). To use it you must have a radio or RDF capable of receiving 194 kc and an *Airman's Guide* (available from the Hydrographic Office), or HO-205, *Radio Navigational Aids—Consolan.* You then tune in, count the dots, look in two tables, and plot a bearing from Nantucket. A better approach is to take United States Coast and Geodetic Survey Chart 70 and preplot on it a number of consolan lines.

Radar. Radar, which could be considered

a "weather-penetrating eye," has not been fully accepted by sailing men as part of their navigating gear. The reason for this may be that this piece of equipment requires quite a bit of room and needs a large special antenna. This could be a source of trouble as far as the sails are concerned. While the gear itself is seldom found on board small sailing craft, it is a good idea to carry a radar reflector on the mast of your boat to enable rescue vessels, especially the Coast Guard, to locate your vessel.

Shoal-water Navigation

Rivers, lakes, bays, and sounds—where so many of us have to keep and use our boats—usually have wide expanses of mighty thin water. To get about on them properly demands an altogether different brand of navigation than is required when using a boat on deep water.

Owning a shallow-draft boat is a help, but not a necessity. The owner of a keel-type auxiliary tends to get himself in less hot water (or should we say shallow water?) than the centerboarder man because his boat's deep draft compels constant vigilance. This is noticed when following the Inland Waterway to and from Florida—shallow-draft boats go aground more often than the deeper ones. So just because your boat draws considerable water, do not hesitate to cruise shallow waterways. If you learn how to handle your boat properly, you will not get into serious difficulty.

Charts give much of the necessary information for piloting shoal water, but you need to know the exact depth of the water at times. The hand lead line is an excellent device for this. It consists of a suitably marked line and a shaped weight. The weight of the lead and length of the line vary on different vessels. A 25-fathom hand lead line with a 5- to 14-pound weight is generally sufficient.

Marking the Line. The line is marked as indicated below to provide a quick method of reading any coastal depth within the range of the length of the line.

Fathoms	Mark
2	2 strips of leather
3	3 strips of leather

Fathoms	Mark
5	White rag
7	Red rag
10	Leather strip with hole
13	3 strips of leather
15	White rag
17	Red rag
20	Cord with 2 knots
25	Cord with 1 knot

Using the Line. The bottom of the lead is hollowed out to allow it to be armed. Arming the lead consists of packing grease or tallow in this hollow. When the lead strikes the bottom, it picks up particles which may be compared with data on the chart showing the nature of the bottom. An excellent check of the boat's position is often secured in this manner. In taking a sounding, the lead is cast well forward so that it will strike the bottom directly below the leadsman as the boat moves slowly through the water. The soundings are reported by the leadsman by calling the fathom depths that are indicated on the line as marks. Depths between marks are estimated. The following are examples of typical reports and corresponding depths.

Report	Depth (in fathoms)
By the mark five	5
And a quarter five	5¼
And a half five	5½
A quarter less six	5¾
By the deep six	6
And a quarter six	6¼
And a half six	6½
A quarter less seven	6¾
By the mark seven	7

Using Soundings to Pilot. A line of soundings may be the only way left to the navigator to determine the yacht's position, especially in fog. A series of soundings is taken at regular intervals throughout a portion of a run while the boat maintains a steady course. These soundings are plotted on a piece of transparent paper and the course line passing through them is labeled. The paper is then moved about on the chart until the sounded depths agree with the charted ones and the course line is properly oriented.

The electronic depth sounder, or depth finder as it is sometimes called, is another way of determining water depths. As was stated in Section II, all depth sounders work in the same manner and consist of the same basic parts—transmitter, transducer, and receiver. They vary in the presentation of the information, which may either be by a flashing red light or a recorded trace on a special graph paper or a direct-reading meter. They may further vary according to their application in shoal, moderately deep, or deep water, the frequency of the sound pulse, number of soundings per minute, voltage, power requirements, and type of transducer.

Here is how the depth sounder operates: The portion of the device which sends out the impulse is a crystal, called a transducer, which is installed in the bottom of the boat. When an electric current is applied to the crystal it flexes, compressing the water and sending the sound wave to the bottom. The returning echo reverses the process, exerting pressure against the crystal, which then produces a trickle of electrical energy. This is instantaneously amplified and sent back to the indicator. The elapsed time is measured against a constant-speed motor and recorded as a flashing light on a dial, a line on a graph, or a meter reading, depending on the device used. The echo returning from a hard, flat bottom is sharp and precise. A rocky bottom deflects the sound waves so that in addition to a well-defined bottom signal, subsequent echoes bounce back as the sound waves ricochet from rock to rock and back up to the surface. A muddy bottom tends to absorb some of the sound and give a diffused echo.

In navigating with a depth sounder, it is well to remember that exact agreement with the chart is rarely found. Such things as the state of the tide, weather conditions, accuracy of the survey of the chart, and the depth of the transducer below the water must be taken into consideration. Every attempt should be made to get a visual bearing or radio-direction-finder bearing when running a "chain of soundings" in navigating. This provides you with a fix from which you may take your next departure. In addition, knowledge of the depth of the water beneath the boat enables the yachtsman to follow known channels between two points. If, for instance, you plan a trip from one marina to another, and you know that there is a 20-foot channel between these two points, then by checking the depth indication on your depth finder while under

way, it becomes relatively easy to stay on course. Any reading on your recorder of less than 20 feet would indicate that you are sailing away from the channel and course correction is required. When charts are available, the yachtsman can often utilize the depth sounder readings to aid in ascertaining his boat's position by comparison with the depths printed on the navigation charts.

Night Navigation

There are not many yachtsmen who sail at night, but there are numbers who are afraid to. The majority of those who do are men who are forced to stay out, and would, if they could get there, rather be in port snug at anchor and enjoying a good sleep or visiting a new yacht club. But outside of these there are a few who enjoy night sailing, and will take a dose of it every chance they get.

In well-charted waters there is little risk of running ashore or of striking shoals or reefs, as the lead or depth finder and the compass or radio direction finder tell the same story by lamplight as they do when the sun is up. The great advantage of night sailing is that it increases your self-confidence as skipper. After a passage through the darkness, when by use of your knowledge you have safely brought your craft into harbor, you feel that you do know something about navigating. Sailing in the daytime, you are constantly able to correct your course by eye, and the compass becomes a mere auxiliary upon which little value is placed as a guide. But at night the compass is at times your sole resource, and must be watched and followed implicitly. Having once followed the needle, and having found that it led you truly to your port, you will have a strong confidence in its guideship, and a firmer and better opinion of your own ability to use its directive powers.

Before darkness falls a thorough check should be made of all necessary clothing, equipment, and navigation aids. All material not necessary for the night run should be stowed to prevent stumbling over obstacles in the dark. Those things you need should be made accessible, ready for use, preferably in an area which can be lighted without interfering with the helmsman's vision. See that the running lights are in good condition and meet navigational requirements, and remember to turn them on before you start. Have your compass light ready and keep a flashlight or cabin light prepared for use if necessary, but do not plan on going along with all cabin lights blazing or with any lights other than navigational lights showing above deck. This might confuse skippers of other boats as well as impair your own vision. Keep in mind that red utility lights will preserve your night vision. Coat bulbs over chart table or compass with red fingernail polish or use red lamps.

Being able to interpret the lights you see around you is as important as making sure that your craft has the proper lights and that they are in good operating condition. Quick recognition of navigational lights will warn you of possible danger and whether you should swing your boat to port or to starboard. For instance, a red and green combination light or a pair of side lights, without any white light showing, indicates that you are directly in front of another sailboat. A red and green combination light with a white light above indicates that a powerboat of less than 26 feet in length is approaching. On inland waterways when a pair of red and green side lights and two white lights are seen, the approaching vessel is in excess of 26 feet. In such cases, the white lights can be used as a range, since they are mounted on the centerline of the vessel. Keep in mind that because the after light is the higher, it is possible to judge the craft's direction by their vertical alignment. When the white lights are in a straight line, the approaching vessel is coming directly toward your boat. When the higher light is to the right, the craft is heading toward your port side; when the higher is to the left, she is bearing toward your starboard. Other possible light arrangements that may be seen can be found in Section II.

When relating the Rules of the Road with the position of an approaching vessel, whether you are under sail or power, remember that when you see a red running light, you are heading into another craft's danger zone. In other words, even when you are under sail and have the right-of-way over a powerboat, it is just good sense to remember the comparison of navigational lights with traffic signals: green means go (right of way) and red

means stop. When under power, of course, you must follow the Rules of the Road as you do in auxiliary operation during daylight. This includes meeting situations when both craft should veer to the right, or starboard, so each can see the other's red light.

If you see only a moving white light, it means one of two things: either you are approaching the other vessel from the stern (you are both traveling in about the same direction), or the other craft is a rowboat, which is not required to carry navigation lights. (On the Great Lakes, it could be that you are being approached by a sailboat from abaft the beam.) A steady white light by itself means that a small boat is at anchor. Larger vessels at anchor show more than one white light (the higher one forward). When passing an anchored vessel, remember that the anchor chain may extend out some distance across your course.

Our country's navigational system employs lights in three different colors—red, green, white—to mark obstructions or channels. The night sailor can determine from the chart what light he wants to find, then search in the appropriate direction until he spots it. This is not always easy. Neon store lights on shore, auto headlights, or street lights reflecting off the water or shining through trees can cause confusion. Since perspective is different at night, use a stop watch to identify lights by their characteristics marked on the chart, and stay in the marked channels.

The compass can help you in channels and rivers as well as in open waters. A good sailor uses the compass to check his boat heading when on large bodies of water even in daytime with land in sight. At night the compass is a necessity on oceans or large bays or lakes unless you are an expert at celestial navigation. The stars can be a help, though, even if you are not an expert. Polaris, the North Star, is the sailor's guide, but you can also use other stars by checking your compass reading and then lining up a star with some point of your boat and keeping it in the same relative position. This is easy on the eyes and does away with the necessity for a continuous light on the compass. You must remember, however, that stars do change their apparent position in the heavens, and every 10 or 15 minutes you should check the compass and change your point of alignment or follow another star.

In a channel or river you may not need the compass if you can see the channel markers, buoys, or banks at all times. But if a marker does not appear when you feel it should, a check on the compass can tell if you are still heading in the right direction or if the current or wind has somehow turned the boat so you are heading for danger. If the compass reading is right for your course, then proceed slowly and the marker will probably appear. Remember that lights sometimes get out of order or are obscured by other objects. This may be the case with the one you seek.

Another method of using the compass in rivers or channels is to chart the courses between buoys and then run this course until the buoy or marker is in sight, always keeping in mind the effect of current and wind direction and those little points of land. If you are in shallow water or think you might be, take soundings, or use a depth finder if you have one on board.

Use your ears as well as your eyes. Listen for engine noises from other boats which might be running without lights; for whistles, horns, bells, breakers, water noises of unusual nature or any other unusual sound. A good hearing aid for listening to sounds at night or in a fog is a megaphone, when the mouthpiece is pressed against your ear. When you cannot hear a distant bell buoy because of wind and sea, go below, press your ear to the hull—listen on each side for the stronger sound.

Radio direction finders are a valuable aid to night cruising. They are easy to operate and can be used to take bearings, fix positions, and to "home in on the beam." If you plan to do much night cruising in open waters they are certainly worth their price.

The skipper who always comes to port at sundown misses one of the most exciting and pleasurable parts of sailing. And the sailor who must be tied up before dark because he is not prepared for it is taking a serious chance, in case circumstances delay his portcoming. With a little preparation and practice, night navigation can be just as accurate as daylight piloting. And the pleasure of a sail under the stars can be unforgettable.

COMMUNICATION AFLOAT

There are various ways to communicate afloat: sound, flashing lights, signal flags, and radiotelephone. The latter is the most dependable.

Radiotelephone

In Section II we discussed the purchasing of radiotelephones. But, before you can transmit, with either a marine or a Citizen's Band phone, you must get a station license from the Federal Communications Commission (FCC). This is a simple matter of filling out an application form, having it notarized, and sending it to the FCC. There is no charge. Your marine electronics dealer should be able to supply the necessary forms and solve any mysteries in the paper work.

One exception is the very-low-power (under 0.1 watt) "handie-talkie" transceiver used on Citizen's Band frequencies. No license is required for this equipment as long as it con-

forms to regulations for *Restricted Radiation Devices,* and as long as it is used only to talk to other similar unlicensed units. But if you intend to use such equipment to contact licensed Citizen's Band units, you must obtain a station license.

The owner of the boat will also need a Restricted Radiotelephone Operator Permit to operate a marine-band radiotelephone. There is no examination or charge for this. However, you must declare that you are a U.S. citizen and that you can write, speak, and understand English, and that you are familiar with treaties, laws, rules, and regulations regarding use of the permit. Unlicensed persons may talk over your marine radiotelephone, but you, as the operator's permit holder, are responsible for what goes on. You make contact with the other stations, supervise the transmissions, make log entries, and sign off.

Apply for your licenses promptly. There is

a waiting period of up to two months for marine radiotelephone station licenses. In case you are caught in a bind, you may get an "interim" ship station license by making application *in person* (yourself or your agent) to the nearest FCC Field Engineering Office.

Operating Procedure. Radiotelephone conversations are not like face-to-face or even shore-telephone talking, where everyone can clack away at once. If two stations try to talk at the same time, neither will hear the other. To prevent pandemonium, there are strict rules on how to get in touch with one another, carry on a conversation, and sign off. Because anyone can listen in, there are also sensible restrictions on your conversation. And, because the primary purpose of the service is to promote safety, priority is given to emergency traffic. While you are required to have and be familiar with the FCC Rules and Regulations pertaining to your service, here are the basic rules:

1. Do not operate transmitter without proper licenses or permits.

2. On the marine band, keep the receiver tuned to the International Calling and Distress frequency (2182 kc) during standby periods.

3. Keep a log of transmissions.

4. On Citizen's Band channels a Conelrad standby must be maintained, but no log is required.

5. No obscene, indecent, or profane language.

6. What you overhear cannot be disclosed to unauthorized persons, or used for your own benefit.

7. No superfluous, false, or deceptive signals.

8. Calls must be identified by the use of station call signs.

9. Stop conversations after 5 minutes; say only that which is necessary, and sign off. Others are waiting.

How to Use the Radiotelephone. Suppose you want to talk to a friend in a boat called the *Gizmo*. Your boat is the *Mary Jane* and your call letters are WZ-9999. Face up to your radiotelephone, turn it on, and switch to the Calling Frequency, 2182 kc. Turn the receiver volume to a comfortable level, and listen, to make sure that you will not interfere with other traffic or that there is no distress situation.

When the air is clear, press the "transmit" button and talk into the microphone like this:

"Gizmo from the *Mary Jane,* WZ-9999, over."

Then you release the "transmit" button and listen. If your friend hears you, he should say:

"Mary Jane. WZ-9999 from the *Gizmo,* WZ-9998, go ahead."

"Switch to 2638," you say. (Or whatever talking frequency is available.)

"Roger" (for "received and understood"), says he.

Both of you switch to the intership frequency specified, repeat the "call-up," and have your talk. At the finish, you again give your boat's name and call letters and say "signing off," or simply "off." Note the time and details of your transmission in your log.

Then you switch back to 2182 kc, listening for possible distress messages. This channel should be "monitored" all the time that the telephone is on, except when you are talking or receiving calls on another frequency. Before using the commercial shore-telephone facilities you must first set up an account for the boat. You can do this by writing or calling up the marine-department business office of the company operating the shore station. To place a call through commercial shore-telephone facilities, you switch to their working frequency, and make the same kind of "call-up," using the name of the city and the words "Marine Operator," i.e., "New York Marine Operator from the *Mary Jane,* WZ-9999, over." Then just follow the operator's instructions. When you are through, make your "sign-off" and return to 2182 kc after logging your call. If you are calling a station from a great distance or if interference is severe, the "call-up" can be repeated up to three times to improve chances of being heard.

It is a good idea to make schedules with your friends or associates with whom you might need to talk; this will make it unnecessary to listen for long periods of time for possible calls. Also, make note of times when your local shore stations broadcast marine weather and warnings, to keep informed of changing conditions.

Emergency Procedure. The word "Mayday" is the international radiotelephone distress signal, corresponding to the Morse Code signal "SOS." The frequency 2182 kc is the international radiotelephone distress channel. Upon hearing the Mayday signal, all stations must stop transmitting immediately until the emergency is over.

Distress calls consist of the word Mayday repeated three times and the name and call letters of the boat. To make sure of getting through, this is repeated three times: The distress message is then transmitted. Its content should be:

1. Name of boat.
2. Position.
3. Nature of the emergency.
4. Nature of the assistance needed.

At sea, the position is given in latitude and longitude. On inland or coastal waters, the bearing and distance from a known point are more convenient.

Any vessel in a position to help the distressed vessel should reply, acknowledging that the Mayday has been received and stating its own position, speed, and estimated time to reach the distressed boat. At this time, more information may be exchanged, such as the description and color of the boats making contact. This helps in recognition. Boats equipped with radio direction finders that work on the marine band can insure speedy contact by taking bearings on the phone signals of the other. Using RDF, it is possible to come right up to another boat even in dense fog.

When a boat is not actually in distress, but it appears that it will be soon, or if someone on board or another boat in sight is in serious difficulty, an "urgent" call may be made. This is identified by the word "Pan" repeated three times.

Messages connected with general safety of navigation, such as warnings of dangerous floating objects or the approach of bad weather, are called "safety" messages. These are broadcast, prefaced by the word "Security" spoken three times.

Lesser emergencies can be taken care of very often by just calling a nearby fuel dock, shipyard, or marina through the shore-telephone station.

Sound Communication

Most primitive, but still good under certain circumstances, are sound signals. A power "bull horn" or electronic hailer is a useful item to assist in speaking to a person on shore or on board another vessel. Amplification of the human voice will permit hailing at greater distances, and in some cases makes it possible where the voice would otherwise be drowned out by the sounds of a storm or the noises of the boat's engines. Some models of radiotelephone equipment have a connection for a loudhailing speaker. In these instances the regular radio microphone and a portion of the radio set pick up and amplify the person's voice. An external weatherproof speaker is all that is additionally required.

In an emergency situation, the universally recognized aural method of sounding the fog signal should give the desired results. While the voice commands may be misunderstood, a continuous or prolonged sounding of your ship's whistle, horn, or bell should indicate just one thing to anyone within hearing distance: a serious effort to attract attention to which all yachtsmen should respond. As detailed in Section IV, whistle signals also play a necessary role in the carrying out of the Rules of Road, as well as in fog operations.

Flashing Lights

Flashing lights, employing combinations of dots and dashes that constitute the International Morse Code, are often used to send messages. Although receiving blinker signals takes practice, it is possible in an emergency at night to slowly spell out a message from a Morse Code chart and send it by flashlight, spotlight, or white range light. In determining the duration of dot and dash signals, the dot is taken as a unit; a dash equals three dots, and the time between any two elements of a symbol is equal to one dot. Between two complete signals, the interval is three dots; between two words or groups, five dots. This spacing of the letters, words, etc., is an important element of successful signaling.

International Morse Code

A	• –	N	– •	1	• – – – –
B	– • • •	O	– – –	2	• • – – –
C	– • – •	P	• – – •	3	• • • – –
D	– • •	Q	– – • –	4	• • • • –
E	•	R	• – •	5	• • • • •
F	• • – •	S	• • •	6	– • • • •
G	– – •	T	–	7	– – • • •
H	• • • •	U	• • –	8	– – – • •
I	• •	V	• • • –	9	– – – – •
J	• – – –	W	• – –	0	– – – – –
K	– • –	X	– • • –		
L	• – • •	Y	– • – –		
M	– –	Z	– – • •		

Signal Flags

In all too many yachting circles, the International Code flags are mainly employed as a decoration for yachts when they dress ship at regattas, on holidays, and so on. While they are certainly attractive for these purposes, they are a great deal more valuable for their basic intent—that of conveying messages from one vessel to another.

Hoists of the International Code flags may be carried at the starboard main spreader or

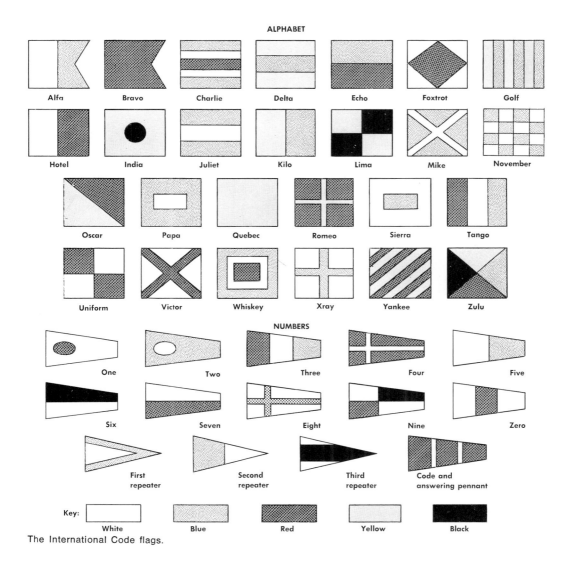

The International Code flags.

yardarm or wherever they may be most easily seen. While many yachtsmen do not carry a set of International Code signal flags aboard their craft, it is important that "urgent and important" flag hoists are understood when they appear. (All larger boats should carry Code flag "T.") The Code comprises forty flags: twenty-six alphabetic flags, ten numeral pennants, one code pennant, and three repeaters. The purpose of the repeaters is to enable the sender to transmit the same letter or number more than once in the same message. The code or answering pennant is used by the receiving vessel to indicate recognition and compliance with the message transmitted. Each flag has a meaning in itself which should be known to everyone who may come in contact with this method of communication. For complete information on all the various flag hoists, we suggest that you purchase a copy of *International Code of Signals, Vol. I, Visual, H.O. Number 87* from the United States Government Printing Office. While it is a very good idea to have this aboard, here are some of the more important flag hoists:

Emergency Signals. For communications with Naval, Coast Guard, or merchant vessels, yachts must use the International Code Book. The following emergency signals are selected from the International Code.

C Yes (affirmative).

F I am disabled—communicate with me.

N No (negative).

O Man overboard.

U You are running into danger.

V I require assistance.

A E I must abandon my vessel.

A N I need a doctor.

C B 4 I require immediate assistance; I am aground.

C B 5 I require immediate assistance; I am drifting.

C B 6 I require immediate assistance; I am on fire.

C B 7 I require immediate assistance; I have sprung a leak.

K Q 1 I am ready to be taken in tow.

N C I am in distress and require immediate assistance.

Z L Your signal has been received but not understood.

The flags are hoisted, the first letter above the second on the same halyard, where they will be most visible. As a general rule, only one hoist should be shown at a time, but each hoist, or set of hoists, should be flown until answered. In answering a flag signal, hoist your answering pennant halfway up as soon as you see the signal, then all the way up when the signal is understood.

Other Uses of Signal Flags. The Code flag "T," commonly known as the transportation flag, may be flown from the starboard spreader or yardarm, or where it can best be seen, to indicate a request for a club lunch. It should be accompanied by three blasts of the horn.

On national holidays, at regattas, and on other special occasions, yachts often dress ship with International Code signal flags. Flag-officers' flags, club burgees, and national flags are not used. The ship is dressed at 8:00 A.M. and remains so dressed from morning to evening colors (while at anchor only). In dressing ship, the yacht ensign is hoisted at the peak or staff aft, and the jack at the jack-staff. Then a rainbow of flags of the International Code is arranged, reaching from the waterline forward to the waterline aft, by way of the bowsprit end to the foretop masthead, then across to the main topmast, and down to the main boom end, allowing several flags to touch the waterline from both the bowsprit end and the main boom end. To keep the flags in position, a weight should be attached to the end of each line. Where there is no bowsprit, flags will start at the stem head. Flags and pennants should be bent on alternately, rather than in an indiscriminate manner. Since there are twice as many letter flags as numeral pennants, it is good practice to follow a sequence of two flags, one pennant, etc., etc., throughout. In order to effect a degree of uniformity in yacht procedure, the following arrangement has been proposed: Starting from forward, AB2, UG1, LE3, JH6, IV5, FL4, DM7, PO third repeater, RN first repeater, ST0(zero), CX9, WQ8, ZY second repeater. The arrangement here proposed is designed to effect a harmonious color pattern throughout. If enough flags are not available for "full dress," the "up and down" dress may be used. The line of flags is strung from the after masthead to the water aft, or on a two-masted vessel, it may be strung from the top of each mast to the water.

Some yacht clubs, as previously stated, have adopted signal codes of their own, which are not in conformity with signals prescribed by the International Code Book. Furthermore, since the practice among the clubs may vary to a certain extent, the interpretation of such club signals depends largely on a knowledge of the local code as prescribed in the club's yearbook. The purpose of the signals prescribed in club codes is principally to provide a means of communication between boats of the club. Most clubs provide that yachts using their own club code should hoist the club burgee over the club code flags; otherwise, absence of the burgee would indicate that the International Code is used.

THE ART OF CRUISING

There are basically two types of cruises: short and distance cruises. The former may be for a day, overnight, or a weekend, and may be in either a day sailer or a cruising-style sailboat. Usually, as described in Section III, day sailers have roomy cockpits, and some have a cuddy cabin which provides a wonderful arrangement for overnighting, protection from the weather, and storage space for gear. If you wish more covered area, especially when at anchor, boom tents are available. Your local marine dealer will be glad to show you the type that is best for your boat and tell you how to install it. You can also rig an awning over the boom, with one end supported by the mast. If you plan to use such an awning, you should test it thoroughly beforehand, as it is not easy to rig one in such a way that it will stand up to wind and rain without letting in drafts and drops of wet. As for sleeping accommodations, there is room generally for one to four persons, depending on the size of the craft. Waterproof sleeping bags generally are recommended, but if you are the rugged type, rolling up in a blanket will provide all the luxury you will need. The fresh air and exercise of the day will make any bed feel soft. If you wish, you can sleep ashore under a tent or in a sleeping bag on the ground. In a pinch, you can empty the boat of all gear, drag her ashore, turn her over, prop up the leeward side, and sleep underneath. This hardly spells comfort, but at least it assures one of shelter in the worst of weather.

In a true cruiser-style sailboat, all the comforts of home (or almost all) are available. It has berths to sleep in, galley space, toilet (head, as it is called at sea) facilities, and stowage lockers for clothing and gear. Generally, as the cruiser-racer becomes larger, and more expensive, the features of "livability" also increase. For more details on this type of boat, see Section III.

Planning a Cruise

All members of the family should engage in all of the cruise planning, and plans should incorporate the widest possible variety of things to do so as to include interest for each member of the cruise party. A lot of things go into making any cruise a happy and memorable experience for everybody aboard. None is more important than first deciding on the right answers to some basic questions such as:

1. *What time of year will we go?* This can make a big difference. For instance, in some sections of the country long-distance cruises should be made in early summer rather than late summer when there is greater likelihood of foggy weather.

2. *How much time is available?* Do not try to cover too much distance or plan too rigid a schedule at the sacrifice of leisurely cruising. More cruises have been ruined for the crew by the skipper's insistence that the boat arrive in a certain place on a particular day. Do not spoil everyone's fun by doing this. Remember that you are out for rest and recreation. Otherwise you will probably arrive back home dead beat and in need of a second vacation. And do not feel that you have to spend every minute of those two weeks aboard the boat. Lay over in some friendly

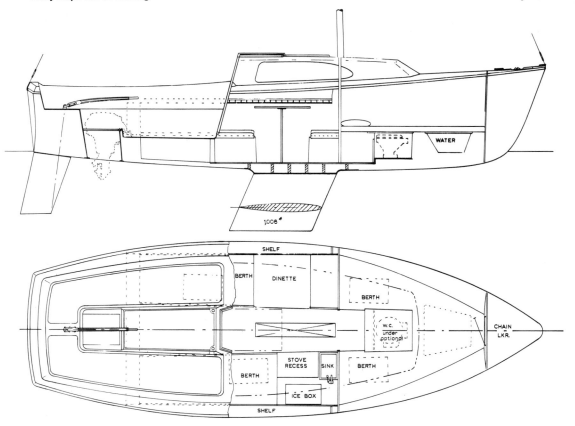

"Floor plan" of a typical 22-foot racer-cruiser.

little harbor for a day or two and go ashore to see the local points of interest, have dinner, and maybe take in a movie or summer stock production. You will find that such a procedure will keep everyone happy on a long cruise.

3. *Are your plans flexible?* Remember that with a sailboat, it is sometimes difficult to judge your speed and time of arrival. However, unless you have an auxiliary on board, you will want to be certain of a harbor within sailing distance before sundown. You should keep in mind that the wind has a general habit of dropping with the sun, and frequently if you have not made port by that time, you will find yourself becalmed for the night within tantalizing view of shore. If you do not make it to the desired port, you should be able to select, from your United States Coast and Geodetic Survey charts, unfamiliar harbors with good assurance of what to ex-

pect in the way of approach, anchorage, and even dock facilities.

4. *What kind of boat will you use?* Water conditions can vary considerably in different parts of the country. Obviously, a small day sailer is apt to be wetter and less comfortable than a large racer-cruiser when waves kick up on a large, open body of water.

5. *What is the objective?* Naturally, if you are out for rest and relaxation, you should pick a very different kind of cruise than if fishing were your chief objective . . . or exploration . . . or sightseeing.

6. *What about supplies en route?* In picking a cruising route, you will want to be sure of sufficient marinas—in the right locations—to get food and other supplies.

7. *What about accommodations?* You will also want to be sure the route selected has the right kind of accommodations for you and your family: Places where you can sleep on

Interior of the 27-foot Tartan.

board . . . or rent a motel, or "boatel," if you prefer the comforts of home.

8. *What about entertainment?* Having a good time is the primary objective of everybody on a cruise. What will that mean in your case? Quiet anchorage to "get away from it all"? Visiting lively boating centers where something is always going on? Visiting waterfront towns where there are movies to see and other things to do? Do you want to visit friends or relatives along the way? It is not difficult to plot a cruise that will include any one or several such forms of entertainment.

9. *Should we take our pets on a cruise?* Since most of our pets are land-based animals, they generally do not care too much for cruising. There are, of course, exceptions. But, unless you have had previous experience in carrying small pets aboard your boat and the animal is used to and enjoys cruising, you are better off to board pets with your local veterinarian.

10. *What about inviting friends?* Remember that there is nothing like a cruise to bring out the traits of a person. For example, that happy-go-lucky fellow from the office may turn out to be a chronic grouch after you have been out a few days. He may want to sleep late when you had planned to start at the crack of dawn each day, or he has his own ideas about where you should cruise, and if you do not follow them, you may get the old silent treatment. There is nothing like the close quarters of a 26-foot sailboat to bring out the good and bad points of your friends and relatives. So play safe and choose your cruising companions with care if you expect to remain on friendly terms after a junket.

Cruising Gear

A good deal of the success of any cruise depends upon having the proper equipment on board. For instance, if you are prepared for it, rough or rainy weather will be part of the adventure. If you are not prepared, the first cold, rainy day can easily douse the spirit of your crew. For this reason, we do not fully subscribe to the old theory of "traveling light." Actually, we believe there is more danger that you will take too little than too much. There is more likelihood that you will neglect your comfort than be ever thoughtful of it. But because every pleasure craft has its limitations for gear storage, the experienced yachtsman knows that what to leave behind is just as important as what to take. The newcomer to cruising should make an inventory of all items he would like to take and should then go over the list several times, eliminating those items not wholly essential to the safety, comfort, and pleasure of those taking the cruise. The gear required by law and for safety was mentioned in Section II, while the navigating equipment was fully discussed earlier in this section.

Cruising Clothes. One place most yachtsmen can travel light is in their cruising clothes. It is not necessary to have a full wardrobe on board for every member of your crew. The growth of automatic laundries along popular cruise routes has been little short of phenomenal lately, and this will allow you to keep clean with a minimum of clothing.

All members of your crew—and this includes the children—should have a suit of foul-weather gear on board. But, when selecting the suits, consider the type of cruising you are going to do and the locale. In general, fabrics used in the better foul-weather suits are light to wear, pliable in varying degrees, do not crack or peel in sun or salt, do not stiffen in cold climates, are odorless, and are impervious to the effects of fuels and most chemicals. The zipper and other fittings on a good suit are made of either noncorroding metal or plastic. In spite of the long-wearing qualities of the fabric in the suit you select, the foul-weather gear deserves to be properly dried after use and the salt rinsed off before prolonged storage.

You must also guard against the sun. As a matter of fact, sunburn can quickly spoil a sailing weekend. The best protection comes with treatment before exposure and moderation of exposure early in the season. New oils, creams, and lotions are reported to completely block out the direct burning rays plus the severe water reflections, or screen them so that tanning progresses slowly. Another point to keep in mind is that every member of the crew should have a pair of good sunglasses.

Before leaving the subject of clothing, remember that suitcases are awkward to store aboard a boat and good luggage may also be damaged by the dampness. Save weight and space by packing all clothing gear in sea or duffel bags. An extra duffel bag or two will be handy for storing soiled clothing and will serve to lug groceries or carry laundry to laundromats.

Galley Gear. The most important item in the galley is the stove. While some cruising sailboats use bottled gas, and a very few have electric ranges, the most popular by far with sailboat people is the alcohol stove. While alcohol stoves are available in several different types and styles, all burn gum-free, denatured ethyl alcohol. Never use menthol (wood) alcohol because it will clog the burners and give off highly poisonous fumes. The alcohol should be stored in metal cans because glass containers could break, spilling the contents into the bilge. Most marine stores package it in metal containers. When filling the tank, be sure to carefully use the filter-equipped funnel, which not only helps prevent spillage, but also traps dirt and lint, which might clog the burners. It goes without saying that the flame should be out and the burners cool when filling the tank.

The maintenance of most marine stoves is an easy task. Keep the outside clean, so that you will not have an unexpected grease fire from the surface accumulation. Occasionally

A suitable dining arrangement aboard a 26-foot cruiser-racer.

tighten the fuel-line connections. Should an alcohol stove start to kick up a little trouble, the first thing to do is to clean out the generator brush. This is a long spiral-wound wire brush through which the fuel passes on its way to the valve. On some models, the brush comes out the front and on others it can be removed in the rear. In either case, the cap is removed first and the brush worked back and forth a few times, then taken out and immersed in a container of clean alcohol, shaking to remove the dirt. Do not slap the brush against any hard surfaces to knock the dirt loose, for this will bend and damage it. Replace the brush and tighten the cap and you will generally find you have cured the trouble.

No galley is too small for a refrigerator. Regardless of the stowage problem on your sailboat, there is a food-cooling arrangement that will suit your needs. There are two basic types: mechanical and nonmechanical. The latter—the kind you fill up with natural ice or chemical "ice"—are adequate for most of us and is the type installed by most sailboat builders. In such iceboxes, generally three or four cans of patent sealed refrigerant that has been prefrozen in your home refrigerator, plus a fifty-cent piece of ice, will keep it cold enough to preserve anything for a three- or four-day period of time. To keep iceboxes smelling sweet and to prevent various foods from picking up the flavor from other foods stored with them, add a mesh bag of charcoal to the box. Periodically replace the charcoal in the bag with a fresh batch. Charcoal can be deodorized and refreshed by heating at high temperature over a stove or in an oven.

While the icebox is still the most popular with sailboat people, the increased use of alternators and generators has made mechanical refrigeration possible. If your kind of sailing justifies mechanical refrigeration, and it is within your budget, there are several such units available, and there is a good possibility that one can be installed in place of your present icebox. A mechanical-refrigeration system has two basic components. One is the evaporator, which is located in the cold compartment. The other is the condensing unit, which is the compressor, condenser, and other parts such as the receiver. This component is located outside the cold compartment and has the moving parts.

Your pots and pans should be of stainless steel, since they are more easily cleansed and are far easier to maintain than other types. (Aluminum is cheaper and is a good second choice.) A pressure cooker will save fuel and, once mastered, will also save cooking time and thus give the first mate more chance to be on deck. If you like toast you can have it readily by getting one of those collapsible top-of-the-burner toasters at any good hardware store; this type of toaster is inexpensive but efficient. If your stove is equipped with an oven, or should you have one of the new portable stove-top burner ovens, there will be many times when cooking while under way will be less of a burden than otherwise. A casserole or other dish placed in the oven is less liable to get into difficulties because of balance problems than if perched on top of a stove. Use plastic glasses and plates to eliminate broken glass and crockery, which can be such a hazard on the water. There are also all sorts of plastic containers for your refrigerator stowage.

When you selected your boat you gave thought, of course, to a fresh-water tank of adequate capacity. The abundance of docks and marinas where fresh water is available in the modern age of the sail almost completely eliminates the possibility of a water shortage except when far offshore or when ocean-racing. Pressure and water-heating equipment is also no longer the problem it was to sailing yachtsmen even a few years ago. Pressure systems, if not already aboard your boat, are easily installed and are not overly expensive. There are several hot-water heating systems available, too. Some boats use a system in which the water is heated by electricity while tied up at a dock and is heated by the auxiliary engine while afloat.

Icepick and its holder, bottle opener, beer-can openers, and a special screw-top jar for matches are essentials, as are a strainer and sufficient sharp knives and mixing spoons, measuring cup, and tongs for grasping hot foods. A chopping board which doubles as a sink cover, and a thermos with pouring spigot are also helpful gear. Take into account the rust factor when selecting these small accessories for the galley. Handles of utility knives, cooking spoons, and forks should be well-connected, or strongly forged. Stainless-steel flatware is best aboard any vessel. Consider tableware and glassware as "tumble-ware," because nowhere do these items undergo as much bouncing, shifting, and bumping as on a boat. Rugged glassware, and plastic or thick restaurant-type plates, can take this punishment. Many seasoned yachtsmen prefer disposable plates and cups.

For the boatkeeping (housekeeping) tasks, be sure to keep on hand a supply of chrome and metal polish, copper wool, stain remover, turpentine, grease solvent, bleach, and furniture polish and oil. But the basic requirements for an efficient galley afloat are to keep things reasonably simple, to keep a careful check on your gear, and if you must cook an elaborate meal, do it while you are safely moored in a harbor or tied up at a pier rather than under way in unpredictable conditions.

The Dinghy. One essential part of your cruising equipment will be the dinghy or tender—whichever you wish to call it. The dinghy can be employed to run errands—to a dock to buy supplies, to take the family crew to a beach for a swim or cookout, to a lobster or fishing boat to buy the makings of a gala dinner, and to go fishing at a good location that may be a short distance from the anchorage. Also, if your boat goes aground, the tender can be used to carry an anchor out so the boat can be kedged free. When equipped with a small outboard motor, a dinghy becomes an auxiliary. If the engine on your auxiliary cruiser conks out—or if powered only by sails, should the wind de-

A dinghy may be towed or stored aboard deck as shown.

part—the tender can tow her into a harbor or up to a dock. If the dinghy is equipped with a sail, it is an extra source of pleasure, especially for the youngsters, but whether rowed, powered, or sailed, the tender widens the horizon for exploration. It can go into little creeks and inlets where larger craft cannot venture. It also provides excellent basic training in seamanship. If the tender is of fiberglass, it will require little maintenance.

On the debit side, any dinghy can be somewhat of a nuisance to tow, and equally a nuisance to stow aboard. In towing, your boat's speed can be cut down as much as half a knot. In running before a following sea, a tender will sometimes try to climb aboard, and the rest of the time there is yanking strain on the painter and the tender's stem. In maneuvering around a dock, there is always the chance that the painter will get wound around your prop. At anchor, with the wind and current in any conflict, the dinghy is always fighting the big boat. The towing problem can be solved to a degree if you purchase a tender that is especially designed for this purpose. There are a couple on the market that are made for use with cruising sailboats and they have proven quite successful.

The best place to "tow" your dinghy is on deck: but if you have not the room nor facilities to stow it on deck or atop the cabin roof, it has to be towed.

Other Cruising Gear. The choice of materials is important for any boat accessory.

For curtains, for example, the only fabric that should be used from a safety standpoint is fiberglass, because it is noncombustible. It is also easy to care for and can be had in a number of designs and attractive colors. Curtains are useful for filtering hot sunlight and are indispensable for privacy. With any but very short curtains you get the trimmest, neatest effect by using rods at both top and bottom. Materials are also important in the choice of the ubiquitous seat cushion. This is probably the most common boat accessory, but it is seldom exploited to full advantage. Nautical quarters are at best compact, and more often crowded, and no accessory that is capable of performing two functions should be allowed to perform just one. It is pretty redundant to sit on nonbuoyant cushions and stuff the probably insufficient storage space that is available with the life preservers required by law and good sense.

The type of bunk that you will sleep on will be predetermined for you by the boat you have purchased. Built-in bunks today are generally equipped with either foam-rubber or air mattresses. The bedding should include at least two mildew-proof synthetic or wool blankets per person. Take along sheets—single-bed size—and small pillows and pillow cases. Always air and dry your bedding on deck the first thing in the morning. Dampness has a habit of getting entrenched aboard a boat—and can become almost incurable unless caught early. Dry all damp bedding and clothing at every opportunity; never stow anything that is wet.

In addition to all the equipment you must have on board for safety and comfort, you may want hobby gear, cameras, fishing tackle, sketch pads, musical instruments, record player, portable TV, and games. Keep them as compact as possible and try to quarter them together. The tackle box for lures, gadget bag for photographic items, etc., is the best arrangement. Also bring along a supply of games to occupy children passengers.

Before Shoving Off

Just like an airline pilot before take off, plan to run through a simple check-off list like the following:

1. Check the weather . . . if possible, at least a day before you plan a cruise. Get to know signs of the weather changes by cloud formations, the sun and moon. Check radio reports and the newspapers for storm warnings. Keep your weather eye peeled at all times.

2. Tell where you are going . . . just as a pilot benefits by filing a flight plan, you add an extra margin of safety to every cruise if, before you go, you leave with a responsible friend or relative, or your local yacht club, a description of your boat and your cruising plans and destination. Then should something happen and you are overdue, this person can make an accurate report to the Coast Guard or local rescue agency so help can reach you without delay. For years the Coast Guard has urged boatmen to follow a procedure of this kind. A "float plan" form has been designed by the Marine Office of America and free pads of this form are available from their offices at 123 William Street, New York, New York 10038.

3. Carry life preservers for all hands . . . this is not only good sense, but mandatory in all areas. Be sure yours are Coast Guard approved. Also make certain that all required gear is on board. All gear should be properly stowed.

4. The proper National Ocean Survey navigational charts . . . lay out your course beforehand on up-to-date charts.

5. If it is vital that you receive mail, check in advance for the names of major marinas or yacht clubs along your cruise route and have mail addressed to you care of these locations. Ask senders to mark envelopes "Please hold for arrival." Also, a number of the major gasoline companies offer mail port service to the cruising yachtsmen. Contact the marine division of the firm whose products you generally use, and ask for a list of their marine service stations on your cruise route. Be sure to inform those writing you to include a return address and the number of days the letter should be held pending your arrival. Yachtsmen expecting mail after their departure from a mailing location may leave their estimated arrival dates at points ahead and the mail port operator will usually be glad to forward letters to meet them.

6. If an auxiliary, check fuel supply . . . fill the tanks and make sure that you have your refuel location picked out. Also be certain that there are no fuel vapor odors, no spills, no leaks.

Cruising Routine

One of the most essential things on any cruise is that the work of your vessel should not be neglected; the lack of day by day boatkeeping and care of the craft can quickly negate all the enjoyment of cruising. There is no question that cruising offers a splendid opportunity for long, lazy hours of sheer relaxation and physical comfort, but when the lazy hours dominate all and the care of your boat is neglected, you make more work for yourself in the end. The easiest way to keep up with the task of boatkeeping, as well as the other duties about the boat, is to conform to an exacting routine. This routine will make the work seem easy and make the boat much more livable. Thus, before starting out on any cruise, set a routine for yourself and your crew (this includes the children). This will make the voyage easier, smoother in operation, less demanding, and safer. Assignment of shipboard duties—anchoring, cooking, boatkeeping, and the like—beforehand gives each crew member time to understand his particular job and prepare for it.

For the average family vacation cruise the routine may be divided into two general departments: navigating and steward's. The navigating department, under the command of the skipper, is responsible for operation of the craft while under way; speed and course; handling of sails and helm; operation of engine (if an auxiliary); and anchorage. The steward's department duties, under the command of the first mate, should include maintaining sufficient food supplies; preparation of meals; obtaining fresh food, ice, smoker's supplies, and liquid refreshments; boatkeeping below deck; making up of berths; replacement of galley and cabin gear; laundry or laundry service; stove maintenance; and ship's mail.

Cruising Records

Keeping a log is considered a dull, dry chore by the majority of yachtsmen who bother with it at all. And yet it can be made a very interesting and even instructive part of cruising if you go at it in the proper way. Actually, the purpose of a log is twofold. First, it is legal and admissible evidence in any court of law should there be any questions arising from accidents, property damage, salvage, etc., and second, it gives a detailed description of a passage and thus becomes valuable in comparing it with other runs, or the same run in adverse or bad weather.

There are many good printed logs available from your local nautical supply dealer. Be sure to keep the log wrapped in oiled silk or neoprene to prevent fog and dampness from ruining it. Do all writing in waterproof ink.

Meals Afloat

On board your yacht, the food you provide can make or break your weekend or cruise, or even just a day's sail. Fine weather afloat cannot make up for poor meals, but when the weather closes in to keep you at anchor, tasty food cradled in good conversation around the cabin table can make you forget a lot of rain on the deck. It takes a great deal of forethought and no little physical effort to produce tempting fare for four or five on a two-burner stove and with a minimum of working area. If you do not understand the job, or do not like it, turn it over to someone who does. It can be a lot of fun, and on the water the results of your labors will be fully appreciated by appetites whetted on fresh air.

Actually, the art of cooking on board is mainly a matter of adroit planning ahead. For instance, many factors enter into your initial grocery list:

1. How many persons are to be served how many meals?
2. How long between ports where you can get fresh supplies?
3. What storage areas do you have, and how much perishable food can be put in your icebox along with the minimum ice you want to carry—allowing plenty for cold drinks?
4. What size and type of stove do you have, and can you plan on oven cooking?
5. What utensils do you have—if you plan a mess of crabs or fresh corn, do you have the pot to cook them in?
6. Finally, what are the food preferences of your crew?

With these ideas in mind, you can devise a series of menus which will include simple, appetizing food, and plenty of it. As a guide in figuring quantities, a table of the approximate needs per man per day which was used successfully on several long passages is as follows:

	Ounces per Man per Day
Meats, poultry, fish	14.5
Beverages (not milk)	4.0
Dairy products (including milk)	22.0
Cereals and bread	13.0
Fruits	8.0
Vegetables	11.0
Soups	3.0
Sweets (sugar, syrup, chocolate, jam)	12.5
	88.0 ounces

or 5½ pounds per man per day

Meat can pose a problem if you do not have sufficient refrigeration space. Smoked meats like hams, bacon, pork butts, and the like can be carried in cool, dry places and will last a reasonably long time. However, you should inspect meat carefully before using it while on a cruise of any length. Salted meats travel best. They must be cooked or soaked in fresh water before the final cooking. You can also utilize the new prefabricated dishes, for example, pot roast, potatoes, and vegetables all cooked on heavy foil plates that can be heated in the oven or on the stove with asbestos mats. Take some heavy pads with you to protect the dining table, or your lap, for these containers are used as plates as well.

In the last few years, a number of prepared meats with no waste have been produced, frozen via a new vacuum process. They come sealed in foil and only need to be soaked in a small amount of fresh water for a matter of minutes before being reconstituted. Then they may be treated like any fresh meat. Several companies now have developed a line of these meats which are fine, especially if you are contemplating a long cruise away from good supply ports. Canned meats are very good, too, under such cruise conditions. For instance, canned hash is always rib-warming, and may be garnished with anything from tartar sauce to catsup.

Actually, canned food is the most important category for meals afloat, which explains why a boat's can opener wears out so frequently.

Canned foods are easy to prepare and when dressed with imagination can also be as delicious as any sophisticated taste could wish. For instance, a short cut to some of the most celebrated recipes can be achieved with a can of soup: condensed soups double for sauces or gravies, can be heated for hot sandwiches, add the flavor and vegetables to a hot stew, serve as a binder for one-dish main courses, and can be used as dressing for salads and vegetables.

When choosing fruit and vegetables such as tomatoes, it is best to select those that are slightly underripe and in firm condition. They need not be refrigerated as long as they are well-covered and protected from buffeting. Carrots, peppers, apples, onions, potatoes, cabbage, and produce of this type will keep for a week, or even two weeks if kept in a cool place. Buy lettuce in firm heads, leaving the tough outside leaves on for protection. Try to keep produce from being buffeted about. Bruises develop into soft spots that will rot easily.

Desserts should be simple, such as canned fruits, cookies, and packaged puddings. A cake may be made at home and brought aboard, or your first mate can make it from a package cake mix. A preheated pie is another welcome dessert. These pies need only 15 minutes to a half hour in an oven before serving.

Boatkeeping Afloat

It is essential that the boat be kept clean and shipshape at all times. This means not just the accommodation quarters but the *entire* boat.

The first rule of good shipboard housekeeping is to have a place for everything and everything in its place. This means you must have storage room—something most small boats do not have enough of. To make the most of the space available, there are several things you can do. For instance, a shelf can often be installed near the ceiling, under the deck, or along the inside of each sleeping berth. This shelf should have a good high rail and, if space permits, should be wide enough to hold spare clothing, oilskins, and other miscellaneous articles. If impracticable to fit a shelf, pullman-berth hammocks make an excellent substitute.

Keep a list of stores on board and a key to their storage locations, so they can be quickly found. If such a scheme is used, you will know what stores are on board and whether they need replenishing and be able to take their weights into consideration.

A well-kept craft calls for a regular daily boatkeeping routine. But, the actual cleaning aboard ship is the same as at home and generally requires the same techniques. The tools are the same, too. While attending to daily boatkeeping routine, you should also make a maintenance check. While cleaning, carefully inspect the plumbing, steering gear, rigging, stoves, etc., and take immediate steps to repair any faulty items.

To make shipboard housekeeping easier, study the following special hints gathered from several "old salts":

1. Use a detergent rather than soap because it will generally clean better in salt water. Also avoid foamy, sudsy cleaners in the galley or around the boat. Fresh rinse water is seldom plentiful aboard little ships; suds do little cleaning and demand lots of rinse. Cleaners high in trisodium phosphate do an excellent job and do not froth too much.

2. Wet bathing suits should be dried or taken off before the wearer enters the sleeping quarters of your floating home. Nothing gives a cabin or bunk a more miserably moist smell than salt-water dampness impregnated in bed clothing.

3. The best way to clean glass windows on shipboard is to wash first with vinegar and water solution. Use paper tissue rather than a cloth. Clean plastic windshields and windows most gingerly. These plastics are soft. Hard rubbing on plastic window surfaces will cause scratching and reduce transparency. Lots of fresh water and very gentle washing with soft cloth or sponge is best, or use one of the special cleaners made for this purpose and follow the manufacturer's instructions. Hard rubbing and abrasive cleaners are *verboten*.

4. Bilges clean easily with one of the bilge solvents available from boating suppliers.

5. Wash varnished work with plain, clean, fresh water or weak soap solution. Varnish may lose gloss if scrubbed with gritty cleaners or strong detergent. Mahogany can be cleaned with lemon oil. A few drops will suffice to clean the varnished surface.

6. Ventilate lockers, drawers, head, and cabin as much as possible. Leave doors and drawers open when you are away from the boat. Lots of light and fresh air reduce rot, mildew, and that smell of dampness. Linens, clothes, and towels are subject to more dampness on the boat than at home. Air them frequently.

7. Keep refrigerator or icebox spotless. If it gets sour and moldy, it will smell up all the food stored inside. Wash the refrigerator interior frequently with soda, ammonia, or bleach solution. When the box is out of operation, keep it wide open; give it plenty of light and air to help it stay sweet. To reduce odors in an icebox, use sheets of transparent plastic (the self-sealing kind) for wrapping melons, cut onions, cheese, and so forth.

8. Use only metal polish meant for boat work, and sold at yacht-supply dealers.

9. Use ammonia as a grease cutter rather than the stronger household preparations. Coffee grounds in a greasy frying pan will absorb most of the grease, making it easy to wash. Take heavy cleaning jobs home when possible. It is lots easier, for example, to boil out and scour a greasy, charred frying pan in the cool convenience of your home kitchen than in the limited quarters of the boat's galley.

10. Shun washing in and around the cabin interior with salt water. The water evaporates leaving a salt film; the salt attracts dampness and makes things feel clammy.

11. To whiten enamel toilet bowls, sinks, etc., fill with water and pour in a little laundry bleach. After a few hours of soaking, even the most stubborn stain will come off.

12. Toy cleaning implements (brooms, carpet sweepers, and the like) stow more easily than the large household ones and are sometimes even more efficient because they will fit into normally impossible angles.

To make your (or your first mate's) boat-keeping tasks easier, you and your crew should develop good living habits afloat. Clean up messes as they are made, and you will never be faced with accumulated work which can spoil the entire cruise.

The best defense against insects is screening. Screen with copper or plastic mesh all portholes, cowl ventilators, hatches, the spill pipe, and all other openings in the cabin.

Carry an insect bomb, spray gun, mosquito-repellent compound, and fly swatter on board, to kill any insect that should get through the screening.

Sea gulls are very real pests in some harbors. To discourage them, keep flags flying whenever possible, or drive a few sharpened brass spikes upward through the truck (at top of mast) to stop them from landing. To remove sea-gull droppings, use cold water, a good paint cleaner, and copper wool.

Children on a Cruise

Children enjoy cruising if they feel that they are a part of it. They should be given routine shipboard chores to do. Older children should be given a chance to show their own seamanship. Provide reading matter, shipboard games, and activities of physical effort —swimming, rowing, and fishing. But also give them a chance to go ashore whenever possible.

Children should be instructed in the art of living aboard ship—use of lights, fresh-water conservation, operation of lavatory, supply storage, and general boating habits. Teach them how to put on a life preserver, how to throw a life ring, how to use a fire extinguisher, how to swim with clothing on, how to give the distress signals, and how to use the other safety devices aboard a boat. The very learning of these important items helps to create shipboard interest.

Actually, owning a yacht in any section of our country can extend anyone's enjoyment

With a catamaran it is possible to do some water skiing.

of water sports immeasurably. The fun of boating can add exciting new horizons to fishing, swimming, photography, skin diving, and racing. Each of these can be done better with a boat, and some sports like water skiing cannot very well be accomplished without some type of craft.

Group Cruising

Most of us cruise alone. We are content with family or invited guests aboard when we "get away from it all." This may be fine if we truly need separation from others. But often we most need relaxation in the presence of others. For this try organized group cruising; not just two or three boats but a gathering of ten or fifteen. Such mass cruises are gaining popularity. Why? The exhilaration of flotilla movement on a selected course, the evening comradeship at moorage or anchorage, the fun of sharing an experience from advance planning to final tie-up—these are the basic pleasures of group cruising.

The increased safety factor, and new formation of lasting friendships—these are the bonuses. Group cruising, incidentally, is a fine activity for weaning the timid skipper from day cruising only to the adventure of extended cruising. Often veteran yachtsmen and qualified skippers, many of them graduates of several sailboat-handling and navigation courses, hesitate to embark upon an extended cruise alone. Yet extended cruising is to sailing as the onion is to hash and as the olive is

to a martini: something that cannot be explained, only savored.

In general, the group cruise is arranged under the auspices of a yacht club or a sailing club, and is open to all the members of that club. Not infrequently such cruises are also invitation affairs, and members of other clubs and sometimes sailboat skippers who are members of no club at all can arrange to be invited. Sometimes group cruises are organized in races from port to port, as described in Section VI. In such cases, however, the essence of a cruise is the really important thing, and the racing merely adds a touch of interest.

While group cruising is usually delightfully informal, a well-organized cruise may have such affairs as clambakes, dinners, dances, and all sorts of pleasant festivities arranged at the different ports. When the anchor is down there is always a great deal of visiting among the different boats, too. All in all, the organized group cruise forms one of the most attractive phases of yachting activities.

Where to Cruise

In cruising the waterways of America, boatmen will want to provide themselves with various types of information. They will want a chart, or a sea-going road map, and they will want the information published by the states explaining their parks, lakes, and recreational facilities. Here are the addresses of departments that will send you the necessary material:

UNITED STATES

Alabama	Information & Education Section, Dept. of Conservation, Montgomery 36104	
Alaska	Division of Tourist & Economic Development, P.O. Box 2391, Juneau 99801	
Arizona	Development Board, 1521 West Jefferson St., Phoenix 85007	
Arkansas	Publicity & Parks Commission, State Capitol, Little Rock 72201	
California	Department of Parks &	

	Recreation, State Capital Bldg., Sacramento 92511
Colorado	Department of Commerce and Development, 600 State Services Bldg., Denver 80203
Connecticut	State Development Commission, State Office Bldg., Hartford 06115
Delaware	State Development Dept., 45 The Green, Dover 19901
Florida	Development Commission,

	Carlton Bldg., Tallahassee 32304
Georgia	State Game & Fish Commission, 401 State Capitol, Atlanta 30303
Hawaii	Hawaii Visitors' Bureau, 2051 Kalakona Ave., Honolulu 96815
Idaho	Dept. of Highways, P.O. Box 829, Boise 83701
Illinois	Division of Park and Memorials, Room 100, State Office Bldg., Springfield 62706
Indiana	Dept. of Conservation, Division of Publicity, State Office Bldg., Indianapolis 46209
Iowa	State Conservation Commission, East Seventh St. and Court Ave., Des Moines 50309
Kansas	Park and Resources Authority, 801 Harrison Ave., Topeka 66612
Kentucky	Director of Public Relations, Dept. of Fish & Wildlife Resources, Frankfort 40601
Louisiana	Dept. of Commerce & Industry, Tourist Information, State Capitol Bldg., Baton Rouge 70804
Maine	State Publicity Bureau, Gateway Circle, Portland 04104
Maryland	Division of Information, Dept. of Economic Development, State Office Bldg., Annapolis 21404
Massachusetts	Dept. of Commerce, 150 Causeway St., Boston 02108
Michigan	Michigan Tourist Council, Lansing 48904
Minnesota	Minnesota Tourist Information, 212 State Office Bldg., St. Paul 55101
Mississippi	Agricultural & Industrial Board, 1104 Woolfolk State Office Bldg., Jackson 39201
Missouri	Division of Resources & Development, Jefferson

Camping and a day sailer go hand in hand.

	Bldg., Jefferson City 65102
Montana	State Highway Commission, Helena 59601
Nebraska	Information & Education Division, Game, Forestation and Parks Commission, State Capitol, Lincoln 68509
Nevada	State Park Commission, Carson City 89706
New Hampshire	State Planning & Development Commission, State House Annex, Concord 03301
New Jersey	Division of Planning & Development, Dept. of Conservation & Economic Development, 520 East State St., Trenton 08625
New Mexico	State Tourist Bureau, State Capitol, Santa Fe 87501
New York	State Dept. of Commerce, 112 State St., Albany 12207
North Carolina	State Advertising Division, Dept. of Conservation & Development, Raleigh 27607
North Dakota	Public Relations Director, Game & Fish Dept., Capitol Bldg., Bismarck 58501
Ohio	Information and Education Section, Dept. of Natural Resources, 1500 Dublin Road, Columbus 43212
Oklahoma	Tourist Division, Planning and Resources Board,

	Oklahoma City 73105	Texas	Highway Dept., Austin 78714
Oregon	Travel Information Division, State Highway Dept., Salem 97310	Utah	Tourist & Publicity Council, State Capitol Bldg., Salt Lake City 84116
Pennsylvania	Travel Development Bureau, Dept. of Commerce, South Office Bldg., State Capitol, Harrisburg 17101	Vermont	Development Commission, State Office Bldg., Montpelier 05602
Rhode Island	Publicity & Recreation Division, Development Council, Roger Williams Bldg., Hayes St., Providence 02908	Virginia	State Chamber of Commerce, Richmond 23213
		Washington	Dept. of Commerce & Economic Development, General Administration Bldg., Olympia 98502
South Carolina	State Chamber of Commerce, P.O. Box 70, Columbia 29202	West Virginia	Industrial & Publicity Commission, State Office Bldg., Charleston 25305
South Dakota	Dept. of Game, Fish & Parks, Pierre 57501	Wisconsin	Conservation Dept., State Office Bldg., Madison 53702
Tennessee	Game & Fish Commission, Information & Educational Section, Cordell Hull Bldg., 6th Ave. N., Nashville 37219	Wyoming	Travel Commission, 213 Capitol Bldg., Cheyenne 82001

CANADIAN PROVINCES

Alberta	Travel Bureau, Legislative Bldg., Edmonton		Provincial Bldg., Halifax
British Columbia	Government Travel Bureau, Dept. of Recreation and Conservation, Victoria	Ontario	Information Branch, Dept. of Travel & Publicity, 67 College St., Toronto
Manitoba	Travel & Publicity Branch, 254 Legislative Bldg., Winnipeg	Prince Edward Island	Travel Bureau, P.O. Box 1087, 252 Prince St., Charlottetown
New Brunswick	Travel Bureau, P.O. Box 1030, Fredericton	Quebec	Provincial Publicity Bureau, 106 Grande-Allée, Quebec
Newfoundland	Tourist Development Board, Fort Townshend, St. John's	Saskatchewan	Tourist Branch, Dept. of Travel & Information, Legislative Annex, Regina
Nova Scotia	Bureau of Information,		

ETIQUETTE AFLOAT

To most sailors a love of boats and the sea is accompanied by a profound respect for and inspiration of those age-old traditions long associated with the sea.

Flag Etiquette

The flying of flags or colors (the term may include all of the flags flown by a vessel or it may refer only to the national or yacht ensign) on sailing and power vessels is a subject governed by custom and tradition, not law. The right of private vessels to fly national colors stems indirectly from the Navy's long traditional use of the stars and stripes. When the Continental Congress established a national flag in June, 1777, it was immediately thereafter flown from naval vessels. As

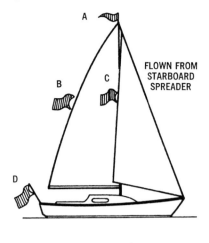

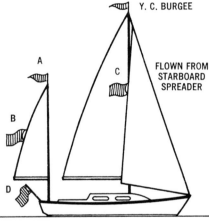

Flag etiquette. Single-masted sailboat: *A*, burgee or private signal; *B*, ensign (under way); *C*, special signals; *D*, ensign (at anchor or under power). Two-masted sailboat—burgee at forward masthead: *A*, private signal; *B*, ensign (underway); *C*, special signal; *D*, ensign (at anchor, under power).

the Navy then and for some time thereafter was supplemented by large numbers of privateersmen, it became customary for these privately owned naval vessels to fly the national standard as well.

The yacht ensign, a Betsy Ross flag with a fouled anchor inside the circle of thirteen white stars, can be flown from yachts instead of the national flag. It was designed by the New York Yacht Club and adopted in 1849 by the Secretary of the Navy as a signal to be flown by certain merchantmen, exempting them from entering and clearing at customs houses. Because of its similarity to the na-

tional flag, it has become the yacht ensign and is today the proper ensign for yachts to fly.

Colors are flown aboard yachts, as they are in naval vessels, from 8 A.M. until sunset while in port. Under way, entering or leaving port, they may be flown whenever there is enough light to distinguish them, but before 8 A.M. or after sunset they should be hauled down immediately after anchoring. Time should be taken from the senior officer present. When in company of a vessel of the United States Navy or Coast Guard, or a shore station of these services, or in the home anchorage of another yacht club, time should be taken from such vessel, station, or club. When under way offshore, colors may be flown whenever required, such as when meeting other vessels. They may also be flown as needed when approaching lightships or nearing foreign shores.

When making colors in the morning, if shorthanded, the ensign is raised first, then the yacht-club burgee. At sunset, colors are executed in the reverse order, if shorthanded. Whenever possible, however, all colors should be raised and lowered simultaneously. Colors should be hoisted smartly but lowered ceremoniously.

The ensign is half-masted only on occasions of national mourning. On Memorial Day, the ensign is half-masted from morning colors to noon. On the death of a yacht-club member, the burgee and private signal only are half-masted on his yacht. The yacht club may also order mourning for a member, in which case the club, other members' yachts at anchor, and other stations should half-mast the burgee only. When the ensign is to be flown at half-mast, it must first be mastheaded and then lowered to half-mast (actually about two-thirds of staff height). Before lowering from half-mast, colors should first be mastheaded and then lowered.

When under sail and under way, fly either ensign at the leech of the mainsail, or when there is more than one mast, at the leech of the aftermost sail, approximately two-thirds the length of the leech above the clew. Under power alone, or when at anchor or made fast, the ensign should be flown from the stern mast of all sailboats.

The club burgee, mentioned earlier, is usually triangular in shape, but sometimes may be swallow-tailed. It is never proper to fly the burgee of more than one yacht club at a time. On any two-masted sailing craft the burgee is carried on the foremost mast and the private signal at the aftermost mast. For example, in a yawl the burgee would be displayed at the mainmast and the private signal from the mizzenmast. On a sloop a burgee is displayed at the mainmast when at anchor; the private signal is flown at the mainmast while under way. The burgee is normally displayed from morning to evening colors. However, the Cruising Club of America has a long-established tradition, only recently incorporated into their bylaws, permitting its members to fly the burgee day and night. This club has no official clubhouse, so each member's boat becomes the informal club station to which all members are welcome at all times, whether for social reasons or for necessity. A yachtsman may carry only the burgee of the clubs of which he is a member.

The owner's private signal, sometimes called the houseflag, is usually swallow-tailed, sometimes rectangular. Any yacht owner, whether or not he is a member of a yacht club, may design and carry a private signal, and have that signal registered in *Lloyd's Register of American Yachts*. If you do not have a private signal and wish to design one, obtain a copy of *Lloyd's Register* and check to see if any of the flags illustrated therein resemble too closely the design you have in mind. Since the basic purpose of the signal is to identify your boat, it should be as simple as possible so that it may be recognized easily at sea. This means that it is best to stick to a simple design, employing no more than three colors. The traditional colors used are dark blue, red, and white. The owner's private signal flag is flown from morning to evening colors.

Good Manners Afloat

Remember that a yachtsman is a gentleman, which means basically that he must have consideration for others. Everett A. Pearson, in his book *The Lure of Sailing,* lists the following points of etiquette and good manners afloat, which should be kept in mind by all sailors:

1. Never wait until the last minute to make clear your intentions of obeying Rules of the Road. Even when aboard a sailboat and you have the right of way over powerboats, do not abuse this right by forcing them into a dangerous situation.

2. Try to anchor clear of lines of traffic and outside of narrow channels. If forced to anchor in a narrow channel, take extra precautions should the tide or wind change. It is always best to anchor in an authorized anchorage or select an anchorage which allows room to swing without fouling other vessels already anchored. Always ask permission before picking up a buoy that does not belong to you. When sailing in a harbor, never have your tender on too long a line.

3. Navigate with care on well-known fishing grounds and keep well clear of fishing vessels. Do not run over fishing stakes or buoys.

4. Do not pass a vessel in distress. When you go out in your yacht, be on the alert and receptive to possible distress signals. In the case of small boats, it is a good idea to investigate any irregular motion or activity. It is better to know that you have not passed up someone in trouble. Also, during the summertime most sailing areas are infested with young sailors who are attempting to learn the sport. Often they may be headed for trouble without knowing it, and it is your duty as a yachtsman to give them a word of advice or a helping hand. Remember that it is a tradition as old as the sea itself that mariners always go to the aid of those in distress.

5. Do not tie up to government buoys or local navigation markers, except in emergencies. Actually, the law forbids any person to interfere with, remove, move, make fast to, or willfully damage any aid to navigation maintained or authorized by the Coast Guard. Violation of this law subjects that person to a fine up to $500.

6. Do not throw garbage or refuse overboard in harbors, or near beaches, or in lakes used for drinking-water supply. (Use shore disposal facilities.) Never throw cans overboard, even in open water, unless punctured at both ends so they will sink.

7. Always be on the alert when passing dredges where divers may be at work and

keep away from areas indicated by the skin-diver's flag.

8. Never land at a private dock or float without invitation, except in an emergency. If your yacht is berthed in a marina or yacht club, other members have equal rights with you, so do not interfere with their berthing spaces. When visiting another yacht club, pull up to the dock or float and inquire as to where you might moor your boat so that you are certain you do not interfere with some regular member's berth. Then properly moor your craft before going ashore. Avoid tying up across club floats. And when anchoring for a swim, or using the bathing facilities of a club, do so quietly, without screams or roughhouse.

9. Do not stare at other yachting parties or into cabins as you pass. If you see a beautiful yacht and wish to look her over, you may do so, but avoid being obvious about it.

10. Never anchor on top of another boat unless there is a good reason for such action. Do not caterwaul or permit your children to do so, and be sure not to keep your radio or phonograph going into the night on quiet evenings in crowded harbors.

11. Always talk to other yachtsmen. Remember there is no snobbishness about our sport. Always greet other yachtsmen—and landlubbers, too—with a wave of the hand or a cheery "good day." Wish them luck and exchange opinions about the weather. To get most fun from sailing you must enter into the camaraderie of the sport.

12. Never presume upon the courtesy of yacht clubs, unless invited, or unless they exchange courtesies with your club. If you de-sire to use the club facilities, inquire first of the steward or attendant as to the club rules and regulations. When you are coming in as a guest at a strange sailing club or yacht club, act as a courteous guest. In general, yachtsmen are quiet, gentlemanly folk. They do not call attention to themselves by loudness or rowdiness. Therefore, it is best not to make yourself obnoxious by being demanding, because even if their courtesy gains the upper hand and you are served as you wish, it will mark you for any future time you may wish to take advantage of the facilities offered by that club.

13. Visiting between yachts that are anchored within easy reach of one another is a common practice. But, there is a ritual to be observed about visiting. Never board another boat without a distinct invitation from the owner. If you do not know the skipper get close enough to his yacht and engage him in conversation, but do not attempt to board until he asks you. Never stay if you are interrupting the work of the vessel.

14. When you anchor in a small port, make friends with the natives. Greet and talk with them while ashore. Their customs and manners are a great deal different from the people of a large city, who make it a rule never to speak to strangers.

15. Do not give uncalled-for advice while a guest on someone else's yacht. Take your orders from the skipper and never try to interfere with the way in which he handles his craft. Courtesy and common sense are the basis of yachting etiquette. If this is kept in mind, the sailor is well on his way to becoming a true yachtsman.

INCREASE YOUR KNOWLEDGE OF THE WEATHER

Weather is, without a doubt, the most important factor in determining the success of any sail, race, or cruise. Men learned long ago that there are definite weather patterns, and by observing existing conditions we are able to predict the weather ahead. In fact, while meteorology—the technical name for the study of the weather—is a highly scientific and complicated business—the weather knowledge you need to have at your fingertips to be a wise sailor can be easily learned.

Visual Indications of the Weather

Weather moves from one place to another, and it sends its signs ahead of it. You do not have to be a meteorologist to read these signs. Actually, nature puts her weather signs right up in the sky for all to see—for example, the colors in the sky itself, the shape and density of the clouds, and the appearance of the sun. Bright blue sky usually means fair weather;

but a dark, gloomy sky means windy weather. A vivid red sky at sunset means fair tomorrow; a vivid red sky at sunrise may mean foul weather that day. There is a great deal of truth in the old proverb: "Red sky at night is the sailor's delight. Red sky in the morning, sailor take warning." Also, a bright yellow sky at sunset presages wind; a pale yellow sky, wet weather.

The sun gives other clues, too. For instance, when the sun comes up out of a gray horizon, chances are that it will be a fair day. A sunset with diffused and glaring white clouds is a good sign that a storm is on its way. A weak, washed-out-looking sun probably means rain in the near future. The moon gives us help, too—that ring, or corona, around it is a sure sign that a storm is on the way.

Good boatmen read clouds like the stars; they recognize them instantly and know what they portend. Clouds have a great variety of shapes which tell many stories. For example, there are four basic cloud weather indications you should recognize:

1. Increasing cloud cover usually means the weather will be worsening.
2. Clouds just moving suggest a storm is approaching.
3. Two or more layers of clouds moving in different directions usually means a storm is pretty close at hand.
4. When general cloudiness is related to the predominant wind direction, it will reveal the exact location of a storm.

It is also important to know *what* clouds you are observing. Basically, they are classified according to their height: cirrus, cirrostratus, and cirrocumulus are considered high clouds (above 20,000 feet); altostratus and altocumulus are called middle clouds (6,500 to 20,000 feet); and stratus, nimbostratus, and stratocumulus are known as low clouds. One type of cloud, cumulonimbus, the thunderhead, belongs to all three height categories, since the cloud begins at the ground and extends upward to great heights—40,000 feet or more. Each type indicates that certain conditions will be soon at hand, as follows:

Cirrus. Detached clouds, delicate and fibrous-looking, which take various forms such as featherlike plumes, curved lines ending in tufts, lines drawn across a blue sky, isolated tufts, and so forth. They are often arranged in bands which cross the sky like meridian lines and, owing to the effect of perspective, converge to a point on the horizon or to two opposite points. Cirrus cloud formations can indicate rain or foul weather when moving rapidly, especially from the southwest. When they thicken, especially with a south wind, and are backed by overcast or gray sky, bad weather can be expected, too. If cirrus clouds move east to west, rain can be predicted in twenty-four hours. Should they build up into an anvil, a thunderstorm is near. Cirrus also can mean fair weather when not increasing, drifting slowly or standing still, and dissolving as the sun rises.

Cirrocumulus. Small globular masses or white flakes, having no shadows, or only very slight shadows, arranged in groups and often in lines. Such clouds indicate changeable weather and can be a sign of rain when driven by northeast and east to south winds.

Cirrostratus. A thin, whitish sheet, sometimes completely covering the sky and giving it a whitish appearance, or at other times presenting, more or less distinctly, a formation like a tangled web. This sheet often produces halos around the sun and moon. These clouds often mean rain when they start to thicken.

Altocumulus. Rather large globular masses, white or grayish, partially shaded, arranged in groups or lines, and often so closely packed that their edges appear confused. The detached masses are generally larger and more compact at the center of the group; at the margin they form into finer flakes. They often spread themselves out in lines in one or two directions. Should they form into a domed shape, a thunderstorm is possible, but when in small, isolated patches, chances for fair weather are good.

Altostratus. A thick sheet of a gray or bluish color, showing a brilliant patch in the neighborhood of the sun or moon. These clouds are like thick cirrostratus but without the halo phenomenon. Rain may fall from altostratus clouds when they grow thick enough and become lower in the sky.

Stratocumulus. Large globular masses or rolls of dark cloud, frequently covering the

CIRROCUMULUS "mackerel sky"
(over 20,000 ft.)

CIRRUS "mares' tails" (over 25,000 ft.)

ALTOSTRATUS (about 19,000 ft.) gray sheet

CIRROSTRATUS (over 20,000 ft.) whitish sheet
often causing halo around sun

CUMULONIMBUS "thunderhead" (thunderstorm
cloud)—can reach height of cirrus

ALTOCUMULUS (over 12,000 ft.) like sheep

STRATOCUMULUS (about 8,000 ft.) dark globular rolls

CUMULUS (over 4,000 ft.)

NIMBOSTRATUS
(about 3,000 ft.)
dark rain cloud

STRATUS (about 1,500 ft.) gray sheet

whole sky, and occasionally giving it a wavy appearance. The layer of stratocumulus is not, as a rule, very thick, and patches of blue sky are often visible through the intervening spaces. All sorts of transitions between this form and altocumulus are observable. It may be distinguished from nimbostratus by its globular or rolled appearance and because it does not bring rain. Stratocumulus usually precede or follow a storm.

Cumulus. These are often called woolpack clouds, thick clouds of which the upper surface is dome-shaped and exhibits protuberances, while the base is horizontal. When these clouds are opposite the sun, the surfaces usually presented to the observer have a greater brilliance than the margins of the protuberances. When the light falls aslant, they give deep shadows; when, on the contrary, the clouds are on the same side as the sun, they appear dark, with bright edges. If they turn gray or black, they are getting all the water they can hold, and a thunderstorm could occur. Also, when they are massing to windward, chances of a storm are good. On the other hand, small, isolated patches of cumulus clouds usually indicate fair weather.

Nimbostratus. Rain clouds; a thick layer of dark clouds, without shape and with ragged edges, from which continued rain generally falls. If the layer of nimbostratus separates into shreds or if small loose clouds are visible floating at a low level underneath a large nimbostratus, they may be described as *fractonimbus,* the "scud" of sailors.

Stratus. A low uniform cloud layer which gives the water a hazy appearance and resembles fog except that these clouds are not resting off the water. They are usually present during a light, steady rain. When this very low layer is broken up into irregular shreds, it is designated *fractostratus;* and it generally indicates a long rainy spell when driven by northeast and east to south winds.

Cumulonimbus. Thunderheads or thunderclouds; heavy masses of clouds rising in the form of mountains, turrets, or anvils; generally they have a sheet or screen of fibrous appearance above, and a mass of clouds similar to nimbostratus underneath. From the base local thundershowers usually fall.

While it is important to be able to identify cloud types, their sequence helps more in making a forecast. The following cloud sequences usually mean the approach of foul yachting weather:

1. Cirrostratus to altocumulus (thunderstorm).
2. Altostratus to altocumulus to nimbostratus or cumulonimbus (thunderstorm).
3. Altocumulus to cumulus (thunderstorm).
4. Cumulus to cumulonimbus (thunderstorm).
5. Cirrus to cirrostratus (thunderstorm).
6. Cirrocumulus to altocumulus to cumulonimbus (thunderstorm).
7. Cirrus to cirrocumulus or cirrostratus (rain).
8. Altostratus to nimbostratus (rain).
9. Stratocumulus to stratus (rain).
10. Cirrus to cirrostratus to altostratus to nimbostratus (rain).

There are also other visual indications to take into consideration. For instance, the weather-savvy sailor knows about the birds too. If you do not, here are some clues that will help you be your own weather prophet, which may save you a rough time afloat. For example, when seabirds and gulls fly out early in the day and go far to seaward, fair weather and moderate wind may be expected. When they hang about the land, or over it, or fly inward screaming, expect a strong wind with stormy weather. Also, most birds perch on wires, tree limbs, or any handy resting spot when bad weather is approaching.

In addition, keep in mind that all weather changes are caused by wind. Weather must move to change. If there is no wind, there will be no weather change. Smoke from factory stacks or smoke trailing from ships is a help in forecasting weather; smoke streaming downward from stacks is a telltale sign of lowering pressure which precedes rain. On the other hand, smoke that rises straight upward is usually a good indication of fair weather ahead.

Aside from the obvious wind indicators, keep your eye on the water for the way puffs and gusts move across the surface. With a little familiarity, you can detect a change in wind strength and direction by the progress of a gust, indicated by moving dark areas on the surface and increased whitecaps. Keep an eye out to windward—the origin of the expression "weather eye"—for the approach of these dark patches. In a harbor with obstructions around it, they may come from radically different directions. On the open sea their variations are usually not as extreme.

Storm Signals

One of the most reliable of all weather signs to watch for and respect while out on the water are the storm signals flown at Coast Guard installations and other locations, such as certain yacht clubs. Check to see if provisions have been made to fly these signals somewhere in your vicinity. If so, make it a point to look for them on every possible occasion. The day and night storm signals with their meanings are as follows:

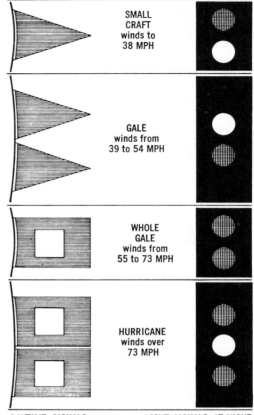

SMALL CRAFT winds to 38 MPH

GALE winds from 39 to 54 MPH

WHOLE GALE winds from 55 to 73 MPH

HURRICANE winds over 73 MPH

DAYTIME SIGNALS   LIGHT SIGNALS AT NIGHT

Storm warnings. Shaded flags and lights are red.

Type of Warning	Day	Night	Forecast
Small craft	One red pennant	Red light above a white light	Winds up to 38 mph (33 knots) and/or sea conditions dangerous to small-craft operations
Gale	Two red pennants	White light above a red light	Winds ranging from 39 to 54 mph (34 to 48 knots)
Whole gale	One square red flag with a black center	Two red lights, one above the other	Winds ranging from 55 to 73 mph (48 to 63 knots)
Hurricane	Two square red flags with black centers	A white light between two red lights	Winds 74 mph (64 knots) and above

Radio Weather Reports

No matter how good you may become at reading man-made and nature's weather signs, do not rely on these alone. A radio set is invaluable for keeping up with local weather forecasts. Even an inexpensive portable radio that will pick up weather reports from regular commercial broadcasting stations is a big help, and one equipped to receive the mariners' weather reports regularly transmitted by the Coast Guard and other government stations is very worthwhile. The Coast Guard broadcasts on 2182 kc, in addition, include notices to mariners and hydrographic information, plus special broadcasts including storm warnings, advisories, and urgent marine information. These are broadcast upon receipt and thereafter on either the odd or the even hour for a period of 6 hours unless canceled or superseded. *Coastal Warning Facilities Charts* list telephone numbers of Weather Bureau and Coast Guard offices plus time, station, and wavelength of these broadcasts. These charts are available through the Superintendent of Documents, Washington, D.C. 20402, for 10 cents each.

In the Great Lakes area, yachtsmen can take advantage of the radiotelephone broadcasts called MAFOR and LAWEB, maintained by the Canadian Meteorological Service and the U.S. Weather Bureau for shipping on the lakes. MAFORs are 24-hour forecasts of wind and weather conditions, given in a simple code. LAWEBs are reports in plain language, every 6 hours, of wind and barometer readings at shore stations and on ships under way.

Yacht owners having radio receivers or direction finders covering the 200- to 415-kc band may be able to pick up interesting and valuable up-to-the-minute weather-data broadcasts by one or more of the Civil Aeronautics Administration airfield control towers in their vicinity. These broadcasts are usually made 15 and 45 minutes after each hour and include current reports on visibility, barometer readings, wind direction and velocity, ceiling heights, sky conditions, weather, temperature, and, as a rule, dew point. These are not forecasts, but offer valuable information on the progress of changes previously forecast.

Certain additional coast stations have been authorized on very high frequencies utilizing frequency modulation. For our coast areas the following stations have been established: all stations authorized in the 152- to 161-mc band may now receive and transmit on the calling and safety frequency at 156.8 mc.

Often your radio can give you tips on the weather even when you are not tuned in on a weather report. For instance, when there is static, your radio is telling you there is an electrical storm somewhere within the range of 25 miles, and the chances are you can expect it to rain within an hour.

Weather Maps

Almost all newspapers carry some type of weather report; and a great many, especially in yachting areas, publish daily weather maps which are based on the Daily Surface Weather Map issued by the Weather Bureau. Sometimes you can find one of these maps on the post office bulletin board, at a Coast Guard station, or at the local airport.

Familiarity with the concept of air masses is essential to understanding and interpreting weather maps. Air masses are large oceans of atmosphere with nearly homogeneous properties throughout, both vertically from the earth's surface and horizontally, along it. They are generated over large areas of land, ice, or water which transmit to the stagnant air mass their own characteristics of temperature, wetness, or dryness. The basic and conflicting air masses are the polar and the tropical, and throughout the year these are alternately backing and filling over much of the continental United States.

As you peer at a weather map or hear a detailed weather forecast, the word *front* will usually be mentioned quite often. A front, in the simplest of terms, could be described as a weather factory. It develops when two different masses of air, each striving to retain its individuality, meet. Cold, dry air from the polar regions flowing south over the United States meets warm, moist air moving northward from the tropics; the two kinds of air do not mix well, so the cold air, being heavier, slides under the warm air and lifts it. A sloping boundary, rather sharply defined, is formed between the two air masses, and this separation is called a front.

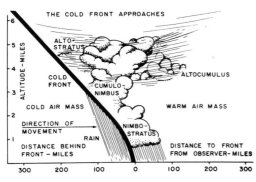

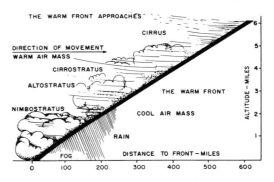

Characteristics of warm and cold fronts.

A *cold front* usually is accompanied by strong, shifting surface winds, squalls, and thunderstorms. Altocumulus clouds, a sign in themselves, may precede a cold front by as much as 300 miles. Cold-front weather is often severe but of short duration. On the other hand, a *warm front* normally brings less violent winds, but the sky will be heavy with great expanses of low clouds. There will be rain, maybe fog and poor visibility. The foul weather accompanying such a front lasts a long while, as a rule, because the system covers a large area and moves slowly.

An *occluded* front is a line along which warm air has been lifted from the earth's surface by the action of the opposing wedges of cold air. This lifting of the warm air often causes precipitation along the entire front. A *stationary front* is an air-mass boundary which shows little or no movement.

Two other terms that are commonly found on weather maps are *high* and *low*. They actually mean high-pressure and low-pressure areas. A high-pressure area is a weather system in which the air pressure, or atmospheric pressure, is high. The air is heavier, colder, and drier. A low, on the other hand, is made up of a mass of low-pressure air that is lighter, warmer, and wetter. In general, lows bring bad weather, because their air contains more moisture. Highs, being made up of colder, drier air, generally bring good weather. Winds are counterclockwise toward the center of low-pressure systems, and clockwise and outward from high-pressure areas.

Our weather, for the most part, flows in a continuous procession from the west to the east. It travels about 700 miles a day in the winter and 500 miles a day in the summer. In other words, as a general rule, tomorrow's weather is always directly to the west of us. As a result, if a town 200 to 300 miles to the west of you is having bad weather tonight, it is a pretty safe bet that you should not plan on doing any sailing tomorrow.

Weather Instruments

Various kinds of instruments are used for gathering the data necessary to forecast weather. Of all of them the barometer—some yachtsmen consider it the next most important instrument to the compass—is by far the most valuable. Unfortunately, although a great many barometers are hung in homes, yacht clubs, and even aboard boats, they are used only as decorations and not for forecasting weather.

The barometer is an instrument used to measure atmospheric pressure. Atmospheric pressure at sea level is approximately 14.7 pounds per square inch; this mean height is expressed as a barometric reading of 29.53 inches of mercury. Variations of the atmospheric pressure serve to indicate changes in weather. In a typical aneroid barometer, the scale is calibrated from 27.5 to 31.5 inches, inclusive. These figures represent inches of mercury, which is the standard means of expressing atmospheric pressure. The black pointer indicates the pressure at any given instant: it is actuated by a shaft-and-linkage arrangement from a metal bellows which expands and contracts as pressure varies. The other indicator is a reference pointer which can be turned by hand to any position on the dial by moving the knurled knob located at the center of the dial face. The reference pointer is used to indicate the pressure at the last reading of the barometer. Although the reading must be recorded, use of the pointer allows a quick visual determination of pressure changes between periodic readings and recordings. In fact, when using a barometer in making weather forecasts, a record of barometric readings made at regular intervals will indicate the pressure being exerted on the earth's surface at the instant of observation. If several readings have been logged, as in the following example, significance may be attached to them.

Time (in hours)	Pressure (in inches)	Change (in inches)
0700	30.02	
0800	30.00	−0.02
0900	29.97	−0.03
1000	29.93	−0.04
1100	29.88	−0.05
1200	29.82	−0.06

Barometric pressure falling at an increasing rate denotes foul weather. A fall of 0.02 inch an hour is a low rate of fall and not particularly disturbing, whereas a fall of 0.05 inch per hour is a high rate and normally indicates stormy weather. Remember that there is a normal daily change in atmospheric pressure. It is usually at its maximum at 1000 (10 A.M.) and 2200 (10 P.M.) each day, and at its minimum about 0400 (4 A.M.) and 1600 (4 P.M.). The variation between minimum and maximum may be as much as 0.05 during 6-hour intervals (about 0.01 inch change per hour). If at 1200 (noon) the

wind is backing east to north and the barometer is continuing to fall at a rapid rate, a severe northeast gale with heavy rain is on its way. On the other hand, given the same barometric reading of 29.82 with the barometer rising rapidly and the wind going to the west, clearing and cooler weather can be expected.

How to Use a Barometer. Here are a few general rules that will help when using the barometer:

1. Foul weather is usually forecast by a *falling* barometer with winds from the east quadrants. Fair and clearing weather is usually forecast by winds shifting to west quadrants with a *rising* barometer.

2. When the wind sets in from points between south and southeast and the barometer *falls steadily,* a storm is approaching from the west or northwest. The center of storm will pass near or north of the observer within 12 to 24 hours and the wind will shift to the northwest by way of south and southwest.

3. When the wind sets in from points between east and northeast and the barometer falls steadily, a storm is approaching from the south or southwest. The storm center will pass near or to the south of the observer within 12 to 24 hours, and the wind will shift to northwest by way of north.

4. The rapidity of the storm's approach and its intensity will be indicated by the rate and amount of the fall of the barometer. The following table provides a ready means of forecasting weather from wind and barometer data.

Wind Direction	Barometer Reduced to Sea Level	Character of Weather
SW to NW	30.10 to 30.20 and steady	Fair, with slight temperature changes for 1 or 2 days
SW to NW	30.10 to 30.20 and rising rapidly	Fair followed within 2 days by rain
SW to NW	30.20 and above and stationary	Continued fair with no decided temperature change
SW to NW	30.20 and above and falling slowly	Slowly rising temperature and fair for 2 days
S to SE	30.10 to 30.20 and falling slowly	Rain within 24 hours
S to SE	30.10 to 30.20 and falling rapidly	Wind increasing in force, with rain within 12 to 24 hours
SE to NE	30.10 to 30.20 and falling slowly	Rain in 12 to 18 hours

Wind Direction	Barometer Reduced to Sea Level	Character of Weather
SE to NE	30.10 to 30.20 and falling rapidly	Increasing wind and rain within 12 hours
E to NE	30.10 and above and falling slowly	In summer, with light winds, rain may not fall for several days In winter, rain in 24 hours
E to NE	30.10 and above and falling fast	In summer, rain probably in 12 hours In winter, rain or snow with increasing winds will often set in when the barometer begins to fall and the wind sets in NE
SE to NE	30.00 or below and falling slowly	Rain will continue 1 or 2 days
SE to NE	30.00 or below and falling rapidly	Rain with high wind, followed within 36 hours by clearing and, in winter, colder
S to SW	30.00 or below and rising slowly	Clearing in a few hours and fair for several days
S to E	29.80 or below and falling rapidly	Severe storm imminent, followed in 24 hours by clearing, and, in winter, colder
E to N	29.80 or below and falling rapidly	Severe NE gale and heavy rain; winter, heavy snow and cold wave
Going to W	29.80 or below and rising rapidly	Clearing and colder

As you can see from this wind-barometer table, atmospheric conditions help to determine future weather conditions. As low barometer readings usually attend stormy weather, and high barometer readings are generally associated with clearing or fair weather, it follows that a falling barometer indicates precipitation and wind, and a rising barometer fair weather or the approach of fair weather. As atmospheric waves, or crests (areas of high pressure), and troughs, or depressions (areas of low pressure), are, by natural laws, caused to assume circular or oval forms, the wind directions with reference to areas of low pressure are spirally and counterclockwise inward toward the region of lowest atmospheric pressure, as indicated by readings of the barometer. Areas of low barometric pressure are, in fact, whirlwinds of greater or less magnitude and intensity, depending upon the steepness of the barometric gradient. Areas of high barometric pressure,

on the contrary, show winds flowing spirally clockwise outward. The wind directions thus produced give rise to, and are responsible for, all local weather signs. The south winds bring warmth, the north winds cold, the east winds, in the middle latitudes, indicate the approach from the westward of an area of low pressure, or storm area, and the west winds show that the storm area has passed to the eastward. The indications of the barometer generally precede the shifts of the wind. This much is shown by local observations.

During the colder months, when the land temperatures are below the water temperatures of the ocean, precipitation will begin along the seaboards when the wind shifts and blows steadily from the water over the land without regard to the height of the barometer. In such cases the moisture in the warm ocean winds is condensed by the cold of the continental area. During the summer months, on the contrary, the onshore winds are not necessarily rain winds, for the reason that they are cooler than the land surfaces and their capacity for moisture is increased by the warmth that is communicated to them by the land surface. In such cases thunderstorms commonly occur when the ocean winds are intercepted by mountain ranges or peaks. If, however, the easterly winds of summer increase in force, with falling barometer, the approach of an area of low barometric pressure from the west is indicated and rain will follow within a day or two.

From the Mississippi and Missouri valleys to the Atlantic Coast, and on the Pacific Coast, rain generally begins on a falling barometer, while in the Rocky Mountain and plateau districts, and on the eastern Rocky Mountain slope, precipitation seldom begins until the barometer begins to rise, after a fall. This is true as regards the eastern half of the country, however, only during the colder months, and in the presence of general storms that may occur at other seasons. In the warmer months summer showers and thunderstorms usually come about the time the barometer turns from falling to rising. It is important to note that during practically the entire year precipitation on the Great Western Plains and in the mountain regions that lie between the Plains and the Pacific Coast districts does not begin until the center of the low-barometer area has passed to the eastward or southward and the wind has shifted to the north quadrants, with rising barometer.

Wind Velocity. Another valuable weather instrument is the anemometer, which is used for measuring wind velocity and, in most cases, wind direction. It is mounted at the masthead with the indicator located near the helm. Some units are designed so that the indicator buzzes and flashes a light the number of times per minute that directly corresponds to the wind velocity in knots; others are direct-reading units. Readings made under way indicate apparent wind speed and direction; they should be corrected for vessel speed and direction to obtain *true* wind readings. When measuring velocity and direction of wind, the high degree of accuracy essential in bearings is not required. It is sufficient if velocity be estimated within one Beaufort number, and direction within 5 percent.

5-0-5s racing in a stiff breeze.

Beaufort Number*	Descriptive term used by U.S. Weather Bureau	Wind mean velocity†		Locations		Probable wave height‡ (in feet)	International Code
		Knots per hour	Miles per hour	Land	Sea		
0	Calm	Less than 1	Less than 1	Calm, smoke rises vertically	Sea like a mirror	0	0
1	Light air	1–3	1–3	Direction of wind shown by smoke drift but not by wind vanes	Ripples with the appearance of scales are formed, but without foam crests	Less than 1	0
2	Light breeze	4–6	4–7	Wind felt on face; leaves rustle; ordinary vanes moved by wind	Small wavelets, still short but more pronounced; crests have a glassy appearance and do not break	Less than 1	1
3	Gentle breeze	7–10	8–12	Leaves and small twigs in constant motion; wind extends light flag	Large wavelets; crests begin to break; foam of glassy appearance; perhaps scattered whitecaps	1–2	2
4	Moderate breeze	11–16	13–18	Raises dust and loose paper; small branches are moved	Moderate waves, becoming longer; fairly frequent whitecaps	2–4	3
5	Fresh breeze	17–21	19–24	Small trees in leaf begin to sway; crested wavelets form on inland waters	Moderate waves, taking a more pronounced long form; many whitecaps are formed (chance of some spray)	4–8	4
6	Strong breeze	22–27	25–31	Large branches in motion; whistling heard in telegraph wires; umbrellas used with difficulty	Large waves begin to form; the white foam crests are more extensive everywhere (probably some spray)	8–13	5
7	Near gale or moderate gale	28–33	32–38	Whole trees in motion; inconvenience felt when walking against wind	Sea heaps up and white foam from breaking waves begins to be blown in streaks along the direction of the wind	13–20	6
8	Gale	34–40	39–46	Breaks twigs off trees; generally impedes progress when walking	Moderately high waves of greater length; edges of crests begin to break into the spindrift; the foam is blown in well-marked streaks along the direction of the wind	13–20	6

9	Strong gale	41–47	47–54	Slight structural damage occurs	High waves; dense streaks of foam along the direction of the wind; crests of waves begin to topple, tumble, and roll over; spray may affect visibility	13–20	6
10	Storm or strong gale	48–55	55–63	Seldom experienced inland; trees uprooted; considerable structural damage occurs	Very high waves with long overhanging crests; the resulting foam, in great patches, is blown in dense streaks along the direction of the wind; on the whole, the surface of the sea takes a white appearance; the tumbling of the sea becomes heavy and shocklike; visibility affected	20–30	7
11	Violent storm or whole gale	56–63	64–74	Very rarely experienced; accompanied by widespread damage	Exceptionally high waves; the sea is completely covered with long white patches of foam lying along the direction of the wind; everywhere the edges of the wave crests are blown into froth, visibility affected	30–45	8
12 to 17	Hurricane	Above 63	Above 74		The air is filled with foam and spray; sea completely white with driving spray; visibility very seriously affected	Over 45	9

* In the era of sailing vessels, Admiral Beaufort introduced a wind scale for judging wind on the sails of a vessel. The Beaufort numbers have since then been correlated into a range of wind velocities, and the scale has continued in universal use for describing wind velocity.

† Velocity equivalent at a standard height of 10 meters above open flat ground.

‡ This portion of the scale is only intended as a guide to show roughly what can be expected in the open sea, remote from land. It should never be used in the reverse way; i.e., for logging or reporting the state of the sea. In enclosed waters, or when near land, with an offshore wind, wave heights will be smaller and the waves steeper.

SAILING AND THE WEATHER

As stated previously several times, weather is most important to sailors, especially the amount of wind. Actually, as mentioned earlier, all wind is derived from pressure differences induced by thermal changes that regularly modify the wind. The sailor needs to understand these basic modifications, as they are often chief causes for the direction and velocity of the surface wind. The nature of the weather-system air flow determines the timing and the likelihood of appearance of the varying daily effects, but the basic pattern is always evident.

Offshore, over water whose temperature is comparatively constant, the variations are slight. Along shore and inshore (where most sailors sail) the variations are marked. "Local knowledge" is largely an understanding of the daily variations in wind flow induced by local land masses. It remains for each sailor to apply this "local knowledge" of daily variation to the circumstances of a particular weather-system air flow, of which there are but nine major varieties, to predict the surface wind flow at a particular time on a particular day.

Temperature changes in the lower layers of the atmosphere are induced from the surface upward by the heating or cooling of the surface. The temperature of the land changes significantly throughout each day, whereas the temperature of the water, unless it is very shallow, varies very little. The surface is heated largely by radiation from the sun. Although the sun's infrared radiation is obstructed by clouds, its major short-wave radiation is not obstructed and thus the surface is heated even under cloud cover, though to a lesser degree. The surface is also heated by conduction, and this becomes most significant with the horizontal flow of air of differing temperature. Cooling of the surface is chiefly by long-wave radiation, which is obstructed by cloud cover. Maximum surface heating thus occurs when the sun is overhead on a clear day, but such a clear sky will also permit maximum cooling during the evening and night. Cloud cover will, on the other hand, reduce heating but delay cooling and thus be associated with less daily variation—cooler days and warmer nights.

Incidentally, one of the most interesting weather phenomena encountered by yachtsmen sailing coastal waters is the movement of land and sea breezes. These are caused by the alternating heating and cooling of coastal land and sea areas. The land, particularly in summer, is warmer than the sea by day and cooler than the sea by night. There is, therefore, a variation in atmospheric pressure over adjoining land and sea areas. This causes a system of littoral breezes which blow landward during the day and seaward during the night. These land and sea breezes usually penetrate to a distance of about 30 miles on and off shore, and extend to a height of a few hundred feet.

The sea breeze begins in the morning hours, from 9 to 11 A.M., as the land warms. In the late afternoon it dies away. In the evening the land breeze springs up and blows gently out to sea until morning. Of course, changes in air temperatures begin at the surface. Mixing of air flow aloft with surface air depends upon breaking the inversion which exists at dawn and which persists until the surface is heated. If the surface is cold (fall, winter, spring) and the weather-system air flow relatively warm (an easterly or southerly on the East Coast), the inversion (warm air aloft above cold air below) will persist unless the cloud cover clears. Even without the sun, however, the land may warm sufficiently to initiate a faint local sea breeze perpendicular to the shore. As the sea breeze is a surface wind, it takes little heating of the land to initiate it. Unless the heating is sufficient to permit thermal columns ashore to break through the inversion, however, it cannot become more general. As cloud cover "burns off" (air temperature at the cloud level rises sufficiently to permit vaporization) in the rising thermals, blue sky appears and the sun shines directly on the surface. This rapidly increases thermal generation, heating aloft, cloud dissipation, and the sea-breeze development. As sea-breeze generation increases, cool surface air flow commences farther and farther offshore and, as it travels greater and greater distances, is increasingly freed of surface friction and veered by the Coriolis force —a deflecting force acting on the wind due to the earth's rotation. This pattern accounts for the characteristic development and shift of the sea breeze from light, perpendicular-to-the-shore flow at noon to strong veered flow at 4 P.M. (in the northern hemisphere).

Variations in an existing sea-breeze flow (or any vertically unstable air flow such as a cold northwesterly) are microrepetitions of this general pattern. Under a cloud cover only a minimal local sea breeze in the few hundred feet below the inversion can develop. This air flowing over a short distance, close to the surface, at low speed is scarcely affected by the Coriolis force and thus is directed perpendicular to the neighboring shore. When the clouds "burn off" and surface heating is increased, the strength, depth, and length of the sea breeze is increased, and therefore the air flow, freed of surface friction, is veered. The water surface exposed directly to the sunshine is heated, thermal columns rise from the water surface, and down drafts of upper air flow appear at the surface. The wind becomes strong and gusty, and surface flow is dragged along with the upper air flow at its speed and direction. Under the cloud cover boats are sailing in a light, shallow, local sea breeze; in the sunshine boats are sailing in a strong, deep, veered flow from aloft.

Tides and Their Effects

Tidal current tables mentioned earlier in this section will predict the time and velocity of flow at a given location with remarkable accuracy, and an evaluation of the cross-section of the water body at various sites in the area will indicate probable local variations in the velocity and direction of surface flow. However, in many areas marked variations from the expected flow behavior often appear. In addition to possible variations from fresh water additions to local tidal flow, wind has a major effect upon surface current.

Current and tide are very important in sailboat racing. In fact, variations in tidal flow consequent to local weather conditions therefore require that the racing waters be in-

spected at the time of the race even after a thorough evaluation of the current tables and the chart has been accomplished. Buoys and anchored vessels in the racing area are the most valuable guides. If the current is not sufficiently strong to create a distinctive eddy down-current of a buoy, a small floating object (which has little or no windage) may be thrown overboard in the vicinity and its movement observed. A stop watch and a reasonable judgment of distance may be utilized to estimate the velocity of flow, but usually an adequate guess may be made with experience. The committee boat is often the best guide. Be particularly alert to the possibility that it is lying to current as well as wind. If so, its degree of deviation from an expected position in relation to the strength of the wind may be a good indication of the velocity and direction of current at the starting line. The position of other anchored boats in relation to their anchors may indicate variations in current velocity in other parts of the course. Periodic observation of anchored vessels is the best indicator of the turn of the tide and may be detected at some distance and considerably in advance of a local change to permit the acquisition of a strategic advantage.

The water is always flowing beneath us and differently in different parts of the racing area. An analysis of the probable variations in velocity and direction of surface flow at different times, on the various legs of the course, is an essential element in planning the strategy of the race.

Of course, you can employ the tidal currents to your advantage at any time. When planning a cruise, for example, keep the following in mind:

1. Try to sail out of a harbor with the ebb and return on the flood.

2. Try to sail up a river going inland on the flood and return to the harbor near the coast on the ebb.

3. Study local conditions to find out where the tide ebbs and flows most strongly, where there are eddy currents and where there is slacker water. If you cannot use the strong current to your best advantage, try to avoid such areas. Remember that currents are named exactly opposite to the winds. Thus, an

easterly current is a current running *to* the east, not *from* the east. The direction of the current is termed the "set" and its velocity the "drift."

Sailing Tactics in Bad Weather

How much more agreeable a cruise can be when it is favored with sunshine and pleasant winds! Inevitably, however, a day will come when the elements decide to go on a rampage, and then all the skill and ability of a skipper are called upon. He may be winding up an extended weekend, and even though the weather has turned bad, he is under the necessity of carrying on to reach his home port so that he may resume his prosaic activities on the morrow.

If there is sufficient advance warning of the approach of bad weather, the wise skipper will take what steps he can to ride out a storm in the quiet shelter of a harbor or bay. The first thing to do is to secure and lash all heavier objects—such as anchors, the dinghy, and the like—so that they will remain where they are put. Then go about and pick up any smaller effects—books, glassware, tools, and what have you—and make certain these are stowed so they cannot come adrift. The best place to care for miscellaneous gear which normally would not be lashed down would be to wrap it in a blanket and then wedge it securely in a corner of the cabin floor. In this way it cannot fall any further and is safe against damage. If time permits, it might also be wise to prepare a few sandwiches and fill a thermos bottle with coffee or perhaps some hot soup. There is no telling in advance how welcome a bit of food may be later on.

You and crew should don foul-weather gear. Also, everyone on deck should wear a short line made fast around his middle and secured to a deck fitting. Many boat people argue against this procedure and subsequently are saved by the line. When the going is really rough everyone on deck must wear a life belt. A man working on the foredeck or some other place where he must move around should wear a line with a snap hook on it. He can use both hands getting forward, and when he gets there he can clip his lifeline to the rigging or a deck fitting. Some newer life belts consist of a harness to be fastened

around the person's body and a strong line or a strap attached to the harness at one end, with a strong snap hook at the other. The length of the line or strap can be adjusted, but should be no longer than necessary to reach a convenient, strong place for attaching the snap hook and allowing reasonable room in which to work. The length between the harness and the place of attachment should not be enough to allow the person to be washed overboard. Should an accident occur, however, the harness should be so designed that the wearer's head will be kept above water if he happens to find himself overboard and being towed alongside the boat. It is a good idea to wear life belts or jackets when sailing at night. Also, attach a flashlight (with good batteries) and a whistle to your life jacket.

It is not wise to lash a life ring to its holder. The horseshoe life buoy is generally thought to be the best type. The buoyed pole with a counterweight and flag is a very important item at sea where there are large waves, because the flag can be seen above the wave tops. The pole should be attached to a life ring, and if a man falls overboard, both pole and ring are thrown over the side instantly. The weighted pole will also tend to prevent the life ring from drifting excessively. It is often a good idea to attach a small drogue (a cone-shaped canvas sea anchor) to a life ring that is not attached to a pole, in order to decrease drift. Obviously, water lights attached to life rings are essential at night. Electric water lights vary in design, but the usual type is equipped with a battery-powered light that shuts off when it is hung upside down. However, the light is turned on when tossed to make a rescue.

Luffing Through a Puff. It will happen very often, even when sailing in good weather, that the breeze will freshen considerably, or a strong puff of wind will strike your boat. This may not be sufficient to make it necessary to reef but will require you to nurse your boat along. If this happens, and the increasing weight of the wind from either of these conditions heels the boat over more than you desire, you can ease the mainsheet until the entire forward part of the sail, the luff, is shaking and only the after two-thirds or so is filled. The jib sheet may also be slacked a little. This will at once ease the pressure, and the boat will recover herself while you sail her along, steering on your course or perhaps more nearly into the wind than you were before. You will, of course, have to watch your boat while in this condition and be ready to put your tiller down still more if the wind continues to increase or if a puff should suddenly fill the sail. In such a case, the boat can be luffed sharply until the puff passes. One can sail a boat a long way with her mainsail only half full; but if there is indication of the wind increasing, or no signs of its slacking off, reefing, as described a little later in this section, is usually advisable for all but the real expert.

In a strong breeze, if a small sailboat is heeling to windward you must pull in the mainsheet. If the boat is heeling to leeward then you must slack off the sheets. In boats under spinnaker if you are heeling to windward pull in the sheet; if heeling to leeward pull in the guy. Try to follow the movements of the sea and do not keep altering the sails if the waves are the cause of heeling; for example, if there is a swell at right angles to the waves which makes you heel.

When luffing, care should be taken to see that the boat is kept moving and that she does not lose headway. A well-balanced boat, as stated earlier, will always respond to the tiller or wheel and will always come up into the wind if the tiller or wheel is let go while the boat is moving. That is why it is always better to slack the sheet when you are sailing close-hauled in a puff or squall and let the wind spill from the luff of the sail rather than to just luff her with the sail trimmed in. But, as long as the boat keeps moving, you can do almost anything with her. If you must come about to change your course, remember that the action of the sea and the height of the waves play an important part in this maneuver. Generally there are three or four steep, high waves, then a series of short rollers, then three or four more steep ones, and so on. The trick is to luff and come about when the seas run low. Do not come around fast, for then there is constant handling of straining sheets. Make a big wide loop broad reaching, then swing to a close reach. Time yourself so that when the seas run low, you quickly come about. When the sails are on the

opposite side let the sheets out (see that they do not snarl) to the point of reaching. Then let out more sheet so as to again run before the wind.

In hard squalls aboard a small sailboat, pull the centerboard half up and keep the boat sailing on a reach. As long as you keep a good speed on the small craft it is then quite difficult to capsize. Even a very hard puff should not capsize a small sailboat because it will be able to slide sideways. Of course it can blow so hard that you cannot keep the boom in the proper position. In this case there is nothing else you can do but to sail far enough by the lee so that the wind gets behind the sail and blows the boom across on its own. Before this happens you should haul in on the mainsheet as much as possible. Watch out that the boom does not hit you as it goes across.

Sailing in Very Strong Winds. There are times when it is necessary to sail or ride out a blow at sea. General information on the various points of sailing in hard winds is given in Section IV. But, when at sea during a real blow, the first step, as the strength of the wind increases, is to reduce sail. The jib must be changed for a smaller one, and the mainsail reefed to balance with the smaller jib and the strengthening wind. If the yacht is only cruising, then this is a relatively simple operation. The jib can be dropped and the boat sailed on the main while another jib is bent on. If racing, however, such a procedure would result in slowing the boat for too long a period, and a faster method of changing headsail must be employed. Actually, some racing yachts have two forestays, enabling a new jib to be bent on and hoisted while continuing to use the old. Where this is not the case, however, the following procedure enables a new jib to be bent on with minimum delay:

1. Take the new jib forward and lash it to the pulpit. Unclip the lower two hanks on the present jib.

2. By means of a spare tackle, fasten the tack to the deck and clip on to the forestay all the hanks of the new jib in the space created by releasing two hanks on the old.

3. Pass the sheets of the new jib aft and through the sheeting blocks. All is now ready for the changeover.

4. Quickly lower the present jib, unclipping the hanks as it comes down. Switch the peak shackle from the old to the new jib and immediately hoist the new jib.

5. When the new jib is set and drawing, the old jib can be unshackled and taken aft to be stowed.

Thanks to technique such as this, reefing forward of the mast is almost a thing of the past. An assortment of jibs to be drawn on to suit the weather is more usual for any craft with a claim to speed. Many cruising boats that have only one jib are often equipped with furling gear. This allows the jib to be rolled along its luff, either completely for stowing or partly for reefing.

Reefing Procedures. There are two basic ways of reefing the mainsail. Most modern sailboats use a variation of roller reefing. The second, older and traditional method, still preferred by some experienced ocean-racing skippers, uses lines and eyes, and does not involve turning the boom. By this we mean that the area of a mainsail is reduced by gathering up some of its foot along the boom and then the surplus sail is bunched along the boom by a series of short lines, called reef points. There may be one, two, or three rows of points permanently attached to the sail in line with eyes (called cringles) in the bolt rope. It is important to remember that the points are only intended for securing the slack of the sail and that it is the end fastenings which should take the strain. With a small sail the material may be pulled down by direct hand hold and secured to the boom end with a loose line. With a larger sail there may be a rope called an earing or pendant, which is fastened to the boom, taken through the roof cringle, down to the eye in the corner of the sail to the hand, giving a purchase. Several turns around the boom or through an eye will secure that end of the sail. At the other end the procedure is rather different because of the slope of the edge of the sail. In a small boat a line may be used in a similar way to the other end to pull down the sail and haul out the line of reef points. Some turns around the boom and through the cringle will secure it.

When both ends are secured, the surplus canvas at the foot of the sail is pulled out and rolled up as neatly as possible, then held,

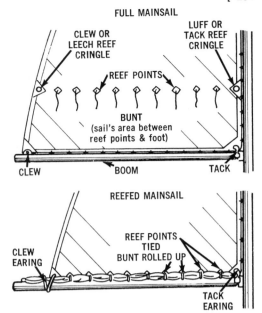

Traditional or conventional reefing.

by bringing the roof points together between the sail and the boom. It is wrong to take them below the boom. The knot used is a reef—this is the job which gave it its name (see the previous section). So that the points can be let go easily, the ends should be turned back to make a bow or slip reef.

In principle, roller reefing is simple and straightforward, and is preferred by most yachtsmen. In theory, the procedure is as follows:

1. Slack away the main halyard slightly. Ease the sheets.

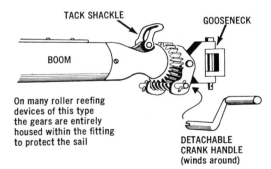

The worm-gear arrangement of a roller-reefing setup. On many roller-reefing devices the gears are entirely housed within the fitting to protect the sail.

2. Insert the roller reefing handle into its socket and commence turning, ensuring that as the sail rolls onto the boom, the luff rope winds evenly.

3. When the slack of the halyard has been taken up, ease it more, and continue winding the reefing gear.

4. Continue until the correct amount of sail has been reefed. Then set mainsheet and continue sailing.

Usually an assistant is needed to see that the sail rolls properly. A little thought will show that the boom must be at right angles to the mast if more than one turn is to be taken without the material piling up at the end. It is usually sufficiently near a right angle in large boats, but in a smaller craft the boom often has to be raised to clear heads, and roller reefing cannot be used to shorten sail very much. If the boom is parallel, although not necessarily round, and the sail cut fairly flat, the sail should roll evenly. If the sail is very full, it would be an advantage to have the boom thicker near the middle. How the boom is turned to reef depends to some extent on the size of the boat and the builder's choice.

Changing the jib and reefing the mainsail are sufficient for a good moderate blow. However, should the wind increase in intensity, the

sails will have to be taken off altogether and replaced by storm gear. This comprises a very small jib and equally small, loose-footed mainsail. Each yacht will have its own system of setting up storm gear, and this should be checked over before leaving port if there is any likelihood of its being needed. Once set, storm gear is controlled in the same manner as a normal suit of sails.

If your boat does not have storm sails and the strong winds increase in velocity and reefing does not help, drop the sails. Actually, if ever in doubt as to the force of wind or whether to carry sail or not, drop the sails for safety; drop the mainsail first as this has greater sail area than a working jib. As the sails come down gather them in, lean on them, and hold them down until they are tied up securely. Then run before the wind under bare poles, or, if you have an auxiliary engine aboard, use it to continue on your course. Remember that it is best to cut through the waves at about a 45-degree angle; adjust your course accordingly, therefore.

Heaving To in Bad Weather. There are times, of course, when the winds have not sufficient velocity to require the dropping of *all* sails, but their strength is still enough to create a degree of concern for the safety of your crew and craft. In such cases it is

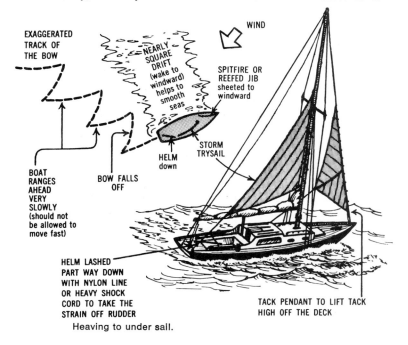

Heaving to under sail.

usually safest and easiest to drop the mainsail and sail with the jib alone. You will be surprised how well you can reach, and, often, how high you can point, with just this one sail. But the best sailing point with such a rig is running before the wind.

On some occasions you will want more exposed sail area so that you can move faster. In such cases, you achieve this with the mainsail alone; however, be prepared to luff if a real strong wind puff comes along. You can luff very quickly with the main alone, because there is a tendency in such an arrangement for the bow to swing into the wind. This, of course, creates a weather helm, so much so that the craft will automatically come up into the wind should you let go of the tiller or wheel.

If close to a lee shore, or a hazard of a kind that could damage the boat, or (the exact reverse) the storm is pushing you out to sea, anchor. Let out as much anchor line as possible so that the boat rides easily and does not drag. If the anchor does drag, or if the water is too deep, trail a sea anchor from the bow to keep your boat heading into the wind. For centuries the technique of "lying to" or "heaving to" has been the ultimate safety resort of mariners caught in weather conditions which prohibit a boat from continuing on her desired course.

A sea anchor is an item that every cruiser-racer should have aboard. It consists of a heavy canvas or Dacron cone perhaps 4 or 5 feet in length, securely lashed to a stainless-steel or galvanized-metal circular rod 20 to 24 inches in diameter. The cone is left open at the small end so that the water funnels through it, and the device furnishes a most effective drag or brake. It does not sink to the bottom but is dragged along just below the surface. Because it is effective as a drag, it is difficult to pull it back aboard when it is no longer needed. For this reason a trip line is attached to the small end, and by this means the sea anchor can be reversed and pulled back aboard when the need for its use no longer exists. Most sailboats, because of their design, will easily ride bow on to the waves with a sea anchor out. If the boat is a yawl, a small trysail, set on the mizzenmast, will do wonders to keep the bow pointed into the wind. Even sloops will ride better if a

riding sail (generally the jib) is set.

The sea anchor is usually tossed over the bow and paid out until it is about two wave lengths away. If it is allowed to drift only one wave length away, it will not be fully effective as the wave carrying the craft and the wave containing the sea anchor will move together, reducing the drag to almost nil. In addition, by paying out plenty of line, the sea anchor also lies deeper in the water, giving an even better "bite" when the pressure comes on to it. As a wave pushes the boat's head off, the weight comes on the line and the drag of the canvas bag full of water pulls her back into the wave, thus holding her head to wind and sea, the most comfortable position in which to heave to.

If you do not have a sea anchor on board, but need one, you will have to improvise a drag of some sort from whatever you can find aboard. Such things as a bucket, a couple of oars lashed together with some canvas, a few life preservers reinforced by oars or boat hooks, or even a dinghy, capsized and full of water—anything which will serve as a drag—will also serve to slow up the rate of drifting and keep the boat headed into the seas and weather. Remember also that the stresses and strains on all this gear at such times are very great, so use line of ample strength, well-protected by chafing gear.

Heaving to is most practical when clear of the shore or other danger, as the boat, when hove to, makes a certain amount of drift to leeward. A yacht should never be close inshore in heavy weather and should head out to sea as soon as the storm develops if shelter is not available. Far more vessels have been lost or damaged trying to make for shelter on a coastline than have foundered in the open sea during a storm.

Sailing in a Fog

While handling a boat under severe storm conditions can sometimes be an ordeal, there are other circumstances, which prevail more frequently, that call for piloting ability. This pertains to operating your sailboat in a fog. Actually, foggy conditions in a crowded harbor are extremely hazardous. An early prediction that fog will occur may aid in avoiding a dangerous situation. Fog results from the cooling of the air that remains at the earth's surface. Air temperature may be cooled in a number of ways.

1. *Warm air flowing over a cold surface.* Fog may form, day or night, when warm moist air flows over water or land surfaces which are cooler than the air.

2. *Radiation fog.* During the day the earth's surface receives and radiates warmth. At night, the incoming heat ceases, but the radiation continues and the earth's surface gets cooler. Although the lowest temperature is reached just before sunrise, fog sometimes forms soon after sunset. Radiation fog is much more common over land than water. It usually burns off within an hour or so after sunrise. If mixed with smoke, it will form a heavy, dark, and greasy smog that will not quickly burn off.

3. *Air moving from low to higher latitude.* Warm moist air moving from a low to a higher latitude may cool to such an extent that fog will form over large areas. This type is more common over sea than land.

Fog is likely to form as the spread between air temperature and dew point decreases. As the temperature approaches the dew point, fog is likely. By the way, the dew point is the temperature at which the moisture suspended in the atmosphere will begin to form dew. The dew point spread is the number of degrees between the actual temperature and the dew point, and it is measured on a device called a hygrometer.

Usually fog is only present in weather with only a very light wind. While this in itself can be a problem for sailboat skippers, there is the added difficulty of reduced visibility and the resultant danger of colliding with other craft or objects. If you have auxiliary power on board, here is surely the time to use it. You do not have to worry about the disgrace—the boys at the yacht club cannot see you because of the fog.

The Rules of the Road definitely call for operating the ship's whistle or a foghorn as a warning signal when under way in a fog. The following sound signals are intended to show, as far as possible, that a boat is present, and its approximate position. Be sure to use the proper signal to identify the action of your craft.

SOUND SIGNALS IN FOG OR IN CONDITIONS OF NO VISIBILITY

Type of Vessel	Method of Signaling	Frequency at intervals of
Vessel under sail* (Both International and Inland Rules)		
Under way, starboard tack	1 blast	1 minute
Under way, port tack	2 blasts in succession	1 minute
Under way, running free	3 blasts in succession	1 minute
Vessel under power†		
Under way (International Rules)	1 long blast	2 minutes
Under way (Inland Rules)	1 long blast	1 minute
Under way but stopped (International Rules)	2 long blasts in succession	2 minutes
Vessel at anchor (Both International‡ and Inland Rules)	Ring ship's bell vigorously for 5 seconds	1 minute
Vessel aground‡ (International Rules)	Basic signal: ring ship's bell vigorously for 5 seconds. In addition, strike three separate and distinct strokes on the bell immediately before and after the basic signal	1 minute

Type of Vessel	Method of Signaling	Frequency at Intervals of
Vessel towing‡ (Both International and Inland Rules)	1 long blast and 2 short blasts in succession	1 minute
Vessel towed (International Rules¶)	1 long blast and 3 short blasts in succession	1 minute
(Inland Rules**)	1 long blast and 2 short blasts in succession	1 minute
Fishing vessel (20 tons or upward) (International Rules)	1 short blast followed by ringing the ship's bell	1 minute

* Signal given on foghorn.
† Signal given on whistle.
‡ On international waters a vessel longer than 350 feet rings a bell in the forward part of the vessel; and a gong, or other different-sounding signal, in the stern, both for about 5 seconds at intervals of about 1 minute. To give additional warning of the possibility of collision by an approaching vessel, a boat also sounds one short, one prolonged, then one short blast of her horn.
¶ Signal given on foghorn or whistle immediately following the signal made by the towing vessel.
** (Optional) Signal given on foghorn immediately following the signal made by the towing vessel.

Since reduced visibility and the uncertainty of what lies ahead are the big problems in sailing through fog, it is necessary that lookouts be posted at bow, stern, and amidships. This assumes, of course, that there are sufficient persons on board to man all the stations. If shorthanded, the bow position is probably the most important. The bow lookout confines his attention particularly to the zone ahead of the boat, and should include the water surface for possible drift, debris, or anything else which might appear. The lookouts on the beam confine their attention to their respective sides, while the lookout at the stern watches for overtaking vessels and any other indications of objects over the stern. (Be sure that you or your crew do not wear the ear flaps down on your foul-weather gear.) Should you hear the signals of another craft, you must be alert to determine the direction from which it comes, as sound is the medium which functions most effectively at such times. Even this may be erratic on occasion, and every care should be taken

to observe that the signal is properly identified. Bell buoys and navigation aids in lighthouses or on shore can also be located by their sound signals. A careful sounding should be taken at known intervals; then a chain of soundings can be plotted which will help a great deal in keeping track of your position. While the usual small boat's running lights are not very powerful, it will help to turn them on because a thin spot in the fog may reveal your presence to the lookout on an approaching vessel who may not be able to hear your fog signals. Some boats that sail in traffic areas carry radar reflectors from their masts so that big vessels can spot them on this piece of electronic navigating gear.

Be sure to keep track of your position on your chart. When in doubt as to where you are, use your sounding lead or electronic depth finder. If you still do not know, you may have to anchor. But keep an alert watch in case of traffic, which may be on or off its course.

SAILING EMERGENCIES

It is a fact that although most emergencies arise as a result of carelessness or negligence, there is always the odd case that is just a matter of bad luck. Whatever the cause, the essential thing about an emergency on board

a boat is the ability of skipper and crew to cope. And to be able to cope with an emergency means to have foreknowledge of what to do in the emergency, and to be prepared when it strikes.

Steps in righting a small capsized sailcraft, such as the Skipjack class boat.

Capsizing and Righting

Capsizing is probably the most common *small*-boat sailing accident. (It is rather difficult to capsize a keel-bottomed racer-cruiser-type boat.) Usually it occurs when least expected. But if you consider a capsize as a part of the fun of sailing, you will be completely safe. That is, of course, if you know what to do.

Most boats capable of being capsized are equipped with built-in flotation to prevent sinking after a capsizing or swamping. The cardinal rule after turning over is to stay with the boat. Even if you are an excellent swimmer, hang onto your capsized boat and do not strike out for a "nearby" shore. Distances can be deceptive when you are in the water, wind and current are hard to predict, and you have a much better chance of being spotted when you are with your boat.

To recover from a capsizing, the overturned boat must be righted or turned upright, and then she can be bailed out. A small nonsailing dinghy will sometimes turn turtle, or completely upside down. However, she can usually be righted easily if you lean backward while gripping the bottom or keel with your fingers and, at the same time, exert pressure downward at the gunwale with your knees or feet. A sailboat is usually more difficult to right because the weight of her mast and wet sails must be lifted out of the water. Most sailboats will lie on their sides with the sails resting on the water's surface, but some with extreme beam or excessive flotation or metal masts which can fill with water may have a tendency to turn turtle. Try not to let any sailboat turn bottom side up because in this position she is very difficult to right, and she is subject to damage. If the water is shoal, her mast may get stuck in the mud. To avoid turning turtle, stand on the centerboard immediately after capsizing. If another crew member is present, have him attach a float, a life preserver for instance, to the masthead. This float should be made fast to the halyard in such a way that the float may be hauled down after the boat is righted and bailed out.

As soon as possible after capsizing, don life jackets. Some small boats carry Coast Guard approved kapok cushions in lieu of life jackets. These cushions may be worn over the chest and stomach with one handle strap around the neck and the other around a leg so that the hands are left free. Do not put one of these cushions on your back as it will tend to float you face down. Although cushions are legally allowed as life preservers, they are inferior to life preservers which are designed for no other purpose.

Not long after capsizing, equipment will begin to float out of the cockpit and start to drift away. Gather up this equipment and lash it or otherwise secure it to the boat, but do not swim any great distance away from the boat in pursuit of a floating object. The bailing bucket should have a lanyard (short rope) in order that it may be tied to the boat. If no rescue craft is in sight or if immediate rescue is impossible, the capsized skipper may drop anchor, but *only* if drift is near an obstruction (bridge, seawall, jetty, etc.). If in open water, forget about anchoring. Once the anchor is out, it can generally be retrieved only by those aboard the rescue craft.

After securing all gear, the sails almost always should be brought down and tied to the boom. Start by releasing the main halyard and pulling the mainsail down the mast toward the boat. It should be loosely furled and stopped, rolled or bundled up and tied to the boom, and also the mainsheet should be pulled tight to prevent the boom from falling down off the deck. Follow the same procedure for the jib and then make all sheets and halyards fast. (Some small sailboats can be righted with sails up. However, if this is done, it is very important that the sheets be slacked before righting.) Take your time during this operation, since it is a fairly difficult job, especially when your sails are flat in the water. Do not tire yourself out while in the water.

Once the sails are down and secured, make sure the centerboard (if she has one) is down as far as possible. Now stand on the far end of the centerboard or keel and take a secure hold of the gunwale or the coaming. While pulling backward, push down with your legs on the centerboard or keel, and the craft should slowly right itself. One of the crew members can help by going to the opposite side of the boat, treading water, and giving the shrouds or mast an initial push upward. Then carefully help one member of the crew to climb into the hull over the stern while the others help to balance the boat and keep it from rolling. The person on board should stay in the center of the craft and bail out the hull as quickly as he can. When the hull is buoyant enough to hold the remaining members of the crew, they should get on board and all should again begin to bail it out completely. If you are alone you may be able to board the boat by climbing over her stern.

Should a rescue craft come along, try to right your boat before accepting help, because a boat coming alongside a capsized sailboat can damage the rigging and get a floating line caught in her propeller. However, if the water is very cold, immediately board the rescue craft, before your boat is righted. The rescue craft should never attempt to tow a capsized boat until she has been righted.

Once the boat is righted and bailed out, the towline should be made fast around the mast and led forward through a bow chock. Great care must be taken not to get the towline wrapped in your propeller when making the final approach. The towline should never be made fast to the quarter of the towing boat, because this will make her exceedingly difficult to steer and cause her to run toward the quarter on which the line is belayed. When possible, belay the towline amidships well forward of the stern of the sailboat. It is well to have a helmsman aboard the boat being towed; she should follow in the wake of the towing boat. Once the towline is belayed, a strain should be taken gradually. The tow should be begun from ahead. Once the towline takes a strain and the boat begins to get way on, power can be increased steadily. All turns should be made gradually. Tow slowly, never at greater than the hull speed of the boat being towed.

The amount of towline will vary with the sea condition. In calm water, several boat lengths should separate the boats, but in a rough sea, considerably more scope should be used. The more scope, the more spring and the less sudden strain on the tow line and towed boat. Although it is desirable to have the two boats in the same position relative to crests and troughs, the sea is seldom regular enough to achieve this condition.

Righting a Capsized Catamaran. Catamarans are more stable than single-hulled planing boats and capsizing is much less prevalent, but it can still happen when boats are being driven to their limit in racing. It is advisable, then, to know how to get sailing again.

Once the boat goes past the point of no return, the crew should slip down the leeward hull without putting weight on the mast, boom, or sail and making sure they always have one hand on the boat. The center plate —or lower plate in a cat with two—should be lowered and the main and jibsheets released. The crew should then slide as far out as possible on the plate.

A permanent lanyard fixed to the forward edge of the bridge deck at the inner edge of each hull should be used to help when righting the hull. The same lanyard helps the crew climb back aboard over the forward end of the bridge deck after righting so they are well advised not to let go of it at all while they are in the water. There is another advantage to the crew's holding on to the special lanyard—the boat cannot sail off on its own when righted, leaving the crestfallen crew bobbing in its wake.

It usually takes 15 to 20 seconds to free the mast and sails from the water, and the crew should stay right out on the end of the plate until this happens. As the boat continues to right itself, the crew should pull themselves in along the plate with the lanyard. The mast will act as a sea anchor while the boat is capsized and will therefore point to windward. Although the wind will help in righting the boat, it will immediately capsize on the opposite side unless the sheets have been properly freed.

When fully righted, the boat may have swung head to wind. In this case you get under way again by using the same method as when "in irons."

Going Aground

There are several types of grounding situations; the several variables include the amount of current, the direction and velocity of wind, the type of bottom, and the state of the tide. Perhaps your boat was forced ashore by wind or current; or perhaps, through faulty piloting on your part, she went upon a shoal. We could go on for hours as to the causes of grounding. It is enough to say that each situation requires different handling depending on the position of the craft, the extent of damage, the kind of assistance anticipated, and gear available on board.

Going aground in tidal waters, for example, may offer no serious problem if the tide is on the flood. An anchor promptly put out in the direction of deep water, with all available scope, will prevent the craft's being carried into shallower water as the tide rises. Then as the tide rises, you may use the pull on the anchor to break the boat free, or use the spinnaker pole or an oar to give a "poling" push. Sometimes a man overboard can shove the boat off a shoal as the tide floods.

Another popular way of getting a grounded yacht off—especially if a keel type—is as follows: As soon as she has grounded, release the sheets. All hands should then be moved to one side of the boat to heel her. If she is heeled sufficiently, the keel will be lifted off and she may be moved off by power or, if it is a weather shore, by sail. If she will not move even when crew are perched right out on the end of the boom in an attempt to heel her over, she will have to be lightened by throwing ashore all equipment and, if possible, internal ballast.

For the small-boat yachtsman, another possible way of freeing a grounded craft is to run a line to the anchor at one side, tie it to the halyard, and pull on the other end of the halyard. As the mast tilts, the boat will heel over, shifting away from the anchor. (All crew members should be on the heeling side.) If the keel breaks free, push or pole the boat into deep water before she hangs up again.

If you have an auxiliary aboard, it is often possible, in both tidal and inland waters, to employ the engine's propeller in a freeing operation if it is clear of the bottom, clear of any obstruction immediately astern, and if it is undamaged. Although the propeller thrust is lessened in reverse, it can still be effective if you time it with a shove from the shoal, a poling push, or a pull on the anchor line set in deep water. (In the latter case, watch the line so it does not foul the propeller.) Employing the rudder, swing the stern slightly from side to side. This frequently gets faster results than a straight reverse pull. It is also often possible to get free by waiting for the wake of a passing vessel to give sufficient lift to break the suction and allow the grounded craft to back off under her own power.

There are times when all these methods will fail and towing by another boat, or boats, will be necessary. Unfortunately, few sailboats are equipped with deck fittings capable of withstanding the towing strain that is sometimes required to break free a keel-bottom boat. While a towing hawser secured to the main bow cleats would most likely hold, it would not permit the towing strain to be applied astern in the proper direction. Since it is usually desirable to have the stern towed off first, the most desirable method of attaching a towing hawser is a bridle. In most cases, the bridle can be rigged by carrying the heaviest available line (double if length permits) completely around the hull from bow to stern just below the level of the deck, suspended in position by lines led across the deck and deckhouse spaced a few feet apart. (Do not forget chafing gear to protect the topsides.) The two ends of the bridle should be secured to each other, outboard of the stern where the hawser will be attached. The pull of the hawser, even under strain, will tend downward, hence the bridle must be particularly well supported in position across the deck aft. Also some provision must be taken for letting the towing hawser go instantly if the applied strain begins to cause damage. One method of doing this is to take three full turns of the hawser around the bridle with a single half hitch on itself in the form of half a bowknot, leaving enough end to bring back on board. A yank on the end will release the half hitch, which frees the hawser.

The actual towing effort itself should await optimum conditions; all preparations should be properly completed and the tide should be at its highest stage. The auxiliary engine, if one is aboard, should not be started until just before the towing effort, to prevent sucking mud or sand into the water intakes. When the pulling strain from the towing vessel is applied, not before, try full throttle in reverse. If the sailboat is not moved the rescuing craft should maintain the strain while reversing an arc from the port quarter to the starboard quarter of the stranded vessel. This maneuver, accomplished by rudder alone, will usually succeed in breaking the suction. Breaking suction can be expedited if the stranded boat is small enough to be rocked by her crew.

Man Overboard

When a man falls overboard, whoever sees him first should shout "Man overboard!" at the top of his lungs to alert the rest of the crew. The nearest man to a life ring, seat cushion, or a life preserver should immediately throw it over the side near the man, but must take care not to hit him. Another crew member should keep his eyes on the man (or water light at night) and point to him continuously. All hands should come on deck, and other crew members should make the boat ready for jibing, especially taking care to slack the running backstay, or for tacking, as the case may be. The helmsman should note his compass course and the time of the accident so that a return course to the victim can be figured, if this becomes necessary.

If a person goes overboard while the boat is sailing with the wind abeam or forward of abeam, the quickest way to get back to your man is by jibing. But sail far enough away to avoid coming upon him in the middle of your turning circle. Approach from the leeward side so that if he is in difficulty, the boat will not drift down on top of him. The mainsail sheet should, if at all possible, be trimmed, then eased off to prevent the boom from slamming violently across, possibly injuring someone in the cockpit or damaging your boat's rigging.

If the accident should occur while the craft is sailing before the wind, you have the choice of two maneuvers to execute the pickup. In

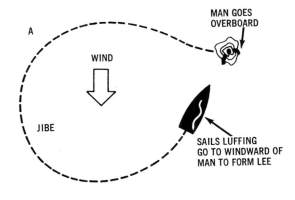

A

WIND

MAN GOES OVERBOARD

JIBE

SAILS LUFFING GO TO WINDWARD OF MAN TO FORM LEE

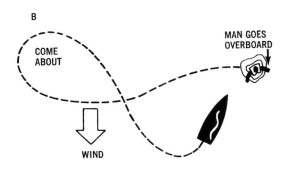

B

COME ABOUT

MAN GOES OVERBOARD

WIND

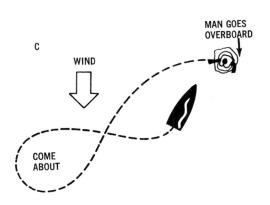

C

WIND

MAN GOES OVERBOARD

COME ABOUT

Procedure for picking up a man overboard. If under power, throw gear into neutral temporarily and swing stern away from victim so that he will not be cut by prop. When picking him up go close to windward of him, put gear in neutral, and drift down to him.

the first maneuver you bring the wind abeam, sail away for a few boat lengths, then bring the craft about and reach back on the other tack and head into the wind. The second procedure is to continue sailing before the wind for a short distance, then tack back. You will generally reach the person in the water on the second tack. The distance you sail before the wind will depend upon how your boat responds, the condition of the water, and the amount of breeze. Through practice and experience in sailing your boat you will be able to obtain the answer to this question. By the way, it would be very wise to practice the pickup maneuvers so that when an accident of this type occurs—which is seldom —you and your crew will know exactly what to do.

Approach your man in the water slowly, spilling the wind from the sail as you go. The sheets should be loose so that the boat is almost dead in the water, and the centerboard should be all the way down during the actual pickup operation to give your craft full stability. Then throw a line to the person overboard and help him in over the stern. Make the rescued party as warm, dry, and comfortable as possible.

The person who falls overboard should concern himself with three important objectives while in the water. First, *keep calm, do not panic.* Second, *keep clear of the rescuing craft.* Third, *keep afloat the easiest way you can.* If you should go overboard while out by yourself, tread water until you see the boat round into the wind, guess where it will stop dead in the wind, then swim for that point.

Fire Afloat

This is undoubtedly the worst hazard encountered on board a boat. Since it almost never occurs in small sailing boats, we shall concentrate on action to be taken with fire on board a cruiser-racer. Having your fire-fighting gear handy and in good condition is the first step in successfully combating fire. Although this equipment might be limited to only one fire extinguisher and a bailer, their availability and proper operating condition could mean the difference between prompt extinguishment and disaster. In addition to having equipment ready in advance, you should think about the action that you would take in case of fire. More can be done in the first minutes than in the following few hours.

Fires are mainly extinguished by one of two methods or a combination of both, namely cooling, smothering, and both cooling and smothering. A fire requires heat as well as oxygen to support combustion. Extinguishing agents such as dry chemical, carbon dioxide, and foam smother and to some extent cool. They are most effective on oil or grease fires when the extinguishing agent is directed at the base of the flames. The fire, if possible, should be approached from upwind so that the breeze will carry the extinguishing agent into the fire. Burning items such as wood, mattresses, and rags are best extinguished by water. For this reason a bailer or bucket can be a most valuable piece of equipment. You will have an unlimited supply of water available on all sides. If the burning object is movable, try to throw it over the side (unless there is risk of burning your hands or clothing). If a fire occurs in a relatively confined space, the closing of hatches, doors, vents, and ports will tend to keep oxygen from fanning the flames. In addition, should the fire be in the engine compartment, shut off the fuel supply.

The maneuvering of your boat will also assist in extinguishing fires. When under way, wind caused by the boat's motion fans the flames. Also, it would make sense to keep the fire downwind—that is, if the fire is aft, head the bow of the boat into the wind; if the fire is forward, put the stern of your boat into the wind. Such action helps to reduce any tendency of the fire to spread to other parts of the boat, and may reduce the hazard of smoke enveloping persons on board.

Since most pleasure-boat fires are caused by, or can be traced to, improper fueling procedures, an auxiliary owner should take *extra* caution when fueling and when starting, especially starting after fueling or after a prolonged absence from the boat. Before fueling, shut off all power, extinguish fires, and cease smoking. Attempt to fuel with the boat heading so that the tanks are to leeward of the companionway. Then the gasoline fumes will be blown away from the boat, *not* down below. Remember that gasoline fumes are heavier than air and will displace the air in the cabin and engine room. When fueling, keep the nozzle of the gasoline hose in contact with the fill pipe to prevent a possible static-electric spark. A static-electric spark can also be caused by running water, so do not fill water tanks at the same time or immediately after filling fuel tanks. Do not spill fuel, and be very careful not to overflow the tank. After fueling, air the boat and run the engine room blower for at least 5 minutes before starting the engine. The higher the humidity and the lighter the breeze, the greater the danger from accumulated gasoline fumes. Open the engine compartment and smell for fumes *in the bilge* before starting.

When securing gasoline engines prior to leaving the boat, shut off the fuel at the tank. This ensures that there will be no leakage from the carburetor into the bilge while the boat is at the mooring.

When starting engines after a long absence, open the engine-room hatch and smell for gasoline fumes in the bilge before energizing any of the systems. Most important, incorporate these precautions into a routine that is *never* varied. Overconfidence and haste are the most usual causes of boat explosions and fires.

Another potential fire hazard on many cruising sailboats is the galley stove. Gimbaled alcohol stoves require that certain precautions should be taken. Garments and towels should not be hung too close to open flames, woodwork and painted surfaces around the stove must be protected or insulated from flames, the stove should be kept clean and grease-free, and care must be taken when filling or priming not to spill fuel. A dry-chemical fire extinguisher is hung near the stove. Minor fires can be smothered with a towel or by pouring salt on the flames. Some people advocate pouring water on flaming alcohol, but this could be dangerous when the boat is heeled, because the water may float the burning alcohol and the fire may flow to a new location. If the cook has a good harness to hold him in his cooking location, there will be less chance of his spilling foods or being thrown against the stove in rough weather.

Obviously, precautions should be taken against smoking around flammable materials, against smoking in bunks, and so forth. A fire at sea is usually a lot more dangerous than a fire in one's home.

Being Lost

When lost, try to reconstruct your dead-reckoning position on the chart by recalling courses, speeds, and times. Follow a straight course and take a chain of soundings at intervals. Try to fit these onto your chart. Head inshore and, when in sight of land, follow the coastline (taking soundings) until a landmark is sighted. Watch for distant steamers and estimate your distance from steamer lanes. The direction of a major city can often be determined with a transistor radio by rotating toward the loudest signal (usually at a right angle to the face of the set). Avoid wasting distress signals if no other vessel is in sight. Do not wander aimlessly, but pursue a direct course toward a landmark. Vary course sharply when you turn. Keep record of course, speed, and time. Do not panic. Patience is your best hope.

First Aid

Accidents can happen anywhere, afloat or ashore. On land it is often possible to get help quickly, but on a boat it is important to be a "do-it-yourself" skipper. Even seemingly harmless falls, cuts, and bruises should be looked after because of possible infection. One caution though about first aid: No matter how expert you may be, the cardinal rule to remember is—do not overtreat the victim!

If you or someone in your crew have had a course in first aid, all well and good. Even so, a first-aid manual (Red Cross or equal) is a must. Every boat should also be equipped with a first-aid kit that is adequate for the number of people normally on board. Keep the entire kit in one container, easily accessible. The plastic or metal waterproof tackle boxes sold in sporting-goods stores make excellent first-aid kits. A suggested first-aid kit for a cruiser-racer with a crew of four to six is given below.

Seasickness. The first indication of seasickness is usually a greenish pallor, followed by yawning, drowsiness, salivation, weakness, loss of attention, deep breathing, cold sweat, giddiness, inability to function, occasionally hiccoughing, dizziness, and vomiting. Following the vomiting the victim may feel a little better temporarily, but this relief is short-lived, and he soon becomes prostrated and continues to be nauseated. He may even think he is going to die, and in most cases probably wishes he were dead.

There are several motion-sickness remedies on the market—Bonine and Dramamine are the most popular. These are frequently effective and need only be taken in doses of one or two tablets a day. If you are susceptible and planning a sail or cruise, consult your doctor. He will recommend one for you. The important point is to take the medication for a day or two in advance of the outing. Almost all medical authorities agree it does little good to begin taking medication after you are aboard.

While the following statement is not very delicate, it is something you should know: The odor of regurgitated material also can be a factor inducing seasickness, as can be

Vaseline gauze	Benadryl tablets*	Darvon compound
Absorbent cotton	Gauze pads (2″ × 2″, 4″ × 4″)	Eye pads
Elastic bandage (3″)	Gauze bandage (2″ and 3″)	Band-aids
Eyecup and dropper	Adhesive and Scotch tape	Q-tips
Thermometer and case	Bandage scissors	Resusitube
Rubbing alcohol	Safety pins	Tweezers
Milk of magnesia	Sunburn cream	Salt tablets
Epsom salts	Hydrogen peroxide	Aspirin
Aromatic spirits of ammonia	Oil of cloves	Glycerine
Bicarbonate of soda	White vaseline	Merthiolate
Codeine*	Penicillin tablets*	Gantrisin tablets*
Paregoric*	Achrostatin*	Insect repellent
	Dramamine or Bonine	Burn ointment

* Requires a prescription from your doctor.
Note: Mark all boxes and jars plainly and be sure to keep out of reach of children.

the various sound effects—those haunting tunes caused by the rapid intake of air into the larynx (a sort of organ pipe in reverse) during vomiting. It is believed that the throaty melodies played by a mamboing stomach can be quite a factor in causing seasickness in otherwise unaffected spectators. In other words, many people have been made ill by watching others with the high heaves. Speaking of seeing, it is a very good idea for those prone to seasickness to wear sunglasses constantly—the best procurable—and always have an extra pair along. Doctors are convinced that a great deal of motion sickness is due to eyestrain. Once under way, reading on board a boat is bad for the eyes.

It is generally agreed that the seasick individual probably benefits most by lying supine with his head flat or just slightly raised. The nearer amidships he stays the better. Sudden movements should be avoided. The victim should not go below, if possible, because fresh air is helpful to him.

Artificial Respiration. You have a good chance to revive the victim if you start artificial respiration within 2 minutes. You have a very poor chance if you wait 10 minutes. But no matter what the time interval, start breathing life into the victim without delay. Have someone else read the following steps to you while you work if you have not already committed them to memory.

1. Put victim on his back. Check to see that victim's mouth is clear of obstructions.

2. Place a folded coat, blanket, etc., under his shoulders to enable the head to tilt back.

3. Grasp and pull jaw open. Keep open to assure air passage.

4. Pinch nostrils shut, take a deep breath, place your mouth over his mouth (with your thumb in his jaw to keep it open). Blow into his mouth until you see his chest rise.

5. Remove mouth and listen for outflow of air.

    Adult—rate is about every 5–6 seconds.
    Child—rate is about every 3 seconds.
    (Use shallow breaths).

6. If first few attempts are unsuccessful—turn victim on side and give several sharp blows between shoulder blades to remove obstruction.

7. Now do it all over again. Frequently the patient, after a temporary recovery of respiration, stops breathing again. Therefore, he must be watched and if natural breathing stops, artificial respiration should be resumed at once.

First Aid for Your Yacht

While a knowledge of first aid to humans is most important, so is it for boats. If proper care of the boat is given and her parts carefully checked each time you go out, chances of a breakdown are slight. But, for example, if you fail to replace a defective stay before you go out, there is always the distinct possibility of its failing and causing you to lose the mast.

As in the case with human first aid, yacht first aid needs a kit of tools and equipment with which to accomplish the best results. The following is a typical small-boat first-aid kit:

S hook
Spare centerboard pennant
Short and long pieces of ⅛-inch line
#8 and #10 wood screws in two lengths
One block with wire pigtail
One small block
Knife
Long-nosed pliers
Screwdriver
Roll of tape
Two sizes of cotter pins
Two small shackles

While the above list is good for a typical small boat, remember that the amount of spare equipment, tools, and repair material will depend on the size of your boat and the nature of her voyage. Therefore, look around your craft and around your boat and imagine what different accidents might happen; then visualize what might be done about them. See that you have the necessary gear in your yacht's first-aid kit to make all repairs.

Rigging Repairs. A broken spar can be very adequately repaired by "fishing" with strips of wood or metal (called "fish") and wire or rope. When making such a jury (makeshift) rig to reinforce a broken spar, remember that the repair depends upon the strength of the material used as a fish, the strength of the lashing, and the firmness of their union. Items used for a fish include boat hooks, oars, the boom crutch, and spinnaker poles. Sometimes two or more fish are used around the damaged spar to hold it tightly together like splints on a broken leg. When using more than one fish, it is usually wise to employ separate lines to hold each piece. Light line or wire, generously and tightly wrapped, is better than a few turns of a heavy one.

If a spreader or shroud fails, the first task is to take the strain off the mast as quickly as possible by jibing or tacking. (If the jib or forestay fails, fall off and run before the wind, while if the backstay goes, luff up.) Then make a temporary repair until a new spreader can be rigged. For instance, a spinnaker pole squared well aft with the shroud attached at the outboard end, and with the pole guyed down forward and aft, will do the job nicely. Similarly, the main halyard might be used

with the pole to replace a parted shroud. Thimbles and wire clamps can be employed to replace a broken true-lock splice or fitting.

If the mast should go over the side, the first task is to get it clear of the boat before it can punch a hole in her hull. If the standing-rigging pins can be removed quickly, do so, because this will allow you to save the wire and turnbuckles and leave just that much more equipment to rig a temporary, or jury, mast with. If you cannot remove the pins, the wire can be cut with wire cutters at the ends. But, always try to save the mast. It and its rigging will make a most effective sea anchor which can be used until the weather moderates. While doing this, it is a good idea to rig fenders or cushions over the side to prevent damage to the hull. When conditions permit, it may be possible to salvage the mast or at least some of the fittings.

The following is a breakdown procedure for a typical racing one-design class boat:

Item Broken	Method to Fix	Other Material Needed
Jib halyard	Use spinnaker halyard	
Forestay	Keep jib up; use spinnaker halyard if necessary	
Jib tack fitting	Tie tack to bow plate or use spare shackle	Small line, knife, shackle
Jib clew fitting	Tie jib to jibsheets	Small line
Spinnaker halyard	If last leg or course is a run, use jib halyard	
Jibsheet	Use anchor line	
Spinnaker pole	Use predrilled paddle	
Spinnaker-pole fitting on mast	Tie small line around mast	Small line
Spinnaker sheet	Use anchor line	Small line
Spinnaker fitting at tack or clew	Tie sheet directly to spinnaker	
Spinnaker-pole topping lift	Tie line to lower spreader	Line
Halyard-winch locking dog in mast base	Crank up sail, and tie handle to mast	Spare crank handle
Jib fairlead block	Tie small block to seat	Small block
Mainsail tack pin broken or lost	Use spare	Spare pin
Main halyard	Drop mast, attach S hook and shackle at truck, reeve anchor line through shackle, step mast, hoist sail	S hook, small shackle

Item Broken	Methods to Fix	Other Materials Needed
Vang block on boom	Use spare	Block with wire tail
Vang line	Use anchor line	
Centerboard pennant	Use spare wire pennant, or rig a two-part pennant with anchor line	Spare pennant
Mainsheet	Use anchor line	
Mainsheet cleat	Attach with larger screws	Supply of #8 and #10 wood screws, screwdriver
Mainsheet block on boom	Use spare block	Block with wire tail
Outhaul fitting	Tie clew to tang	Small line
Traveler	Tie lower main block to transom hole	Line
Tiller breaks in middle	Make a splice using spinnaker pole	Roll of tape
Batten	Splice with tape or carry spare	

At sea when cruising continuously for days at a time, rigging gets a lot more wear than one would ordinarily think. Metals can become fatigued from the constant motion, and lines that are rubbed can soon chafe through. Chafe is a major enemy at sea, and chafing gear must be applied to any running rigging where it touches a spar or lifeline, etc. Chafing gear must be checked and adjusted continually.

If the headstay should part while beating, bear off immediately so that you are running dead before the wind. Do not lower the jib right away because its wire luff will help hold the mast forward. Set up the forestay at once, if it is not already rigged. Fasten one or two masthead halyards to the stem head, and tighten these halyards so that they pull the masthead forward. Lower the mainsail and reef it to the point where its head is no higher than the forestay's point of attachment to the mast. If a spare headstay is carried, then this may be rigged when the weather permits. Otherwise, perhaps the wire jib halyard can be rigged as a jury headstay. The upper end of the halyard might be held to the masthead with wire clamps, and in moderate or light weather a large jib could be hoisted with a spinnaker halyard. Needless to say, spares of every size turnbuckle should be car-

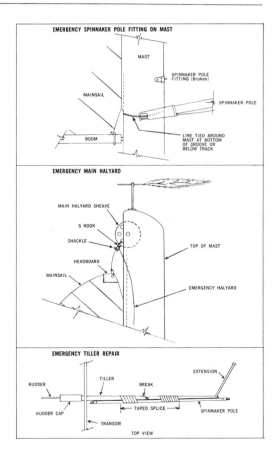

ried because these will often break before the wire stay breaks.

If any of the main shrouds should break on the boat's windward side, tack immediately so that the strain will be put on the opposite shrouds. This maneuver, quickly done, might save the mast. If the mast should happen to break (a very unlikely occurrence if the rigging is regularly inspected), the mast will usually fall over the side. In this case the broken spar should be hauled aboard as soon as possible because in rough seas, it can pound a hole in the hull. This is where the required rigging cutters will come in handy. At sea in heavy weather it is always a good idea to glance at the lee shrouds immediately before tacking to see that none are loose. Masts have been lost needlessly because of failure to check the lee rigging before tacking.

Should the permanent backstay break, round up into the wind at once. Simultaneously set up the running backstays and haul the mainsail in flat. Then lower the jib to take the strain off the head of the mast. If a jury backstay is rigged, do not set the spinnaker, as this can put a great strain on the backstays.

The chance of breaking a stay is rather remote if the rigging is thoroughly inspected. It is not enough to do this before going to sea. Inspections should also take place regularly while at sea. Every few days, when weather permits, a man should be hauled up to the head of the mast in a bosun's chair so that he can check stays, mast sheaves, blocks, pins, tangs, splices, swages, halyards, etc. Hauling a man up the mast at sea when the boat is rolling can be a dangerous operation. Every precaution should be taken. It is important that the man going aloft is lashed in his seat in such a way that he cannot possibly fall even if he is knocked unconscious.

A chafed rope halyard should be replaced long before it has a chance to chafe through. It is often possible to replace a halyard without going aloft by marrying the new halyard to the old one. (This is done by placing the ends of the two halyards end to end, and sewing them together in that position.) Then the old halyard can be unrove from the deck, and the new halyard will follow the old one through the block.

Spinnaker halyards are particularly sus-

Dismasting is a tough spot for any crew.

ceptible to chafe aloft but this chafe can be reduced by taking the hauling part of the halyard to leeward of the headstay so that the halyard will not cross the headstay and chafe on it.

Loss or Disablement of a Rudder. If you should lose the use of your boat's rudder, a substitute "blade" can be found by employing a door, hatch cover, oar, table leaf, or a combination of these nailed together. This blade is then lashed to the transom and used like the steering-sweep installations employed on life boats at sea.

Another possible way to steer a small boat that has lost her rudder is to use a drag at the stern; for instance, by towing a bucket. When the drag is located in the center of the stern, the craft will go straight ahead. When you wish to make her turn, haul the drag to the side to which you desire to turn.

Hull Repair. As stated earlier, the foresighted skipper going far from shore should always provide his boat with a stock of spare parts and the necessary materials for emergency repairs, and this includes repairs to the hull. The fiberglass-boat owner should, therefore, avail himself of a repair kit of glass and resin. These kits can be purchased from a marine hardware store or plastics supply house and usually contain the following items:

Fiberglass cloth—several square yards
Fiberglass tape 6 inches wide—10 yards
Polyester resin—at least a quart in pint
   cans

Fiberglass mat—1 square yard
Epoxy cement—several tubes

The cloth and mat would be largely useful for taking care of fracture or a hole. The tape can be enormously useful—perhaps for restoring a fractured spar or temporarily stopping a leak in a pipe or the cold end of the exhaust tube. Polyester resin is easiest to handle under field conditions because it will wet the glass rapidly and cure more quickly than epoxy. The epoxy cement can be considered as a "super" glue or solder and has many obvious applications.

Quite obviously, accidents do not always occur in such a convenient way that this recommended repair kit can be immediately employed. That is to say, you cannot apply a patch to the hull when you are rolling in a sea or when it is raining and cold. You may have to apply some ingenuity and special techniques to protect the watertight integrity of the boat until you can get into a sheltered spot and then use the fiberglass repair materials. Impromptu techniques have been employed by seamen for generations—stuffing the hole with a rag, pillow, or mattress is one example; a collision mat is another. The latter would be a sail, mattress, or similar object, pulled and held in place under the hull by ropes to its corners, one or more of which must go under the keel to the far side of the boat. Pressure of water will help hold an outside patch in place.

It would even be possible in certain circumstances to drill through the fiberglass hull and bolt in place a makeshift dam constructed from any available wooden member in the boat.

Collision. In event of a serious collision, check the gravity of the damage before separating vessels. Stand by to help other craft unless your vessel or passengers are in danger. If other bow has penetrated your craft, be prepared to plug the fracture immediately on separation of boats. Nail canvas patch over serious break with wood strips. Distribute weight to get hole out of water during repairs. Shore up mattresses against break on inside. If boat is in sinking condition, get all passengers in life jackets. If other boat is sinking, you must stand by and give aid, no matter how serious your damage.

Taking On Water. When taking on water, pump promptly and search for the leak. If a break in hull, drive rags in with wood wedges. If leaking seacock or adjacent pipe, wind with rubber tape. If seam has opened, drive in oakum or twisted small material. If a large hole, cover from outside with canvas, or canvas and plastic seat cushion, tacking canvas snugly to hull. If hole is at waterline, turn boat to other side so damage rides out of water.

Plugged Head. When the ship's head (toilet) is plugged, apply suction with plumber's helper (rubber plunger). Probe and twist with wire coat hanger. Work vent lever slowly. Shut off incoming water. Remove blockage (usually wadded paper) in pieces. Bail head with tin and bucket to facilitate working. If no other remedy, disassemble the valve and clear, making sure the vent seacock is shut off to prevent entry of water.

Lighting Problems. Most modern sailboat cruisers have an electrical system consisting of a 12-volt alternator and battery. Such a system allows for sufficient interior cabin lighting fixtures, plus the navigational and anchor lights required by law. But remember that the battery must be kept charged, and if you do not use your auxiliary's engine, you must use your lights sparingly. Many sailors who do not like to use their engines when cruising will run them while at anchor to recharge the batteries. By reading the specific gravity of the battery with a hydrometer, it is easy to tell at a glance its state of discharge. A battery is fully charged when the hydrometer reads 1.275. It is fully discharged when the hydrometer reads 1.100. Also make sure that the battery's electrolyte is checked at regular intervals. Even in the dry-charge batteries, where the electrolyte is coated on the internal plates, the distilled-water level must be maintained. And, no matter what type of battery you buy, it is eventually going to wear out. The internal plates deteriorate naturally due to chemical action.

Engine Failure. If your auxiliary's engine fails, check the fuel system for: clogged filter, clogged or damaged fuel line, needle valve stuck, choke stuck, out of gas. Check ignition system for: fouled or cracked plugs or loose plug wires, shorting ignition wires, cracked distributor cap, bad points, bad rotor, loose plug, worn coil. (Keep spare

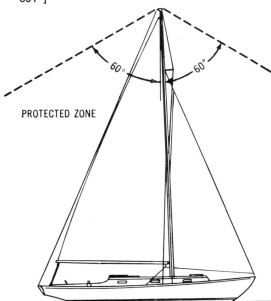

PROTECTED ZONE

To prevent a boat from being struck by lightning it is wise to create a "cone of protection" whose sides run down from the terminal at 60° from the vertical. Every object and person within the cone is virtually immune to lightning. If the cone's apex is high enough, the whole boat is protected. *A boat with a metal mast* needs only to have the mast properly grounded. Copper wire at least ⅛ inch in diameter, or an equivalent copper tube or strip, should be run from the mast's lowest point to the nearest ground, i.e., a metal connection on the hull below the water-line. A radiotelephone ground plate is good; an iron keel or metal through-hull fitting may be used; a through-bolt can be fitted and the ground wire secured to its inner end. Any ungrounded object projecting above the metal mast should be electrically bonded to it. *With a wooden mast,* a short, pointed spire of heavy copper (No. 8 cable or larger) should be attached so that it projects at least 6 inches above the masthead. This creates an air terminal which in turn must be grounded—commonly by connecting it to the wire stay leading most directly downward and then running a grounding wire from the stay's lower terminal to underwater metal, as above. Any continuous metal sail tracks on spars should be wired to the main ground.

plugs, points, rotor, coil, and distributor cap on board for replacements.) For more details on servicing, check the instruction manual that comes with your engine.

Distress Signals

Searching for a craft in distress can be a rather quick and easy job or a difficult and lengthy procedure, depending upon the amount and accuracy of the information given to the rescuing ships. Thus you must know the recognized distress signals and have the proper gear on board to send them. This signaling equipment is not a minimum legal requirement; your needs of this type must be based upon the waters in which your boat sails and the size of your craft.

As mentioned in Section II, more and more cruising sailboats are being equipped with radiotelephones. This is possibly the best way to summon aid since merchant vessels, pleasure craft, and Coast Guard ships and stations listen on 2182 kilocycles on the radiotelephone band. This is a calling and distress frequency. A vessel calling "Mayday" (code for needing emergency assistance) stands an excellent chance of receiving help quickly. Though 2738 or 2638 kilocycles may not be busy and may bring assistance sooner, in an emergency you may use any available frequency to indicate your need for help. The Coast Guard has available a 4- by 5-inch cardboard placard called *Distress Information Sheet* for posting near your radiotelephone. These placards, which give the information desired by rescuers, can be had at most Coast Guard units, or from their headquarters in Washington, D.C. 20402.

Since many searching craft today are equipped with radar and because boats made of fiberglass do not make the best radar targets, the locating of a radar reflector such as the small collapsible type (available at most marine suppliers) high on the mast of a disabled boat will increase the chance of radar detection and rescue. While almost any signal that will attract attention and bring help is a satisfactory distress signal, there are known or recognized distress signals that will greatly enhance your chances of obtaining assistance. The most commonly recognized distress signals are as follows:

1. Most widely recognized distress signal is "SOS." This, in Morse Code, is made with three dots, three dashes, three dots. Besides radio, it can be sent by sound signals—three short, space, three long, space, three short blasts on a horn; or by visual signal—three short, three long, three short flashes of a light.

2. Send the emergency signal word "Mayday" repeatedly on your radiotelephone and

then follow the procedure given earlier in this section.

3. A gun or other explosive, fired at intervals of about one minute.

4. Continuous sounding of fog horn, bell, or whistle.

5. Rockets or shells burning red flares. In commercial kits, some flares have parachutes attached to keep them in the air longer.

6. Flames at night and heavy black smoke by day, such as from oil burned in a metal bucket or equivalent. Use oil or kerosene— *never gasoline.*

7. Reverse your flag or ensign so that it flies upside down.

8. Fly a white cloth from the highest point on your boat. The International Code flags NC, or a square flag with a basket, a box, or a bell-shaped object above or below it on your boat's mast are also well-known daytime distress signals.

9. An old fisherman's distress signal is a pair of oilskin trousers or any other conspicuous and incongruous object hung in rigging.

10. The most recent distress signal for small craft, as proposed by the Coast Guard, is as follows: the boat operator stands and repeatedly—and slowly—raises and lowers his arms outstretched to each side. This signal is distinctive and not likely to be mistaken for a greeting. As the Coast Guard recom-mends, "To be as effective as possible, this signal should be given from the highest vantage point on the boat, with consideration given to color contrasts."

Abandoning Ship

Most boats involved in casualties will continue to remain afloat indefinitely. If it becomes necessary to abandon your boat due to fire, swamping, capsizing, or other emergencies, do not leave the area. Generally a damaged boat can be sighted more readily than a person in the water, and it may help to keep you afloat. Also, as previously stated, distance over water is deceptive. Usually the estimated distance is much shorter than the actual distance. Keep your head and restrain your initial impulse to swim ashore. Calmly weigh the facts of the situation, such as injuries to passengers, the proximity of shore, and your swimming abilities, before deciding your course of action. But remember that in 999 cases out of 1,000 it is best to stay with your boat.

If there is time before abandoning ship, don your life preserver and give distress signals. Do not foolishly waste signaling devices when a small likelihood of assistance exists. Wait until you sight someone or something. If your boat is equipped with a radiotelephone, a distress message should be sent.

SAILBOAT MAINTENANCE

Proper maintenance not only preserves the asset you so happily have in your sailboat, but it makes a great deal of difference in safety, fun, and comfort. Most maintenance work may be divided into three time categories: going out of commission, fitting-out, and sailing-season care.

Going Out of Commission

As is true of all boat maintenance work, there are two aspects to your fall layup procedure—one corrective, the other preventive. Your boat, first, has served through the season with inevitable wear and tear, despite your maintenance work. Second, lying idle through the winter—probably out of her ele-ment—she will suffer further exposure which in many ways can be more severe than her exposure in service. To restore the wear and tear loss is one job, and to preserve and protect her from deterioration through the winter ahead is the other.

Selection of Storage. Large sailboats with heavy keels, spars, and riggings are sometimes kept afloat during the winter months. However, today, most of the modern cruiser-racer-type sailboats are stored ashore in boatyards, while day-cruiser or small-craft owners tend to store them at home. There are several factors that you must consider before you make your choice.

Storage afloat requires a well-protected berth or anchorage. It should be one sheltered from heavy seas, high winds, and disturbances from commercial traffic, yet one where a daily check is assured. If any danger of ice damage exists, this alone is enough to arrange for storage ashore. Remember that a fiberglass molded boat, because of its impact resistance and resiliency, will break through thick ice without being damaged. Generally the determining factor is whether the engine has power enough to push through the ice formation. Surface scratches may occur to the plastic finish after repeated contact with sharp ice, but it is surprising how minor the effects are. The plastic is very slippery and the hull yields and releases itself quite readily.

Storage afloat is easier and more natural in more southerly waters. In any event all boats stored afloat should first be hauled, and, after draining all the piping and plumbing, through-hull connections should be securely plugged from the outside before the boats are again waterborne.

It is quite true that storage afloat avoids all risk of faulty blocking, avoids any drying out of wooden bottom planking, and perhaps lessens the risk of fire. However, the latter thought needs to be qualified, for internal moisture accumulations may cause serious damage to mechanical equipment, and this may well invite the reentry of a serious fire peril by efforts to provide a little periodic heat. If you decide on wet storage, follow the general laying-up and engine care (if you have an auxiliary) given later in this section. Also check with local boating people for the best areas for wet storage and their specific tips for that region. But, keep in mind that the decision to store afloat or ashore should be on the basis of what is best for the boat and not on the immediately involved economics.

Whether you store your boat in the open or in a shed is almost a question of personal preference. Obviously, your boat will weather less in inside storage, and this will be a particularly important factor if she is adorned with a great deal of exposed varnish. Painted exteriors should not suffer greatly in the open unless the sun is likely to be hot, and in the South all boats ashore should be under cover. If your leanings are toward wet storage but you cannot find the proper facilities, outside storage is your logical alternative. Here your boat is exposed to something like the conditions met afloat and with normal moisture or rainfall will not dry out as much as she would inside. On the contrary, hull types described above as entirely unsuited to wet storage are best laid up in dry buildings, for they will be better preserved if completely dry.

Shun the jerry-built fire trap which may collapse in a fresh breeze. It is better for your boat to suffer a little weathering than to run the risk of her being crushed and punctured by the sagging timbers of the storage shed. If you wish to prolong your cruising this fall or have plans for early spring and want to be overboard ahead of the others, you may have to be content with an open berth due to congestion in the sheds, which are usually filled first. Some boat owners believe in the moving air outside, which they feel produces a natural and adequate circulation under their winter covers, while others argue that no cover at all is better, even in the still inside air, for the entire interior can be thrown open for ventilation.

Finally, the relative cost of each type of storage will again influence your decision, as well as the length of time the boat will be out of commission. Remember, too, that some of the work you plan to do, whether immediately, through the winter, or in the spring, may be prohibited by yard rules except in outdoor sections of the yard.

In most areas where boating is a widely popular sport, you will have at least a limited choice of boatyards. This selection, possibly with some slight compromises, will have to be worked into your plans. When you have decided what you want for your boat—and for yourself—try to find a good yard which provides both. The points on which you yield should not be significant ones and should prejudice, if anything, your own convenience rather than your boat's physical well-being. Some things to consider are:

1. Convenience of location (not the first consideration).

2. Cost (also should not be of primary importance).

3. Covered, open, or shed storage.

4. Nearness of caustic fumes or discoloring dirt and soot.

5. Supervision. Fire and theft protection.

6. Competence of staff.

7. Ability and facilities to do your own work.

8. Extent to which staff stands ready to assist.

In most good boatyards, particularly in areas where there is a well-organized marine trades association, storage and work done while the craft is laid up are on a flat-rate basis. In other words, storage is so much per foot, winterizing the engine is a specific amount for the size and type of engine, and so on. There is a definite charge listed for nearly every possible job—painting, repairing damaged parts and sails, etc.—you could want done. Go over every detail with the yardmaster and draw up a contract with *exact* details as to what is to be done and the cost. (In most yards, for the owner who is so inclined and who has the time, there are many things he can do to keep yard charges down.) When the contract is agreed to and signed by both of you, it is generally possible to budget accordingly, and you and the yard will know just where each one stands as far as spring accounts receivable. But, remember that there is one thing no one ever guarantees, and that is the date your sailboat will go back into the water in the spring. This is controlled solely by the gods of the weather and the strange things that go on at all boatyards.

Proper Shoring or Cradle Supports. After the boat has been hauled out, the essential requirement of adequate blocking and shoring is the provision of such well-distributed and steady support that it approaches the condition provided by the water when the boat is afloat. If it does not do so, there is a good likelihood some permanent deformation of the hull may occur. Most modern sailboats, especially those of fiberglass, are designed so that the hull weight can be supported by keel blocks while stored ashore. Exceptions to this rule are some hulls used strictly for racing and a few centerboard boats that are stored in cradles built to conform to the special shape of their hulls.

There are, of course, many suitable systems of crib-work and if they provide the essential requirement of adequate support uniformly distributed, they need not be questioned. For instance, the shipping cradles for small cruisers, if well preserved and reinforced, have been found to provide good hull support for layup purposes. They have properly placed chocks which are fitted to bear evenly on bottom contours from bilges or chines to keels at strong points of the hull. The only problems in such instances are to see that boats are properly placed in their cradles, and that the cradles are not set on soft ground. A few additional thoughts are:

1. All average-size boats should have three keel blocks, one in the area of greatest concentration of weight, one near the fore foot and one in the area of the dead wood.

2. Larger craft, dependent upon type, length, and hull structural strength, may need more than three keel blocks.

3. Boats with long overhangs should have special shoring for such sections to prevent sag, which could well lead to a permanent hog.

4. Many of our modern, wide-stern, hard-chine cruisers are so constructed that blocking and shoring support should be distributed along the chines and bottoms, particularly in the aft quarters which may have considerable overhang.

5. Setting shores directly on the ground or doing the same with short keel blocks is hazardous practice. Both may settle if the ground becomes muddy from rain, or in the spring as the frost loosens the ground. This can cause uneven support and potential hull trouble.

6. Keel blocks and shores should be set at strong points of the hull structure.

Small sailboats that are normally transported to and from the water on towed trailers usually present no problem to amateur boat handlers. The hauling, moving, and blocking up for storage of heavier craft, however, is not work for unskilled individuals, and is best done by skilled boatyard personnel. Remember that unless the job is done properly, damage to hulls may result from strain and distortion.

Stripping and Cleaning. As soon as possible after hauling, your boat's bottom must be scrubbed clean. While most yards do this for you, it is imperative that she be thoroughly clean. Even if an antifouling paint has been used, it is likely that a film of scum has built up. This film is not easy to remove if allowed to dry. If any barnacles have fixed themselves to the bottom, knock them off with a scraper, and use a little sandpaper to rid the surface of the hard shell which may still hold fast. Barnacles seem to fuse to a fiberglass surface which has not been protected by antifouling paint. They will not damage the fiberglass hull, but are a nuisance.

Algae or scum which will not come free in the washing procedure is easily removed with bronze-wool pads (use the finer grades). Scouring pads are very effective. Fiberglass hulls which have been in dirty water for an extended period may show staining on an unpainted bottom, and perhaps up to a few inches above the waterline. It is naturally most visible on a white hull. A fine bronze-wool pad dusted with kitchen cleanser will do the job in most cases. However, if this treatment does not yield satisfactory results, the owner will have to consider paint on the bottom and a painted boot top to restore the desired appearance to the topsides. Washing down the topsides, deck, and interior is an optional procedure, but if done when the boat is hauled out, cleaning in the spring will be easier.

The colored-pigment finish on a fiberglass boat is designed to hold its luster and appearance for a number of years. Although it is quite durable, it should receive reasonable care. Wash it with soap and water whenever dirt accumulates. Apply car wax to preserve the finish and make the surface easier to keep clean. Do not apply wax to those areas to be painted, as paint will not adhere to a wax film. It is also recommended that interior surfaces be given the same treatment. Any wood surfaces should be cleaned, too, to remove salt traces.

As the boat is cleaned, look for evidence of galvanic action, worm infestation, broken fastenings, areas of suspiciously hollow planking, and other faults which will have to be corrected before you go afloat next season. An exhaustive hull survey in the spring will round out what you learn now, but serious defects should be discovered early and remedial steps taken.

The preliminary job when you go aboard is to complete the job of stripping your boat clean of all movable items of equipment and stores. A systematic approach to this operation will probably result in the most expeditious and efficient results. Perhaps beginning in the forepeak and working aft toward the cockpit will be best for your boat. Your cockpit will also serve well as a sorting place. To avoid making a tiresome number of trips up and down the ladder or scaffolding with small loads, arrange in the cockpit a number of cartons or light boxes, each labeled to receive a specific type of stores with a large one for trash. This will avoid later sorting and also prevent the loss of small items of gear.

If any interior items—blankets, curtains, etc.—need cleaning, it should be done in the fall. All furnishing items that are not being stored at home should be neatly folded and wrapped in paper with moth flakes (when necessary) before being placed in the boatyard's storage locker. It is also advisable either to wrap or to cover the mattresses and cushions with plastic or canvas to protect them from dirt. Sails should also be washed, dried, and stored in a well-ventilated location (further details on sail care are given later in this section). Any sails that need repairs should be sent to the sailmaker in the fall. Also order any new sails you need at this time. You will avoid delays that occur in the spring.

Make certain to remove all bottled goods and food; bottled goods left aboard may freeze and break, while food will attract insects and mice. Wash out the icebox with soap and water and leave it open for the winter. Open all sea cocks in the plumbing system to let the water drain out. The toilet pump and water tanks particularly require special attention. All electronic equipment—depth finder, radiotelephone, direction finder, etc.—should be removed from the boat. If you are not thoroughly familiar with this kind of work, have the yard remove the instruments; they should be stored in a dry place, preferably in a heated room. Also be sure to remove all navigational gear, books and charts, lifesaving gear, and all similar items. Air chambers (flotation compartments) ought to be checked to see that water has not accumulated from condensation or as a result of a small pinhole.

Check all lines—ground tackle and mooring lines, standing and running rigging—for wear. Place any needed lines on your shopping list. Inspect all deck hardware, too, since it takes a beating from exposure to salt-laden sea air. Remove fittings with pitted chrome and have them replated. It is cheaper than buying new hardware each year. But if the deck chocks or cleats are chewed up or too small, replace them with new ones that will reduce chafe on the anchor or mooring lines. Set aside blocks, snap hooks, sail hanks, turnbuckles, and other working hardware for cleaning up, lubricating, and overhaul during the long winter evenings.

Cowl vents, bitts, cleats, chocks, porthole rims, guard strips, grab rails, and other fixed equipment were probably highly polished when you sent your boat ashore. An hour or so spent now applying a dampproof coating will save you hours of laborious rubbing with a strong cleaner in the spring, and may even prevent irrevocable damage to the luster and surface. Noncarbolic vaseline is effective, and several commercial products are recommended for this specific purpose. The same treatment is also due the threads and surfaces of deck fill plates, turnbuckles and their threaded shafts, instrument-panel switches and trim, electric outlets, and all other metals subject to corrosion. Winches, fairleads, jam cleats, and similar equipment fitted with moving parts are probably sufficiently lubricated internally to last until they are overhauled in the spring, but they should be coated externally in such a way as to prevent moisture entering them. Whatever coating is used is probably capable of soiling objects which come in contact with it, so it should be applied with some care and be suitably shielded. A detergent or kerosene will remove it in the spring.

Wire standing rigging or lifelines, if left on board and subject to weathering or to salt air, can be preserved by brushing on one of the elastic rust-preventive films recently developed. The heavier compounds marketed for this purpose are intended for commercial service and, being dirty and greasy, are usually unsuited to pleasure-boat use. If you do use them, however, a sharply underlined note should be made early in your spring work list to clean all shrouds and stays thoroughly to avoid staining sails and halyards.

With the work of laying up your boat, you are probably inclined to neglect your long-suffering dinghy. It deserves attention and proper storage if it is to serve another season. A good plan is to store it at home where, on dismal winter weekends, you will find much pleasure and satisfaction in overhauling it. The need to savor again, from time to time through the off season, the pleasures of boating is thus partly filled, if only remotely.

Preparing Engines for Winter Storage. The owner of an auxiliary has an added responsibility—the engine. Failure to give your engine proper protection through the winter storage season will cause irreparable damage and will contribute more than many seasons of hard use to its premature collapse. For this reason, the most vital part of the layup work of an auxiliary is that of securing your engine. For the actual step by step procedure, follow the instructions given in the manual for your engine.

Winter Cover. If you have chosen outside storage, a complete, well-designed canvas or composite cover is a very worthwhile and vital investment in the future of your boat. It should provide thorough upward ventilation against sweat and dampness, while still giving protection against dirt and weather. Strong enough of itself to resist high winds and the weight of rain and snow, there should be no necessity for it to bear unduly on fragile parts or to chafe excessively against paint and varnish work. Remember, too, that some cover and lanyard materials will alternately draw taut and stretch as they become wet and dry.

With most large boats, the first task is to set up the frame; if a new frame is built by the boatyard, be sure that it is marked immediately. Each rafter should be marked. A good system is to label them in numerical order, as Port 1, 2, 3, and so on. The ridgepole should be marked with a corresponding number where each of the rafters is to be placed. A frame that is properly marked will go together a great deal more quickly than one that is not. Be sure to pad the lower ends of the rafters where they rest on the rail or rail cap, to prevent any possible chafing.

The best winter cover is one tailored by a sailmaker to fit the frame and shape of your boat. Since this is usually a rather expensive proposition, the cover most extensively found is a tarpaulin which simply covers the frame and the boat and is tied underneath to prevent it blowing away. While a big tarpaulin is pretty difficult to handle, one man can do it, however, if he goes about it the proper way. Stretch out the tarpaulin beside the boat, flaking it down so that it lies in accordion pleats with one edge uppermost. Then go on the boat and lift one corner aboard, then work along that edge, pulling the edge up and over the ridge pole of your frame, lifting it up little by little. You will have no trouble getting it up and in place. Do not try to take it all aboard at once. A tarpaulin should come well down over the topsides and extend at least slightly below the waterline. Never lash the cover down too tightly; allow for shrinkage when the canvas is wet. If you fail to do this, the grommets will tear out before the winter is over. Before lacing up the flap, make certain that the ports, hatches, and locker doors are open to assure thorough ventilation of the hull.

Fitting-Out

When you start the spring fitting-out depends on three factors: how much work you plan to do, what amount of work you plan for the boatyard to do, and, of course, the weather. With the latter in mind, do not be in a rush to remove the winter cover completely. A great deal of the inside work can be done with it in place. When a portion of the cover is taken off to do a specific job, it should be replaced before nightfall or in the event of a shower. When the cover is completely taken off, make certain that it is thoroughly dry before you store it away. Gather up all the framework and be sure that it is correctly marked with the name of your boat so that it can be located easily in the fall. It should be stored in a location designated by the boatyard. If this is not done, the chances are you will never see it again.

Painting Your Boat. As soon as weather permits, check all painted and varnished surfaces carefully, from spar top to keel line, hosing down the exterior with fresh water. On cabin craft, assure as much as possible free circulation of air throughout the hull. Foul, stagnant air often promotes mold and mildew.

All cracked, blistered, peeled, or scaled paint should be removed thoroughly, with

particular attention to parts of the hull below the waterline. The secret is to get down to a good, sound surface before you even think about applying new coats of paint or varnish, for the final finish will be only as good as the substrate on which it is coated. Also be sure that all surfaces are free of dirt, grease, and oil. Sandpaper wood surfaces to remove imperfections and insure adhesion over old finishes. Remove rust from metal surfaces by sandpapering or wire brushing, and then wash the metal with mineral spirits, kerosene, or washing compound, and prime. Carefully calk all wood seams with non-hardening seam compound.

Once the surfaces are ready for refinishing, begin work at the top and work down for best results. Usual order is standing spars, cabin exteriors, cabin interiors, decks and deck equipment, topsides, bottom and finally, boot top—although if you are anxious to launch the boat, you can just as well start with the hull and then do the rest of the topside work once you have it in the water.

Since most paint products will not give good results if the temperature of the air is below 45 degrees or if the weather is damp, wait for a fairly warm, dry day before painting or varnishing. Use only the very best marine paints and varnishes; cheap paint will not stand up to marine use. Choose a well-known brand and follow the manufacturer's instructions.

Bare iron or steel surfaces should be primed with a good red-lead or zinc-chromate primer, which provides an excellent foundation for finish coats. On galvanized surfaces, use a primer formulated for use on that type of metal. Fast-drying, hard-surface alkyd enamels, available in many colors, in addition to white and black, make excellent long-wearing, weather-resistant topside finishes.

Hulls require extra care if the boat owner is to get not only the ultimate in protection but also a sleek, clean surface that provides a minimum of resistance or friction in the water and thereby contributes to the craft's speed. Where marine growths or algae are a problem, use an antifouling bottom paint, available in such attractive colors as bright blue, submarine copper bronze, red, green, copper red, and vinyl red.

One type of antifouling bottom paint is

formulated on the well-known eroding principle, which means that it sloughs off at a controlled rate to prevent the build-up of marine growths. A second type is based on a vinyl formulation that provides a tough, flexible film approaching that of hard racing bottom paints. Both types contain ingredients which keep active toxic materials on the paint surface in sufficient quantities to control marine growth effectively. Painting schedules should be arranged to meet manufacturer's requirements as to launch time.

Fiberglass bottoms, of course, require special treatment. Previously finished surfaces should be cleaned with a detergent or solvent wash and—if free from cracks, peeling, or other film failures—refinished with fiberglass primer. This is a fast-drying material which should be sanded before it reaches ultimate hardness—within 4 to 6 hours. Any of the antifouling bottom paints can then be applied over it.

If fiberglass is applied to an old hull, allow the plastic to cure for 5 to 7 days before applying any finish, then start with a fiberglass primer. Two or more coats of primer may be required to insure complete filling over nonuniform surfaces before the final antifouling paint is applied.

Vinyl bottom paint, incidentally, acts as its own primer on wood, and a minimum of two coats should be used on new surfaces, allowing 1 to 2 hours' drying between coats. On steel hulls, multiple coats of submarine zinc-chromate metal primer should be applied as a base for the vinyl bottom paint.

Not too many years ago there was only one type of varnish that was fit to be used on boats—spar varnish. Every boatyard had its own secret formula for thinning and heating the varnish before and during application, and a whole lore surrounding the way to put it on. Today most of that hocus-pocus has gone by the board because modern varnishes are compounded to be supertough and easy to apply. In fact, on most properly prepared surfaces, you cannot go far wrong if you just take off the lid and go to it. These new varnish formulas have ingredients to withstand sun, salt, and ultraviolet rays. Silicone resins give them greater ability to shed water, too.

Besides the more conventional new varnishes, most of which have a polyurethane base, you might want to use the really supertough epoxy resin varnish for those parts of your boat that take the most beating and soaking. Although these epoxies are all they claim to be, there is a string attached to their use—the wood has to be bare. And, you have to sand the old finish off. Varnish remover leaves a film of wax that will not let the epoxy varnish bond well. You cannot get the wax off with turpentine either. If you try to burn off the finish, oil from the old varnish soaks into the wood and you are in trouble again. So if you are going to use epoxy, prepare yourself for some extensive sanding.

No matter what kind of varnish you use, preparation of the surface is probably the most important step in the finishing process. If the finish on your spars, rudder, floorboards, etc., is in pretty good condition, you can probably get by with simply adding a coat or two to the existing finish. Start by washing everything to be refinished with a warm detergent solution. Rinse with clean water and let dry. If you have used any wax, wash it off with a rag liberally dampened with turpentine. As with the other paint finishing materials, be sure to apply varnish as directed by its manufacturer.

General Inspection. When going over the hull, examine all deck hardware such as chocks, bitts, cleats, winches, ringbolts, sheet travelers, stanchions, and fairleads; tighten all fastenings; free all scuppers and other water drains; check hatches; clean all brightwork and protect with polish applied as directed by the manufacturer; make sure all portholes and doors are in good condition; check ventilators; replace hardware as necessary; and clean all metal and protect with polish. Before yachts were equipped with the various electronic devices found aboard many modern sailboats, little difficulty was experienced with electrolytic action on propellers, shafts, struts, and hull fittings. Therefore, after hauling out your boat, check for any signs of electrolysis. If you do not find any, do not do anything other than to replace zinc plates that may have been eaten away. When replacing these plates, be sure that they are bonded to the strut, or other underwater fitting which they are installed to protect, with a copper strap or mounted on the fitting itself. On the other hand, should your boat show that she is affected by electrolytic action, then by all means have an expert at the boatyard attempt to find the trouble and take care of it. If neglected, electrolysis can cause great damage to underwater fittings and fastenings.

Speaking of electronic equipment: Tune, fix, and fit it out on your boat, by all means, but do not tinker and experiment beyond your technical proficiency or the capability of your tools. It is rather silly to play around with gear you know little about and then pay a professional to repair your own damage. Therefore, if you lack experience in electronic work, stick to simple service operations cited in the technical or owner's manuals. All other work should be done by professionals.

It is most important to check the steering tiller or wheel, cables, sheaves, and worm or quadrant. Examine pintles, gudgeons, linkage, and steering-gear fittings, and lubricate where necessary. Inspect rudder stock for wear and rudder blade for warpage. Connect up the plumbing, flush out the tanks, and fill them sufficiently to check your basin pumps and other fixtures. If you have the yard do this, give the order early in the spring so that the job can be completed before you give the interior the final touches and cleaning. Clean the galley, head, bunks, and lockers. Refinish any interior surfaces that need it. Restock the galley, and return all gear that you took off when laying her up.

Preparing the Engine. The auxiliary-engine work should also be completed as soon as possible. This is usually a dirty job; and the sooner it is finished, the better. Final checking and tuning up, of course, should not be done until after the boat is in the water. If you have stored the boat in a good boatyard, have the mechanic there check over your engine and let him decide what should be done to put the engine into top running condition. If you place limitations on the engine work to be done, that is all the mechanic will do, and you will have no grounds for complaint if your engine gives trouble during the season because other necessary work was not done.

Electrical System. Since the batteries were probably removed from the boat during winter layup, they should be checked with a hydrometer before being placed aboard. The hydrometer should indicate a fully charged

condition for each cell. If any cell has a low reading have your battery service station determine the source of trouble. Do not start the season with a poor battery. Storage batteries are expensive, but if given reasonable care during the period of use as well as during winter layup, they should last for several years. This is particularly true of standard brands that are designed for marine service.

Inspect main switch panel, and clean all terminals. Examine all wiring for worn insulation and replace if worn. Check all navigating lights, cabin lights, and all other electrical equipment, and if they do not operate properly, take the necessary action to make sure that they do.

Tuning the Rigging. Getting aluminum booms and masts ready to go is a lot easier than preparing wooden booms and masts, but they should get some attention. Aluminum is subject to oxidation and eventual pitting. To prevent this, give it a liberal coat of a good commercial automobile wax. But, if you have an anodized mast or boom, just wash it, wax it, and forget it. Heavy buffing with wire wool will just wear away the anodized finish. Any splits or dents should be very carefully checked, and if the mast is found unsound, it should be replaced. It usually is not a good idea to start the sailing season with defective masts or booms. Wooden masts and booms should be very carefully inspected, and painted or varnished as necessary. Apply either of these finishing materials as directed by the manufacturer.

After checking and refinishing of the spars is completed, inspect all rigging hardware to make sure that it is secure. Also look at sheaves and clevis pins for wear and replace if they show an appreciable amount of wear. Another piece of hardware that needs attention is the sail track. Besides seeing that it is solidly fastened, make sure all the joints are properly aligned and the whole track lubricated. A simple test is to shove a single slide from end to end. On masts up to 30-odd feet, it should make it with one shove. If it does, you can be sure of getting the sail down in a hurry when you really need to. When making any hardware replacements, never put bronze fittings on an aluminum spar. Use stainless steel or plastic.

If the rigging was marked when it was removed from the spar or if you are thoroughly familiar with the rigging, it will be an easy task to put it back on. Be sure you have not overlooked any cotter pins in the rigging, and make certain that the ends of the cotter pins are properly turned back to prevent tearing the sails. (Where pins come into direct contact with the sails, it is wise to cover them with tape.) Vertical clevis pins should have their heads on top so that if the cotter pin does work loose the pin will stay in by gravity. Screw-pin shackles aloft should be avoided. Inspect shrouds, lazy jacks, struts, stays, chain plates, spreaders, and topping lifts. All swaged fittings should be examined with the greatest of care, preferably with a magnifying glass. Any visible longitudinal fracture in the sleeve is cause to discard the shroud or stay. This may sound drastic, but wide experience has shown that once the sleeve has fractured, it is useless and the wire may pull out at any time. A good way to prevent splitting is to put a little epoxy glue around the neck of the sleeve so that water cannot run down inside and cause rust to split the fitting. The wire itself should be looked over and replaced if wear is found. The running rigging also deserves equal attention. Here the deficiencies are usually pretty obvious. Any line that appears in poor condition should be retired to a position of less responsibility, such as fender lines.

It is a good idea to do all this work before the mast is stepped. Also check the electric wiring to the spreader and masthead lights to be sure connections are tight and the bulbs are good. Make certain that the wind pennant and anemometer are installed before the mast is stepped. Check the turnbuckles to be sure they work freely. Actually, anything else that you can do to have everything in good shape and ready for the riggers will save them time, and will reduce the cost to you of stepping the spar. For example, once the spar is stepped and the shrouds are in place, make sure that the standing rigging is properly adjusted. In some boatyards, you can leave the problem of adjustment to the riggers, but it is a good idea to do it yourself, because you are probably more familiar with the amount of tension the shrouds should have. Whether you or the rigger makes the final adjustments, a general rule to follow is

that the uppers and intermediates should be fairly taut, and the lowers just tight enough to leave a little sag in the wire. The forestay should be quite taut so that headsails will not sag off to leeward. While adjusting the rigging, sight up along the sail track to be sure the mast is straight and set the shrouds accordingly. It is wise to tape over all cotter pins in the turnbuckles. Also, when putting in the mast wedges, do not drive them in hard; just a few taps of the mallet is sufficient. It is best to place as even a strain as possible on them all around the spar. More on tuning the rigging of racing sailboats can be found in Section IV.

Launching. When the day to go overboard arrives, arrange to be the last man below decks, to assure yourself that the bilge plugs are in and locked and that all sea cocks are closed. You should also board your boat promptly after she is waterborne, to look for leaks. If your job was well done, only a moderate seepage will appear, and that will soon stop. It will probably be necessary to take up on the new shaft packing from time to time.

After launching it is wise to allow a little time before stowing your gear and fitting out the accommodations. In this interval there is one vital job to be done carefully, precisely, and thoroughly. The gas tank and fuel line remain to be tested before the battery is in place. Fill the tank a little at a time and check each connection, each fitting, each gasket, and during the test—until you are convinced that the entire system is sound—permit no source of ignition near the boat. Here, more than in any part of your spring work, may your future hinge on conscientious attention to the most minute details.

When the engine has been tuned up and there is no further evidence of leaks beyond those which you have learned to expect, you can squeegee down any soiled paint, wash varnish, polish port lights and windows, get carpets, mattresses, curtains, and bedding aboard, and stow your new spare parts and personal gear. Before you set sail, make sure all safety gear is on board and is in good or operative condition. Check your ground tackle carefully; and examine your mooring, including anchor, chain, buoy, and pendant, before setting it in place. This should mark the finish of your labor, and the beginning of your fun.

If you started early enough and have planned well on the basis of a thorough preliminary survey, you should be afloat on schedule, weeks ahead of the improvident boat owner who turned out in the late spring with abundant energy but no organization. But one final word: After a shakedown cruise the chances are that the rigging will need retuning or readjustment. In fact, after sailing in any heavy blow, some checkup is necessary, even in well-stretched riggings. Actually the most important thing to remember about tuning your rigging in order to get the most out of your boat is that tuning rigging is a process that never ends. The framework that presents your sails to the breeze is just as critical as how you trim your sheets—perhaps more so.

Sail Care. The maintenance demands of modern sails are minimal. Soap and water is sufficient to remove most stains. Harsher chemicals may affect the sail finish and may even result in setting the stain. After washing, rinse with clean water by hose while the sails are hung loosely outdoors on a quiet day. If they become really bad or are too big to handle they should go to the sailmaker for a complete washing. Not only can a sail's shape be improved but also its life can be extended. While clean sails may make the boat go a little faster and will last a little longer, the psychological advantage of a new-looking sail is also worth something. Before you set a main or jib be sure the mast and boom and rigging have had a thorough going-over. Aluminum spars especially seem to pick up an oily dirt that is almost impossible to remove from Dacron. Wipe down shrouds and stays as well as the mast during the season and you will be astounded at the filth you take off. Also, if you always wash down decks as soon as you get aboard, your sails will stay whiter. Remember that oil and grease spots can be removed with most commercial cleaning fluids.

Two-, three-, and four-ounce Dacron as well as spinnaker nylon can be temporarily mended with spinnaker repair tape or white rigging tape. Pressed with the finger on both sides of a tear or open seam, the tape in most cases will hold until the sail can be taken to

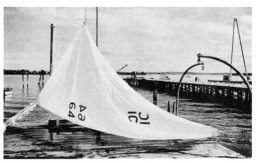

Steps to keep any sail in excellent condition: (*top*) Fresh-water rinse is good remedy for accumulation of salt. Residue of repeated salt-water exposure can increase abrasion within fabric and can attract moisture from air. Light scrubbing with water and detergent is preferred cleaning sequence. More rigorous methods, including use of solvent cleaners, should be avoided. (*bottom*) Accordion-type fold can limit excessive creasing during bagging and storage of sails, which can be more damaging than heavy use under sail. Excessive crushing and creasing can limit effectiveness of hard-finished fabrics.

be repaired. It is usually better to leave the sewing to an experienced machine operator or sailmaker so that no puckers or hard spots are sewn in. The cruising-boat owner cannot rely on repair tape except for spinnakers and other sails of spinnaker cloth. There are three basic sewing repairs that can be easily learned and applied with needles, a palm, Dacron thread, and some scraps of Dacron. The first is the overhand, or round, stitch for closing seams, darning very small holes, and repairing tears of about an inch. For a longer tear, but one not at a point of great tension, the herringbone stitch is excellent. The third possible repair is the patch. More permanent repairs should be made, in all three methods, later by sending the sail to the sailmaker.

Chafe is a problem common to everyone who uses sails. The stitching of a Dacron sail remains exposed and is susceptible to damage from any contact. How nice it was with cotton, where the thread could find protection in the soft fabric! The small-boat racers who have gone to grooved spars must continually check the headboard and clew for chafe. (The use of wax on the luff rope will probably help somewhat with this problem.) The shrouds take a toll on seam stitching every time the main is eased for a run. When track slides are used, the seizings normally do not last more than a season or two at most, and many sailmakers are now using small shackles. Headsails, especially the overlapping variety, show signs of chafe around the clew and lower leech after surprisingly few heavy-weather races because of contact with shrouds and mast on every tack.

The cruising-boat owner has all the chafe problems of the one-design racer and many more of his own. He does have the advantage of rigging rollers on his shrouds (too much windage for the little boat) to help his headsails around, but spinnaker-pole fittings and winches on the mast offset this help. He must also continually watch his jib hanks, especially the lowest one, as tremendous strain is exerted along the foot of big genoas. Chafing patches should be installed by your sailmaker where the genoa foot breaks over the lifelines, where it meets the shrouds, and also aloft on the leech where the spreader makes contact. Usually it is best to set the genoa and mark the areas that need to be protected before placing patches.

The fact than an ocean racer or coastwise cruiser might run before the wind for days rather than hours emphasizes the need to guard against chafe. A mainsail wearing on a spreader, lee shroud, or running backstay, or a slatting topping lift for this length of time is bound to be damaged. A boom vang will help to quiet the main and keep it off the spreader. The lift should be made of vinyl-covered wire. A number of systems are used for controlling the lift; one system is a combination double wheel that goes up the permanent backstay as the boom is eased. The use of a long piece of shock cord running from the lift to the tack area of the main is

another. With the latter it is necessary to change the shock cord to the windward side each time you tack, but the extra effort pays dividends in the long run. No boat owner can afford to wait until the end of the season to inspect his sails for chafe—it should be a constant routine.

It does sails no good to allow them to slat unnecessarily. Not only does slatting wear the stitching but it also weakens the cloth itself by causing the threads of which it is made to rub one against the other. Moreover, excessive slatting is likely to tear batten pockets which, in turn, may result in battens being lost or broken. If you must dry sails on a windy day, do not hoist them. Instead, spread them out on deck, loosely bunched so the air and sunshine can do their work. Two things you should avoid, however, with Dacron sails are extreme heat (like lighted cigarettes) and sharp creases.

Battens can also be a special headache to the offshore racing man, because Dacron is rougher than cotton. The stiffer material not only helps break wooden battens but it then lets the rough edges chafe through in short order. One method of overcoming this problem is to run white rigging or medical tape down both edges and then wrap the entire batten from one end to the other. The tape, besides keeping the batten from splintering, will act as a guard against chafe. Whether you tape your battens or not, it is a good idea to give them a couple of coats of varnish so that they will not pick up moisture and encourage mildew in the batten pockets. Most mildew found on Dacron sails has been in and around batten pockets, and was very likely caused when sails were furled without being dried after a sail in wet weather.

Both nylon and polyesters resist sunlight attack, but storage or covering is still advised after use. Even hulls of glass-reinforced plastic are affected if left exposed long enough. A sailmaker's advice to use a cover on a mainsail left furled on its boom should not be taken as an indication that modern sailcloth is sensitive to sunlight. But before leaving the subject of sails, it may be a good idea to say a word or two about sail bags and covers. As a rule, it is best to have them made of the same type of material as the sails. There are fabrics coated with impervious plastic or rubberlike coatings which look fine and are

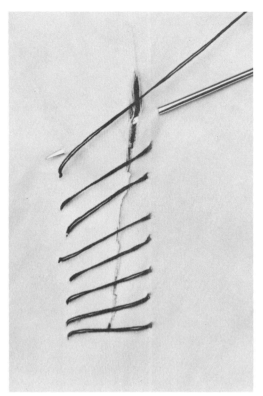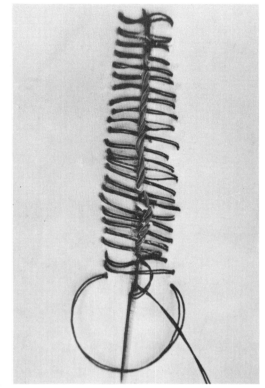

Sail repairs should be made by your sailmaker. Minor tears, however, can be temporarily repaired with thread of Dacron. The overhand stitch (left) is best for small tears and holes and for closing opened seams. Tears longer than one inch, but not at a point of great tension, can be repaired with herringbone stitch (right). On lighter sails of Dacron (under 4 ounces) a temporary repair can be made with spinnaker repair tape or white rigging tape. This will generally hold until the sail can be taken in for professional repair.

supposed to be—and doubtless are—waterproof. But these do not permit the air to circulate freely about a sail, with the result that mildew frequently appears. (Although mildew does modern sailcloth no harm, it makes it look bad.) The best bags and covers are those that are slightly porous so that the sails can breathe. Sail covers that do not fit too tightly are best. The closure used at the bottom should permit air to get in and circulate around the sail.

Midseason Care

Sailboat maintenance is a year-round job. Most of us give our boats the needed time in the fall to haul them up properly and during the winter and spring to fit them out in the best possible way. This is all good. However, all too many of us think that the summer is for sailing only and drop all maintenance work. For instance, you should check all rope and wire splices, spinnaker halyard, spin-

naker guys, main and jibsheets. All wire rigging should be examined for broken strands and fatigue, especially where the wire passes over sheaves. If strands fly out when the wire is bent, the wire probably needs replacing. If it looks rusty, it may not require replacing at once but should be inspected frequently. The rigging and the wire halyards should be run through a greasy rag occasionally, but not too much grease should be used for the grease will be transferred to the sails. Wire rope can also be protected by finishing it with aluminum paint that has been thinned with turpentine and linseed oil. The linseed oil penetrates to lubricate the rope internally. Oil all blocks occasionally to insure that the sheets run freely. Much of the material covered earlier in the chapter deals with points that must be constantly checked. For care and maintenance during the sailing season itself is just as important as that given during the fall layup and spring fitting-out.

SECTION VI

The Lure of Racing

Racing is sailing at its most critical. Actually it requires more pure sailing skill and nerve than any other branch of the sport, and if you can prove yourself able to hold your own as a racing skipper, you can with confidence undertake any other kind of sailing. In fact, almost everyone who sails has thought at one time or another of racing just to test himself against the other fellow. While you may get your boat for the fun of sailing, for the quiet relaxation, and for the satisfaction of going places propelled by the wind alone, you—often to your own surprise—find yourself drawn into racing.

There are various types of races, and a sailor who might be a champ on an inshore-course race event may be a chump in an offshore distance contest where basic seamanship and navigation are much more vital. Really, one of the many wonderful lures of sailboat racing is that there is a race to suit the taste of every sailor. There are races for male and female, young and old, summer and winter. The boats, as stated earlier, vary in size and style. For example, the Yacht Racing Association of Long Island Sound schedules regular races for more than thirty-six different types of sailing craft, while the Narragansett Bay area has well over thirty. But regardless of the many types of hulls, there are two major classifications of racing in which a group of sailboats race against each other as individuals (not as a team):

Class-boat racing—between boats of the same class, racing on even terms. In this boat-for-boat race between nearly identical craft, the boat with the fastest elapsed time from start to finish, or the first boat over the finish line, wins the race.

Handicap racing—between boats of different types handicapped by some type of time-allowance system to make all boats as evenly matched as possible. With the resulting handicap rating, sloops, cutters, yawls, ketches, and schooners are able to compete evenly against each other regardless of size. That is, the winning boat is the one with the best corrected time, or the best time for sailing the course after handicap corrections have been made.

CLASS-BOAT RACING

Class-boat racing is by far the most popular in the United States. There are races of this type on almost every sound, bay, lake, and river on the North American continent.

Sailing Instructions

The sailing instructions in the race circular and the advertisement of the race, if one is made, may contain valuable information that should be studied, especially when the race is being sailed at an unfamiliar location. These sailing instructions, prepared in writing by the race committee, include the following matters: the starting signals and their scheduled times; starting line; finish line; and the order in which the turning marks of each course are to be passed and the side on which each mark is to be passed, with a de-

scription of each mark. The instructions also cover such of the following matters as may be appropriate: the date and place of the races; the classes to race; possible courses; eligibility and entry requirements; measurement certificates; the signals used to designate courses other than the only prescribed or regular course; any government buoys or other objects required to be passed on a specified side; whether buoys will bound the

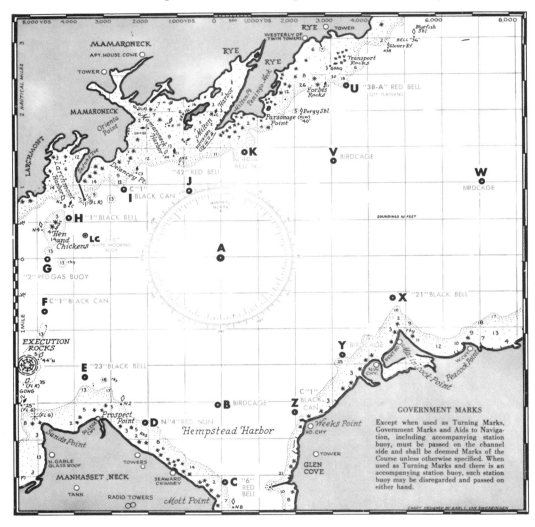

SPECIAL Y.R.A. MARKS

* A YRA Birdcage Starting Buoy, 2060 yards from Scotch Caps Red Bell "42" on a line to Weeks Point Black Can C "1."

* Equipped with radar reflector.

B YRA Hempstead Birdcage (284° Mag. from HO CHY, Weeks Point, 2600 yrds.).

V YRA Birdcage off Parsonage Point (168° Mag. from Westerly of Twin Towers, Rye, 3500 yards).

* W YRA Cage on a line from Starting Mark "A" and halfway to Whistle Buoy "32-A" (131° Mag. from Westerly of Twin Towers, Rye, 6200 yards).

Y YRA Birdcage on a line halfway between "X" and "Z."

A well-prepared set of sailing instructions as they appear in a typical race circular.

SIGNAL SHAPES

ON STATION AT START
3 Red Cylinders

RECALL SIGNAL
(White Cylinder with red Band) with 1 blast of horn for each yacht recalled.

ON STATION AT FINISH
3 Blue Cylinders

SPECIAL CODE FLAGS

GENERAL RECALL SIGNAL
(First Repeater and 2 guns) Entire Class recalled for fresh Start on next signal.

COURSE CHANGE
(Code Flag "L" and 2 guns or horns) Signal will be displayed until the Division affected has started. A Course Change for any Class cannot be made after the Warning Gun for that Class.

MISSING MARK SIGNAL
(Code Flag "M") When displayed on temporary Mark or launch, means round this instead of Mark originally signalled.

CHANGING LINE
(Code Flag "Q") Waved on a mobile staff indicates change of angle and/or length of Starting or Finishing line.

SHORTENED COURSE
(Code Flag "S" and 2 guns) May be used only at last Mark of Course originally signalled.

LIFE JACKETS
When Code Flag "D" (yellow and blue bars) is displayed with two guns or horns, skippers and crews of all Classes starting while the signal remains displayed shall wear vest-type non-inflatable life jackets throughout the race.

POSTPONEMENT AND CANCELLATIONS

POSTPONEMENT
(Answering Pennant and 2 guns) All Classes not started are postponed for intervals of 5 minutes. The next signal shall be the Warning for the Class that would have started if there had been no Postponement.

CANCELLATION
(Code Flag "N" over First Repeater and 3 guns) All Classes not started cancelled.
(Code "N" placard under Division numeral) Division cancelled.

ABANDONMENT
(Code Flag "N" and 3 guns) All Classes including those already started abandoned.

STARTING TIMES

	TIME — P.M.	CLASS	SIGNAL CYLINDERS
WARNING	1:20		1 Yellow
PREPARATORY	1:25		1 Blue
DIVISION I	1:30	Etchells 22	1 Red
	1:35	International	2 Yellow
	1:40	Shields	2 Blue
	1:45	210	2 Red
	1:50	"S"	1 Yellow
	1:55	Soling	1 Blue
DIVISION II	2:00	Tempest, Star	1 Red
DIVISION III	2:05	Ensign	2 Yellow
	2:10	Rhodes 19	2 Blue
	2:15	Rainbow, Triton, Electra, Ariel Commander, Rhodes 18, Day Sailer, All Other Classes	2 Red
DIVISION IV	2:20	Lightning	1 Yellow

NO RACE 3:00 P.M. Unless the initial Warning Signal is made at or before 3:00 P.M., all races for that day are cancelled.

TIME LIMIT 5:30 P.M. The Finish of one yacht in a Class by this time constitutes a race for that Class.

LIFE JACKETS: It is the responsibility of skippers and crews in all Classes to wear vest-type non-inflatable life jackets whenever conditions warrant whether or not Code Flag "D" is displayed.

POSTPONED TIME LIMIT 6:00 P.M. For any Class that has had a Postponed Start.

After the first Preparatory Signal, all Classes must keep completely clear of the Starting line until their own Preparatory Signal. The penalty can be disqualification.

Yachts must not cross Starting and/or Finishing Line between yellow flag on Committee Boat and adjacent mark or buoy except when maneuvering for a start or starting or when finishing and clearing the course.

Yachts withdrawing or abandoning the race should report to the Race Committee without crossing the Finish Line or to the Clubhouse by telephone.

COURSE SIGNALS

Normally courses will be signalled as shown at right 10 minutes before start of that Division.

Courses may consist of 1, 2 or more Government, YRA or Special Marks.

I	II	III	IV
D	D	D	
F	J	½ K	
J	K		
K			

If shorter legs are indicated, the Committee Boat or Launch may place special turning marker on a line between Start and any one of the above Government or YRA Marks. Special turning marker will be flagged with the Code Flag of the letter assigned to that Mark. The Committee Boat will signal such Marks, i.e.:

½ K — means Special Mark will be at approximately ½ the distance from start to "K."

All Marks signalled must be left on the same hand as starting mark. Upon finishing, a yacht must cross finish line from direction of preceding mark.

RACING RULES

The RACING RULES OF THE NAYRU, 1969, shall apply except as modified herein and by the Y.R.A. Championship Rules (see Year Book). In addition all Classes must conform to their own Class Rules as filed with the Y.R.A.

MODIFICATIONS

4 — Signals — 8.2(b) — Start after General Recall (see inside).

25.1 & 2   — Sail Nos., Letters & Emblems: "Class Rules, as filed with the YRA of LIS shall take precedence."

68.3   — Protests: Modified as below. 77 — Appeals procedure: See below.

PROTESTS

A protest should be hailed to the Race Committee after finishing and must be put in writing to the Race Committee involved, according to the NAYRU Rules, and postmarked or delivered no later than the first weekday following the Race. NAYRU Standard Protest Form should be used. The protest will be disallowed unless the protestor contacts the Race Committee within one week following filing of the protest to arrange a hearing.

APPEALS

Decisions involving solely the interpretations of the Racing Rules by the Race Committee first hearing the Protest may be appealed within 10 days of the announcement from that Race Committee of its decision. Such Appeal must be in writing on the Standard Protest Form, or in the form thereof, accompanied by a deposit of $25.00 and filed with the APPEALS COMMITTEE, YACHT RACING ASSOCIATION OF L.I.S.

ABANDONING THE RACE

In heavy weather conditions yachts abandoning the race shall report as soon as possible either to the Committee Boat or by telephone — see front page for Yacht Club number.

COX-SPRAGUE SCORING SYSTEM
as recommended by Y.R.A. of L.I.S.

No. of Starters →	2	3	4	5	6	7	8	9	10	11	12	13	14	15	16	17	18	19	20 or More	Place
	10	31	43	52	60	66	72	76	80	84	87	90	92	94	96	97	98	99	100	1
	4	25	37	46	54	60	66	70	74	78	81	84	86	88	90	91	92	93	94	2
	(0)	21	33	42	50	56	62	66	70	74	77	80	82	84	86	87	88	89	90	3
		(17)	29	38	46	52	58	62	66	70	73	76	78	80	82	83	84	85	86	4
			(26)	35	43	49	55	59	63	67	70	73	75	77	79	80	81	82	83	5
				(32)	40	46	52	56	60	64	67	70	72	74	76	77	78	79	80	6
					(38)	44	50	54	58	62	65	68	70	72	74	75	76	77	78	7
						(42)	48	52	56	60	63	66	68	70	72	73	74	75	76	8
							(46)	50	54	58	61	64	66	68	70	71	72	73	74	9
								(48)	52	56	59	62	64	66	68	69	70	71	72	10
									(50)	54	57	60	62	64	66	67	68	69	70	11
										(52)	55	58	60	62	64	65	66	67	68	12
											(53)	56	58	60	62	63	64	65	66	13
												(55)	57	59	61	62	63	64	65	14
													(56)	58	60	61	62	63	64	15
														(57)	59	60	61	62	63	16
															(58)	59	60	61	62	17
																(58)	59	60	61	18
																	(58)	59	60	19
																		(58)	59	20

Pts in ( ) are for DNF & Disq.

Place	Pts.		Place	Pts.		Place	Pts.
21	58		31	48		41	38
22	57		32	47		42	37
23	56		33	46		43	36
24	55		34	45		etc.	etc.
25	54		35	44			
26	53		36	43			
27	52		37	42			
28	51		38	41			
29	50		39	40			
30	49		40	39			

For additional information, other YRA schedules, scores, Bay Racing activity, Distance schedules, etc. Phone or Write

Yacht Racing Association of Long Island Sound

37 West 44th Street, New York, N. Y. 10036 • 212 MU 2-3284

starting area (if so, they do not rank as marks); special method of recall; time allowance; special time limit; prizes; the scoring system; special time limit for protests; and any special provisions and signals. These written instructions make it possible for you to form a mental picture of the race course and to lay racing plans in advance.

Racing Courses

What is a course for a yacht race? In its barest essentials it is a start, a place to go, and a finish. The start is usually a line to be crossed, although occasionally the start is made with the yachts at their moorings or anchored. The place to go is sometimes, as in some ocean races, nothing more than a statement about the finish, in which case the only marks may be the marks of the starting and finishing lines. In most cases, however, there are from one to half a dozen or more marks which yachts are required to round, thereby establishing a minimum distance which each yacht must sail. Complete freedom to sail wherever there is water is frequently restricted, usually but not always for safety reasons, by designating additional marks which must be passed on a stated side. And finally the finish, like the usual start, always seems to be a line to be crossed, although in rare circumstances it may be only one point.

As a rule, there are two basic types of courses: the closed course and the point-to-point course. The latter is from one geographic location to another and is generally used in distance or offshore handicap events. This type of racing may turn out to be a run, reach, or beat the entire length, or it may be some combination of these points of sailing depending on the wind direction with respect to the particular course. The closed course, on the other hand, has its start and finish in the same or approximately the same location and is deliberately planned to have a variety of points of sailing, and at least one beating leg is considered essential.

While a few class or one-design races are run from one geographic point to another, the majority of regattas are held on closed courses that are windward-leeward, triangular, or some combination of the two. The former has

its first leg a near dead beat to a windward turning mark and then a run back to the starting point. Some windward-leeward courses have an initial short windward leg to the mark, then a long run to another mark to leeward of the starting line, and finally a short beat back to the starting area which then becomes the finish line.

In the conventional triangular course, the arrangement is such that three major marks are employed to make each leg of the course the side of a triangle. This course is a good test of skill since it requires sailing to windward, reaching, and sailing before the wind. Boats start the race by crossing the line between a white flag on the committee boat or station and the starting mark, and they finish by crossing a line formed by a white flag on the committee boat or station and the starting mark. Generally the race course is so arranged that the first leg requires a beat to windward. This spreads the boats out a little and minimizes, to some degree, traffic jams at the first mark. Some courses are twice around the triangle.

A popular course is the so-called Gold Cup course, which is a windward-leeward followed by a triangle. In class national championship the "modified" Gold Cup course is often used. This also consists of five legs, with the starting and finishing at the same mark. The first three legs are generally around a triangle, starting with a windward leg followed by two reaching legs; the fourth leg is usually a repetition of the first leg to windward; while the fifth leg is a return downwind to the finish line at the starting mark.

Another course frequently employed is the Olympic one, which is a triangle followed by a windward-leeward course with an extra windward leg. There are a few other course arrangements employed by race committees —generally based on local factors—but usually a course is announced in two parts. Sometimes the notice of the race or the sailing instructions announces a single course, but usually the sailing instructions provide for several courses and then on race day the race committee selects and announces one of them for that particular day.

Establishment of a Racing Course. Generally, there are four bases for the establishment of yacht-racing courses:

WINDWARD-LEEWARD COURSES

TRIANGULAR COURSE

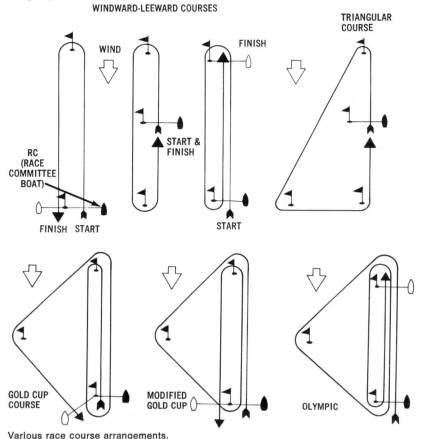

Various race course arrangements.

1. Government marks (buoys, beacons, lighthouses, lightships).
2. Permanently moored, or located, club marks.
3. Combinations of government and private marks.
4. Temporary marks located in position especially for a specific race.

Under the first three classifications, two types of courses as just stated are usually possible:

1. Prearranged or preselected courses arbitrarily laid out from different combinations of marks properly identified on the racing instructions by assigned letters of the alphabet. The course combinations carry numbers.
2. Flexible courses using the same buoys in varying combinations depending upon the whims of the weather, the committee, or both.

When temporary marks are set out (tall, moored flag stakes, or inflatable rings and pylons in the new high-visibility colors are best), their locations are indicated by flag hoists giving compass directions to the first mark, from there to the second, and thence home—assuming the course is triangular; if it is windward-leeward, the direction of the first mark should suffice.

Actually, as referred to in the rules of racing, there are three kinds of marks—line marks, rounding marks, and guide marks. Each has a distinct function. Line marks establish the ends of the starting and finishing lines. Rounding marks determine the minimum distance a yacht must sail. Guide marks restrict the area available to the yachts. In setting up courses in the sailing instructions, it will minimize problems to deal with each type of mark separately.

The starting and finishing lines need only a brief reference. It is sufficient to designate clearly their general location and the marks which establish them.

In establishing what is ordinarily thought of as the course—the minimum required distance, determined by the rounding marks—it is important, as indicated above, to treat the rounding marks by themselves (whether selective or fixed courses are used) and then to deal with guide marks separately. With selective courses it is usual to list first all rounding, turning, or course marks (or just marks—whichever phrase is customary locally) and then follow with a paragraph about guide marks. If, as is common, some guide marks are also occasionally used as rounding marks, confusion is avoided by starting the guide-mark instructions with the phrase "except when designated as rounding marks [for example] all government marks shall be passed on the channel side."

This same separate treatment can be used to advantage with fixed courses. If, however, it is deemed desirable to include the pertinent guide marks in the description of each fixed course, it is still important to treat them separately. To use a simple course for illustration, suppose Course A goes north to mark X and returns, with dangerous rocks, marked by Nun 4, lying off the shore to the west. If course A is designated as "Nun 4(P), X(P), Nun 4(S)" (P = port; S = starboard), there is nothing in the sailing instructions to indicate whether Nun 4 is a guide mark or is to be rounded twice—in fact, the implication is the latter, since it is referred to twice in the same manner as what is obviously a rounding mark. However, if Course A is designated as "X(P) . . . on both legs leave Nun 4 to seaward," it is clear that Nun 4 is a guide mark.

Should you ever have anything to do with the arrangement of a course, remember that the most successful sailboat races are sailed for the benefit of the skippers. It is one sport in which the spectator is not considered, and a great many of the biggest regattas are held away from shore solely with the idea of making the race a fair test of skill and not a matter of knowing all the little slants and vagaries of wind and current along the shore. Sailboat races are to be won by fair sailing and superior seamanship, and the idea is to give the contestants every possible chance at fair sailing.

Scoring Yacht Races

Yacht racing is a curious sport. There is *no* single method of "keeping score" accepted by all the "players."

The purpose of any scoring system is to provide a race committee with an accepted and fair procedure for selecting the winner of a series of yacht races. The fairness of these procedures is not usually questioned until two different systems are found which would result in the selection of different winners from the same set of race results. The problem that must then be considered by the race committee is one of determining which, if any, of the possible scoring systems is "fair" in that its use will result in the selection of the best skipper as the first-place trophy winner. Of course, if every race were a complete contest in itself, there would be no need for complicated scoring systems (and some are really complicated). But because every race is not important enough to carry a prize, a system of scoring must be devised by which the award goes to the boat with the best performance over a series of races running perhaps over a weekend, or a week, or even over the entire season. The placings are determined according to the total number of points earned by each boat during a series of races. Let us take a look at some of the more common scoring systems.

Low-point System. Boats get the number of points in each race corresponding to their finishing position. For example, a boat will receive 1 point for first place, 2 points for second place, 3 points for third place, etc. All boats not finishing a race (d.n.f.) receive points equaling the number of boats starting the race plus 1; if disqualified (d.s.q.), plus 2. The series winner is the boat with the lowest number of points.

High-point System. Points for a race are awarded on the basis of 1 point for finishing and 1 point for each yacht defeated; also, ¼ point additional is given for first place. The basis for point award is the total number of registered entries. The entry with the greatest total points is the winner of the series. In the case of a dead heat, each boat receives the number of points normally awarded to the higher finishing positions. A boat that does not finish a race or a contestant who is disqualified receives no points whatsoever for the race.

New Olympic Scoring System. This system, which was first used in the 1968 Olympic Games, is as follows:

There are seven races for each class, of which the best six for each yacht are counted for her total points. Any yacht which does not start or which starts within the meaning of the rules and does not finish or any yacht which commits a breach of the rules but retires within reasonable time receives points for a last-place finish, that is to say, for the finishing place equal to the number of yachts entered in her class. Any yacht which commits a breach of the rules but fails to retire within reasonable time or is disqualified pursuant to the provisions of international racing Rule 72 or 73 (see below) scores four points more than for a last-place finish.

Each yacht scores points in each race as follows:

First place	0
Second place	3
Third place	5.7
Fourth place	8
Fifth place	10
Sixth place	11.7
Seventh place and thereafter	The place plus six

Lowest total score wins.

When the international jury (i.e., judges or race committee) decides that a yacht is entitled to the relief granted by Rule 12, *Yacht Unduly Prejudiced,* an equitable arrangement may be deemed to be the awarding to the yacht whose finishing position has been materially prejudiced of points for that race equal to the average points, to the nearest tenth of a point, of her best five races.

In the event of a tie on total points between two or more yachts, the tie is broken in favor of the yacht or yachts with the most first places, and if any such yachts remain tied, the most second places and so on, if necessary, for the six races which count for total points. If this method fails to resolve the tie, the tie stands as the final placings of the series.

Old Olympic Scoring System. This system, which was employed in Olympic Games before 1968, underscored stellar performances rather than consistent placing. The bonuses in points for placing at or near the top are a constant incentive to place well rather than be satisfied with a modest but consistent performance. Furthermore, the added advantage of being scored only on the best six of one's seven races makes for a more lively contest for the top placers. Only after suffering a very poor score in one race will a promising competitor begin to become slightly conservative, and even then he must place near the top of the fleet in order to accumulate a substantial score.

An indication of how the scoring works can be gained from the following two examples:

I. *In a 40-boat fleet*	II. *In a 20-boat fleet*
1703—First	1402—First
1402—Second	1101—Second
1226—Third	925—Third
1101—Fourth	800—Fourth
1004—Fifth	703—Fifth
703—Tenth	402—Tenth
527—Fifteenth	226—Fifteenth
402—Twentieth	101—Twentieth
305—Twenty-fifth	
226—Thirtieth	
153—Thirty-fifth	
101—Fortieth	

The scoring formula is: 101 plus 1,000 log A minus 1,000 log N, where A equals the total number of yachts starting in the race, and N equals the yacht's finishing position. Any yacht disqualified receives no points. Yachts which retire and do not finish each receive the points for the last boat in the class, calculated on the basis of the number of starters. In the event of a tie of points between two or more yachts, the number of times each tied yacht has beaten the other tied yacht shall decide. If still equal, the highest number of the highest placing prevails. Should neither of these methods resolve the tie, then the tied yachts sail a deciding race.

While this so-called "curve" system—the *new* Olympic, high-point and low-point systems are known as "straight-line," or premium, systems—is no longer employed in the Olympics, it is used by several racing associations.

Snipe Scoring System. Some one-design

Many big associations, such as the Snipe class shown, have their own scoring rules.

class associations, such as the International Snipe Class Racing Association, have their own scoring methods. In the Snipe system—which allows competition between Snipe owners of different clubs even though these clubs do not actually race against one another—points are awarded to the boats according to the order in which they finish, irrespective of the number of boats in the race. But, for a race to count in this curve scoring system, there must be at least five boats taking part and the course must be at least 2½ miles long. In order to encourage skippers to race as often as possible, a bonus of 10 points per race up to fifteen races is added to the average score. But to equalize things between clubs with long racing seasons and those with short ones, the scores are averaged. In the following table the left-hand column in each case represents the finish place of the boat and the right-hand column the points awarded. A

boat that does not finish or is disqualified for a rule infraction is given the points for last place. Thus, if there are seven boats in a race and one fails to finish, it will receive the points for seventh place. In a race for seven boats, if three fail to finish or are disqualified, all three get seventh-place points. Boats that fail to finish or are disqualified receive the 10-point bonus.

1.	1,600	11.	900	21.	400	31.	100
2.	1,521	12.	841	22.	361	32.	81
3.	1,444	13.	784	23.	324	33.	64
4.	1,369	14.	729	24.	289	34.	49
5.	1,296	15.	676	25.	256	35.	36
6.	1,225	16.	625	26.	225	36.	25
7.	1,156	17.	576	27.	196	37.	16
8.	1,089	18.	529	28.	169	38.	9
9.	1,024	19.	484	29.	144	39.	4
10.	961	20.	441	30.	121	40.	1

The following example shows how the points are determined:

Boat No. 000

May	30:	Fourth place	1,369	10 bonus
June	4:	Second place	1,521	10 bonus
June	18:	Third place	1,444	10 bonus
July	2:	First place	1,600	10 bonus
July	4:	First place	1,600	10 bonus
July	16:	Fourth place	1,369	10 bonus
July	22:	First place	1,600	10 bonus
			10,503 (total points)	70 (total bonus)

Divided by 7 (number of races) = average 1,500.4
Total average points = 1,570.4

Let us assume that the skipper and his boat race the rest of the season and take part in twenty events with a total point count of 28,549. This sum is then divided by 20 to give a season's average of 1,427.4 points. To find the season's total average points, add 150 (10 bonus points for each race up to 15) and we have 1,577.4 points.

There are several other scoring systems plus many variations employed by different yacht clubs and class associations. Each system is designed to reward slightly different types of excellence. One may place greater emphasis on consistency, another may permit dropping out the poorest race of a given series, or a d.n.f. or d.s.q. may be penalized more in one system than another. Of course, when racing, you must follow the scoring system designated by the sponsor or the one-design class in which you sail.

Yacht Racing Rules

To oversimplify, yacht racing rules are framed with two objectives: *safety* and *sportsmanship.* We say this is an oversimplification because it takes a lot of study and years of experience to really understand this complex body of law of the sport; that is, to become a real authority.

The full set of Racing Rules of the International Yacht Racing Union (IYRU) as adopted by the North American Yacht Racing Union (NAYRU) are given here in this section. No changes in these rules are contemplated until 1973. Actually, the IYRU rules permit certain changes and additions by national authorities. In order to assist North American yachtsmen when racing abroad and visiting yachtsmen when racing here, rules so changed or added have been identified by placing a star (☆) in the margin beside them.

The IYRU rules are divided into six parts. It is most important to become very familiar with the sailing rules in Part IV. A beginner should read through all the easy rules several times and then concentrate on Part IV one rule at a time. Get thoroughly familiar with the basic rules in Part IV before going on to the others in detail. But keep in mind that the rules of Part IV do *not* apply in any way to a vessel which is neither intending to race nor racing; such vessel shall be treated in accordance with the International Regulations for Preventing Collisions at Sea or Government Right-of-Way Rules (see Section IV) applicable in the area concerned. Also remember that in translating and interpreting *all* IYRU racing rules, it shall be understood that the word "shall" is mandatory, whereas the word "should" is directive and not mandatory, and the words "can" and "may" are permissive.

While the complete set of NAYRU Racing Rules appear here, specific *class* racing rules may be obtained from the secretary of the class.

1969 CHANGES

As in 1965, the 1969 rules include a good many small changes for consistency and better understanding.

The most important changes of substance are in rule 40 and the related new rules 45 and 52.1. Also new are rules 42.3(b), 42.3(e)(ii), 51.1(c), 65 and 66.

Some less important changes of substance are to be found in the definition of Clear Astern and Clear Ahead; Overlap and in rules 35, 42.1(b), 43.1, 53.2 and 62.

Race Committees may be interested in noting among other things the changes in signals (particularly L, N over X and N over 1st Repeater) and in rules 4.4(d), 8.2(a), 72.1 and 73.2 ("orally") and the omission of former rule 28.

N·A·Y·R·U

THE
YACHT RACING RULES
INCLUDING
TEAM RACING RULES
OF THE
INTERNATIONAL YACHT
RACING UNION
AS ADOPTED BY THE
NORTH AMERICAN
YACHT RACING UNION
1969

(No changes contemplated until 1973)

NORTH AMERICAN YACHT RACING UNION
37 WEST 44TH STREET   NEW YORK, N.Y. 10036

FOREWORD

Effective April 1, 1969, the North American Yacht Racing Union has adopted as its official racing rules the racing rules, including the team racing rules, of the International Yacht Racing Union. No changes are contemplated until 1973.

The I.Y.R.U. rules permit certain changes and additions by national authorities. In order to assist North American yachtsmen when racing abroad and visiting yachtsmen when racing here, rules so changed or added have been identified by placing a star (☆) in the margin beside them.

Of the twenty-four rules listed in this paragraph the following eight rules have been changed by the N.A.Y.R.U. and have been starred (☆) except rule 72.4 which has been deleted. The I.Y.R.U. text of these rules is given in Appendix III.

4.1 "AP", 8.1, 18, 25.2, 28, 72.4, 77, 78.

The following sixteen rules have not been changed by the N.A.Y.R.U. other than to be printed without the phrase "unless otherwise prescribed (or if so prescribed) by the national authority" or words to that effect:

1.4, 2(j), 3.1, 3.2(b)(xvi), 4.2, 4.4(a), 8.2(a)(ii), 8.2(b), 10, 23, 24, 52.1, 54.2, 56, 57, 62.

All the above twenty-four rules should be checked for differences when sailing under the jurisdiction of another national authority.

The following four starred (☆) rules have been added by

---

the N.A.Y.R.U. on matters not covered by I.Y.R.U. rules: 21A, 51.6, 53.2, 55A.

North American yachtsmen will find the above information of significance to them only when racing under the jurisdiction of another national authority. For racing under the jurisdiction of the N.A.Y.R.U. the starred (☆) rules are to be treated like any other rules.

TABLE OF CONTENTS

Rule
63 Anchoring and Making Fast
64 Aground or Foul of an Obstruction
65 Skin Friction
66 Increasing Stability

Part VI—PROTESTS, DISQUALIFICATIONS AND APPEALS
68 Protests
69 Refusal of a Protest
70 Hearings
71 Decisions
72 Disqualification after Protest
73 Disqualification without Protest
74 Penalties for Gross Infringement of Rules

Rule
75 Persons Interested not to take part in Decision
76 Expenses Incurred by Protest
77 Appeals

TEAM RACING RULES
Appendix I—Amateur
Appendix II—"Pumping" Sails, "Ooching" and "Rocking"
Appendix III—I.Y.R.U. Rules before changes prescribed by the N.A.Y.R.U.
Appendix IV—International Rules of the Road
Protest Committee Procedure

PART I
DEFINITIONS

*When a term defined in Part I is used in its defined sense it is printed in **bold** type. All definitions and italicized notes rank as rules.*

Racing—A yacht is **racing** from her preparatory signal until she has either **finished** and cleared the finishing line and finishing **marks** or retired, or until the race has been **cancelled**, **postponed** or **abandoned**, except that in match or team races, the sailing instructions may prescribe that a yacht is **racing** from any specified time before the preparatory signal.

Starting—A yacht **starts** when, after her starting signal, any part of her hull, crew or equipment first crosses the starting line in the direction of the first mark.

Finishing—A yacht **finishes** when any part of her hull, or of her crew or equipment in normal position, crosses the finishing line from the direction of the last mark.

Luffing—Altering course towards the wind until head to wind.

Tacking—A yacht is **tacking** from the moment she is beyond head to wind until she has **borne away**, if beating to windward, to a **close-hauled** course; if not beating to windward, to the course on which her mainsail has filled.

Bearing Away—Altering course away from the wind until a yacht begins to **jibe**.

Jibing—A yacht begins to **jibe** at the moment when, with the wind aft, the foot of her mainsail crosses her centre line and completes the **jibe** when the mainsail has filled on the other **tack.**

On a Tack—A yacht is **on a tack** except when she is **tacking** or **jibing**. A yacht is on the **tack** (**starboard** or **port**) corresponding to her **windward** side.

Close-hauled—A yacht is **close-hauled** when sailing by the wind as close as she can lie with advantage in working to windward.

Clear Astern and **Clear Ahead**; **Overlap**—A yacht is **clear astern** of another when her hull and equipment in normal position are abaft an imaginary line projected abeam from the aftermost point of the other's hull and equipment in normal position. The other yacht is **clear ahead**. The yachts **overlap** if neither is **clear astern**; or if, although one is **clear astern**, an intervening yacht **overlaps** both of them. The terms **clear astern**, **clear ahead** and **overlap** apply to yachts on opposite **tacks** only when they are subject to rule 42, Rounding or Passing Marks and Obstructions.

Leeward and Windward—The **leeward** side of a yacht is that on which she is, or, if **luffing** head to wind, was, carrying her mainsail. The opposite side is the **windward** side.

When neither of two yachts on the same **tack** is **clear astern**, the one on the **leeward** side of the other is the **leeward yacht**. The other is the **windward yacht**.

Proper course—A **proper course** is any course which a yacht might sail after the starting signal, in the absence of the other yacht or yachts affected, to **finish** as quickly as possible. The course sailed before **luffing** or **bearing away** is presumably, but not necessarily, that yacht's **proper course**. There is no **proper course** before the starting signal.

Mark—A **mark** is any object specified in the sailing instructions which a yacht must round or pass on a required side.

Obstruction—An **obstruction** is any object, including craft under way, large enough to require a yacht, if not less than one overall length away from it, to make a substantial alteration of course to pass on one side or the other, or any object which can be passed on one side only, including a buoy when the yacht in question cannot safely pass between it and the shoal or object which it marks.

Cancellation—A **cancelled** race is one which the race committee decides will not be sailed thereafter.

Postponement—A **postponed** race is one which is not started at its scheduled time and which can be sailed at any time the race committee may decide.

Abandonment—An **abandoned** race is one which the race committee declares void at any time after the starting signal, and which can be re-sailed at its discretion.

PART II
MANAGEMENT OF RACES
Authority and Duties of Race Committee

The rules of Part II deal with the duties and responsibilities of the race committee in conducting a race, the meaning of signals made by it and of other actions taken by it.

1—General Authority of Race Committee and Judges

1. All races shall be arranged, conducted and judged by a race committee under the direction of the sponsoring organization, except as may be provided under rule 1.2. The race committee may delegate the conduct of a race, the hearing and deciding of protests or any other of its responsibilities to one or more sub-committees which, if appointed, will hereinafter be included in the term "race committee" wherever it is used.

2. For a special regatta or series, the sponsoring organization may provide for a jury or judges to hear and decide protests and to have supervision over the conduct of the races, in which case the race committee shall be subject to the direction of the jury or judges to the extent provided by the sponsoring organization.

3. All yachts entered or **racing** shall be subject to the direction and control of the race committee, but it shall be the sole responsibility of each yacht to decide whether or not to **start** or to continue to **race**.

4. The race committee may reject any entry without stating the reason.

5. The race committee shall be governed by these rules, by the prescriptions of its national authority, by the sailing instructions, by approved class rules (but it may refuse to recognize any class rule which conflicts with these rules) and, when applicable, by the international team racing rules, and shall decide all questions in accordance therewith.

2—Notice of Race

The notice of a race or regatta shall contain the following information:—

(a) That the race or races will be sailed under the **rules** of the I.Y.R.U. and the prescriptions of the national authority concerned.

(b) The date and place of the regatta and **the time of** the start of the first race and, if possible, succeeding races.

(c) The class or classes for which races will be given.

The notice shall also cover such of the following matters as may be appropriate:—

(d) Any special instructions, subject to rule 3.1, which may vary or add to these rules or class rules.

(e) Any restrictions or conditions regarding entries and numbers of starters or competitors.

(f) The address to which entries shall be sent, the date on which they close, the amount of entrance fees, if any, and any other entry requirements.

(g) Particulars and number of prizes.
(h) Time and place for receiving sailing instructions.
(i) Scoring system.
(j) That for the purpose of determining the result of a race which is one of a series of races in a competition, decisions of protests shall not be subject to appeal if it is essential to establish the results promptly.

3—The Sailing Instructions

1. **Status**—These rules shall be supplemented by written sailing instructions which shall rank as rules and may alter a rule by specific reference to it, but except in accordance with rule 3.2(b)(ii) they shall not alter Parts I and IV of these rules ; provided however, that this restriction shall not preclude the right of developing and testing proposed rule changes in local regattas.

2. **Contents**—(a) The sailing instructions shall contain the following information :—

(i) That the race or races will be sailed under the rules of the I.Y.R.U. and the prescriptions of the national authority concerned.
(ii) The course or courses to be sailed or a list of **marks** or courses from which the course or courses will be selected, describing all **marks** and stating the order in which and the side on which each is to be rounded or passed.
(iii) The course signals.
(iv) The classes to race and class signals, if any.
(v) Time of start for each class.
(vi) Starting line and starting area if used.
(vii) Finishing line and any special instructions for shortening the course or for **finishing** a shortened course. (Where possible the sailing instructions for **finishing** a shortened course should not differ from those laid down for **finishing** the full course.)
(viii) Time limit, if any, for **finishing.**
(ix) Scoring system, if not previously announced in writing, including the method, if any, for breaking ties.

(b) The sailing instructions shall also cover such of the following matters as may be appropriate :—

(i) The date and place of the race or races.
(ii) When the race is to continue after sunset, the time or place, if any, at which the International Regulations for Preventing Collisions at Sea, or Government Right-of-Way Rules, shall replace the corresponding rules of Part IV, and the night signals the committee boat will display.
(iii) Any special instructions, subject to rule 3.1, which may vary or add to these rules, or class rules, and any special signals.
(iv) Eligibility ; entry ; measurement certificate ; declaration.
(v) Any special instruction or signal, if any, regarding the carrying on board and wearing of personal buoyancy.
(vi) Names, sail numbers and letters and ratings of the yachts entered.
(vii) Any special instructions governing the methods of starting and recall.
(viii) Recall numbers or letters, if used, of the yachts entered.
(ix) Time allowances.
(x) Length of course or courses.
(xi) Method by which competitors will be notified of any change of course.
(xii) Information on tides and currents.
(xiii) Prizes.
(xiv) Any special time limit within which, and address at which, the declaration that all rules have been observed, if required, or written protest shall be lodged, and the prescribed fee, if any, which shall accompany the latter.
(xv) Time and place at which protests will be heard.
(xvi) That for the purpose of determining the result of a race which is one of a series of races in a com-

petition, decisions of protests shall not be subject to appeal if it is essential to establish the results promptly.
(xvii) Whether races **postponed** or **abandoned** for the day will be sailed later and, if so, when and where.
(xviii) Disposition to be made of a yacht appearing at the start alone in her class.

3. **Distribution**—The sailing instructions shall be available to each yacht entitled to race.

4. **Changes**—The race committee may change the sailing instructions by notice, in writing if practicable, given to each yacht affected not later than the warning signal of her class.

5. **Oral Instructions**—Oral instructions shall not be given except in accordance with procedure specifically set out in the sailing instructions.

4—Signals

1. **International Code Flag Signals**—Unless otherwise prescribed in the sailing instructions, the following International Code flags shall be used as indicated :

☆   "AP", Answering Pennant—Postponement Signal.
When displayed alone means :—
"All races not started are postponed until later in the day. The warning signal will be made 30 seconds after this signal is lowered."
When displayed over the letter "A" means :—
"All races not started are postponed to a later date."
When displayed over a class signal means :—
"The above signals apply to the designated class only."
"B"—Protest signal.
When displayed by a yacht means :—
"I intend to lodge a protest."
"L"—When displayed means :—
"Come within hail." or "Follow Me."
"M"—Mark Signal.
When displayed on a buoy, vessel, or other object, means :—
"Round or pass the object displaying this signal instead of the mark which it replaces."
"N"—Abandonment Signal.
When displayed alone, means :—
"All races are abandoned."
When displayed over a class signal, means :—
"The designated race is abandoned."
"N over X"—Abandonment and Re-Sail Signal.
When displayed alone, means :—
"All races are abandoned and will shortly be re-sailed. Watch for fresh starting signals."
When displayed over a class signal, means :—
"The designated race is abandoned and will shortly be re-sailed. Watch for fresh starting signals."
"N over First Repeater"—Cancellation Signal.
When displayed alone means :—
"All races are cancelled."
When displayed over a class signal means :—
"All races are cancelled."
When displayed over a class signal means :—
"The designated race is cancelled."
"P"—Preparatory Signal.
When displayed means :—
"The class designated by the warning signal will start in 5 minutes exactly."
"R"—Reverse Course Signal.
When displayed alone, means :—
"Sail the course prescribed in the sailing instructions in the reverse direction."
When displayed over a course signal, means :—
"Sail the designated course in the reverse direction."
"S"—Shorten Course Signal.
When displayed alone
(a) at or near the starting line, means :—
"All classes shall sail the shortened course prescribed in the sailing instructions."
(b) at or near the finishing line, means :—
"All classes shall **finish** the race either at the prescribed finishing line at the end of the round still to be completed by the leading

yacht, or in any other manner prescribed in the sailing instructions under rule 3.2(a)(vii)."

(c) elsewhere, means:—
"All classes shall finish between the nearby mark and the committee boat."

When displayed over a class signal, this signal applies to the designated class only.
"1st Repeater"—General Recall Signal.
When displayed, means:—
"The class is recalled for a fresh start as provided in sailing instructions."

2. **Signaling the Course**—The race committee shall either make the appropriate course signal or otherwise designate the course before or with the warning signal.

3. **Changing the Course**—The course for a class which has not **started** may be changed:—

(a) by displaying the appropriate **postponement** signal and indicating the new course before or with the warning signal to be displayed after the lowering of the **postponement** signal; or

(b) by displaying a course signal or by removing and substituting a course signal before or with the warning signal.

(The race committee should use method (a) when a change of course involves either shifting the committee boat or other starting mark, or requires a change of sails which cannot reasonably be completed within the 5-minute period before the preparatory signal is made.)

4. **Signals for Starting a Race**

(a) Unless otherwise prescribed in the sailing instructions, the signals for starting a race shall be made at 5-minute intervals exactly, and shall be either:—

(i) *Warning Signal* — Class flag broken out or distinctive signal displayed.

Preparatory Signal — Code flag "P" broken out or distinctive signal displayed.

Starting Signal — Both warning and preparatory signals lowered.

In system (i) when classes are started:—

(a) at ten-minute intervals, the warning signal for each succeeding class shall be broken out or displayed at the starting signal of the preceding class, and

(b) at five-minute intervals, the preparatory signal for the first class to start shall be left flying or displayed until the last class has started. The warning signal for each succeeding class shall be broken out or displayed at the preparatory signal of the preceding class, or

(ii) *Warning Signal* — White shape.
Preparatory Signal — Blue shape.
Starting Signal — Red shape.
first class to start

In system (ii) each signal shall be lowered 30 seconds before the hoisting of the next, and in starting yachts by classes, the starting signal for each class shall be the preparatory signal for the next.

(b) Although rule 4.4(a) specifies 5-minute intervals between signals, this shall not interfere with the power of a race committee to start a series of races at any intervals which it considers desirable.

(c) A warning signal shall not be made before its scheduled time, except with the consent of all yachts entitled to race.

(d) Should a significant error be made in the timing of the interval between any of the signals for starting a race, the recommended procedure is to have a general recall, **abandonment** or post-ponement of the race whose start is directly affected by the error and a corresponding **postponement** of succeeding races. Unless otherwise prescribed in the sailing instructions a new warning signal shall be made. When the race is not recalled, **abandoned** or **postponed** after an error in the timing of the interval, each succeeding signal shall be made at the correct interval from the preceding signal.

5. **Finishing Signals**—Blue flag or shape. When displayed at the finish, means:—"The committee boat is on station at the finishing line."

6. **Other Signals**—The sailing instructions shall designate any other special signals and shall explain their meaning.

7. **Calling Attention to Signals**—Whenever the race committee makes a signal, except "R" or "S" before the warning signal, it shall call attention to its action as follows:—

Three guns or other sound signals when displaying "N", "N over X", or "N over 1st Repeater".

Two guns or other sound signals when displaying the "1st Repeater", "AP", or "S".

One gun or other sound signal when making any other signal.

8. **Visual Signal to Govern**—Times shall be taken from the visual starting signals, and a failure or mistiming of a gun or other sound signal shall be disregarded.

5—Cancelling, Postponing or Abandoning a Race and Shortening Course

1. The race committee:—
(a) before the starting signal may shorten the course or **cancel** or **postpone** a race for any reason, and
(b) after the starting signal may shorten the course by finishing a race at any rounding **mark** or **cancel** or **abandon** a race because of foul weather endangering the yachts, or because of insufficient wind, or because a **mark** is missing or has shifted or for other reasons directly affecting safety or the fairness of the competition.

2. After a **postponement** the ordinary starting signals prescribed in rule 4.4(a) shall be used, and the postponement signal, if a general one, shall be hauled down before the first warning or course signal is made.

3. The race committee shall notify all yachts concerned by signal or otherwise when and where a race **postponed** or **abandoned** will be sailed.

6—Starting and Finishing Lines

The starting and finishing lines shall be either:—
(a) A line between a **mark** and a mast or staff on the committee boat or station clearly identified in the sailing instructions;
(b) a line between two **marks**; or
(c) the extension of a line through two stationary posts, with or without a **mark** at or near its outer limit, inside which the yachts shall pass.

For types (a) and (c) of starting or finishing lines the sailing instructions may also provide a **mark** at or near the inner end of the line, in which case yachts shall pass between it and the outer **mark**.

7—Start of a Race

1. **Starting Area**—The sailing instructions may define a starting area which may be bounded by buoys; if so, they shall not rank as **marks**.

2. **Timing the Start**—The start of a yacht shall be timed from her starting signal.

8—Recalls

☆ 1. Yachts' sail numbers shall be used as recall numbers except that the Race Committee may instead allot a suitable recall number or letter to each yacht in accordance with rule 3.2(b)(viii).

2.(a) When, at her starting signal, any part of a yacht's hull, crew or equipment is over the starting line or its extensions, or she is subject to rule 51.1(c) and has not returned to the right side of the starting line around one of the starting **marks**, the race committee shall either:

　　　(ı) display her recall number or letter as soon
　　　　　as possible and make a suitable sound, or
　　　(ii) follow such other procedure as may be pre-
　　　　　scribed in the sailing instructions.
　(b) When there is either a number of unidentified pre-
　　　mature starters, or an error in starting pro-
　　　cedure, the race committee may make a general
　　　recall signal in accordance with rules 4.1, "1st
　　　Repeater", and 4.7. Unless otherwise prescribed
　　　in the sailing instructions, a fresh warning and
　　　preparatory signal shall be given. Rule infringe-
　　　ments before the preparatory signal for the new
　　　start shall not be cause for disqualification.
3. As soon as a recalled yacht has wholly returned to the
right side of the starting line or its extensions, the race
committee shall so inform her by removing her recall number if displayed; if not, by hail if practicable or in some
other manner prescribed in the sailing instructions.

9—Marks
1. **Mark Missing**
　(a) When any **mark** either is missing or has shifted,
　　　the race committee shall, if possible, replace it
　　　in its stated position, or substitute a new one
　　　with similar characteristics or a buoy or vessel
　　　displaying the letter "M" of the International
　　　Code—the **mark** signal.
　(b) If it is impossible either to replace the **mark** or to
　　　substitute a new one in time for the yachts to
　　　round or pass it, the race committee may, at its
　　　discretion, act in accordance with rule 5.1.
2. **Mark Unseen**—When races are sailed in fog or at
night, dead reckoning alone should not necessarily be accepted as evidence that a **mark** has been rounded or passed.

10—Finishing
Unless otherwise prescribed in the sailing instructions, in
races where there is a time limit, one yacht **finishing** within
the prescribed limit shall make the race valid for all other
yachts in that race.

11—Ties
When there is a tie at the finish of a race, either actual or
on corrected times, the points for the place for which the
yachts have tied and for the place immediately below shall
be added together and divided equally. When two or more
yachts tie for a trophy or prize in either a single race or a
series, the yachts so tied should, if possible, sail a deciding
race; if not, either the tie shall be broken by a method
established under rule 3.2(a)(ix), or the yachts so tied shall
either receive equal prizes or share the prize.

12—Yacht Materially Prejudiced
When the race committee decides that, through no fault
of her own, the finishing position of a yacht has been materially prejudiced; by rendering assistance in accordance
with rule 58, Rendering Assistance; by being disabled by
another yacht which should have kept clear; or by an action
or omission of the race committee, it may **cancel** or **abandon** the race or make such other arrangement as it deems
equitable.

13—Re-Sailed Races
When a race is to be re-sailed:—
1. All yachts entered in the original race shall be eligible
to sail in the re-sailed race.
2. Subject to the entry requirements of the original race,
and at the discretion of the race committee, new entries may
be accepted.
3. Rule infringements in the original race shall not be
cause for disqualification.
4. The race committee shall notify the yachts concerned
when and where the race will be re-sailed.

14—Award of Prizes, Places and Points
Before awarding the prizes, the race committee shall be
satisfied that all yachts whose finishing positions affect the
awards have complied with the racing rules and sailing instructions. It is recommended that the sailing instructions
require the member in charge of each yacht to submit within
a stated time after she has **finished** a race a signed declaration to the effect that "all the rules and sailing instructions were

obeyed in the race (or races) on (date or dates of race or
races)".

(Numbers 15, 16, and 17 are spare numbers.)

PART III
GENERAL REQUIREMENTS
Owner's Responsibilities for Qualifying his Yacht

*A yacht intending to race shall, to avoid subsequent
disqualification, comply with the rules of Part III
before her preparatory signal and, when applicable,
while racing.*

18—Entries
☆　　Entries shall be made as required by the notice of the
race or by the sailing instructions.

19—Measurement Certificates
Every yacht entering a race shall hold such valid measurement or rating certificate as may be required by the
national authority or other duly authorized body, by her
class rules, by the notice of the race, or by the sailing instructions and she shall adhere to the conditions upon which
such certificate was based.

20—Ownership of Yachts
1. Unless otherwise prescribed in the conditions of entry,
a yacht shall be eligible to compete only when she is either
owned by or on charter to and has been entered by a yacht
or sailing club recognized by a national authority or a member or members thereof.

2. Two or more yachts owned or chartered wholly or in
part by the same body or person shall not compete in the
same race without the previous consent of the race committee.

21—Member on Board
Every yacht shall have on board a member of a yacht or
sailing club recognized by a national authority to be in
charge of the yacht as owner or owner's representative.

21A—Crew
☆　　1. NUMBER IN CREW—Except as otherwise provided
in class rules, the total crew of a yacht, including the skipper,
shall not exceed: 2, for yachts with less than 100 square
feet of sail area; 3, for yachts with 100 or more, and less
than 200, square feet of sail area; and for yachts with 200
or more square feet of sail area, 1 for every 250 square feet
of sail area and fraction thereof plus 3. Sail area is the total
area entered in a yacht's measurement certificate or otherwise arrived at and used in the final formula determining
her rating.

☆　　COUNTING WOMEN AS CREW—Except as otherwise
provided in class rules, on yachts of more than 25 feet waterline length, women not taking any active part in handling the
yacht do not count as crew. On smaller yachts, women
count as crew.

22—Shifting Ballast
1. **General Restrictions.** Floorboards shall be kept down;
bulkheads and doors left standing; ladders, stairways and
water tanks left in place; all cabin, galley and forecastle
fixtures and fittings kept on board; all movable ballast shall
be properly stowed under the floorboards or in lockers and
no dead weight shall be shifted.

2. **Shipping, Unshipping or Shifting Ballast; Water.** No
ballast, whether movable or fixed, shall be shipped, un-
shipped or shifted, nor shall any water be taken or discharged except for ordinary ship's use, from 9 p.m. of the
day before the race until the yacht is no longer **racing**,
except that bilge water may be removed at any time.

23—Anchor

Unless otherwise prescribed by her class rules, every yacht shall carry on board an anchor and chain or rope of suitable size.

24—Life-Saving Equipment

Unless otherwise prescribed by her class rules, every yacht, except one which has sufficient buoyancy to support the crew in case of accident, shall carry adequate life-saving equipment for all persons on board, one item of which shall be ready for immediate use.

25—Sail Numbers, Letters and Emblems

1. Every yacht of an international class recognized by the I.Y.R.U. shall carry on her mainsail:—

(a) When racing in foreign waters a letter or letters showing her nationality, thus:—

A	Argentine	L	Finland
AL	Algeria	LE	Lebanon
AR	United Arab Republic	LX	Luxembourg
B	Belgium	M	Hungary
BA	Bahamas	MA	Morocco
BL	Brazil	MG	Madagascar
BU	Bulgaria	MO	Monaco
CA	Cambodia	MX	Mexico
CB	Colombia	MY	Malasia
CY	Ceylon	N	Norway
CZ	Czechoslovakia	NK	Democratic People's Republic of Korea
D	Denmark		
E	Spain		
EC	Ecuador	OE	Austria
F	France	P	Portugal
G	West Germany	PH	The Philippine
GO	East Germany	PR	Puerto Rico
GR	Greece	PU	Peru
GU	Guatemala	PZ	Poland
H	Holland	RC	Cuba
HA	Netherland Antilles	RI	Indonesia
		RM	Roumania
I	Italy	S	Sweden
IR	Republic of Ireland	SA	South Africa
IS	Israel	SE	Senegal
J	Japan	SL	El Salvador
		SR	Union of Soviet Socialist Republics
K	United Kingdom		
KA	Australia		
KB	Bermuda	T	Tunisia
KBA	Barbados	TA	Republic of China (Taiwan)
KC	Canada		
KG	British Guiana	TH	Thailand
KGB	Gibraltar	TK	Turkey
KH	Hong Kong	U	Uruguay
KI	India	US	United States of America
KJ	Jamaica		
KK	Kenya		
KR	Rhodesia	V	Venezuela
KS	Singapore	VI	U.S. Virgin I.
KT	West Indies	X	Chile
KZ	New Zealand	Y	Yugoslavia
KZA	Zambia	Z	Switzerland

(b) A number, letter or emblem showing the class to which the yacht belongs.

(c) Number of yacht:—

A distinguishing number allotted by her own national authority. In the case of a self-administered international class, the number may be allotted by the class owners' association.

Assuming a five-point-five metre yacht belonging to the Argentine Republic to be alloted number 3 by the Argentine national authority, her sail shall be marked:

$$5.5$$
$$A3$$

When there is insufficient space to place the letter or letters showing the yacht's nationality in front of her allotted number, it shall be placed above the number.

(d) The sail numbers, letters and emblems shall be placed on both sides of the mainsail, at approximately two-thirds of the height of the sail above the boom, so that the lowest number shows when the sail is fully reefed. Sail numbers, letters and emblems shall sharply contrast in color with the sail and shall be placed at different heights on the two sides of the sail, those on the starboard side being uppermost, to avoid confusion owing to translucency of the sail. The sail numbers only, shall be similarly placed on both sides of the spinnaker, but at approximately half height.

(e) The following sizes for numbers and letters are prescribed:—

Size of Numbers and Letters on Sails for the Several Classes Recognized by the I.Y.R.U.

Class	Minimum height of figure and letters		Minimum width occupied by each figure except Figure 1		Minimum thickness of every portion of each figure or letter		Minimum space between adjoining figures	
	Metres.	Ins.	Metres.	Ins.	Metres.	Ins.	Metres.	Ins.
12 Metre ..	0.66	(26)	0.46	(18)	0.10	(4)	0.15	(6)
13.5 and 15 Metre Cruiser Racer	0.66	(26)	0.43	(17)	0.10	(4)	0.15	(6)
10.5 and 12 Metre Cruiser Racer ..	0.56	(22)	0.33	(14)	0.10	(4)	0.12	(5)
9 Metre Cruiser Racer	0.50	(20)	0.33	(13)	0.075	(3)	0.10	(4)
7 and 8 Metre Cruiser Racer	0.45	(18)	0.30	(12)	0.075	(3)	0.10	(4)
8 Metre ..	0.50	(20)	0.36	(14)				
6 Metre ..								
5.5 Metre ..								
30 sq. Metre ..	0.46	(18)	0.30	(12)	0.075	(3)	0.10	(4)
22 sq. Metre ..								
Dragon ..								
Soling ..								
"C" Catamaran ..								
Star ..	0.38	(15)	0.25	(10)	0.064	(2½)	0.10	(4)
Tempest ..								
Flying Dutchman ..								
Tornado Catamaran ..								
Australis Catamaran..								
505 ..								
12 sq. Metre Sharpie								
Lightning ..	0.30	(12)	0.20	(8)				
Finn ..								
14 ft. Dinghy ..								
Vaurien ..								
Cadet ..	0.23	(9)	0.15	(6)				
Snipe ..								

☆ 2.(a) Unless otherwise authorized by the Race Committee or provided by class rules, a yacht not in one of the classes above shall carry her class number, letter or emblem and her racing number on her mainsail and spinnaker, as provided above, except that the only size requirement shall be that the numbers, letters and emblems shall be not be less than 10 inches in height for yachts under 22 feet waterline length, not less than 15 inches in height for yachts 22 feet to 32 feet waterline and not less than 18 inches in height for yachts over 32 feet waterline length.

☆ (b) Offshore racing yachts shall carry N.A.Y.R.U. numbers on mainsails, spinnakers and all overlapping headsails, effective January 1, 1970.

3. A yacht shall not be disqualified for failing to comply with the provisions of rule 25 without prior warning and adequate opportunity to make correction.

26—Advertisements

A yacht shall not carry any form of advertisement on her hull or equipment, except that:

(*a*) Not more than one sailmaker's mark, if any, shall be placed on each side of the sail, not more than than 15 per cent of the length of its foot from the tack, and

(*b*) builders' marks may be placed on the hull, spars or equipment.

Such marks (or plates) shall fit within a square not exceeding 15 x 15 cms. (6 x 6 ins.).

27—Forestays and Jib Tacks

Unless otherwise prescribed in the class rules, forestays and jib tacks (not including spinnaker staysails when not **close-hauled**) shall be fixed approximately in the center-line of the yacht.

28—Flags

☆   A yacht may display her private signal on the leech of her mainsail or from her mizzen mast head, and a wind indicator of a solid color or a feather. Other flags shall not be displayed except for signaling. A yacht shall not be disqualified for failing to comply with the provisions of this rule without warning and adequate opportunity to make correction.

(Numbers 29 and 30 are spare numbers.)

PART IV

SAILING RULES WHEN YACHTS MEET

Helmsman's Rights and Obligations Concerning Right of Way

The rules of Part IV apply only between yachts which either are intending to race or are racing in the same or different races, and, except when rule 3.2(b) (ii) applies, replace the International Regulations for Preventing Collisions at Sea or Government Right-of-Way Rules applicable to the area concerned, from the time a yacht intending to race begins to sail about in the vicinity of the starting line until she has either finished or retired and has left the vicinity of the course.

SECTION A—RULES WHICH ALWAYS APPLY

31—Disqualification

1. A yacht may be disqualified for infringing a rule of Part IV only when the infringement occurs while she is **racing**, whether or not a collision results.

2. A yacht may be disqualified before or after she is **racing** for seriously hindering a yacht which is **racing**, or for infringing the sailing instructions.

32—Avoiding Collisions

A right-of-way yacht which makes no attempt to avoid **a** collision resulting in serious damage may be disqualified **as** well as the other yacht.

33—Retiring from Race

A yacht which realizes she has infringed a racing rule or a sailing instruction should retire promptly; but, when **she** persists in **racing**, other yachts shall continue to accord her such rights as she may have under the rules of Part IV.

34—Limitations on the Right-of-Way Yacht to Alter Course

When one yacht is required to keep clear of another, **the** right-of-way yacht shall not (except to the extent permitted by rule 38.1, Right-of-way Yacht Luffing after Starting), so alter course as to prevent the other yacht from keeping clear; or to obstruct her while so doing.

35—Hailing

A right-of-way yacht, except when **luffing** under rule 38.1, Luffing after Starting, should hail before or when making an alteration of course which may not be foreseen by the other yacht or when claiming the establishment or termination of an **overlap** at a **mark** or **obstruction**.

SECTION B—OPPOSITE TACK RULE

36—Fundamental Rule

A **port-tack** yacht shall keep clear of a **starboard-tack** yacht.

SECTION C—SAME TACK RULES

37—Fundamental Rules

1. A **windward yacht** shall keep clear of a **leeward yacht**.

2. A yacht **clear astern** shall keep clear of a yacht **clear ahead**.

3. A yacht which establishes an **overlap** to **leeward** from **clear astern** shall allow the **windward yacht** ample room and opportunity to keep clear, and during the existence of that **overlap** the **leeward yacht** shall not sail above her **proper course**.

38—Right-of-Way Yacht Luffing after Starting

1. **Luffing Rights and Limitations.** After she has **started** and cleared the starting line, a yacht **clear ahead** or a **leeward yacht** may **luff** as she pleases, except that:—

A **leeward yacht** shall not sail above her **proper course** while an **overlap** exists if, at any time during its existence, the helmsman of the **windward yacht** (when sighting abeam from his normal **station** and sailing no higher than the **leeward yacht**) has been abreast or forward of the mainmast of the **leeward yacht**.

2. **Overlap Limitations.** For the purpose of this rule: An **overlap** does not exist unless the yachts are clearly within two overall lengths of the longer yacht: and an **overlap** which exists between two yachts when the leading yacht **starts**, or when one or both of them completes a **tack** or **jibe**, shall be regarded as a new **overlap** beginning at that time.

3. **Hailing to Stop or Prevent a Luff.** When there is doubt, the **leeward yacht** may assume that she has the right to **luff** unless the helmsman of the **windward yacht** has hailed "Mast Abeam", or words to that effect. The **leeward yacht** shall be governed by such hail, and, if she deems it improper, her only remedy is to protest.

4. **Curtailing a Luff.** The **windward yacht** shall not cause a **luff** to be curtailed because of her proximity to the **leeward yacht** unless an **obstruction**, a third yacht or other object restricts her ability to respond.

5. **Luffing Two or More Yachts.** A yacht shall not **luff** unless she has the right to **luff** all yachts which would be affected by her **luff**, in which case they shall all respond even if an intervening yacht or yachts would not otherwise have the right to **luff**.

39—Sailing Below a Proper Course

A yacht which is on a free leg of the course shall not sail below her **proper course** when she is clearly within three of her overall lengths of either a **leeward yacht** or a yacht **clear astern** which is steering a course to pass to **leeward**.

40—Right-of-Way Luffing before Starting

Before a yacht has **started** and cleared the starting line, any **luff** on her part which causes another yacht to have to alter course to avoid a collision shall be carried out slowly and in such a way so as to give the **windward yacht** room and opportunity to keep clear, but before her starting signal, the **leeward yacht** shall not so **luff** above a **close-hauled** course, unless the helmsman of the **windward yacht** (sighting abeam from his normal **station**) is abaft the mainmast of the **leeward yacht**. Rules 38.3, Hailing to Stop or Prevent a Luff; 38.4, Curtailing a Luff; and 38.5, Luffing Two or more Yachts, also apply.

SECTION D—CHANGING TACK RULES

41—Tacking or Jibing

1. A yacht which is either **tacking** or **jibing** shall keep clear of a yacht **on a tack**.

2. A yacht shall neither **tack** nor **jibe** into a position which will give her right of way unless she does so far enough from a yacht **on a tack** to enable this yacht to keep clear without having to begin to alter her course until after the **tack** or **jibe** has been completed.

3. A yacht which **tacks** or **jibes** has the onus of satisfying the race committee that she completed her **tack** or **jibe** in accordance with rule 41.2.

4. When two yachts are both **tacking** or both **jibing** at the same time, the one on the other's **port** side shall keep clear.

SECTION E—RULES OF EXCEPTION AND SPECIAL APPLICATION

When a rule of this section applies, to the extent to which it explicitly provides rights and obligations, it over-rides any conflicting rule of Part IV which precedes it except the rules of Section A—Rules Which Always Apply.

42—Rounding or Passing Marks and Obstructions

When yachts either on the same **tack** or, after **starting** and clearing the starting line, on opposite **tacks**, are about to round or pass a **mark** on the same required side or an **obstruction** on the same side :—

When Overlapped

1.(*a*) An outside yacht shall give each yacht **overlapping** her on the inside, room to round or pass it, except as provided in rules 42.1(c),(d) and (e). Room includes room to **tack** or **jibe** when either is an integral part of the rounding or passing manoeuvre.

(*b*) When an inside yacht of two or more **overlapped** yachts on opposite **tacks** will have to **jibe** in rounding a **mark** in order most directly to assume a **proper course** to the next **mark,** she shall **jibe** at the first reasonable opportunity.

(*c*) When two yachts on opposite **tacks** are on a beat or when one of them will have to **tack** either to round the **mark** or to avoid the **obstruction,** as between each other rule 42.1(a) shall not apply and they are subject to rules 36, Opposite Tack Fundamental Rule, and 41, Tacking or Jibing.

(*d*) An outside **leeward yacht** with luffing rights may take an inside yacht to windward of a **mark** provided that she hails to that effect and begins to **luff** before she is within two of her overall lengths of the **mark** and provided that she also passes to windward of it.

(*e*) When approaching the starting line to **start,** a leeward yacht shall be under no obligation to give any **windward yacht** room to pass to leeward of a starting **mark** surrounded by navigable water; but, after the starting signal, a **leeward yacht** shall not deprive a **windward yacht** of room at such a **mark** by sailing either above the first **mark** or above **close-hauled.**

When Clear Astern and Clear Ahead

2.(*a*) A yacht **clear astern** shall keep clear in anticipation of and during the rounding or passing manoeuvre when the yacht **clear ahead** remains on the same **tack** or jibes.

(*b*) A yacht **clear ahead** which **tacks** to round a **mark** is subject to rule 41, Tacking or Jibing, but a yacht **clear astern** shall not **luff** above **close-hauled** so as to prevent the yacht **clear ahead** from **tacking.**

Restrictions on Establishing and Maintaining an Overlap

3.(*a*) A yacht **clear astern** shall not establish an inside **overlap** and be entitled to room under rule 42.1(a) when the yacht **clear ahead** :—
(i) is within two of her overall lengths of the **mark** or **obstruction,** except as provided in rules 42.3(b) and 42.3(c) ; or
(ii) is unable to give the required room.

(*b*) The two lengths determinative of rule 42.3(a)(i) shall not apply to yachts, of which one has **tacked** in the vicinity of a **mark,** unless when the **tack** is completed the yachts are clearly more than two overall lengths from the **mark.**

(*c*) A yacht **clear astern** may establish an **overlap** between the yacht **clear ahead** and a continuing **obstruction** such as a shoal or the shore, only when there is room for her to do so in safety.

(*d*) (i) A yacht **clear ahead** shall be under no obligation to give room to a yacht **clear astern** before an **overlap** is established.
(ii) A yacht which claims an inside **overlap** has the onus of satisfying the race committee that the **overlap** was established in proper time.

(*e*) (i) When an outside yacht is **overlapped** at the time she comes within two of her overall lengths of a **mark,** she shall continue to be bound by rule 42.1(a) to give room as required even though the **overlap** may thereafter be broken.
(ii) An outside yacht which claims to have broken an **overlap** has the onus of satisfying the race committee that she became **clear ahead** when she was more than two of her overall lengths from the **mark.**

43—Close-Hauled, Hailing for Room to Tack at Obstructions

1. **Hailing.** When two **close-hauled** yachts are on the same **tack** and safe pilotage requires the yacht **clear ahead** or the **leeward yacht** to make a substantial alteration of course to clear an **obstruction,** and if she intends to **tack,** but cannot **tack** without colliding with the other yacht, she shall hail the other yacht for room to **tack,** but she shall not hail and **tack** simultaneously.

2. **Responding.** The hailed yacht at the earliest possible moment after the hail shall either :—
(*a*) **tack,** in which case, the hailing yacht shall begin to **tack** either :—
(i) before the hailed yacht has completed her **tack,** or
(ii) if she cannot then **tack** without colliding with the hailed yacht, immediately she is able to **tack, or**
(*b*) reply "You **tack**", or words to that effect, if in her opinion she can keep clear without **tacking** or after postponing her **tack.** In this case :—
(i) the hailing yacht shall immediately **tack** and
(ii) the hailed yacht shall keep clear.
(iii) The onus shall lie on the hailed yacht which replied "You **tack**" to satisfy the race committee that she kept clear.

3. **Limitation on Right to Room**
(*a*) When the **obstruction** is a **mark** which the hailed yacht can fetch, the hailing yacht shall not be entitled to room to **tack** and the hailed yacht shall immediately so inform the hailing yacht.
(*b*) If, thereafter, the hailing yacht again hails for room to **tack,** she shall, after receiving it, retire immediately.
(*c*) If, after having refused to respond to a hail under rule 43.3(a), the hailed yacht fails to fetch, she shall retire immediately.

44—Yachts Returning to Start

1.(*a*) A premature starter when returning to **start,** or a yacht working into position from the wrong side of the starting line or its extensions, when the starting signal is made, shall keep clear of all yachts which are **starting,** or have **started,** correctly, until she is wholly on the right side of the starting line or its extensions.
(*b*) Thereafter, she shall be accorded the rights under the rules of Part IV of a yacht which is **starting** correctly ; but if she thereby acquires right of way over another yacht which is **starting** correctly, she shall allow that yacht ample room and opportunity to keep clear.

2. A premature starter while continuing to sail the course and until it is obvious that she is returning to **start,** shall be accorded the rights under the rules of Part IV of a yacht which has **started.**

45—Yachts Re-rounding after Touching a Mark

1. A yacht which has touched a **mark** and is about to correct her error in accordance with rule 52.1, Touching a Mark, shall keep clear of all other yachts which are about to round or pass it or have rounded or passed it correctly, until she has rounded it completely and has cleared it and is on a **proper course** to the next **mark**.

2. A yacht which has touched a **mark**, while continuing to sail the course and until it is obvious that she is returning to round it completely in accordance with rule 52.1, Touching a Mark, shall be accorded rights under the rules of Part IV.

SECTION F—WHEN NOT UNDER WAY

46—Anchored, Aground or Capsized

1. A yacht under way shall keep clear of another yacht **racing** which is anchored, aground or capsized. Of two anchored yachts, the one which anchored later shall keep clear, except that a yacht which is dragging shall keep clear of one which is not.

2. A yacht anchored or aground shall indicate the fact to any yacht which may be in danger of fouling her. Unless the size of the yachts or the weather conditions make some other signal necessary a hail is sufficient indication.

3. A yacht shall not be penalized for fouling a yacht in distress which she is attempting to assist or a yacht which goes aground or capsizes immediately ahead of her.

(Numbers 47 and 48 are spare numbers.)

PART V
OTHER SAILING RULES

Obligations of Helmsman and Crew in Handling a Yacht

Except for rule 49, a yacht is subject to the rules of Part V only while she is racing.

49—Fair Sailing

A yacht shall attempt to win a race only by fair sailing, superior speed and skill, and, except in team races, by individual effort. However, a yacht may be disqualified under this rule only in the case of a clear-cut violation of the above principles and only if no other rule applies.

50—Ranking as a Starter

A yacht which sails about in the vicinity of the starting line between her preparatory and starting signals shall rank as a starter, even if she does not **start**.

51—Sailing the Course

1.(a) A yacht shall **start** and **finish** only as prescribed in the starting and finishing definitions, even if the committee boat is anchored on the side of the starting or finishing **mark** opposite to that prescribed in the sailing instructions.

(b) Unless otherwise prescribed in the sailing instructions, a yacht which either crosses prematurely, or is on the wrong side of the starting line, or its extensions, at the starting signal, shall return and **start** in accordance with the definition.

(c) Unless otherwise prescribed in the sailing instructions, when after a general recall, any part of a yacht's hull, crew or equipment is over the starting line during the minute before her starting signal, she shall thereafter pass on the course side of and around one of the starting **marks** and cross the starting line in the direction of the first **mark**.

(d) Failure of a yacht to see or hear her recall notification shall not relieve her of her obligation to **start** correctly.

2. A yacht shall sail the course so as to round or **pass** each **mark** on the required side in correct sequence, and so that a string representing her wake from the time she **starts** until she **finishes** would, when drawn taut, lie on the required side of each **mark**.

3. A **mark** has a required side for a yacht as long as she is on a leg which it begins, bounds or ends. A starting **mark**

begins to have a required side for a yacht when she **starts**. A finishing **mark** ceases to have a required side for a yacht as soon as she **finishes**.

4. A yacht which rounds or passes a **mark** on the wrong side may correct her error by making her course conform to the requirements of rule 51.2.

5. It is not necessary for a yacht to cross the finishing line completely. After **finishing** she may clear it in either direction.

☆ 6. In the absence of the Race Committee, a yacht shall take her own time when she finishes, and report the time taken to the Race Committee as soon as possible. If there is no longer an established finishing line, the finishing line shall be a line extending from the required side of the finishing **mark** at right angles to the last leg of the course, and 100 yards long or as much longer as may be necessary to insure adequate depth of water in crossing it.

52—Touching a Mark

1. A yacht which either :—
   (a) touches :—
      (i) a starting **mark** before **starting** ;
      (ii) a **mark** which begins, bounds or ends the leg of the course on which she is sailing ; or
      (iii) a finishing **mark** after **finishing**, or
   (b) causes a **mark** vessel to shift to avoid being touched,

shall retire immediately, unless she claims that she was wrongfully compelled to touch it by another yacht, in which case she shall protest. However, unless otherwise prescribed in the sailing instructions, when the **mark** is surrounded by navigable water, a yacht may correct her error by making one complete rounding of the **mark**, leaving it on the required side without touching it, in addition to rounding or passing it as required to sail the course. In the case of a **mark** at the starboard end of the starting or finishing line, such complete rounding shall be clockwise, and at the port end of a starting or finishing line anti-clockwise.

2. For the purposes of rule 52.1: Every ordinary part of a **mark** ranks as part of it, including a flag, flagpole, boom or hoisted boat, but excluding ground tackle and any object either accidentally or temporarily attached to it.

53—Fog Signals and Lights

1. Every yacht shall observe the International Regulations for Preventing Collisions at Sea or Government Rules for fog signals and, as a minimum, the carrying of lights at night.

☆ 2. The use of additional special purpose lights such as masthead, spreader or jib luff lights shall not constitute grounds for protest.

54—Setting and Sheeting Sails

1. **Changing Sails.** While changing headsails and spinnakers a replacing sail may be fully set and trimmed before the sail it replaces is taken in, but only one mainsail and, except when changing, only one spinnaker shall be carried set.

2. **Sheeting Sails to Spars.** Unless otherwise prescribed by the class rules, any sail may be sheeted to or led above a boom regularly used for a working sail and permanently attached to the mast to which the head of the working sail is set, but no sails shall be sheeted over or through outriggers. An outrigger is any fitting so placed, except as permitted in the first sentence of rule 54.2, that it could exert outward pressure on a sheet at a point from which, with the yacht upright, a vertical line would fall outside the hull or deck planking at that point, or outside such other position as class rules prescribe. For the purpose of this rule : Bulwarks, rails and rubbing strakes are not part of the hull or deck planking. A boom of a boomed foresail which requires no adjustment when **tacking** is not an outrigger.

3. **Spinnaker, Spinnaker Pole.** A spinnaker shall not be set without a pole. The tack of a spinnaker when set and drawing shall be in close proximity to the outboard end of a spinnaker pole. Any headsail may be attached to a spinnaker pole provided a spinnaker is not set. A sail tacked down abaft the foremost mast is not a headsail. Only one

spinnaker pole shall be used at a time and when in use shall be carried only on the side of the foremost mast opposite to the main boom and shall be fixed to the mast. Rule 54.3 shall not apply when shifting a spinnaker pole or sail attached thereto.

55—Owner Steering Another Yacht
An owner shall not steer any yacht other than his own in a race wherein his own yacht competes, without the previous consent of the race committee.

55A—Paid Hand Steering
☆   A paid hand shall not steer a yacht of less than 32 feet waterline length.

56—Boarding
Unless otherwise prescribed in the sailing instructions, no person shall board a yacht except for the purpose of rule 58, Rendering Assistance, or to attend an injured or ill member of the crew or temporarily as one of the crew of a vessel fouled.

57—Leaving, Man Overboard
Unless otherwise prescribed in the sailing instructions, no person on board a yacht when her preparatory signal was made shall leave, unless injured or ill, or for the purposes of rule 58, Rendering Assistance, except that any member of the crew may fall overboard or leave her to swim, stand on the bottom as a means of anchoring, haul her out ashore to effect repairs, reef sails or bail out, or help her to get clear after grounding or fouling another vessel or object, provided that this person is back on board before the yacht continues in the race.

58—Rendering Assistance
Every yacht shall render all possible assistance to any vessel or person in peril, when in a position to do so.

59—Outside Assistance
Except as permitted by rules 56, Boarding, 58, Rendering Assistance, and 64, Aground or Foul of an Obstruction, a yacht shall neither receive outside assistance nor use any gear other than that on board when her preparatory signal was made.

60—Means of Propulsion
A yacht shall be propelled only by the natural action of the wind on the sails, spars and hull, and water on the hull, and shall not pump, "ooch" or rock, as described in Appendix 2, nor check way by abnormal means, except for the purpose of rule 58, Rendering Assistance, or of recovering a man who has accidentally fallen overboard. An oar, paddle or other object may be used in emergency for steering. An anchor may be sent out in a boat only as permitted by rule 64, Aground or Foul of an Obstruction.

61—Sounding
Any means of sounding may be used provided rule 60, Means of Propulsion, is not infringed.

62—Manual Power
A yacht shall use manual power only, except that a power winch or windlass may be used in weighing anchor or in getting clear after running aground or fouling any object, and a power bilge pump may be used in an auxiliary yacht.

63—Anchoring and Making Fast
1. A yacht may anchor. Means of anchoring may include the crew standing on the bottom and any weight lowered to the bottom. A yacht shall recover any anchor or weight used, and any chain or rope attached to it, before continuing in the race, unless after making every effort she finds recovery impossible. In this case she shall report the circumstances to the race committee, which may disqualify her if it considers the loss due either to inadequate gear or to insufficient effort to recover it.
2. A yacht shall be afloat and off moorings, before her preparatory signal, but may be anchored, and shall not

thereafter make fast or be made fast by means other than anchoring, nor be hauled out, except for the purpose of rule 64, Aground or Foul of an Obstruction, or to effect repairs, reef sails or bail out.

64—Aground or Foul of an Obstruction
A yacht, after grounding or fouling another vessel or other object, is subject to rule 62, Manual Power, and may, in getting clear, use her own anchors, boats, ropes, spars and other gear; may send out an anchor in a boat; may be refloated by her crew going overboard either to stand on the bottom or to go ashore to push off; but may receive outside assistance only from the crew of the vessel fouled. A yacht shall recover all her own gear used in getting clear before continuing in the race.

65—Skin Friction
A yacht shall not eject or release from a container any substance (such as polymer) the purpose of which is, or could be, to reduce the frictional resistance of the hull by altering the character of the flow of water inside the boundary layer.

66—Increasing Stability
Unless otherwise prescribed by her class rules or in the sailing instructions, a yacht shall not use any device, such as a trapeze or plank, to project outboard the weight of any of the crew, nor, when a yacht is equipped with lifelines, shall any member of the crew station any part of his torso outside them, other than temporarily.

(Number 67 is a spare number.)

PART VI
PROTESTS, DISQUALIFICATIONS AND APPEALS

68—Protests
1. A yacht can protest against any other yacht, except that a protest for an alleged infringement of the rules of Part IV can be made only by a yacht directly involved in, or witnessing an incident.

2. A protest occurring between yachts competing in separate races sponsored by different clubs shall be heard by a combined committee of both clubs.

3.(a) A protest for an infringement of the rules or sailing instructions occurring during a race shall be signified by showing a flag (International Code flag "B" is always acceptable, irrespective of any other provisions in the sailing instructions) conspicuously in the rigging of the protesting yacht at the first reasonable opportunity and keeping it flying until she has **finished** or retired, or if the first reasonable opportunity occurs after **finishing**, until acknowledged by the race committee. In the case of a yacht sailed singlehanded, it will be sufficient if the flag (whether displayed in the rigging or not) is brought to the notice of the yacht protested against as soon as possible after the incident and to the race committee when the protesting yacht **finishes**.

(b) A yacht which has no knowledge of the facts justifying a protest until after she has **finished** or retired may nevertheless protest without having shown a protest flag.

(c) A protesting yacht shall try to inform the yacht protested against that a protest will be lodged.

(d) Such a protest shall be in writing and signed by the owner or his representative, and should state :—
(i) The date, time and whereabouts of the incident.
(ii) The particular rule or rules or sailing instructions alleged to have been infringed.
(iii) A statement of the facts.
(iv) Unless irrelevant, a diagram of the incident.

(e) Unless otherwise prescribed in the sailing instructions a protesting yacht shall deliver, or if that is not possible, mail her protest to the race committee:

  (i) within two hours of the time she **finishes** the race, or within such time as may have been prescribed in the sailing instructions under rule 3.2(b)(xiv), unless the race committee should have reason to extend these time limits, or

  (ii) should she not **finish** the race, within such a time as the race committee may consider reasonable in the circumstances of the case. A protest shall be accompanied by such fee, if any, as may have been prescribed in the sailing instructions under rule 3.2(b)(xiv).

(f) The race committee shall allow any omissions in the details required by rule 68.3(d) to be remedied at a later time.

4.(a) A protest that a measurement, scantling or flotation rule has been infringed while **racing**, or that a classification or rating certificate is for any reason invalid, shall be lodged with the race committee not later than 6 p.m. on the day following the race. The race committee shall send a copy of the protest to the yacht protested against and, should there appear to be reasonable grounds for the protest, it shall refer the question to an authority qualified to decide such questions.

(b) The race committee, in making its decision, shall be governed by the determination of such authority. Copies of such decision shall be sent to all yachts involved.

5.(a) A yacht which claims that her chances of winning a prize have been prejudiced by an action or omission of the race committee, may seek redress from the race committee in accordance with the requirements for a protest provided in rules 68.3(d), (e) and (f).

(b) When the race committee decides that such action or omission was prejudicial, and that the result of the race was altered thereby, it shall cancel or **abandon** the race, or make such other arrangement as it deems equitable.

6. A protest made in writing shall not be withdrawn, but shall be decided by the race committee, unless prior to the hearing full responsibility is acknowledged by one or more yachts.

69—Refusal of a Protest

1. When the race committee decides that a protest does not conform to the requirements of rule 68, Protests, it shall inform the protesting yacht that her protest will not be heard and of the reasons for such decision.

2. Such a decision shall not be reached without giving the protesting yacht all opportunity of bringing evidence that the requirements of rule 68, Protests, were complied with.

70—Hearings

1. When the race committee decides that a protest conforms to all the requirements of rule 68, Protests, it shall call a hearing as soon as possible. The protest, or a copy of it, shall be made available to all yachts involved, and each shall be notified, in writing if practicable, of the time and place set for the hearing. A reasonable time shall be allowed for the preparation of defense. At the hearing, the race committee shall take the evidence presented by the parties to the protest and such other evidence as it may consider necessary. The parties to the protest, or a representative of each, shall have the right to be present, but all others, except one witness at a time while testifying, may be excluded. A yacht other than one named in the protest, which is involved in that protest, shall have all the privileges of yachts originally named in it.

2. A yacht shall not be penalized without a hearing, except as provided in rule 73.1(a), Disqualification without Protest.

3. Failure on the part of any of the interested parties or a representative to make an effort to attend the hearing of

the protest may justify the race committee in deciding the protest as it thinks fit without a full hearing.

71—Decisions

The race committee shall make its decision promptly after the hearing. Each decision shall be communicated to the parties involved, and shall state fully the facts and grounds on which it is based and shall specify the rules, if any, infringed. If requested by any of the parties, such decision shall be given in writing and shall include the race committee's diagram. The findings of the race committee as to the facts involved shall be final.

72—Disqualification after Protest

1. When the race committee, after hearing a protest or acting under rule 73, Disqualification without Protest, or any appeal authority, is satisfied:—

  (a) that a yacht has infringed any of these rules or the sailing instructions, or

  (b) that in consequence of her neglect of any of these rules or the sailing instructions she has compelled other yachts to infringe any of these rules or the sailing instructions,

she shall be disqualified unless the sailing instructions applicable to that race provide some other penalty. Such disqualification or other penalty shall be imposed, irrespective of whether the rule or sailing instruction which led to the disqualification or penalty was mentioned in the protest, or the yacht which was at fault was mentioned or protested against, e.g., the protesting yacht or a third yacht might be disqualified and the protested yacht absolved.

2. For the purpose of awarding points in a series, a retirement after an infringement of any of these rules or the sailing instructions shall not rank as a disqualification. This penalty can be imposed only in accordance with rules 72, Disqualification after Protest, and 73, Disqualification without Protest.

3. When a yacht either is disqualified or has retired, the next in order shall be awarded her place.

73—Disqualification without Protest

1.(a) A yacht which fails either to **start** or to **finish** may be disqualified without protest or hearing, after the conclusion of the race, except that she shall be entitled to a hearing, provided she satisfies the race committee that an error may have been made.

(b) A yacht so penalized shall be informed of the action taken, either by letter or by notification in the racing results.

2. When the race committee:—

  (a) sees an apparent infringement by a yacht of any of these rules or the sailing instructions (except as provided in rule 73.1), or

  (b) receives a report not later than the same day from a witness who was neither competing in the race, nor otherwise an interested party, alleging such an infringement, or

  (c) has reasonable grounds for supposing from the evidence at the hearing of a valid protest, that any yacht involved in the incident may have committed such an infringement,

it may notify such yacht thereof orally, or if that is not possible, in writing, delivered or mailed not later than one day after:—

  (i) the finish of the race, or
  (ii) the receipt of the report, or
  (iii) the hearing of the protest.

Such notice shall contain a statement of the pertinent facts and of the particular rule or rules or sailing instructions believed to have been infringed, and the race committee shall act thereon in the same manner as if it had been a protest made by a competitor.

74—Penalties for Gross Infringement of Rules

1. When a gross infringement of any of these rules or the sailing instructions is proved against the owner, the owner's representative, the helmsman or sailing master of a yacht, such persons may be disqualified by the national authority, for any period it may think fit, from either steer-

ing or sailing in a yacht in any race held under its jurisdiction.

2. Notice of any penalty adjudged under this rule shall be communicated to the I.Y.R.U. which shall inform all national authorities.

75—Persons Interested not to take part in Decision

No member of either a race committee or of any appeals authority shall take part in the discussion or decision upon any disputed question in which he is an interested party, but this does not preclude him from giving evidence in such a case.

76—Expenses Incurred by Protest

Unless otherwise prescribed by the race committee, the fees and expenses entailed by a protest or measurement or classification shall be paid by the unsuccessful party.

77—Appeals

☆ 1. LIMITATIONS ON RIGHT TO APPEAL—Appeals involving solely the interpretation of the racing rules may be taken to the Appeals Committee of the Union for final determination:

   a. if the Club is a member of the Union but is not a member of a local association belonging to the Union, by an owner or his representative from a decision of the Race Committee;

   b. if the Club is a member of a local association belonging to the Union, by an owner or his representative or by the Race Committee from a decision of the local association.

2. PREPARATION OF APPEAL PAPERS—All appeals shall be in writing and shall set forth the grounds of the appeal and be signed by the appellant. They shall be filed with the Secretary of the Union by the body rendering the decision appealed from, within thirty days after the decision is announced, together with—

   (a) a copy of the sailing instructions;

   (b) a copy of the protest or request for redress;

   (c) the names of the yachts represented at the hearing, and of any yacht duly notified of the hearing, but not represented, and the name and address of the representative of each of said yachts;

   (d) a copy of the decision of the Race Committee containing a full statement of the facts found by it;

   (e) an official diagram prepared by the Race Committee in accordance with the facts found by it and signed by it and showing, (i) the course to the next mark or, if close by, the mark itself and its required side, (ii) the direction and velocity of the wind, (iii) the set of the current, if any, and (iv) the position or positions and tracks of the yachts involved;

   (f) a copy of the decision, if any, of the local association.

3. DECISION OF APPEALS COMMITTEE—Decisions of the Appeals Committee shall be in writing and the grounds of each decision shall be specified therein. Each decision shall be filed with the Secretary of the Union, who shall send copies thereof to all parties to the infringement and appeal.

TEAM RACING RULES

Team racing shall be sailed under the yacht racing rules of the International Yacht Racing Union as adopted by the North American Yacht Racing Union supplemented as follows:

SAILING RULES

1. A yacht may manoeuvre against a yacht sailing another leg of the course only if she can do so while sailing a proper course relative to the leg which she herself is sailing.

2. Except to protect her own or a team mate's finishing position, a yacht in one team which is completing the last leg of the course shall not manoeuvre against a yacht in another team which has no opponent astern of her.

3. Right of way may be waived by team mates, provided that by so doing an opponent is not baulked; but the benefits of rule 12, Yacht Materially Prejudiced, shall not be available to a yacht damaged by contact between team mates.

4. When two overlapping yachts on the same tack are in the act of rounding or passing on the required side of a mark at which their proper course changes:

   (a) If the leeward yacht is inside, she may, if she has luffing rights hold her course or luff. If she does not have luffing rights, she shall promptly assume her proper course to the next mark whether or not she has to jibe:

   (b) If the windward yacht is inside, she shall promptly luff up to her proper course to the next mark, or if she cannot assume such proper course without tacking and does not choose to tack, she shall promptly luff up to close-hauled. This clause does not restrict a leeward yacht's right to luff under rule 38, Luffing after Starting.

SCORING

5. **Each Race**

   (a) Yachts shall score three-quarters of a point for first place, two points for second place, three points for third place, and so on.

   (b) A yacht which infringes any rule and retires with reasonable promptness shall score one point more than the number of yachts in the race, but if her retirement is tardy, or if she fails to retire and is subsequently disqualified, she shall score four points more than the number of yachts in the race.

   (c) A yacht which infringes a rule shortly before or when finishing shall be considered to have retired with reasonable promptness if she notifies the race committee of her retirement as soon as is reasonably practicable.

   (d) A yacht which does not finish for a reason other than an infringement shall score points equal to the number of starters in the race, except as provided in (e)

   (e) After all the yachts of one team have finished or retired, the Race Committee may stop the race and allot to each yacht of the other team which is still racing and underway the points she would have received had she finished.

   (f) The team with the lowest total point score shall be the winner of the race.

6. **The Series**

   (a) When only two teams are competing, the team winning the greater number of races sailed shall be the winner of the series.

   (b) When three or more teams are competing in a series consisting of races each of which is between two teams, the team winning the greatest number of races shall be the winner.

   (c) When three or more teams are all competing in each race the team with the lowest total point score in all races sailed shall be the winner.

7. **Breaking Ties**

   (a) When two or more teams are tied because of each having won the same number of races, if practicable the tie should be resolved by a sail off.

   (b) If there is a tie when more than two teams are competing, the team which has beaten the other tied team or teams in the most races shall be the winner. Failing this, the team with the lowest point score in all races sailed shall be the winner. When teams tie with only two teams competing and a sail off is impracticable, the tie shall be broken in favor of the winner of the last race.

ADDENDUM

RULES RECOMMENDED TO APPLY WHEN THE HOME TEAM FURNISHES ALL RACING YACHTS

A. ASSIGNMENT OF YACHTS: The home team shall furnish the visiting team with a list of the yachts to be used and of the sail numbers assigned to each yacht for the match. The home team shall divide these yachts into as many equal groups as there are competing teams and these groups shall be drawn for by lot for the first race. Skipper assignment to the yachts shall then be made as each team decides for itself, except that a skipper shall not at any time sail his own yacht. The groups of yachts shall be exchanged between races so that, as far as possible, each group will be sailed in turn by each team. In a two team match after an even number of races, if either team requests that the yachts be regrouped, the home team shall re-divide them into new groups which shall be drawn for by lot; except that for the final odd race of a two team match, the visiting team may select the group it wishes to sail.

B. ASSIGNMENT OF SAILS: If sails as well as yachts are furnished by the home team, the sails used by each yacht in the first race shall be used by her throughout the series and the substitution of a spare or extra sail shall not be permitted unless because of damage or for some other valid reason, a change is approved by the Jury or Judges after notification to both teams.

C. GROUP IDENTIFICATION: One group shall carry no marking. The second group shall carry dark colored strips or pennants, and additional groups shall carry light or differently colored strips or pennants. Strips or pennants should usually be furnished by the home team and should be attached to the same conspicuous place on each boat of a group, such as the after end of the main boom or permanent backstay.

D. BREAKDOWNS: When a breakdown results in substantial loss, the Jury or Judges shall decide whether or not it was the fault of the crew. In general, a breakdown caused by defective equipment, or the result of a foul by an opponent shall not be deemed the fault of the crew, and a breakdown caused by careless handling or capsizing shall be. In case of doubt, the doubt shall be resolved in favor of the crew.

E. If the Jury or Judges decide that the breakdown was not the fault of the crew and that a reasonably competent crew could not have remedied the defect in time to prevent substantial loss, they shall cancel the race, or order it to be resailed, or award the breakdown yacht the number of points she would have received had she finished in the same position in the race she held when she broke down. In case of doubt as to her position when she broke down, the doubt shall be resolved against her.

F. SPARES: The home team shall be prepared to furnish one or more extra yachts and sails to replace any which, in the opinion of the Jury or Judges, are unfit for use in the remaining races.

APPENDIX I

Amateur

1. For the purpose of international yacht races in which yachts entering are required to have one or more amateurs on board, and in other races with similar requirements, an amateur is a yachtsman who engages in yacht racing as a pastime as distinguished from a means of obtaining a livelihood. No yachtsman shall lose amateur status by reason of the fact that his livelihood is derived from designing or constructing any boats or parts of boats, or accessories of boats, or sails or from other professions associated with the sea and ships.

2. Any yachtsman whose amateur status is questioned or is in doubt, may apply to the national authority of the country of his residence for recognition of his amateur status. Any such applicant may be required to provide such particulars and evidence and to pay such fee as the national authority may prescribe. Recognition may be suspended or cancelled by the national authority by which it was granted.

3. The permanent committee of the International Yacht Racing Union, or any tribunal nominated by the chairman of that committee, may review the decision of any authority

as to the amateur status of a yachtsman for the purpose of competing in international races.

4. For the purposes of participation in the Olympic Games an amateur is required to conform to the eligibility rules of the International Olympic Committee. Information on these eligibility requirements is available from all national authorities.

APPENDIX II

"Pumping" Sails, "Ooching" and "Rocking"

"Pumping" consists of frequent rapid trimming of sails with no particular reference to a change in true or apparent wind direction. To promote planing or surfing, rapid trimming of sails need not be considered "pumping".

The purpose of this interpretation of rule 60 is to prevent "fanning" one's boat around the course by flapping the sail similar to a bird's wing in flight. "Pumping" or frequent, quickly-repeated trimming and releasing of the mainsail to increase propulsion is not allowed and is not "the natural action of the wind on the sails".

Where surfing or planing conditions exist, however, rule 60 allows taking advantage of "the natural action of water on the hull" through the rapid trimming of sails and adjustment of helm to promote (initiate) surfing or planing.

The test is whether or not the conditions are such that by rapid trimming of sails a boat could be started surfing or planing. A skipper challenged for "pumping" will have to prove, through the performance either of his own boat or of other boats, that surfing or planing conditions existed, and that the frequency of his rapid trimming was geared to the irregular or cyclical wave forms rather than to a regular rhythmic pattern.

Note that the interpretation refers to "promoting" and not to "maintaining" surfing or planing. Once a boat has started surfing or planing on a particular set of wave forms, from then on she must let the natural action of wind and water propel her without further rapid trimming and releasing of the sails.

Rapid trimming when approaching marks or the finishing line or other critical points should be consistent with that which was practiced throughout the leg.

"Ooching", which consists of lunging forward and stopping abruptly, falls in the same category as "pumping".

"Rocking" consists of persistently rolling a yacht from side to side.

APPENDIX III

INTERNATIONAL YACHT RACING UNION RULES BEFORE CHANGES PRESCRIBED BY THE N.A.Y.R.U

(For use only when racing outside of the jurisdiction of the N.A.Y.R.U.)

4—Signals

1. **International Code Flag Signals**
   "AP"—Answering Pendant, Postponement Signal.
   When displayed alone over a class signal, means:—
   "The scheduled time of the start of the designated race is postponed 15 minutes."
   (This postponement can be extended indefinitely in 15-minute intervals by dipping and rehoisting the signal.)
   When displayed over 1 ball or shape over a class signal, means:—
   "The scheduled time of the start of the designated race is postponed 30 minutes."
   (This postponement can be extended indefinitely by the addition of 1 ball or shape for every 15 minutes.)
   When displayed over one of the numeral pendants 1 to 9 over a class signal, means:—
   "The scheduled time of the start of the designated race is postponed 1 hour, 2 hours, etc."

When displayed over the letter "A" over a class signal, means :—
"The designated race is **postponed** to a later date."
When any of the above signals is displayed without a class signal below, means :—
"The whole sailing programme is **postponed** in accordance with the signal made."

8—Recalls

1. Unless otherwise prescribed by the national authority or in the sailing instructions, the race committee may allot a recall number or letter to each yacht, in accordance with rule 3.2(b)(viii), using yachts' sail numbers or letters when practicable.

18—Entries

Unless otherwise prescribed by the national authority or by the Race Committee in either the notice or the sailing instructions, entries shall be made in the following form :—

FORM OF ENTRY

To the Secretary..*Club*
   Please enter the yacht...*for*
the..........................*race, on the*.........................
Her distinguishing flag is..
her sail numbers and letters are................, *her rig is*...............
the color of her hull is..
and her rating or class is..

I agree to be bound by the rules of the I.Y.R.U., by the prescriptions of the national authority under which this race is sailed, by the sailing instructions and by the class rules.
   Signed .... *Date* ....
      (*Owner or owner's representative*)
            Name ....
            Address ....
            Telephone No. ....
            Club ....

Entrance fee enclosed

25—Sail Numbers, Letters and Emblems

2. Other yachts shall comply with the rules of their national authority or class in regard to the allotment, carrying and size of sail numbers, letters and emblems, which rules should, so far as they may be applicable, conform to the above requirements.

28—Flags

A national authority may prescribe the flag usage which shall be observed by yachts under its jurisdiction.

72—Disqualification After Protest

4. The question of damages arising from an infringement of any of these rules or the sailing instructions shall be governed by the prescriptions, if any, of the national authority.

77—Appeals

1. Unless otherwise prescribed by the national authority which has recognized the sponsoring organization concerned, an appeal against the decision of a race committee shall be governed by rules 77, Appeals, and 78, Particulars to be Furnished in Appeals.

2. Unless otherwise prescribed by the national authority or in the sailing instructions (subject to rule 2(j) or 3.2(b) (xvi)), a protest which has been decided by the race committee shall be referred to the national authority solely on a question of interpretation of these rules, within such period after the receipt of the race committee's decision, as the national authority may decide :—
   (a) when the race committee, at its own instance, thinks proper to do so, or
   (b) when any of the parties involved in the protest makes application for such reference.
This reference shall be accompanied by such deposit as the national authority may prescribe, payable by the appellant, to be forfeited to the funds of the national authority in the event of the appeal being dismissed.

3. The national authority shall have power to uphold or reverse the decision of the race committee, and if it is of opinion, from the facts found by it, that a

yacht involved in a protest has infringed an applicable rule, it shall disqualify her, irrespective of whether the rule or sailing instruction which led to such disqualification was mentioned in the protest.

4. The decision of the national authority, which shall be final, shall be communicated in writing to all interested parties.

5. In the Olympic Games and such other international regattas as may be specially approved by the I.Y.R.U., the decisions of the race committee, jury or judges shall be final.

6. An appeal once lodged with the national authority shall not be withdrawn.

78—Particulars to be Furnished in Appeals

1. The reference to the national authority shall be in writing and shall contain the following particulars, in order, so far as they are applicable :—
   (a) A copy of the notice of the race and the sailing instructions furnished to the yachts.
   (b) A copy of the protest, or protests, if any, prepared in accordance with rule 68.3(d), and all other written statements which may have been put in by the parties.
   (c) The observations of the race committee thereon, a full statement of the facts found, its decision and the grounds thereof.
   (d) An official diagram prepared by the race committee in accordance with the facts found by it, showing :—
      (i) The course to the next **mark**, or, if close by, the **mark** itself with the required side ;
      (ii) the direction and force of the wind ;
      (iii) the set and strength of the current, if any ;
      (iv) the depth of water, if relevant ; and
      (v) the positions and courses of all the yachts involved.
      (vi) Where possible, yachts should be shown sailing from the bottom of the diagram towards the top.
   (e) The grounds of the appeal, to be supplied by either :—
      (i) the race committee under rule 77.2(a) ; or
      (ii) the appellant under rule 77.2(b).
   (f) Observations, if any, upon the appeal by the race committee or any of the parties.

2. The race committee shall notify all parties that an appeal will be lodged and shall invite them to make any observations upon it. Any such observation shall be forwarded with the appeal.

APPENDIX IV

EXCERPTS FROM THE INTERNATIONAL REGULATIONS FOR PREVENTING COLLISIONS AT SEA—1963

(Commonly called the International Rules of the Road)

PART B.—LIGHTS AND SHAPES

Rule 5

(b) In addition to the lights prescribed in section (a), a sailing vessel may carry on the top of the foremast two lights in a vertical line one over the other, sufficiently separated so as to be clearly distinguished. The upper light shall be red and the lower light shall be green. Both lights shall be constructed and fixed as prescribed in rule 2(a)(i) and shall be visible at a distance of at least 2 miles.
[NOTE : 2(a)(i) calls for a light "to show an unbroken light over an arc of the horizon of 225° so fixed as to show from right ahead to 2 points abaft the beam on either side."]

Rule 12

Every vessel or seaplane on the water may, if necessary in order to attract attention, in addition to the lights which she is by these rules required to carry, show a flare up light or use a detonating or other efficient sound signal that cannot be mistaken for any signal authorized elsewhere under these rules.

PART D.—STEERING AND SAILING RULES
Preliminary

1. *In obeying and construing these rules, any action taken should be positive, in ample time, and with due regard to the observance of good seamanship.*

2. *Risk of collision can, when circumstances permit, be ascertained by carefully watching the compass bearing of an approaching vessel. If the bearing does not appreciably change, such risk should be deemed to exist.*

4. *Rules 17 to 24 apply only to vessels in sight of one another.*

Rule 17

(a) When two sailing vessels are approaching one another, so as to involve risk of collision, one of them shall keep out of the way of the other as follows:

(i) When each has the wind on a different side, the vessel which has the wind on the port side shall keep out of the way of the other.

(ii) When both have the wind on the same side, the vessel which is to windward shall keep out of the way of the vessel which is to leeward.

(b) For the purposes of this rule the windward side shall be deemed to be the side opposite to that on which the mainsail is carried or, in the case of a square-rigged vessel, the side opposite to that on which the largest fore-and-aft sail is carried.

Rule 20

(a) When a power-driven vessel and a sailing vessel are proceeding in such directions as to involve risk of collision, except as provided for in rules 24 and 26, the power-driven vessel shall keep out of the way of the sailing vessel.

(b) This rule shall not give to a sailing vessel the right to hamper, in a narrow channel, the safe passage of a power-driven vessel which can navigate only inside such channel.

Rule 22

Every vessel which is directed by these rules to keep out of the way of another vessel shall, so far as possible, take positive early action to comply with this obligation, and shall, if the circumstances of the case admit, avoid crossing ahead of the other.

Rule 24

(a) Notwithstanding anything contained in these rules, every vessel overtaking any other shall keep out of the way of the overtaken vessel.

(b) Every vessel coming up with another vessel from any direction more than 22½° (2 points) abaft her beam, i.e., in such a position, with reference to the vessel which she is overtaking, that at night she would be unable to see either of that vessel's sidelights, shall be deemed to be an overtaking vessel; and no subsequent alteration of the bearing between the two vessels shall make the overtaking vessel a crossing vessel within the meaning of these rules, or relieve her of the duty of keeping clear of the overtaken vessel until she is finally past and clear.

(c) If the overtaking vessel cannot determine with certainty whether she is forward of or abaft this direction from the other vessel, she shall assume that she is an overtaking vessel and keep out of the way.

Rule 26

All vessels not engaged in fishing, except vessels to which the provisions of rule 4 apply, shall, when underway, keep out of the way of vessels engaged in fishing.

The International Rules apply to vessels on the high seas. The Inland Rules apply to vessels on inland waters including coastal areas.

Copies of the complete regulations, both International and Inland, may be obtained from the United States Coast Guard.

PROTEST COMMITTEE PROCEDURE
in Outline Form

Rules Concerning Protests—68, 69, 70, 71, 72, 73 and 75.

Preliminaries

1. Note on the protest the time it is received.

2. Determine whether the protest contains the information called for by rule 68.3(d) in sufficient detail to identify the incident and to tell the recipient what the protest is about. If not, ask the protestor to supply the information (rule 68.3(f)).

3. Inquire whether the protestor flew a protest flag in accordance with rule 68.3(a) unless rule 68.3(b) applies or the protestor is seeking redress under rule 68.5(a) and note his answer on the protest.

4. Inquire whether the protestor tried to inform the yacht(s) protested against (the protestee(s)) that a protest would be lodged (rule 68.3(c)) and note his answer on the protest.

5. Unless rule 69 applies, promptly notify the protestee(s).

6. Hold a hearing as soon as possible when the protest conforms to the requirements of rule 68 (see 1, 2 and 3 above). Notify the representative of each yacht involved of the time and place of the hearing (rule 70.1).

The Hearing

1. The representative of each yacht involved in the incident is entitled to be present throughout the hearing. All others, except one witness at a time while testifying, may be excluded (rule 70.1).

2. Read to the meeting the protest and any other written statement there may be about the incident (such as an account of it from the protestee).

3. Have first the protestor and then the protestee(s) give their accounts of the incident. Each may question the other(s). Questions by the Protest Committee, except for clarifying details, are preferably deferred until all accounts have been presented. Models are helpful. Positions before and after the incident itself are often helpful.

4. Invite the protestor and then the protestee to call witnesses. They may be questioned by the protestor and protestees as well as by the Committee.

5. Invite first the protestor and then the protestee to make a final statement of his case, including any application or interpretation of the rules to the incident as he sees it.

Decision

1. The Protest Committee, after dismissing those involved in the incident, should decide what the relevant facts are.

2. The Committee should then apply the rules and reach a decision as to who, if anyone, infringed a rule and what rule was infringed (rule 71).

3. Having reached a decision, it should record both the findings of fact and the decision in writing, recall the protestor and protestee and read to them the decision (rule 71).

4. Any party involved is entitled to a copy of the decision (rule 71), signed by the Chairman of the Protest Committee. A copy should also be filed with the Committee records.

N.B. The Protest Committee referred to above may be the Race Committee, Judges appointed for the event in which the incident occurred or a Protest Committee established by the Race Committee for the express purpose of handling protests.

Standard Protest Forms are available from the N.A.Y.R.U. at $1.25 for sets of 25.

RACE COMMITTEE SIGNALS
See Rule 4

AP—Answering Pennant, Postponement Signal

L—Come Within Hail or Follow Me

M—Mark Signal

N—Abandonment Signal

N over X—Abandonment and Re-Sail Signal

N over 1st Repeater—Cancellation Signal

R—Reverse Course Signal

S—Shortened Course Signal

1st Repeater—General Recall Signal

Know Your Racing Committee

There is a factor, affecting to a greater or lesser extent the outcome of every yacht race, that is unknown to many skippers and disregarded by most of the rest of them. This factor is the difference between the way the participating sailors see their race and the view taken by the race committee. You would hardly believe they were dealing with the same sport.

Not enough racing skippers serve on com-mittees. As a skipper, you should try to do a stint on the race committee once in awhile—not only as a public service but as an eye-opener. You may make several interesting discoveries, such as: Your friends on the committee are not as stupid as you thought they were; the committee is faced with many difficult and sometimes insoluble problems; and finally (and most important), the committee's view of the race may help your future racing performance by warning you of what to expect and helping you to think in the way the race committee is thinking and thus to outguess your competitors. That is, "know your enemy" or at least attempt to analyze in advance how they will handle their problems. Their problems and how they administer the race may well determine its outcome. In planning your tactics and strategy, one of the most

Racing rules are followed even in *big* races, such as America's Cup event. In the 1970 race, a foul occurred as shown here. With seconds to go, *Gretel II* appeared to have *Intrepid* squeezed out. The gun went off and *Intrepid* held her course. (1) As shown, *Intrepid* kept coming while *Gretel* appeared to harden up. (2) The point of impact. Note *Gretel*'s genoa to windward. (3) *Intrepid* hardens up and *Gretel* falls away. (4) *Intrepid* clears the line with *Gretel*'s genoa still amidships.

important determinations is whether the race committee will behave competently or incompetently, whether they think like racing sailors or bingo players!

The conditions and the race instructions should be thoroughly analyzed before the race, and if any ambiguities exist, the committee should be questioned at the skipper's meeting or afloat before the preparatory signal. It is essential to understand fully how the course will be signaled, what marks will be used, whether any similar marks exist which might be confusing, and how the course will be established. Although it may be impossible to obtain all the answers you may wish to ask from the committee in advance or from "friendly" competitors, remembering to ask the questions of your crew (if no one with any knowledge is available) will at least force you to consider the various and frequently amazing solutions which the committee may reach.

RACING TACTICS

The most interesting part of racing is the tactics, and by this we mean the way the competitor places himself in relation to the other competitors, the marks, the course, the current, and the wind. You can sail as fast as you like and have the best possible technique, but if you do not have a plan of tactics you probably won't do well. In other words, a really clever tactician can often win against helmsmen who are actually sailing their boats faster.

In order to be a successful tactician you must train yourself to sense in advance the type of situation that is likely to develop. You have to weigh instantly the various possibilities and then select your own tactics from the answers.

The greatest advantage is experience. The reason why so many older helmsmen are so hard to beat is that they have stored up so many race-course situations in their minds that they automatically make the right decisions.

Unless you are always thinking ahead you may tack, for example, on a heading shift, as one is often taught to do, when this would put you immediately in the wind shadow of another boat. Then you would have to tack back again and, while this would certainly slow your boat, it might also put you in an even worse situation. In fact, lack of forethought could lose you ten places in as many seconds in a hot fleet.

The Start

No part of a race more consistently determines which yachts will have a chance of winning and which will not than the start. Usually a good start will assure a position at the front of the fleet at the weather mark, barring poor speed or bad guessing on wind shifts. Usually a good start is a necessary part of winning. Usually the same skippers get the best starts time after time. Why?

Starting should be the easiest part of your yachting game to improve—it does not take super speed or a fantastic spinnaker hand on the crew or a mind like a computer predicting 5-degree wind shifts—only the ability to follow a rather consistent starting plan and lots of practice to improve your boat handling and time-distance judgment, plus some flexibility in adjusting to the presence of other boats.

As previously mentioned, the starting line is an imaginary line between two points, usually a mark and a committee boat. The mark may be a fixed channel marker or buoy or a special mark, often a flag mounted in a small rowboat, temporarily put into position by the organization sponsoring the race. The committee boat may be any kind of craft with a mast from which flags and shapes (usually balls, cylinders, and cones) can be hoisted. Of course the boat must be large enough to accommodate several members of the race committee from the sponsoring yacht club. Usually, but not always, the starting-line marker is placed so that it is passed on the same side as the course turning marks are passed. In other words, all marks are usually left on the same side.

The ideal starting line is one that is set approximately square (90 degrees) to the wind. (If there is any variation, the left-hand end of the line should be set slightly closer to the

Driving across the starting line on the first leg of a Gold Cup course. These International One-Designs beat for the windward mark.

first mark than the right-hand end. This variation should not exceed 10 degrees with the first leg of the course, the direction to the first mark being nearly a dead beat to windward.) This ideal is theoretically possible to achieve with a closed-course race, but it is usually not possible on a point-to-point course unless the wind happens to blow from exactly the right direction. Of course, the first mark may not always lie dead to windward, but the important thing is that the line be square to the wind. The object of such a line is that neither end of the line is favored, so that competitors will not be bunched or jammed together at one end. If the current or some other factor makes one end of the line more attractive, then the line should be slanted slightly away from the right angle to the wind in order to make both ends equally attractive.

This principle holds true on reaching and running starts as well. It is highly desirable to have the starting boats evenly spread out along the line no matter what the point of sailing. Windward starts are preferable, because all the boats rarely arrive at the first mark at almost the same time, as so often happens with reaching and running starts.

Even on a closed course, the ideal starting line is often very difficult to set because of last-minute wind shifts which cause the line to be slanted away from the 90-degree angle to the wind. In fact, even though the race committee makes a great effort to get a perfect line, more often than not one end will be slightly more favored than the other.

The following system is customarily used to start a race: at precisely 10 minutes before the start, a *warning* signal is given from the

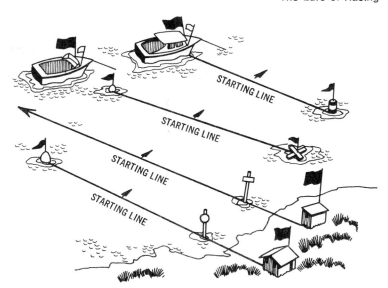

Several starting-line arrangements.

committee boat. This signal is given audibly, with a gun or whistle, and at the same time it is given visibly with the hoisting of a flag or shape. Exactly 4½ minutes later, the warning shape, which is usually white, is hauled down; and 30 seconds later another signal is given audibly and visibly with a gun or whistle and the hoisting of another flag or shape. This is called the *preparatory* signal and the flag or shape is usually colored blue. Four and one-half minutes later, the preparatory shape is hauled down; and 30 seconds after this, the *start* signal is given with the hoisting of the starting shape or flag, usually colored red, and the sounding of the whistle or gun. Actually, the visual signal gives the exact time of the start, because a starting gun can misfire.

Racing skippers try to reach the line just as the starting signal is made. The ideal or perfect start is one that is made at the favored spot on the line, with the boat sailing at top speed and just touching the line as the signal is hoisted and the gun is fired. Of course, this is an ideal that is very difficult to achieve.

Planning the Start. The most important thing to remember about the start is that the initial warning signal of the start is given a long time before the actual start of the race. By the time the gun goes off, the race can almost be over for the skipper who is in the wrong place on the line. To add to the problem, there are very few right places on the line. There are many average places, and a whole crowd of poor places.

The right place on the line needs an analysis. The perfect start consists of hitting the line right on the gun, with a full head of steam, with clear air, with the ability to tack if tacking is indicated, at the favored end of the line, with knowledge of what the wind will do, with knowledge of currents and other local phenomena, and with the boat carefully tuned. Add to this a complete understanding of the rules, and a mental list of the "hot" boats in the fleet by number and color.

The morning of the race be sure to study local conditions with care. While your crew is stepping the mast, washing the bottom, and doing their other crew duties, you may appear to be doing nothing but strolling around the club and acting like a poorly dressed bum. This is the way skippers are supposed to look —but you are really planning and getting ready for the start. You look over the course, analyze the location of clumps of trees, and other objects that may influence the wind. You talk to members of the home club and try to find out about currents, sand bars, stumps of trees below the surface, places where the wind plays tricks, and in general to try to get a "feel" for the location. If you can, try to pump the local fleet champ in another class. Since he has no ax to grind, he *may* give you the straight information. The most reliable dope, however, will probably be based on your own observations or from a government chart.

Study the wind. The map in the local paper will show you the possibility of fronts coming through. A low front scheduled to go through will have about the same effect in this locale as it would have in your home waters, which you are thoroughly familiar with. Find out the relative strength of the wind, and estimate whether it will be on the increase or decrease. Time the wind shifts to get the regular pattern and the duration of the steady periods. This information you will need out on the course as you begin starting maneuvers.

About three hours before the race, take the boat for a short trip. This will give you a chance to check that the crew has everything aboard, that the knot in the end of the mainsheet is properly tied, that the forestay is under the desired tension, and that a good supply of cigarettes is on board. Keep checking the wind during this period to see if it is beginning to act temperamental and change its pattern. Look over the local conditions that you have heard about to be sure that somebody did not change the layout by growing a clump of pine trees overnight. Get back to the dock no later than two hours before the race is to start.

Go back to the registration desk, get a copy of the instructions, and find how the committee is going to run the event. Learn the course signals, and make your crew do the same. If the committee says modified Gold Cup course, ask them what they mean and insist that they draw you a diagram. One committee's modified Gold Cup course is the next committee's "twice around" with an extra beat.

Find out at the registration desk whom you are racing against and, if you know the fleet, try to spot the top ten contenders. These are the skippers you have to beat to take home the award. Get their sail numbers and the colors of their boats. This may help later on. If during the race you spot four boats going off alone on what looks like a gamble, it may not be a gamble if they are all from your top-ten group and smart enough to do something that the rest of the fleet does not know about.

While you are doing all these things, keep checking the wind.

About one hour before, get your crew ready, make the final check on the boat, and get out on the course. First, sail out to the vicinity of the starting line and do not wander too far away from that area. Keep checking the direction, strength, and shift pattern of the wind in the starting area. Run your crew through a loosening up series of exercises on every point of sailing—beating, reaching, and running. As soon as the line is set, go to the windward end, and time how long it takes you to reach down the full length of the line. On the way, sailing right down the line, get a compass reading of the line. Now harden up on starboard and get a compass reading of your heading. If the difference between these readings is over 45 degrees, the starboard tack will be the favored tack. If the difference is less than 45 degrees, the port tack will be favored. Go through this timing run and compass check again and again to keep informed about shifting patterns in the wind.

Head for the upwind side of the committee boat, in order to be close by when the 10-minute gun is fired. When the gun goes off, start the stop watch and have the crew member who is handling the watch advise you of the time remaining every 30 seconds down to the 5 minutes. From then on, your timekeeper should call the time every 15 seconds.

During this period before the actual start you should make another check on wind direction and decide which tack is going to be the best. With this knowledge, you can determine where you want to start. If starboard is favored, a windward-end start is indicated. If port is favored, a leeward-end start will be best. This assumes that the mark that you are heading for is close to directly upwind of the starting-line center. If the weather mark is to one side of the course, and the initial weather leg is short, this will influence your plan about which end to start on.

Selecting the Starting Position. Choosing the proper starting spot on the line is one of the keys to successful starting. There is a simple rule for choosing the favored end when the line is not square to the wind. With the boat near the center of the starting line, luff up until the boat is headed directly into the eye of the wind, and the bow will point closer to one end of the line than the other. The end that is closer to the boat's heading when she is head to wind is the favored end of the line. A boat making a well-timed start at the favored end is always ahead of boats making well-timed starts anywhere else on the line. In choosing the favored end, however, one has to be careful about a last-minute wind shift which might favor the opposite end. If you are ahead but to leeward of a competitor, you gain if the shift is a header, but you lose if the shift is a lift.

It is usually more prudent to start on a *starboard tack* because you have the right of way and can force port-tack boats about in converging situations. Thus most sailors always start on a starboard tack. But, there are a *few* occasions when it pays to take a chance and try a port-tack start, especially if it is late in a series and you need a brilliant race to get back in contention.

A port-tack start should also be considered if strategy indicates that the "right" way to go after the start is on port tack. Even if you have to go under several yachts on starboard tack, you will be the first boat going in the correct direction and are almost certain to overcome the early deficit.

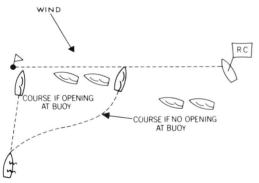

The port-tack start.

A port-tack start becomes even more inviting if the line also favors the leeward end. Only one or two yachts can get a good starboard-tack start. The others will be backwinded and even the leader will have to wait until he draws out before tacking to port. In a small fleet or a fleet with timid starters, you might be able to start right at the buoy end and cross the whole fleet. In a large and keen fleet this will seldom work, as someone on

starboard tack is apt to be right at the buoy as the gun goes. Still there is a way to try for the "perfect" port-tack start and then modify it if there is no opening at the buoy. Approach the buoy end on port tack some distance back of the line and with say one minute to go, be 30 seconds sailing time from the line. If it then appears there will be an opening at the buoy, kill way for 30 seconds and then go for it. If, as will more often be the case, it appears there will be no opening, reach off down the line looking for a hole to shoot through behind several starboard-tack yachts. Usually you can find such a hole and at the gun will be off in the right direction with clear air and a big smile on your face.

When choosing the favored starting spot on the line, there are factors to be considered other than what position will put you ahead of your competitors at that particular moment. The racing skipper must decide where he wants to go immediately after the start. He may, for example, wish to go offshore if the current is favorable and there appears to be a better breeze away from the land, or he may want to tack inshore to get into smoother water and to escape a foul current.

Another tremendously important consideration is where the starter should go to get clean, undisturbed wind. A boat's speed can be greatly harmed by the disturbed air (backwind and wind shadows) from other boats, and this is particularly true in the vicinity of a crowded starting line. A boat that makes a well-timed start at the line's favored end will usually get clean air. At the windward end of the line (when on the starboard tack of a windward start), a boat can usually get clear wind even if she gets a bad start, because she can promptly tack into undisturbed wind soon after crossing the line. If she gets a bad start at the line's leeward end, she may not be able to tack, but she may be able to bear off slightly and foot into clean air. Of course, if all the starting boats are headed, this will put the leeward boat in the most favored position. In the event that the line is square to the wind and the starters are bunched at each end, there might be cleaner air in the middle; but when starting in the line's middle, it is usually difficult to bear off into less disturbed air and also difficult to tack for clean air. If several races have been run before the one in which you are entered, watch the boats in them closely and see what their behavior is at the windward or leeward end of the starting line.

Now let us consider the techniques of starting at the three spots on the line—flag end, committee-boat end, and somewhere in between.

1. *The flag end.* The moves are easy. Pass the flag end on starboard going away with anywhere from 1½ to 3 minutes left. Tack or jibe so as to return on port tack passing the flag with around 30 seconds left. Plan to tack ahead of the first starboard boat, stall until you can trim in, and be at the flag at the gun.

Four times out of five it will go smoothly and just as described. The fifth time there will be complications, which can be of two kinds. If the first starboard tackers are very early and are going to cross before the start, you will have to either tack into the first hole that does appear or, better in most cases, remain on port tack and go through the first hole that develops. Actually, the danger in trying

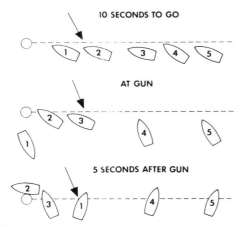

10 SECONDS TO GO

AT GUN

5 SECONDS AFTER GUN

The close-port start.

for the position at the port end of the line is that you might make a miscalculation and not be able to get around the mark, or will be too soon and have no place to go to kill time. However, you must keep in mind that on such a line everyone will be tacking onto port at the earliest opportunity. Therefore, you will be safe most of the time to do a tight jibe with a few seconds to go and head for the line on port tack just after the gun, as

boat 1 has done in the diagrams. This sounds dangerous, but nine times out of ten you will find a hole will open up for you. Boats will be tacking onto port with little way on and you will come steaming up astern and sail past them before they are squared away. If by any chance the hole does not open, you can safely lay off and go under a few sterns. On the other hand, if you try to squeeze past the buoy without enough room, you will almost surely end up on top of it, as boat 2 has done, and if you head up to kill time you will be over the line too soon.

The second complication occurs when a few other skippers (almost always the best ones in the fleet) are also trying the same technique. It usually turns into a waiting game to see who can be last past the flag on port and still have room to tack to leeward of the line of starters. The best advice we have is to wait until the latest you feel you can handle the moves. Then go for the line of starters on port. If you judge correctly, anybody waiting until after you will be too late to tack or will be unable to make the mark after tacking.

2. *The weather-end start at the committee boat.* The most important key is this: sailboats which are stalled out or nearly stalled out go sideways pretty fast, and have to go sideways a little more to get moving—this means that *often* (not always) a hole develops at the committee boat at the last minute.

The moves are these—first, put yourself on starboard tack to weather of the lay line to the committee boat well ahead of time—for example, with 2 minutes to go you are in a position to make the line in 20 seconds sailing full speed. Stop your boat (all sails luffing). You will drift sideways and forward, and if you have placed your boat correctly you will move slowly up to the committee boat, reaching a spot just off her transom with 3 or 4 seconds to go, when you can sheet in and be off.

The smaller and less aggressive the fleet, the later you can position yourself and the faster you can move into position off the stern. Remember, because you are moving faster you make less leeway, so keep closer to the lay line.

Problems are these: it begins to appear as if the boat to leeward of you did a better job

A 13-boat start breaks away from the starting line in the first race of a recent PC national championship.

of placing himself, and is going to be able to cross less than a boat width from the committee boat. *Slow down* until he is clear ahead. If necessary, repeat this for as many boats as you have to. This can happen on a very crowded weather end when you have misjudged badly in placing yourself to drift onto the lay line. Start a little late. With good boat handling, you can be third or fourth in line and still prevent those ahead from tacking until you do (this ensures clear air, the primary goal of all starts).

A second problem: again you misjudged, and placed yourself too far to leeward to lay the committee boat, thus creating a hole to weather. If you have time and room, two quick tacks can turn a miserable start into an excellent one. At first you will have some difficulty in judging from what point your boat will just lay the committee boat when in a stalled (or semistalled) state. With practice you will get better, and probably be surprised how often there is a big hole at the committee boat.

3. *In-between start.* When you do not want to start at either end of the line—probably around 10 percent of your starts, as the ends of the line provide the most advantage of

position and clear air—we have the third kind of start.

Clear air and good speed are crucial to on-the-line starts. You should stay on port tack until the last minute or so before the gun, as port gives you much freedom of movement and choice of your starting slot. When you see an open spot in the line of starboard tackers, preferably with sailors of average ability to windward and to leeward, tack into it so you have clear air on starboard. Follow the standard technique of keeping close to the boat on your weather side, and luffing (slowly) several times to clear out an opening to leeward, into which you can drive for speed and clear air during the last 2 or 3 seconds before the start. Do not let the boats on either side get ahead of you—this can be disastrous.

Starting Technique. Once the starting spot on the line is selected, the next problem to cope with is how to hit the line with sufficient headway when the starting gun is fired. There might be considered five fundamental techniques for arriving at the line as the starting signal is made: (1) the timed start, (2) sitting on the line, (3) running the line, (4) the dip start, and (5) the barging start. There are

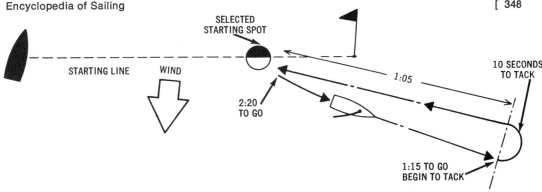

The timed start.

certain special occasions when any of these techniques or a combination of some of them might be used; but by and large, the timed start is generally the most effective and the safest.

In the case of large, heavy yachts it is vital to have good headway at the start, and this requires a long approach to the line on a fast point of sailing. To accomplish this a *timed start* is essential. The particular method of timing described here is often referred to as a Vanderbilt start, after Harold K. Vanderbilt, who used it to such good effect on J boats and other large yachts.

The procedure is to record the time you cross the line in the wrong direction, calculate the time it takes to tack or jibe and thereby determine when you should head back for the start. Say you cross the line with 5 minutes left and it takes your boat 20 seconds to reverse course. Then sail away for 2 minutes 20 seconds and jibe with 2 minutes 40 seconds left. After taking 20 seconds to jibe you will have 2 minutes 20 seconds to get back to the line. It is important to remember:

1. If possible, return on the same point of sailing as you left the line.
2. If there is a fair current on the approach to the line, head back later.
3. If you anticipate any blanketing on the return, head back sooner.

To assist in figuring the mathematics, prepare a card telling you when to head back for various times of crossing the line in the wrong direction. If you can calculate in your head during the stress of a start, *add* the time it takes to jibe and reverse course to the time remaining when you leave the line. Then di-

vide by two and the result is the time to head back. The timed start is not recommended for small light boats, but for heavy ones which require time to gain headway, it is essential.

In most racing classes helmsmen have developed the technique of luffing up to the starting line, sheeting in with a few seconds to go, and hitting the line at the gun. With big fleets this has become almost the only way to get a reasonable start on a well-set line in a true wind. The big danger in this type of crowded start is in finding, as the gun goes, that there is a boat in a close "safe leeward" position. Because of the density of the fleet it will probably be impossible to tack onto port to clear your wind for some time, at least without having to dip under several sterns. Many experienced big-fleet skippers have developed a technique which keeps them out of this difficulty. This is how it works: when luffing up toward the line with boats all around doing the same thing, wait until about 15 seconds to go, then swoop up to wind-

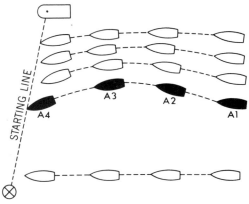

A squeeze play.

ward, gently forcing the boats above you to squeeze up. This will leave a hole to leeward of you, so that with about 5 seconds to go you may drop down, quickly gain speed, and hit the line going fast with no one too close underneath.

The method takes practice and the timing will depend on how quickly the boat will pick up speed after it is laid off for the line. The type of boat, the wind strength, and the sea conditions will determine this. A word of caution: While you are swooping up to clear out a hole to drop down into, be sure no one shoots across your stern and fills the hole before you have had a chance to use it.

The second starting technique, sitting on the line, is sometimes used when racing small, light dinghies. In this case, the starter approaches the line early, perhaps a minute before the gun, lets his sails luff to kill speed, and then trims them in immediately prior to gunfire. This can be dangerous when right of way boats establish an overlap to leeward.

Sometimes a change in the racing rules alters tactics. And such is the case in the 1969 version of Rule 40. Now, before the start, a leeward yacht may luff up to a close-hauled course even if she has the barest of overlaps on a yacht to windward of her. This change will make it risky to camp right on the line with sails shaking. If you do, you are apt to be shoved over the line early as yacht *A* is being luffed into a premature start by yacht *B* in the diagram.

A safer tactic at the start, if you wish to stall on the line awaiting the gun, is to assume a position well to leeward of it. Then, if a yacht with a slight overlap to leeward of you

starts to luff, you have room to respond to her now-legal luff without being forced over the starting line prematurely. Yacht *C* illustrates the safe way of camping to leeward of a line. Assume a position *at least as far* to leeward of it as *C* has in order to be safe.

The other three starting techniques should be used rarely and with great caution. When running the line a boat arrives at the line early and to windward of the desired starting spot. Her sheets are then eased, and she reaches along parallel to the line until just before the gun fires, at which time her sheets are trimmed and she is headed up onto her proper course. This method has the advantage that the boat has good headway when she hits the line as the gun is fired. However, there are two disadvantages in running the line. First, you have to keep clear of any boat to leeward on a close-hauled course. In the process you might well be forced over early. Second, and of perhaps greater importance, if you are right on the line you cannot sharpen up until the gun goes. As a result, right after the start you are still reaching instead of making the best advantage to windward.

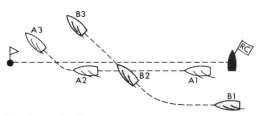

Stay below the line.

It is well to reach along the line to insure not being late, but do so parallel to the line and a length or two below it. If a boat to leeward of you forces you up you will have room to respond. But best of all, when the gun goes you can be headed in the right direction. Swing up on the wind 10, 15, or 20 seconds before the gun (depending on your distance from the line or the size of your boat), with the aim of hitting the line precisely on time. The diagram shows how this tactic gives *B* a jump on *A*, which was reaching down the line. In the drawing the gun goes at stage *A*2 and *B*2. This tactic will not work so well in a large fleet due to blanketing, but

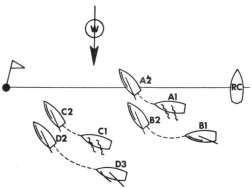

Do not camp right on the line.

try it whenever possible to get that all-important jump at the start.

Especially in large fleets of centerboarders or other fast-accelerating boats, the *dip start* can sometimes be the answer. It is a bit risky, it takes guts, but the rewards are often worth it. The bulk of the fleet will doubtless be camped on the line for a minute or more before the gun, killing way and trying to open a gap between their own boat and the one ahead of them. With just seconds to go all will trim in and go for the line, but many will either be backwinded or blanketed by a faster moving boat passing to windward. The dip start can often help you find an area of free air. Here is how to do it. Station yourself a length or two above the line with a couple of minutes to go. Kill your way and look to leeward to see where the fleet is jamming and where the gaps are. If you see a large gap, pick up speed and swoop down into it and onto the right side of the line well before the gun. If no large gaps exist, wait in hopes of one developing just before gunfire. Then shortly before the fleet as a whole trims in go for it, pick up speed, dip down into the hole someone else has so carefully created. Time your swoop to get on the right side of the line only seconds before the gun. By reaching down you will have higher speed and even if backwinded may break through.

WIND

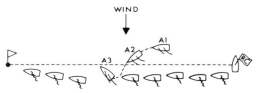

The dip start.

Dangers are the fact that you have to keep clear of the leeward boats, might find no hole to dip into, and will be a premature starter. But more often you can spot a gap which someone else has nurtured and which you can claim for your very own. Or perhaps from your vantage point you can see that the other starters are not up to the line, often the case when starting against a foul current, when the dip start is most effective. But make sure there is no one-minute rule in effect before starting this one.

The barging start is also dangerous. When a boat illegally barges, she attempts to force her way between the starting mark and another competitor. However, it is perfectly legal to start on the wrong side of the danger line, as boats *B* are doing in the diagram, provided there are no boats close or overlapping you to leeward. The danger lines shown in the diagram represent the course to the first mark for a reaching start or the close-hauled course for a windward start.

In order to understand the barging start thoroughly, it is necessary to learn Racing Rule 42, which deals with rounding or passing marks or obstructions. Rule 42.1 covers various rounding situations when boats are overlapped, and Rule 42.1(*e*) is the anti-barging rule. In most cases, when two boats are overlapped rounding or passing a mark, the outside boat must give the inside boat room to pass the mark on the correct side. An important exception is the antibarging rule, which says that the windward boat *cannot* claim room from an overlapping leeward boat. However, the rule goes on to say that the leeward boat may not sail above her course to the first mark on a reaching or running start or luff above a close-hauled course on a windward start after the starting signal has been made. Before the signal, the leeward boat may sail higher, and if she is close enough to the mark, she may squeeze out windward boats after the signal provided she does not sail above her close-hauled course or her course to the next mark.

Match-race Starts. The primary offensive intent in a match race between two boats is to keep the opponent away from the line or at least the preferred end of the line until insufficient time remains for him to reach the line on time. The corollary of this intent is that the offensive boat must stay between his opponent and the desired point on the line, ever ready to "get there first."

To best achieve this, 5 or 10 minutes before the start, get on the other boat's stern. If close enough, you might be able to block him from tacking or jibing back to the line. When time has run out, you can return to the line and the boat you had been tailing will have to follow in your wake and eat dirty air. If you feel your boat is faster, do all your prestart maneuvering below the line and not beyond either end of it. This minimizes the

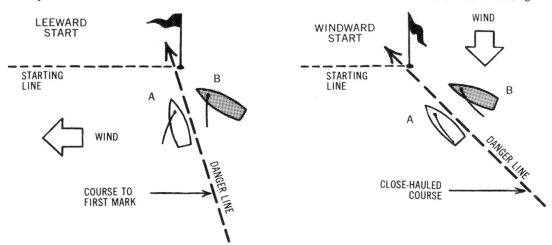

Barging: In both cases B is barging illegally because she is trying to get room at the starting mark. A does not have to give room to B, but A cannot head above her course to the first mark (or her close-hauled course when beating) after the starting signal before she has crossed the starting line.

chance of being blocked and makes it easier to get clear air. If you are slower, then maneuver beyond the extremities of the line and do everything possible to block the other boat.

If the opponent is not aggressive and intends a conventional start, the port-tack approach is advantageous. Port tack is unrestricted by balking limitations and therefore permits greater freedom of maneuver. When the leeward end of the line is favored, a reaching approach permits crossing ahead of the major opponent, if an opening appears, or if not, crossing his transom with clear air on the tack. When the weather end is favored, the port-tack approach permits tacking beneath the opponent and starting on his lee bow.

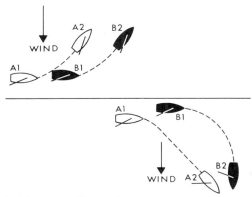

Match-race starting tactics.

When the opponent is aggressive, a more forceful technique may be required. If he voluntarily sails away from the line so that a relatively high-speed return will be required, tacking ahead and blanketing or backwinding will provide the desired starting advantage. Riding the opponent's transom after the 5-minute gun (or sooner if necessary) will often insure this type of control. From behind, the opponent's movements can be countered and he can be continually forced ahead, preferably to a position beyond the range of his ability to return with the gun. As soon as an overlap to leeward is established, the trailing boat acquires right of way and the leading boat must speed up to keep clear. Once forced too far from the line in either direction, the trailing boat can tack away and reach the line in the lead.

The defense, of course, becomes, with practice, more effective than the offense. The intention of the leading boat is to return before being forced too far from the line, to time his breakaway maneuver for an ideal return run. At any time the leading boat can jibe away, but, if early, the following boat can continue the controlled follow or if late, can tack inside and ahead. If the following boat is slightly to weather, intending to prevent a tack to return to the line, a sudden slowup can catch him unaware, permit a luff head to wind, and force him about before he desires. If the following boat is slightly to

A good start in this Geary 18 race permitted boat 1017 to put way ahead of the rest of the bunched-up fleet.

leeward, prodding the leading boat ahead, a sudden slowup can catch him pinned to leeward, permit a tack away, and a return to the line in the covering position, to windward.

Once started, if you are ahead govern your tactics to the actions of the other boat, letting him go off alone only if you are *sure* he is going the wrong way, and even then do not let him go completely. Stay pretty much between him and the next mark. If behind, try tacking duels and jibing duels. Keep the pressure on. Do not go off on the "wrong" tack hoping for a break. It will hardly ever work.

The Windward Leg

It is difficult to remember, in the heat of starting, the power and extent of the backwind effect from a boat to leeward. Any boat within two boat lengths to leeward and as far aft as the mast abeam position, and certainly any boat to leeward that is bow to bow, as well as any boat ahead and to leeward, is seriously hindering the windward boat. The blanket zone of the windward yacht, on the other hand, extends only as a rapidly narrowing cone, never wider than the boat's length, aft and to leeward. There can be no question

that the leeward boat is far safer herself and far more dangerous to her competitors. Thus, we should always remember to avoid boats to leeward like the plague and always seek to be to leeward ourselves.

Even when the weather end of the line is heavily favored, a leeward boat, even crossing the line perpendicularly, has clear air herself and is seriously backwinding her neighbors to windward. Although this is usually recognized in leeward-end-favored starts, when only the single boat at the leeward-end buoy will have clear air, it is commonly overlooked by the barging fleet approaching the weather mark when this end is furthest upwind.

In many circumstances it may be sufficient to approach the line slowly with time to spare, periodically luffing the boats to weather so as to keep your lee side free. Often, however, wiser competitors will shoot across your stern at the last moment to establish a protected position close to leeward. For this reason it is better to hang back a bit so as to retain this initiative yourself, and then, with but seconds to go, to bear away at high speed and shoot into a safe lee-bow position. In order to be able to achieve this, of course, it is essential not to be caught hanging by a gang of leeward boats and preferably to be far enough down from a favored weather end to be able to find this amount of maneuvering room.

Once the choice is made, every effort of hiking and sail trim must be expended to insure not only maintenance of the safe leeward position but freedom from boats further to leeward. If it has been possible to find the ideal opening from which no boat further to leeward can produce a significant backwind effect, one can afford to ease sheets, bear off a bit, and drive her out of the mob. As more frequently there are one or more boats at various distances to leeward which are producing a harmful effect, it becomes necessary to develop every inch of possible lift to windward with maximum forward drive, keeping her "right on edge," every muscle and every perceptive brain cell tuned to the utmost effectiveness. This is no time for planning the approach to the mark, let alone worrying that the spinnaker pole is adrift; no time for the crew to adjust the board or discuss the next expected shift. These are the seconds that try men's souls—and backs— and those in the fleet that make the effort and sail their boats emerge with the lead and the race, as their less determined competitors flounder helplessly in the backwind.

Often, races are won and lost on the first quarter of the first leg. Often races so lost are lost so disastrously that they offset an entire sequence of top finishes. A bad start in the wrong spot without clear air can always account for a disaster, but presuming a good start in the right spot with clear air, the race can still be lost by sailing a few hundred yards in the wrong direction.

Experience shows that it may sometimes be impossible to tack at the desired moment, but this should be infrequent if the start is properly planned and appropriate slowing or bearing away is utilized before the tack. The more frequent problem is failure or inability to look around to see how the race is developing.

All too often races are lost by getting ahead and thereafter covering too closely. In the early stages of a fleet race it seldom pays for the leader to attempt to cover the fleet. If part of the fleet goes on one tack, part on the other, and the leader tries to cover both

by going up the middle, he is almost sure to wind up behind one group or the other, sometimes both. It is often a mistake also to take the tack your closest pursuer is on. By all means do so if you think it is the faster tack. But often the boat closest to you takes that tack in hopes of splitting with you. If you think it is the wrong tack, do not cover the nearest boats. Instead sail your own race, and if your judgment is sound you will widen your lead. Late in a race it is well to consolidate a lead by covering the boat or boats nearest to you, but do not do it blindly.

Even in a match race there are times when you should let the boat behind go. If she tacks onto what appears to be an unfavorable slant, do not go with her right away. She has taken that tack to clear her wind, without worrying about it being an unfavorable one, assuming no doubt you will cover. If you do not and the tack is unfavorable, it is a great opportunity to work out a big lead. If the tack remains unfavorable, the boat behind will be forced to tack again and follow you, thus losing not only by virtue of the poor slant, but also because of having taken two extra tacks. Do not overdo this not covering in a match race. After the boat astern has been on the "unfavorable" tack for several minutes, you better go over with her. It just might not remain unfavorable. The thing to remember, however, is not to be a slave to theory— "when ahead cover the boat astern and stay between her and the mark." It is usually a prudent thing to do, but there are times when you can get an unbeatable lead by *not* covering.

When trying to really "hang one" on a

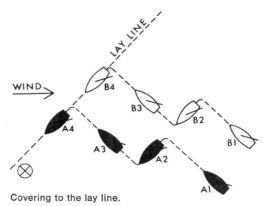

Covering to the lay line.

competitor on a weather leg, work your opponent out to the lay line and then he has little chance of escape. To do this put a "loose" cover on him on one tack and a "tight" cover on him on the other tack. In the diagram boat *A* is concerned only with getting to the windward mark ahead of *B*. When covering *B* on port tack, *A* leaves *B* free air so that *B* is inclined to stay on port. If *B* tacks onto starboard, *A* should put a "tight" cover on her. That means *A* should tack so that she is drastically affecting *B*'s wind. *B* will have to tack again or drop back rapidly, or she might try to stay on starboard by bearing off to gain speed and break through *A*'s wind shadow; but *A* should bear off the same amount to stay in the same relative position and thus encourage *B* to tack. By continuing these tactics *A* will soon force *B* to the starboard-tack lay line. Then *A* can tack directly ahead of *B* and shoot backwind at her all the way to the mark. *B*'s choices are then (1) she can put in another short tack on port, which will mean that she has overstood and has also tacked twice more than *A*, or (2) she can try to gain free air by bearing off. Of course *B* should do everything she can to keep from being worked out to the lay line, but *A* can discourage this, by making one tack inviting and the other most uninviting.

If you are being covered closely while sailing to windward, either in a match race or because the skipper ahead is determined to beat you, you have got to get clear air fast. You may be able to get it either by bearing off and driving or by a false tack, but if these tactics fail there is an almost surefire way not only to get clear air, but also to get on the opposite tack from your tormentor. Make several tacks in quick succession (usually three will be sufficient). By tacking before gaining full headway you will lose ground, but you will wind up on opposite tacks from the boat ahead. Thereafter you can keep out of phase with him by tacking each time he tacks and will thereby retain clear air. The illustration shows how *B* has managed to get on opposite tacks from *A*. Now she has to sail faster to make up the lost ground, but she has clear air with which to do it.

Although normally associated with match racing, the *false tack* is also a useful device to have in your bag of tricks for fleet racing. Frequently a series, or an individual race, will come down to a two-boat contest—a situation where one boat must beat a certain other boat in order to win. In such cases a tacking duel is almost certain to take place, and of course the false tack is a device used for the boat being covered in a tacking duel to break loose from the cover. In the dia-

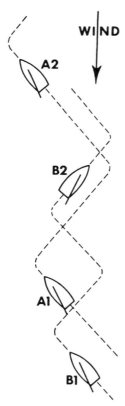

To break a cover.

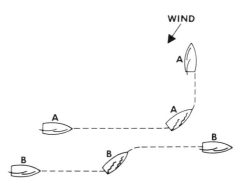

The false tack.

gram boat *B* is being covered, tack for tack, by boat *A*. It is necessary for *B* to allow two or three tacks to take place before she tries the false tack. This is to lull *A* into a sense of security so that he will be surprised by the false tack. In making the false tack be sure to do everything just as it would be done if the tack were to be completed. Of course the crew must be tipped off as to what's going on. If the boat has a jib, the crew must be sure not to let it get aback, but must ease it off so that it luffs. If the jib gets caught aback it might be impossible for the helmsman to get back to the original tack, and in any case the boat will be unduly slowed down. If the boats are within hearing range the normal orders for tacking must be given, so that those on boat *A* will have no reason to suspect anything out of the ordinary. The helmsman of *B* should make sure he is being watched by his opponents as he pushes the tiller down, as *A* must respond very quickly if the false tack is to work. If *A* does not cover immediately it is best to go through with the tack and try the false-tack ruse again later. But if *A* responds quickly the helmsman of *B* should begin immediately to slow down his turn, but wait until *A* is past head to wind before pulling his boat back to its original course.

When a tight series boils down to a match between two top boats, regardless of where they finish in the final race, one must beat the other in order to take the series. Under such circumstances the competitor who finds himself being sat on by his foe should keep in mind that the other boats in the race can be used to help spring him into clear wind. In the situation pictured, boat *A* is being closely

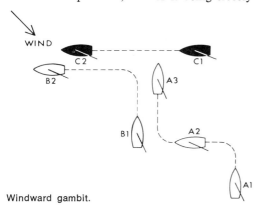

Windward gambit.

covered by boat *B*. Boat *A* waits until his rival is approaching a third boat, *C,* which is on starboard tack, and then *A* tacks. Boat *B* has a choice. He may lay off under boat *C,* in which case he has lost his windward berth and *A* will be able to escape onto starboard tack well clear of *B*. Or boat *B* may tack on *C*'s lee bow to cover *A*. Boat *A* may then wait until she has way on and tack back onto port (*A*3). Boat *B* is then unable to tack without running the risk of fouling *C,* or without laying away off to go under *C,* in which case she will end up in *A*'s backwind. And if *C* decided to tack out of *B*'s backwind, boat *B* would not be able to tack onto port without sailing in *C*'s dirty air.

There are other ways of entangling one competitor with another in order to get yourself into the clear, and the helmsman who is racing to beat a specific boat in the fleet should always be looking for such opportunities.

No attempt should be made to lay the mark from a great distance (whether close covering or not). It is always better to tack short of the lay line (unless the mark is close); the loss from two additional tacks is usually less than from overstanding. Once on the lay line or near it, the leg becomes a "one-leg beat," and the proper tactical position for a "one-leg beat" is ahead and to leeward. Ahead and to leeward provides gains in either a lift or a header and completely controls the boat close on the weather quarter. The ideal solution to covering on the lay line is to make the final approach in the close-ahead to leeward position. Actually the vulnerable positions when approaching the lay line are ahead and to windward, dead ahead, and ahead to leeward. Unless a tack is made short of the lay line, the lee-bow position and tactical advantage will be lost on the approach to the mark. The situation should be manipulated well short of the lay line so that the lay line is reached in the abeam or astern to windward position to facilitate the final lee-bow tack. Of course, all of the above must be modified when the mark is close aboard. Then the paramount concern is to make a tack which will permit rounding the mark. The final lee-bow tack is still preferable and is best acquired from an abeam or astern to windward position, but it should not be

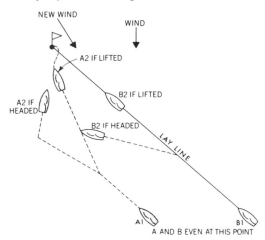

NEW WIND

WIND

A2 IF LIFTED

B2 IF LIFTED

A2 IF HEADED

B2 IF HEADED

LAY LINE

A1   B1

A AND B EVEN AT THIS POINT

Do not sail to the lay line.

sought unless it permits laying the mark. That is, when beating to windward, except when near the mark, it seldom pays to sail all the way to the lay line. There are many reasons why. When behind several boats, if you go all the way to the lay line before tacking, other boats are apt to tack on you and you will be unable to get clear air by tacking again without overstanding. But even when leading, unless covering one close pursuer, it is better to tack short. The accompanying diagram shows why boats which go to the lay line will lose ground unless the wind holds absolutely steady. If the wind fairs they will overstand and boats which tacked short will fetch. If it heads, boats which tacked short will be able to cross on the other tack well ahead of any boats which went right to the lay line. And then there is a third consideration—with a mile or more to go, it is almost impossible to tack at precisely the right instant to fetch the mark. Unless there is an obviously better wind right at the lay line or unless a match-race tactical situation exists, *always* tack short. Nine times out of ten you will gain by so doing.

Rounding Marks

In starts with between 30 and 200 boats it is very important to start thinking about rounding the mark when you are on the windward beat. If you have to leave the first mark to starboard, there is no need to be

afraid of using the port side of the course because by overstanding the mark a little you are certain of being able to round it. It often pays to overstand the mark a little, rather than being caught in the starboard-tack queue sailing directly for the mark.

It is different when the weather mark has to be rounded to port, for in this case it is essential to keep over on to the starboard side of the course, because, if you have to come to the mark on port tack, you risk not being able to find room to round the mark, owing to the long queue of starboard-tack boats approaching the mark. You can easily lose ten, twenty, or thirty places through this error because even if you are able to find a hole through which you can pass and then tack, you may not be able to do so owing to the cut-up wind caused by so many boats to windward.

In small fleets you will be fairly well spread out at the first mark and therefore you do not have to think too far ahead about the rounding maneuver. You can easily lose speed when rounding a mark, but if you do it correctly in light winds you can actually gain speed because as you luff up toward the wind its speed will increase.

In most cases when rounding a mark with other boats, try to maneuver to be on the inside at the mark so that you have the right of way. However, if you plan to squeeze into the inside position on a boat ahead of you, be very careful not to establish your overlap when the boat ahead is very close to the mark. Rule 42 deals with rounding or passing marks or obstructions, and this should be studied carefully. Rule 42.3(*a*) says, "A yacht *clear astern* shall not establish an inside *overlap* and be entitled to room under Rule 42.1(*a*) when the yacht *clear ahead:* (i) is within two of her own lengths of the *mark* or *obstruction,* except as provided in Rule 42.3(*b*); or (ii) is unable to give the required room."

There is a definite technique to rounding marks. A turn which is too sharp will kill your boat's way; thus the turn should be fairly gradual. This is more true for big boats than for small ones. If you are not overlapped by other boats, do not approach the mark very closely when first beginning to make your turn, but cut close to the mark after the turn has been almost completed. This is im-

Here is the inevitable "busy" at the marks as the Lido 14 fleet clusters around the leeward mark in one of their class races.

portant when turning onto a windward leg, in order that boats behind cannot sail up on your windward quarter in an attempt to clear your backwind. You should try to keep boats following you directly behind you or slightly to leeward. When turning onto a leeward leg, keep to windward of your close competitors so that you can blanket them.

When making the actual turn, attempt to do so as smoothly as possible, because if your boat becomes jammed around with a quick thrust of the tiller, she loses both speed and headway. While the turn should be close to the buoy, it should not be too close, for any boat that strikes a mark of the course is immediately disqualified. For this reason, a good rule is to steer wide of the mark on its near side, then head up smartly on the far side as the turn is completed. A boat finishing a turn close to the mark may be able to slip inside to windward of someone ahead who has sagged off. When a turn is begun too wide,

however, it is an open invitation for a trailing boat to sneak inside, closer to the mark. Should current be a factor on the course, be sure to use it to your best advantage when rounding a mark.

When two boats have overstood the weather mark and are coming in to round it side by side, the outside boat can sometimes manage to reverse the expected order of rounding by working up to the close-astern position. In the diagram, A and B are approaching the mark with started sheets. If she continues as in position 1 B will be on the outside of the turn, and therefore behind after rounding. So B squeezes up under A and when blanketed, pops quickly through into clear air directly astern of her competitor (position 2). Being on a close reach, rather than hard on the wind, will mean that B will not be unduly hampered by backwind. By staying close astern, B can prevent A from tacking to round the mark (tacking too close aboard). A will

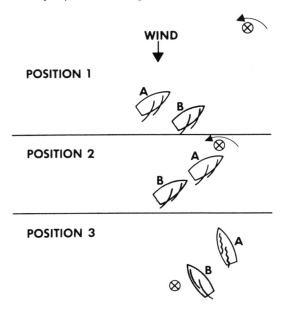

POSITION 1

POSITION 2

POSITION 3

Reversing the order.

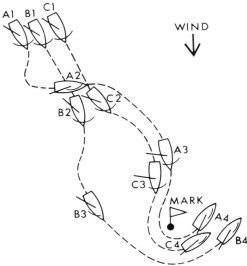

Rounding leeward marks.

have to wait for *B* to round before following (position 3).

In a crossing situation such as the one shown below, the tactics of the port-tack yacht *A* depend on the proximity of the next mark. She cannot quite cross the starboard-tack boat but can tack on her lee bow and gain a safe leeward. This is the preferred tactic if the mark is some distance away and well upwind. Suppose, however, the port-tack boat can nearly fetch the mark, as in the case

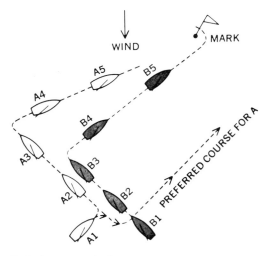

To tack, or go under?

shown. Then if she tacks and even if she gets a "safe" leeward, yacht *B* may be able to hold on long enough to keep yacht *A* from tacking for the mark without overstanding. Yacht *B*, when able to fetch, can then tack first and will doubtless round first, as shown in the diagram. In such a situation, yacht *A* would have been far better off to bear off and go under yacht *B*'s stern as indicated by the preferred course for *A*. A subsequent lift might enable her to fetch the mark, a header will put her ahead, and in any event, if the two boats converge on the mark on opposite tacks, this time yacht *A* will be on starboard tack.

When approaching a leeward mark in a closely bunched fleet it is important not to be caught on the outside, overlapped by boats inside. Plan ahead, therefore, for the inside overlap, provided you do not lose too much distance fighting for it. As shown above, *A*1 is in an apparently hopeless position. She therefore kills way and loses distance so as to be able to reach across the sterns of *B* and *C*. Having a closer sailing angle she goes faster and establishes an overlap on both *B* and *C* shortly after position 2. It is vital that this overlap be established before *C* is within two lengths of the mark. If not, *A* would not be entitled to room. *C* tries to keep *A* from gaining an overlap but is not quick enough. *B*, seeing *C* head up, bears off, gains clear air, comes reaching for the mark at good speed,

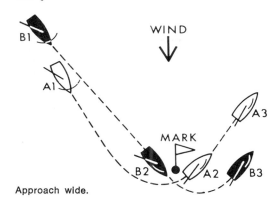

Approach wide.

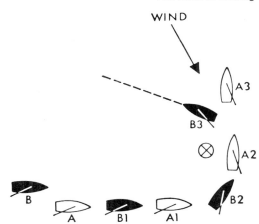

Controlling from behind.

breaks through *A* and *C*'s wind shadow, and rounds in good shape. *A* has turned a "hopeless" situation into the best position, *B* has improved her lot and *C*, which was in the driver's seat with just ten lengths to go, is now in the tank.

When approaching a leeward mark and closely pursued, plan your approach to permit rounding in the most advantageous position relative to the other boat. Unless fearful of the boat astern gaining an overlap, head to leeward of the mark to take it wide on the approach course. This permits you to leave the mark very close aboard on the new course. *A* in the diagram has done it perfectly and ends up directly on *B*'s wind, even though *B* rounded as sharply as she could after arriving at the mark. *A*'s course also gave her more time to trim for windward work. Unless *B* felt she had a good chance of gaining an overlap, she should have followed in *A*'s wake. True, she would then end up backwinded after rounding but upon tacking would get clear air more easily than she would from the position shown in the diagram.

When approaching a leeward mark close behind a competitor and there is a weather leg to follow, every effort should be made to establish an inside overlap so that you may be in control of the situation after the mark is rounded. However, if you know it will be advantageous to tack immediately after rounding, it is possible to sacrifice the inside overlap and control the situation from astern. If you have tried for the overlap and have just failed to establish it, the danger is that in escaping from the inside trap, where you

have no rights, you will swing too far to the outside and end up, after rounding, behind and to leeward of the leading boat. This must be avoided especially when an early tack is indicated, as it will mean that your opponent is not only ahead, but is also free to tack and thereby consolidate and increase his lead.

In the diagram, *B* has just failed to gain an overlap at the required distance (two lengths) from the mark. She immediately swings to leeward but *keeps astern* of *A*. She then bears up again so as to round the mark directly behind, but very close to her opponent. In this way *B* makes it impossible for *A* to come about for fear of tacking too close aboard (Rule 41.1). As soon as she is clear of the mark, *B* may go over to the desired tack and be clear of *A*. *A* is then faced with the choice of tacking and having *B* in a safe leeward position or of remaining on the less desirable tack until she is well clear of *B*'s influence.

In modern racing courses there are usually two or more weather legs, and frequently the final leg is to windward. So it becomes very important to plan that beat to windward before rounding onto it. The sharp helmsman knows before he starts the last weather leg which tack will be the best to be on, and he must make every effort to see that he is able to get onto it. When the racing is tight, it is often better to let another boat round the lee mark ahead of you, even though you could easily prevent it.

In the diagram the boats are heading for the lee mark on the normal buoys-to-port

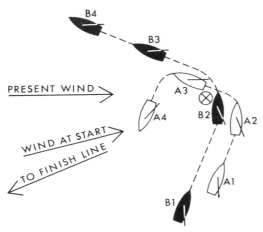

PRESENT WIND

WIND AT START

TO FINISH LINE

Leeward-mark strategy.

course. The starboard tack will be favored after rounding due to a wind shift which has made that tack much closer to the course to the finish line. Boat *A* could easily keep boat *B* from gaining an overlap (1) by luffing slightly and then bearing off to round with *B* in her wake. But *B* would be so close that *A* would not then be free to tack onto starboard.

So *A* allows *B* to get the overlap (2). *A* takes the mark wide on the near side and close on the far side of the turn. In this way *A* controls the situation by preventing *B* from getting onto starboard tack first (3). *A* is free to tack right away. *A* is then in the driver's seat. If *B* tacks right after *A*, she will be in danger of having *A* establish a "safe leeward" position. If *B* stays on port for a while, and the wind continues to shift in the direction it has already shifted, *A* will have a good chance of fetching the mark while *B* will have overstood. If the wind comes back to where it was at the start of the race, *A* will be in a position to take full advantage of the shift by tacking on it, while *B* will be far off to leeward.

As fleets grow bigger and racing keener, the "infighting" becomes an ever-increasing part of the game. And, of course, the most frequent places on the course for pile-ups are at the downwind marks. Here the fleet, or great portions of it, frequently will arrive strung out abreast, with more boats being brought up astern on a puff and trying to find their way into the lineup. When approaching a mark (let us say the jibe mark of an Olym-

The girls aboard these Moth class boats know how to take the mark close!

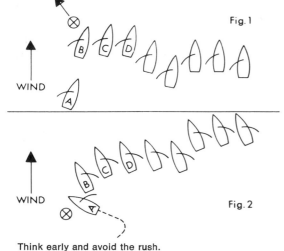

Fig. 1

Fig. 2

Think early and avoid the rush.

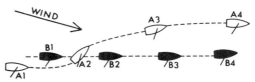

Timing the pass.

pic course) and such a pile-up is developing, the wise helmsman will do his thinking early and avoid the rush. The best place to be is on the inside; but remember that overlaps must be established before the first of the two boats in question has reached a point two lengths from the mark. If you are coming up from astern you must be sure you are going to establish that overlap soon enough. Otherwise you will suddenly find there is no place to go except on the wrong side of the mark, or to the outside of the stack.

When attainment of the overlap is doubtful, it is best to stay astern of the line of boats (Fig. 1) and try to get to weather of them *after* the mark has been rounded. Best results can be attained (if you start *early* enough) by veering out to windward, jibing astern of the lineup, and then cutting the buoy close just after the inside boat has rounded (Fig. 2). If this maneuver is timed properly, the boat that was trailing may be able to pick off all the boats that were ahead of her, because by sailing at a sharper wind angle both before and after her jibe, she should be going considerably faster than the others as the jumble unsorts.

Reaching and Running

On a reach or run many skippers consider that these legs have little effect on the outcome of a race, but very often it is during

these portions that there are real opportunities for ground-gaining. On a reach keep your wind clear and head no higher than the next mark. If possible, steer to leeward of it so that you are in a good position to gain speed by heading up, but make sure to compensate for any current taking you off course. Avoid getting entangled in a luffing match that might permit other craft astern to go ahead of you. When passing boats, be sure to allow enough clearance so that they will have trouble in covering or luffing you.

The boom vang is very valuable in this leg of a race. It should be set up before reaching the weather mark. With a boom vang, such as one described in Section II, the boom and sail swing as a unit and the sail is held in one plane. This allows the sail to be eased further off than would otherwise be possible. Without the downwind pull of the vang, the mainsail will luff first aloft, and the entire sail must be trimmed to meet this condition. With it down, the luff occurs simultaneously along the entire hoist. A spinnaker can also be employed effectively on broad reaches. While quite often it may be hard to judge on the prior leg if your boat should carry the spinnaker on the next, prepare to set it anyway, and save the actual decision until the turn has been made and the angle of the wind on the new course can be fully determined. The latter is most important. For instance, on a close reach, a spinnaker is generally more of a liability than a help because it will drag the boat to leeward, off the proper course.

Being too eager to get ahead on a broad reach or run, however, can result in being behind again when it counts. While running or broad reaching for the finish, or for that important last leeward mark before the final beat, it is wise to consider carefully the opportune time to pass a competitor. There are two dangers in attacking too early: (1) You may end up in a luffing match that will last all the way down the leg and cost you several

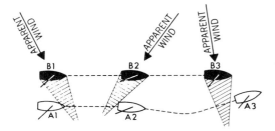

Dodging the wind shadow.

places, and (2) you may simply put yourself in a position where your competitor can pass you again before the mark is reached. The place to wait is in the opposition's wake, or just to leeward of it (position 1). Do not work to weather or you will cause him to steer high to keep his wind clear and both of you will end up having to run off or jibe for the mark. As you get close (within 100 yards for small boats) to the mark (or finish line), pick a time when there is a bit of a puff, and when the competitor is not looking at you, to suddenly angle to windward across his stern (position 2). In this way you will have three advantages: (1) You will have the puff first, (2) you will have a sharper wind angle, and (3) you will blanket your competitor just when he should be getting the puff. With excellent timing (and a bit of laxness on the part of the competition) you may gain "mastline" before he has a chance to luff; but in any case you should have a good enough spurt to get through even if he does luff. The object of waiting until late in the leg is that the other helmsman may hesitate to luff when close to the mark for fear of getting involved in an awkward position where he would have difficulty heading back down to the mark, or difficulty in giving room to the boat which has just established an overlap. And by passing him late in the game, you do not give him time to pull the same maneuver on you.

In planing classes, passing another boat on a reach affords opportunities not found in displacement boats. These are (1) the quick bursts of speed which can mean that you may suddenly be going twice as fast as a competitor, and (2) the sudden radical change in apparent wind which the increased speed produces. In puffy, strong winds it is possible to get past another boat on a broad reach by sailing through its lee, a maneuver which is virtually impossible in nonplaning boats. At position 1, boat *A* is two lengths to leeward of boat *B;* the apparent wind is aft of the beam and boat *A* has sailed right up to the point where the wind shadow from boat *B* is preventing her from breaking through to leeward. At position 2 the wind has increased and both boats have begun to plane, now traveling nearly twice as fast as before. The increased speed immediately brings the apparent wind forward of abeam and suddenly the wind shadow of boat *B* falls astern of boat *A*. The leeward boat must be very sharply handled to make this tactic pay off as there is a danger that as soon as the wind dies again the windward boat's wind shadow will once more fall on or ahead of the leeward boat. If the puff stays for some time *A* should blast forward on the fastest point of sailing, whether it is higher or lower than *B*'s course, so that when the wind dies she will remain in clear air. If the puff appears to be of short duration *A* should sharpen up quickly as the wind begins to die and thus gain speed by having a better angle. The apparent wind will not leap aft suddenly, but will come around slowly as the boats slow down; so by angling up to prevent slowing, *A* should be able to keep the wind ahead long enough to ensure being clear when she falls back to her normal course.

The boat should usually be set on her best lines at a slight heel. In light air, the crew sits to leeward to give the boat this heel. But in heavy weather the leeward rail should be clear of the water, with the crew riding to windward and perhaps the mainsail luffing to spill a little unnecessary wind. Long before reaching the mark, you should plan to be the inside boat at the buoy, and sail the course accordingly. You should try to establish an overlap on the boat nearest you, so that you will be entitled to buoy room, and in addition, be the windward boat after you have rounded.

When racing downwind the use of the spinnaker is most important. But, to obtain the most from it, you must know how fast the spinnaker can be set up at the beginning of the leg and how long it can be kept aloft before dousing at the end. When this big sail is pulling, it adds so much speed that the crew which gets it up first has an excellent chance

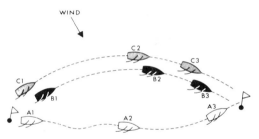

Avoid going high on a reach.

you expect the wind to increase later on in the leg, it will usually pay to sail either on the rhumb line or slightly below it. Ride off in each puff to get below the direct course, come up in the lulls, but average a bit below the rhumb line. This course provides a sufficient gap between you and the bulk of the fleet to windward to insure clear air. It will not look good at first, but stick to it. As the mark is neared you will reach up on a fast course and should break through. This tactic is especially effective if the wind lightens toward the end of the leg, but should work in steady winds, too, since your course for the leg will be more direct.

If unable to round the weather mark with a long lead, the major concern downwind is to stay out from under the boats behind. Not only the nearby blanketing boat may overtake but, while you are stopped, several others may take over the blanket and slip by. As on all offwind legs, working to leeward initially is the ideal tactical solution and this should be attempted whenever feasible.

If a dense cloud of sail is following close astern as you round, however, it may be far wiser to immediately luff well to weather of the rhumb line to discourage anyone's attempting or being capable of blanketing thereafter. The unfortunate problem in luffing at all is that there always seems to be

to pass others. Actually this leg of the race presents opportunities to run up on those ahead, blanket their wind with the spinnaker, and perhaps pass them. In other words, you should try to blanket others ahead and avoid being blanketed by those behind. In most instances, try to sail a straight-line course. The vast majority of boats do sail high on the reach. Leaders tend to in order to keep boats from passing them to windward. Tail-enders do in hopes of passing with clear air. And virtually all do because except in strong air boats go faster close reaching than broad reaching and the sight of boats going faster by sailing high of course is usually too much to resist. But all these boats must come back down to the mark eventually and when they do they will slow down. Therefore, unless there is a better wind to windward or unless

Thistles on the reach. Note boats 1109 and 818 are having a hard time trying to reach up to the mark.

someone who wants to go even higher, so that, once started, there seems to be no limit. If the course is a run, it may be wise to assume the jibe opposite to that assumed by the majority and/or to tack downwind. This is a valuable technique if used under the following limitations: (1) without deviation further from the rhumb line than necessary to keep clear wind or sails drawing well, (2) not in moderate or heavy winds when boats are at displacement hull speed dead downwind, and (3) not against a significant current.

Defensive tactics under spinnaker are primarily the avoidance of the wind shadows of following boats. Watch the masthead fly carefully to insure against sailing into a position or allowing a competitor to sail into a position which may produce wind interference.

Never cross in front of another boat while tacking downwind—after a wind shift, to reach a favored side of the course, or for any other reason. If a change in course or a jibe is necessary to prevent sailing by the lee, check to be certain that the change will not sail you into a blanket. Sail no higher than necessary to keep your wind clear; always let the follower work a little further upwind so that his resultant course will be slower than your own. What goes up must come down.

Offensive tactics under spinnaker obviously are based upon blanketing boats ahead. Watch the masthead fly of the boat being attacked. Stay directly between her and her apparent wind. Blanket cones of sails at the stall extend for at least five boat lengths, but narrow to a point at the extremity so that continuous accurate boat manipulation, in terms of the observed masthead fly, is essential. Never try to pass close to leeward except at the finish or the completion of a leg when the few feet ahead before the blanket becomes effective may be extremely valuable. Never try to pass close to windward either, as you are likely to be luffed out of the race. Attempt the final stage of the pass from close aboard, high on the wind, moving rapidly and away from the overtaken boat so that as she rounds up for the luff she will almost immediately be "mast abeam."

Wind and Racing

In light air strategy is the significant consideration. Where is the wind? Where should

one sail to find it first and keep it longest? What is the effect of the current? Where does one sail to attain or avoid its effects first and longest? Any wind, from any direction, in any boat is better than no wind in the fastest possible boat. All boats of the same class are basically equal in light air; the heaviest, mossiest dogs drift with the gold platers and, if taken to the wind first, will win the race. Boat handling is of secondary importance; it is essential to keep her moving with sheets freed and hull trimmed to offer the least resistance. Tactics need only to be considered in the negative sense that the least involvement with other boats in light air the better.

In moderate air boat speed becomes the dominant consideration. Boat speed results from a combination of boat development and boat handling to improve forward thrust—primarily good sails—and to decrease air and water resistance—decreased windage, weight, and skin friction. But as the boat speed of different hulls varies little at maximum displacement speed, tactical advantages become significant. The right tack referable to wind shifts, the good start, the overlap at the proper time become crucial factors. Slow boats (almost) always lose in moderate air; no amount of sailing skill will alter their maximum potential speed. Slow boats lose, but only boats whose tactics are effective win.

Heavy weather is the test of the seaman. Strategy and tactics are of little significance. And the "fast" boat may be far behind. In heavy air boat handling is everything. Keeping her on her feet and keeping her moving, not necessarily pointing, to windward and keeping her planing, regardless (almost) of the direction of the next mark, off the wind is all that matters. Speed differences of two- and threefold can be seen between well and poorly handled boats in a breeze—when everyone has more power than he can use. So remember:

1. In light air—*strategy*—find the wind and keep her moving in free air.

2. In moderate air—*boat speed and tactics* —a fast boat and a sharp mind.

3. In heavy air—*boat handling*—experience, daring, and drive.

Light-weather Technique. As a summary, here are some basic points to remember when racing in *light weather:*

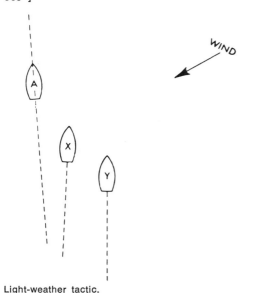

Light-weather tactic.

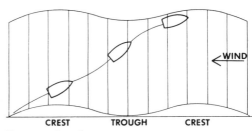

Heavy-weather tip.

1. Keep still to avoid shaking wind from the sail.

2. Reduce wetted surface by heeling the boat or depressing the bow.

3. Make sails as full as possible by easing the outhaul and Cunningham eye (or raising the gooseneck) of the main and by easing sheet and halyard (or downhaul) of the jib. Move jib leads forward.

4. Do not stray too far from the starting line as there is danger that if the wind drops more, you will not make it in time.

5. On reaches, be sure not to get high of the course, as you will suffer greatly if you have to run off before the wind to get down to the mark.

6. On runs do not head straight downwind, but angle off to one side or the other to keep speed up. This will result in tacking downwind, and the lighter the air, the more likely this tactic will pay off.

7. Try not to become involved in tacking duels, or to get caught in bad air. Any slowing down in light winds is harder to recover from, as your boat will not pick up speed quickly.

8. When going to windward in light airs avoid pointing too high (as *X* and *Y* are doing). Lay off a bit (*A*) and keep moving.

Heavy-weather Technique. Here are some basic points to remember when racing in *heavy weather:*

1. Try to sail your boat upright (except in

scow classes). It will have more drive, and both sails and centerboard (or keel) will be more efficient.

2. Flatten sails by pulling the main to the block bands, and tightening the Cunningham eye to eliminate wrinkles along the luff. Pull fullness out of the middle of the sail. Let the traveler off a few inches. Tighten the jib luff, move the sheet leads aft (or outboard), and sheet harder.

3. Before the start, check over sails and rigging to be sure everything is secure. Sail upwind for several minutes to get the feel of the boat. Then be sure the boat is dry in time to begin starting maneuvers.

4. When sailing upwind, try to point up on wave crests and off in troughs. Feather up in puffs to keep the boat flat. Keep as much crew weight as possible as far out over the weather rail as they can hang it.

5. On reaches, keep the boat flat to reduce helm and induce planing or surfing. Avoid going high, of course, as you might end up having to run straight down in a hard puff. Sail low in puffs and keep up speed in lulls by sailing a bit higher.

6. On runs, sail straight for the next mark unless the wind is very strong, in which case sail as low as you dare. And be careful of the spectacular "jibe broach." When the time comes to get over to the mark, choose a lull and a flat spot in the sea to jibe. Or if it's really screaming, get the boat up to a close reach, let the board down, and bring her about.

Against the Current

When racing in a stream, tidal or otherwise, the major determinant of victory will be the current. The general principles which are recognized are that when the current is adverse one should sail out of its strength as rapidly as possible and stay out of it for as much of the leg as possible; and that if the current is favorable one should sail into its strength as soon as possible and stay in it for as much of the leg as possible. The principles are understood, but their significance is usually underestimated.

Current is of greatest importance on the beat for three reasons: (1) More time is spent on the beat for an equivalent length of course than on any other leg, (2) there is a greater possibility of major variation in current strength between boats at the extremities of each tack than on any other leg, and (3) boat speed over the bottom and through the air will vary on each tack and thus create greater boat-speed differentials than on any other leg. Adverse current multiplies this significance as it increases the time spent in these conditions and thereby multiplies the differential effects upon boats in various positions on the leg. The dramatic effects of current in determining the outcome of a race are most obvious in light air (because of the increased duration of exposure), but are significant at all times regardless of the wind strength.

Success in yacht racing is dependent upon establishing and functioning under a set of priorities which determine *when* to do what. A priority of significance must be determined for current so that other strategic and tactical considerations can be properly correlated; in general, greater strength of current, its adverse set, and its presence on the beat increase its priority for consideration. When its strength outweighs other considerations, as when sailing against the current on a light-air beat, immediate course adjustment must be made. The start should be made from a position close to, or even above the line, at the end with the least current (being certain that the mark can be laid) on the tack which will take the boat into the area of least current. If there is a shore or other limitation which prevents sailing to the lay line on this tack, short tacks up the shore, avoiding the main tidal flow, are essential. Cross immediately (unless the current is significantly less upstream) to the side of the main current flow on which the weather mark is located so that the final approach to the mark is in the most favorable conditions. If no limitations exist, sail out of the current to the lay line on a

single hitch, remembering that because of the adverse current the lay line will be considerably above the 90-degree line to the initial tack course.

Tacking is extremely dangerous in adverse tide as significant losses in windward distance occur with each maneuver; thus, if possible, it should only be done once and then as far out of the tide as possible. No compromise which requires additional tacks further into the current than the competitors should be undertaken, regardless of disturbed-air need to cover, or other tactical considerations. Let the competition be the first to tack out, the first to test the current out in mainstream; it often pays to be a little behind so as to observe the leaders peel off and be swept away, thus to judge the optimal lay-line approach.

Once out in the major current approaching the mark, boats on the cross-tide tack may be moving at two, three, or more times the speed of boats on the uptide tack. Indeed, boats having approached across tide, unable to achieve any forward progress at all after tacking to the uptide tack, may have to watch their competitors who continued but a few feet beyond them on the initial tack sweep above them and round the mark well in the lead.

This difference in boat speed on the two tacks is the major determinant of the racing results in these conditions, so every precaution should be taken to insure that the uptide tack is taken entirely out of the main current and that nothing remains but rounding once the mark is reached. Sailing 100 yards too far before tacking for the cross-tide approach is a negligible loss compared to tacking 10 yards too early and being unable to make any forward progress at all uptide in the vicinity of the mark. If a tack must be made to round, there must, of course, be at least enough wind to permit some progress uptide; it may pay if the wind is extremely light to hang back, proceeding on the cross-tack approach very slowly and waiting for the necessary puff to swoop down and around.

Once you are out in the current, it may be too late to get back; the decision to initiate the cross-tide approach tack is the crucial one. Not only does the uptide boat have markedly reduced boat speed over the bottom but markedly reduced boat speed through the air, further reducing her apparent wind. She is thus helpless against the properly executed approach of a cross-tide boat coming down on a puff.

Frostbite Racing

Sailboat racing can be a year-round sport, even in northern states. The hardy sailors who race in the winter are known as "frostbiters." Starting as a lark in the early 30's, frostbiting is now a serious and popular sport. Many of the leading sailors of larger boats in the summer sail little dinghies in the winter, with the result that top-flight competition is the rule.

Long Island Sound, Cape Cod, Lake Michigan, and Puget Sound are just a few of the frostbite centers, and it takes a freezeover of the harbors or a blizzard to stop the sport. The location of the fleet determines the amount of action. For example, the established frostbiting fleets in the New York area operate only once a week, usually on Sunday

afternoons, and in the period of three hours the race committee will jam in a half dozen or more races around short courses.

The seasons can be long ones, beginning in October and carrying into April. With 24 weekend dates and an average of six races an afternoon, this means a skipper can enrich his experience 144 times a winter. Unless he is an avid traveler, he will never get to that many starting lines in summer.

Most frostbiting is done in little one-design dinghies such as Penguins, Interclubs, Dyer Dinks, Turnabouts, Roosters, Snowbirds, Kites, O.K. Dinghies, El Toros, Tech Dinghies, Dyer Dhows, and Sabots. They can easily be dry-sailed, meaning hauled out of the water on trailers or carried on top of an auto or in the back of a station wagon, to and from the races. This solves the problem of winter dockage and permits the boat to escape the ravages of ice. Also their size and simplicity (cat-rigged) make them inexpensive.

The frostbiting racing course is generally no longer than three-fourths of a mile, averag-

Dyer Dhows sail in a Mamaroneck Frostbite Association regatta.

ing half a mile, windward-leeward-windward, or triangular in shape. The start is signaled by a series of blasts from a horn, whistle, or cannon. (One club uses a prerecorded phonograph record that calls out the number of seconds to go before each signal.) In the frequent instances of wholesale barging and premature starting, the racing committee is generally empowered to call the whole thing off and demand a new start. No regattas should be held in winds blowing over 15 knots. In conditions of 10 to 15 knots, courses should be set which require no jibing. Most dinghies will capsize long before they will jibe in a good breeze. The regatta should end at the discretion of the race committee or most certainly one to two hours before sunset.

Certain ground rules and precautions are generally observed in order to promote safety. It is bitter cold, of course, when a boat capsizes—as they frequently do—but a frostbiting rule requires any boat in the vicinity of a capsized one to go to the latter's aid immediately. It is the universal rule of never sailing without a "crash boat" to fish out those who do go over that has kept the frostbiters' safety record intact—there has never been a fatality in over thirty years of this type of racing.

One stays amazingly warm because the physical exertion in sailing a small boat is sufficient to keep skipper and crew warm, except—of course—on the coldest days. Sensible clothing helps immensely—for example, insulated underwear (the type skiers and hunters use), wool socks, good foul-weather gear, etc. When outfitted properly against the elements, you are ready to take part in the northerner's answer to a Florida or Southern California winter.

Team Racing

With the sport of racing growing rapidly in recent years, more and more yachtsmen are being introduced to a very exciting type of racing—team racing. Here is a brief outline of how teams race.

Type of Boat. Any evenly matched one-design class.

Type of Course. Best of all is a right triangle with the right angle at the windward mark. On the first round the triangle is completed, and on the second round the second mark is omitted (i.e., a windward-leeward second round). Such a course provides every point of sailing—dead beat, beam reach, broad reach, and dead run—with a second windward leg for good measure.

Racing Rules. IYRU racing rules are followed, plus the team racing rules.

Scoring of Team Races. In each individual race, 1 point for every boat you beat, 4 points for sailing the course, and an extra ¼ point for the winner. (In team racing, as opposed to fleet racing, it is important to have the same increment of 1 point between all finishing positions from first to last.) For a series of team races there are two possible methods of scoring:

1. Race by Race: The winning team is the first to win two races out of a possible three, or three out of a possible five, or four out of a possible seven. Each race is scored separately. This method brings out the best in team racing and team tactics.

2. Total Points Carried Forward: The number of races is specified in advance. Each team's points are added up, race by race, the team with the greater total at the end of the final race being declared the winner. This method should be discouraged because one flukey day, or a disablement or disqualification, can easily decide the whole series.

Mathematical Considerations. In a match between two four-boat teams, calculations of the possible scoring combinations show (barring disablement or disqualification) that there are 70 ways for a team to finish—35 ways of winning, and likewise 35 ways of losing. Of the 35 ways to win, 28 of the 35 include first place. Thus the first boat to finish is theoretically on the winning side four times out of five. In practice, however, these odds do not quite hold, because after the leading boat finishes, the other team then has four boats with which to "gang up" on the remaining three. Under certain conditions this numerical advantage toward the end of a race may prove decisive, thus considerably minimizing the theoretical importance of first place. If the first two boats to finish are of the same team, it is impossible for that team to lose, barring disablement or disqualification. This one-two finish is known as the "big double." If first place goes to your opponents, there are only 7 out of 35 ways for your team to win, and 6 of these 7 require both second and third places. This two-three finish is known as the "little double." If a boat withdraws after fouling, or is disabled, this makes your team lose the race (theoretically) four times out of five. In practice, the penalty for your team is even more severe, because your opponents then have a numerical advantage of four boats against your three. Last place is almost as bad a handicap because the last-place boat causes your team to lose the race five times out of seven.

In view of these mathematical peculiarities of the scoring system, it is most important for your team to keep from fouling, keep out of last place, and secure first place—in about that order. Do not forget that if your team at any time needs 2 more points, you can win if only one of your boats passes an opponent, because when you gain a point your opponents likewise lose a point—a net gain of 2 for you.

Racing Tactics. The oft-enunciated principles of successful team racing are:

1. Get first.
2. Do not get last.
3. Cover (the appropriate opponent).
4. Do not make major mistakes.

And from these principles derives almost all else. Application implies an aggressive, confident attitude which is fundamental to team-racing success. The principles remain the same when success is unlikely, but their application is significantly altered.

To "get first" each member of the team with a reasonable chance of winning should attempt to break away for that purpose. Early conflicts with the opposition must be avoided. The best end of the starting line must be determined and the best boat must be there with the gun. Even more important is the selection of the strategically advantageous side of the course and the acquisition of a breakaway position to reach it—first. Once in front, the leaders must concentrate on staying there with no thought for their mates until the final leg. The opposition must be prevented from getting first by preventing them from getting the best start and by covering them carefully thereafter. If one opponent is exceptionally fast he should be controlled at the start,

forced to make a late or poorly positioned start, or at least prevented from sailing to the preferable side of the course.

To avoid being last each member of the team should get a good, if not the best, start in clear air. An immediate breakaway should be attempted if covered so as to avoid further loss. Even the boat in last place must stay with her fleet, should not take long chances, and avoid the lay lines until late in the beat. Help will be available later, but will be useless if the tail-ender is far astern. Only on the last leg when all else has failed is the big gamble justified. If a weak opponent is last he should be kept there by careful covering and, if possible, by carrying him even farther away, but the covering boat should not drop too far behind the fleet. If the opponents are superior, a more aggressive starting technique must be utilized. One boat should be forced over the line early or away from the line so as to insure that an opponent is last. If one of their better boats can be held back, he should be closely covered and forced if possible to the disadvantageous side of the beat.

Once out on the course, the situation should be analyzed and the position score calculated. Members of the leading team who are themselves leading their nearest opponents should push on for the best strategic course while covering these opponents. Boats behind should attempt to break away, but not by assuming an obviously less advantageous course. Cover should be changed between teammates as indicated by developments to control the most similarly performing opponent. In general the fastest boat should cover the fastest opponent, the slowest boat the slowest opponent. A slower boat may, of course, assume a distant coverage of a faster boat which is sailing a significantly disadvantageous course. Unless the capabilities of the opposition are well understood, as for instance late in a team match series, it is better to delay the choice of opponent to cover until out on the beat. When behind in series score, aggressive control may be justified from the 5-minute gun.

An appropriate manipulation of cover is achieved through resolution of "sandwiches" when the team is behind or in danger of falling behind. Whenever an opponent is "sandwiched" between two teammates, it is possible to improve the team position by maneuvering the opponent so as to let the trailing teammate through. The leading boat may carry the opponent to an overstanding position on the beat, force him beyond or on the wrong side of a turning mark, or luff him off course on a reach or run until his teammate can take the lead.

A leading boat may resolve a "sandwich" and stop an opponent most effectively on the beat. If she waits at the leeward mark, dead ahead or after two quick tacks, dead to windward, she should thereafter, by tacking and bearing away as needed, be able to control the following boat throughout the entire windward leg. Sail flapping by the leader increases the air disturbance about the follower to a point which virtually stops her. Control of this kind is so effective, if carefully conducted, that an opponent may be dropped from second or third all the way to last as successive teammates break through. Only a one-two combination is safe against this tactic, as a one-three can easily be converted into a losing one-last. Following teammates must be alert to this technique and not allow themselves to become so involved with other opponents that they are not close enough to profit from it.

Gains are possible when two boats of one team are close astern of one member of the opposing team. To windward, frequent tacking by one member of the pair may slow the covering leader so that the teammate can break through to the lead. On the reach, luring the leader into a luffing match may provide a similar opportunity for a teammate to break ahead. On the run, blanketing by one may provide the needed opening for the other. Unless a teammate is close at hand, however, such tactics should be avoided inasmuch as loss by the attacking boat is almost certain.

"Finish-line" or final-leg control on the reach to recover a winning combination is ineffective unless teammates are close at hand to capitalize on brief flowing and deviation by luffing. Starboard-port crosses as a desperate finale are ineffective, unless unnoticed, as the starboard boat must hold an undeviating course in order not to balk, and the post boat may maneuver as she wishes. Variations in speed by the starboard boat are legal, however.

Luffing should be utilized when opponents are close aboard to windward. This situation obtains after a lee-bow tack on the windward leg and when a windward boat seeks an inside overlap on a mark approach. In the latter case the luff must be completed prior to entering the "two-boat-length circle" or if not, the "outside" boat must go with the "inside" boat to the wrong side and past the mark. It is essential, if so doing, for the luffing boat to allow enough room above the mark to permit a jibe back without hitting the mark as soon as the luffed boat attempts to tack away.

Finally, and particularly in team racing, major mistakes must be avoided. Commission of major errors is the usual reason for not winning in ordinary racing and may be tolerable where first or nothing is the object. But in team racing every boat is of equal significance and major mistakes are no more tolerable by the last boat than by the first. Most significantly, team racing is "team" racing. Every action of every member of the team is equally important to the final result. Winning is the only goal and every sacrifice may and should be made to this end. The score must be constantly reviewed. If the team is behind on the last legs even first place must be relinquished to achieve the victory.

Protests and Appeals

"A yacht which realizes she has infringed a racing rule or a sailing instruction should retire promptly." Such a yacht which does not retire should be protested. Protests are usually the consequence of ignorance (it is still surprising how many otherwise competent racing sailors do not know the rules) or carelessness.

If an incident occurs which results in the failure of a yacht or yachts to comply with the rules, the following solutions are possible and recommended. If the helmsman of one yacht recognizes that he was wrong, he withdraws. If he is ignorant and does not withdraw, he should be protested—to assist education, if for no other purpose. If the helmsman of one yacht recognizes that he arrived at this sorry situation because he was careless, he should withdraw unless he is certain that despite his carelessness he did not violate the rules. When there is doubt and the cause is carelessness, he should withdraw. If the incident arose from a planned maneuver, he should carry on and reconsider. Acting impulsively can produce an inappropriate withdrawal as readily as an inappropriate maneuver. If after due consideration, it is evident that a foul was committed, he should withdraw. If in doubt he should sail on and let the protest committee decide.

Mistakes are made and when they are, the question of the psychology involved arises. Occasionally a disqualification is deliberate: when the pressure becomes too great, some take the easiest way out, which is equivalent to suicide. More frequently a conflict suddenly erupts which is viewed in an opposite manner by two competitors. The aggressor is acting out, "I'll show you that I'm in command"; the victim is reacting, "You can't do this to me." As racing sailors are competitors, this conflict is a common one and the underlying basis of many protests. A port-tack boat approaches the weather mark against a stream of starboard tackers on the lay line. He swings his bow almost upon the transom of one boat and completes his tack 6 feet ahead of the bow of the next in line. The port tacker is saying (to himself), "I have a perfect right to be here; I am ahead of this next boat." The second starboard tacker is shouting (so all can hear), "You tacked too close! You have no right to tack there!" ("You can't do this to me!")

Protest committees must keep in mind that this psychic background underlies much of what they are compelled to hear. The protestor after drawing his diagram and writing his version of the facts might well add, "He can't do this to me!" The "innocent" competitor after preparing his statement might well add, "But I was only doing what was justified" (by my construction of the world as it should be!). Yachtsmen are gentlemen; they do *not* knowingly lie. But they can reconstruct the situation in an image which portrays more their view of a "just" world than a real one!

A protest can be made by any competitor against any other competitor and should a protest occur between yachts competing in a race sponsored by two clubs or more, the case is heard by a combined committee of these clubs. A helmsman who wishes to protest must do his best to tell the other yacht that a protest will be lodged. This is only fair because the "accused" then has as good a chance of remembering the circumstances

of the case as the helmsman who is making the protest. For this reason a protest flag has to be flown conspicuously in the rigging at the first reasonable opportunity and must be kept flying until the protestor has finished his race (also as a warning to the officer of the day) unless the competitor's boat was dismasted, capsized, or sunk. Even in this case, however, the protesting helmsman must make an effort to find and warn the other yachtsmen concerned.

The protest flag must be either a flag or a burgee or a rectangular piece of material no smaller than the distinguishing flag usually flown by the protesting yacht. In the case of a yacht being sailed single-handed it might be difficult for the helmsman with only one pair of hands to hoist a protest flag, so it is considered enough if the flag is brought to the notice of the other helmsman (for example, by waving it) as soon as possible after the incident and to the committee when the finishing line is crossed at the finish. If a yacht fails to observe this rule the race committee must refuse to accept the protest but they may still bring one on their own initiative under certain circumstances.

Full information on protests, disqualifications, and appeals is given in Part VI of the NAYRU rules, together with an outline form for protest-committee procedures. Of course, each party to a protest presumably comes to the hearing believing that he behaved satisfactorily and that the other should be disqualified. The committee, recognizing the emotional involvement of each, must obtain the facts or at least some mutually agreed upon version of the real situation. The committee wants to reach a decision and perceives itself as an impartial judge capable of reaching a just conclusion. If the committee is in fact impartial, the party which presents the best evidence that it met the requirements of the rules will be exonerated and the other disqualified. If the committee instead perceives that it is a dispenser of "justice," it will fall into the dilemma of the parties to the protest, substituting a personal construction of propriety for the criteria of the rules.

A good protest committee is always courteous; each participant in the hearing should be properly introduced to every other. Adequate opportunity should be given to each party and each witness to fully present his recollection of the situation. Opportunity should be given for each party to cross-examine the other and to cross-examine each witness and, of course, each party should be permitted to be present throughout the entire hearing. The chairman should maintain complete control; no interruptions should be permitted; testimony, cross-examination, and questioning should be arranged in their proper order. An opportunity should be given for each party to present a summation of his case at the termination of the hearing.

Never initiate a protest unless you are confident that the committee will be a good one; then rely completely upon it. Never preach to a protest committee; they view themselves as judges and need to live up to their role. Be humble, but confident. Be courteous: wait your turn, do not interrupt, treat the other party with respect. The more gentlemanly you appear, the more reliance will be placed upon your testimony. Demonstrate that you thoroughly understand the rule involved (do a little homework). During your testimony state the criteria which must be used to decide the protest and indicate that you understand that the burden of proof is upon you to prove your case (if so). (Do not indicate that the burden of proof is on the other party; if so, the committee knows it.) Present your testimony so as to establish the requirements for proof. Be precise; indicate no doubt about timing, point of collision, relationships between boats prior to the incident. Indicate, if appropriate, that you were better able than the other party to observe the circumstances of the incident. Do not coach your crew or other witnesses beyond an agreement upon the basic facts of the situation; the committee is bound to be skeptical of a story which is too "pat." In summation indicate that you clearly understand the criteria which the committee will use in their judgment and that you have fully complied with them.

Selecting Your Crew

In the old days the yacht skipper, true and accepted gentleman that he was, had his boat worked by a collection of paid hands, often a raffish lot with whom he had little in common and with whom he associated as little as possible. On top of this, the skipper sometimes had a social standing which gave his word the impact of law on or off the boat, and the depth of his purse directly reflected the sailing quality of his crew.

Today's skipper and crew are a different lot, and the skipper-crew relationship is very much changed. Today's skipper is one of the crew. He has to rely, not on his purse, but on his own interest in the sport and his own personality to gather and keep a good crew, and he sails with them in friendly association.

The skipper today has another advantage over his one-man-band ancestor. He has the opportunity to build up a team of people devoted to the sport—a team with racing experience and an understanding of yacht racing which may match his own. To get the best out of his craft, he should try to attract such people, and he must strive to use their talents fully—their minds as well as their rope-pulling ability.

If your existing crew setup does not allow for "thinking boats" creatively, change it so that it does. Thinking crewmen are the ones you want aboard. At the least, the crew you choose should have the ability to seek out and keep abreast of other people's ideas, and of general developments in the sport. We have suggested that on the water the crew should jump to a skipper's command. By this we mean they should do so whether or not they think at the time that the command is wise. But they should be encouraged to make suggestions, even in the boat, provided their timing is right. Chipping in when things are happening fast will not help at all and this applies no matter how well-meaning the suggestion is or, as may be subsequently proved, how well-merited it may be. Any interruption during a hectic moment can only confuse the man or men already given an instruction. Often it will make the rest of the crew hesitate so the skipper has to repeat what he wants done, and time is lost.

In short, on occasions of crisis the crew should *act,* and do any talking later. Perhaps there will be a chance further along the course, but more likely the best place for a post mortem of any incident will be when everyone is back on shore. Ashore is where the skipper and crew should get together, regularly, and in full democratic forum, to review the race and see what can be learned from it. The club bar is the usual place. Crew meetings like these are best held immediately after the race when details are fresh in mind and when there is a full week to do whatever is needed—whether it is a major refit or re-tuning, or simply the need for one (or all) to take another long look at the rules of racing.

Shore discussions also have benefits that go beyond achieving any immediate practical aim. They help each crewman to feel more a part of the team—the togetherness of it, if you like—and the discussions will stimulate those vital ideas.

Two more standards by which we can measure the potential of the crew we want as permanent hands are temperament and keen-ness. By temperament, we mean the ability to respond under racing pressure without any outbursts of emotion. Emotion is contagious and one excited or excitable man can unsettle an entire crew. The man who cannot contain his feelings is not for you. Remember, too, that the skipper should encourage the level-headed approach to racing by his own example. He can indicate urgency by his tone of voice, but ideally never anger. (It follows that violent "seamanlike" phrases achieve no long-term good. They may help relieve the skipper's tension, but the man who says, "Get that blank jib sheet blankwell on!" has merely taken too long to give a simple command.)

The skipper will have his best chance to judge crew keenness during a racing reverse, when the hope for a win is low. When a yacht is not sailing well, a sort of inertia can pervade all on board. The whole race effort can seem futile, and all anybody wants to do is get ashore and forget about it. A keen skipper —and he must be keen to deserve keen people with him—will buck this feeling, fast. Even if he is not sure what is wrong with the boat, he has to smash the lassitude engulfing the crew and get better results from the yacht. He must do something to get the crew with it again—adjust the jib lead, perhaps, or the main traveler or the backstay tension. To do nothing is to capitulate. Those of the crew who are really keen will show their colors at a time like this, making their own suggestions and enthusiastically doing whatever the skipper asks of them. You can judge enthusiasm on shore too. Watch a crewman's reaction when he is asked to do one of the more un-pleasant jobs. Perhaps the bottom has to be scrubbed on a cheerless day, or a torn spinnaker has to be taken to a sailmaker in an outer suburb. You will soon be able to pick the really keen man, and he is the person you need the most. The keen newcomer you can train is worth any two with a mint of experience who are the tired "I-know-all-about-that" type who are not 100 percent with you. You do him a favor if you let him gravitate to whatever yacht his attitude warrants.

Let us accept now that we have found the men we want—the men with potential. The next step is to build them into an ace crew. There are several aspects to consider. First comes morale. A simple way to starting out with a team spirit is to adopt a crew uniform. There is hardly a man alive who is not proud to be in a neat, well-turned-out group, and psychologists can measure the improved results such pride brings.

Make sure everybody aboard the boat knows exactly what his job is. Confusion is the direct product of doubt, and each man should have his specific duties and responsibilities, beginning on shore, checking the gear, rigging the boat, and working the craft while on the water. Set crew members should handle the jib and mainsheets. Only one man should handle the stop watch (he and the skipper should have worked out beforehand how he should call, and he must stick to it). Another in the crew can be lookout, another responsible for spinnaker halyard, or sheet, or guy. If you have only one or two in the crew, all these duties will have to be split among the men available. If you have a large yacht, it is handy before the start to have a lookout in the bow, who with his own stop watch can direct the skipper to drive forward or ease up in the last few seconds before the gun.

The most important thing is that the duties are clearly divided, no one should jump to do the appointed task of another man unless asked, although it is always a good idea for one crewman to be ready to backstop for another if needed. Ideally, a yacht is sailed by people with experience in every position aboard. The fuller the understanding each man has of what is involved, the better he will be. When there are no races, go sailing with the sole aim of switching the crew about. And give each man a spell at the helm.

The skipper should want his men to know just what weight there can be on the helm during a shy spinnaker run, or if the kite and mainsheet are not eased smartly in a squall. He should want them to see and feel the amount of way a yacht loses when a jib is fouled in tacking or sheeted home late. Only the skipper can see and feel these things because the crew is heads down while it is going on.

The skipper, of course, owes the crew one major debt, which only he can pay. He must provide a racing unit, hull and gear, that is reliable enough to give the crew a fighting chance of winning. We have all heard, seen, or even been on a boat that would have taken the winning gun except the main halyard or jibsheet parted. Unless the breakage rammed home to the skipper the need for good gear and constant checks, he is lucky if he has kept the same crew or had later success. It all boils down to this: If the skipper cannot stand the checkbook pain of keeping his craft up to scratch, he might as well buy a more modest racer.

The Corinthians. Incidentally, the subject of selecting a crew would not be complete without a word about the Corinthians. Whether you are a sailing enthusiast on the lookout for a berth or own a boat and need a crew, if you are a member of the Corinthians you just call up the crewing office and state your requirements. It is almost that simple. This remarkable group of amateur seafarers is dedicated to serving the needs of boatless crews and crewless skippers, and its crewing committee is kept busy year-round matching men and ships.

The Corinthians were formed in 1934 by Carleton S. Cooke and Frederick M. Delano, who felt that there was a definite need for a different kind of yachting organization and were inspired somewhat by The Little Ships Club in England. In the 1930's, as now, more and more yachtsmen were finding it difficult to crew their boats with professionals; and at the same time many good amateur sailors, who were not yet in a position to own boats, had trouble getting afloat. To help solve the problem, the Corinthians were incorporated as a nonprofit, member association in the State of New York. In the succeeding years they have more than lived up to the objective set forth in their constitution: "to promote sailing, to encourage good fellowship among yachtsmen, afloat and ashore, to assist yacht-owner members to obtain competent and congenial crews, and to assist non-yacht-owning members to obtain desirable berths." But in addition to crewing their own boats and other people's, the Corinthians sponsor a spring and a fall rendezvous afloat, followed by a dinner ashore at a convenient yacht club. Recently the rendezvous has been preceded by a handicap race. This is not a racing club, however, and the events have been kept very informal. Wives and families are cordially invited to every rendezvous, and participate with enthusiasm.

The Corinthians have demonstrated that there is a real need for this type of crewing association, over and above the recognized functions of a regular yacht club. There are other similar organizations—one may be in your sailing area—and there is room for many more. In business, a good "sale" is one which benefits both buyer and seller. In boating, good "sails" are often the result of mixing crewless skippers with boatless sailing enthusiasts. A club that accomplishes this kind of an affiliation will always be popular with yachtsmen.

Crewman's Checklist

So much for the duties of the skipper. Here is a checklist of advice which we hope will be of value in helping the crewman help his skipper win more races:

1. Learn the correct names for each part of the boat and her rigging.
2. Read the race circular carefully and discuss it with your skipper.
3. Learn all the race signals.
4. Study the rules of racing (NAYRU rules).
5. Check all gear at the dock and be sure everything is shipshape before the start of the race.
6. Watch the wind for clues of approaching wind shifts.
7. Report positions of other boats, progress of other boats, course shifts and sail changes of other boats, imminent gear failure—anything at all that the

skipper may not have noticed himself.

8. Work hard at trimming the boat and do things the skipper's way.

9. Learn to use the compass in racing.

10. Keep things shipshape during the race and treat the equipment as if you owned it.

11. Stick around after the race and help with the postrace cleanup.

12. Remember, yacht racing is supposed to be fun. If all the hard work, discomfort, technical jargon, and competition strikes you as something less than good

sport, there is probably nothing wrong with you. It is just that you are not cut out for yacht racing. If, on the other hand, it does not throw you, stick with it and sooner or later you will start to win your share.

So, if you do not own a boat, but love to sail, do not be bashful. Ask to crew. All you need is a desire to win, agility, brains, weight, some experience, dexterity, strength, ability to concentrate, a congenial personality, and fortitude. Everything else the skipper provides.

HANDICAP AND DISTANCE RACING

As was stated earlier in this section, racing can be done either level (even-up) or handicapped. As we said, most one-design class races are sailed without handicap, although some yacht clubs and racing associations work out a system of some type by which a boat that wins a race incurs a handicap penalty in the next. Actually, when such a method is used, the skipper is handicapped rather than the boat since the boats are one-designs. Handicaps, however, become necessary when boats of different sail area and hull size race against each other. When this occurs there are two main systems employed: (1) handicaps by "time-on-time"; and (2) handicaps by "time-on-distance."

In the time-on-time system the allowance is calculated at a given number of seconds or minutes per hour of the finishing time either of the leading boat, or more often, of the individual boat which is receiving the handicap. Time-on-distance system is calculated according to the length of the course.

Both handicap systems have their faults and under some weather conditions each may favor one boat over another boat. For example, the time-on-time system generally gives an advantage to the small boat should the race be sailed in light-air conditions with periods of calm; for its time allowance over the larger craft increases while both are becalmed. In a time-on-distance race, on the other hand, no more allowance is given if the course is a dead beat against strong winds than if the course were a straight run in good weather the entire way.

Whether a race is based on time-on-distance (NAYRU time-allowance tables) or time-on-time (RORC rules), many different rating formulas have been devised to establish what handicap one boat should receive against another. In general, they cater to a class of boats more or less uniform in design and sail area. With the NAYRU time-allowance system, the scale is based on the rating and distance sailed, which gives a fixed time allowance regardless of the elapsed time of the race —a time which will vary under different sailing conditions.

Measurement Rules and Time Allowance

The three principal handicap rules for racing cruisers used in America are the CCA (Cruising Club of America), IOR (International Offshore Rating), and MORC (Midget Ocean Racing Club) rules. Two other rules of some popularity are the Off Sounding Club (OSC) and the Storm Trysail Club (STC) rules. The MORC was formerly for boats under 24 feet LOA, but the size limit was extended and now includes boats up to 30 feet LOA. Yachts racing under this rule are customarily divided into two classes: division A, for boats 24 feet but under 30 feet LOA, and division B, for those under 24 feet LOA. The CCA rule is generally for boats between 30 and 73 feet LOA. In some racing areas such as Southern California (MORF—Midget Ocean Racing Fleet—the organization that controls small cruiser boats in that region), however, boats under 30 feet (with a rated

The start of an ocean race from Miami to Montego Bay, Jamaica—a distance of 811 miles. This photo shows *Kailoa II,* right, and *Windward Passage,* left, battling for the early lead.

length of perhaps over 22 feet) are allowed to race under the CCA rule; and so in this case these small boats may have an option to race under CCA or MORC. Of course, it is up to the race sponsoring organization to choose the handicap rule, but the great majority of important races in the United States presently use the MORC for small boats and the CCA for larger boats.

Handicapping of cruising yachts of various sizes and types for equitable racing revolved hopefully around methods to evaluate the factors influencing speed and to relate these by a time-allowance table or system. On the basis of present knowledge the factors which influence speed of displacement hulls may be considered to include both *drive* and *drag* factors.

Under the heading of drive factors may be included:

1. *Sail area*—the horsepower driving the yacht. Some consideration should be given to the arrangement of the sail plan or rig.
2. *Length*—or sailing length of the yacht— the effective length or size of a yacht under conditions of sailing. Length is generally considered the most fundamental measure of a boat's speed.
3. *Stability*—the ability of the yacht to carry sail effectively.

Under the heading of drag factors may be included:

1. *Wetted surface*—the frictional resistance of the hull and appendage moving through water.
2. *Wavemaking*—the drag resulting from the forces expended in wavemaking by the hull in moving through the water.

Cruiser-racers often race on closed courses, too. Here MORC Triton class boats maneuver around windward mark.

3. *Other forms* of drag as from *induced drag* afforded by the hull and the appendage; the drag resulting from heeling and the drag resulting from propellers, shafts, apertures, and skegs.

Other factors that are important and readily measurable are displacement (or hull depth), beam, draft, stability, freeboard, and rig. As stated previously, the most fundamental measure of a boat's speed is her sailing length, because the square root of this measurement approximates her easily attained top speed (at a speed-length ratio of 1.0) when sailing full and by in moderate winds. Sail area is equally important, because this is the driving or motivating force, and displacement or hull depth with beam, considered as resistance, can be thought of as the bulk or weight to be moved. In the various measurement formulas, sail area (SA) is expressed as a square root because this is a surface or square measurement; while displacement (disp. or D or P), expressed as volume or cubic measurement, is shown in the formulas as a cube root. Or, the rated lengths of racer-cruisers of different sizes vary with the square roots of their sail area and the cube roots of their displacement.

The rating formulas give a rated length in feet (R) which is then applied to time-allowance tables to obtain the actual handicap time for a particular race. This will be discussed later. Yachts assigned a rating under the rules mentioned in this chapter must be measured by official measurers approved by the race or rule sponsoring organization or club.

The Cruising Club of America Measurement Rule. While yacht designers, builders, and owners continue their efforts to develop boats which sail faster than their ratings call for, the existing CCA rule reflects periodic adjustments of measurements to compensate for the ingenuity of yacht designers in taking advantage of loopholes in the rules that preceded it. In the spirit of fair racing, all of us should vow to uphold the CCA's *Spirit of the Rule* statement, which reads as follows:

It is the intent of CCA Measurement Rule

to make it possible for yachtsmen to race seaworthy cruising boats of various designs, types, and construction on a fair and equitable basis. The rules are not, and can never be, perfect. In order that the rules may serve this purpose, yachtsmen themselves must interpret them in keeping with the *Spirit of the Rule*. No infringement of the *Spirit of the Rule* nor any method of reducing the rating of any yacht by utilizing questionable, unreasonable, or unsafe methods will be acceptable; and the Club will not issue a rating certificate to any yacht owner who in any manner attempts to defeat the purpose for which this rule is intended. All Race Committees conducting races under this Measurement Rule are strongly urged to require that any unusual practice in rig, hull, ballast, or other factors not covered specifically within these rules be reported to the Race Committee for a ruling, and in any case, be subject to protest. The test of said ruling shall be whether or not, in the opinion of the Race Committee, the practice would give unfair advantage or in any way violate or circumvent the intent of the rule.

The measurement rule of the CCA is a formula for correcting the waterline length of a boat to obtain a rated length. It takes into consideration the principal factors which affect the potential speed of a boat. It endeavors to correct for differences in design which tend to increase or decrease the speed of a boat in relation to a standard, so that in applying these corrections, all boats in a race will be on an equitable basis as far as these factors are concerned. For instance, the power to drive a boat through the water is obtained from the sails, and therefore more sail area, or a more efficient sail plan, will increase speed, while the reverse is true with less sail area or a less efficient sail plan. The formula endeavors to correct for variations in sails and to convert variations from a standard, or base, into a change in waterline length. However, displacement, or the weight of a boat, offers resistance to hull movement through the water, and therefore the rule endeavors to allow for variations from a standard or base displacement by giving a credit or reduction in waterline length when displacement is greater than a standard, and by giving a penalty or increase in waterline length

when displacement is less than a standard. Similarly, beam affects the speed of a boat. As a general rule, an increase in beam increases wave making resistance, and it also increases wetted surface, thus increasing skin-friction resistance. However, it must be realized that if a boat has insufficient beam it cannot properly carry her sails and therefore will suffer when on the wind. The formula provides for a decrease in the waterline length for increased beam above a standard, or for an increase in the waterline length for decreased beam below a standard. Also, the draft of a boat has a considerable effect on speed. A boat with light draft may benefit by having less wetted surface, whereas a deep draft lowers the center of gravity, thus adding to stability and sail-carrying capacity, as well as perhaps giving a more effective lateral plane, or better performance to windward.

Although corrections for these factors, plus corrections for freeboard, propeller type and location, centerboards, and iron versus lead keels are important and necessary, there are direct calculations by themselves as to their effect on speed and on rating. However, stability is a very important factor in determining the sailing qualities of a boat, as it involves the combined effect of many of the other factors. It is therefore necessary to devise a formula to take stability into consideration in order that variations in it may be properly evaluated. This results in some of the more complicated calculations of the measurement rule for translating stability into the effect on speed and rating. Ballast-to-displacement ratios and measured beam-to-beam ratios are needed from which is derived a correction factor to rating. For instance, more ballast or more beam increases the stability of a boat and results in a penalty correction to rating, but the corresponding increase in displacement on beam derived by their respective formulas increases the resistance of the hull through the water, and results in a credit correction to the rating; so that a loss in one adjustment may be offset to some extent by a gain in another. Therefore, in the final calculation of the rating, the plus-and-minus corrections for all the factors are summed up and applied in the rating formula to determine the rated length of the boat.

The complete rule details are given in a booklet published by the CCA and obtainable from the Cruising Club of America, 25 Broadway, New York, N.Y. 10004, for a fee of $2. This booklet should be studied prior to measuring, especially the sections that explain the owner's preparation of the hull and rig for measurement and the owner's responsibility after measurement.

The International Offshore Rating Rule. The IOR (International Offshore Rule) is the newest measurement in practice and is, for the most part, a compromise between the rules of the American CCA and the British RORC (Royal Ocean Racing Club). Sail rating and measurements are quite similar to those of the CCA, but hull measurements are more closely related to those of the RORC.

A copy of the booklet *International Offshore Rule—IOR Mark II* may be obtained at a cost of $2.50 from the North American Yacht Racing Union, Offshore Office, 198 New York Avenue, Huntington, N.Y. 11743.

Also similar to RORC practice is the new rule's use of hull-depth measurements together with beam instead of displacement as an assessment of hull resistance. Stability is measured by an inclining test similar to that of the CCA.

"Is the IOR better than the CCA rule?" "Will the IOR be adaptable enough to negate the effect of any loopholes which may develop in the future?" "Are there features of the IOR which are exploitable?" "Will the IOR favor light or heavy boats?" "Will my boat's IOR rating be higher or lower than its CCA rating?" "Will my chief competitors be better off than I?" "Will I have to alter my boat to conform to the IOR?" These and similar questions can only be answered when the International Offshore Rule has had a chance to function.

The Midget Ocean Racing Club Rule. As stated in Section I, the Midget Ocean Racing Club (MORC) was inspired by the Junior Offshore Group (JOG), a British club devoted to racing small boats offshore. Founded in 1950, JOG retained the Royal Ocean Racing Club's measurement rule to which they added some rigid safety rules of their own, as befits small vessels on a body of water like the English Channel, covering stability, flota-

tion, cockpit volume, and companionway-area limitations, and they published a list of mandatory equipment, such as personal lifelines for each crew member, life jackets, and distress flares. Originally the JOG only concerned itself with vessels in the 16- to 20-foot waterline-length category, but to accommodate owners of boats directly above this and less than 24-foot waterline length, the bottom limit of the RORC classes, they later established JOG-IV for this new group and JOG-V for their formerly exclusive membership. JOG-V is further limited to vessels with RORC ratings between 12.0 and 18.0, though no restriction of rating exists for JOG-IV.

Although operating without a great deal of publicity, the Midget Ocean Racing Club has been functioning since 1954 solely to promote and administer the racing of well-found, small cruising boats. Until 1959 this organization catered only to boats not exceeding 24 feet in overall length, but was then expanded to include boats under 30 feet overall when a definite need for expansion was evidenced. All boats compete for open fleet prizes, but the fleet in turn is divided into two classes: Class B for boats up to 24 feet overall length and Class A for those over that dimension and under 30 feet.

The MORC very wisely did not follow the JOG example of adopting the major existing local measurement rule, which in the United States would have certainly been that of the Cruising Club of America. While the CCA rule is undoubtedly a fine one for its intended purpose, very strange things occur when it is applied to vessels much under 30 feet overall, and some even stranger types of vessels would be fostered by it. The MORC was very fortunate to have among its charter members naval architect William Shaw. It was Shaw, with the help of Olin Stephens, who drafted the new measurement rule which directly administered to the needs of the new club. This MORC measurement rule was definitely molded on the pattern of the CCA rule but problems of scale and ease of measurement were always clearly in mind. The rule was so successful that only in 1959 were minor modifications necessary and these only concerned the introduction of a constant to bring ratings more closely in line with actual waterline lengths, provision of a more equitable method of measuring draft on the keel-centerboard types, and refinement of the propeller allowance formula. The rules were modified slightly in 1970.

With safety a top-priority consideration in activity involving small boats on open water, the MORC instituted and rigidly enforces several safety requirements. Boats must be self-righting and outfitted with either a self-bailing or watertight cockpit. When the measurer is not satisfied as to the ultimate stability of a vessel, he may insist on a stability test, which is the physical act of placing the boat on her beam's end and observing whether or not she is capable of righting herself. This is frequently much easier said than done when the overall length approaches 30 feet. The cubage limitations for both the self-bailing and the watertight cockpits are reasonable enough so that alterations are an unlikely requirement on most cruisers. Other than the insistence on personal lifelines for each member of the crew and a choice between either built-in flotation with a resultant positive buoyancy of 250 pounds or the carrying of a bottle-inflated rubber life raft, the balance of the MORC safety requirements are roughly equivalent to those of the U.S. Coast Guard for vessels of this size.

A copy of the *MORC Measurement Rule and Safety Requirements* can be obtained from the National Secretary of the Midget Ocean Racing Club, 10 Catherwood Crescent, Huntington Station, N.Y., 11745, for $1.

The Off Soundings Club Rule. Although relatively informal and used less often than the other rules we have discussed, the OSC is a good rule to look at first, because it is quite simple, and it incorporates only a few handicapping fundamentals. Measurements for this rule are quite easily made, because neither displacement nor a direct calculation of stability is involved.

The OSC rule gives great credit for beam, and it often favors some light displacement types of sailboats to such an extent that many times these are relegated to a special class. The rule works best for boats of similar type.

OSC rules state that the hull measurements are "to be made with yacht afloat, completely rigged and with all sails to be used when racing on board stowed in the normal racing stowage position. Working jib and main to be rigged or stowed in working position. Water and fuel tanks must be full and pressure should be up. Bilges or sump tanks shall be empty. All equipment necessary to support a weekend cruise (other than optional consumable supplies) shall be on board. All equipment which will be aboard while racing must be aboard and in the place occupied while racing." Details of the OSC measurement rules may be obtained from Off Soundings Club, 99 Nassau Street, New York, N.Y. 10013.

The Storm Trysail Club Rule. Another simple but quite commonly used rule was the 1963 Storm Trysail Club one. Since its inception in 1948, the rule had steadily grown in popularity, especially in the northeastern United States. The Storm Trysail Club put into effect a new, more complicated handicap rule in the spring of 1968. It may take a few years of racing under the new rule to determine the new STC rule's accuracy and fairness. A copy of this rule may be had by writing to The Storm Trysail Club, 37 West 44 Street, New York, N.Y. 10036.

Time-allowance Tables

When a yacht's rated length in feet (R) has been determined, it is applied to time-allowance tables to obtain the handicap for any given race. The commonly used tables, as previously stated, are the NAYRU Time Allowance Tables. These tables, which have been employed since 1908, are based on the assumption that, considering the average summer winds experienced while racing over a triangular course, the rate at which boats draw apart approximates 0.6 of the time differences between the boats when their speeds are equal to the square roots of their ratings.

To find the allowance a yacht of any given rating should receive from a larger one, take the figure to be found opposite the smaller rating from the table, from this subtract the figure opposite the measurement of the larger yacht; and the difference, multiplied by the number of nautical miles in the course, is the amount of time allowance due the smaller vessel, in seconds and hundredths of a second. Example:

Boat *A*—rating 36.7

Boat *B*—rating 42.3

Course length 600 nautical miles

Boat *A* allowance from table (for 36.7) = 140.55 seconds per mile

Boat *B* allowance from table (42.3) = 112.25 seconds per mile

Boat *B* allows Boat *A* (subtract *B* allowance from *A* allowance) 28.3 seconds per mile

In the race (600 nautical miles) *B* allows *A* 600 × 28.3 seconds, or 3 hours 36 minutes 7 seconds.

The table is based upon the assumption that, under average racing conditions, a yacht of rating measurement *R* will sail one nautical mile in the number of seconds given by the formula

$$\frac{2{,}160}{\sqrt{R}} + 183.64$$

The allowance per mile between yachts of different ratings will therefore be given by

$$\frac{2{,}160}{r} - \frac{2{,}160}{R}$$

in which *R* is the rating measurement of the larger yacht and *r* that of the smaller yacht.

Relative-speed Handicap Systems

The relative-speed handicaps, such as the Portsmouth and Pacific Handicap systems, are developed on the relative speed of the competing yachts by statistically analyzing their performance under varying racing conditions.

Pacific Handicap Racing Fleet Rule. Under the Pacific Handicap Racing Fleet (PHRF) rule, for instance, a boat is given an arbitrary rating by a handicapper, an experienced sailor or designer qualified to judge boat speed and performance. This rating is later adjusted to reflect actual performance after the boat begins racing. One difficulty with a rule of this type is perhaps that it reflects the vicissitudes of skipper performance; nevertheless the rule is said to work well.

Portsmouth System. In 1961 clubs of the Dixie Inland Yacht Racing Association inquired of S. Zillwood Milledge (one of the prime movers in convincing the Royal Yacht-

ing Association in England of the validity of Portsmouth Yardsticks) how Portsmouth Numbers could be used for mixed fleets. The principle was simple: to get corrected time (*CT*) one divided the elapsed time (*ET*) by a boat's Portsmouth Number (*N*) over 100, i.e., $CT = (100ET/N)$. But like many simple procedures, considerable research and experience precedes proficiency. These clubs of the DIYRA have now provided that background.

Portsmouth Numbers, until developed to the reliability of a rating (±0.5) are empirical. Only after testing and confirmation can a new or approximate number become classified as a rating. DIYRA experience has shown that the average for boats with well-established fleets under a variety of weather conditions over the year comes out the same as the previous Portsmouth rating. For example, the ratings for Flying Dutchman, Snipe, Windmill, and Shark in 1969 were 78, 93, 94, and 66. The averages based on 112, 47, 72, and 28 races in 1970 were 78.5, 93.1, 94.3, and 67.9 respectively. When there is but one or two of a class in a region, then a "skipper factor" is included in the Portsmouth Number for that boat. As the skipper's skill improves he is favored under this system.

Some boats have a wider range of performance over the spectrum of wind conditions than others. As presently practiced the Portsmouth Number system does not compensate for a change in relative performance with wind velocity. Racing multi- and mono-hulled boats together in a handicap fleet is rarely satisfactory because of the special characteristics of multihulls over a wide range of wind velocities.

The records are only now becoming sufficiently comprehensive for a correlation of the Portsmouth Number and wind velocity to be developed. The Portsmouth Number Committee of DIYRA will be working on this project.

With the exceptions noted, the results of racing mixed fleets based upon Portsmouth handicapping has been very satisfactory. Finishes are generally decided by seconds; no one class dominates open-class competition. The discerning skipper can normally see mistakes he made reflected in the corrected times.

TABLE 1 – TIME ALLOWANCES IN SECONDS PER MILE FOR TENTHS OF A FOOT RATING

RATING	.0	.1	.2	.3	.4	.5	.6	.7	.8	.9
10.	467.05	463.66	460.32	457.03	453.79	450.59	447.44	444.33	441.27	438.25
11.	435.26	432.32	429.42	426.56	423.74	420.95	418.20	415.48	412.80	410.15
12.	407.54	404.96	402.41	399.89	397.40	394.94	392.51	390.11	387.74	385.39
13.	383.08	380.79	378.52	376.28	374.07	371.88	369.71	367.57	365.45	363.36
14.	361.28	359.23	357.20	355.20	353.21	351.24	349.30	347.37	345.47	343.58
15.	341.71	339.86	338.03	336.21	334.42	332.64	330.88	329.13	327.41	325.70
16.	324.00	322.32	320.66	319.01	317.37	315.76	314.15	312.56	310.99	309.42
17.	307.88	306.34	304.82	303.31	301.82	300.34	298.87	297.41	295.97	294.54
18.	293.12	291.71	290.31	288.93	287.55	286.19	284.84	283.50	282.17	280.85
19.	279.54	278.24	276.95	275.67	274.40	273.14	271.89	270.65	269.42	268.20
20.	266.99	265.79	264.59	263.41	262.23	261.06	259.90	258.75	257.61	256.48
21.	255.35	254.23	253.12	252.02	250.92	249.84	248.76	247.69	246.62	245.56
22.	244.51	243.47	242.43	241.41	240.38	239.37	238.36	237.36	236.36	235.37
23.	234.39	233.42	232.45	231.48	230.53	229.57	228.63	227.69	226.76	225.83
24.	224.91	223.99	223.08	222.18	221.28	220.39	219.50	218.62	217.74	216.87
25.	216.00	215.14	214.28	213.43	212.58	211.74	210.91	210.08	209.25	208.43
26.	207.61	206.80	205.99	205.19	204.39	203.60	202.81	202.02	201.24	200.46
27.	199.69	198.92	198.16	197.40	196.65	195.90	195.15	194.41	193.67	192.93
28.	192.20	191.47	190.75	190.03	189.32	188.61	187.90	187.19	186.49	185.80
29.	185.10	184.41	183.73	183.04	182.36	181.69	181.02	180.35	179.68	179.02
30.	178.36	177.70	177.05	176.40	175.76	175.11	174.47	173.84	173.20	172.57
31.	171.95	171.32	170.70	170.08	169.47	168.86	168.25	167.64	167.04	166.44
32.	165.84	165.24	164.65	164.06	163.47	162.89	162.31	161.73	161.15	160.58
33.	160.01	159.44	158.87	158.31	157.75	157.19	156.64	156.08	155.53	154.98
34.	154.44	153.89	153.35	152.81	152.28	151.74	151.21	150.68	150.15	149.63
35.	149.11	148.59	148.07	147.55	147.04	146.53	146.02	145.51	145.00	144.50
36.	144.00	143.50	143.00	142.51	142.02	141.53	141.04	140.55	140.07	139.58
37.	139.10	138.62	138.15	137.67	137.20	136.73	136.26	135.79	135.32	134.86
38.	134.40	133.94	133.48	133.02	132.57	132.12	131.66	131.21	130.77	130.32
39.	129.88	129.43	128.99	128.55	128.12	127.68	127.25	126.81	126.38	125.95
40.	125.53	125.10	124.68	124.25	123.83	123.41	122.99	122.58	122.16	121.75
41.	121.34	120.92	120.52	120.11	119.70	119.30	118.89	118.49	118.09	117.69
42.	117.30	116.90	116.50	116.11	115.72	115.33	114.94	114.55	114.17	113.78
43.	113.40	113.01	112.63	112.25	111.88	111.50	111.12	110.75	110.37	110.00
44.	109.63	109.26	108.89	108.53	108.16	107.80	107.43	107.07	106.71	106.35
45.	105.99	105.64	105.28	104.93	104.57	104.22	103.87	103.52	103.17	102.82
46.	102.47	102.13	101.78	101.44	101.10	100.76	100.42	100.08	99.74	99.40
47.	99.07	98.73	98.40	98.07	97.74	97.41	97.08	96.75	96.42	96.09
48.	95.77	95.44	95.12	94.80	94.48	94.16	93.84	93.52	93.20	92.89
49.	92.57	92.26	91.94	91.63	91.32	91.01	90.70	90.39	90.08	89.78
50.	89.47	89.17	88.86	88.56	88.26	87.95	87.65	87.35	87.06	86.76
51.	86.46	86.16	85.87	85.57	85.28	84.99	84.70	84.41	84.12	83.83
52.	83.54	83.25	82.96	82.68	82.39	82.11	81.82	81.54	81.26	80.98
53.	80.70	80.42	80.14	79.86	79.59	79.31	79.03	78.76	78.48	78.21
54.	77.94	77.67	77.40	77.13	76.86	76.59	76.32	76.05	75.79	75.52
55.	75.25	74.99	74.73	74.46	74.20	73.94	73.68	73.42	73.16	72.90
56.	72.64	72.38	72.13	71.87	71.62	71.36	71.11	70.85	70.60	70.35
57.	70.10	69.85	69.60	69.35	69.10	68.85	68.60	68.36	68.11	67.87
58.	67.62	67.38	67.13	66.89	66.65	66.41	66.17	65.93	65.69	65.45
59.	65.21	64.97	64.73	64.50	64.26	64.02	63.79	63.55	63.32	63.09
60.	62.85	62.62	62.39	62.16	61.93	61.70	61.47	61.24	61.01	60.79
61.	60.56	60.33	60.11	59.88	59.66	59.43	59.21	58.99	58.76	58.54
62.	58.32	58.10	57.88	57.66	57.44	57.22	57.00	56.78	56.57	56.35
63.	56.13	55.92	55.70	55.49	55.27	55.06	54.85	54.64	54.42	54.21
64.	54.00	53.79	53.58	53.37	53.16	52.95	52.74	52.54	52.33	52.12
65.	51.92	51.71	51.50	51.30	51.09	50.89	50.69	50.48	50.28	50.08
66.	49.88	49.68	49.48	49.28	49.08	48.88	48.68	48.48	48.28	48.08
67.	47.89	47.69	47.49	47.30	47.10	46.91	46.71	46.52	46.32	46.13
68.	45.94	45.75	45.55	45.36	45.17	44.98	44.79	44.60	44.41	44.22
69.	44.03	43.85	43.66	43.47	43.28	43.10	42.91	42.72	42.54	42.35
70.	42.17	41.99	41.80	41.62	41.43	41.25	41.07	40.89	40.71	40.53
71.	40.34	40.16	39.98	39.80	39.63	39.45	39.27	39.09	38.91	38.74
72.	38.56	38.38	38.21	38.03	37.85	37.68	37.50	37.33	37.16	36.98
73.	36.81	36.64	36.46	36.29	36.12	35.95	35.78	35.61	35.43	35.26
74.	35.09	34.93	34.76	34.59	34.42	34.25	34.08	33.92	33.75	33.58
75.	33.42	33.25	33.08	32.92	32.75	32.59	32.42	32.26	32.10	31.93
76.	31.77	31.61	31.44	31.28	31.12	30.96	30.80	30.64	30.48	30.31
77.	30.15	30.00	29.84	29.68	29.52	29.36	29.20	29.04	28.89	28.73
78.	28.57	28.42	28.26	28.10	27.95	27.79	27.64	27.48	27.33	27.17
79.	27.02	26.87	26.71	26.56	26.41	26.25	26.10	25.95	25.80	25.65
80.	25.50	25.34	25.19	25.04	24.89	24.74	24.59	24.45	24.30	24.15
81.	24.00	23.85	23.70	23.56	23.41	23.26	23.12	22.97	22.82	22.68
82.	22.53	22.39	22.24	22.10	21.95	21.81	21.66	21.52	21.38	21.23
83.	21.09	20.95	20.81	20.66	20.52	20.38	20.24	20.10	19.96	19.82
84.	19.68	19.54	19.40	19.26	19.12	18.98	18.84	18.70	18.56	18.42
85.	18.28	18.15	18.01	17.87	17.74	17.60	17.46	17.33	17.19	17.05
86.	16.92	16.78	16.65	16.51	16.38	16.24	16.11	15.98	15.84	15.71
87.	15.58	15.44	15.31	15.18	15.05	14.91	14.78	14.65	14.52	14.39
88.	14.26	14.13	14.00	13.87	13.74	13.61	13.48	13.35	13.22	13.09
89.	12.96	12.83	12.70	12.57	12.45	12.32	12.19	12.06	11.94	11.81
90.	11.68	11.56	11.43	11.31	11.18	11.05	10.93	10.80	10.68	10.55
91.	10.43	10.31	10.18	10.06	9.93	9.81	9.69	9.56	9.44	9.32
92.	9.20	9.07	8.95	8.83	8.71	8.59	8.46	8.34	8.22	8.10
93.	7.98	7.86	7.74	7.62	7.50	7.38	7.26	7.14	7.02	6.91
94.	6.79	6.67	6.55	6.43	6.31	6.20	6.08	5.96	5.84	5.73
95.	5.61	5.49	5.38	5.26	5.15	5.03	4.91	4.80	4.68	4.57
96.	4.45	4.34	4.22	4.11	4.00	3.88	3.77	3.65	3.54	3.43
97.	3.31	3.20	3.09	2.98	2.86	2.75	2.64	2.53	2.42	2.30
98.	2.19	2.08	1.97	1.86	1.75	1.64	1.53	1.42	1.31	1.20
99.	1.09	.98	.87	.76	.65	.54	.43	.32	.22	.11

Time-allowance table.

Compilation of Portsmouth Numbers for Handicapping Yachts

Monohull Classes					
Beetle	124	Javelin, O'Day	108	Ski	110
Blue Bird	(122)	Jet 14	95	Skipjack	95
Blue Jay	105	Jolly Boat	82	Skylark	98
Bull's Eye	(106)	Kenn 11	111	Snark	(108)
Butterfly	104	Kestrel	92	Snipe	93
C Scow	83	Kite*	98	Soling	88
Cadet	129	Knarr	94	South Coast 21	(96)
Celebrity	89	Korsar	89	Sparkler	126
Chatauqua (12-foot)	105	Lehman 12	100	Sprite	114
Clipper 20	93	Lido 14	98	Star	82
Columbia 5.5 Meter	86	Lightning	87	Sunfish*	106
Comet	93	Lone Star 13	103	Super Satellite	(96)
Crescent (CB)	100	Lone Star 16	101	Tech Dinghy	(109)
D Scow	82	Luders 16	89	Thistle	83
Day Sailer	97	M-16 Scow	88	Tibron	(129)
Demon	94	M-20 Scow	75	Upstart	104
Dragon	89	MC Scow	94	U.S. One Design	91
Dyer Delta	90	Marauder	(100)	Victory	93
E Scow	73	Mariner	(102)	Viking	98
El Toro	138	Meteor	(112)	Vivacity	108
Ensign	97	Missile	91	Wesort	124
Enterprise	98	Mobjack	85	Whistler	112
Explorer	97	Moth*	106	Widgeon	(110)
Finn	90	Mustang (17-foot)	99	Windmill	94
Fireball	87	Mystic	113	Y-Flyer	88
Firefly	100	National One Design	97	Zephyr	101
Five-O-Five	80	OK Dinghy	97		
Flying Dutchman	78	Optimist Pram	144	**Catamarans**	
Flying Fifteen	89	Ospray O'Day	116	A Lion	75
Flying Junior	98	Osprey Mk II and III	85	Aquacat 12	97
Flying Saucer	(104)	Peanut	122	B Lion	67
Flying Scot	88	Penguin	111	Cal Cat	93
Flying Tern	101	Picnic (17-foot)	106	Catalina Cat	72
420	97	Rainbow	97	Catfish	96
Gannet	99	Raven	80	Cheetah Cat II	81
Geary (18-foot)	(91)	Rebel	94	Cougar Mk II	72
GP (14-foot)	103	Regatta	(106)	Cougar Mk III	71
Hampton	89	Renegade (CB)	(125)	DC 14	76
Hawk	104	Rhodes Bantam	97	Malibu Outrigger	76
Highlander	83	Rhodes 19 (keel)	94	Pacific Cat	64
Hogden	98	Sailfish*	(108)	Phoenix	68
Holiday Jr.	(116)	Sea Scouter	117	Shark	66
Interlake	90	Sea Sport 12	113	Shearwater Mk II	75
International 110	88	Seaviewer	125	Shearwater Mk IV	71
International 210	83	Scorpion*	106	Thai Mk IV	66
International (14-foot)	88	Shields One Design	85	Tiger Cat	73
International Tempest	79	Silhouette II	116	V4 Cat	(90)
		Skate	117		

* Applied when single-handed.
Numbers in parentheses are based on limited data.

Distance-racing Tips and Strategy

While the sport of offshore distance or ocean racing has many things in common with inshore racing around the buoys, it has one major difference: the result does *not* depend solely on speed. Navigation, for instance, plays a most important part in it, for if the fastest craft misses a few marks or bearings, she might finish among the "also rans." For this reason, the navigator is perhaps the most important member of the crew, although the cook cannot be considered to be far behind; for if—as Napoleon is supposed to have stated—an army marches on its stomach, the crew of an ocean (distance) racing yacht sails on theirs. For real long races, it is a great asset to have a dependable full-time navigator. But for the average offshore race it is best for the skipper to do all the navigation work, because both the strategy and tactics of offshore racing are closely connected with the navigation. Unfortunately, under this arrangement the skipper has no one to blame but himself if the next mark does not appear right on the nose.

Equipment Lists. The primary consideration in an ocean race should be safety. It is easier than you might think to lose a man overboard at night in a rough sea, and if accidents happen offshore, prompt help is usually difficult to get. For this reason, safety equipment is very important and the NAYRU equipment lists—given on pages 95–97—should be met.

Offshore-racing Numbering System. In 1970, according to NAYRU racing regulations, class numbers had to be replaced for yachts racing in offshore events by assigned NAYRU numbers which should be affixed to the mainsails, spinnakers, and all overlapping headsails. Class insignia, however, may continue to be displayed.

Blocks of numbers are assigned on an area basis and are issued either by the NAYRU or by local associations as follows:

0001–4999: from Halifax to Corpus Christi including Lake Ontario and Lake Erie (contact NAYRU, 37 West 44 Street, New York N.Y. 10036)
4000–4250: Lake Yacht Racing Association—yachts in Ontario
5000–5999: Detroit River Yachting Association
6000–6999: Lake Michigan Yachting Association excluding Lake Huron
7000–7999: Southern California Yachting Association
8000–8999: Yacht Racing Association of San Francisco Bay
9000–9999: Pacific International Yachting Association and Hawaii Yacht Racing Association

When an area has used up its assigned block of numbers it adds as a prefix the digits 1, 2, etc., so that in the case of the Detroit River YA, for example, numbers 15000–15999 will be issued followed successively by 25000–25999, and so forth. A yacht which *permanently* transfers from one area to another should contact the issuing organization in her new area for a new number.

The Crew. Although all racing is a team effort, in short races the skipper is the most important member of the crew. His start has a great bearing on the outcome, strategy is largely based on his quick tactical decisions, and he usually has the helm for most of the time. In distance racing, however, other members of the crew gain importance. There is less emphasis on the start, most members of the crew must take their trick at the helm; and although strategy is the skipper's responsibility, other members of the crew are conferred with and consulted before major decisions are made. In fact, it is usually the judgment of the weather expert or the navigator that influences the skipper's decisions.

Signing on a qualified crew is vital to the success of a distance race. A few inexperienced crew members may be taken if there is an ample number of veterans aboard. However, the novices should be thoroughly investigated for susceptibility to seasickness, and they should be given ocean-racing instruction and training before the race. All new crew members whether experienced or not should be thoroughly familiar with every aspect of the boat. An attempt should be made to acquire a number of good helmsmen, because no one helmsman, regardless of his skill, should be allowed to steer for too long a period. If so, he will become tired and lose judgment and effectiveness.

Certain of the crew have definite specialties—like the previously mentioned cook and navigator. Other members should be able helmsmen, sail handlers, and seamen; but even these men should have knowledge of, or should be encouraged to specialize in, one or more useful subjects. For instance, there should be a weather specialist, a medic or someone with a good knowledge of first aid, at least one member with mechanical and electrical aptitude, a carpenter, an expert on marlinspike seamanship, and so forth. Of course, the perfect crew is hard to find, but regardless of experience and skills the single most important ingredient for an ocean-racing crew is probably enthusiasm.

On most ocean races, the deck watch is on

duty four hours and off four hours. This is commonly referred to as the "two-watch" or "watch-and-watch" system. In order to avoid the rotation sequence that would bring the same watch on duty at the same times each day, one of the four-hour periods is divided into two *dog watches*. These are two-hour watches, customarily from 1600 to 1800 and from 1800 to 2000, for the specific purpose of alternating watch hours each day. Another popular watch schedule is the *Swedish system,* which divides the day into five watches: 0200–0600, 0600–1200, 1200–1800, 1800–2200, and 2200–0200.

This method gives six-hour watches during daylight, four-hour watches at night, and automatically alternates watches daily. Quite often the navigator is not required to stand watches, and in some cases the skipper does not stand regular watches. Each watch should have a capable watch officer. Incidentally, while the ideal crew should be made up of members with even tempers and free from complexes, this is not always possible. If two men's temperaments tend to clash, be sure that they are *not* scheduled on the same watch.

Soon after the start of a long-distance race, although excitement is high, it is a good idea to settle down into a regular routine. It is important from the outset to combat fatigue. This is the ever-present enemy of the ocean-racing sailor. Fatigue causes carelessness, poor judgment, and laziness which can lose races, cause accidents, and even endanger lives. An adequate crew should be carried so that the boat can be tacked and her headsails changed without rousing out the watch below. It is important that the crew get plenty of rest and sleep. If anyone has trouble sleeping, he might try using ear plugs or an eye mask or perhaps even a mild sedative.

Before the Race. Before sailing in an ocean race, a boat should be thoroughly surveyed and inspected. Most sponsoring yacht clubs require a superficial inspection, but most such inspections are far from complete. The spars and rigging should receive particular attention. Look for the shifting of tangs, for bent bolts, worn pins, or any deformation of wood or metal. See that all tracks on the mast, deck, and rail are securely fastened. All tracks should be through-bolted wherever possible at major points of stress. Also, wherever pos-

sible, all cleats and other fittings should be through-bolted. Inspect very carefully the spreaders and the masthead. See that the spreaders are securely fastened and that wire halyards cannot possibly jump out of their sheaves. Double-check the spinnaker halyard blocks and swivels, because these take tremendous strain. It is always wise to have spare halyards rigged in case one parts from chafing. See that all stays and shrouds are fitted with toggles. Also see that most halyards or at least the essential ones are fitted with downhauls (light lines attached to the halyard ends so that they can be pulled down in case a halyard shackle breaks or the head pulls out of a sail and leaves the halyard end aloft).

An important aspect of inspecting the boat that relates to speed rather than safety is an inspection of the bottom surface. The hull should be as smooth and fair as possible. Slime and marine growth on the bottom, especially barnacles, are disastrous to boat speed. A foul bottom can make a difference of many hours on a distance race. Before racing in a major ocean race, the boat should be hauled and her bottom cleaned. Particular attention should be given to the bottom of the keel, as this is an area that is often neglected. If the boat cannot be hauled, the crew should go overboard and scrub her bottom with stiff brushes. Before starting the race do not fail to see that the two blades of the propeller are lined up directly behind the keel, in the position of least drag. The shaft should be marked so that the propeller position for sailing can be noted by looking at the shaft from aboard the boat. Quite often this position can be noted by looking at the shaft keyways. If the propeller is out of position, it can be corrected by turning the shaft by hand. Once in position, the shaft must be locked (with the gear shift or shaft lock) to prevent inadvertent turning.

Sailing Tactics. The actual sailing procedures of ocean racing are the same as those when cruising (Section V), while the strategy and tactics involved in a distance race are basically similar to those of a short race (given earlier in this section), but there are subtle differences. The start of a distance race is, of course, very important, but it is not as crucial as in a short, closed-course race around the buoys. In long ocean races there is a greater dependence on general weather forecasts. Navigation plays a greater role in the distance race, as previously stated, and there is less boat-for-boat racing and emphasis on covering tactics. By and large, each skipper sails his own race.

Although the start is not as vital in a 600-mile race as in one 20 miles long, the start is always important. Distance races have been won and lost by minutes and even seconds. However, it seems ridiculous to attempt a split second start at the risk of fouling when there are perhaps four or five days of racing to come. The important thing is to start in clear air. More often than not, a distant point-to-point race will have a reaching start. In such a case, the smaller boats or late starters will often be subjected to the disturbed wind of the leaders. Do not follow in the wakes of those boats ahead unless they are far ahead. It is usually best to drive or head up until you reach clear air. Quite often when there is a long starting line with competitors bunched at the windward end, it pays to try a leeward-end start with a "full head of steam." In this way, perhaps you can get a safe leeward position, and if you are overtaken by a large boat close to windward, you can usually bear off below her wind shadow. It seldom pays to split tacks on a reaching start. Even if your wind is disturbed temporarily, boats will soon disperse.

The general weather picture certainly must be carefully considered in a distance race. Weather maps should be meticulously studied before the race. Most ocean racers do not have the facilities, nor their crew the inclination, to pick up the vast number of radio weather reports (some of which are in code) necessary to draft their own complete daily weather maps during the progress of a race. However, forecasts based on the information available just before the start can predict weather over the following few days with reasonable accuracy. These predictions can be substantiated or modified by tuning in, as often as possible, to the regular forecasts on commercial stations or reports from airports.

Everyone knows that weather reports are not entirely reliable, and therefore they should not be absolutely depended on. Do not make a drastic alteration in a normally sensible course to gamble on a probable weather change. If the risk is such that a predicted change which fails to materialize costs you only a few miles or even hours, it may pay to take the risk. However, if the nonmaterialization could seriously damage your chances of doing well in the race, do not take the risk. In other words, where the weather is concerned, do not climb out on a limb. Make slight alterations in the course in an attempt to take advantage of weather predictions, but do not risk everything.

Any course alterations on the rhumb line (the straight-line course on a Mercator chart) will not amount to any great change in the total distance to be covered if you are far from your destination, but a similar course alteration close to your destination will add considerably to the total distance remaining. Another thing to keep in mind if you are attempting to follow a rhumb-line course is that your *present* rhumb line is a straight line from where you are, at the moment, to the finish line. Do not feel that you necessarily have to get back to the original (start-to-finish) rhumb line. This original course may have been the shortest one at the time of the start, but it is not later on in the race if you are not located on that line.

With some skippers, the desire to stick to the rhumb line becomes almost an obsession. Do not become overly concerned with a straight-line course especially in the early stages of the race. The important thing is to keep your boat moving even if it is not in the exact direction of the finish line. If, for example, you have a close-hauled course to the finish and you pinch up in an attempt to fetch, a competitor near you who eases or cracks the sheets and sails full and by on a nonfetching course will almost always beat you. The reason for this is that there will probably be a general wind shift later on that will either lift and allow your competitor to fetch, or else will head you both, allowing neither of you to fetch. In the latter case, this shift will put you directly astern of your competitor, because (as you will recall from earlier in this section) a heading shift favors the leeward leading boat. The same principle often applies when you are reaching or running. If you are sailing a course which gives you an effective angle with the wind, especially when the spinnaker is set, do not worry about straying from the rhumb line, because the chances are that the wind will shift or change velocity later on. Use the wind you have to best advantage while you have it.

One of the keys to successful distance racing is the maintaining of the best possible speed, not only through choosing the right course, but through continual attention to such factors as sail trim and helmsmanship. It is easy to let down on these matters when there are no other competitors in sight, but an attempt should be made to sail the boat just as though she were racing around the buoys. Not only should sheets be adjusted for every wind change, but also outhauls, downhauls, and leads should be adjusted. It is of the utmost importance that the boat be reefed when there is a need for it and that appropriate headsails are carried. There is a common tendency to procrastinate when it comes to sail changes. Sails are usually reefed and unreefed too late, and headsails are not changed with enough frequency.

When the wind moderates while you are carrying a number 3 genoa, it is easy to be lazy and rationalize that the wind will freshen again after a while, but in most cases the number 1 genoa should be set. If properly done, a headsail change does not waste much time. On any boat with a double head rig, the forestaysail is set as an interim sail to prevent excessive speed loss while the jib is down. Before the original jib is lowered, its two lower hanks are unsnapped and the substitute jib is hanked onto the headstay beneath the original jib. A new set of sheets are bent to the substitute jib, and of course they are properly led. Then the original jib is lowered, and its hanks are unsnapped as it comes down. The halyard is quickly shifted to the substitute jib and this is immediately hoisted. In a strong breeze, it sometimes pays to stop the substitute jib with light line, similar to the way a spinnaker is stopped. Then after the jib is hoisted, the stops can be broken by hauling back on the sheet. Of course, after the new jib has been hoisted and sheeted, the forestaysail may be lowered if so desired. On a short closed-course race it is often not advisable to change jibs, because the time wasted is too great when compared with the time spent on a course leg; but on a distance race, the best sails for the conditions of the mo-

ment should be used, and this often means reasonably frequent sail changes.

The questions of how hard to drive a boat and how long to carry on in bad weather are very difficult to answer. When these questions arise the skipper must carefully consider the trend of the weather, the behavior of his boat, the condition of the boat and her equipment, and the ability of his crew. If the weather appears to be growing worse, the boat is becoming difficult to manage, and there have been a number of gear failures and jury repairs; and/or if some of the crew are sick, tired, or inexperienced, then it is time to reduce sail drastically. As weather conditions get worse, sail should be reduced accordingly. At first you might shift to a smaller genoa, then to a double head rig, with working jib, and forestaysail, then take in the mizzen and reef the mainsail. A further wind increase might call for the storm trysail with the forestaysail, storm jib, and mizzen. If it blows even harder, you might reduce sail further to the double head rig and mizzen. This is the smallest rig under which the boat will perform well to windward. If even further sail reduction is necessary, you would have the choice of either trysail and forestaysail, or forestaysail and mizzen. The boat will handle well under either of these minimum rigs, but cannot be expected to drive to windward with so little sail. Under conditions that would warrant such sail reduction, the boat should be eased along and held as near as possible on course. However, if she shows any alarming tendencies to bury the lee rail, or broach to when running or reaching, or frequently to take solid green water on deck, she should be put on the easiest, most comfortable course, and her speed should be further slowed.

In gale-force winds, the boat might be run before the wind under a storm jib trimmed flat or, in extreme conditions, under bare poles with lines and cables towed astern to slow her speed. If a running course should take you away from the direction of the finish line, then you might try *heaving to* (stopping speed under counteracting sails with the bow near the wind). This might be done under a storm trysail and a storm jib backed (trimmed to windward) with the helm lashed all the way down. Finding the best means of heaving to will take a little experimentation. The boat should lie reasonably comfortably, and she should not be allowed to forereach (move ahead) with any speed. Get ready for bad weather early; the simplest task on deck becomes extraordinarily difficult in a gale, and an undone rigging chore may lead to a serious casualty.

To the basic strategic elements of sailing—wind, current, and often waves—ocean racing *sometimes* adds another: ocean swells. These significantly affect the apparent wind and create a marked difference in performance between tacks. That is, when sailing to windward against the direction of the swell movement, the boat rapidly crosses successive crests and swells. As forward speed increases in the backward moving water of the trough, the apparent wind increases markedly. The boat surges ahead and tends to heel as both driving force and heeling force increase abruptly. As the sails will tolerate a much lower angle of incidence at higher wind speeds and forward speed is available without regard to windward direction, the boat can be headed up abruptly in the troughs (actually as soon as the crest passes beneath the hull) to gain significant distance to windward. As forward speed and apparent wind decrease in the crest of the swell, driving force and heeling force decreases. The sails no longer tolerate the low angle of incidence utilized in the trough; instead they luff as the boat slows and comes erect. To reduce this slowing and inefficient luffing the boat must be headed off to increase the angle of incidence and the aerodynamic force available. In a small boat the crew will have to hike hard in each trough, move inboard in each crest; in all boats, marked variations in heading must be utilized to maintain sail efficiency and to make optimal progress to weather. The technique is, of course, essentially the opposite of that used to deal with a chop in heavy air.

One tack will provide a more favorable relation to the swells than the other if the swells are not moving directly downwind (as they rarely are). Occasionally in a southerly the swells may be met on the lee bow. Under these circumstances the boat can and should be headed up in the crests and must be headed off in the troughs when the apparent wind moves abruptly ahead. Boats on a tack which tends to meet the swells nearly head on will be exposed to abrupt and frequently recurrent variations in the strength and direction of the apparent wind which may be impossible to compensate for through heading changes. The opportunity to move to windward in the troughs is partially blocked by the shift of the apparent wind direction forward and the slowing effect of the crests is accentuated by shift of the apparent wind direction aft (to a degree which may produce stalling). Boats on a tack which tends to meet the swells more obliquely will meet fewer swells per unit of time and have more time to adjust to each segment of the swell. As the apparent wind increases in the troughs, its direction shifts aft, further improving the opportunity to head and move to windward. The crest will produce an obvious header as the boat slows and the apparent wind moves ahead but can be managed satisfactorily in the additional time available. One tack is almost always better oriented to the swells than the other.

Another key to successful distance racing is the ability to keep a boat moving at her best at night. This is not easy. In the dark, some competent daytime helmsmen become disoriented, and sail trimming is often neglected. On downwind courses at night, steering is done by compass primarily. In this case, the helmsman usually tries to steer the straightest course; at least he should not let his heading wander excessively. It is not easy to steer a straight compass course with a following or quartering sea, when the boat has a tendency to yaw. The helmsman must attempt to "catch" the boat before she swings past her proper heading. The common mistake of beginners is to turn the helm too late and to overcorrect. Proper steering at night with the sea running takes practice and the helmsman's full attention.

Beginners often become disoriented when steering with a compass at night, because of a lack of distinct visible reference points. On a clear night it is sometimes wise to pick out a star somewhere ahead that can be lined up with the mast or rigging for a check point. Sometimes a beginner becomes almost hypnotized by the compass so that it seems as though the compass card moves while the boat remains stationary. However, it must always be kept in mind that the card stands still and the lubber line is what really moves.

It is important that the binnacle light not be too bright, because this can be blinding to the helmsman when he has to look away from the compass. Red binnacle lights are the least damaging to night vision. Those crew members in the cabin should be careful to use a minimum of light so as not to blind the helmsman (and of course so that they will not disturb off-watch sleepers or use more electrical power than necessary).

When sailing to windward at night, the helmsman must depend to a lesser degree on his sense of sight and to a greater degree on some of the senses discussed in Section IV, sound, feel, balance, and the helm touch. He must determine when the boat is moving at her best to windward by listening to the bow wave, sensing the liveliness of the boat, and feeling the balance of the helm. He senses when to bear off or head up by listening to the rattling of the sail slides, by feeling any wind changes on his face, and by using his sense of balance in detecting any changes in the angle of heel.

Although there is less emphasis on the visual aspects of helmsmanship when sailing at night, the sense of sight should not be discounted altogether. When there is a moon, sails can often be seen fairly well. Also the luff of a sail can be occasionally checked with a flashlight that is not overly bright. White ribbon telltales should be substituted for those of light line. Although the compass is not used as much when beating, it should constantly be consulted to see that you are sailing the generally proper course close-hauled and to detect wind shifts. If you were headed southeast on the starboard tack, for example, you should be sailing roughly southwest on the port tack, barring any permanent wind shift. Also, of course, the navigator is usually interested in your "average" heading for his dead reckoning. There is a normal tendency to pinch a boat at night because the boat's

speed usually sounds and feels greater than it actually is, and heavy night air can cause the misjudging of wind strength.

When one helmsman relieves another, the new man, just going on watch, should have plenty of time to get oriented and to let his eyes become adjusted to the dark. The new helmsman should watch the one he is relieving for several minutes before taking the wheel to see how the boat is being steered and to study how the compass heading averages. The helmsman to be relieved should give the new man all pertinent information, such as the course he is trying to make good, the location of other boats, the steering characteristics, what sails are set, what preventers are rigged, or any special problems that might be met.

Sails should constantly be trimmed at night just as they are in the daytime. It is easy to become complacent in this respect after dark, but boat speed will suffer far more than one might think from apathetic attention to trim. Sails can be checked by stationing a man forward to check the headsails (when weather permits), by occasionally shining a dim flashlight on the sails, or by use of the spreader lights once in a while, and by noting the proper daylight trim points and lead positions. It is often a help to mark the sheets with pieces of white tape at proper positions of trim for various points of sailing.

When carrying the spinnaker at night, keep the wind well on the quarter, so there is little danger of the sail being blanketed by the mainsail. On this point of sailing in a good breeze the sheet should be trimmed a little more than usual to guard against the sail collapsing at the luff. A man should be standing by the sheet at all times, ready to give it a quick pull in the event of collapse. Naturally, the helmsman should be ready to bear off when the sail first begins to break at the luff.

All racing boats should be equipped with not only the NAYRU Racing Rules, but also the complete International and Inland Rules of the Road (see Section II).

SECTION VII

Sailing Competition

Although yachting is one of the youngest sports in the world, it was also one of the first to enjoy major international competition. Toward the middle of the last century, as previously stated in Section I, a syndicate of members of the New York Yacht Club headed by Commodore John C. Stevens commissioned George Speers—designer of the "whirlwind" rowing shell of 1838—to build a 110-ton racing yacht, the *America*. They sailed the *America* across the ocean to England, in 1851, to compete for the Hundred Guinea Cup put up by the Royal Yacht Club for the annual 60-mile race around the Isle of Wight. Actually, the Hundred Guinea Cup —also known as the Royal Yacht Squadron Cup and Queen's Cup—was not a cup at all, but rather a bottomless, baroque silver ewer, built by the London silversmiths R. and S. Gerard. Its original cost was about $510.

The America's Cup Regatta is the forerunner of all international sailboat racing. In fact, the Cup is the world's oldest *international* sporting trophy. Most historical details of the various races have been covered in Section I; let us look at some of the basic facts of the America's Cup Race.

The America's Cup

Many aspects of Cup competition have changed over the years. In 1870 only one race decided the winner, while in 1871 four victories were necessary. From 1876 to 1920 three victories were necessary. From 1920 to the present, a yacht must have won four match races to capture the Cup. Each boat has the right to request a "lay," or off, day after each completed or canceled race.

Since 1958 the yachts have had to be of the 12-Meter class. The three challenge series before then (in 1930, 1934, and 1937) were sailed in yachts of the J class. Before that, any design could be used, and time allowances were agreed upon.

As discussed in Section VI, the 12-Meter class is designed to the International Rule of Measurement, which is basically expressed by the following formula: $L + 2D + \sqrt{SA} \div 2.37 = 12$ meters. Twelve meters equals 39.37 feet, and the result of the formula must not equal more than 39.37, which is the rating. In the formula, L is the corrected length at approximately 7 inches above the waterline; D is the girth difference (or the remainder between a "chain measurement" from deck to deck under the keel at the widest point and a "skin measurement," which follows all the cross-sectional contours at the same point. SA is the mainsail plus 85 percent of the fore triangle, and F is the freeboard. The yachts are raced, as a rule, by crews consisting of 11 men each.

Originally the Cup races were sailed in the

mouth of New York Harbor where local knowledge of winds and currents supposedly favored the defender. In 1930 the match was moved to Newport, R.I., and the races started at a special buoy 7 miles south-southeast of Brenton Reef Light well away from the harbor entrance. Here, in the open ocean, there are no quirks in the environment that affect either challenger or defender adversely.

Since 1964 the yachts sail the so-called Olympic course. It is 24.3 miles long and has six legs and is always started to windward. There are three windward legs of 4.5 miles each, two reaching legs of 3.15 miles each, and a downwind leg of 4.5 miles. The magnetic course to the first mark is signaled by code flags from the race-committee boat. Marks of the course are passed on the same side the yachts pass the starting buoy. In 1958 and 1962 the course alternated from a 24-mile windward-leeward to a 24-mile triangular course. From 1893 through 1937 the length was 30 miles. From 1870 through the 1880's the average course ran from 37.5 to 32.3 miles. The longest race was the first one, about 58 miles around the Isle of Wight.

Under the present rules the start is between the America's Cup buoy and the race-committee boat. Under normal conditions the following timetable is followed: Course signals are hoisted at 11:50 A.M. The warning gun is fired at 12:00 and one yellow cylinder is hoisted; the preparatory signal is fired at 12:05 and one blue cylinder is hoisted; the start is signaled at 12:10 and one red cylinder is hoisted. If a yacht starts prematurely, the committee sounds one blast of the horn and displays the letters indicating the nationality of the vessel.

The race committee of the New York Yacht Club conducts the races. They may postpone a race in case of fog, if there is too little or too much wind, or if the course is obstructed. They may not start a race after 2:10 P.M. Also, if neither yacht completes the course in 6 hours, the race will be resailed. The match is decided by the best four out of seven races. The actual racing is done under the New York Yacht Club racing rules, which are almost identical to the North American Yacht Racing Union rules, and form the basis of most tactical maneuvers of the contest.

Since 1851, England, Canada, Scotland, and Australia have unsuccessfully challenged to win the "old mug." A list of defenders and challengers follows:

The crew of the *Intrepid* celebrate their victory over *Gretel II* in the final race of 1970 America's Cup series.

Year	Winner for U.S., Owner	U.S. Skipper	Losing Boat, Owner, Country of Challenging Club	Challenging Skipper	Race Score: U.S.– Challenger
1851	*America* John C. Stevens Syndicate	Richard Brown	*Aurora* and 16 others, England	T. LeMerchant and others	1–0
1870	*Magic* and 22 others	Andrew Comstock and others	*Cambria,* James Ashbury, England	J. Tannock	1–0
1871	*Columbia* and *Sappho* Franklin Osgood and Wm. P. Douglass (respectively)	Nelson Comstock and Sam Greenwood (respectively)	*Livonia,* James Ashbury, England	J. R. Woods	4–1
1876	*Madeleine* John S. Dickerson	Josephus Williams	*Countess of Dufferin,* Maj. Charles Gifford Syndicate, Canada	J. E. Wellsworth	2–0
1881	*Mischief* Joseph R. Busk	Nathaniel Clark	*Atalanta,* Capt. Alex Cuthbert, Canada	A. Cuthbert	2–0
1885	*Puritan* J. Malcolm Forbes Syndicate	Aubrey Crocker	*Genesta,* Sir Richard Sutton, England	John Carter	2–0
1886	*Mayflower* Gen. Charles J. Paine	Martin V. B. Stone	*Galatea* Lt. William Henn, R.N., England	Dan Bradford	2–0
1887	*Volunteer* Gen. Chas. J. Paine	Henry C. Haff	*Thistle* James Bell, Scotland	John Barr	2–0
1893	*Vigilant* C. Oliver Iselin Syndicate	William Hansen	*Valkyrie II* Lord Dunraven, England	William Cranfield	3–0
1895	*Defender* C. O. Iselin Syndicate	Henry C. Haff	*Valkyrie III* Lord Dunraven, England	William Cranfield	3–0
1899	*Columbia* J. P. Morgan–C. O. Iselin Syndicate	Charles Barr	*Shamrock* Sir Thomas Lipton, Northern Ireland	A. Hogarth	3–0
1901	*Columbia* E. D. Morgan Syndicate	Charles Barr	*Shamrock II* Sir Thomas Lipton, Northern Ireland	Edward A. Sycamore	3–0
1903	*Reliance* Cornelius Vanderbilt– C. O. Iselin Syndicate	Charles Barr	*Shamrock III* Sir Thomas Lipton, Northern Ireland	Robert Wringe	3–0
1920	*Resolute* Henry Walters–R. W. Emmonds Syndicate	Charles F. Adams II	*Shamrock IV* Sir Thomas Lipton, Northern Ireland	William Burton	3–2
1930	*Enterprise* Winthrop Aldrich–H. S. Vanderbilt Syndicate	Harold S. Vanderbilt	*Shamrock V* Sir Thomas Lipton, Northern Ireland	Ernest Heard	4–0

Year	Winner for U.S., Owner	U.S. Skipper	Losing Boat, Owner, Country of Challenging Club	Challenging Skipper	Race Score: U.S.— Challenger
1934	*Rainbow* H. S. Vanderbilt Syndicate	Harold S. Vanderbilt	*Endeavor* T. O. M. Sopwith, England	T. O. M. Sopwith	4–2
1937	*Ranger* H. S. Vanderbilt Syndicate	Harold S. Vanderbilt	*Endeavor II* T. O. M. Sopwith, England	T. O. M. Sopwith	4–0
1958	*Columbia* Henry Sears, B. Cunningham Syndicate	Briggs S. Cunningham	*Sceptre,* Royal Yacht Squadron and Syndicate, England	Lt. Comdr. Graham Mann, R.N.	4–0
1962	*Weatherly* Henry Mercer, Arnold Frese, Cornelius Walsh	Emil Mosbacher, Jr.	*Gretel,* Sir Frank Packer and Syndicate, Australia	Alexander Sturrock	4–1
1964	*Constellation* Walter Gubelmann, Eric Ridder and Syndicate	Robert N. Bavier, Jr.	*Sovereign,* James A. J. Boyden, England	Peter Scott	4–0
1967	*Intrepid* Intrepid Syndicate	Emil Mosbacher, Jr.	*Dame Pattie* Emil Christensen and Syndicate, Australia	Alexander Sturrock	4–0
1970	*Intrepid* William Strawbridge and Briggs Dalzell Syndicate	William Ficker	*Gretel II* Sir Frank Packer and Syndicate, Australia	James Hardy	4–1

Totals (Matches and Participants)

22 matches (first win in 1851 and 21 United States defenses)	2 Canadian boats
	1 Scottish boat
44 different American boats (including 23 in 1870)	72 separate races including 1851 match
27 English boats (including 17 in 1851)	64 races won by the United States
5 boats from Northern Ireland	3 races won by England
3 boats from Australia	2 races won by Northern Ireland
	2 races won by Australia

Elimination trials for America's Cup began in 1881. United States contenders eliminated in trials are as follows:

1881 *Pocahontas, Gracie,* and *Hildegard*
1885 *Priscilla, Gracie,* and *Bedouin*
1886 *Atlantic, Puritan,* and *Priscilla*
1887 *Mayflower*
1893 *Pilgrim, Colonia,* and *Jubilee*
1895 *Vigilant*
1899 *Defender*
1901 *Constitution* and *Independence*
1903 *Columbia* and *Constitution*
1920 *Vanitie* and *Defiance*
1930 *Weetamoe, Yankee,* and *Whirlwind*
1934 *Yankee, Weetamoe,* and *Vanitie*
1937 *Yankee* and *Rainbow*
1958 *Vim, Weatherly,* and *Easterner*
1962 *Nefertiti, Columbia,* and *Easterner*
1964 *American Eagle, Columbia, Nefertiti,* and *Easterner*
1967 *American Eagle, Columbia,* and *Constellation*
1970 *Heritage, Valiant,* and *Weatherly*

Olympic Games

Adverse weather conditions forced the cancelation of all the scheduled yachting events at the first of the modern Olympic Games in Greece in 1896. The first Olympic yachting championships were contested in France in 1900. The boats entered in the first several Games were formula sailboats of 6 to 12 meters; they were heavy, cumbersome, and expensive, and consequently registrations were few. Until 1920 almost all the sailing medals were won by Norway, Sweden, England, and the Netherlands. The exceptions were the Swiss *Lerina,* winner in Le Havre in 1900, and the French *Mac Miche,* winner in 1912 at Stockholm.

The Games of the VIII Olympiad, held in Paris in 1924, marked the rise of the small monotype sailboat, which conformed to precise specifications and was economically available to all. Thereafter, registrations became more numerous.

The Star class one-design boat first appeared in the Games at Los Angeles, California, in 1932. Since that time the practice of the International Sailing Union and the Olympic Committees has been to hold the regattas for boats in various International Classes, as follows:

1. Formula sailboats
2. Fixed-keel sailboats with three crew members

3. Bulb-keel sailboats
4. Centerboard sailboats with two crew members
5. Sailboats with a crew of one

The sailboat selected for each type for the 1972 Games at Kiel, Germany, is described in Section III.

It was not until 1928 that a United States team competed for the coveted Olympic yachting medals. Prior to World War II there was an average of five yachting events on each Olympic program—including none in 1904 and an astronomical fifteen classes in 1920. The United States Olympic yachtsmen, who won their first gold medals in 1932, have now won a total of ten Olympic yachting championships. But Norway heads the list of all-time Olympic yachting triumphs with fourteen gold medals, seven of them won in 1920 alone. England ranks third with nine gold medals, while Sweden is close behind with eight. A rundown of Olympic boats and their skippers follows:

Finn leaders in 1968 Olympic Games just after rounding the windward mark. Boat number 40 is Peter Barrett of the United States.

Class	Number of Entries	Gold (1st)	Silver (2nd)	Bronze (3rd)
6-Meter				
1900	2	*Lerina* H. de Pourtales Switzerland	Name not listed M. Wiesner Germany	
1908	5	*Dormy* G. V. Laws Great Britain	*Zut* L. Huybrechts Belgium	*Guyoni* A. Delagrave France
1912	9	*Mac Miche* O. Thube France	*Nurding II* O. Reedz-Thott Denmark	*Kerstin* D. Brostrom Sweden
1920 (new classification)	2	*Lo* Andreas Bracke Norway	*Tan-Fe-Pah* L. Huybrechts Belgium	
1920 (old classification)	4	*Edelweiss II* E. Corneille Belgium	*Marmi II* Leif Ericsen Norway	*Stella* H. Agersborg Norway
1924	9	*Elisabeth V* Eugen Lunde Norway	*Bonzo* W. Vett Denmark	*Willem Six* J. R. Carp Netherlands
1928	13	*Norma* Prince Olav Norway	*Hi-Hi* M. Wett Denmark	*Tutti V* E. Fahle Estonia
1932	3	*Bisslie* Tore Holm Sweden	*Gallant* Frederic Conant United States	*Caprice* Philip Rogers Canada
1936	12	*Lalage* M. A. Bellville Great Britain	*Lully* M. Konow Norway	*Maybe* Sven Salen Sweden
1948	11	*Llanoria* Herman Whiton United States	*Djinn* E. Sieburger Argentina	*Ali Baba II* Tore Holm Sweden
1952	11	*Llanoria* Herman Whiton United States	*Elisabeth X* F. Ferner Norway	*Ralia* E. Westerlund Finland
6.5-Meter				
1920	2	*Oranje* J. R. Carp Netherlands	*Rose Pompon* A. Weil France	
7-Meter				
1908	1	*Heroine* C. J. Rivett-Carnac Great Britain		
1920	1	*Ancora* Dorothy Winifred Great Britain		
8-Meter				
1900	2	*Olle* J. Exshaw Great Britain	*Susse* Skipper not listed France	
1908	5	*Cobweb* Blair Cochrane Great Britain	*Vinga* C. L. Hellstrom Sweden	*Sorais* Duchess of Westminster Great Britain

Class	Number of Entries	Gold (1st)	Silver (2nd)	Bronze (3rd)
1912	8	*Taifun* Thoralf Glad Norway	*Sans Atout* B. Heyman Sweden	*Lucky Girl* B. Tallberg Finland
1920	3 (new)	*Sildra* Magnus Konow Norway	*Lyn II* Jens Salvesen Norway	*Antwerpia V* Skipper not listed Norway
1920	2 (old)	*Irene* August Ringvold Norway	*Fornebo* M. N. Nielsen Norway	
1924	6	*Bera* August Ringvold Norway	*Emily* E. E. Jacob Great Britain	*Namoussa* G. Breguet France
1928	8	*L'Aile* Mme. V. Heriot France	*Hollandia* Wit de Dedes Netherlands	*Sylvia* J. Sandblom Sweden
1932	4	*Angelita* Owen Churchill United States	*Santa Maria* C. Maitland Canada	
1936	10	*Italia* Leone Reggio Italy	*Silja* O. Ditlev-Simonsen Norway	*Germania* H. Howaldt Germany
10-Meter 1900	3	*Ashenbrodel* M. Weisner Germany	*Scotia* M. M. Gretton Great Britain	*Crabe II* F. Baudrier France
1912	4	*Kitty* Nils Asp Sweden	*Nina* H. Wahl Finland	*Gallia II* A. Vishnegradsky Russia
1920	1 (new)	*Mosk II* Willy Gilbert Norway		
1920	1 (old)	*Eleda* Erik Herseth Norway		
Over 10-Meter 1900	3	*Esteril* France	*Rozen* France	*Quand-même* France
12-Meter 1908	2	*Hera* T. C. Glen-Coats Great Britain	*Mouchette* Charles MacIver Great Britain	
1912	3	*Magda IV* Alfred Larson Norway	*Erna Signe* Nils Persson Sweden	*Heatherbell* E. Krogius Finland
1920	1 (new)	*Heira* Johan Friele Norway		
1920	1 (old)	*Atalanta* Henrik Ostervold Norway		

Class	Number of Entries	Gold (1st)	Silver (2nd)	Bronze (3rd)
30-Meter				
1920	1	*Kullan* Gosta Lundquist Sweden		
40-Meter				
1920	2	*Sif* Tore Holm Sweden	*Elsie* G. Svensson Sweden	
18-Foot Centerboard Boat				
1920	1	*Brat* Skipper not listed Netherlands		
5.5-Meter				
1952	16	*Complex II* Dr. Britton Chance United States	*Encore* Peder Lunde Finland	*Hojiva* Folke Wassen Sweden
1956	10	*Rush V* Lars Thorn Sweden	*Vision* Robert Perry Great Britain	*Buraddoo* Alexander Sturrock Australia
1960	19	*Minotaur* George O'Day United States	*Web II* William Berntsen Denmark	*Ballerina IV* Henri Copponex Switzerland
1964	15	*Barenjoey* William Northam Australia	*Rush VII* Lars Thorn Sweden	*Bingo* J. McNamara United States
1968	14	*Wasa IV* Ulf Sundelin Sweden	*Toucan IX* Louis Noverraz Switzerland	*Yomen XIII* Robin Aisher Great Britain
Dragon				
1948	11	*Pan* Thor Thorvaldsen Norway	*Slaghoken* Folke Bohlin Sweden	*Snap* William Berntsen Denmark
1952	17	*Pan* Thor Thorvaldsen Norway	*Tornado* Per Gedda Sweden	*Gustel X* Theodor Thomsen Germany
1956	16	*Slaghoken II* Folke Bohlin Sweden	*Tip* Ole Berntsen Denmark	*Bluebottle* Graham Mann Great Britain
1960	27	*Nirefs* Prince Constantine Greece	*Tango* Jorge Chavez Salas Argentina	*Venilia* Antonio Cosentino Italy
1964	23	*White Lady* Ole Berntsen Denmark	*Mutafo* P. Ahrendt Germany	*Aphrodite* Lowell North United States
1968	23	*Williwaw* George Friedricks United States	Name not listed Aage Birch Denmark	Name not listed Paul Borowski Germany
Star				
1932	7	*Jupiter* Gilbert Gray United States	*Joy* Colin Ratsey Great Britain	*Swedish Star* Gunnar Asther Sweden

Class	Number of Entries	Gold (1st)	Silver (2nd)	Bronze (3rd)
1936	12	*Wannesee* Dr. Peter Bischoff Germany	*Sunshine* Arved Laurin Sweden	*Bemm II* Adrianus Mass Netherlands
1948	17	*Hilarius* Hilary Smart United States	*Kurush II* Carlos de Cardenas Cuba	*Starita* Adrianus Mass Netherlands
1952	21	*Merope* Agostino Straulino Italy	*Comanche* John Reid United States	*Espadarte* F. de Andrade Portugal
1956	12	*Kathleen* Herbert Williams United States	*Merope III* Agostino Straulino Italy	*Gem IV* Durward Knowles Bahamas
1960	26	*Tornado* Timir Pinegin U.S.S.R.	*Ma Lindo* Mario Quina Portugal	*Shrew II* William Parks United States
1964	17	*Genn* Durward Knowles Bahamas	*Glider* Richard Stearns United States	*Humbug V* P. Pettersson Sweden
1968	20	*North Star* Lowell North United States	*Sirene* Peder Lunde Norway	*Romance* Franco Cavallo Italy

Swallow

Class	Number of Entries	Gold (1st)	Silver (2nd)	Bronze (3rd)
1948	14	*Swift* Stewart Morris Great Britain	*Symphony* D. de Almaida-Bello Portugal	*Migrant* L. Pirie United States

Sharpie (12 Square Meter)

Class	Number of Entries	Gold (1st)	Silver (2nd)	Bronze (3rd)
1956	13	*Jest* P. G. Mander New Zealand	*Falcon IV* R. L. Tasker Australia	*Chuckles* J. R. Blackall Great Britain

Flying Dutchman

Class	Number of Entries	Gold (1st)	Silver (2nd)	Bronze (3rd)
1960	31	*Sirene* Peder Lunde Norway	*Skum* Hans Fogh Denmark	*Macky VI* Rolf Mulka Germany
1964	21	*Pandora* Helman Pederson New Zealand	*Lady C* Keith Musto Great Britain	*Widgeon* Harry Melges, Jr. United States
1968	30	*Superdocious* Rodney Pattison Great Britain	*Leda* Ullrich Libor Germany	Name not listed Reinaldo Conrad Brazil

Monotype

Class	Number of Entries	Gold (1st)	Silver (2nd)	Bronze (3rd)
1920	2	*Beatriss III* A. E. Van der Biesen Netherlands	*Boreas* Skipper not given Netherlands	
1924	17	Leon Huybrechts Belgium	Henrik Robert Norway	Hans Dittmar Finland
1928	10	Sven Thorell Sweden	Henrik Robert Norway	Bertil Broman Finland
1932	11	Jacques LeBrun France	J. Maas Netherlands	S. Cansino Spain

Class	Number of Entries	Gold (1st)	Silver (2nd)	Bronze (3rd)
1936	25	*Nurnberg* D. Kagchelland Netherlands	*Rostock* W. Krogmann Germany	*Potsdam* Peter Scott Great Britain
Firefly 1948	21	Paul Elvstrom Denmark	Ralph Evans, Jr. United States	J. DeJong Netherlands
Finn 1952	28	Paul Elvstrom Denmark	Charles Currey Great Britain	G. Sarby Sweden
1956	20	Paul Elvstrom Denmark	Andre Nelis Belgium	John Marvin United States
1960	35	Paul Elvstrom Denmark	Aleksandr Tyukelov U.S.S.R.	Andre Nelis Belgium
1964	33	Willi Kuhweide Germany	Peter Barrett United States	Henning Wind Denmark
1968	36	Valentin Mankin U.S.S.R.	Hubert Randaschl Austria	Fabio Albarelli Italy

The Snipe class winners in 1963: First, Ralph Conrad (Brazil); second, Eleanor M. Huggins (United States); third, Pedro J. Dates (Argentina). The other three are crewmen for the winners.

Pan-American Games

These games, which are held the year prior to the Olympic Games, were first held in Buenos Aires, Argentina, in 1951. Yachting's history in the Pan-American Games—which includes teams from North, South, and Central America—has been rather sporadic. Sailing was included in the first games but only in two classes: Snipe and Star. The United States team did not include sailors, and Brazil won in Stars while Argentina and Brazil finished one-two in what was evidently a two-boat Snipe fleet.

For the second games yachting was omitted altogether. As in the Olympics, on which the Pan-American Games are closely patterned, the host country has some choice in determining which sports shall be included. Doubtless the poor turnout for the 1951 events in Argentina led Mexico to exclude yachting in 1955. By 1959 in Chicago sailing was up to full strength—at least in number of participating classes. All seven Pan-American classes —the five Olympic classes plus Lightning and Snipe—were invited. Some classes had as few as three entries, but at least all were represented.

In the 1963 games the seven classes were again scheduled, but this time the extreme distances to São Paulo and consequent high shipping costs and inconvenience proved major hurdles for some of the classes. All fleets were rather small in size, and the 5.5-Meter series had to be canceled because only the United States had registered an entry. For the fifth games in Canada, there were four classes represented. Winning countries and skippers over the years were:

Class	Gold (1st)	Silver (2nd)	Bronze (3rd)
Star			
1951	Brazil R. Bueno	Argentina J. Brauer	Chile A. Hurtado
1959	Bahamas D. Knowles	Cuba A. Cardenas	United States G. Comer
1963	United States R. Stearns	Mexico C. Branif	Brazil H. Adler
Snipe			
1951	Argentina C. Castex	Brazil J. R. Maligo	
1959	Brazil R. Conrad	Cuba G. Diaz	United States R. Tillman
1963	Brazil R. Conrad	United States E. M. Huggins	Argentina P. J. Dates
1967	Brazil N. Piccole	United States A. Levinson	Bermuda E. Simmons
1971	Brazil P. Reinhard	United States A. Diaz	Argentina L. Orella
Flying Dutchman			
1959	United States H. Sindle	Canada A. MacDonald	West Indies Federation B. Kirkconnell
1963	Brazil J. Roderbourg	United States P. Duane	Canada T. Zegers
Finn			
1959	Bahamas K. Alburg	Argentina E. Berisso	United States W. McLean
1963	Brazil H. Domschke	United States P. Barrett	Uruguay P. Garra
1967	Brazil J. Bruder	United States C. Van Duyne	Canada A. J. Clark
1971	Brazil J. Bruder	United States C. Van Duyne	Argentina Skipper not given

Class	Gold (1st)	Silver (2nd)	Bronze (3rd)
Lightning			
1959	Brazil E. Schmidt	Ecuador E. Plaza	United States H. Nickels
1963	United States T. Allen	Brazil E. Schmidt	Argentina A. Migone
1967	United States B. Goldsmith	Brazil R. A. DaMatta	Argentina A. Migone
1971	Brazil M. Buckup	United States T. Allen	Canada D. Allen
Dragon			
1959	Argentina J. Sakas	United States W. Swindeman	Canada A. Massey
1963	Argentina J. Salas	Canada S. MacDonald	United States R. Smith
5.5-Meter			
1959	United States G. O'Day	Canada M. Gould	Ecuador E. Estrada

The 37-foot yawl *Burgoo* won the 1964 Newport-Bermuda race.

Southern Star, largest boat to sail in a Newport-Bermuda race since the 1930's, eases through a calm patch with her monstrous spinnaker barely drawing, eventually to finish third after the wind returned. *Southern Star,* a scratch boat for the 149-boat fleet, sailed with a 23-man crew, perhaps the largest crew ever in a Bermuda race.

Newport-Bermuda Race

While there were several Brooklyn (Gravesend Bay) to Bermuda races before World War I, the present Bermuda classic was started in 1923. Since 1924 it has been sailed biennially in June between Brenton Reef Tower off Newport, R.I., and Mount Hill Light on St. David's Head, Bermuda. This 635-mile event, open to sailing yachts and under the rules of the Cruising Club of America, is sponsored by the CCA and the Royal Bermuda Yacht Club.

The fastest passage in any Newport-Bermuda race was 70 hours 11 minutes 40 seconds by *Bolero* in 1956. The 73-foot yawl was sailed by Sven Salen, of Sweden, but was beaten by *Finisterre* on corrected time. The slowest time was 121 hours 13 minutes 12 seconds, made by the Class A yacht *Venturer* in 1960. Again *Finisterre* was the winner on corrected time. Other winners of the Newport-Bermuda race are:

1923 *Malabar IV,* schooner, John Alden, corrected time 85:34:40, 22 starters
1924 *Memory,* yawl, R. N. Bavier, corrected time 98:07:41, 14 starters, 3 classes
1926 *Malabar VII,* schooner, John Alden, corrected time 116:04:37, 16 starters, 2 classes

1928 *Rugosa II,* yawl, Russell Grinnell, corrected time 96:19:43, 25 starters, 4 classes

1930 *Malay,* schooner, R. W. Ferris, corrected time 84:20:19, 42 starters, 2 classes

1932 *Malabar X,* schooner, R. I. Gale, John Alden, corrected time 69:48:48, 27 starters, 2 classes

1934 *Edlu,* sloop, R. J. Schaefer, corrected time 69:42:58, 29 starters, 3 classes

1936 *Kirawan,* cutter, R. P. Baruch, corrected time 103:15:40, 44 starters, 3 classes

1946 *Gesture,* sloop, A. H. Fuller, corrected time 95:10:20, 31 starters, 2 classes

1948 *Baruna,* yawl, Henry C. Taylor, corrected time 86:59:10, 36 starters, 2 classes

1950 *Argyll,* yawl, William T. Moore, corrected time 74:05:59, 54 starters, 3 classes

1952 *Carina,* yawl, Richard Nye, corrected time 88:05:47, 58 starters, 3 classes

1954 *Malay,* yawl, D. D. Strohmeier, corrected time 99:40:29, 77 starters, 4 classes

1956 *Finisterre,* yawl, Carleton Mitchell, corrected time 64:00:00, 89 starters, 4 classes

1958 *Finisterre,* yawl, Carleton Mitchell, corrected time 79:03:38, 111 starters, 4 classes

1960 *Finisterre,* yawl, Carleton Mitchell, corrected time 102:58:52, 135 starters, 5 classes

1962 *Nina,* schooner, DeCoursey Fales, corrected time 74:45:31, 131 starters, 5 classes

1964 *Burgoo,* yawl, Milton Ernstof, corrected time 80:50:07, 143 starters, 5 classes

1966 *Thunderbird,* sloop, Vincent Learson, corrected time 95:23:20, 167 starters, 6 classes

1968 *Robin,* yawl, Frederick Hood, corrected time 78:04:19, 152 starters, 6 classes

1970 *Carina,* sloop, Richard S. Nye, corrected time 79:42:04, 149 starters, 6 classes

Onion Patch Trophy

The Onion Patch Trophy is awarded in international team competition which is sponsored by the Royal Bermuda Yacht Club and the Cruising Club of America in conjunction with the Seawanhaka Corinthian and Ida Lewis Yacht Clubs. It is run prior to the Newport-Bermuda race and includes this event. Only yachts accepted for the Newport-Bermuda race are eligible for the Onion Patch series, which consists usually of four races. In 1970, there were four competing nations—Argentina, Bermuda, Great Britain, and the United States—and the first race in this series carried twelve yachts—three from each nation—from a starting in Long Island Sound off Oyster Bay, N.Y., around Block Island to Newport, R.I. The second and third races were on a 25-mile closed course off Newport. The fourth race is the Newport-Bermuda race itself. Past winners of the Onion Patch Trophy are:

Year	Winning Nation	Year	Winning Nation
1964	United States	1968	United States
1966	Great Britain	1970	United States

Annapolis-Newport Race

Sailed in June every other year, alternating with the Newport-Bermuda race, the Annapolis (Maryland) to Newport (R.I.) ocean race is 473 miles long and is sponsored by the New York Yacht Club, the Annapolis Yacht Club, and the U.S. Naval Academy Sailing Squadron. From 1947, when the prized Blue Water Bowl was first presented to the winner of this event, to 1953, the race was run Newport to Annapolis. In 1955, the course was New London (Conn.) to Annapolis. Since 1957, the racing fleet has sailed the Annapolis-Newport course.

Prior to World War II there were other races between New London and Gibson Island in Chesapeake Bay. Actually, the first race of this type was run between Brooklyn and Hampton, Va., in 1905 and was won by the schooner *Tamerlane.* Winners of the Blue Water Bowl for the best corrected time are as follows:

1947 *Alar,* David Z. Bailey, 36 starters, 2 classes

1949 *Alar,* David Z. Bailey, 40 starters, 3 classes

1951 *Baruna,* Henry C. Taylor, 32 starters, 3 classes

1953 *Bolero,* John N. Brown, 30 starters, 3 classes

1955 *Actea,* Henry Sears, 27 starters, 3 classes

1957 *Harrier,* Jesse M. Bontecou, 48 starters, 3 classes

1959 *Caper,* H. Irving Pratt, 71 starters, 3 classes

1961 *Reindeer,* E. Newbold Smith, 86 starters, 3 classes

1963 *Dyna,* Clayton Ewing, 88 starters, 4 classes

1965 *Dyna,* Clayton Ewing, 93 starters, 5 classes

1967 *Lancetina,* Juan Cameloo, 91 starters, 5 classes

1969 *American Eagle,* R. E. Turner III, 84 starters, 5 classes

1971 *Sorcery,* James E. Baldwin, 91 starters, 5 classes

Transpacific Race

This sailing yacht race is now held every odd-numbered year in July, going from Los Angeles to Honolulu. It is sponsored by the Transpacific Yacht Racing Association. Previous winners are:

1906 *Lurline,* 86′3″, schooner, H. H. Sinclair, 3 starters

1908 *Lurline,* 86′3″, schooner, H. H. Sinclair, 4 starters

1910   *Hawaii,* 69'9", schooner, Hawaii YC, 3 starters
1912   *Lurline,* 86'3", schooner, A. E. Davis, 4 starters
1923   *Diablo,* 46', schooner, A. Pedder, 4 starters
1925   *Mariner,* 78', schooner, L. A. Norris, 4 starters (San Francisco to Tahiti)
1926   *Invader,* 95', schooner, Don Lee, 6 starters
1928   *Teva,* 56', yawl, Clem Stone, 6 starters
1930   *Enchantress,* 136', schooner, Morgan Adams, 4 starters
1932   *Fayth,* 39', ketch, William McNutt, 2 starters
1934   *Manuiwa,* 46', schooner, H. G. Dillingham, 12 starters
1936   *Dorade,* 51', yawl, James Flood, 22 starters
1939   *Blitzen,* 55'9", cutter, R. J. Reynolds, 26 starters
1941   *Escapade,* 46'5", sloop, D. Walter Elliott, 7 starters
1947   *Dolphin II,* 70'4", schooner, Frank Morgan, 34 starters
1949   *Kitten,* 46', sloop, Fred Lyon, 24 starters

1951   *Sea Witch,* 36', ketch, A. L. McCormick, 27 starters
1953   *Staghound,* 39'3", ketch, Ira P. Fulmor, 32 starters
1955   *Staghound,* 39'3", ketch, Ira P. Fulmor, 53 starters
1957   *Legend,* 50', sloop, Charles Ullman, 34 starters
1959   *Nalu II,* 46'1", sloop, Peter Grant, 41 starters
1961   *Nam Sang,* 66'3", cutter, A. B. Robbs, Jr., 41 starters
1963   *Islander,* 40', sloop, Thomas Corkett, 32 starters
1965   *Psyche,* 39'6", sloop, Don Salisbury, 55 starters
1967   *Holiday II,* Cal 40, sloop, Robert E. Allan III, 71 starters
1969   *Argonaut,* Cal 40, sloop, Jon Andron, 72 starters
1971   *Windward Passage,* 73' ketch, Mark Johnson, 69 starters

Windward Passage crosses line at Diamond Head with only chute and mainsail in gusty wind to be first to finish in 25th Transpac race. She lost on corrected time to *Holiday II.*

Transatlantic Race

The first transatlantic race was in 1866 when James Gordon Bennett's *Henrietta* won, sailing from Sandy Hook to the Isle of Wight. The longest of the various courses used for this race was about 4,200 miles, from Havana, Cuba, to San Sebastian, Spain. In general, the eligibility requirements are similar to the requirements for the 1968 Newport-Bermuda race. The race is open to any yacht meeting such requirements whose owner or charterer is a member of a recognized yacht club.

Former winners of this event are as follows:

1866 *Henrietta,* James Gordon Bennett (United States); schooner, 107 feet; Sandy Hook to Isle of Wight; 3 starters; 13 days 21 hours 45 minutes

1870 *Cambria,* James Ashbury (Great Britain); schooner, 108 feet; Daunt Rock, Ireland, to Sandy Hook; 2 starters; 23 days 5 hours 17 minutes

1887 *Coronet,* Rufus T. Bush (United States); schooner, 133 feet; Sandy Hook to Cork; 2 starters; 14 days 19 hours 3 minutes

1905 *Atlantic,* Wilson Marshall (United States); schooner, 185 feet; Sandy Hook to Lizard Light, England; 11 starters; 12 days 4 hours 1 minute

1928 *Elena,* William B. Bell (United States); schooner, 136 feet; Ambrose Lightship to Santander, Spain; 5 starters, 16 days 19 hours 50 minutes

1931 *Dorade,* Olin J. Stevens and Roderick Stevens, Jr. (United States); yawl, 52 feet; Newport to Plymouth, England; 10 starters; 17 days 1 hour 15 minutes; corrected time 15 days 2 hours 46 minutes

1935 *Stormy Weather,* Philip Leboutillier (United States); yawl, 54 feet; Newport to Bergen, Norway; 6 starters; 19 days 5 hours 32 minutes; corrected time 17 days 6 hours 8 minutes

1936 *Roland von Bremen,* Franz Perlia (Germany); yawl, 59 feet, Bermuda to Bremen, Germany; 9 starters, 20 days 37 hours 49 minutes

1950 *Cohoe,* K. Adlard Coles (Great Britain); sloop, 32 feet; Bermuda to Plymouth, England; 5 starters; 21 days 9 hours 14 minutes

1951 *Malabar XIII,* Kennon Jewett (United States); ketch, 53 feet; Havana to San Sebastian, Spain; 4 starters; 29 days 26 minutes

1952 *Samuel Pepys,* Royal Naval Sailing Association (Great Britain); Lt. Cmdr. Erroll Bruce; Bermuda to Plymouth, England; 5 starters; 17 days 5 hours 4 minutes

The start of Class A of the transatlantic race from Bermuda to Travemunde, West Germany, in 1968, finds four of the largest entries crossing the line. From left, *Stormvogel, Kialoa II, Ondine,* the Italian entry *Stella Polare,* and the *Germania VI.* The race was won by *Indigo* (not shown).

1955 *Carina,* Richard S. Nye (United States); yawl, 53 feet; Newport to Marstrand, Sweden; 7 starters; 20 days 8 hours 16 minutes 28 seconds

1956 *Mare Nostrum,* Enrique Urrutia (Spain); yawl, 72 feet; Havana to San Sebastian, Spain; 5 starters; 28 days 5 hours 42 minutes

1957 *Carina,* Richard S. Nye (United States); yawl, 53 feet; Newport to Santander, Spain; 19 days 13 hours 28 minutes 47.5 seconds; corrected time 18 days 2 hours 13 minutes 47.5 seconds

1960 *Figaro,* William T. Snaith (United States); yawl, 47 feet; Bermuda to The Skaw lightship, Sweden; time not available

1963 *Ondine,* Sumner A. Long (United States); yawl, 57 feet; Newport to Plymouth, England; 14 starters; 18 days 7 hours 46 minutes 29 seconds; corrected time 12 days 13 hours 40 minutes 56 seconds

1966 *Ondine,* Sumner A. Long (United States); yawl, 57 feet; Bermuda to Denmark; 42 starters; 17 days 7 hours 31 minutes 6 seconds; corrected time 14 days 18 hours 28 minutes 56 seconds

1968 *Indigo,* S. K. Wellman (United States); yawl; Bermuda to Travemunde, Germany; 32 starters; corrected time 17 days 11 hours 59 minutes 21 seconds

1969 *Kialoa II,* John B. Kilroy (United States); yawl; Newport to Cork, Ireland; 12 days 5 hours 43 minutes; corrected time 12 days 21 hours 6 minutes

Tina, owned by E. R. Stettinius and sailed brilliantly by Richard E. Carter, won the One-Ton Cup in 1966.

La Coupe Internationale du Cercle de la Voile de Paris (C.V.P.)

The cup is given as a prize for an international race presented to the so-called one-ton restricted class, from whence its English surname, One-Ton Cup, under which it became famous throughout the world. Sailed for the first time in 1899 in Meulan, on the River Seine, it was won by *Belouga,* sailed by Eugene Laverne and the Michelet brothers, defeating the English challenger *Vectis* of the Island Sailing Club. From 1899 to 1906, the story of the One-Ton Cup was a French-English business, sailed by turns on the River Seine and on the Solent with, in 1901, the participation of the Italian challenger *Dai-Dai,* and in 1906 the German *N.R.V.*

In 1907 the first International Rating system was born and the cup was assigned to the International 6-Meter class. The cup was held by the Norddeutscher Regatta Verein until 1912, when it was won by the Royal Thames Yacht Club. It remained during World War I in London's Knightsbridge Hotel window.

When the war was over, the cup was assigned to the 6.5-Meter class, but in 1924 it was returned to 6-Meter yachts. In 1962 the last 6-Meter race for the C.V.P. Cup was held.

In 1965 the cup was revitalized as a handicapped event with yachts measured to the Royal Ocean Racing Club formula. (Prior events were sailed scratch, without corrected time.) Countries were invited to enter up to three yachts each, all of which must rate at no more than 22 feet RORC rule and fit the accommodation requirements of the IYRU 8-Meter cruiser-racer class. In addition, unlike former rules which made it strictly an offshore event and was not completed until one of the competitors had won three races, the new regulations stated that there would be three races—to start with an inshore event of some 30 to 35 miles. The next day would see the start of a 250-mile race around a triangle. Two days after yachts returned from this event there would be a final short race like the first. Yachts score individually, the long race counting double, and the highest scoring individual yacht wins the trophy.

Beginning in 1970 only yachts rating 27.5 feet or less under the IOR rule are eligible for the cup. As a rule the races are conducted by the country having won the previous year. For example, the 1971 competition was held in Auckland, New Zealand, and consisted of five races as follows:

1. Three 30-mile races on an Olympic course.
2. One triangular course race of 150 miles in Hauraki Gulf.
3. One ocean race of about 300 miles. This race counted double points.

Previous winning yachts and their countries were:

	Winner	Other Competitors
1899	*Belouga* (France)	*Vectis* (Great Britain)
1900	*Sidi* (France)	*Scotia* (Great Britain)
1901	*Scotia II* (Great Britain)	Two nations
1902	*Scotia III* (Great Britain)	*August* (France)
1903	*Chocolat* (France)	*Iris* (Great Britain)
1906	*Feu Follet* (France)	*N.R.V.* (Germany)
1907	*Onkel Adolph* (Germany)	Four nations
1908	*Windspiel XI* (Germany)	Three nations
1909	*Windspiel XII* (Germany)	Three nations
1910	*Agnes II* (Sweden)	Six nations
1911	*Windspiel XV* (Germany)	Seven nations
1912	*Bunty* (Great Britain)	Eight nations
1913	*Cremona* (Great Britain)	Six nations
1920	*Cordella* (Great Britain)	Two nations
1921	*Cordella* (Great Britain)	Three nations
1922	*Cordella* (Great Britain)	Three nations
1923	*Cordella* (Great Britain)	*Qui Va* (France)
1924	*Holland's Hope* (Holland)	Four nations
1925	*Princess Juliana* (Holland)	Two nations
1926	*Zenith* (Great Britain)	Three nations
1927	*Petite Aile II* (France)	*Dana* (Great Britain)

	Winner	Other Competitors
1928	*Yara III* (France)	*Windy* (Sweden)
1929	*Bissbi* (Sweden)	Two nations
1930	*Bissbi* (Sweden)	Eight nations
1931	*Bissbi* (Sweden)	Three nations
1932	*Abu* (Norway)	Three nations
1933	*Varg V* (Norway)	Six nations
1934	*White Lady* (Norway)	Three nations
1935	*Jan III* (Sweden)	Five nations
1936	*Tidsfordrif* (Sweden)	Two nations
1937	*Tidsfordrif II* (Sweden)	Three nations
1938	*Norna VI* (Norway)	Four nations
1939	*Noreg III* (Norway)	Four nations
1946	*May Be VI* (Sweden)	*Apache* (Norway)
1947	*May Be VI* (Sweden)	*Ragnhild* (Norway)
1948	*May Be VI* (Sweden)	*Tokus III* (Norway)
1949	*Trickson VI* (Sweden)	Four nations
1950	*May Be VI* (Sweden)	Three nations
1952	*Llanoria* (United States)	*May Be VII* (Sweden)
1953	*Ylliam VIII* (Switzerland)	Seven nations
1954	*Ylliam IX* (Switzerland)	*Elghi* (France)
1955	*Ylliam IX* (Switzerland)	Five nations
1956	*Ylliam IX* (Switzerland)	Three nations
1957	*Llanoria* (United States)	Five nations
1958	*Royal Thames* (Great Britain)	Five nations
1959	*May Be VIII* (Sweden)	Five nations
1960	*Elghi III* (France)	Two nations
1961	*Elghi III* (France)	Three nations
1962	*Elghi II* (France)	Three nations
1965	*Diana III* (Denmark)	Eight nations
1966	*Tina* (United States)	Nine nations
1967	*Optimist* (Germany)	Ten nations
1968	*Optimist* (Germany)	Eleven nations
1969	*Rainbow II* (New Zealand)	Eight nations
1971	*Stormy Petrel* (Australia)	Nine nations

Coupe Internationale Atlantique (Half-Ton Cup)

Competition for the Coupe Internationale Atlantique, commonly referred to as the Half-Ton Cup, is almost unknown on the west-side of the Atlantic yet in Europe it has outstripped the One-Ton Cup in popularity.

The Half-Ton Cup is raced for in boats rating at the top of the Junior Offshore Group (JOG) limit. They race without handicap and must have RORC ratings of not more than 18.0 feet. The boats must have specified minimum cruising accommodations (although they need not have engines of any kind). They average around 30 feet overall, 22½ feet waterline, and about 10,000 pounds dis-

placement. Costs, so far, have stayed lower than $15,000, which is about half the cost of a minimum One-Ton Cupper.

In the beginning there were four races: an inshore race, two Olympic courses, and an offshore race. In 1969 a five-race series with one throw-out was adopted—the fifth race being an additional inshore event. In 1970 the second inshore race was changed to a short offshore race. Scoring was one point each for the inshore and Olympic courses, one and a half points for the short offshore race, and two points for the long offshore race.

Winners of the Half-Ton Cup are as follows:

Year	Name	Class	Owner	Designer	Country
1967	*Safari*	Arpege	Serge Lindales	Michel Dufour	France
1968	*Dame d'Troise*	Super Challenger	Michel Perroud	Andre Mauric	France
1969	*Scampi*	Scampi	Peter Norlin	Peter Norlin	Sweden
1970	*Scampi II*	Scampi	Peter Norlin	Peter Norlin	Sweden
1971	*Scampi III*	Scampi	Peter Norlin	Peter Norlin	Sweden

Quarter-Ton Cup

The Quarter-Ton Cup is the smallest and the least known as yet of the "ton cup" races. Its name has no specific connotation. Rather, it is a derivation of the One-Ton Cup, reflecting a desire to produce boats about one-quarter the size of One-Ton Cup yachts. The contenders race in small, series-built, family-type cruiser-racers which have waterline lengths of 18 to 21 feet. These are "everyman" boats which builders can spew out in hundreds per year at reasonable prices. Such boats can be fully equipped with the best equipment and sails available for about $8,000 each. The boats are raced with a crew of three or four, and the series is now becoming as competitive as any Olympic class.

Only two major factors now control entry: that the boat measure 18 feet (5.5 meters) under the IOR and that there are at least three boats built from this design. There are some interior measurements and equipment inventories which must be adhered to, but these are only to stop designers from sacrificing living accommodations aboard for pure speed and to ensure that the boats conform to safety regulations.

Unlike the One-Ton Cup, which restricts entries to three per country, the two smaller cups do not have participant restrictions. One-Ton national teams are chosen to fight it out for a national prize, but in each of the Half- and Quarter-Ton series all who had boat, crew, and a desire to sail were allowed to compete. The result is that these races have attracted wide interest. They do not require an owner to enter a grueling and expensive series of trials in order to participate. In other words, the object of the Half-Ton and the Quarter-Ton series is to select the best all-around boat and crew. This has been achieved by having a variety of races and by insisting that the same crew sail the boat in each of the races—no specialists for the inshore races with other specialists for offshore. There are no nationality restrictions, thereby allowing picking up of local crew members (such as a navigator for local knowledge), but once the crew has raced in one race, there can be no changes except for extenuating circumstances. Courses of racing and scoring system for the Quarter-Ton Cup are the same as for the Half-Ton. Previous winners of the Quarter-Ton Cup are as follows:

Year	Name	Class	Helmsman	Designers	Country
1966	*Spirit*	Spirit	Andre Nelis	E. G. Van deStadt	Belgium
1967	*Spirit*	Spirit	Andre Nelis	E. G. Van deStadt	Belgium
1968	*Piraiha II*	Challenger	Hans Kortehans	Andre Mauris and Jacques Gaubert	Netherlands
1969	*Listang*	Listang	Ullrich Libor	Klaus and Karl Felt	Germany
1970	*Fleur d'Ecume*	Ecume d'Mer	Laurent Cordelle	J. M. Finot	France

Admiral's Cup

The Admiral's Cup competition started in 1957 as a biennial event held during Fastnet Race years (odd-numbered) in the English Channel. It is open to a selected team of three yachts of more than 30 feet waterline (RORC Class II minimum) from each participating country. The cup is awarded to the team with the best score from a series of inshore and offshore events preceding and during Cowes Week in Great Britain.

Actually, the Admiral's series embraces four races. It starts with the RORC's 230-mile Channel race (this counts double points). It continues with the two main Cowes Week events for yachts over 30 feet at the water-line—the Britannia Cup and the New York Yacht Club Challenge Cup, both of around 30 miles. These each count single points. Then, finally, comes the main event, the 605-mile Fastnet Race, which starts from Cowes toward the end of the week, takes the boats around the Fastnet Rock off southern Ireland, and ends in Plymouth. This race counts triple. Each country fields three yachts, and the country with the most points wins.

Winning countries of the Admiral's Cup are:

1957	Great Britain	1965	Great Britain
1959	Great Britain	1967	Australia
1961	United States	1969	United States
1963	Great Britain	1971	Great Britain

Fastnet Race

As previously stated, the *big* event of the biennial Cowes Week in Great Britain is the Fastnet Race. Since the records of the Royal Ocean Racing Club were destroyed by bombing during World War II, the following list is not complete as to corrected times of some races:

1925 *Jolie Brise,* Lt. Cmdr. E. G. Martin, Great Britain, 168:57:30
1926 *Ilex,* Royal Engineer Yacht Club, Great Britain, 86:44:52
1927 *Tally Ho,* Lord Stalbridge, Great Britain
1928 *Nina,* Paul Hammond, United States, 101:48:20
1929 *Jolie Brise,* Robert Somerset, Great Britain
1930 *Jolie Brise,* Robert Somerset, Great Britain
1931 *Dorade,* R. Stephens, United States, 82:38:33
1933 *Dorade,* R. and O. J. Stephens, United States, 124:59:15
1935 *Stormy Weather,* P. LeBoutillier, United States
1937 *Zeearend,* C. Bruynzeel, Netherlands, 85:29:00
1939 *Bloodhound,* I. Bell, United States
1947 *Myth of Malham,* Capt. J. Illingworth, RN, Great Britain, 112:13:54
1951 *Yeoman,* O. A. Aisher, Great Britain, 99:07:02
1953 *Favona,* Sir Michael Newton, Great Britain, 96:11:26
1955 *Carina,* R. S. Nye, United States, 81:43:32
1957 *Carina,* R. S. Nye, United States, 92:55:50
1959 *Anitra,* Sven Hansen, Sweden, 97:02:52
1961 *Zwerver,* W. N. H. van der Vorm, Netherlands, 81:32:03
1963 *Clarion of Wight,* D. Boyer and D. Miller, Great Britain, 86:34:13
1965 *Rabbit,* R. E. Carter, United States, 86:01:46
1967 *Pen-Duick III,* E. Tabarly, France, 78:39:19
1969 *Red Rooster,* R. E. Carter, United States, 91:38:37
1971 *Ragamuffin,* S. Fischer, Australia, 76:08:38

Captain James Cook Trophy

This trophy is an Admiral's Cup type competition in JOG/MORC boats (under 24 feet waterline), with three boats from each country racing as a team. The trophy was donated by the JOG Association of Australia and is raced in the English Channel every other year. Winning countries are as follows:

1968 France   1970 Australia

International Catamaran Challenge Cup Trophy (Little America's Cup)

In 1961, after correspondence concerning the ability of Britain or America to design the fastest catamarans, the Chapman Sands Sailing Club of Essex in England issued a challenge for a series of races against an American catamaran to be run along the lines of the America's Cup. A set of rules was drawn up requiring a maximum sail area of 300 square feet, a maximum length of 25 feet, and a maximum beam of 14 feet. The Seacliff Yacht Club of Long Island took on the defense for the Eastern Multihull Sailing Association of America (which had accepted the challenge), presented a trophy, and organized the trials and the series.

In 1964—when the C-class received its official status as an international class—all International Catamaran Challenge Cup events were raced on C-class catamarans. Winners of the Cup since 1961 are as follows:

Year	Winner	Loser	Score
1961	*Hellcat II,* Great Britain	*Wildcat,* United States	4 to 1
1962	*Hellcat II,* Great Britain	*Beverly,* United States	4 to 1
1963	*Hellcat III S,* Great Britain	*Quest,* Australia	4 to 0
1964	*Emma Hamilton,* Great Britain	*Sealion,* United States	4 to 1
1965	*Emma Hamilton,* Great Britain	*Quest II,* Australia	4 to 1
1966	*Lady Helmsman,* Great Britain	*Gamecock,* United States	4 to 2
1967	*Lady Helmsman,* Great Britain	*Quest III, Australia*	4 to 1
1968	*Lady Helmsman,* Great Britain	*Yankee Flyer,* United States	4 to 2
1969	*Opus III,* Denmark	*Ocelot,* Great Britain	4 to 3
1970	*Quest III,* Australia	*Sleipner,* Denmark	4 to 3

The Canada's Cup

The Canada's Cup is known as the America's Cup of the Great Lakes. In 1896 the sloop *Canada* won this cup at Toledo, Ohio, and then it was offered by the Royal Canadian Yacht Club of Toronto as a Challenge Cup. In 1967 the deed of gift was changed and now specifies that the match-race series be sailed in CCA-measured boats of not more than 37 feet rating. The contest had been held in 8-Meters in the previous few challenges.

The match series between a yacht from the United States and one from Canada is decided by the winning of three out of the five races. However, in 1969 an innovation in the series was made in that the third race was a long-distance race (about 200 miles), which was scored as two of the five races. The shorter events were raced on a 30-mile Olympic course.

The record of the Canada's Cup is as follows:

Year	Winner	Loser	Score
1896	*Canada,* Royal Canadian Yacht Club	*Vencedor,* Chicago Yacht Club	2 to 0
1899	*Genesee,* Chicago Yacht Club	*Beaver,* Royal Canadian Yacht Club	3 to 0
1901	*Invader,* Royal Canadian Yacht Club	*Cadillac,* Chicago Yacht Club	3 to 2
1903	*Irondequoit,* Rochester Yacht Club	*Strathcona,* Royal Canadian Yacht Club	3 to 1
1905	*Iroquois,* Rochester Yacht Club	*Temeraire,* Royal Canadian Yacht Club	3 to 2
1907	*Seneca,* Rochester Yacht Club	*Adele,* Royal Canadian Yacht Club	3 to 0
1930	*Thisbe,* Rochester Yacht Club	*Quest,* Royal Canadian Yacht Club	3 to 2
1932	*Conewago,* Rochester Yacht Club	*Invader II,* Royal Canadian Yacht Club	3 to 1
1934	*Conewago,* Rochester Yacht Club	*Invader II,* Royal Canadian Yacht Club	3 to 0
1954	*Venture II,* Royal Canadian Yacht Club	*Iskareen,* Rochester Yacht Club	3 to 1
1969	*Manitou,* Royal Canadian Yacht Club	*Niagara,* Cleveland Yacht Club	4 to 0

The 1966 Little America's Cup series between *Lady Helmsman* (Great Britain) and *Gamecock* (United States). *Lady Helmsman* won 4 to 2.

Chicago-Mackinac Race

This 333-mile freshwater sailboat race is sponsored annually by the Chicago Yacht Club in July. In 1927 the race was reorganized into divisions: sail (universal) and cruising. In 1952 the Chicago-Mackinac race fleet was changed into six "sections" and two "divisions." The first three sections (larger boats) made up Division I and the next three Division II. In 1971 the race fleet was divided into eight sections, four divisions. The Jack Ritchie Trophy—marked with an asterisk in the following winners list—is given for the best corrected time in the fleet.

1898 *Vanenna,* sloop, W. R. Crawford
1904 *Vencedor,* sloop, Fred A. Price
1905 *Mistral,* schooner, Dwight Lawrence

1906 *Vanadis,* yawl, George S. Steers
1907 *Vencedor,* sloop, George Tramel
1908 *Valmore,* schooner, William Thompson
1909 *Valmore,* schooner, William Thompson
1910 *Valmore,* schooner, William Thompson
1911 *Mavourneen,* sloop, E. M. Mills
1912 *Polaris,* yawl, J. O. Heyworth
1913 *Olympian,* sloop, J. O. Heyworth (syndicate)
1914 *Olympian,* sloop, Frank Snite, Roy Barcal
1915 *Leda,* sloop, George Currier
1916 *Intrepid,* sloop, Frank Snite, Roy Barcal
1921 *Virginia,* sloop, Carlos Alling
1922 *Intrepid,* sloop, Donald Prather, Vernon Farrell
1923 *Virginia,* sloop, J. A. Hadwiger
1924 *Sari,* sloop, Benj. Carpenter, Jr.
1925 *Virginia,* sloop, J. A. Hadwiger
1926 *Intrepid,* sloop, Donald Prather
1927 *Siren* (Universal Division), sloop, A. E. Karas, L. L. Karas, W. L. Latimer
     Shalamar (Cruising Division), ketch, M. G. Herbert
1928 *Siren* (U.D.), sloop, A. E. Karas, L. L. Karas
     Comet (C.D.), yawl, H. D. Beaumont
1929 *Blue Moon* (U.D.), schooner, H. T. Simmons
     Bagheera (C.D.), schooner, R. P. Benedict
1930 *Siren* (U.D.), sloop, A. E. Karas, L. L. Karas
     Cynthia (C.D.), yawl, J. L. Williamson
1931 *Siren* (U.D.), sloop, A. E. Karas, L. L. Karas
     Elizabeth (C.D.), schooner, L. A. Williams
1932 *Princess* (U.D.), sloop, E. Jedrzykowski, C. A. Kallgren
     Bagheera (C.D.), schooner, R. P. Benedict
1933 *Siren* (U.D.), sloop, A. E. Karas, L. L. Karas
     Chimon (C.D.), schooner, H. K. Hill
1934 *Princess* (U.D.), sloop, E. Jedrzykowski, C. A. Kallgren
     Elizabeth (C.D.), schooner, L. A. Williams
1935 *Princess* (U.D.), sloop, E. Jedrzykowski, C. A. Kallgren
     Elizabeth (C.D.), schooner, L. A. Williams
1936 *Hope* (U.D.), sloop, E. Karnstedt
     Rubaiyat (C.D.), cutter, N. Rubinkam
1937 *Revenge* (U.D.), cutter, Blair Walliser, Ken Griffin
     Rubaiyat (C.D.), cutter, N. Rubinkam
1938 *Hope* (U.D.), sloop, E. Karnstedt
     Manitou (C.D.), yawl, James Lowe
1939 *Gloriant* (U.D.), sloop, A. M. Herrmann
     Bangalore (C.D.), cutter, E. B. Lumbard
1940 *Lively Lady* (U.D.), sloop, Otto Dreher
     Bangalore (C.D.), cutter, E. B. Lumbard
1941 *Lively Lady* (U.D.), sloop, Otto Dreher
     Breeze (C.D.), yawl, S. D. Scott
1942 *Falcon II* (U.D.), sloop, L. L. Karas, Clare Udell
     White Cloud (C.D.), cutter, C. E. Sorenson
1943 *Gloriant* (U.D.), cutter, C. E. Sorenson
     Lassie (C.D.), cutter, William Lawrie
1944 *Falcon II* (U.D.), sloop, Clare Udell
     Bangalore Too (C.D.), yawl, John D. Kinsey
1945 *Cara Mia* (U.D.), sloop, L. L. Karas
     Bangalore Too (C.D.), yawl, John D. Kinsey, E. M. Lumbard

1946 *Spindle* (U.D.), sloop, Vitas Thomas
     Blitzen (C.D.), cutter, Ernie Grates, Murray Knapp
1947 *Cara Mia* (U.D.), sloop, L. L. Karas
     Royona III (C.D.), J. B. Ford, Jr.
1948 *Cara Mia* (U.D.), yawl, L. L. Karas
     Taltohna (C.D.), cutter, Edgar Tolman, Jr.
1949 *Cara Mia* (U.D.), yawl, L. L. Karas
     Taltohna (C.D.), cutter, Edgar Tolman, Jr.
1950 *Gale* (U.D.), sloop, Harry Nye, Jr.
     Fleetwood (C.D.), ketch, Nicholas Geib
1951 *Gale* (U.D.), sloop, Harry Nye, Jr.
     Escapade (C.D.), yawl, Wendell Anderson
1952 *Tahuna* (1st Division), yawl, P. C. McNulty
     Fleetwood (2nd Division), yawl, N. Geib
1953 *Gypsy* (1st Division), yawl, J. Schoendorf
     Fleetwood (2nd Division), yawl, N. Geib
1954 *Taltohna* (1st Division), cutter, Edgar Tolman, Jr.
     Fleetwood (2nd Division), yawl, Nicholas Geib
1955 *Revelry* (1st Division), cutter, Norman Sarns
     Rangoon (2nd Division), yawl, A. E. Stern, Jr.
1956 *Copperhead* (1st Division), yawl, Charles Kotovoc
     Fleetwood (2nd Division), yawl, Nicholas Geib
1957 *Dyna* (1st Division), yawl, Clayton Ewing
     Meteor III (2nd Division), sloop, Henry Burkhard
1958 *Dyna* (1st Division), yawl, Clayton Ewing
     Rangoon, (2nd Division), yawl, D. Silberman, Jr., A. E. Stern
1959 *Barb* (1st Division), cutter, Dr. David Axelrod
     Feather (2nd Division), yawl, William Peacock
1960 *Freebooter* (1st Division), sloop, Mac and Bob Pohn
     Dauntless II (2nd Division), sloop, Thomas Hanson
1961 *Greetings* (1st Division), sloop, Win Tice
     Blue Horizon (2nd Division), sloop, Dick Kaup
1962 *Flame* (1st Division), James Doane
     Sixth Girl (2nd Division), sloop, Joseph Krueger
1963 **Blitzen* (1st Division), cutter, Tom and William Schoendorf
     Meteor III (2nd Division), sloop, Henry Burkhard
1964 *X-Barb* (1st Division), cutter, Dr. David Axelrod
     *Talisman (2nd Division), sloop, George Quandee
1965 **Blitzen* (1st Division), cutter, Tom and William Schoendorf
     Challenge (2nd Division), sloop, Bob Rothchild
1966 **Blitzen* (1st Division), cutter, Tom and William Schoendorf
     Bantu (2nd Division), sloop, Dick Richheimer
1967 **Diavolo* (1st Division), sloop, Alfred E. Stern, Jr.
     Flying Buffalo (2nd Division), sloop, Maury Declercq, Karl Ness
1968 **Comanche* (1st Division), sloop, Schoendorf Brothers
     Decision (2nd Division), yawl, David W. Howell

1969 *Bay Bea (1st Division), sloop, Patrick F. Haggerty
Flying Buffalo (2nd Division), sloop, Maury Declercq, Karl Ness
1970 *Dora (1st Division), sloop, Lynn A. Williams
Decision (2nd Division), sloop, David W. Howell
1971 *Endurance (1st Division), sloop, Roger Derusha
Glory Bea III (2nd Division), sloop, James Curlin
Decision (3rd Division), sloop, David Howell
Goblin (4th Division), sloop, Lindy Thomas

Acapulco Race

Sponsor of this famous 1,430-mile sail is the San Diego Yacht Club, which runs it from San Diego Harbor to Acapulco, Mexico, every even-numbered year, in February. Previous winners are as follows:

Year	Yacht	Owner
1950	Conejo	Wolf Schoeborn
1952	Fairweather	Fred J. Allen
1954	Aventide	Stephen Newmark
1956	Carousel	Ashley G. Brown
1958	Pursuit	Howard Ahmanson
1960	Kialoa	James B. Kilroy
1962	Carousel	Ashley G. Brown
1964	Sirius II	Howard Ahamson
1966	Ondine	Sumner A. Long
1968	Kialoa II	James B. Kilroy
1970	Yellow Jacket	Terrell Greene

World Ocean Racing Championship

In 1969 the St. Petersburg (Florida) Yacht Club established a three-year competition for a world's championship for ocean-racing yachts. A low-point system is used, with seven out of nineteen possible races counted. Of the nineteen, two are mandatory, the St. Petersburg to Ft. Lauderdale race and the Miami to Montego Bay, Jamaica, race; the other five are optional, but one must be of more than 1,000 miles. While seven races *must* be sailed to qualify for the trophy, more may be sailed and the best seven will count. Corrected-time fleet position will be the basis for scoring. The boat and the owner (or charterer) must be the same for the three-year period, but the rig and rating may vary.

The sanctioned nineteen races are: St. Petersburg to Ft. Lauderdale (compulsory); Miami to Jamaica (compulsory); Transatlantic; Newport to Bermuda; Fastnet (England); Plymouth (England) to La Rochelle (France); Annapolis, Maryland, to Newport, Rhode Island; San Pedro, California, to Honolulu; Skaw Race (Sweden); Sydney to Hobart (Australia); Hobart to Auckland (New Zealand); Hong Kong to Manila; Buenos Aires to Rio; Giraglia Race (Italy); San Diego to Acapulco; Chicago to Mackinac; Aegean Sea Rally; Piraeus to Rhodes Race (Greece); and Marblehead, Mass., to Halifax, Nova Scotia.

Ensenada Race

The Ensenada International Yacht Race is often billed as the world's biggest sailboat contest, and so far no one has seen fit to dispute the claim. In 1968 there were 580 boats entered for the overnight jaunt (about 130 miles) from Newport, California, to Ensenada, on Mexico's Baja Peninsula. This event is sponsored by the Newport Ocean Sailing Association, on the weekend closest to May 5, each year. Winners of the President of Mexico Trophy—awarded to overall ocean-racing winners—are as follows:

Year	Number of Starters	Winner and Owner	Yacht Affiliation
1949	134	Kitten, Fred Lyons	Newport Harbor Yacht Club
1950	138	Scandia, Hebert Erickson	Balboa Yacht Club
1951	139	Mara, Barney Huber	Balboa Yacht Club
1952	138	Mara, Barney Huber	Balboa Yacht Club
1953	139	Bagatelle, W. Zinsmeyer	Los Angeles Yacht Club
1954	172	Sirius, H. Ahamson	Newport Harbor Yacht Club
1955	178	Carousel, Ash G. Brown	San Diego Yacht Club
1956	197	Cynjo, Gordon A. Alles	Lido Isle Yacht Club
1957	236	Renegade, Hale Field	Los Angeles Yacht Club
1958	294	Nam Sang, Louis Statham	Los Angeles Yacht Club
1959	320	Carousel, Ash G. Brown	San Diego Yacht Club
1960	364	Bravata, E. Bourne and D. Stewart	Cabrillo Yacht Club
1961	403	Choleta, Keith Lister	San Diego Yacht Club
1962	265	Cheerio, R. C. Bradley	San Diego Yacht Club

Year	Number of Starters	Winner and Owner	Yacht Affiliation
1963	345	*Vela*, H. Riley, E. McDonald, and V. Landis	Lido Isle Yacht Club
1964	412	*Kialoa II*, John B. Kilroy	Newport Harbor Yacht Club
1965	471	*Hilaria*, Jack Baillie	Balboa Yacht Club
1966	538	*Pace III*, W. Gearhart	Offshore Cruising Club
1967	543	*Redhead*, Larry Maio	San Diego Yacht Club
1968	580	*Aquarius*, John Holiday	Long Beach Yacht Club
1969	558	*Balandra*, J. McClaire	Lido Isle Yacht Club
1970	564	*Encore*, Fred McDonald	Newport Harbor Yacht Club
1971	560	*Aquarius*, John Holiday	Long Beach Yacht Club

Congressional Cup

A round-robin match-racing event among the nation's top sailors (usually ten) is sponsored each year by the Long Beach (California) Yacht Club. The trophy for this invitational series was presented by the United States Congress in 1965. Winners of the cup and their yacht clubs are as follows:

1965	Gerry Driscoll, San Diego YC, *Blue Marlin*
1966	Gerry Driscoll, San Diego YC, *Blue Marlin*
1967	Scott H. Allan, Newport Harbor YC, *Madrugador*
1968	Robert E. Allan III, Los Angeles YC, *Holliday Too*
1969	Henry Sprague III, U.S. Naval YC, *Madrugador*
1970	Argyle Campbell, Balboa YC, *Kuuipo*
1971	Thomas Pickard, Long Beach YC, *Bellwether*

Comanche, a 42-foot stock cruiser-racer, won the 1968 Chicago-Mackinac race and was named the Boat of the Year on Lake Michigan.

Southern Ocean Racing Conference

The Southern Ocean Racing Conference (SORC) championship has become recognized as one of the best series of offshore events in the world. It vies with such institutions as the Admiral's Cup series and is unique in many respects. The attraction of a tropical siren's song to yachtsmen from New York and Chicago is obvious, but the SORC also draws racers from Florida's rival sunshine land, Southern California, and the closer-by Gulf Coast ports of Texas and Louisiana—where good sailing is a year-round sport. The main attractions of the SORC are good race courses and top-level competition. There are six different races which comprise the series (only five count for the overall championship).

The SORC is open to "seaworthy, single-hulled yachts" between 30 and 75 feet overall length. There is no entry fee, and entries close four days before the start of each race.

Each boat must have a valid CCA certificate, and the NAYRU time-allowance tables are used for handicaps. The distances published are those used to calculate time allowances and will be at slight variance with the actual rhumb-line mileages.

The scoring system is unique and requires some explanation. Each race is weighted according to its distance so that winning a long race has more value than winning a short one. The St. Petersburg–Fort Lauderdale and Miami-Nassau races each count 35 percent of the total SORC score. Next in importance are the St. Petersburg–Venice and Miami–West End races, either of which is counted at 15 percent of the total score. The two shortest races, the Lipton Cup and Nassau Cup races, count 7½ percent each. Points are awarded on the basis of 1,000 for first place, 990 for second, 980 for third, etc., multiplied by the appropriate weighted percentage of the race. The system is effective but cumbersome—particularly for the contestants. Winners for the past five years are as follows:

Pace III (center), a Columbia 50, first overall winner of the 1966 Newport to Ensenada International Yacht Race approaching the finish line. She is flanked by scratch boat *Serena* of San Francisco YC (right) and the Catamaran *Imual* of Lido Isle YC.

Event	Yacht	Owner
1967		
St. Petersburg–Ft. Lauderdale	*Chubasco*	Arnold D. Haskell
St. Petersburg–Venice	*Red Jacket*	Perry Connolly
Lipton Cup	*Red Jacket*	Perry Connolly
Miami-Lucaya	*Circe II*	R. D. Wollsey
Miami-Nassau	*Solution*	Thor Ramsing
Nassau Cup	*Panacea*	J. M. Elkard
SORC Champion	*Guinevere*	George M. Moffet, Jr.
1968		
St. Petersburg–Ft. Lauderdale	*Red Jacket*	Perry Connolly
St. Petersburg–Venice	*Rage*	Homer Denius
Lipton Cup	*Red Jacket*	Perry Connolly
Miami–West End	*Panacea*	J. M. Elkard
Miami-Nassau	*Nina*	Lee Creekmore
Nassau Cup	*Rage*	Homer Denius
SORC Champion	*Red Jacket*	Perry Connolly

The distinctive spinnaker quickly identifies 1970 Congressional Cup entrant Ted Hood of New York YC aboard Columbia 50 sloop *Cygnus* as it moves downwind ahead of Tom Fisher and his Great Lakes crew.

Event	Yacht	Owner
1969		
St. Petersburg–Venice	*Windward Passage*	Robert E. Johnson
St. Petersburg–Ft. Lauderdale	*American Eagle*	R. E. Turner III
Miami-Lucaya	*Touché*	Dr. Herbert Virgin
Lipton Cup	*Stampede*	Roland Becker
		George Dewar
Miami-Nassau	*Lively Lady II*	Mike Shea
Nassau Cup	*Windward Passage*	Robert E. Johnson
SORC Champion	*Salty Tiger*	Jack Powell and
		Wally Frank
1970		
St. Petersburg–Venice	*American Eagle*	R. E. Turner III
St. Petersburg–Ft. Lauderdale	*Equation*	Jack Potter
Miami-Lucaya	*Inferno*	James McHugh
Lipton Cup	*American Eagle*	R. E. Turner III
Miami-Nassau	*American Eagle*	R. E. Turner III
Nassau Cup	*American Eagle*	R. E. Turner III
SORC Champion	*American Eagle*	R. E. Turner III
1971		
St. Petersburg–Venice	*Sorcery*	James Baldwin
St. Petersburg–Ft. Lauderdale	*American Eagle*	R. E. Turner III
Miami-Lucaya	*Nepenthe*	T. V. Learson
Lipton Cup	*Panacea*	Jack Eckerd
Miami-Nassau	*Running Tide*	J. Isbrandtsen
Nassau Cup	*Dora*	Lynn Williams
SORC Champion	*Running Tide*	J. Isbrandtsen

One of the big winners in the SORC: *American Eagle.*

Other Major Distance Sailing Races

It is impossible, of course, to list all the distance sailing races held in the world. Here, however, is a list of major distance sailing events and their winners from 1966:

Event	Yacht	Owner
1966		
San Francisco–Newport (Calif.)	*Sally Lightfoot*	Wayne Kocher
Jacksonville-Savannah	*Fluff*	Sherrill Poulnot
Toronto-Rochester	*Red Jacket*	Perry Connolly
Skaw Race (Denmark)	*Ticonderoga*	Robert F. Johnson
Bermuda–Virginia Cape	*Huntress*	Morton Engel
New Orleans–Isla Mujeres	*Cal Gal*	Fred Maudlin
Port Huron–Mackinac	*Flying Buffalo*	Maury Declercq and Karl Ness
Block Island Race	*Kialoa*	J. B. Kilroy
Stamford YC Vineyard Race	*Thunderbird*	T. Vincent Learson
Cape May–Brenton Reef	*Dyna*	Clayton Ewing
Monhegan Island Race	*Robin Too*	Ted Hood
Swiftsure Race	*Terna*	Per Christofersen
Gulfport-Pensacola	*Goslin*	William Hayes
Edlu Trophy Race	*Thunderhead*	Paul Hoffman
Buckner Cup	*Montgomery Street*	Elly Dowd
Sydney-Hobart Race	*Cadence*	James Mason
Tampa–Tarpon Springs	*Panacea*	J. M. Eckhard
San Clemente Race	*Blue Marlin*	Max Smith
MORC Block Island Race	*Pickpocket*	E. Junn
Los Angeles–Mazatlan	*Debutante*	William Polly
San Diego–Ensenada	*Salacia*	Thomas Corketts
1967		
Miami–Montego Bay	*Vamoose*	R. E. Turner III
Long Beach–La Paz	*Conquest*	W. C. Polly
San Diego–Ensenada	*Auspicious*	Rob Batcher
Marblehead-Halifax	*Nina*	U.S. Merchant Marine Academy
Bayview-Mackinac	*Escapade*	Peter Grimm
Block Island Race (Storm Trysail)	*Palawan*	Thomas J. Watson
Stamford YC Vineyard Race	*Baccarat*	George Coumantaros
Monhegan Island Race	*Palawan*	Arthur K. Watson
Swiftsure Race	*Mara*	William Buchan
Vashon Island Race	*Mara*	William Buchan
Tri-Island Series	*Mara*	William Buchan
Gulfport-Pensacola	*Tiare*	Temple Brown, M. J. Hartson III
Biloxi–Isla Mujeres	*Tiare*	Temple Brown, M. J. Hartson III
Edlu Trophy Race	*Carina*	Richard S. Nye
Buckner Cup	*L'Allegro*	Rod Parks
Sydney-Hobart Race	*Rainbow II*	Chris Bouzaid
1968		
Los Angeles–Tahiti Race	*Aranji*	Henry Wheeler
San Diego–Ensenada	*Hilaria*	Dave Callender
Block Island Race (Storm Trysail)	*Inverness*	R. W. McCullough
Stamford YC Vineyard Race	*Windquest*	A. Justin Wasley
Monhegan Island Race	*Palawan*	Thomas J. Watson
Swiftsure Race	*Mistral*	J. C. Baillargeon
Stratford Shoal—City Island YC	*Sitzmark IV*	Walter Neuman
Stratford Shoal–Riverside YC	*Nike*	J. Christopher Meyer
Edlu Trophy	*Resistance*	N.Y.S. Maritime College
Stratford Shoal–Indian Harbor YC	*Quicksilver*	George Eddy
Port Huron–Mackinac	*Hilaria*	Hugh Scaddelle

Event	Yacht	Owner
Buenos Aires–Rio de Janeiro	*Ondine*	Sumner A. Long
Marina Del Rey–San Diego	*Jano III*	R. M. Kahn
Singlehanded Transatlantic, Plymouth, England–Newport, R.I.	*Sir Thomas Lipton*	Geoffrey Williams
Cartegna-Kingston	*Cocoban*	Not listed
China Sea	*Snow Goose IV*	Eric Holm
Sandy Hook–Chesapeake Bay	*Sitzmark IV*	Walter Neuman
Multihull Transpacific	*Polynesian Concept*	Buddy Ebsen
Victoria-Maui	*Porpoise III*	F. R. Killam
MORC Block Island	*Turkey*	Walter Fink
Sydney-Hobart	*Koomooloo*	Dennis O'Neil

1969

Event	Yacht	Owner
Singlehanded Transpacific (San Francisco–Tokyo)	*Pen-Duick V*	Eric Tabarly
Miami–Montego Bay	*Flyway*	Ogden R. Reid
St. Petersburg–Isla Mujeres	*Stampede*	Roland Becker
Vachon Island	*Nor'wester*	Doug Footh, Ken Browne, Joe Williams
Edlu	*The Hawk*	Ideal Partnership
Block Island (Storm Trysail)	*Ergo*	Conrad Jones
Swiftsure	*Diamond Head*	Henry L. Kotkins
New York–Bermuda Multihull	*Surf*	Martin Pollard
Marina Del Rey–San Diego	*Westerly*	Mark Segal, Ron Kaplan, Jerry Tannenberg
Transpacific (San Pedro–Honolulu)	*Argonaut*	Jon Andron
Marblehead-Halifax	*Summertime*	Irwin Tyson
Aegean Rally	*Errante*	John Vatis
Port Huron–Mackinac	*Diavolo*	Peter Stearn
Trans-Lake Superior	*Tigress*	George Lyon
Monhegan Island	*Salty Tiger*	Jack Powell, Wally Frank
Stamford YC–Vineyard	*Decibel*	Richard D. Lemmerman
Stratford Shoal–City Island YC	*Windbourne IV*	Harold B. Oldak
San Diego–Ensenada	*Serena*	Ken Wallis
Stratford Shoal–Indian Harbor YC	*Shearwater*	Thomas Young
Long Beach–La Paz	*Concerto*	John J. Hall
Chicago-Mackinac	*Bay Bea*	Pat Haggerty
San Francisco–Newport	*Grendal*	George Olson
Sydney-Hobart	*Morning Cloud*	Edward Heath

1970

Event	Yacht	Owner
China Sea Race	*Chita III*	Hiroaki Yoshida
Ft. Lauderdale–Charleston	*Jemel*	Charles Slingluff
St. Petersburg–Isla Mujeres	*Hombre*	Bruce Bidwell, Hugh Obrentz
Isla Mujeres–Naples	*American Eagle*	Ted Turner
Newport-Ensenada	*Encore*	Fred MacDonald
Galveston–Vera Cruz	*Utopia*	Gerald Smith
Vashon Island	*Mara*	William Buchan, Jr.
Edlu	*Sonny*	Albert D. Phelps, Jr.
Block Island (Storm Trysail)	*Ondine*	Sumner A. Long
Gulf of Farallones	*Arriba*	Bill Clute
Swiftsure	*Endless Summer*	George O'Brien
Cape May–Newport	*Jubilee III*	U.S. Naval Academy
San Diego–Papeete	*Widgeon*	G. Norman Bacon
San Francisco–Santa Barbara	*Quicksilver*	J. Greenlaw
Victoria-Maui	*Graybeard*	Lol Killam

Event	Yacht	Owner
Marina Del Rey–San Diego	*Adventure*	Jim Foyer
Multihull Transpac (Los Angeles–Diamond Head)	*Sea Bird*	Bob Hanel
Stratford Shoal–Riverside YC	*Challenge*	Bruce Lockwood, Allen Berrien, Barrows Peale
Bayview-Mackinac	*Charisma*	Jesse Phillips
Aegean Rally	*Errante*	John Vatis
Monhegan Island Race	*Gesture*	James L. Madden
Stamford Y.C.–Vineyard	*Carina*	Richard S. Nye
Stratford Shoal–City Island YC	*Thunderhead*	Paul Hoffman
Sandy Hook–Chesapeake Bay	*Salty Tiger*	Jack Powell, Wally Frank
San Diego–Ensenada	*Hilaria*	Ed Callender
Los Angeles–Mazatlan	*L'Allegro*	Roderick Park
Sydney-Hobart	*Pacha*	R. Crighton-Brown

One-Design Sailing Championships

As described in Section III, there are more than a thousand classes of sailboats in the world and a good majority have class championships. In this book we have selected the more popular classes and have listed the champions (national unless noted) since 1966:

Class	Skipper
1966	
Aqua Cat	Louis Banks East Norwalk, Conn.
Atlantic	Dr. T. G. Kantor Cedar Point YC
B Lion	Dave Boulter Toronto, Canada
Blue Jay	Billy Pagels Sayville, N.Y.
Cal 20	Dave Heggie King Harbor YC (Calif.)
Cal 24	Peter Ebling Cabrillo Beach YC (Calif.)
Cape Cod Mercury (keel)	John Bowers Scituate, Mass.
Cape Cod Mercury (centerboard)	Robert Early Boston, Mass.
Comet (International)	C. Thomas Wright Toledo, Ohio
Comet (Junior)	Art Ellis Weekapaug, R.I.
Cougar Catamaran	Arthur Murray Cedarhurst, N.Y.

Class	Skipper
Day Sailer	Wendell Davis Squantum, Mass.
DC-14	Dick and Dan Kix Miller Summit, N.J.
Dragon (European)	Buddy Friederichs New Orleans, La.
Duster	Peter Mullen Riverton, N.J.
Ensign	James Fulton Larchmont, N.Y.
E Scow	Runyon Colie Mantoloking, N.Y.
Finn (North America)	Peter Barrett Newport Harbor, Calif.
Finn (European)	H. Raudaschl Austria
Flying Junior (North America)	Robert Levine Manhasset Bay, N.Y.
5-0-5 (World)	Jim Hardy Australia
5-0-5 (North America)	Dr. Dennis Surtees Palo Alto YC (Calif.)
5.5-Meter (World)	Paul Elvstrom Hellerup, Denmark
5.5-Meter (United States)	Bill Luders Stamford, Conn.
Flying Dutchman (North America)	Dick Pitcher Royal Burnham YC (England)
Flying Dutchman	Bud Melges Zenda, Wis.
Flying Scot	Bill Wickes Toledo, Ohio

Class	Skipper	Class	Skipper
Flying Tern	Dr. H. M. K. Peddie Hallowell, Me.	Lightning (North America)	Bob Seidlemann Cherry Hill, N.J.
420 (World)	Francis Mouvet France	Luders 16 (International)	Charles Eshleman New Orleans, La.
420 (National and North America)	Charles Munitz	M Scow	Ed Smith Geneva, Ind.
GP 14	Jim Joss Cooper River YC (N.J.)	M-20	Bill Reier Lake Geneva, Wis.
Interlake	Art Barrie Toledo, Ohio	Mercury	Pat Bradley, Fresno, Calif., and Dick Thompson, Redwood City, Calif. (tied)
International 14	Baird Bardarson Seattle, Wash.	Moth	Doug Halsey St. Petersburg, Fla.
International 110	Chuck Rudinsky Boston, Mass.	Moth (Women)	Joan Filsinger Stone Harbor YC (N.J.)
International 210	Michael Cuddy Barrington, R.I.	Moth (Junior)	Bill Packer Ocean City YC (N.J.)
Jet 14	Max Culpepper Stratford, N.Y.	National One-Design	John and Roy Christianson Milwaukee, Wis.
Lido 14	Harris Hartman Mission Bay YC (Calif.)	OK Dinghy	Brian Thomas Mission Bay YC (Calif.)
Lido 14 (Junior)	Chris Drake Mission Bay YC (Calif.)	Pacific Catamaran	Hilyard Brown Cabrillo Beach YC (Calif.)

Day Sailers in their Nationals.

Class	Skipper	Class	Skipper
Peanut	Lou Jones West Islip, N.Y.	Scorpion	William Westerman Lancaster, Pa.
Pioneer	Ned Lawson	Shark Catamaran	Steve Dashew Los Angeles, Calif.
Penguin (International Senior)	Cliff Campbell Beachwood YC (N.J.)	Shields	Dave Smalley Rye, N.Y.
Penguin (International Junior)	Christiano Pontes Brasilia, Brazil	Snipe	Earl Elms San Diego, Calif.
Rainbow	George Maloney Wilmette, Ill.	Star (World)	Paul Elvstrom Hellerup, Denmark
Raven	Myers Noell Miami, Fla.	Star (North America)	Donald Trask San Francisco, Calif.
Rebel	Perry Brittain Dallas, Texas	Super Sailfish	Chuck Millington Plymouth, Mass.
Rhodes Bantam	Mark Gardner Erie, Pa.	Thistle	Walt Stubner East Hartford, Conn.
Rhodes 18	Henry Guard Greenwich Cove, Conn.	Town	Herbert Bruce Nahant, Mass.
Sabot (Senior)	Brian Thomas San Diego, Calif.	Triton	Stanley Mach Seacliff YC (N.Y.)
Sabot (Junior)	Alex Kimball Alamitos Bay YC (Calif.)	Y-Flyer	Gerald Callahan Oxford, Ohio

Start of the Mercury class Nationals.

Class	Skipper	Class	Skipper
1967		Celebrity	Joe Corbi
Amphibi-Con	Dr. Ethan Sims		Indian River YC
	Burlington, Vt.	Comet	Talbot Ingram
Aqua Cat	Jim Hazard	(International)	Shrewsbury, N.J.
	Swarthmore, Pa.	Comet	Isaac Braddock
Atlantic	Dr. T. G. Kantor	(Junior)	Namequoit, Mass.
	Cedar Point YC	DC-14	Jack and John Cormack
A Lion	Greer Ellis		Manlius, N.Y.
	Larchmont, N.Y.	Dragon	Bud Friedrichs
B Lion	Dave Boulter	(World)	New Orleans, La.
	Toronto, Canada	Ensign	Benjamin H. Byron, Jr.
Blue Jay	Bill Canning		Riverside, Conn.
	Groton, Conn.	E Scow	Brad Robinson
Bull's Eye	Mark and Henry Cohen		Minnetonka, Minn.
	Marblehead, Mass.	Finn	Arwed Von Gruenwaldt
Butterfly	Nick Coates	(European)	Sweden
	Lotawana, Mo.	Flying Junior	Hank Jotz
Cal 20	Les Marshall		San Francisco, Calif.
	Mission Bay YC (Calif.)	5-0-5	B. Moret and R. March
Cal 24	Pete Ebeling	(World)	France
Cape Cod Mercury	John Bowers	5-0-5	Sandy Van Zandt, Noank,
(keel)	Scituate Harbor, Mass.	(North America)	Conn., and Bill Healy, Ni-
Cape Cod Mercury	Robert Early		antic, Conn.
(centerboard)	Boston, Mass.		

The fleet leaving the weather mark in the National Butterfly Championship.

Class	Skipper	Class	Skipper
5.5-Meter	Don McNamara Boston, Mass.	Mercury	Douglas Baird Fresno, Calif.
Flying Dutchman	Bud Melges Lake Geneva, Wis.	Mobjack	Charles Ulmer, Jr. City Island, N.Y.
Flying Dutchman (World)	John Oakeley England	Moth (International)	Blair Fletcher Cherry Hill, N.J.
Flying Scot (North America)	Sandy Douglass Oakland, Md.	Moth	Lee Creekmore Miami, Fla.
Flying Tern	Randy Sprague Newton, N.J.	Moth (Women)	Joan Filsinger Stone Harbor YC (N.J.)
420 (World)	Michael Rogiers Belgium	Moth (Junior)	John Menz Wildwood, N.J.
420 (National and North America)	Jerry Drew Little Silver, N.J.	National One-Design	Roy Christianson Milwaukee, Wis.
Geary 18 (International)	Felix Moiteret Seattle, Wash.	OK Dinghy	Brian Thomas Mission Bay YC (Calif.)
Gemini	M. Moore Provincetown, Mass.	Pacific Catamaran	Phil Chase California YC
GP 14	Jim Joss Cooper River YC (N.J.)	Peanut	Axel Paulsen West Islip, N.Y.
Highlander (International)	Romeyn Everdell Concord, Mass.	Penguin (International Senior)	Robert and Beverly Smith Thousand Oaks, Calif.
International One-Design (World)	William Withnall Marblehead, Mass.	Penguin (International Junior)	Christiano Pontes and Jose Paradeda Brasilia, Brazil
International 110	Terry Ryan San Diego, Calif.	Raven	Bob Sellers Grosse Pointe, Mich.
International 210	Morton Bromfield Boston, Mass.	Rhodes Bantam	Paul Valigosky Toledo, Ohio
Islander 32	Bill Wetherill San Diego, Calif.	Rhodes 18	Ken Olsen Port Dennis YC (Mass.)
Jet 14	Hansi Bonn Chatham, N.J.	Rhodes 19	Dr. Robert Stine Mobile, Ala.
Jollyboat (all titles)	David Curtis Not listed	Robin	Ed Baltzell Philadelphia, Pa.
Lido 14	Harry Wood Alamitos Bay, Calif.	Schock 25	Jim Crabtree King Harbor YC (Calif.)
Lido 14 (Junior)	Mark Mason Newport Harbor, Calif.	Shields	Dick and Jim Sykes Port Washington, N.Y.
Lightning (North America)	Bruce Goldsmith Chicago, Ill.	6-Meter (North America)	Sunny Vynne Seattle, Wash.
Lightning (World)	Lou Pocharski Marblehead, Mass.	Snipe	Earl Elms San Diego, Calif.
Luders 16 (International)	Graham Ross Chicago, Ill.	Snipe (World)	Nelson Piccolo Porto Alegre, Brazil
M-20	Tom Gunderson Delavan, Wis.	Star (World)	Paul Elvstrom Hellerup, Denmark

Class	Skipper	Class	Skipper
Star (North America)	Alan Holt Seattle, Wash.	*1968* Amphibi-Con	Bill Dickinson Not listed
Tempest	Charles Ulmer, Jr. City Island, N.Y.	Aqua Cat	Duncan MacLane Newton, Conn.
Tempest (World)	Cliff Norbury and Roger Knight England	A Lion	Greer Ellis Larchmont, N.Y.
Thistle	Peter Brodes Brooklyn, N.Y.	B Lion	Dave Boulter Toronto, Canada
Town	Nathan Nichols Marblehead, Mass.	Blue Jay	John Whittle Shrewsbury YC (N.J.)
Wayfarer (North America)	Pete Bassin Kitchener, Ont.	Bull's Eye	Ingersoll Cunningham Beverly YC (Mass.)
Woodpussy	Dick Waschenfeld Fair Haven, N.J.	Butterfly	Duane and Irene Pierson White Lake, Mich.
Windmill	Paul Gernhardt Overland Park, Kansas	Cal 20	Henry Schofield Alamitos Bay YC
		Cal 24	Dave Johnson Not listed
Windmill (International)	John Bear Bradenton Beach, Fla.	Cal 28	Glenn Thorpe California YC
Y-Flyer (North America)	John Baker Savannah, Ga.	Cape Cod Mercury (keel)	Steven Mehl Satuit BC

A Windmill fleet on the move.

Class	Skipper	Class	Skipper
Cape Cod Mercury (centerboard)	Robert Early Boston, Mass.	Finn	Joerg Bruder Brazil
Celebrity	John Stratton Penn Manor SA	Finn (North America)	Carl Van Duyne Mantoloking YC
Comet (International)	Don McPherson Ithaca, N.Y.	Finn (European)	Arne Akerson Gevele, Sweden
Cottontail	Jim McAllister Stamford YC	Flying Junior	Steve Lewis Berkeley, Calif.
Day Sailer	Mike and Barbara Dunmire Arlete, Calif.	5-0-5 (World)	M. Troupel and F. Lanaverre France
DC-14	James Peterson Not listed	5.5-Meter	F. Gardner Cox Villanova, Pa.
Dragon (European)	Y. Animisov Russia	Flying Dutchman (North America)	Tom Allen Buffalo, N.Y.
Dragon (North America)	O. J. Young New Orleans, La.	Flying Scot (North America)	Franklin Bloomer Riverside YC
Ensign	Marvin Kapilow Not listed	Flying Tern	John Bradley Manchester YC (Mass.)
Dragon Gold Cup	Aage Birch Denmark	420 (World)	F. Bourdereau France
E Scow	Brad Robinson Minnetonka, Minn.	420 (National and North America)	Bill Simmons Annapolis, Md.

Brisk breezes and smooth waters bunch 24 young skippers from six nations in one of the tightly fought heats for the sixth International Optimist Dinghy Regatta in 1968. Sweden won first place, Denmark second, United States third in the sailing competition, which also attracted teams from England, Finland, and West Germany.

Class	Skipper	Class	Skipper
Geary 18 (International)	Jon Arden Santa Barbara, Calif.	Snipe	Earl Elms Mission Bay YC
GP 14 (North America)	Blair Fletcher Ocean City YC	Star (North America)	Tom Blackaller St. Francis YC
Highlander	Jack Clark Duxbury, Mass.	Tempest	William E. Kelly Larchmont, N.Y.
International One-Design (World)	Jonathan Wales Marblehead, Mass.	Tempest (World)	William E. Kelly Larchmont, N.Y.
Jet 14	Hansi Bonn Lavalette YC (N.J.)	Thistle	Dennis Clark Seattle, Wash.
Jollyboat (all titles)	Clint McKim Marblehead, Mass., and Roger Byrne Melbourne, Australia (co-champions)	Thunderbird	Toni Redstone Middle Harbor YC
		Town	Donald Stoddard Not listed
420 (Junior)	Peter Zona Squantum YC	210	Kenneth Drewry Not listed
Lido 14	Ed Rodriques Alamitos Bay, Calif.	Woodpussy	Don Colyer Navesink SS
Lightning (North America)	Tom Allen Buffalo, N.Y.	Windmill	Dr. Pat Hamilton Miami, Fla.
Luders 16 (International)	Jerome T. Coe Not listed	Y-Flyer (North America)	Gerald Callahan Trenton, Ohio
M-20	Bill Freytag Lake Geneva YC	*1969* Albacore	Jack Langmaid Oshawa, Ontario
Mercury	Doug Baird Fresno YC	Albacore (North America)	Dan Owen Royal Canadian YC (Ontario)
Mobjack	Peter W. Camp Not listed	Atlantic	Joe Olson Niantic YC (Conn.)
Moth	Doug Halsey St. Petersburg YC (Fla.)	B Lion	Dave Boulter Toronto, Ontario
National One-Design	Alan Lemke Milwaukee, Wis.	B Lion (North America)	Don McNair Niantic, Conn.
OK Dinghy	Chris Boome St. Francis YC	Barnegat 17	Ernie Dean Toms River YC (N.J.)
Pacific Catamaran	Joe and Ed Davis Mission Bay YC	Blue Jay	Todd Field Port Washington YC (N.Y.)
Peanut	Louis Jones Long Island YC	Bull's Eye	Henderson Inches, Jr. Mattapoisett YC (Mass.)
Raven	Bruce McKeige Manhasset Bay YC (N.Y.)	Butterfly	Nick Coates Aspen, Colo.
Rebel	George Carr Clark Lake YC (Mich.)	Cal 20	Norm Baxter Kaneohe YC (Hawaii)
Rhodes 19	Art Anderson St. Petersburg YC	Cal 40	Ken Croan Los Angeles YC
Robin	Chip Stark Corinthian YC	Cape Cod Knockabout	John J. Valois Woods Hole YC (Mass.)
Shields	Jim and Dick Sykes Port Washington, N.Y.	Cape Cod Mercury (keel)	James Anthrem Nahant BC (Mass.)

Class	Skipper	Class	Skipper
Cape Cod Mercury (centerboard)	George McInnis Community BC (Mass.)	E Scow	Bud Melges Lake Geneva YC (Wis.)
Celebrity	Mort and Richard Sork Not listed	El Toro (North America Senior)	Mark Briggman San Jose, Calif.
Comet (Junior)	Rick Warren Surf City YC (N.J.)	El Toro (North America Intermediate)	Robert Nelson Lake Merritt SC (Calif.)
Comet (North America)	Carl Chapman Avalon YC (N.J.)	El Toro (North America Junior)	Greg Paxton San Jose, Calif.
Comet (International)	Talbott Ingram Shrewsbury YC (N.J.)	Endeavor	George Haine California YC
Coronado 15	Henry Sprague III Long Beach, Calif.	Ensign	Albert Weiser Fall River, Mass.
Coronado 25	Henry Sprague III Long Beach, Calif.	Enterprise	Jim Hoffman King Harbor YC (Calif.)
Cottontail	Bruce Kennedy Narrasketuck YC (N.Y.)	Etchells 22	Timothea S. Larr Seawanhaka Corinthian YC (N.Y.)
Day Sailer (North America)	Edwin Richardson Corinthian YC (Mass.)	Finn	Joerg Bruder Sao Paulo, Brazil
Dragon (North America)	Bill Henry Corinthian YC (Wash.)	Finn (North America)	Gordon Bowers Not listed
Dragon (European)	Axel Holm Denmark	Fireball	John Lovett Cleveland, Ohio
Dragon (World)	Bob Mosbacher United States		
Duster	Dave Styer Riverton YC (N.J.)		

The start of first race for the 1969 B Lion National Championship.

Class	Skipper	Class	Skipper
Fireball (North America)	Robert Griggs Edgewater YC (Ohio)	International 110	Mike Cuddy Providence, R.I.
5-0-5 (North America)	Dennis Surtees Los Altos, Calif.	International Tempest	Andrew T. Kostanecki Noroton YC (Conn.)
5-0-5 (World)	Vic Deschamps and Larry Marks England	International Tempest (World)	Cliff Norbury England
5.5-Meter	Ted Turner Atlanta, Ga.	International 210	Douglass MacGregor Hingham, Mass.
5.5-Meter (World)	Jean-Marie Le Guillou France	Jet 14 (Junior)	David Eck Pines Lake SC (N.J.)
Flying Dutchman	Chris Chatain Wilmette, Ill.	Jet 14	Hans Bonn Lavallette YC (N.J.)
Flying Dutchman (North America)	Roger Green Toronto, Ontario	Jollyboat (North America)	Clint McKim Marblehead, Mass.
Flying Dutchman (World)	Rodney Pattison England	Kite	Peter Parker Newport Harbor YC (Calif.)
Flying Junior	Steve and Randy Lewis Berkeley, Calif.	Lido 14 (Junior)	Kurt Wiese Balboa YC (Calif.)
Flying Junior (North America)	Ian McAllister Ottawa, Ontario	Lido 14	Dave Ullman Balboa YC (Calif.)
Flying Junior (World)	Duuk van Heel Holland	Lightning (North America)	Tom Allen Buffalo, N.Y.
Flying Scot (North America)	Jack Laird Panama City, Fla.	Luders 16 (International)	Graham Ross Chicago, Ill.
Flying Tern	John Bradley Manchester, Mass.	M-20	Bill Freytag Lake Geneva, Wis.
420 (Junior)	Eric Sorensen Greenwich, Conn.	Mariner	Bill Finkle Wantagh, N.Y.
420 (World)	Z. Karmel Israel	Mercury	Doug Baird San Jose, Calif.
Geary 18 (International)	Felix Moiteret Seattle, Wash.	Mobjack	David Berger Potomac River SA
Gemini	Bill Curby Newton, Mass.	Moth	Doug Halsey St. Petersburg YC (Fla.)
GP-14	Al Hopkin Ocean City YC (N.J.)	Moth (Women)	Carol Zimmerman Sea Isle City YC (N.J.)
Hampton One-Design	Eddie Williams Hampton YC (Va.)	Moth (Junior)	John Moscowitz Cooper River YC (N.J.)
Highlander (International)	Tom Smith Hoover YC (Ohio)	Moth (World)	David McKay Australia
Hobie Catamaran	R. Paul Allen Bahia Corinthian YC (Calif.)	National One-Design	Bill Steel Leland, Mich.
Interlake	Dave White Columbus, Ohio	OK Dinghy	Emery Kamps Fort Lauderdale, Fla.
International One-Design (World)	Bert Damner San Francisco YC (Calif.)	OK Dinghy (North America)	Gene Coleman Sequoia YC (Calif.)
		OK Dinghy (World)	Kent Carlsson Sweden

Class	Skipper	Class	Skipper
Pacific Catamaran	Norm Marchment Malibu YC (Calif.)	Star (World)	Pelle Petterson Sweden
Peanut	Kurt Finni Youngstown, Ohio	Sunfish (North America Senior Singles)	Carl Knight Mamaroneck, N.Y.
Penguin (International Junior)	Gregorio Pontes Brazil	Sunfish (North America Senior Doubles)	John Cort Roxbury, Mass.
Penguin (International)	Robert Johnstone Skokie, Ill.	Super Sailfish (Junior Singles)	Ken Evans Smoke Rise SC (N.J.)
Pram	Scooter Kinsey Fort Myers, Fla.	Super Sailfish (Senior Singles)	Jack Evans, Jr. Smoke Rise SC (N.J.)
Rainbow	Richard Hasse Wilmette, Ill.	Thistle	Jim Miller Oyster Bay, N.Y.
Raven	Bill Pagels Sayville Wet Pants (N.Y. Assoc.)	Tornado	Bruce Stewart Cabrillo Beach YC (Calif.)
Rebel	Ed Fromme Toledo, Ohio	Triton	Gene Yates Sausalito YC (Calif.)
Rhodes Bantam	C. K. Bloomer Newark, N.Y.	Victory	Homer Deming Mission Bay YC (Calif.)
Rhodes 19	Richard Saltmarsh New Bedford YC (Mass.)	Wayfarer	Fred Ungers Detroit, Mich.
Robin	Bob Seybold Brant Beach, N.J.	Wayfarer (North America)	Mike Schoenborn Queen City YC (Toronto)
Santana 22	Tom Leweck California YC	Windmill (International)	Ed Laviano Bellport, N.Y.
Shark Catamaran	Al Perrin Canandaigua, N.Y.	Y-Flyer	Martin B. Jones, Jr. Columbia, S.C.
Shields	Patrick O'Neal Larchmont YC (N.Y.)	Y-Flyer (International)	Randall Swan Charleston, S.C.
Skimmer	Barney Warner Mission Bay YC (Calif.)	*1970* A Scow	Bill Perrigo Pewaukee, Wis.
Skipjack	Phil Ransome Hayes, Va.	Albacore	Dave Wallerstein Washington, D.C.
Snipe (Junior)	Augustin Diaz Miami, Fla.	Albacore (North America)	Donald Barnes Royal Hamilton YC (Ontario)
Snipe	Earl Elms Mission Bay YC (Calif.)	Aqua Cat	Duncan MacLane Locust Valley, N.Y.
Snipe (World)	Earl Elms Mission Bay YC (Calif.)	Atlantic	Lou Michaels Cedar Point YC (Conn.)
Soling (North America)	John Dane New Orleans, La.	B Lion	Dave Boulter Toronto, Ontario
Soling (World)	Paul Elvstrom Denmark	Blue Jay	Bill Pagels Sayville, N.Y.
Star (North America)	Barton Beck Los Angeles, Calif.	Bull's Eye	Edward Brainard Not listed
Star (Europe)	Borje Larsson Sweden	Butterfly	Ande Holly Muskegon, Mich.

Class	Skipper	Class	Skipper
C-Lark	Rick Martin Univ. of Washington YC	Coronado 25 (World)	Ray Miller Palo Alto YC (Calif.)
Cal 20	Bud Gardner King Harbor YC (Calif.)	Cottontail	Reginald Page Stamford, Conn.
Cal 28	Ray Corbett Cabrillo Beach YC (Calif.)	Cougar Catamaran	James Bryant Memphis, Tenn.
Cal 2-30	Don Bekins San Francisco YC	DC-14	James Peterson Not listed
Cal 40	Jon Andron Los Angeles YC	Day Sailer (North America)	Louis Wagoner Fresno, Calif.
Cape Cod Mercury (centerboard)	Ed Shaw Community Boating of Boston	Dragon	Bill Henry Seattle, Wash.
Cape Cod Mercury (keel)	Jim Antrim Nahant, Mass.	Dragon (North America)	Buddy Friedrichs, Jr. New Orleans, La.
Celebrity	Ed Lippman Penn Manor SA	Dragon (European)	Paul Borowski East Germany
Columbia 26	Don Wilson Bahia Corinthian YC (Calif.)	Duster	Jim Walter, Jr. Pine Lakes SC (N.J.)
Columbia 50	Robert Grant Newport Harbor YC (Calif.)	E Scow	Bill Allen Lake Minnetonka, Minn.
Comet (Junior)	Scott Williams Stone Harbor, N.J.	El Toro (North America Junior)	Jim Maloney San Jose SC (Calif.)
Comet (North America)	Don McPherson Ithaca, N.Y.	El Toro (North America Intermediate)	Bill Gerth San Jose SC (Calif.)
Comet (Internatonal)	Jack Boehringer Cooper River, N.J.	El Toro (North America Senior)	Henry Jotz Lake Merritt SC (Calif.)
Coronado 15	Tom McLaughlin Mission Bay YC (Calif.)		

Albacore class boats at their North American Championships.

Class	Skipper	Class	Skipper
Endeavor	Tom Moore South Shore SC (Calif.)	470 (World)	Yves and Harve Carré France
Ensign	Rollin Whyte Narragansett Bay, R.I.	GP-14	Carl Chapman Avalon YC (N.J.)
Enterprise	Hugh Warnock Seal Beach YC (Calif.)	GP-14 (North America)	Bill Blumenstein Cooper River YC (N.J.)
Ericson 26	Emil Karawan South Bay YRC (Calif.)	Hampton One-Design	Lou Michaels Cedar Point YC (Conn.)
Ericson 30	Don Hanhart King Harbor YC (Calif.)	Highlander	Tom Smith Columbus, Ohio
Etchells 22	Timothea and Dave Larr Seawanhaka Corinthian YC (N.Y.)	Hobie Catamaran	Cappy Sheeley Waikiki YC (Hawaii)
Excalibur 26	Bill Hartge Huntington Harbor YC (Calif.)	International 14	Baird Bardarson Seattle, Wash.
Finn	Bob Andre San Diego, Calif.	International One-Design (World)	Stuart B. Rowe, Jr. Horseshoe Harbor YC (N.Y.)
Finn (North America)	Carl Van Duyne Naval Academy S.S.	International 110	Mark O'Connor Marblehead, Mass.
Finn (European)	Thomas Lundquist Sweden	International Tempest	John and James Linville Larchmont, N.Y.
Fireball	O. H. Rodgers Tampa, Fla.	International 210	Norman Cressy Marblehead, Mass.
Fireball (North America)	Peter Bateman England	Jet 14 (Junior)	Chad McLoughlin Saratoga Lake YC (N.Y.)
5-0-5 (North America)	Dennis Surtees Palo Alto YC (Calif.)	Jet 14	Peter Jones Washington, D.C.
5.5-Meter	Ted Turner Atlanta, Ga.	Jollyboat	Jo Ann Mayer Marblehead, Mass.
5.5-Meter (World)	David Forbes Australia	Kite	C. E. Williams Bahia Corinthian YC (Calif.)
Flying Dutchman	Hans Fogh Royal Canadian YC (Ont.)	Lido 14 (Junior)	Dovell Smith Newport Beach, Calif.
Flying Dutchman (North America)	David Croshere California YC	Lido 14	Dave Ullman Balboa YC (Calif.)
Flying Dutchman (World)	Rodney Patterson England	Lightning (North America)	Tom Allen Buffalo, N.Y.
Flying Junior	Fred Paxton San Jose, Calif.	Luders 16 (International)	Leroy Sutherland Newport Beach, Calif.
Flying Scot (North America)	Paul Schreck Lillian, Ala.	M Scow	Jane Pegel Chicago, Ill.
Flying Tern (International)	George Baird Sagamore YC (N.Y.)	M-20	Bill Freytag Lake Geneva, Wis.
420	Steve Mehl Not listed	Mariner	Al Czajkowski Worcester, Mass.
420 (World)	John Gilder Australia	Mercury	Roger Roessler Santa Barbara YC (Calif.)
470	Peter Barrett Pewaukee, Wis.	Mobjack	Robert S. Perry, Jr. Crofton, Md.

Class	Skipper
Moth (North America Junior)	Andy Lawson Surf City YC (N.J.)
Moth (North America Women)	Kathy Mullen Surf City YC (N.J.)
Moth (North America Senior)	Bob Patterson Sea Isle City YC (N.J.)
National One-Design (World)	John Makielski South Bend, Ind.
OK Dinghy	Dennis Clark Corinthian YC (Wash.)
OK Dinghy (North America)	Gary Carlin Not listed
OK Dinghy (World)	Kent Carlsson Sweden
Pacific Catamaran	Paul Allen Bahia Corinthian YC (Calif.)
Pram (Junior)	Craif Haas Coral Reef YC (Fla.)
Pram	Scooter Kinsey Fort Myers, Fla.
Rainbow	Alfred Fay Annapolis, Md.
Raven	Bill Pagels Sayville, N.Y.
Rebel	Jack Bartlett Hurton Portage YC
Rhodes Bantam (International)	Sebald Korn Owasco YC (N.Y.)
Rhodes 19	Martha Martin San Francisco YC
Robin	Charles Kipp Little Egg Harbor YC (N.J.)
Sabot	Hank Schofield Alamitos Bay YC (Calif.)
Sailfish (Junior)	Bill Cofer Hampton YC (Va.)
Sailfish (Senior)	Jack Evans, Jr. Smoke Rise SC (N.J.)
Santana 27	Glenn Reed South Shore SC (Calif.)
Shark Catamaran	Stan Woodruff Detroit, Mich.
Shields	Lance McCabe Balboa YC (Calif.)

Class	Skipper
6-Meter (North America)	Tom Blackaller San Francisco, Calif.
Skimmer	William Movius Mission Bay YC (Calif.)
Skipjack (North America)	Barry Lewis San Diego, Calif.
Snipe	Earl Elms San Diego, Calif.
Snipe (North America	August Diaz Miami, Fla.
Soling (North America)	Dave Curtis Marblehead, Mass.
Soling (World)	Stig Wennerstrom Sweden
Star (North America)	Durward Knowles Nassau, Bahamas
Star (World)	Bill Buchan United States
Sunfish (North America Junior)	Jeff Howell Rio Piedras, Puerto Rico
Sunfish (North America Senior Singles)	Dick Griffith St. Thomas, U.S. Virgin Islands
Sunfish (North America Senior Doubles)	Arden Farey Winnetka YC (Ill.)
Sunfish (World)	Gary Hoyt San Juan, Puerto Rico
Thistle	Kent Foster Cincinnati, Ohio
Thunderbird (World)	Tony Parkes Australia
Wayfarer	Larry Bacow Pontiac, Mich.
Windmill	Richard Schmidt Greenbelt, Md.
Windmill (International)	John Dane III New Orleans, La.

Yachting's One-of-a-Kind Regatta

The One-of-a-Kind regatta was begun in 1949 by *Yachting* magazine to create a venue where skippers of different one-design classes could settle their "my boat is better than your boat" differences. While several other similar events have sprung up in various areas, the

Yachting classic is the best known. At present, four of the five divisions race over a 10-statute-mile Olympic-style course consisting of a triangle followed by a beat and a run. Division V, for cruising auxiliaries up to 30 feet in length, sails on an adjoining course. The other four divisions are as follows: Division I, multihulls (catamarans and trimarans) and large scows; Division II, trapeze centerboarders and small scows; Division III, conventional centerboarders; and Division IV, racing keelboats. The overall winner is picked on the basis of comparative performance within a division. Since each class of boat in the regatta is different from the others in terms of size and sail area, the boats are rated on the basis of a formula utilizing overall length, waterline length, and sail area. From these ratings, judges determine winners in each division as well as the overall regatta winner. Previous winning classes and the skippers are as follows:

Year	Place	Winners
1949	Noroton, Conn.	Overall and elapsed: E Scow, Runyon Colie
1952	Riverside, Conn.	Overall: C Scow, William Freytag Elapsed: E Scow, Runyon Colie
1954	Riverside, Conn.	Overall: 5-0-5, Eric Olsen Elapsed: E Scow, Harry Melges
1959	Coconut Grove, Fla.	Overall: Tigercat, Eric Olsen Elapsed: A Scow, Harry Melges
1963	Coconut Grove, Fla.	Overall and elapsed: Beverly Class C catamaran, Van Alan Clark
1966	St. Petersburg, Fla.	Overall: International 14, Dr. Stuart Walker Elapsed: A Scow, William Bentsen
1969	Chicago, Ill.	Overall: Thistle, James Miller Elapsed: Wildwind Class D catamaran, Charles Tobias

America's Teacup

This is a one-of-a-kind event for monohull class boats priced less than $1,000 and class multihulls below $1,200. Sponsored by *One-Design & Offshore Yachtsman,* the name is not intended as a flippant reference to that big mug which is raced for by big boats, but rather chosen to describe a truly North American gathering of the smaller kind of racing sailboats. The 1970 overall winners in the various categories are as follows:

Division	I	(Multihulls): Hobie Cat 14
Division	II	(Planing centerboard): Laser and Banshee (tied)
Division	III	(Scows): Scamp
Division	IV	(Boardboats): Sunfish
Division	V	(Canoes): Sawyer Canoe
Division	VI	(Day sailers): Ghost 13
Division	VII	(Dinghies): Montgomery Dinghy

Sears Cup (Junior Sailing Championship)

The Sears Cup was first placed in competition in the year 1921 by Commodore Herbert M. Sears of the Eastern Yacht Club, Marblehead, Mass., as a trophy emblematic of the Junior Sailing Championship to be competed for annually by youths between fifteen and eighteen years of age, whose parents or guardians were members of Massachusetts yacht clubs.

In 1922 the restriction, in regard to contestants being members of a yacht club in the state of Massachusetts, was removed and crews from the Larchmont Yacht Club, the Seawanhaka Corinthian Yacht Club, and the Cedarhurst Yacht Club, were invited to compete.

The Eastern Yacht Club continued to conduct a series of matches for the cup each year up to and including 1930. In 1931 the deed of gift was changed so that thereafter the contests have been conducted under the direction of the North American Yacht Racing Union. The cup has now been deeded to the NAYRU with the executive committee acting as trustees. By action taken by the executive committee in January, 1951, final races for the Sears Cup can be conducted by a yacht club located anywhere in North America. In 1955 the West Coast was included as an area, and in 1956 California was specially named as an area.

The deed of gift and trust agreement provides in effect that competition for the cup shall be open to crews of three boys or girls who have reached their thirteenth birthday and have not reached their eighteenth birthday by September 1 of the year in which they compete and who are members or whose parents are members of a recognized yacht club in North America. Here are winning yacht clubs and skippers since its start in 1921:

1921	Pleon Yacht Club, R. S. Thayer
1922	Larchmont Yacht Club, Arthur Knapp, Jr.
1923	Duxbury Yacht Club, Raymond Hunt
1924	Pleon Yacht Club, H. B. Thayer, Jr.
1925	Duxbury Yacht Club, Raymond Hunt
1926	Duxbury Yacht Club, John S. Wilbor
1927	Chatham Yacht Club, C. Ashley Hardy, Jr.
1928	Beverly Yacht Club, William B. Cudahy
1929	Bar Harbor Yacht Club, William B. Cudahy
1930	Vineyard Haven Yacht Club, William S. Cox
1931	Beverly Yacht Club, Michael Cudahy
1932	Eastern Yacht Club, Chandler Hovey, Jr.
1933	Vineyard Haven YC, Frank B. Jewett, Jr.
1934	Vineyard Haven YC, Frank B. Jewett, Jr.
1935	Vineyard Haven Yacht Club, John H. Ware, Jr.
1936	Vineyard Haven Yacht Club, John H. Ware, Jr.
1937	Pequot Yacht Club, Charles P. Stetson
1938	Pequot Yacht Club, Robert E. Gordon
1939	Annisquam Yacht Club, Richard W. Mechem
1940	Eastern Yacht Club, Robert E. Coulson
1941	Eastern Yacht Club, Robert E. Coulson
1946	Stage Harbour Yacht Club, William R. McClay
1947	The Buzzards Yacht Club, Michael Jackson
1948	Vineyard Haven Yacht Club, Douglas Cassel
1949	Cohasset Yacht Club, Kingsley Durant
1950	Pleon Yacht Club, Kingsley Durant
1951	Rocky Point Sailing Club, George Reichhelm
1952	Indian Harbor Yacht Club, Martin A. Purcell
1953	Sandusky Sailing Club, Dave Ortmann

Boats in America's Teacup get ready to sail.

1954	Kingston Yacht Club, Harry D. M. Jemmett
1955	Royal Canadian Yacht Club, A. R. Lennox
1956	Seattle Corinthian Yacht Club, Alan Holt
1957	Pequot Yacht Club, John Merrifield
1958	Noroton Yacht Club, Kevin Jaffe
1959	Hudson Yacht Club, John Welch
1960	Royal Vancouver Yacht Club, David Miller
1961	Pleon Yacht Club, Steven Wales
1962	Newport Harbor YC, Henry Sprague, III
1963	Milford Yacht Club, Whit Batchelor
1964	Corinthian YC, Marblehead, Robert E. Doyle
1965	Corinthian YC, Marblehead, Robert E. Doyle
1966	Monmouth Boat Club, Robert Held
1967	Southern Yacht Club, John Dane, III
1968	Galveston Bay Cruising Assoc., John Kolius
1969	Noroton Yacht Club, Manton D. Scott
1970	Houston Yacht Club, Daniel Williams

Adams Trophy (Women's North American Sailing Championship)

The original trophy, emblematic of the Women's Sailing Championship, was the Hodder Cup, placed in competition by Commodore James R. Hodder of the Boston Yacht Club in 1924 and was won by the Cohasset Yacht Club. Thereafter in 1925, Charles Francis Adams presented a cup in honor of his wife, and it was retired in 1929, having been won three times by the Cohasset Yacht Club, Cohasset, Mass.

In 1930 the Indian Harbor Yacht Club retired the trophy again, and a perpetual Challenge Trophy was placed in competition by Mrs. Charles Francis Adams. In 1951, when the American Yacht Club at Rye, N.Y., burned down, the trophy was destroyed, and then replaced by Henry S. Morgan, son-in-law of Mrs. Adams, with assistance from the American Yacht Club and the Women's National Yacht Racing Association. Here are the winners since its start in 1924:

1924	Cohasset Yacht Club, Ruth Sears
1925	Cohasset Yacht Club, Ruth Sears
1926	Cohasset Yacht Club, Jessie Bancroft
1927	Indian Harbor Yacht Club, Lorna Whittelsey
1928	Indian Harbor Yacht Club, Lorna Whittelsey
1929	Cohasset Yacht Club, Frances Williams
1930	Indian Harbor Yacht Club, Lorna Whittelsey
1931	Indian Harbor Yacht Club, Lorna Whittelsey
1932	Edgartown Yacht Club, Clair Dinsmore
1933	Cohasset Yacht Club, Ruth Sears

The 1963 Sears competition went right down to the wire before the series winner was decided. In this second race *Mantoloking* and *Milford* near the finish line as the judges keep a careful watch. *Mantoloking* was the winner of this race in Ensign class boats.

1934   Indian Harbor Yacht Club, Lorna Whittelsey
1935   Cohasset Yacht Club, Frances McElwain
1936   Cohasset Yacht Club, Frances McElwain
1937   Cohasset Yacht Club, Frances McElwain
1939   American Yacht Club, Sylvia Shethar
1940   American Yacht Club, Sylvia Shethar
1941   Riverside Yacht Club, Lois MacIntyre
1946   Edgartown Yacht Club, Virginia Weston Besse
1947   American Yacht Club, Sylvia Shethar Everdell
1948   Larchmont Yacht Club, Aileen Sheilds
1949   Portland Yacht Club, Jane Smith
1950   American Yacht Club, Allegra Knapp Mertz
1951   Seal Harbor Yacht Club, Jane Smith
1952   Manhasset Bay Yacht Club, Pat Hinman
1953   Riverside Yacht Club, Judy Webb
1954   American Yacht Club, Allegra Knapp Mertz
1955   Manhasset Bay Yacht Club, Toni Monetti
1956   Fort Worth Boat Club, Glen Hill Lattimore
1957   Chicago Yacht Club, Jane Pegel
1958   American Yacht Club, Nancy Underhill Meade
1959   American Yacht Club, Allegra Knapp Mertz
1960   Delray Beach Yacht Club, Pat Duane
1961   Seawanhaka Yacht Club, Timothea Schneider
1962   Noroton Yacht Club, Susan W. Sinclair
1963   American Yacht Club, Allegra Knapp Mertz
1964   Lake Geneva (Wisconsin) YC, Jane Pegel
1965   Seawanhaka YC, Timothea Schneider Larr
1966   Corinthian Yacht Club, Seattle, Jerie Clark
1967   Indian Harbor Yacht Club, Betty Weed Foulk
1968   Monmouth Boat Club, June Methot
1969   Mantoloking Yacht Club, Jan O'Malley
1970   Mantoloking Yacht Club, Jan O'Malley

Clifford D. Mallory Cup (North American Sailing Championship)

In 1952, yachtsmen for the first time competed for a North American Sailing Championship. The trophy, the Clifford D. Mallory Cup, for this important new event was presented by the family of the late Clifford D. Mallory, first president of the North American Yacht Racing Union. Twenty of the twenty-three member associations of the NAYRU entered crews in the first event, the eight finalists meeting at Mystic, Conn. The winner and first North American Sailing Champion was Cornelius Shields, representing the Yacht Racing Association of Long Island Sound.

The series in 1952 was open only to men eighteen years of age and older. In 1953 the regulations were changed to permit crew members to be either male or female. The skipper, however, must be a man. The winning skippers are as follows:

1952   YRA of Long Island Sound, Cornelius Shields
1953   Gulf YA, Eugene H. Walet III

The Mallory Cup quarter-finals in 1968 were sailed in Tempest class boats.

1954	Gulf YA, Eugene H. Walet III
1955	Pacific International YA, William Buchan, Jr.
1956	YRU of Massachusetts Bay, Fred E. Hood
1957	YRU of Massachusetts Bay, George D. O'Day
1958	Texas YA, Robert Mosbacher
1959	Inland Lake YA, Harry C. Melges, Jr.
1960	Inland Lake YA, Harry C. Melges, Jr.
1961	Inland Lake YA, Harry C. Melges, Jr.
1962	Inland Lake YA, James S. Payton
1963	YRA of San Francisco Bay, James DeWitt
1964	Gulf YA, G. Shelby Fredrichs, Jr.
1965	YRA of Long Island Sound, Cornelius Shields, Jr.
1966	YRA of Long Island Sound, William S. Cox, Jr.
1967	Barnegat Bay YRA, Clifford W. Campbell
1968	Southern Massachusetts YRA, James H. Hunt
1969	YRA of Long Island Sound, Graham M. Hall
1970	Dixie Inland YA, Dr. John Jennings

George D. O'Day Trophy (North American Single-Handed Championship)

In 1962 George D. O'Day awarded to the NAYRU a trophy known as the George D. O'Day Trophy. The trophy is to be sailed for in single-handed boats and the winner is to be known as the North American Single-Handed Champion.

Competition is open to representatives of yacht racing associations belonging to the NAYRU and also to yachtsmen and women representing the Inter-Collegiate Yacht Racing Association. The trophy was first sailed for in 1962, in Finns on Long Island Sound. Winners follow:

1962	Peter J. Barrett, Madison, Wis.
1963	Henry Sprague, III, Newport Beach, Calif.
1964	Robert Andre, San Diego, Calif.
1965	Colin Park, Vancouver, B.C.
1966	Norman D. Freeman, Ithaca Yacht Club
1967	Charles Barthrop, U.S. Merchant Marine Academy
1968	Gordon Bowers, Jr., Minnetonka YC, Minn.
1969	Gordon Bowers, Jr., Minnetonka YC, Minn.
1970	Robert E. Doyle, Marblehead, Mass.

Prince of Wales Bowl (North American Inter-Club Match-Race Championship)

Match-race competition for the Prince of Wales Bowl started in 1931 at the Acadia Yacht Club under the sponsorship of the Royal Nova Scotia Yacht Squadron. Competition was held for crews under nineteen years of age among clubs on the Eastern Seaboard. The trophy was permanently retired by the Vineyard Haven Yacht Club in 1937. In 1965 the Vineyard Haven Yacht Club restored the Prince of Wales Bowl to active competition as a perpetual trophy for inter-club match racing in North America. The first two winners in the current series were champions of the Southern Massachusetts Yacht Racing Association; from 1967 on the winners were North American champions. Although competition is between clubs, the skipper of the crew winning the North American finals is the North American Yacht Racing Union Champion:

Winners of Original Series

1931	Pleon Yacht Club
1932	Beverly Yacht Club
1933	Eastern Yacht Club
1934	Vineyard Haven Yacht Club
1935	Vineyard Haven Yacht Club
1936	Eastern Point Yacht Club
1937	Vineyard Haven Yacht Club

Winners of Current Series

1965	Beverly Yacht Club, Charles Shumway
1966	Nantucket Yacht Club, Peter Jost
1967	Newport Harbor Yacht Club, Scott Allan
1968	Newport Harbor Yacht Club, Burke Sawyer
1969	Quissett Yacht Club, E. M. Burt
1970	St. Petersburg YC, Dr. John Jennings

Nathanael G. Herreshoff Trophy

The Nathanael G. Herreshoff Trophy, which was donated by the National Association of Engine & Boat Manufacturers, is awarded annually by the North American Yacht Racing Union to the individual who, in the opinion of a NAYRU selection committee, has contributed most during the past year to the sport of sailing in North America, whether as skipper, crewman, designer, builder, writer, or in any other activity connected with the sport. Winners are as follows:

1957	Henry Sears
1958	Henry S. Morgan
1960	George D. O'Day
1961	James M. Trenary
1962	Julian K. Roosevelt
1963	R. S. Stevenson
1964	Olin J. Stephens II
1965	Leonard Munn Fowle
1966	Allegra Knapp Mertz
1967	Everett B. Morris
1968	Harold Stirling Vanderbilt
1969	Paul H. Smart
1970	F. Gregg Bemis

St. Petersburg Yacht Club Trophy

The St. Petersburg Yacht Club Trophy is awarded annually to the North American Yacht Club which does the best job of running a championship regatta for a major one-design class. This trophy, for which *One-Design & Offshore Yachtsman* magazine serves as trustee, has been awarded to:

1967	Royal Canadian Yacht Club, Toronto
1968	Alamitos Bay Yacht Club, Long Beach, Calif.
1969	Long Beach Yacht Club, Long Beach, Calif.
1970	Not awarded

Martini & Rossi's Yachtsman and Yachtswoman of the Year Awards

These annual awards are made to the outstanding sailing man and woman for the year as selected by a panel of distinguished yachting writers. Former winners were:

1961	Harry C. Melges, Jr.
	Timothea Schneider
1962	Emil Mosbacher, Jr.
	Susan W. Sinclair
1963	Joseph Duplin
	Allegra Knapp Mertz

1964	Robert N. Bavier, Jr.
	Jane Pegel
1965	Richard L. Tillman
	Timothea Schneider Larr
1966	William S. Cox
	Jerie L. Clark
1967	Emil Mosbacher, Jr.
	Betty Weed Foulk
1968	Lowell North
	Jane Methot
1969	Robert F. Johnson
	Jan Chance O'Malley
1970	R. E. Turner III
	Jan Chance O'Malley

Henry A. Morss Trophy

The Morss Trophy is awarded to the winner of Inter-Collegiate Yacht Racing Association of North America dinghy championship finals. When the Dinghy Championship was launched in 1937 at the Charles River Basin in front of the campus of Massachusetts Institute of Technology, Cambridge, Mass., the ICYRA numbered eight colleges. Now its rolls total over a hundred. The finalists for the Morss Trophy must survive a series of district eliminations. At present there are eight districts: Northwest, Ontario, South Atlantic, Southeastern Atlantic, Middle Atlantic, Midwest, New England, and Pacific Coast. Past winners are as follows:

OK Dinghy fleet charges over the starting line in the 1965 O'Day Trophy Championship, which pitted top United States and Canadian sailors in a nine-race series. Canadian Colin Park won the trophy.

Year	Winner	Year	Winner
1937	MIT	1954	MIT
1938	MIT	1955	MIT
1939	MIT	1956	Navy
1940	Princeton	1957	Navy
1941	Princeton	1958	MIT
1942	Brown	1959	Harvard
1943	MIT	1960	Coast Guard Academy
1944	Coast Guard Academy	1961	MIT
		1962	Coast Guard Academy
1945	MIT	1963	Princeton
1946	MIT	1964	British Columbia
1947	Yale	1965	Rhode Island
1948	Brown	1966	Coast Guard Academy
1949	*Yale	1967	U. of Southern California
1950	Yale	1968	San Diego State
1951	MIT	1969	San Diego State
1952	Harvard	1970	U. of Southern California
1953	Harvard	1971	U. of Southern California

* First championship under reorganized ICYRA of North America.

Robert M. Allan Sr. Trophy

This award is given to the high-point skipper during the Inter-Collegiate Yacht Racing Association dinghy championship. Past winners and schools are as follows:

1937	C. R. Colie, Jr., MIT
1938	S. Allbright, Dartmouth
1939	C. R. Colie, Jr., MIT
1940	L. A. Romagna, Brown
1941	L. A. Romagna, Brown
1942	L. A. Romagna, Brown
1943	H. Boericke, MIT
1944	A. E. Fontaine, Coast Guard Academy
1945	C. K. Bloomer, MIT
1946	C. M. Hunt, Jr., MIT
1947	R. E. Monetti, Yale
1948	R. E. Monetti, Yale
1949	R. E. Coulson, Yale
1950	R. E. Monetti, Yale
1951	R. D. Nuherson, MIT
1952	C. S. Hoppin, Harvard
1953	C. S. Hoppin, Harvard
1954	A. J. de Berc, MIT
	L. J. Bedford, UCLA
1955	F. A. Brooks, MIT
1956	J. P. Googe, Navy
1957	J. P. Googe, Navy
1958	W. S. Widnall, MIT
1959	W. G. Saltonstall, Harvard
1960	R. E. Marshall, Ohio State
1961	D. E. Nelson, MIT
1962	J. T. Wuestneck, Coast Guard Academy
1963	E. A. Greenberg, Princeton
1964	G. W. Vandervort, San Diego State
1965	H. G. Schofield, California State

1966	J. T. Ingham, Coast Guard Academy
1967	H. G. Schofield, California State
1968	E. O. Butler, San Diego State
1969	J. Dane III, Tulane
1970	T. P. Hogan, Southern California
1971	R. Whyte, Rhode Island

Walter C. Wood Trophy

This trophy, honoring one of the principal founders of college dinghy racing, is given to the winner of the ICYRA intersectional team races. Previous winners are as follows:

1960	Middle Atlantic ISA
1961	Middle Atlantic ISA
1962	Pacific Coast ICYRA
1963	New England ISA
1964	Pacific Coast IYRA
1965	New England ISA
1966	New England ISA
1967	Pacific Coast IYRA
1968	Pacific Coast IYRA
1969	Pacific Coast IYRA
1970	New England ISA
1971	Pacific Coast IYRA

Glen S. Foster Trophy

This trophy is awarded the winner of ICYRA's single-handed championship and has been given to the following:

1963	William S. Cox, Princeton
1964	Steven Martin, Coast Guard Academy
1965	Robert H. Purrington, Princeton
1966	Carl Van Duyne, Princeton
1967	Henry Sprague, U. of Southern California
1968	Frederick V. Minson, Coast Guard Academy
1969	Thomas J. McLaughlin, San Diego State
1970	Robert E. Doyle, Harvard
1971	William Campbell, Naval Academy

The McMillan Cup

Modern United States intercollegiate sailing started back in 1928 when Princeton, led by Arthur Knapp, defeated Harvard and Yale at racing one-design 8-Meters off the Pequot YC, Southport, Conn. In the next two years, Cornell, Dartmouth, and Williams joined the sport and Hugh McMillan offered the lovely piece of Tiffany silver, known as the McMillan Cup, although the inscription omits the name. Though its overall intercollegiate championship significance declined with the 1936–50 advent of dinghy racing—in which many more colleges could engage—the Mc-

Millan Cup remains a coveted prize, almost a "Holy Grail," for Middle Atlantic and New England colleges. In 1950, the United States Naval Academy offered their 44-foot Luders yawls for this ICYRA competition. Since that time, the regatta has been raced aboard these vessels by the various college crews and is a regular Chesapeake Bay event. Winners of the McMillan Cup over the years are as follows:

1930	Princeton	1950	Brown
1931	Princeton	1951	MIT
1932	Harvard	1952	Williams
1933	Dartmouth	1953	MIT
1934	Harvard	1954	Cornell
1935	Princeton	1955	Naval Academy
1936	Princeton	1956	Brown
1937	Yale	1957	Coast Guard Academy
1938	Harvard	1958	Naval Academy
1939	Williams	1959	Princeton
1940	Williams	1960	Williams
1941	Dartmouth	1961	Naval Academy
1942	Dartmouth	1962	Babson College
1943	MIT	1963	Yale
1944	Harvard	1964	Babson College
1945	Coast Guard	1965	Princeton
	Academy	1966	Tufts
1946	MIT	1967	Tufts
1947	Yale	1968	Yale
1948	Yale	1969	Brown
1949	Princeton	1970	Rhode Island

John F. Kennedy Memorial Trophy

In 1965 the United States Naval Academy received permission from the Kennedy family to name a regatta in honor of the late President. It is the first truly nationwide intercollegiate sailing competition to be held in *large* yachts. The event is modeled on the McMillan Cup competition. (In 1938 a Harvard team on which the late President and his late brother Joseph were skippers won the McMillan Cup off Wianno, Mass.)

Winning schools and their skippers are as follows:

1965	Harvard, Edwin Butler
1966	Naval Academy, Robert L. Hamilton, Jr.
1967	Stanford, Robert M. Allan, Jr.
1968	Stanford, Tom McCarthy
1969	Cornell, David R. McFaull
1970	Tulane, John Dane III
1971	Tulane, John Dane III

Douglas Cup

The Douglas Cup features match racing and there are usually seven races, each divided into four matches, as leading crews of the ICYRA challenge for a huge silver cup. Winning schools are as follows:

1966	California State at Long Beach
1967	British Columbia University
1968	University of Southern California
1969	Tulane
1970	Tulane

All-America Sailing Team

1968

Edward O. Butler, San Diego State; Argyle Campbell, U. of Southern California; Christopher C. Chatain, Michigan; David M. Coit, Yale; David A. Curtis, Tufts; Richard T. Doyle, Notre Dame; Timothy P. Hogan, U. of Southern California; James T. Ingham, Coast Guard Academy; Thomas W. McLaughlin, San Diego State; Arthur Messinger, N.Y. Maritime; John F. Meyer, Michigan; Richard Mayerrose, Jr., N.Y. Maritime; Frederick V. Minson, Coast Guard Academy; G. Arthur Seaver III, Tulane; and Christopher T. Seaver, Yale.

1969

Thomas E. Bernard, Coast Guard Academy; Edward O. Butler, San Diego State; Argyle Campbell, U. of Southern California; David M. Coit, Yale; John Dane III, Tulane; Richard T. Doyle, Notre Dame; Robert E. Doyle, Harvard; Timothy P. Hogan, U. of Southern California; Andrew L. Johnston, Princeton; R. DuBose Joslin, Naval Academy; Thomas W. McLaughlin, San Diego State; Richard Mayerrose, Jr., N.Y. Maritime; Stephen D. Milligan, MIT; Daniel M. Rugg III, Naval Academy; and Christopher T. Seaver, Yale.

1970

Thomas E. Bernard, Coast Guard; Edward O. Butler, San Diego State; Argyle Campbell, U. of Southern California; John Dane III, Tulane; Richard T. Doyle, Notre Dame; Robert E. Doyle, Harvard; Thomas Dykstra, Rhode Island; Timothy P. Hogan, U. of

Southern California; Paul G. Hunricks, San Diego State; David W. McComb, MIT; Arthur L. Messinger, N.Y. Maritime; John F. Myer, Michigan; Richard Mayerrose, Jr., N.Y. Maritime; Daniel M. Rugg III, Naval Academy; Christopher T. Seaver, Yale.

1971

E. Louise Anstey, U. of Victoria; Henry Bossett, U. of Rhode Island; Edward O. Butler, San Diego State; Argyle Campbell, U. of Southern California; William Campbell, Naval Academy; Robert W. Crossley, U. of British Columbia; John Dane III, Tulane; Robert E. Doyle, Harvard; Frederick G. Hanselman, Ohio Wesleyan; Paul Hunrichs, San Diego State; Gary Jobson, N.Y. Maritime; Abbott L. Reeve, Harvard; Charles T. White, Michigan State; Rollin Whyte, U. of Rhode Island; and Jonathan Wright, U.S. Merchant Marine Academy.

Intercollegiate Sailing Hall of Fame

Collegiate sailors have been honored for their work and competitive record in intercollegiate sailing by election to the Intercollegiate Sailing Hall of Fame at the U.S. Naval Academy. The elections to the Hall of Fame from college sailing's past are made by an Inter-Collegiate Racing Association of North America selection committee.

The following were selected in 1969: Leonard M. Fowle, Harvard '30; Robert M. Allan, Jr., Stanford University '41; Peter J. Barrett, Wisconsin '57; C. Runyon Colie, Jr., MIT '40; F. Gardner Cox, Jr., Princeton '41; Glen S. Foster II, Brown '52; Arthur Knapp, Jr., Princeton '28; Emil "Bus" Mosbacher,

Jr., Dartmouth '43; George O'Day, Harvard '45; William S. Cox, Jr., Princeton '63; Carter G. Ford, Harvard '63; Richard M. Rose, Princeton '60; Graham M. Hall, U.S. Merchant Marine Academy '64; Colin N. Park, British Columbia '64; and Walter C. Wood, MIT '17.

Yachtsmen named in 1970 are as follows: Henry H. Anderson, Jr., Yale '43; Harold Brown, Jr., Boston University '59; William S. Cox, Sr., Princeton '35; Terry L. Cronberg, MIT '66; A. Wallace Everest, Jr., Boston University '59; G. Shelby Friedrichs, Sr., Tulane '33; Bruce G. Goldsmith, Michigan '58; Lt. James P. Googe, Jr., USN, Navy '57; Edward A. Greenberg, Princeton '63; Charles S. Hoppin, Harvard '53; Robert E. Monetti, Yale '50; Lowell O. North, San Diego State and University of California at Berkeley '51; Leonard A. Romagna, Brown '42; Cornelius A. Shields, Sr., and Charles R. Ulmer, Navy '61.

Everett B. Morris Memorial Trophy

Awarded to the "college sailor of the year," this trophy is given in recognition of all-around contributions to intercollegiate sailing, and is named in honor of the late Everett B. Morris, former yachting editor of the *New York Herald-Tribune* and editor of *Motor Boating* magazine. Winners of the Trophy are:

1968   Scott H. Allan, U. of Southern California
1969   Timothy P. Hogan, U. of Southern California
1970   Richard T. Doyle, Notre Dame
1971   Jonathan Wright, U.S. Merchant Marine Academy

SECTION VIII

Glossary of Sailing Terms

A congressman who was speaking at the dedication of an aircraft carrier kept referring to "this boat." Navy people present were mortified, because the carrier weighed 45,000 tons and a vessel of this size is called a *ship*.

Nevertheless, the point of division between *boats* and *ships* has never been precisely defined. A vessel large enough to carry one or more boats is usually a ship, but this rule is not hard and fast. Nearly all pleasure craft, however, are best described as *boats*.

It is true that the sailing world has its own vocabulary. Many of its words are confusing to the landsman. For example, a *sheet* is a *line*, not a *sail*. Remember that a length of cordage, used on a sailboat, is called a *line*. When cordage is coiled, as in a store or a storeroom, it is called *rope*. There are exceptions, however, to this rule—a topmast is hoisted and lowered with a *top rope,* not a *top line*. But *rope* in use at sea is nearly always a line.

Familiarity with the following nautical terms, most of which refer to sailing boats, will be useful.

Aback. The set of a boat's sails with the wind on the leeward instead of windward side.

Afterguard. On a large racing sailboat, the helmsman, navigator, and others who are normally aft rather than handling sail or doing other work forward.

After sails. Sails bent to masts abaft the foremast.

Aground. When the hull or keel of a boat touches the bottom.

Ahead. Toward the bow of a boat, or in front of a boat.

Ahoy. Greeting used to hail another boat.

Ahull. Of a boat, with all sails lowered—usually for riding out a gale in open water. Such a boat is said to be *lying ahull*.

Aid to navigation. A chartered mark to assist navigators, such as buoys, beacons, lights, radio beacons, etc.

Airfoil. A surface formed to obtain reaction on its sides from the air through which it moves.

Alee. The side of a boat or object away from the direction of the wind.

All aback. When all the sails are aback.

All fast. Indication that rope is secured.

All hands. The entire crew.

All in the wind. A boat pointing too high, causing all sails to shake.

Allowance. The time, measured in seconds per nautical mile, which a sailing boat of higher rating (see *rating*) gives up to a boat of lower rating in a race.

All standing. To be fully equipped and in use. Also, a sailboat running before the wind with all sails set.

Aloft. Up above; up in the rigging or up the mast.

Alongside. Side by side a vessel; by the side of.

Alow. Below deck.

Altocumulus clouds. A cloud formation at about 20,000 feet, advancing ahead of a cold front.

Altostratus clouds. A continuous layer of clouds

at a height ranging from 20,000 to 30,000 feet that usually precedes a warm front and follows a cold front.

Amidships. Toward the center of the vessel.

Anchor. A device so shaped as to grip the sea bottom; secured to line from a craft to hold her in a desired position.

Anchorage. A sheltered place or area where boats can anchor or moor without interfering with harbor traffic.

Anchor bed. A securely made fitting on each side of the forecastle, used for storing stocked anchors. Same as *billboard*.

Anchor bell. The bell rung according to the Rules of the Road when at anchor during fog.

Anchor lights. Riding lights required to be carried by vessel at anchor.

Anchor warp. The rope used in small boats when anchoring.

Anemometer. An instrument to measure the velocity of the wind.

Angle of heel. Of a sailboat, its angle from the vertical at a given moment, depending on the strength of wind, point of sailing, and stability of the hull.

Answering pennant. The pennant used to acknowledge a signal.

Anticyclone. An area of comparatively high atmospheric pressure, with winds rotating clockwise around the center.

Antifouling paint. Contains chemicals which discourage growth of marine life (barnacles, etc.) on the bottoms of boats.

Apparent wind. The direction from which the wind appears to blow when aboard a boat in motion.

Ashore. On or to the shore.

Aspect ratio. The length of the luff of a sail compared with the length of its foot.

Astern. To the rear of a boat or behind a boat.

Athwartships. At right angles to the fore-and-aft line of a vessel; across the vessel.

Atrip. An anchor is atrip when it is raised above bottom. A sail is atrip when ready for trimming.

Auxiliary. A power plant used as secondary propulsion in a vessel. Also a small motor used to drive pumps, generators, etc.

Avast. Hold fast; as in "avast heaving."

Awash. Immersed in water that passes over the side of a boat when it is heeling.

Aweather. To windward, toward the weather side.

Aweigh. Describes an anchor raised from the bottom.

Awning. Canvas covering boat or deck for protection from sun or rain.

Aye. Yes; an affirmative reply to any order, or "I understand."

Azimuth. Angular distance of an object from a fixed point measured on a horizon circle in a clockwise direction.

Back. Of a vessel, to make sternway. Of wind, to shift in a counterclockwise direction.

Back a sail. To hold a sail so that the wind will blow aft against its forward side, slowing or butting the boat or forcing her back.

Backboard. Vertical board rest used for helmsman's back.

Backstays. Rigging wires that lead from mast top aft to the ship's sides.

Back wash. The churning water thrown aft by the propeller.

Back wind. Back winds on a sail throw wind on leeward side.

Baggy. Of a sail, to hang more or less slack from edges that are stretched taut.

Bail. To bail a boat is to throw the water out of it.

Bald-headed. Of a gaff-rigged boat sailing without a topmast.

Ballast. Heavy material, usually lead or iron, placed in the bottom of some boats to give stability. Also, weight at foot of keel.

Balloon jib. Larger and looser-cut sail than a genoa used on a reach or a broad reach.

Balloon sail. Generic term for any large, light sail used in racing or cruising to replace or supplement the working sails when reaching or running. A common example is the balloon jib (also called reaching jib), a triangular racing sail which may be even bigger than the outsize genoa jib and is used primarily for reaching in light to moderate weather. Other examples include the balloon foresail, balloon jib topsail, balloon spinnaker, and balloon topsail.

Bar. A ridge or succession of ridges of sand or other substances, especially such a formation extending across the mouth of a river or harbor, and which may obstruct navigation.

Bare poles. With all sails down.

Bare sailing. Sailing with sheets too far in.

Barging. Forcing one's way illegally between the starting mark and boats to leeward.

Bark. A three-masted sailing vessel square-rigged on the fore and main, and fore-and-aft rigged on the mizzen.

Bar keel. Solid-metal external keel.

Barkentine. A three-masted sailing vessel, square-rigged on the fore while it is fore-and-aft rigged on the main and mizzen.

Barnacle. A small shellfish that fastens itself to the bottom of your yacht.

Barometer. An instrument used to register or measure the atmosphere's pressure.

Batten. A thin wooden, metal, or plastic strip

placed in a pocket in the leech of a sail to help hold its form.

Batten down. To secure or to make watertight; said of hatches and cargo.

Batten pockets. The long, narrow "tube" of sailcloth into which the battens slide.

Beacon. A navigational aid or mark, usually placed on land, to warn boats of danger.

Beam. The maximum width measurement of a vessel. Also, in radio, a signal transmitted along a narrow course for use in direction finding.

Beam sea. A sea at right angles to a vessel's course.

Beam wind. A wind which blows athwart a boat's fore-and-aft line.

Bear. To *bear down* is to approach from windward. To *bear off* or *bear away* is to uphelm and run more to leeward. The latter also means to keep clear of, as another boat.

Bear in. To approach an object or shore.

Bearing. The direction of one object to another.

Bear up. Steer closer to the direction of the wind, shore, or object.

Beat. To sail toward the direction from which the wind blows by making a series of tacks while sailing close-hauled.

Beaufort Scale. A table used for describing the velocity of the wind.

Becalm. A vessel is becalmed when the sails hang limp and lifeless because of no wind.

Becket. A temporary tie or lashing, most commonly a short piece of rope with a knot at one end and an eye at the other. Also, an eye or loop made with fiber or wire rope.

Before the wind. Having the wind coming from aft.

Belay. To make fast to a cleat or pin. Also, to change an order.

Belaying pin. A wooden or iron pin fitting into a rail upon which to secure ropes.

Bell buoy. A buoy with a bell actuated by the sea.

Belly. Fullness of sail when swelled out by wind.

Below. Under the deck.

Bend. To fasten a sail to the boom and mast. Also, to fasten one rope to another.

Bending shackle. A device which connects chain cable to the anchor ring.

Bermuda rig. Triangular-sail rig, as opposed to a gaff rig; same as jib-headed rig, *Marconi* rig, and *Bermudian* rig.

Berth. The dock or anchorage occupied by a boat. Also, the place where a person sleeps.

Bight. The bend or loop in a rope. Also, a bend in a coastline or in a river.

Bilge. That part inside the hull above and around the keel where water will collect.

Curved part of hull below the waterline.

Bilge water. Water that collects in the bilge.

Bill. The point at the extremity of a fluke of an anchor.

Billboard. See *anchor bed*.

Binnacle. A stand with receptacle containing the compass and compensating magnets.

Bitter end. The extreme end of a line.

Bitts. Vertical posts extending above the deck to which mooring lines are made fast.

Blanketed. When a sail is between the wind and another sail, the latter cannot get the wind and is said to be blanketed. One boat can blanket another boat by sailing between it and the wind.

Blinker signaling. The transmission of optical signals by the Morse Code, using fixed electric lamps or portable signaling lamps.

Block. Pulley consisting of a frame in which is set one or more sheaves (shivs) or rollers. Lines are run over these rollers.

Board. A tack or leg to windward when beating.

Boardboat. Any of various small sailboats whose hulls resemble a surfboard. Also called a *sailboard*.

Boat boom. Swings from boat's side when at anchor to secure dinghy.

Boat hook. A device for catching hold of a ringbolt or grab line when coming alongside a pier or picking up a mooring.

Bobstays. A stay from the end of a bowsprit to a boat's stem near the waterline.

Bolt rope. The rope surrounding a sail and to which the material is sewed.

Bonnet. Extra canvas piece secured to foot of jib by lacings.

Boom. The spar to which the foot of the sail is attached with lacing, slides, or groove.

Boom crutch. A frame in which the boom rests when the boat is at anchor. Also called *boom crotch*.

Boom horse. Same as *boom crutch*. A curved metal fitting made into the shape of a band, on which a sheet block travels. Same as *traveler*.

Boom jack. A rope or tackle rigged to exert a downward pull on the boom.

Boomkin. A short spar projecting from the stern to which the mizzen or jigger is secured. Also called *bumpkin*.

Boom vang. A tackle secured to the boom to prevent it from lifting on a reach or run, and to flatten the sail.

Boot top. A narrow stripe of paint at the waterline.

Bosun's chair. A seat of canvas or wood in which a man working aloft is swung.

Bound wind. Adverse headwind which keeps sailboat in port.

Bow. The forward end of a boat.

Bow breast. A forward mooring line used in docking.

Bow line. A docking or mooring line led forward through a bow chock.

Bowline. A knot used to form an eye or loop in the end of a line.

Bow painter. Forward line leading from boat to buoy or other boat.

Bowse. To pull upon a tackle.

Bowsprit. A spar extending forward from the bow to which jibs and stays are made fast.

Brackish. Mixture of fresh and salt water.

Brails. An arrangement by which the leech of a fore-and-aft sail can be hauled to the mast for quick furling.

Brail up. To furl a sail by means of brails.

Breakers. Waves caused by ledges, bars, and shoals.

Break ground. To lift anchor from bottom.

Break off. To stop.

Break out. To bring something out of stowage, such as a sail from a bag.

Break shear. Refers to a vessel that is restless at anchor due to force of wind or current.

Breakwater. An artificial embankment to protect anchorages or harbor entrances. Also, a low bulkhead forward on a boat to prevent seas from coming aft.

Breast, breast line. Mooring lines leading roughly at right angles from ship's sides.

Breast the sea. To meet a swell or waves head on.

Bridge. A short deck running from side to side of the vessel, fitted out for control and navigation of the craft.

Bridle. Rope span with ends secured for sheet block to ride on.

Brigantine. A two-masted sailing vessel, square-rigged on the foremast, fore-and-aft rigged on the mainmast; sometimes carries a square main topsail.

Brightwork. Varnished wood and polished brass or chrome.

Bring about. To reverse direction.

Bring to. The act of stopping a boat by bringing her head up into the wind.

Bring up. To come to a sudden standstill, as a boat striking an unexpected obstacle.

Broach. A vessel running downwind inadvertently swings broadside to the wind. Dangerous in high seas.

Broad before the wind. With sails flung out, before the wind; sailing downwind.

Broad reach. Any point of sailing between a beam reach and a quartering wind.

Broadside. The entire side of a vessel.

Bulkhead. A partition or wall below decks.

Bull rope. Shock cord leading from bowsprit end to mooring buoy to keep buoy from bumping boat when wind and tide are opposed.

Bull the buoy. To bump a buoy with the side of a vessel.

Bulwark. The extension of the hull sides above the deck.

Bumboat. A peddler's boat that comes alongside in a port.

Bumper. A resilient object or material on piers or landings to protect boats alongside from chafe or breakage.

Bunk. Sleeping berth; same as a bed.

Bunt. Middle of sail.

Buoy. Any floating object anchored in one place to show position.

Buoyage. A system of buoys and marks to aid your course.

Buoyancy. Upward pressure of the water exerted on the hull equal to the hull's displacement.

Burdened vessel. A craft required to keep clear of a vessel holding the right of way.

Burgee. A small swallow-tailed or triangular flag identifying the owner or the yacht club to which he belongs.

By the board. Overboard.

By the lee. Running with the wind on the same side as the boom.

By the luff. The purposeful flapping of the mainsail in a strong wind.

By the run. Let go altogether.

By the wind. Sailing close-hauled.

Cabin. A room used for living space.

Cable. A large, strong rope, used for mooring a ship. As a unit of length, a cable is usually 120 fathoms.

Calk. To make seams watertight by filling them with cotton, oakum, or similar material.

Camber. A curvature upward.

Cam cleat. A fitting that has interlocking teeth on springs (cams) instead of prongs to secure the rope. It is especially useful when speed is all important, as on sheets, since a quick pull down and toward you secures the rope, and an upward jerk releases it.

Can. A cylindrical black buoy having an odd number; found on the port side of a channel as you proceed away from the ocean.

Canvas. General term covering all sails on a boat. Also, the strong fabric used to cover decks.

Capsize. Upset; turn over.

Capstan. A mechanical device used for hoisting anchors or other heavy objects.

Cardinal points. Four main points of a compass.

Careen. A vessel placed on her side so that work may be carried out on her underwater parts.

Carry away. To break or tear loose.

Carry on. Carry all sails possible.

Carvel. A smooth-planked hull.

Cast. To throw.

Cast off. To let go a line.

Cat. The tackle used to hoist the anchor up to the cathead.

Catamaran. A twin-hulled boat.

Catboat. A sailboat with a single fore-and-aft sail.

Cathead. Timbers projecting from bow to secure anchor.

Catspaw. Little wind ruffling the water.

Centerboard. A keel-like device that can be hoisted or lowered in a well, or trunk, to act as a keel in shoal-draft boats.

Centerboard pennant. Rope used for lowering and raising the centerboard.

Centerboard trunk. Wooden framing in center of cockpit to contain centerboard when it is pulled up.

Chafe. To damage by rubbing.

Chafing gear. Canvas, plastic, or other similar material secured about a line or sheet to protect it from abrasion and wear.

Chain plates. Metal plates bolted to the side of a boat to which shrouds are attached to support rigging.

Channel. The deeper portion of a water area, with buoyage supposedly marked to guide boats with some appreciable draft safely through shoal water.

Chart. The proper term for a nautical map.

Cheeks. The projections on each side of a mast, upon which the trestletrees rest; side of block.

Chine. The line where the sides of a boat intersect the bottom. A "hard" chine is sharply angled; a "nontrip" chine makes the transition between vertical and horizontal in two bends; a "soft" chine is rounded.

Chock. A device affixed to the deck used as a guide for anchor or mooring line.

Chock-a-block. If two blocks of a tackle rest firmly against each other.

Chop. Short, irregular waves, usually caused by meeting of tides, or meeting of current and wind.

Chow. Food, or a meal.

Chronometer. A highly accurate clock used by navigators.

Cirrus. Wispy cloud formation, which is the first warning of an approaching warm front.

Claw off. To clear a lee shore.

Cleat. A wood or metal fitting for securing a line without a hitch.

Clew. The aftermost corner of the sail.

Clew outhaul. Tackle for stretching the foot of a sail out along the boom.

Clinker. Lapstrake planked (hull), planks overlapping like clapboards.

Close-hauled. Sailing as close to the wind as possible.

Close reach. A point of sailing between a beam reach and a beat. Same as a *fine reach*.

Close-winded. Describes a craft capable of sailing very close to the wind.

Clove hitch. A practical knot for securing a mooring line quickly.

Club. Spar on bottom of staysail or topsail.

Club-footed. A type of jib which is bent to a club.

Coachroof. A raised cabin roof to give additional space.

Coaming. The raised protection around a cockpit.

Cockpit. The space at a lower level than the deck in which the tiller or wheel is located.

Coffeegrinder. A type of sheet winch used on larger offshore racers and 12-Meters. It has an upright pedestal with two handles and can be worked from a standing position by one or two crew members.

Coil. To lay down a line in circular turns.

Colors. The ceremony of hoisting the national flag at 8 A.M. The lowering at sunset is called *making colors*.

Come about. To bring the boat from one tack to the other when sailing into the wind.

Come up into the wind. Steer toward the direction from which the wind is coming.

Companion. Wooden covering over staircase to a cabin.

Companionway. A staircase to a cabin or below.

Compass. Magnetized needle attached to a circular compass card that tends to point to the magnetic north.

Compass card. A calibrated card which has the points of the compass.

Compass rose. A graduated circle printed on a chart that has the points of the compass.

Compensate. Correcting a compass to allow for local magnetic attraction so that it will point as nearly as possible to magnetic north.

Cone. Signal displayed on sailboat under power and sail.

Consol/consolan. A directional radio beacon in the 190- to 194-kilocycle band from which bearing information is obtained by counting the dots and dashes heard in a cycle of operation.

Cordage. General term for all ropes made from fibers.

Corinthian. A term used to describe an amateur

sailor; used primarily to describe a member of a racing crew.

Corrected time. A boat's elapsed time minus her time allowance. In any race where time allowances are given, corrected time determines the winner.

Course. Direction sailed as measured by the compass.

Course protractor. Device for determining a boat's course on a chart.

Cover. To keep between an opponent and the next turning mark, or between an opponent and the direction from which the wind is coming. It is what a leading boat does to prevent a trailing boat from passing.

Cow's-tail. Frayed rope end.

Crabbing. Making leeway, moving sideways through the water.

Cradle. A frame used to hold a boat when she is hauled out of the water.

Craft. General term for small vessels.

Crank, cranky. A boat that heels too easily.

Crest. The top part of a wave.

Cringle. A ring sewn into the sail through which a line can be passed at tack, head, or clew.

Cross bearings. The bearings of two or more objects, crossing each other at the position of the observer.

Crosstrees. Spreaders fitted to the mast to take the shrouds.

Crown. The center point of an anchor where the arms join the shank.

Cruiser. Any boat having arrangements for living aboard.

Crutch. Support for boom when sails are furled.

Cuddy. A small cabin or protective cover over the fore part of the cockpit.

Cumulonimbus. The thunderstorm cloud.

Cumulus. The fair-weather cloud, recognized by its powder-puff appearance.

Cunningham eye. A hole made in a sail—when a rope looped through the hole is pulled on, or released, the sail is respectively flattened or made more full. Usually two are fitted, one controlling the luff and the other the foot. Same as *Cunningham hole.*

Current. The continuous movement of water in a certain direction.

Cutter. A single-masted sailboat in which the mast is set amidships.

Cutwater. Foremost part of bow or stem.

Daggerboard. A type of centerboard which does not pivot on a hinge, but is raised and lowered vertically in the trunk. Same as *daggerplate.*

Danger buoy. Buoy marking danger spot or area.

Davits. Devices of timber or metal, with sheaves or blocks at their ends, projecting over a vessel's sides or stern, to hoist up a small boat.

Davy Jones' locker. The bottom of the sea.

Day sailer. A boat used for day sailing, as opposed to a boat in which one could cruise overnight or longer. An open boat, without living accommodation.

Day's work. Record of noon-to-noon navigation work to determine a ship's position.

Dead ahead. Directly ahead of a boat's course.

Dead astern. Directly astern of a boat's course.

Dead before the wind. When the wind is directly behind the boat, and the mainsail and boom are all the way out at right angles to the mast.

Deadeye. A round, flat wooden block with three holes but no sheaves, through which shroud lanyards are received.

Deadlight. Glass permanently set in a cabin or deck to admit light below.

Dead men. Neglected old loose ends of a rope.

Dead reckoning. Determining a boat's position at sea by noting the course sailed and the distance covered.

Dead rope. Line not led through a block or sheave.

Dead run. A run when the wind is directly behind the boat.

Dead water. The eddy under a vessel's counter when not in motion.

Deck. A platform covering or extending horizontally across a boat. The floor.

Deck. To dress up.

Declination. The angular distance of a heavenly body from the celestial equator measured either northward or southward on an hour circle.

Deep six. Where you send an unwanted object when you throw it overboard.

Departure. The distance due east or due west made by a boat on its course.

Derelict. An abandoned ship.

Deviation. An error of compass caused by the proximity of magnetic materials.

Dew point. The point at which a given amount of air becomes saturated, condensation forms, and fog begins.

Dinghy. A small rowing boat that occasionally is rigged with a sail. Also called *tender* or *dink.*

Dip. To salute or signal by means of hoisting and then lowering.

Dismantle. To strip a vessel of spars, masts, and rigging.

Dismast. To remove a ship's mast(s).

Displacement. The weight of water displaced by a boat.

Distress signal. Methods by which a boat can draw attention to its distress.

Dividers. Instrument used chiefly for measuring distances or coordinates on a chart.

Dock. Generally the water next to a pier, but

usually used to designate any platform at which boats may come alongside.

Dodger. A screen of cloth or other material, fitted up as a shelter or protection.

Dog. Metal fitting used to close hatches, covers, etc.

Dog vane. A small strip of bunting attached to the rigging to indicate the direction of wind.

Dolphin. A mooring buoy or spar.

Dory. A rowboat with a flat, narrow bottom and high freeboard noted for seaworthiness.

Double ender. Any boat that is pointed at both bow and stern.

Doubling. Sailing around point of land; overlapping parts of two masts.

Douse. To take in or lower a sail. Also, to put out a light.

Downhaul. A tackle or single line by which a sail is hauled down.

Down helm. To bring a boat up into the wind. Same as *up helm*.

Downwind. To leeward.

Down with the sun. The recommended way of coiling a line by following the sun's path through the sky.

Draft. Depth of water to deepest part of hull or keel. Also, the fullness, or "belly," of a sail.

Drag. A retarding force caused by friction between the water and the hull.

Draw. A sail draws when filled with wind, while a boat draws enough water to float her.

Drift. The leeway of a boat.

Drift. To move along with the tide or current.

Drift lead. A lead weight on a line dropped from an anchored vessel to indicate if she is starting to drag.

Drive. To carry all canvas possible in a heavy wind.

Drogue. A canvas cone used forward as a sea anchor.

Drop. The depth of a sail as measured from head to foot amidships.

Dry rot. Decay of wood.

Dry sailing. Keeping a boat out of water when not in use.

Earing. A line used to secure a corner of a sail to a spar; short line securing reefed sail to boom.

Ease. To let out the sheet to relieve the pressure on the sail and perhaps spill some wind.

Ease in. To go slowly.

Ease off. To allow a boat to run slightly to leeward of its most windward course.

Ease the helm. To permit the tiller to regress a little after being close-hauled.

Ease the sheet. To let out the rope that controls a sail.

Ease up. To let up gently.

Easing-out line. The line used to hold back a strain on something being eased out to prevent it from going out too quickly.

Ebb. The outgoing tide.

Eddy. A current of water or air running against the main current, especially one moving circularly.

Edge away. Sail off the wind from the course steered.

Ensign. A national flag flown on a boat.

Entry. The flare of the hull at the stem. *Fine entry* means a sharp bow.

Even keel. Floating level.

Eye. Loop of rope; any kind of round hole for leading or fastening a rope.

Eyebolt. A bolt with an eye at the end.

Eyelet hole. A hole made in a sail for cringle or roband to go through.

Eye of the wind. The exact direction from which the wind is coming.

Eye splice. A kind of splice made at the end of a rope.

Fag. A rope is fagged when the end is untwisted.

Fair. The wind "fairs" when it strikes the sails from a more favorable angle, from further aft, making it possible for the boat to point higher.

Fairlead. An eyelet fitting which changes the direction of a sheet or halyard led through it.

Fair tide. Current running with vessel.

Fairway. A navigable channel.

Fake. To lay a coil of line in such a way that it will run out freely. Same as *flake.*

Fall. The part of a tackle to which the power is applied in hoisting.

Falling glass. Lowering barometer pressure.

Fall off. To head the boat away or to go away from the direction of the wind; head to leeward.

False keel. Protective wood strip bolted outside main keel.

Fanning. Used to describe a sailboat making little headway in light airs.

Fast. To secure.

Fathom. A nautical measurement for the depth of water. One fathom is equal to 6 feet.

Feather. To allow wind to spill from a sail so that it flutters, to use only the wind you want when there is too much available.

Fend. To push off.

Fender. Bumper hung over the boat's side to prevent chafing when tied up.

Fetch. When a craft sailing to windward can make her objective without another tack.

Fetching the mark. The proper movement of the boat to bring her about so that she is pointed directly at the windward mark on her final tack of a leg. Same as *laying a mark*.

Fiberglass. Glass drawn into extremely thin filaments (18/10,000 to 38/10,000 of an inch in diameter) which nonetheless have greater tensile strength than steel. Because of this quality, plastics reinforced with fiberglass are increasingly used in building, covering, and repairing sailing craft. A fiberglass boat actually is one constructed of such a plastic (usually a polyester-resin type), with the fiberglass constituting perhaps a third of its content by volume.

Fid. A tapered, pointed tool for spreading the strands of rope when splicing.

Fiddle block. A pulley that has two superimposed sheaves, the upper one being larger than the lower. Similar to a *sister block*.

Figure-eight knot. A knot shaped like an eight; helps prevent a line from unreeving.

Fill. To become full of wind.

Fill away. A sailboat gathering headway on a new tack or the sails filling out as the bow goes past the eye of the wind.

Fisherman's bend. A knot used to bend a line to a ring; also called *anchor bend*.

Fisherman's knot. Joins two lines together, forming one knot.

Fisherman's staysail. A large topsail as used in schooners, set above a main staysail.

Fit out. Preparing a boat for launching or an extended trip.

Fittings. Hardware.

Fix. To find a boat's position by celestial or land observation.

Flare. A device used for signaling, particularly to indicate distress. Also, the outward curve or slant of a boat's sides, from bilge to deck line.

Flashing light. A light (chart symbol: F1) that shows one or more flashes at regular intervals, the duration of light always being less than the duration of darkness. Also, a system of signaling in which dots and dashes, as used in the International Morse Code, are represented by light flashes of appropriate duration; also called *blinker*.

Flat. Hauled all the way in, said of a sail.

Flat-aback. When a sail is blown with its convex surface toward the stern.

Flat calm. No wind pressure.

Flat-cut. A type of sailmaking which reduces draft for heavy-weather use, permitting more sail area to be carried and closer sailing to windward.

Flatten in. Haul in on sheets.

Flaw. Sudden short burst of wind.

Floorboards. Wooden boards or slattings, sometimes removable, covering the bottom of a boat for protection and dryness.

Flotation. Air tanks or other similar devices or materials which help to prevent a swamped boat from sinking.

Flotsam. Floating debris.

Flow. Spilling the wind by easing the sheets. Also, the area of deepest curve in a sail.

Flowing sheets. Sailboat running before the wind with sheets that are eased.

Fluke. The entire point of an anchor, composed of the bill and palm at the end of an arm.

Flush deck. A type of design in which no house protrudes above deck, and the cabin beams extend full width.

Fly. Small pennant at the top of the mast to indicate direction of the wind.

Flying. Not fastened or furled, as a sail.

Fog. Reduced visibility from moisture in the air.

Fog signals. System of sound signals given forth by vessel during fog, as prescribed by the Rules of the Road.

Following sea. When the waves approach from astern of the boat.

Foot. The lower edge of a sail.

Foot. To move through the water at good speed.

Footline. A light rope inserted into the foot of a sail which when drawn tight will increase the fullness of the sail and when released will flatten it.

Fore. In or toward the bow of a boat.

Fore-and-aft. In the direction of the keel, from front to back. Also, a sailboat's sailing rig.

Forecastle. The forward part of the boat below the deck (pronounced *fok-s'l*).

Foredeck. The deck, or that part of the deck, in the forward part of a boat. Also called *forward deck*.

Forefoot. The forward part of the keel, adjoining the lower part of the stem.

Foremast. Forward mast of a sailing vessel having two or more masts.

Forereach. The movement or shooting ahead a sailboat makes when going about or luffing into the eye of the wind.

Foresail. The first working sail immediately forward of the mainsail (pronounced *for-s'l*).

Forestay. Supporting rope or wire from the mast to the bow.

Forestaysail. A foresail bent on a stay (pronounced *for-stay-s'l*).

Forge ahead. Shoot ahead when going in stays or coming to anchor.

Forward quarter spring line. A dock line attached to the quarter of a boat and led ashore to be secured alongside the bow.

Foul. Not clean; entangled or clogged.

Foul hawse. Twisted anchor lines.

Foul wind. One that is blowing against the course of the boat.

Founder. When a boat is swamped and begins to sink.

Frame. Skeleton of a ship.

Free. Sailing with the wind anywhere from abeam to due aft. Also means to cast off, untangle, permit to run easily.

Freeboard. The distance from the top of the hull to the water.

Fresh breeze. Wind of 17 to 21 knots velocity.

Freshen. When the wind gains in strength.

Full and by. Sailing as close to the wind as possible with all sails full.

Full spread. All sails set.

Furl. To roll up a sail tightly on a boom or spar.

Furling gear. Any mechanical device for furling a sail.

Gaff. Spar hoisted on the aft side of the mast to support the head of a sail, hence gaff-rigged. Also a long-handled instrument used to lift hooked fish from the water.

Gaff-headed. A sail having its head bent to a gaff; any sail with which a gaff is used.

Gaff topsail. A triangular sail set over a gaff which is set from a topmast.

Gaff vang. Line going to gaff peak used to steady the gaff.

Gale. Hard wind.

Galley. A nautical kitchen.

Gangplank. A movable bridge on which to get from the dock or pier to a boat or vice versa.

Gangway. That part of boat's side where people pass in and out of the boat. Also, a command meaning "Get out of the way!"

Gantline. Line rove through a single block that is secured aloft, and used for hoisting sails or for other articles.

Garland. Strap or rope secured to spar when hoisting it aboard.

Gasket. A piece of rope or canvas used to secure a furled sail.

Gather way. The motion of moving forward as the wind fills the sails.

Gear. A general term embracing all rigging or boat equipment.

Genoa. A large, overlapping jib or headsail which reaches the top of the forestay and whose clew overlaps the mainsail. It is the principal power source on a modern racing sloop when beating. Also called *jenny*.

Ghoster. A sailboat capable of comparatively good speed in very light air.

Ghosting. A boat making headway when there is no apparent wind.

Gig. Usually the officers' boat; long light boat with two masts.

Gimbal. A device used for suspending the compass so that it will remain level.

Gimlet. To turn anything around on its end.

Girt. To moor a boat with a tight line to guard against force of tide or wind.

Give way. An order to a boat's crew to begin pulling. A command to stay clear of another vessel.

Go about. To change tack to windward.

Go large. Sail with the wind near the quarter.

Gong buoy. A navigational buoy that gives a gong sound, motivated by the rocking of the buoy.

Gooseneck. A metal device that secures the boom to the mast.

Goosewinged. Describes a sailboat sailing wing and wing. Also, the result of accidental jibe with gaff rig, when boom and gaff are on different sides.

Gores. The angles at one or both ends of cloths that increase the breadth of a sail.

Goring cloths. Pieces of cloth cut on the bias and added to the breadth of a sail.

Grafting. Guarding a rope by weaving yarns together to cover it.

Granny knot. A square knot improperly tied.

Grapnel. A cluster of curved hooks at the end of a shank, the other end of which has a ring for the attachment of a line. It is primarily used for snagging and bringing up objects from the bottom.

Grappling irons. Odd-shaped irons used to hold vessels fast.

Grating. A built-up wooden platform containing drain holes and for covering hatches in good weather.

Great-circle course. A great circle is formed on the surface of the globe by a plane which passes through the center of the earth. A course on a great circle provides the shortest distance between two points.

Gripe. To tend to come into the wind, to carry a hard-weather helm.

Grommet. A metal ring fastened in a sail. Also, a ring made of rope.

Groove. Narrow opening running the length of the mast or boom into which the rope-reinforced edge of the mainsail is inserted and thus bent.

Grounding. Running ashore.

Ground tackle. Anchor, cable, etc., used to secure a boat to her moorings.

Gudgeon. A fitting attached to the hull into which the rudder's pintles are inserted.

Gunkholing. Shallow-water sailing.

Gunwale. The rail of the boat at deck level.

Gusset. A piece of canvas let in to increase width or to strengthen.

Gust. A quick, temporary increase in wind strength.

Guy. A rope or wire used to steady or support.

Hail. To speak or call to someone aboard your craft or another vessel.

Half hitch. Single underhand loop used to fasten

a rope to a post or other stationary object.

Halyard. A line used to hoist sails. Also referred to as *halliard* or *haliard*.

Hand. A member of the crew.

Hand lead. A small lead used for sounding in waterways.

Handsomely. With care and caution.

Hank. To attach to a stay.

Harbor of refuge. An anchorage safe from storms.

Hard-alee! A command to come about.

Hard aweather. To put the tiller up as in changing course from close-hauled to a reach or broad reach without changing tack.

Hard down. To put the tiller as far to leeward as possible.

Harden. To remove the luffing next to the mast in the sail by filling it with wind, either by heading the boat away from the wind or pulling in the sail. Same as *harden up*.

Hard over. Placement of the wheel, or tiller, when it is put over as far as possible to one side or the other.

Hatch. An opening in a deck with a cover.

Haul. To draw a boat out of the water on to land.

Haul to windward. When sailing free, to bring a sailboat up into the wind.

Haul your wind. To sail closer to the wind.

Hawk. Wind indicator at the top of the mast.

Hawse block. Wooden block set into hawse hole when at sea.

Hawser. A heavy line used for towing a boat or for mooring.

Head. The wind "heads" when it comes from further ahead.

Head. A shipboard toilet. Also, the top of a sail or the top of the mast.

Headboard. The fitting at the head of a sail with holes to receive the shackle of the halyard.

Head down. To point the boat away from the direction of the wind; to head to leeward.

Header. A sudden wind shift toward the bow.

Heading. Direction of sailing.

Head into the wind. To point the boat directly into the wind.

Head off. To direct the boat away from the wind, usually when the sail is luffing in order to make it full. Same as *head down*.

Headsails. All sails forward of the mast.

Head sea. Waves lashing the boat on the bow.

Headsheets. The sheets of the headsails.

Headstay. Wire from the bow supporting the mast (same as *forestay*).

Head up. To luff.

Headway. Moving ahead.

Heave. To haul or pull together, to draw on, to throw.

Heave away. To cast away.

Heave in. To haul in.

Heave short. To haul in on the cable until the vessel is nearly over her anchor.

Heave taut. To haul in until a line is taut with strain.

Heave to. To position a vessel's bow to the wind and hold it there (after which she is *hove to*).

Heaving line. A strong, lightweight rope one end of which is formed into a weighted ball, or "monkey fist." After the ball is thrown over the water to a recipient on shore or on another vessel, the heaving line is used to haul over a heavier "working" line.

Heel. The tilt, tip, listing, or laying over of a boat, usually due to the wind.

Helm. The tiller or wheel by which the rudder is controlled.

Helm down. When the tiller is pushed away from the wind. Same as *helm alee*.

Helm port. The hole in the counter through which the rudder head passes.

Helmsman. The hand who steers.

High. To windward.

High and dry. A vessel that is above the watermark.

Hike. To lean out to windward to counteract excessive heeling.

Hiking seat. A board that can be slid out on either side as a perch for a hiking skipper or crew member when racing to windward. Also called *sliding seat* or *hiking board*.

Hiking stick. An extension to the tiller to let the helmsman control the latter while hiking out in a race. The stick usually is swiveled on the tiller's end and used at right angles to it.

Hiking strap. Either of two fore-and-aft straps attached to the floorboards or centerboard trunk so a crew member can support himself by hooking his feet under one of them when he is hiking out in a race.

Hitch. A simple knot, used for temporarily fastening a rope.

Hogged. Describes a hull drooped at the ends due to incorrect support when stored for the winter.

Hoist. The vertical edge of a sail. To hoist is to haul aloft.

Hold. The interior of a vessel where the cargo is stowed.

Hold. To dig in the anchor so that it will not drag.

Hook. An anchor.

Horn. Prong of a cleat.

Horseshoe. A life preserver designed in a horseshoe shape which can be worn under the arms as potential support for arms and head.

Hounds. The place on the mast where the forestays and shrouds come together.

House. The part of the mast below the deck.

Hove down. Excessive heeling. Also, process of having bottom scraped.

Hull. The main body of the boat.

Hull speed. The theoretical maximum speed of the hull; the square root of the waterline length "times" 1.4.

Inboard. Inside a hull.

Inhaul. Line used to haul in the clew.

In irons. A boat is in irons when she is in the wind's eye and, having lost all headway, will not go off on either tack.

Inshore. Toward the shore.

In stays. When a boat is in the wind's eye while going from one tack to another.

Internal. Any line which is led inside a hollow spar.

International code of signals. The system of signal flags adopted between ships and shore internationally, that can be decoded in any language.

In the wind. Pointing too high into the wind resulting in some wind being spilled from the sails.

Irish pennant. An untidy loose end of a rope.

Jam cleat. A fitting designed with a V-shaped throat between the prong and its base so that when a line is pulled tight (or "jammed"), it is held fast without need for further tying. Never put a line on top of a jam cleat.

Jaws. Semicircular or U-shaped end on boom or gaff which fits around the mast.

Jetty. A pier or wharf built expressly for boats.

Jib. A triangular sail set forward of the mast.

Jib boom. A boom or spar extension beyond the bowsprit used for setting of additional headsails.

Jibe. When running, to bring the wind on the other quarter so that the boom swings over. Same as *gybe*.

Jibe-ho! Command issued by the skipper to show that he is starting the act of jibing.

Jib halyard. Line by which the jib is pulled up and down.

Jib-headed. A sailing rig that has all sails triangular.

Jib lead. The deck fitting which leads the jibsheet to the hand controlling it.

Jibsheet. The line that leads from the lower aft end of the jib to the cockpit. It controls the angle at which the sail is set.

Jibstay. Forward stay (forestay or headstay) on which the jib is hoisted.

Jigger. Another name for the mizzen on a ketch or yawl.

Jog along. To go slowly.

Jumbo. A very large forestaysail, usually set on a boom.

Jumper stay. A trusslike stay on the upper forward side of the mast.

Jury. A term used for making a temporary or makeshift rig. For example, a *jury rig* is any kind of a temporary rig that can be used to take a dismasted sailboat back to port.

Kedge. A small anchor.

Kedging. To move a boat by hauling it up to an anchor.

Keel. The backbone of a boat running fore and aft. Also, finlike member projecting down from hull to provide resistance to leeway, often weighted at its foot to control heeling.

Keel boat. A craft with a fixed keel that extends below the hull.

Keep away. Change to safer course, away from the wind.

Keep her full. An order to keep the sails filled.

Keep her luff. To sail close-hauled.

Keep her off. Command to continue sailing further from the wind.

Keep her so. An order to steady on the course.

Kentledge. Pig iron, as laid out in a vessel for ballast.

Ketch. A two-masted sailing vessel with smaller aftermast stepped forward of the sternpost.

Kick. The abrupt movement of a vessel's stern when helm or power is applied.

Kicker. A line led from the middle of the spinnaker pole to a cleat in the cockpit to prevent the pole flying upward under wind pressure. Same as *kicking strap*.

Kite. A colloquialism for spinnaker.

Knot. Nautical unit of speed—6,080 feet, or one nautical mile, per hour. Same as *admiralty knot*.

Labor. To roll or pitch heavily in a seaway.

Lacing. Lines used to fix sail to spar or mast.

Laid up. To be in dry dock.

Land breeze. Evening breeze coming from land to sea.

Landlocked. To be entirely surrounded by land.

Landmark. A distinct or familiar mark or object on shore.

Lanyard. A term used to describe any line but primarily used for a line fastened to an article, such as a pail, whistle, knife, or other small tool, for purposes of securing it.

Lapstrake. A type of hull construction with strakes overlapping in shingle fashion; also known as clinker or clinker-built.

Lash. To bind or secure an object with a line.

Latchings. Loops on head rope of bonnet by which it is laced to foot of sail.

Lateen. A triangular sail with a comparatively short luff, bent to a yard that is set obliquely to the mast.

Lateral resistance. The ability of a hull, by means of the area of submerged surfaces, to resist being driven sidewise by the wind.

Latitude. Distance in degrees north or south of the equator.

Launch. To set a boat afloat. Also a small boat usually used for transporting people within a harbor.

Lay. To bring.

Lay, lie. To place and to be in a place, and all their forms, are used almost interchangeably by sailors, more often incorrectly than correctly by shore usage. To come or to go.

Lay aft. An order to go toward the stern of a boat.

Lay forward. An order to go toward the bow of a boat.

Lay line. An imaginary line which brings a close-hauled boat directly to the mark. (Same as *fetch line;* see *fetching the mark.*)

Lay off. To rule off a course.

Layup. Protecting the boat during winter storage, etc.

Lazarette. A small space below deck, usually aft, where spare parts are kept.

Lazy guy. Rigging to steady the boom to prevent a jibe in rough sea.

Lazy jacks. A bridle of light line leading from the topping lift or mast of a sailboat down to the boom. Fitted one on each side of the sail, lazy jacks hold the sail as it is lowered, keep it from falling on the deck and make it in effect self-furling. Same as *boom guys.*

Lead. A small piece of lead or other heavy object with marked-off *leadline* attached, used to determine depth of water.

Leading edge. Forward part of a sail.

Leading wind. A fair wind. Applied to a wind abeam or quartering.

League. Distance measurement of 3 nautical miles.

Lee. The side sheltered from the wind. The side away from the wind on a ship is called the lee side.

Leeboards. Boards projecting from the bilges to provide lateral resistance.

Leech. The after edge of a fore-and-aft sail.

Leech line. A rope used for adjusting the fullness of a sail.

Lee helm. When the position of the helm necessary to keep a boat on her course is toward the lee side.

Lee-ho! The skipper's announcement that the helm has been put down for sailboat to come about.

Lee shore. The shore toward which the wind is blowing. Not to be confused with the lee of a shore.

Leeward. The direction which is away from the wind.

Leeway. Movement to leeward under pressure of wind.

Left rudder. The command to turn the wheel to the left.

Leg. Brace to keep stranded boat upright.

Let draw. Fill sail on desired tack.

Let fly. Drop the sheets.

Let go. To drop anchor.

Let her off. Command to head farther from the wind.

Let her up. Order to point higher into the wind.

Lie to. To remain as near stationary as possible while headed into the wind; some sailboats can be adjusted to this, alternately filling and luffing.

Life boat. A small ship's boat for emergency use.

Life buoy. A buoyant ring for saving lives, usually made of cork.

Lifeline. A wire or rope rigged around the deck of a vessel for the safety of the crew.

Life preserver. A buoyant safety device worn by a person to keep afloat.

Life raft. Float made of cork, plastic, canvas, or rubber.

Life ring. A ring-shaped life preserver designed to be thrown or dropped to a person in the water. It is made of cork covered with canvas, or of synthetic material, with a light line around it so the ring can be thrown easily or attached to a heaving line.

Lift. A rope or tackle, going from the yardarms to the masthead, to support and move the yard. Also, term given to a sail when the wind strikes on the leech and raises it slightly.

Lighten up. To slack away.

Limber holes. Holes bored horizontally in the frames of the boat near the bottom to allow water in the bilge to drain to the lowest point, where it can be pumped out.

Line. A term for any rope used aboard a boat.

List. A boat is said to list when it is leaning at an angle due to excess weight on one side.

Ljüngstrom rig. A unique sailboat rig with a single triangular sail attached along its vertical axis to a rotating, unstayed mast. Also called *twin-wing rig.*

LOA. Length overall; refers to the longest measurement of the boat as compared to the length at the waterline.

Locker. A storage compartment on a boat. A box, wardrobe, or chest. A *chain locker* is a compartment where chain cables are kept, while a boatswain's locker is where rigging and small stuff are kept. A *hanging locker* is a closet sufficiently large for hanging clothing.

Log. A speed-measuring device which when hung astern rotates and registers on a dial. Same as *patent log.*

Logbook. Record book or sheet of a vessel's activities: course, destination, time, speed, distances traveled, fuel consumed, weather, wind, and other items of importance.

Long board. Long tack.

Longitude. A measurement of distance expressed in degrees east and west of the meridian of Greenwich, England.

Lookout. A crewman positioned in the bow or aloft for the purpose of observing and reporting conditions and objects seen.

Loose-footed. A sail (fore-and-aft) not secured along the foot to a boom.

Loran. A system of long-range radio navigation based on the measurement of the difference in time of reception of signals from a pair of shore transmitters. Measurements are made with a special loran receiver.

Low. Area of low pressure.

Lubber. A beginner.

Lubber line. The fore-and-aft line of a compass.

Luff. The forward edge of a sail. When sailing sharply into the wind, the luff of a sail trembles, or luffs. To luff is also to bring the boat's head to the wind.

Luff, keep your. Order to luff.

Luff her. Order to bring sailboat into the wind.

Luff rope. Line sewn into the luff of a sail.

Lug. A fore-and-aft sail, almost square in shape, bent to a yard, and slung to leeward of the mast, when hoisted and set, with its tack well forward. Used in various rigs, and referred to as a standing, dipping, or balanced lug.

Lull. Period of calm.

Lunch hook. A small, light anchor for use during short stays, like eating lunch.

LWL (or DWL). Length waterline, waterline length, load waterline; the length of the boat along its waterline.

Lying to. Keeping a boat stationary with her head in the wind, usually by means of a sea anchor.

Mackerel sky. Banded altocumulus clouds, seen in advance of a storm.

Magnetic course. A course with reference to the magnetic north pole in the area covered by the chart.

Main. The most important, such as main deck, mainmast, mainsail.

Mainsail. The largest regular sail on a modern sailboat (pronounced *mains'l*).

Mainsheet. The line for controlling the main boom.

Main topsail. A triangular sail set above a gaff-headed mainsail, with peak hoisted to the topmast truck, clew hauled out to the gaff, and the luff set up by means of a tack downhaul.

Main truck. The top of the mainmast; specifically, a circular wood piece containing sheaves for hoisting flag halyards.

Make fast. To secure a line.

Make sail. To set sail.

Man-ropes. Steadying ropes used in going up and down vessel's side or ladder.

Man the boat. Order to climb into a rowboat.

Marconi rig. Employs tall triangular jib-headed sails, as distinguished from the gaff rig.

Mares' tails. Tufted cirrus clouds at high altitude; the first indication of approaching warm front.

Marina. A place that offers dockage, services, and facilities to all types of pleasure craft.

Mark. Markings on a lead line which show the depths visually or by feeling. Also any kind of distinguishable buoy placed in position to mark anything, a race for example. Same as *marker buoy.*

Marl. To wind or twist a small line or rope around another.

Marline. A tarred, small line used for lashings, whipping, etc.

Marlinspike. A pointed wooden or steel instrument used to open up the strands of rope and wire.

Martingale. Short perpendicular spar extending from bowsprit, used for counteracting pull of headstays.

Mast. The vertical spar supporting the booms, sails, etc.

Mast box. A box or cup into which the mast fits in any boat where the mast is stepped on deck.

Mast butt. The lower end of the mast.

Master. The captain or man in charge of a boat. Same as *skipper.*

Masthead. The top of a mast.

Mast partners. Heavy deck beams housing the mast and taking the strain from it.

Mast step. Frame or slot to secure lower end of mast.

Mate. One of master's assistants. On a family boat, the first mate is usually the wife.

Mayday! The distress call used on marine radio-telephone in case of immediate danger (from the French word *"M'aidez"* meaning "Help me").

Mean low water. The average depth at low tide.

Measurement rule. A formula for rating sailboats of similar but not identical dimensions so that they may race together, either on equal terms or on a handicap basis.

Mend. To refurl an improperly furled sail, to rebend a sail to a boom.

Meridian. A measurement of geographical location; any point on a half circle drawn between the North and South Poles.

Messenger. A light line used to haul over a heavier rope or cable.

Metacenter. The point of intersection of the vertical through the center of buoyancy of a hull, and a line drawn through the new center of buoyancy when the hull is heeled; as long as the metacenter is above the center of gravity, the boat will not capsize.

Mid-channel buoy. Buoy to be passed on either side.

Midships. The broadest part of the boat.

Mile. At sea the nautical mile is the length of one minute or 6,080 feet.

Miss stays. To be unable to go about; to get into irons, or stays.

Mitchboard. Boom crutch on rail to support boom when sail is lowered.

Mizzen. The shorter mast aft on a yawl or ketch. Same as *mizzenmast*.

Mizzen sail. A sail set from the mizzenmast.

Mizzen staysail. A triangular sail bent to a temporary stay from the mizzenmast to the deck or with a wire luff set up in similar fashion.

Molded-plywood hull. One made by gluing successive layers of thin wood together over a male mold.

Monkey block. Small single block which swivels.

Monkey fist. Knot worked in end of heaving line.

Monkey rail. A low rail around the stern.

Moor. To secure a boat to an object such as a dock, buoy, post, etc.

Mooring. A place where a boat is permanently anchored. Usually consists of a chain, buoy, pennant, and an anchor.

Mooring line. An anchor line or a dockline, depending on how and where the vessel is moored.

Motor sailer. A compromise-designed boat using both sail and motor power. The ratio of time used between sail and motor power is 50 to 50 to 85 to 15 percent. In some situations both engine and wind power are used.

Multihull. Generic term for any vessel with more than one hull. Among sailing craft this normally means one of three types: the catamaran (twin hulls); the proa, or outrigger (main hull, smaller side float); or the trimaran (main hull, floats on each side).

Mushroom anchor. An anchor with a circular cup in place of flukes, designed to be used as a permanent mooring on a mud bottom; with time, the anchor becomes deeply imbedded and has excellent holding power.

Nautical mile. 6,080 feet—therefore a mile over water is farther than over land (5,280 feet).

Navigable. Water that is deep enough to permit passage of boats.

Navigating lights. Required lights at sea.

Navigation. The science of determining a boat's position and safely conducting it from one place to another by means of charts, instruments, and/or the stars.

Neap tide. The least tide in a lunar month; its results are the lowest high water and the highest low water.

Near. Close to the wind.

Nimbus. Storm clouds.

Nose. Stem of a vessel; the wind is on the nose when it blows directly from where you want to go in a sailboat.

Nose-ender. A wind from dead ahead.

Nothing off. Helm order to keep her as close to the wind or as near on course as she is, and not let her pay off.

Nun buoy. A conical buoy, colored red, that is always on the right or starboard side of a channel when entering from seaward.

Oakum. Old, tarred rope strands used for stuffing into openings between boards of hull to prevent leakage.

Occulting. Disappearing and reappearing, used of a navigational light at sea; an occulting light is a recurring light with longer periods of light than of darkness (in contrast to a *flashing* light).

Off. To seaward of, outside of; away from, as, the wind is off shore.

Off and on. Stand toward land and off again, on different tacks.

Offing. To seaward but a safe distance from the shore.

Offsets. Naval-architect measurements used to lay out boat's lines.

Offshore wind. The wind when it is blowing from the shore.

Off the wind. Sailing downwind or before the wind.

Oilskins. A term generally used for all waterproof clothing.

On a wind. To sail close-hauled.

One-design class boat. Boat built to uniform specifications and measurements so that it is comparable to all the other boats in that class for competitive purposes.

On the beam. At any distance from a ship at right angles to her.

On the bow. Within the angle from right ahead to 45 degrees on either side.

On the quarter. On a bearing midway between abeam and astern.

Open. Unprotected anchorage; away from shelter; a boat without decking.

Open hawse. Riding to two anchors without swivel or crossing each other.

Outboard. Beyond a boat's side or hull.

Outfoot. One vessel sailing faster than another.

Outhaul. A line used to haul the clew of a sail out to the end of the boom.

Out of trim. Improperly ballasted.

Outpoint. To sail closer to the wind than another sailboat.

Overall. The extreme fore-and-aft measurement of a boat.

Overcorrecting. Swinging the wheel or helm farther than necessary to bring a boat back on course, usually carrying the lubber line well past the desired point.

Overfall. Seas breaking due to currents over a shallow area.

Overhang. Any part of a boat extending beyond the waterline at the bow and stern.

Overhatted. Sailing vessel which is oversparred.

Overhaul. To gain on another boat.

Overlap. The position of two boats when the one overtaking is within two overall lengths of the other boat.

Overrigged. Heavier sailing gear than necessary.

Oversparred. Carrying a taller mast, longer boom, etc., than she needs.

Overstand. To sail beyond an object, such as a buoy.

Overtake. To catch up with and pass another boat; to overhaul.

Owner's flag. The private signal of a boat owner; usually of his own design.

Painter. Bow line by which a small boat is towed or made fast to a mooring.

Palm. Leather fitting over hand to thrust needle through sailcloth.

Pan! Pan! Pan! An urgent radiotelephone message concerning the safety of a vessel and/or her crew, neither of which is in immediate danger of loss.

Para-anchor. Parachute surface anchor for deep water. Also called a drogue.

Parachute. Another name for a balloon spinnaker.

Parachute flare. A distress signal. A small parachute carrying a bright red flare is fired to a height making it widely visible as it floats down slowly.

Parallel rules. A pair of straight edges fastened together so that the distance between them may be changed while their edges remain parallel. Used for transferring lines from one part of a chart to another.

Parallels. Lines of latitude going around the earth's surface parallel to the equator.

Parcel. To cover a line by winding it with strips of canvas to protect the line at a point of wear (such as a chock).

Parrel. A line for confining a spar to a mast; a parrel for the jaws of a gaff usually is fitted with wooden rollers to prevent binding as the throat of the sail is hoisted. Same as *parral.*

Partners. Strengthening boards to help support something set through an opening in the deck, such as a mast or bitt.

Pass. To take securing turns with a lashing or rope.

Passage. Sailing from one port or place to another.

Pay off. To turn the bow away from the wind.

Pay out. To let out a line.

Peak. Highest point of a gaff-rigged sail.

Peak halyard. Rope which hoists the peak.

Peak outhaul. A line for pulling the peak of a sail out toward the end of the gaff.

Pelorus. A compass card fitted with sighting vanes and used for taking bearings.

Pennant. A length of line. Also, a small, narrow flag.

Permanent backstay. One that clears boom.

Pick-up buoy. A small buoy secured to a line leading from a mooring buoy, and fitted with an eye or bail for picking it up with a boat hook when arriving at the anchorage.

Pier. A structure built out into the water to serve as a landing place for boats. Same as *jetty* or *wharf.*

Pile. Thick pole or post, as for a dock, driven into the sea bottom and projecting above the water to hold up a dock or pier.

Piling. Vertical timbers or logs driven into the sea bottom to form a support for a dock or to act as a breakwater.

Pilot. A man qualified and licensed to direct ships in and out of a harbor.

Piloting. The act or technique of guiding a vessel and fixing her position by means of visible landmarks and aids to navigation (lighthouses, buoys, etc.), coastal or inland navigational charts, relevant publications, and various instruments. It is distinct from offshore navigation, though by definition both are included in navigation, overall.

Pin. The axis on which a sheave turns. Wood or metal to belay ropes to.

Pinch. When sailing into the wind, to pull the sail in too tight or head the bow of the boat into the wind too much, so that the sail begins to luff and the boat becomes sluggish and does not foot well.

Pin rail. A rail bored with holes to accept be-laying pins; also called *fife rail.*

Pintle. Metal braces or hooks upon which a stern-mounted rudder swings.

Pipe up. When the wind increases in velocity.

Pitch. The fore-and-aft motion of a boat. Also, the angle of the propeller blades.

Pitch-pole. To turn a boat end over end.

Plain sails. Regular working sails.

Planing. When a boat rides on top of the water.

Planing hull. A hull that is capable of planing.

Planing speed. The speed at which a planing hull rises to the surface.

Plot. Applying calculation to a chart.

Point. One thirty-second of a circle.

Points of sailing. Direction of boat in relation to the wind. The three basic points are running, reaching, and beating.

Point up. To sail more or less close to the wind.

Pole mast. One-piece mast; highest mast on ship.

Poop. A deck abaft the mizzen and above the after deck.

Pooped. Boarded from astern by a breaking wave.

Porpoise. When a boat rides with the bow up and out of the water.

Port. The left side of a boat, looking toward the bow. Also, a harbor or place where vessels enter and leave, as for commerce.

Porthole. Hole or window in the side of a boat.

Port tack. A sailboat is on the port tack when the wind is coming over the port side.

Pound. To strike the waves with jarring force, a characteristic of some hulls.

Pram. A small dinghy, usually rectangular in shape.

Prevailing wind. The usual wind direction for the area and season.

Preventer. A rope added for the purpose of supporting or restraining.

Privileged vessel. One which has the right of way.

Prow. The part of the bow which extends up and out from the waterline.

Pulpit rail. Guard equipment at bow.

Punt. A small, rectangular, flat-bottomed boat or dinghy.

Purchase. Any rigging consisting of two or more blocks used to hoist a heavy weight.

Put to sea. To leave port.

Quarter. The after part of a boat's side; that part of a craft which lies within 45 degrees from the stern, known as the port quarter or starboard quarter.

Quartering. Coming from a point back of the middle (the beam) and not directly astern of a boat; coming over the quarter, said of wind or waves; also, sailing with the wind coming over the quarter.

Quarter point. One-fourth of the angular distance between any two of the 32 points of the compass.

Quarters. Living and sleeping areas of a vessel.

Quay. Wharf used to unload cargo.

Race. A very strong tidal current created when two tides of a different strength meet.

Radar. Electronic equipment for the detection of objects and measurement of their bearing and distance by their reflection of radio signals.

Rail. The outer edge of the deck.

Raise. To bring an object on the horizon into view.

Rake. The inclination sternward of a mast from the vertical.

Range alongside. Come close abeam of another boat.

Range lights. Vertical white lights indicating vessel's direction. Generally not employed on sailing vessels.

Range of cable. A quantity of cable, ready for letting go the anchor or paying out.

Rap full. Sailing with all sails filled with wind.

Rating. The figure assigned to a sailboat after her dimensions have been measured and applied to one of the formulas known as measurement rules.

Ratlines. Lines running fore and aft between shrouds, used as a ladder in going aloft.

Rattail. Tapered end of a rope, such as the end of a bolt rope in the edge of a sail.

Reach. All sailing points between running and close-hauled. *Close reach,* sailing nearly close-hauled with sheets just eased. *Beam reach,* sailing with the wind abeam. *Broad reach,* sailing with the wind abaft the beam and with sails well out on the quarter.

Reaching jib. Large jib used usually in racing when on a broad reach, one of the light sails.

Ready about! Last warning given by the helmsman that he is going to turn the bow of the boat into the wind, so that the boom and sail swing across the boat, and go on the other tack.

Ready to jibe! Skipper's command to warn the crew and passengers that he is preparing to jibe.

Reckoning. Calculation of a boat's position.

Reef. To reduce sail area by partly lowering sail and securing the surplus material to the boom. Also, a chain of rock or coral, or ridge of sand lying at or near the surface of the water.

Reef band. A band of stout canvas sewed across the sail, with reef points in it, and earings at each end.

Reef cringle. Metal eye in sail for reefing.

Reef knot. Same as square knot.

Reef point. Small rope running through the lower part of a sail and used for taking a reef; they are placed several inches apart in one, two, or three horizontal lines starting a foot or two above the boom. Same as *reefing point*.

Reef tackle. Tackle used to haul out foot of sail.

Reeve. To pass a line through block or fairlead.

Regatta. Series of boat races, and attendant festivities arranged by a yacht club or other organization.

Relieving tackle. A tackle hooked to the tiller, to steer by in the case of accident to the wheel or tiller ropes.

Render. Cause a rope to slide or run freely through a block.

Rhumb line. A course that crosses all meridians at the same angle.

Ride. To lie at anchor.

Ride out. To weather out a storm safely whether at anchor or under way.

Rig. Arrangement of a boat's sails, masts, and rigging. Also, to put in proper order for working or use.

Rigging. A general term applying to all lines, shrouds, and stays necessary to spars and sails.

Right. To turn upright, as in righting a capsized boat.

Right of way. The legal authority for one boat to hold its direction while the other gives way.

Right rudder. The command to turn the wheel to the right.

Ring. Ring at upper end of anchor to which cable is bent.

Ringbolt. Eyebolt used for leading running rigging.

Rips. Short, steep waves, indicating the meeting of two tidal currents or crosscurrents.

Rip tide. A running tide, rising as it flows, and breaking in ripples.

Roach. Outward curve of the leech of a sail.

Roband. A piece of line used to hold a sail to the end of a spar.

Rode. An anchor line.

Roll. The transverse or athwartship rotation of a hull in sea.

Roller reef. Reef made by rolling the bottom of the sail around the boom with a twisting device on the boom.

Rope. Technically, cord made of fibers or wire twisted together, but in the operation of a sailboat a rope becomes a line.

Rotten stop. Lightweight string or thread to tie up a sail temporarily that can be easily broken with a tug to break out the sail.

Round down. To haul tackle so lower block will come down.

Round in. To haul in on a rope.

Rounding. A length of rope, hove around a spar or larger rope.

Round up. To haul up on a tackle.

Rudder. A flat member attached under the hull or to the stern which controls the course of the boat.

Rules of the Road. The international regulations for regulating traffic and for preventing collisions at sea.

Run. Sailing course with the wind astern and the sails and boom let out at right angles to the boat.

Run free. To sail with the wind behind the boat, to sail before the wind; to run.

Runners. Stays that support a mast when running before the wind.

Running. Sailing before the wind.

Running backstays. A temporary backstay set up to windward as a boat comes about and the leeward one is slacked off.

Running lights. Lights carried by a vessel under way; they are required by law.

Running rigging. The lines, such as halyards and sheets, that are used in the setting and trimming of sails.

Saddles. Wood brackets secured to lower part of mast for boom to rest on.

Safety pin. A pin attached to the shank chain of an anchor and inserted in the stock to hold it in position.

Sag. To drift off course. A boat improperly cradled by end supports during storage is said to sag in the middle.

Sail. Flexible vertical airfoil using wind pressure to propel a sailboat.

Sailing free. Going to windward but not pointing as high as possible, sailing below the optimum angle. Same as *sailing low*.

Sailing high. Sailing as close to the wind as possible.

Sailing trim. Most efficient trim of sails.

Sail track. T-shaped metal strip running the length of the mast or boom onto which the sail is fitted by means of lugs or slides sewn along its edge.

Scale. To climb up.

Scandalize. To make the area of certain sails smaller, generally because of a storm. Dropping the peak, on a gaff-rigged sail; tying the corners on a small sail.

Scantling. The measure of width and thickness of frames, planking, or other elements of a wooden boat's hull. For racing sailboats raced under a measurement rule, scantlings may be specified along with other dimensions, sail area, etc.

Scend. Boat lifting to a swell or seaway.

Schooner. A sailboat with two or more masts in which the mainmast is behind the smaller one or ones.

Scope. The length of mooring or anchor line in use.

Scow. Flat-bottomed boat with square unpointed ends; the broad boats are scow-type sailboats. The class-boat scow differs from other classes not only by its blunt ends, but also by its use of two bilge boards, one on each side, instead of a centerboard.

Screw. A boat's propeller. Also, the twist in a sail where it matches its angle to the different angle in wind encountered about 20 feet above the surface of the water.

Scud. To run before the wind in a storm.

Scull. To impel a boat by one oar at the stern.

Scupper. A drain or opening through the rail, gunwale, or planking of a boat to permit accumulated water to flow overboard.

Scuttle. To cut or bore holes in a vessel to make her sink.

Scuttlebutt. Gossip.

Sea anchor. A drag device, usually canvas, used to keep a boat headed into the wind during very heavy weather.

Sea buoy. Last buoy as a boat leaves the channel going out to sea.

Seacock. A drain.

Seagoing. A vessel capable of going to sea. Same as *seaworthy.*

Sea-kindly. Performing well in rough weather.

Sea room. Space for maneuvering without danger of colliding or going aground.

Seaway. Area with rough or moderate sea running.

Secure. To make fast.

Secure for sea. Order for extra lashings on all movable objects.

Seizing. A means of binding two parts of rope together to keep them secure.

Serve. To wind tightly, as rope, with small stuff such as marline in order to protect it against chafe and weather.

Set. To lay out or prescribe, as to set a course on which to sail. To hoist and spread to the wind, as to set the sails. Manner in which a sail is pulled up and fastened to its spars.

Set a course. To steer.

Set up. To tighten or make taut the last few inches of a halyard when raising the sail.

Sextant. An instrument used in navigation which determines altitude of sun or stars.

Shackle. A U-shaped metal fastener with a pin across the open end.

Shake. Sails shake when wind is spilled such as when pointing too high and luffing.

Shakedown. A trial cruise to test boat's condition.

Shake out. To let out a reef. Also, to hoist the sails.

Shank. Long part of an anchor.

She. Correct nautical pronoun to use when referring to a boat.

Sheathing. A casing or covering on the bottom of a vessel.

Sheave. A wheel inside a block or masthead.

Sheepshank. Type of knot, used for temporary shortening of a line.

Sheer. Sudden change in course.

Sheer. The curve of the deck or gunwale viewed from the side. Also called *sheerline.*

Sheer off. Bear away.

Sheerpole. A metal rod secured horizontally at the foot of a mast's standing rigging, to prevent the shrouds from turning or untwisting.

Sheet. A line used to trim a sail.

Sheet anchor. A spare anchor.

Sheet bend. Type of knot.

Sheet block. *See block.*

Shift. To change.

Shipshape. Well-kept, orderly, clean.

Shiver. To shake the wind out of a sail by bracing it so that the wind strikes upon the leech.

Shoal. An underwater hill or sandbar whose top is near the surface. Also, shallow water.

Shock cord. An elastic rope that can be speedily fastened and unfastened.

Shoot. To "coast" into the wind on momentum, as when coming to a pier or mooring.

Shore. The coast or land adjacent to the sea. A timber or other prop placed in position to act as a support; to shore up.

Short board. Short tack.

Shorten. Reduce sail area by reefing or dropping sail.

Shove off. To push off a boat from alongside.

Shroud. Standing rigging, usually of wire, running from the mast to the sides of a boat to support the mast.

Sideslip. To slide sideways through the water; make leeway.

Single-sticker. One-masted vessel.

Sister ship. Another ship of similar class, line, design, or name.

Skeg. A triangular vertical projection below the after end of a boat's keel, designed to increase the boat's lateral resistance and directional stability. The rudder often is attached to a skeg.

Skiff. Small, lightweight rowboat or sailboat.

Skin. The outside part of a sail when it is furled. Also, outer planking of a vessel.

Skin friction. Surface resistance of a hull as it passes through the water.

Skylight. A glazed framework built in a deck to admit light and air.

Skyscraper. Triangular skysail.

Slack. To ease off a line.

Slack water. Period at high or low tide when water is not in motion.

Slant of wind. Favorable wind change.

Slat. To flap noisily, as idle sails or halyards against a mast.

Slew. To turn anything about its axis.

Slide. Small metal lug fastened at intervals to the front edge and bottom of the mainsail to attach it to mast and boom, and enable the sail to be pulled up, on, or along the sail track.

Sling. To set in ropes, so as to put on a tackle to hoist or lower it.

Slings. The ropes used for securing the center of a yard to the mast. Also, a large rope fitted so as to go around anything which is to be hoisted or lowered.

Slip. The space between two wharves or piers where a boat can be moved.

Slip the mooring. To cast off from the mooring.

Sloop. A single-masted sailboat in which the mast is set forward of amidships.

Slot effect. Wind passing through the opening between overlapping jib and mainsail results in increased pressure differential between the windward and leeward sides of the mainsail.

Small stuff. While it technically means any line or rope less than one inch in diameter, it usually implies twine, marline, etc.

Snap hook. Metal device with spring catch to attach one thing to another.

Snatch block. A block with an open or hinged sheave, enabling it to be used quickly without reeving a line through the swallow.

Snotter. The bellshaped spinnaker-pole fitting used on many small boats. Same as *spinnaker-pole bell*.

Snub. To check or stop suddenly, as a line.

Snug down. Reduce sail, close hatches, secure loose objects before a blow.

Snugged down. Under small but comfortable sail area.

Soft eye. Eye at end of rope that does not contain a metal thimble.

Sound. To measure the depth of water.

Sounding. Charted depth.

Spanker. The gaff-rigged sail set on a mizzen mast. Same as *driver*.

Spanking breeze. Good wind coming over stern or quarter.

Spar. Mast, boom, spinnaker pole, etc.

Spar buoy. A tall buoy used as an aid to navigation.

Spell. To relieve another.

Spencer. A loose-footed sail set abaft a mast with its head extended.

Spider band or hoop. A metal band around a mast, or spar, fitted with eyes to take the shackles of shrouds, guys, etc.; on a mast it may also carry belaying pins for the running gear.

Spill the wind. To cause the sail to lose its wind, and to flap or luff by turning the bow into the wind or by releasing the rope which controls the mainsail so that the wind no longer fills the sail. To luff.

Spinnaker. A large, light headsail used when a boat is sailing before the wind or on a reach.

Spinnaker boom or pole. Spar for the large light sail, the spinnaker.

Spinnaker-pole lift. Line from mast to middle part of a spinnaker pole to hold it in place; spinnaker lift.

Spitfire. The small storm jib, specially made of strong canvas.

Splice. To join rope by tucking the strands together, such as short, long, eye, and back splice, etc.

Spreader. A horizontal strut to which shrouds or stays are attached, to support the mast and spread rigging.

Spring. To crack or split a mast. To spring a leak is to begin to leak. To spring a luff is to force a vessel close to the wind, in sailing.

Spring lines. Additional docking lines used to prevent a boat from moving.

Sprit. Spar for a spritsail.

Spritsail. Four-sided sail differing from a gaff-rig sail in that the sprit (a pole) extends diagonally from the lower part of the mast across the sail to hold up the outer corner, the peak.

Squall. Sudden gust of wind, likely to make your boat heel.

Square. Yards are squared when they are horizontal and at right angles with the keel.

Square away. To ease the sheets when going on to a reach or run—the opposite to *harden up*.

Square-rigged. Having squaresails like an old-time ship.

Square-sail. A temporary sail, set at the foremast of a schooner or the mainmast of a sloop, when going before the wind.

Stability. Tendency of a boat to return to an upright position after being heeled. A *stiff* boat is very stable, while a *cranky* or *tender* boat heels easily.

Staff. Upright pole on which a light or flag is affixed.

Stanchion. Upright pillar to support guard rails, awnings, etc.

Stand by! An order employed to alert crewmen.

Stand in. Approach.

Standing part. The part of a line made fast to something.

Standing rigging. The shrouds and stays as well as other rigging which are not moved in working a boat.

Stand off. Keep away; wait clear of any position.

Stand on. Maintain one's course and speed.

Starboard. The right side of a boat, looking toward the bow.

Starboard tack. Sailing with the wind coming from the right side; the sail is on the left, or port, side.

Start. To ease, to loosen.

Starving. Sailing so high when going to weather that the sails are not properly filled with wind; pinching.

Stay. Wire rigging running fore and aft from mast. Also, a change of tack. Also see *in stays.*

Staysail. A fore-and-aft triangular sail set upon a stay after of the forestay.

Steady. To maintain a given course.

Steerageway. Sufficient forward speed to allow rudder control.

Stem. More or less vertical timber at bow; boat's entering edge.

Stem the tide. Sailing against current yet still making some headway.

Step. A socket that holds the base of the mast; hence, to step.

Stern. The after part of a boat.

Stern staff. A short pole for flying the ensign aft.

Sternway. Moving in reverse.

Stiff. Describes a boat that doesn't heel readily.

Stock. On some types of anchor (known collectively as stocked anchors), a crosspiece at the end of the shank opposite the arms. Its purpose is to hold the anchor in such a position that one of the flukes will bury itself in the ground.

Stop. A narrow band of canvas, piece of rope, or shock cord used in furling a sail.

Stopper. Short rope, device, or knot to hold something in place temporarily or to check a rope from running.

Stopper knot. Last knot on rope to stop it running through block.

Storm canvas, storm sails. Strong small sails for very windy weather, usually not part of a small boat's gear.

Storm jib. A small triangular sail at the bow of the boat, used in very heavy weather.

Storm trysail. A heavy, flat-cut triangular sail hoisted in place of the mainsail to heave to and ride out a blow; other sails, such as mainsails and jibs, are also cut flat of heavy canvas for storm use.

Stow. To put away.

Strake. A row of planks in a hull.

Strike. To lower.

Strip. To take apart.

Strut. Support or brace.

Suction bailers. Various devices which drain water from small boats. Also called *self-bailers.*

Swab. Rope mop.

Swallow. The space between the sheave and shell of a block, through which a rope is rove.

Swamp. To fill with water.

Sway. To hoist aloft.

Sway up, sweat up. To pull up as tight as possible.

Swell. A heavy undulation of the sea, caused by strong wind blowing at a distance; it is often a warning signal of a major storm.

Swivel. A rotating fitting used to prevent a line from winding up.

Tabernacle. The deck housing (usually a raised socket or post) for the heel of a mast, often pivoted or hinged so that the mast can be lowered when passing under obstructions.

Tack. The lower forward corner of a sail. Also, to proceed to windward by sailing on alternate courses so that the wind is first on one side of the boat and then on the other; a windward course.

Tack downhaul. A line or tackle for putting a downward strain on the luff of a sail.

Tackle. A system of blocks and ropes arranged for hauling.

Tackline. Signal halyards. Line to haul down tack of gaff topsail.

Tail. A rope fixed to the end of a wire for ease of handling.

Tail off. To pick up the end of a line and haul on it.

Tail on. To pull on a rope.

Take in. To lower a sail; to stow a sail.

Take off. To remove sail.

Tang. A metal mast fitting to which a stay is attached.

Telltale. Any pennant, feather, or piece of wool at the masthead or on the shrouds which indicates wind direction. Same as *masthead pennants.*

Tender. A small boat employed to go back and

forth to the shore from a larger boat. Also, describing a boat that heels readily.

Tenon. The heel of a mast, shaped to fit into the step.

Thimble. A metal or plastic eyelet set in an eye splice in rope or wire.

Throat. Upper corner nearest mast of a four-cornered, or gaff-rigged, sail. *Throat halyard* is the rope by which the sail at the inner end of the gaff is pulled up.

Thwarts. The seats going across a small boat.

Thwartships. Across the boat from side to side.

Tide. Commonly, it is used to describe the inflow and outflow of ocean water caused by the gravitational influences of moon and sun.

Tideway. Part of channel where current is strongest.

Tight. A boat that does not leak.

Tiller. A bar connected with the rudder head. By this bar the rudder is moved as desired.

Toggle. A pin placed through the bight or eye of a rope, block strap, or bolt, to keep it in its place, or to put the bight or eye of another rope upon, securing them together.

Top. A platform at the head of a lower mast, resting on the trestletrees. Also, to raise one end of, as a boom, by hoisting on its topping lift.

Top-heavy. Too heavy aloft.

Top light. Signal light carried to top.

Top lining. Lining to prevent chafe against top edge on after part of sail.

Topmarks. Distinguishing marks placed on buoys, beacons, etc.

Topmast. Second mast above deck.

Topping lift. A line that takes the weight of the boom while the sail is being set.

Top rope. The rope used for sending topmasts up and down.

Topsail. On a gaff-rigged sailboat, the triangular fore-and-aft sail set above the gaff.

Topside. On deck.

Touch. To luff a sailboat until the leech is also luffing.

Tow. To pull behind a boat.

Track. The course of a boat. Also, the groove or slide on the mast or boom by which a sail is attached.

Transom. The stern facing of the hull.

Trapeze. Wire and belt device to enable crew to hike out to windward so as to balance the boat when she heels.

Traveler. A metal rod or track for sheets to slide athwartships rather than having a sheet block coming to a cleat; if rope or wire is substituted for a metal rod it becomes a bridle. Same as *boom horse*.

Trestletrees. Supports running fore and aft on a lower masthead to support the top, crosstrees, and topmast.

Triatic stay. Stay connecting mainmast and foremast.

Trice. Haul up.

Trick. A period of duty at the helm.

Trim. To set a sail in correct relation to the wind by means of a sheet. Also, the way a boat floats on the water—on an even keel, heeled over, or down by the bow or stern.

Trimaran. A craft that has three hulls.

Trim tab. An adjustable horizontal plate, usually of wood or metal, attached to the bottom of a boat's transom to improve her trim and provide a more comfortable ride. Same as an *elevator*. Also, a small hinged section of the trailing edge of a rudder which may be set at an angle to the rudder itself, by controls within the boat, to counteract the pull of a weather or lee helm against the tiller or steering wheel.

Tripping line. A line attached to the crown of an anchor for recovering it if it should become fouled or jammed; also, a line attached to the apex of a drogue or sea anchor for releasing the drag or hauling it in.

Trough. The valley between the crests of two waves.

Truck. A cap for a masthead, sometimes containing sheaves for flag halyards.

True course. A course steered by a boat's compass that has been corrected for deviation and variation.

True wind. Direction the wind blows on dock differing from apparent wind under way.

Trunk. The housing for a centerboard.

Trunnion hoop. A hinged hoop fitted to the cap of a mast to contain the mast next above it.

Trysail. Small rugged mainsail for stormy weather.

Tumble home. The inward curve or slant of a boat's sides, from the turn of the bilge to the deck line.

Tune. To make changes or adjustments in the boat, its rigging, fittings, or sails to bring about better performance.

Turnbuckle. A device used to maintain correct tension on standing rigging.

Turn turtle. Capsizing by turning over completely with the mast pointing to the bottom.

Turtle. A bag in which a spinnaker can be stowed with the head and tacks attached to halyard, sheet, and guy.

Unbend. To cast adrift or untie.

Under bare poles. With no sails set.

Underlay. To make the "last" tack too early so

that the mark cannot be rounded without another tack.

Under the lee. Protected from the wind—by land, by another boat, or by any object.

Undertow. Offshore current noticeable in the surf.

Under way. A vessel in motion when not aground, made fast to the shore, or at anchor.

Unfurl. To unfold a sail, flag, etc.

Union. The upper inner corner of an ensign. The rest of the flag is called the *fly*. The union of the U.S. ensign is a blue field with white stars and the fly is composed of alternate white and red stripes.

Union-down. The situation of a flag when it is hoisted upside down, bringing the union down instead of up. Used as a signal of distress.

Union jack. A small flag, containing only the union, without the fly, usually hoisted at the bowsprit-cap.

Unreeve. To pull a rope out from any block or sheave.

Unship. To remove something from its proper place.

Up. Toward the direction of the wind.

Up anchor. Order to weigh, or hoist up, the anchor.

Uphill. To windward.

Upwind. Toward the direction from which the wind is blowing.

Vane. A weathercock.

Vang. A line to steady the boom when off the wind.

Variation. The difference in degrees between true and magnetic north.

V-bottom. A hull with bilges forming a V-section from chines to keel.

Veer. A change of direction, as in the wind.

Veer and haul. To alternately slack up and haul away.

Veering wind. A shifting wind.

Wake. The foamy path of disturbed water left behind a moving boat.

Warp. To move a boat into a desired position by manipulating lines extended to shore, dock, etc.

Wash. The waves made by a boat moving through the water.

Watch. Working shifts aboard ship.

Waterline. Imaginary line around the hull at the surface when boat is on an even keel—sometimes painted on a boat's side indicating the proper trim.

Waterlogged. Swamped but afloat.

Way. Movement through the water.

Wear. To turn away from the wind, jibe.

Weather. Windward side of a sailboat. Also, to pass safely to windward of object without changing tack.

Weather helm. A sailboat wanting to come up into the wind.

Weatherly ship. One making little leeway working to windward.

Weather shore. Shore onto which the wind blows.

Weather tide. Wind and current going same direction.

Weigh. To lift up, as an anchor or mast.

Well-found. Well-equipped.

Wetted surface. The total submerged area of a hull.

Wheel. Steering device on larger boats, in place of the tiller.

Whip. To whip a line is to bind the strands of its end with yard or cord.

Whisker pole. A light spar extending from the mast and used to hold the jib out when off the wind.

Whiskers. Crosstrees on a bowsprit.

Whistle buoy. A buoy having a whistle actuated by water movement.

Wide berth. To give room.

Winch. A mechanical device to give increased hauling power on a line.

Windage. The amount of sail area presented as a target to the wind.

Windbound. Unable to sail because of contrary winds.

Windlass. A winch for hauling in cable, etc. Also called *capstan*.

Wind-rode. Riding head to wind at anchor, when the wind overcomes the tide.

Wind's eye. Exact direction from which the wind is blowing.

Wind shadow. The turbulent air directly to leeward of a sail.

Windward. Toward the wind.

Wing and wing. Running before a wind with sails set both sides.

Wire luff. A luff in which the usual bolt rope is replaced by a wire rope to provide strength when the sail is not bent to a stay.

Withe. An iron band fitted on the end of a boom or mast, with a ring or eye to it, through which another boom or mast or rigging is made fast.

Work, work to windward. To beat; to tack; to sail close-hauled, on the wind.

Working sails. Regular sails on a boat, used in ordinary weather.

Wring. To bend or strain a mast by setting the rigging up too taut.

Wung out. Sailing with mainsail set one side

and foresail set the other side, so that one will not blanket the other. Same as *goosewing* and *wing and wing*.

Yacht. General term for a boat used solely for the personal pleasure of the owner.

Yard. The spar from which a square sail is suspended.

Yardarm. Tapering end of a yard.

Yaw. To swing off course (usually due to heavy seas) without regard for the position of the rudder.

Yaw angle. The angular difference between a boat's centerline and her actual course made good owing to her making leeway or crabbing but not including any effects of current. Same as *angle of leeway*.

Yawl. A sailboat similar to ketch but with smaller aftermast stepped abaft the tiller or wheel.

Yoke. Piece across the top of a rudder with which to control it.

Yoke lines. Rope leading from either end of rudder yoke to turn rudder.

Zenith. The part of the celestial sphere which is exactly overhead.

Zephyr. The west wind.

Zigzag sailing. Sailing continuously on alternate tacks.

Illustration Credits are listed by page numbers; all other illustrations courtesy of One-Design Yachtsman, Inc.

72 73 74 75 10 9 8 7 6 5 4 3 2